EVANGELICAL FREE WILL

Evangelical Free Will

*Philipp Melanchthon's Doctrinal
Journey on the Origins of Faith*

GREGORY B. GRAYBILL

OXFORD

UNIVERSITY PRESS

OXFORD
UNIVERSITY PRESS

Great Clarendon Street, Oxford OX2 6DP

Oxford University Press is a department of the University of Oxford.
It furthers the University's objective of excellence in research, scholarship,
and education by publishing worldwide in

Oxford New York

Auckland Cape Town Dar es Salaam Hong Kong Karachi
Kuala Lumpur Madrid Melbourne Mexico City Nairobi
New Delhi Shanghai Taipei Toronto

With offices in

Argentina Austria Brazil Chile Czech Republic France Greece
Guatemala Hungary Italy Japan Poland Portugal Singapore
South Korea Switzerland Thailand Turkey Ukraine Vietnam

Oxford is a registered trade mark of Oxford University Press
in the UK and in certain other countries

Published in the United States
by Oxford University Press Inc., New York

© Gregory B. Graybill 2010

The moral rights of the author have been asserted
Database right Oxford University Press (maker)

First published 2010

British Library Cataloguing in Publication Data
Data available

Library of Congress Cataloging in Publication Data
Library of Congress Control Number: 2010925609

Typeset by SPI Publisher Services, Pondicherry, India
Printed in Great Britain
on acid-free paper by
MPG Books Group, Bodmin and King's Lynn

ISBN 978–0–19–958948–7

3 5 7 9 10 8 6 4 2

Dominus illuminatio mea
Soli Deo gloria

Preface

> '*Listen! A sower went out to sow. And as he sowed, some seed fell on the path, and the birds came and ate it up. Other seed fell on rocky ground, where it did not have much soil, and it sprang up quickly, since it had no depth of soil. And when the sun rose, it was scorched; and since it had no root, it withered away. Other seed fell among thorns, and the thorns grew up and choked it, and it yielded no grain. Other seed fell into good soil and brought forth grain, growing up and increasing and yielding thirty and sixty and a hundredfold.' And he said, 'Let anyone with ears to hear listen!'* (Mark 4.3–9 NRSV)

When a crowd hears the message of salvation in Jesus Christ, some believe it, and others do not. From a committed Christian perspective, the obvious question is *Why? What is the origin of faith in Christ?* Philipp Melanchthon wrestled with this issue throughout his life, and this book is an account of that struggle.

This study is addressed to the scholarly practitioners of historical theology. It is an attempt to make a contribution to our understanding of Melanchthon and, through him, Lutheranism. Perhaps it will also have some bearing on our view of the wider flowering of Protestant theology. That is up to the reader to decide.

More significantly, as far as I am concerned, this book is also addressed to Bible-believing Christians. Both the Scriptures and the issue of the origins of faith that Melanchthon encountered are still with us today. Where *does* faith come from? How one answers this question has apologetic, evangelistic, and pastoral implications. By entering vicariously into one man's struggle with this issue, believers may thereby enter into their own.

Gregory B. Graybill

Acknowledgements

My first acknowledgement is to the LORD God, without whom this project would have been impossible, and to whom all praise is ever due.

I am grateful to my supervisor, Graham Tomlin, for his able guidance, both through the M.St. and through the D.Phil. More than any other person, he was vital to the success of the original thesis, on which this book is based.

Several people have been invaluable teachers and aides to me in understanding various languages: Analiese van den Dikkenberg (German), Jeremy Duff (Greek), Christine Eckhard-Black (German), Anna Fields (Swedish), Philip Johnston (Hebrew), Rhidian Jones (Latin), Nabil Shehadi (French), and Wolfgang von Ungen Sternberg (German). John Pearce kept me abreast of Lutheran research on Melanchthon in America, and Timothy Wengert kindly critiqued some of my early ideas on this thesis via email, as did Sachiko Kusukawa in relation to Melanchthon's view of paradox. To Prof. Wengert I owe a special debt of gratitude. Over the last number of years, he has, over email, answered many of my questions, both large and small, related to all things Melanchthon. His replies were invariably speedy, and thorough. I am also grateful to Ron Frost and Karl Heinz zur Mühlen for discussing some of the ideas of this thesis with me in person. Peter Sanlon gave me some good feedback on Augustine. Sarita McCaw very helpfully read and commented upon some of the early chapters of this thesis, and my late mother, Pat Graybill, proofread the whole thing. My mother-in-law, Mary Caroline Hunt, and my wife, Cathryn, have also helped me greatly in proofreading.

I further wish to extend my thanks to the staffs of the Bodleian Library, Taylorian Institute, Oxford Theology Faculty Library, Wycliffe Hall Library, Princeton Theological Seminary Library, Pittsburgh Theological Seminary Library, the Library of the University of Michigan, the Burgettstown Public Library, and the Carnegie Library of Pittsburgh. Without them, I could not have done this project.

It would be remiss of me to fail to mention Roger Mohrlang of Whitworth College (now University), who was influential in my coming to Oxford and to Wycliffe. He has encouraged me in both faith and academics. Likewise, I owe much to Dale Bruner, who set me on the path toward Reformation studies early in my undergraduate years. In addition to Graham, I also owe a debt of gratitude to Alister McGrath and Peter (Aggarwal) MacPherson, who both taught me much about the Reformation during my M.St. studies immediately preceding this thesis. Further, I wish to thank my D.Phil. examiners, Diarmaid MacCulloch of the University of Oxford, and Tony Lane of London Bible College. Extra gratitude goes to Prof. MacCulloch for his patience in serving as my advisor at Oxford University Press. Also at Oxford University Press, I am indebted to Tom Perridge, Elizabeth Robottom, Jenny Wagstaffe, Sophie Goldsworth, Emma Barber, Tessa Eaton, Carolyn McAndrew and David Sanders. Thanks, too, go to the anonymous reader who so vigorously critiqued my manuscript.

I am also grateful for the encouragement and support of my two congregations, whom I have served as pastor since 2004: Langeloth Community Presbyterian Church, and Cross Creek United Presbyterian Church. They have been generous in study leave, and tolerant of my academic pursuits taking place alongside the busy rounds of parish ministry.

I offer my thanks to the numerous friends, relatives, and colleagues who have encouraged me over the course of this work. Special regards go to my family, for all their support at every stage in this project spanning more than ten years. I am grateful to my late parents, Blair and Pat Graybill; to my brother, Jon Graybill; and most of all to my good wife, Cathryn.

Of course, all the mistakes are mine, and all the glory belongs to God.

Contents

Abbreviations

Ann. Rom.	Philipp Melanchthon, *Annotationes Philippi Melanchthonis in Epistolam Pauli ad Romanos unam, et ad Corintios duas* (Argentorati: Iohannem Heruagium, 1523).
Ap.	*Apologia Confessionis*
ARC	Georg Pfeilschifter, ed., *Acta reformationis Catholicae ecclesiam Germaniae concernentia saeculi XVI. Die Reformverhandlungen des deutschen Episkopats von 1520 bis 1570,* 6 vols. (Regensburg: F. Pustet, 1959–).
ARG	*Archiv für Reformationsgeschichte*
AW	John Duns Scotus, *God and Creatures: The Quodlibetal Questions,* ed. and trans. Felix Alluntis and Allan B. Wolter (Princeton: Princeton University Press, 1975).
Bds	Heinrich Ernst Bindseil, ed., *Philippi Melanchthonis epistolae, iudicia, consilia, testimonia aliorumque ad eum epistolae quae in Corpus Reformatorum desiderantur* (Halle, 1874).
BoC	Robert Kolb and Timothy J. Wengert, eds., Charles Arand et al., trans., *The Book of Concord: The Confessions of the Evangelical Lutheran Church* (Minneapolis: Fortress, 2000). *Cf. Tapp. below.*
BSLK	*Die Bekenntnisschriften der evangelisch-lutherischen Kirche/ herausgegeben im Gedenkjahr der Augsburgischen Konfession 1930* (Göttingen: Vandenhoeck & Ruprecht, 1952).
CA	*Confessio Augustana*
Capita	Philipp Melanchthon, *Rerum theologicarum capita seu Loci fere sunt, c.*1519–20. The CR editors also place it under the heading of *Lucubratiuncula Philippi Mel.* CR 21.11–46.
CChr	*Corpus Christianorum: Series Latina* (Turnholt, 1953–).
CO	John Calvin, *Ioannis Calvini opera quae supersunt omnia,* ed. Guilielmus Baum, Eduardus Cunitz, and Eduardus Reuss, 59 vols. (Brunsvigae: C. A. Schwetschke, 1863–1900).
CR	Philipp Melanchthon, *Corpus Reformatorum: Philippi Melanthonis opera quae supersunt omnia,* ed. K. Bretschneider and H. Bindseil, 28 vols. (Halle: Schwetschke, 1834–60).

CSEL	*Corpus Scriptorum Ecclesiasticorum Latinorum* (Vienna 1886–).
CT	Schroeder, H. J., trans., *Canons and Decrees of the Council of Trent: Original Text with English Translation* (London: B. Herder Book Co., 1941).
Delius	Martin Luther, *Martin Luther: Studienausgabe*, ed. Hans Ulrich-Delius (Berlin: Evangelische Verlagsanstalt, 1979–99).
DLA	*De libero arbitrio*
DSA	*De servo arbitrio*
EAS	Desiderius Erasmus, *Ausgewählte Schriften: Ausgabe in acht Bänden: Lateinisch und Deutsch*, ed. Werner Welzig, 8 vols. (Darmstadt: Wissenschaftliche Buchgesellschaft, 1968–80).
EE	Desiderius Erasmus, *Opus epistolarum Des. Erasmi Roterodami*, ed. P. S. Allen et al., 12 vols. (Oxonii: Typographeo Clarendoniano, 1906–58).
GA	Gregory of Rimini, *Gregorii Ariminensis OESA Lectura super primum et secundum Sententiarum*, ed. A. Damasus Trapp, 7 vols. (Berlin: W. de Gruyter, 1978).
Heubtartikel	Philipp Melanchthon, *Heubtartikel Christlicher Lere: Melanchthons deutsche Fassung seiner* Loci Theologici *nach dem Autograph und dem Originaldruck von 1553*, ed. Ralf Jennett and Johannes Schilling (Leipzig: Evangelische Verlagsanstalt, 2002). (Citations are given according to the page number listed at the bottom of each page.)
Hill	Philipp Melanchthon, *Melanchthon: Selected Writings*, trans. Charles Leander Hill, ed. Elmer Ellsworth Flack and Lowell J. Satre (Minneapolis: Augsburg, 1962).
Hiob	Johann Staupitz, *Staupitz, Tübinger Predigten*, Quellen und Forschungen zur Reformationsgeschichte 8, ed. Georg Buchwald and Ernst Wolf (Leipzig, 1927).
JEH	*Journal of Ecclesiastical History*
Keen	*A Melanchthon Reader*, trans. and ed. Ralph Keen, American University Studies, Series VII, Theology and Religion 41 (New York: Peter Lang, 1988).
Kn.	Johann Staupitz, *Johannis Staupitii, opera quae reperiri poterunt omnia: Deutsche Schriften*, ed. J. K. F. Knaake, vol. 1 (Potsdam, 1867).

LB   Desiderius Erasmus, *Opera omnia Desiderii Erasmi Rotero-dami*, ed. Joannes Clericus, 10 vols. (Lugduni Batavorum, 1703–6).

LCC   *Library of Christian Classics*, ed. John Baillie et al., 26 vols. (Philadelphia: Westminister, 1950–69).

Lenz   Philipp I, Landgraf von Hessen, *Briefwechsel Landgraf Philipp's des Grossmüthigen von Hessen mit Bucer*, ed. Max Lenz (Leipzig: S. Hirzel, 1880–91).

Libellus   Johann Staupitz, *Libellus de executione eterne predestinationis* (Nuremberg, 1517).

LW   Martin Luther, *Luther's Works: American Edition*, ed. Jaroslav Pelikan and Helmut Lehmann, 55 vols. (Saint Louis/Philadelphia: Concordia/Fortress, 1955–86).

MBW   Philipp Melanchthon, *Melanchthons Briefwechsel: Kritische und kommentierte Gesamtausgabe*, ed. Heinz Scheible, 10 vols. to date (Stuttgart: Frommann-Holzboog, 1977–). For example, MBW 1.163 means *Melanchthons Briefwechsel*, volume 1, letter number 163. MBW gives summaries of Melanchthon's letters, while the *Texte* volumes (abbreviated as T, below) provide the actual text.

MSA   Philipp Melanchthon, *Melanchthons Werke in Auswahl [Studiensausgabe]*, ed. R. Stupperich, 7 vols. (Gütersloh: Gerd Mohn, 1951–75).

OER   Hans J. Hillerbrand, ed., *The Oxford Encyclopedia of the Reformation*, 4 vols. (New York: Oxford University Press, 1996).

OLD   P. G. W. Glare, ed., *Oxford Latin Dictionary* (Oxford: Clarendon Press, 1982).

OTh   William Ockham, *Opera theologica*, ed. Gedeon Gál et al., 9 vols. (1967–84).

I Pet.   Martin Luther, *Epistel S. Petri gepredigt und ausgelegt. Erste Bearbeitung*, 1523. LW 30.1–145. WA 12.260–399.

II Pet.   Martin Luther, *Der ander Epistel S. Petri und eine S. Judas gepredigt und ausgelegt*, 1523/4. LW 30.147–99. WA 14.16–74.

PL   J. P. Migne, ed., *Patrologia cursus completus, series Latina*, 221 vols. (Paris, 1844–79).

PW   John Duns Scotus, *Philosophical Writings: A Selection*, ed. and trans. Allan B. Wolter (Indianapolis: Hackett, 1987).

Scholia 1528	Philipp Melanchthon, *Scholia in Epistolam Pauli ad Colossenses, recognita ab autore* (Wittenberg: Joseph Klug, 1528).
ST	Thomas Aquinas, *Summa Theologiae: Latin Text and English Translation, Introductions, Notes, Appendices and Glossaries,* ed. Cornelius Ernst et al., 61 vols. (London: Blackfriars, 1963–80).
Staupitz I	Johann Staupitz, *Sämtliche Schriften, Abhandlungen, Predigten, Zeugnisse. Tübinger Predigten,* ed. Lothar Graf zu Dohna and Richard Wetzel, vol. 1 (Berlin: De Gruyter, 1987).
Staupitz II	Johann Staupitz, *Sämtliche Schriften, Abhandlungen, Predigten, Zeugnisse. Libellus de exsecutione aeternae praedestinationis,* ed. Lothar Graf zu Dohna and Richard Wetzel, vol. 2 (Berlin: De Gruyter, 1987).
Summa	Philipp Melanchthon, *Pauli ad Romanos Epistolae Summa,* c.1519. CR 21.56–60.
Suppl. Mel.	Philipp Melanchthon, *Supplementa Melanchthoniana. Werke Philipp Melanchthons die im Corpus Reformatorum vermisst werden,* ed. O. Clemen (Leipzig, 1910–29).
T	Philipp Melanchthon, *Melanchthons Briefwechsel: Texte,* ed. Heinz Scheible, 9 vols. to date (Stuttgart: Frommann-Holzboog, 1977–). For example, T 1.163.3–5 means *Texte* volume 1, letter number (*not* page number) 163, lines 3–5 (see also MBW above).
Tapp.	Theodore G. Tappert, ed. and trans., *The Book of Concord: The Confessions of the Evangelical Lutheran Church* (Philadelphia: Fortress, 1959). *Cf. BoC, above.*
Theologica Institutio	*Theologica Institutio Philippi Melanchthonis in Epistolam Pauli ad Romanos,* c.1519. CR 21.49–60.
TRE	Gerhard Krause and Gerhard Müller, eds., *Theologische Realenzyklopädie,* 36 vols. (Berlin and New York: Walter de Gruyter, 1977–).
Vatican	John Duns Scotus, *Opera Omnia,* ed. C. Belić et al. (Vatican City: Typis Polyglottis Vaticanis, 1950–).
WA	Martin Luther, *D. Martin Luthers Werke: Kritische Gesamtausgabe* (Weimar: H. Böhlau, 1883–).
WABr	Martin Luther, *D. Martin Luthers Werke: Kritische Gesamtausgabe. Briefwechsel* (Weimar: H. Böhlaus Nachfolger, 1930–).

WATr   Martin Luther, *D. Martin Luthers Werke: Kritische Gesamtausgabe. Tischreden*, 6. vols. (Weimar: H. Böhlaus Nachfolger, 1912–21).

WADB   Martin Luther, *D. Martin Luthers Werke: Kritische Gesamtausgabe. Deutsche Bibel*, 12 vols. (Weimar: H. Böhlaus Nachfolger, 1906–61).

Wadding   John Duns Scotus, *Opera Omnia*, ed. Luke Wadding, 12 vols. (Lyon: Durand, 1639).

Part I

Foundations

1

Introduction

Theology played a crucial role in western civilization in the sixteenth century, and one of the most influential theologians of the age was a diminutive man named Philipp Melanchthon. One engraving of him reads, 'Although he was small of body, he was great of skill.'[1] Melanchthon was a leading Reformation teacher on the key issue of salvation, writing passionately that people were justified by faith alone—that on account of Christ's death and resurrection, believers were declared innocent before God, as in a court of law.[2] As the years went by, his evolving thought on the *origins* of each individual's saving faith in Jesus Christ caused quite a stir, and his line of thought can still be seen today among many evangelical Christians. So, for those who take the Bible as the inspired Word of God, where *does* the decision of faith come from? What was Melanchthon's answer at the beginning of his life? What was he teaching by the end, and what brought him from one position to the other? As we trace the evolution of Melanchthon's thought on free will, we will get a glimpse not only of one of the great issues of sixteenth-century theology, but also of an ongoing debate within the modern evangelical mind—for the Bible of the sixteenth century is essentially the same as the Bible of the twenty-first century, and whether or not one believes it personally, it continues to exert a strong influence on modern society—if not so much in western Europe anymore, then certainly still in North America, and, increasingly, in Asia, Africa, and South America.

PHILIPP MELANCHTHON

In the introduction to his biography of Melanchthon, Heinz Scheible affirms that the question of free will is perhaps the central problem in the life,

---

[1] The full inscription reads as follows: 'Corpore parvus erat sed maximus arte philippus, Quam bene Germanis sic Philo mela fuit.' For a photo, see Diarmaid MacCulloch, *The Reformation* (New York: Viking, 2004), 137.
[2] The phrase associated with this formulation is 'forensic justification'.

thought, and faith of Melanchthon[3]—a man who was not just a private individual, but a figure of continuing significance. Melanchthon was the codifier of Lutheran theology (in the *Loci communes, or Commonplaces*), the author of its most famous confession (the *Augsburg Confession*), and the chief educator, the *Preceptor Germaniae,* of a whole generation of the Lutheran church, and of Germany more widely. He was a humanist without parallel (except perhaps in the great Erasmus), for he was a master of ancient languages, rhetoric, dialectics, and the writings of Greek and Roman antiquity. He also read widely in many other disciplines. With Luther, he was one of the founders (or revivers) of evangelical Protestant and Augustinian doctrine. Scheible comments, 'That we so often name Luther and Melanchthon in the same breath indicates the great debt we owe to both for shaping their age—a fact no one disputes.'[4] Yet Melanchthon should not be viewed merely as Luther's sidekick. Melanchthon is significant in his own right, and the present study will show his independence from Luther. As Euan Cameron remarks, one historical distortion is that 'Melanchthon is too often judged by whether he was a "good" or "faithful" follower of Luther. . . . Yet Melanchthon aspired to be a scriptural Christian, not a "Lutheran". . . . His theological legacy deserves to be evaluated on its own terms, as much as that of say, Calvin or Zwingli.'[5] In total, Melanchthon represents a vital link in the history of Christian theology, and his teachings on salvation have helped shape Protestant orthodoxy and identity, most substantially through the *Augsburg Confession* and the *Loci communes.*

MELANCHTHON'S CHANGING THOUGHT ON SALVATION

Melanchthon's teachings on salvation did not remain consistent over the course of his theological career (from 1519 to his death in 1560), particularly in relation to the question of who is saved, and how that salvation is appropriated. Peter Fraenkel writes, 'There can be little doubt that Melanchthon's views evolved considerably on some points, primarily on the question of Free Will.'[6] Early in his career, Melanchthon spoke about the total determination

---

[3] *Melanchthon: Eine Biographie* (Munich: C. H. Beck, 1997), 10.

[4] Scheible, 'Luther and Melanchthon', *Lutheran Quarterly* 4 (1990), 317.

[5] 'Philipp Melanchthon: Image and Substance', *JEH* 48 (1997), 706, cf. 722. See also Robert Kolb, *Bound Choice, Election, and Wittenberg Theological Method* (Grand Rapids: Eerdmans, 2005), 71.

[6] Peter Fraenkel, *Testimonia Patrum: The Function of the Patristic Argument in the Theology of Philip Melanchthon* (Geneva: Droz, 1961), 24. For a contrasting position, see Scheible, 'Luther and Melanchthon', 324.

of God, and how God, before all time, chose who would be saved, apart from anything the individual human being had ever said, done, or believed. However, by the end of his career, Melanchthon still taught that God's role in salvation was imperative (both in his saving work in Christ, and later, through the Word and Holy Spirit in bringing the message to the individual), but that salvation could be accepted or rejected by a free choice of the human will. No longer did God determine who would be saved, but now all individuals had to choose for themselves.[7]

The question of who is saved, and how a saving faith arises in that individual, is a central concern of Christian doctrine. Is the human will free, or is it bound? Did God choose me, or was I free to choose *him*? The aim of this book is to trace the evolution of Melanchthon's thought on this question, noting both how his teaching changed and seeking to explain why. This endeavour has value both for the history of ideas, and for a better understanding of the roots and development of Protestantism. In the sixteenth century, the question of the will's role in conversion was an issue of central importance—Luther viewed it as the key to his theology, Erasmus chose it as the one issue on which to attack Luther, and Calvin also saw it as a vital aspect of Christian theology. Melanchthon, in finding a new position on the freedom of the will, set himself apart from Luther, Erasmus, and Calvin, and established a uniquely Protestant conception of free will—*evangelical* free will.

FRAMING THE QUESTION

A study of the nature and freedom of the human will requires careful definition and limitation in order to remain manageable. One can speak of free will[8]

---

[7] Michael Rogness is in the distinct minority in arguing that Melanchthon's soteriology (especially regarding the origins of faith) at the end of his life remained essentially unchanged from his early position. See his *Philip Melanchthon: Reformer Without Honor* (Minneapolis: Augsburg, 1969), esp. pp. 126–8, on 'the synergistic controversy'. I will return to conversation with Rogness later in this volume. Similarly, Kolb, in *Bound Choice* (e.g. p. 101), sees Melanchthon, even at the end of his life, as holding in tension God's total responsibility for salvation with human total responsibility for responding to God's Word. I disagree with Kolb's assessment, and will seek to demonstrate in this book how Melanchthon *resolved* that tension through a doctrinal formulation I call evangelical free will.

[8] In sixteenth-century Latin-language discussions on free will, two distinct yet related words frequently crop up: *arbitrium* and *voluntas*. As Richard Müller writes, 'The will [*voluntas*] is the faculty that chooses; *arbitrium* is the capacity of will to make a choice or decision' (p. 330). See his in-depth discussions under his entries on *liberum arbitrium* and *voluntas* in his *Dictionary of Latin and Greek Theological Terms: Drawn Principally from Protestant Scholastic Theology* (Grand Rapids: Baker/Paternoster, 1985). Accordingly, throughout this book, I have chosen to translate *voluntas* as 'will', and *arbitrium* as 'choice'.

in three separate though interrelated spheres within Christian doctrine—contingency, conversion, and good works. First, one can think of the freedom of the will in a philosophical sense, dealing with every action in the universe. Does God determine all events, from the falling of a particular leaf from a particular tree at a particular moment, to the fall of Constantinople? Does genuine contingency exist in the course of human (and heavenly) events? Second, one can speak of free will in a very narrowly defined theological sense, relating specifically to the doctrine of justification. How does one receive salvation? Is it a gift from God, or an independent choice of the individual? Is it somehow both? Third, one can speak of free will in relation to the works of Christians following the acquisition of faith. How is the will involved in doing good works? What role does the Holy Spirit play?

To cover all three of these major aspects of the question of the freedom of the will would be a task too large for a single volume. My present aim, therefore, is to focus on the second area of free will—that is, the role of the will as specifically related to justification. It will be necessary at times to mention Melanchthon's thought on the other two areas of free will (contingency and good works), but discussions in these areas will be utilized solely for the purpose of aiding in the main task—understanding the evolution of Melanchthon's thought on the role of the will in justification. This is a distinctively *theological* study, which will focus heavily on Melanchthon's theological writings. Full treatments of contingency or the relationship of will and works deserve separate studies in their own right, and some of these works would more appropriately belong within the realm of *philosophy*, as opposed to my distinctively *theological* focus.[9]

METHOD

The present study is a systematic, chronological exploration of Philipp Melanchthon's doctrinal journey on the origins of faith, as represented in his major theological works and personal correspondence. No other study of

[9] For a philosophical approach, see H. Gerhards, 'Die Entwicklung des Problems der Willensfreiheit bei Philipp Melanchthon', dissertation (Rheinischen Friedrich Wilhelms-Universität, 1955). See also Wolfgang Matz, *Der befreite Mensch: Die Willenslehre in der Theologie Philipp Melanchthons* (Göttingen: Vandenhoeck & Ruprecht, 2001). For an approach that focuses on Melanchthon's view of works, see Timothy J. Wengert, *Law and Gospel: Philip Melanchthon's Debate with John Agricola of Eisleben over Poenitentia* (Carlisle: Paternoster, 1997). See also Carl E. Maxcey, *Bona Opera: A Study in the Development of the Doctrine in Philip Melanchthon* (Nieuwkoop: B. de Graaf, 1980).

which I am aware has taken this tack.[10] Helmut Gerhards' dissertation takes a self-consciously *philosophical* approach (the thesis was tendered within the Faculty of Philosophy), and his main concern is contingency, rather than free will in relation to justification.[11] Hartmut Günther's study takes a more theological approach than Gerhards', meaning that he focuses on Melanchthon's doctrine of the will in justification. However, Günther puts a heavy emphasis on Melanchthon's role in the debate on free will between Luther and Erasmus, to the point of paying little attention to a thorough examination of the internal dynamic of Melanchthon's own theology and how his presuppositions drove the shifts in his thought as much as (or perhaps more than) external stimuli. Further, Günther spends little time working on Melanchthon's thought between 1535 and 1560, while the present study takes into account Melanchthon's theological works and controversies during this period. My work builds upon and expands Günther's contribution (but dissents from his conclusions). Within the English-language literature on Melanchthon, Timothy Wengert is currently one of the most prolific writers (along with Robert Kolb). Wengert's book on Melanchthon's view of free will is important, but it only deals with a single work: Melanchthon's *Scholia in Epistolam Pauli ad Colossenses*. Wolfgang Matz's German-language work does overlap with the present study, but he, like Gerhards, often focuses strongly on philosophical writings such as the various versions of *De anima*, while the present work will concentrate on the theological writings. Further, Matz concentrates more on the freedom of the will in doing good works, rather than on the will's role in conversion. Finally, Kolb examines Melanchthon's changing thought in a number of sections, but is more concerned with telling a broader story.

ARGUMENT

In a survey of the literature on Melanchthon on the will, one finds in the mid-nineteenth century that Melanchthon scholars were reluctant to draw a distinction between Luther and Melanchthon. Writers such as Friedrich Galle, Herrlinger, and Heinrich Heppe tended to gloss over the differences

---

[10] For comparable studies, see Gerhards; Hartmut Oskar Günther, 'Die Entwicklung der Willenslehre Melanchthons in der Auseinandersetzung mit Luther und Erasmus', dissertation (Friedrich-Alexander Universität, 1963); Wengert, *Human Freedom, Christian Righteousness: Philip Melanchthon's Exegetical Dispute with Erasmus of Rotterdam* (New York: Oxford University Press, 1998); Matz; and Kolb, *Bound Choice.*
[11] Gerhards, 9.

between the two. At the beginning of the twentieth century, however, scholars began to pay more attention to Melanchthon's unique position on the will in relation to Luther. In 1912, Otto Ritschl highlighted the differences between the two men, but opined that Melanchthon was content to acquiesce to Luther. In the 1920s, Reinhold Seeberg and Karl Holl argued that Melanchthon had distorted and harmed Luther's view of justification.[12] Similarly, in 1931, Hans Engelland maintained that it was impossible to bring the theologies of Luther and Melanchthon into harmony.[13] By the mid-1930s, the consensus of the Reformation scholars already mentioned was that Melanchthon deviated from Luther in the nature of the will and justification, and these writers seemed content to pursue the subject no further. However, even if one prefers Luther's view of justification and the will over his younger colleague's, Melanchthon's position remains important to understand, for it represents an implicit criticism of Luther's theology. Melanchthon began with Luther's position, and eventually moved to something else. By following the journey, one may get a good view of the internal dynamics of Luther's doctrine, in addition to tracing one man's struggle with one of the most ancient and important questions of Christian doctrine.

In the mid-twentieth century, Melanchthon scholarship tailed off in the face of the consensus that Melanchthon had deviated from Luther. Then, in the second half of the century (and moving into the twenty-first) a few individuals began to explore the question of how Melanchthon differed from Luther, and why. The most important studies have already been mentioned, and I have shown how they differ in approach from the present work. However, these writers, as well as many others, have put forth ideas as to why Melanchthon's view on the will changed. It will be helpful to survey these

[12] I have begun the survey of the literature here with the nineteenth century. However, the reader should be aware that the relationship between Melanchthon's doctrine of the will and Luther's has been an issue among Lutherans since the sixteenth century. Bearing this in mind, it should be noted that the opinion of Seeberg and others that Melanchthon distorted and harmed Luther's view of justification is not a new position, but rather harks back to an opinion first proffered in the 1500s.

[13] See Gerhards' good survey of the literature of the nineteenth and early twentieth centuries on Melanchthon's view of the will, pp. 2–6. Friedrich Galle, *Versuch einer Charakteristik Melanchthons als Theologen und einer Entwicklung seines Lehrbegriffs* (Halle: Johann Friedrich Lippert, 1840). Herrlinger (first name not given), *Die Theologie Melanchthons in ihrer geschichtlichen Entwicklung und im Zusammenhange mit der Lehrgeschichte und Kulturbewegung der Reformation* (Gotha: Friedrich Andreas Perthes, 1897). Heinrich Heppe, *Dogmatik des deutschen Protestantismus im 16. Jahrhundert* (Gotha: F. A. Perthes, 1857). Otto Ritschl, 'Die Entwicklung der Rechtfertigungslehre Melanchthons bis zum Jahr 1527', *Theologische Studien und Kritiken* 85 (1912). Reinhold Seeberg, *Lehrbuch der Dogmengeschichte*, 4 vols. (Erlangen: A. Deichert, 1920). Karl Holl, *Gesammelte Aufsätze zur Kirchengeschichte*, 3 vols. (Tübingen: J. C. B. Mohr, 1928). Hans Engelland, *Melanchthon, Glauben und Handeln* (Munich: C. Kaiser, 1931).

theories in order to develop a useful context in which to anchor my own conclusions.

Convinced by Erasmus

A common theory in the literature about Melanchthon's changing thought on free will is that he simply found himself persuaded by the arguments of Erasmus in *De libero arbitrio* διατριβή *sive collatio* (1524),[14] and the *Hyperaspistes diatribae adversus servum arbitrium Martini Lutheri* (1526).[15] Friedrich Loofs and Karl Zickendraht came to this conclusion early in the twentieth century.[16] More recently, C. P. Williams advocates this theory, arguing, 'On predestination and free will [Melanchthon] leaned more towards Erasmus.'[17] Oswald Bayer concurs.[18] Robert Stupperich, also, consistently puts forward the same idea in clear language.[19] Wilhelm Maurer and J. A. O. Preus also advance the idea that Melanchthon was persuaded by Erasmus on the doctrine of the will, though with the addition that in the 1520s Melanchthon's humanism re-emerged and made him more amenable to Erasmus' ideas. In relation to this idea, Maurer and Preus represent a bridge to the next major school of thought in Melanchthon literature on why Philipp's thought on free will changed.[20]

---

[14] LCC 17.35–97. The original Latin can be found in EAS 4.1–195, which also contains a parallel German translation.

[15] EAS 4.197–675 (Book I). The title for Luther's work, *De servo arbitrio*, most likely derived from Augustine, who, in his controversy with Julian of Eclanum, wrote, 'Sed vos festinatis, et praesumptionem vestram festinando praecipitatis. Hic enim vultis hominem perfici, atque utinam Dei dono, et non libero, vel potius servo propriae voluntatis arbitrio.' *Contra Iulianum haeresis Pelagianae defensorem* II.viii.23. PL 44.689. See Alister E. McGrath, *Iustitia Dei: A History of the Christian Doctrine of Justification*, 2nd edn. (Cambridge: Cambridge University Press, 1998), 25. For more on Augustine's use of the phrase *servum arbitrium*, see Harry J. McSorley, *Luther: Right or Wrong? An Ecumenical-Theological Study of Luther's Major Work, The Bondage of the Will* (New York: Newman Press, 1969), 90–3.

[16] Friedrich Loofs, *Leitfaden zum Studium der Dogmengeschichte* (Halle: Max Niemeyer, 1906), 837–8. Karl Zickendraht, *Der Streit zwischen Erasmus und Luther über die Willensfreiheit* (Leipzig: J. C. Hinrichs, 1909), 177.

[17] C. P. Williams, 'Melanchthon, Philip', in *New Dictionary of Theology*, ed. Sinclair B. Ferguson et al. (Leicester: Inter-Varsity Press, 1988), 419.

[18] Oswald Bayer, 'Freedom? The Anthropological Concepts in Luther and Melanchthon Compared', *Harvard Theological Review* 91 (1998), 380.

[19] e.g. in *Der Humanismus und die Wiedervereinigung der Konfessionen* (Leipzig: M. Heinsius, 1936), 21. See also his *Melanchthon*, trans. Robert H. Fisher (London: Lutterworth Press, 1965), 67.

[20] Wilhelm Maurer, *Der junge Melanchthon: zwischen Humanismus und Reformation*, 2 vols. (Göttingen: Vandenhoeck & Ruprecht, 1967–9). See esp. 1.5. See also Maurer, 'Melanchthons Anteil am Streit zwischen Luther und Erasmus', *ARG* 49 (1958), 89–114, esp. p. 101. Cf. J. A. O. Preus, Introduction to Philipp Melanchthon, *Loci Communes 1543 Philip Melanchthon*, trans. J. A. O. Preus (St Louis: Concordia, 1992), 11.

The Influence of Philosophy

The second major argument in the literature is not necessarily mutually exclusive of the one just mentioned. This second argument (to which Maurer and Preus hinted) is that Melanchthon's humanism from his early days (before 1518) resurfaced, causing him to re-evaluate his theology. In other words, from the 1520s onwards, Melanchthon returned to a philosophically informed theology to which he had (presumably) subscribed before he met Luther. Adolf Sperl, Wilhelm Neuser, J. R. Schneider, Gerhards, E. P. Meijering, Bengt Hägglund, Günther, Alfons Brüls, and Oliver Olson all support this thesis.[21] Olson, in the best imitation of a tabloid headline, writes, '[Melanchthon] was tampering not just with the method, but also the *content* of theology. Was Melanchthon thus making a pact with Satan?'[22] Here, instead of Erasmus, it was metaphysical Aristotelian philosophy incorporated into theology that caused Melanchthon's shift. A variation of this argument can be found in Hans Engelland and J. Noryskiwicz, both of whom maintain that Melanchthon eventually came to accept some of the arguments of scholastic theology,[23] and hence returned to a Catholic position on free will.

The Internal Dynamic of Melanchthon's Own Theology

A third and weaker strand in the literature involves the idea that Melanchthon changed his mind on free will independently of humanism, scholasticism, philosophy, or Erasmus. The internal dynamic of his own theological system, when thought through to its logical conclusions, was the primary motivating factor in Melanchthon's shifting thought on free will. Clyde Manschreck takes

---

[21] Adolf Sperl, *Melanchthon zwischen Humanismus und Reformation* (Munich: Chr. Kaiser Verlag, 1959), 107. Wilhelm Neuser, *Der Ansatz der Theologie Philipp Melanchthons* (Neukirchen Kr. Moers: Verlag der Buchhandlung des Erziehungsvereins, 1957), 155–9. John R. Schneider, *Philip Melanchthon's Rhetorical Construal of Biblical Authority: Oratio Sacra* (Lewiston, NY: Mellen, 1990), 217. Gerhards, 11. E. P. Meijering, *Melanchthon and Patristic Thought: The Doctrines of Christ and Grace, the Trinity, and the Creation* (Leiden: E. J. Brill, 1983), 138. Bengt Hägglund, *De homine: människouppfattningen i äldre luthersk tradition* (Lund: C. W. K. Gleerup, 1959), 209. Günther, 120. Alfons Brüls, *Die Entwicklung der Gotteslehre beim jungen Melanchthon, 1518–1535, Untersuchungen zur Kirchengeschichte* (Bielefeld: Luther-Verlag, 1975), 33.

[22] Oliver K. Olson, *Matthias Flacius and the Survival of Luther's Reform* (Wiesbaden: Harassowitz, 2002), 44.

[23] Engelland, Introduction to *Melanchthon on Christian Doctrine: 1555 Loci Communes*, ed. Clyde L. Manschreck (New York: Oxford University Press, 1982), xxvi. J. Noryskiewicz, 'Melanchthons ethische Prinzipienlehre und ihr Verhältnis zur Moral der Scholastik', dissertation (Münster, 1904).

this position: 'Philip changed his early views [on free will] because he saw the moral and psychological dangers of extreme predestinarianism, and because he had seen the actual experiences of anxiety and response of Christians in conversion. Yet he did not wish to detract from the Holy Spirit or from the Word, nor to imply works righteousness.'[24] Similarly, Diarmaid MacCulloch has attributed Melanchthon's shift on free will to a withdrawal from the logic of double predestination, combined with a reaction to antinomianism, especially as observed at Wittenberg in 1521–2.[25] Kolb takes a similar position, citing Melanchthon's desire to affirm genuine human responsibility, and to absolve God of blame for evil.[26] Wengert, also, assumes that Melanchthon's thought changed from within, based on an incorporation of Luther's political theology into the realm of soteriology.[27]

Melanchthon's Internal Dynamic, Leading to Evangelical Free Will

In this book, I will argue against the popular view in the literature that Melanchthon simply went over to Erasmus. Melanchthon always considered himself to be on Luther's side, and in his personal correspondence, Melanchthon was clear in his denunciation of Erasmus' writings on the will. Likewise, I will also argue against the second popular view—that is, that Melanchthon's early humanism resurfaced in the late 1520s, and led him to change his theology. Melanchthon's works clearly show his desire to separate philosophy from theology, even in the late 1520s and in the 1530s. Melanchthon valued the ideas of humanism (i.e. clarity, eloquence of expression, and going back to the original sources), but he always strove to keep philosophical metaphysics separate from theology, for the philosophy of the ancients, no matter how eloquently expressed, was derived from fallen human reason alone. Theology properly found its origins in the authority and revelation of God himself. The only way in which humanism and philosophy might have affected Melanchthon's theology would have been through grammar, rhetoric, and dialectics. Melanchthon viewed Scripture as divine rhetoric (as J. R. Schneider rightly argues[28]), and hence it was to be interpreted according to the ancient rules of

---

[24] Clyde L. Manschreck, *Melanchthon: The Quiet Reformer* (New York: Abingdon Press, 1958), 301.

[25] *The Reformation*, 338, 340.

[26] See, for example, *Bound Choice*, 97–102.

[27] Wengert, *Human Freedom, Christian Righteousness*. This argument can be found throughout the book, but see especially chapters 6 and 7.

[28] This is his thesis in *Oratio sacra*.

rhetoric, which came from Aristotle. However, this argument from grammar, rhetoric, and dialectics could not fully explain Melanchthon's shifting thought on free will, and hence can only function as an ancillary or contributory factor.

Indeed, Manschreck, MacCulloch, Kolb, and Wengert are on the right track in their explanations of the evolution of Melanchthon's thought on free will, but each only argues for a part of the case, and none of them gives the overall subject the full treatment it deserves. In *The Quiet Reformer*, Manschreck maintains (without evidence) that Melanchthon's thought on free will changed as a result of his meditations upon the negative implications of extreme predestinarianism.[29] MacCulloch makes his point in passing, in the midst of a work painting the broad sweep of the Reformation over a vast tableau of years and nations. Kolb, while accurately identifying a number of the internal motivating factors of Melanchthon's shift, has limited space to focus on Melanchthon, and also presents Philipp's final position as an antinomy of divine responsibility *and* human responsibility,[30] which (while attractive to this author, as a pastor and believer) leaves out some important nuances of Melanchthon's mature thought. Wengert, basing his ideas on Melanchthon's *Scholia in Epistolam Pauli ad Colossenses* in its several editions, maintains that Melanchthon's thought on free will evolved due to an incorporation of Luther's two-kingdoms theology into his soteriology. The actual case is more complex than either Manschreck or Wengert assumes. The issue of predestination (or more accurately, reprobation) did play a significant role in Melanchthon's changing thought, but so did the problem of evil, the question of the origins of sin, and Melanchthon's exegetical methods. Luther's two-kingdoms theology did factor into how Melanchthon changed his views of the governance of God in the 1520s, yet so did Melanchthon's own thoughts on natural law and the problems of antinomianism. Manschreck and Wengert each present a partial solution to the reasons for why Melanchthon evolved on his understanding of free will, and each makes his comments within works dedicated to other purposes (Manschreck's ideas are put forth in passing in a biography of Melanchthon, and Wengert's arguments come in a book specifically focusing on Melanchthon's view of free will in his *Scholia in Epistolam Pauli ad Colossenses*). In the present work, I will take the thoughts of Manschreck, MacCulloch, Kolb, and Wengert into account, add the problems of theodicy and a natural law ethical imperative, consider the role of rhetoric and dialectics in Melanchthon's argumentation, and examine in detail the

---

[29] Manschreck, *The Quiet Reformer*, 301.
[30] e.g. *Bound Choice*, p. 101. Kolb frequently describes Melanchthon's mature thought as juxtaposing 'God's total responsibility and human total responsibility'.

combination and catalization of all these factors systematically and chrono-
logically throughout Melanchthon's major theological writings and correspondence over the course of his entire theological career. This project is
intended as an original endeavour which offers a more complete explanation
of the development of Melanchthon's thought on free will than has previously
been tendered. Hopefully, the final result will be a clear portrait of Melanchthon's movement within the Lutheran theology of his time towards a new,
distinctively Protestant, evangelical doctrine of free will.

2

Doctrinal Prologue

INTRODUCTION

In order to set the stage for a careful examination of Melanchthon's doctrinal journey on the origins of faith, it is worth investigating some of the major strands of thought which came down to Melanchthon. Of course, such a topic in its entirety is much too vast suitably to be investigated in a single chapter. Nevertheless, in this chapter, I will focus on some of the greater lights of the ages, to put Melanchthon's doctrines into the context of an ongoing historical conversation, to better understand the origins of his thought and how he used, altered, or discarded the teachings of those before him. Beginning with Augustine, we shall proceed to Peter Lombard, Thomas Aquinas, Duns Scotus, William of Ockham, Gregory of Rimini, Gabriel Biel, Johann von Staupitz, and finally, Erasmus, through whom we shall enter into the sixteenth century, and make our approach in the following chapter to Luther and Melanchthon.

AUGUSTINE: 354–430

Second only to the Bible, Luther and Melanchthon routinely appealed to the writings of Augustine.[1] As influential as Augustine's theology has proved to be throughout the course of Christian history, his ideas did not spring into place fully formed. Over time, his thought grew and evolved. In the end, it was his mature, fully developed theology that would have the greatest impact on subsequent generations, and as a result, this later theology will be the primary concern of the present brief examination.

---

[1] The most important biography of Augustine remains Peter Brown's *Augustine of Hippo* (London: Faber & Faber, 1967). But see also Carol Harrison, *Rethinking Augustine's Early Theology: An Argument for Continuity* (Oxford: Oxford University Press, 2006), and Serge Lancel, *Saint Augustine*, trans. Antonia Nevill (London: SCM Press, 2002).

While Augustine's later theology (especially in controversy with the Pela
gians) was the most important for understanding his views on the will's role
in justification, the dispute with the Manicheans earlier in his career also had
some bearing on his eventual formation of his doctrine of the will. The
Manicheans insisted that all things occurred necessarily, that is, that all things
were determined. Augustine abhorred this teaching (to which he had in his
youth adhered), for it made God responsible for sin and evil. Consequently,
Augustine vigorously opposed the Manicheans in works such as *De libero* ↙
arbitrio.[2] Later in life, when he revisited this work in his *Retractiones*, Augustine wrote, 'We took up this discussion in order to refute those who deny that
the origin of evil lies in the free choice of the will and therefore contend that
we should blame evil on God, the Creator of all natures.'[3] People genuinely
did have free will in what they did. Even though God foreknew what choices
people would make, that foreknowledge did not infringe upon the genuine
freedom of those human actions.[4] In fact, God's foreknowledge of future
events had no more effect on them than does memory upon past events.[5] God
had given people free will, meaning they could live good or bad lives, and they
could be judged accordingly.[6] Augustine thus affirmed what I have defined in
my introduction as the free will of contingency, and on this position he
remained firm and unchanging throughout his life.

In the beginning, taught Augustine, Adam and Eve were created with
original righteousness. They were without sin. The full range of both good

[2] This opposition to determinism was the main point of Augustine's anti-Manichean polemic, *De libero arbitrio*. PL 32.1221–1310. CChr 29.205–321. This work is also available in English
translation: *On Free Choice of the Will*, trans. Thomas Williams (Indianapolis: Hackett, 1993).
Another English translation can be found in LCC 6.102–217. Other major anti-Manichean
writings included *De moribus ecclesiae Catholicae et de moribus Manichaeorum* (PL 32.1309–78),
De Genesi contra Manichaeos (PL 34.173–220), *De duabus animabus contra Manichaeos* (CSEL
25.51–80, PL 42.93–112), *Contra Adimandum Manichaei discipulum* (CSEL 25.115–90,
PL 42.129–72), *Contra epistolam Manichaei quam vocant Fundamenti* (CSEL 25.193–248,
PL 42.173–206), *Contra Faustum Manichaeum* (CSEL 25.251–797, PL 42.207–518), *De actis
cum Felice Manichaeo* (CSEL 25.801–52, PL 42.519–52), *De natura boni contra Manichaeos*
(CSEL 25.855–89, PL 42.552–72, LCC 6.324–38), and *Contra Secundinum Manichaeum* (CSEL
25.905–47, PL 42.577–602).
[3] Trans. Williams, 124. *Retractiones* I.ix.2. CChr 57.23.19–21. Eugene TeSelle adds, 'The
heritage of sin is the result of human freedom, not of divine ordering. Although God by some
device could have prevented the fall of angels and men, Augustine thinks, he permitted it out of
respect for creaturely freedom and for the sake of the good that could be brought out of it.'
Augustine the Theologian (New York: Herder and Herder, 1970), 319.
[4] *De libero arbitrio* III.3.6–4.10. *De civitate Dei* V.8–10. See also TeSelle, 314.
[5] *De civitate Dei* V.9. PL 41.148–52. *De libero arbitrio* III.3.6–8. PL 32.1273–5. *In Joannis
Evangelium tractatus CXXIV* 53.4. PL 35.1776. See also Eugène Portalié, *A Guide to the Thought
of Saint Augustine*, trans. Ralph J. Bastian (London: Burns & Oates, 1960), 180.
[6] *De spiritu et littera*. CSEL 60.159.12–13; 60.216.20–1.

and evil choices lay open before them,[7] for God desired that mankind serve him freely, rather than under compulsion.[8] Of course, this glorious freedom was entirely predicated on God's grace: his operating (or prevenient) grace established human natural powers in a state of integrity; and God's cooperating (or subsequent) grace came into play when righteous human beings freely grasped his aid.[9] Then, when Adam and Eve transgressed, God removed both operating and cooperating grace. Consequently, human free choices were reduced from both good *and* evil to being exclusively evil.[10] The will came into captivity to wickedness, and while it still had freedom, it was only free to commit different varieties of sin.[11] Further, because Adam and Eve were the progenitors of the entire human race, all humanity became subject to the same sinful bent as they.[12] This was original sin. All human beings were now inevitably sinners,[13] both by imputation through Adam, and also through each individual making creative, free choices to embrace sin in many personalized, unique ways.

This stain of original sin cut off freely acting, wicked humans from relationship with the holy God. This relationship, moreover, could not be rectified by fallen human beings, because, free though they were, the attitudes and actions necessary for union with God now lay beyond the scope of the free choices available to people. Augustine wrote, 'Human beings cannot pick themselves up voluntarily—that is, by their own free choice—as they fell voluntarily.'[14] Also, 'Without God's help we cannot by

---

[7] *Enchiridion de fide, spe, et charitate ad Laurentium,* cvii. PL 40.282. TeSelle's translation (p. 315): 'Man was created upright, and in such a way that he could remain in that rectitude—though not without divine aid—but could go astray from his own choice.'

[8] *De vera religione,* 14. PL 34.133–4. See Norman L. Geisler, ed., *What Augustine Says* (Grand Rapids: Baker, 1982), 153. For an English translation, see J. H. S. Burleigh, ed. and trans., *Augustine: Earlier Writings* (Philadelphia: Westminster, 1953).

[9] TeSelle, 315–16.

[10] *Ad Simplicianum de diversis quaestionibus* I.ii.21. CChr 44.53.740–2. PL 40.126. *Sermones* 156.11–12. PL 38.856. The soul lost its mastery over the body: *De civitate Dei* XIII.13. Geisler, ed., 121. *Enchiridion* cvi. PL 40.281–2. Geisler, ed., 160.

[11] *Contra duas epistolas Pelagianorum* II.v.9. *De correptione et gratiae* II.xxxi. *Enchiridion* xxx. PL 40.246–7. Geisler, ed., 160. *De civitate Dei* XV.21. For a broader discussion of this subject, see Alister E. McGrath, *Iustitia Dei,* 23–8. See also McGrath, *Christian Theology: An Introduction,* 2nd edn. (Oxford: Blackwell, 1998), 427: 'Free will really does exist; it is, however distorted by sin.'

[12] *Confessions* 5.9. *De natura et gratia contra Pelagium* 3, 5. *Epistolae* 143.6; 166.iii.7. *De peccatorum meritis et remissione et de baptismo parvulorum* I.xiii. *De civitate Dei* XIV.1; XIII.14; XXII.22.

[13] 'No one has anything of himself except deceit and sin.' Augustine, *In Joannis Evangelium tractatus CXXIV* 5.1. PL 35.1414. Translation by Portalié, 195.

[14] Trans. Williams, 129. *Retractiones* I.ix.6. CChr 57.29.176–7.

free will overcome the temptations of this life.'[15] Human beings could freely choose to do many things, but achieving their own justification in the sight of the holy God was not one of them. Left to their own devices, all were doomed to hell. For a sinner to be saved, the grace of God was absolutely necessary.

Augustine defined grace as 'an internal and secret power, wonderful and ineffable',[16] by which God operated in people's hearts.[17] Grace was the free gift of God,[18] and it was the means by which he saved people. McGrath summarizes: 'Augustine held "grace" to be the unmerited or undeserved gift of God, by which God voluntarily breaks the hold of sin upon humanity. Redemption is possible only as a divine gift. It is not something which we can achieve ourselves, but is something which has to be done for us. Augustine thus emphasizes that the resources of salvation are located outside of humanity, in God himself. It is God who initiates the process of salvation, not men or women.'[19] *God* initiated salvation, and not human beings.[20] Humans had free will, but for them to be saved, God had to act.

When God decided to save an individual he first used prevenient (literally, 'coming-before') grace to stir that person's heart. Through his prevenient grace, God began to work in the souls and wills of those whom he had decided to save.[21] Following his prevenient grace inevitably came God's *operative* grace. That is, God directly caused the individual to have faith in him. As Kelly notes, 'Even the initial motions of faith are inspired in our hearts by Him.'[22] Further, 'Augustine acknowledges that God's omnipotent will, operating on our wills by grace, is irresistible.'[23] Faith

---

[15] Trans. J. N. D. Kelly, *Early Christian Doctrines* (London: Adam & Charles Black, 1977), 366. *Enarrationes in Psalmos* 89.4. PL 37.1142.

[16] *De gratia Christi et de peccato originali contra Pelagium et Coelestium* 25. PL 44.373–4. See also Kelly, 366; Geisler, ed., 171.

[17] Ibid.

[18] 'Gratuita Dei gratia sunt'. *Epistola 186 ad Paulinum*. PL 33.325.

[19] McGrath, *Christian Theology*, 22.

[20] As TeSelle says (p. 179), 'Man receives from God, then, both the act of willing and the power to do what is willed.' *Ad Simplicianus* q. II.10, 12. Further, God gave his grace solely for his own reasons, without consideration for (always insufficient) human merit. *De peccatorum meritis et remissione* I.21.29–22.32.

[21] *Enchiridion* xxxii. PL 40.247–8. LCC 7.337–412. *De natura et gratia ad Timasium et Jacobum: contra Pelagium* 35. PL 44.263–4.

[22] Kelly, 367. *Ad Simplicianum de diversis quaestionibus* I.ii.10. CChr 44.34–5. PL 40.116–17. *De gratia et libero arbitrio ad Valentinum et cum illo monachos* 29. PL 44.898.

[23] Kelly, 368. *De correptione et gratia ad eumdem Valentinum et cum illos monachos adrumetinos* 45. PL 44.943–4. Portalié, a Jesuit, shows concern to differentiate Augustine's doctrine of effective calling from the Reformed doctrine of irresistible grace (e.g. p. 179). He goes to great pains to show that Augustine's view of God's call is effective, though non-coercive—assuming that the Reformed doctrine is that God *is* coercive in his call. Yet, this is not necessarily the case, for a Reformed understanding of how God calls one to faith is actually quite congenial to Augustine's views, in that both agree that the decision of faith is inevitable for God's elect.

was a gift, given by God to the individual.[24] It did *not* originate in a person's free will.[25]

While faith did not originate in a person's will, faith operated *through* an individual's will. Augustine declared, 'And since, as I have said, all good things—the great, the intermediate, and the lowest goods—are from God, it follows that the right use of our free will, which is virtue and is included among the great goods, is also from God.'[26] Again, 'You must simply hold with unshaken faith that every good thing that you perceive or understand or in any way know is from God.'[27] Yet, Augustine taught that God does not work salvation in people as though they were stones or animals devoid of reason and will.[28] Rather, the effect of grace was to give a victorious delight (*victrix delectatio*) in the good.[29] For those to whom God chose to give faith, he would arrange and influence their lives and experiences to bring them to the point at which they would seize upon faith as a free choice of their wills.[30] God effectively *gave* faith as a gift by causing people to *choose* faith in him through their wills.[31] This choice of faith was inevitable, yet not coerced.[32]

Phil 2:13

---

[24] *Ad Simplicianum de diversis quaestionibus* I.ii.12. CChr 44.53.740–2.

[25] *Retractiones* I.ix.6.

[26] Trans. Williams, 129. *Retractiones* I.ix.6. PL 57.28–9.171–4.

[27] Trans. Williams, 127. *Retractiones* I.ix.4. PL 57.27.121–3.

[28] *De peccatorum meritis et remissione* II.5–6. TeSelle, 283.

[29] *De peccatorum meritis et remissione* II.17.27. TeSelle, 286. This is a theme that Staupitz would later emphasize (see the section on Staupitz below).

[30] *De correptione et gratia ad eumdem Valentinum et cum illos monachos adrumetinos* 45. PL 44.943–4. See also *Ad Simplicianum de diversis quaestionibus* I.ii.13. CChr 44.37–8. PL 40.118–19. *De spiritu et littera* 60. PL 44.240–1. Sometimes this is referred to as a 'congruous calling', in that God, in a non-coercive fashion, works in the life of the elect individual in order to lead her to faith through a series of events that will function congruently with her own inclinations and disposition, resulting in a *free* decision to put her faith in Jesus Christ. *Ad Simplicianus* q. II.13. Cf. TeSelle, 179.

[31] Kelly (p. 368) puts it like this: 'To be more explicit, God knows in advance under the influence of what motives this or that particular will will freely consent to what He proposes for it, and arranges things accordingly. Thus grace accommodates itself to each individual's situation and character, and Augustine can claim that, for all the power of grace, it rests with the recipient's will to accept or reject it.' TeSelle calls this *vocatio effectrix* (p. 179), and notes that Roman Catholic theologians often call this 'efficacious grace' (ibid.). He, too, gives a good summary (p. 179): 'The willing or not willing . . . is our own, but we cannot will anything at all unless something comes before the mind delighting and attracting the affections, and what will come before the mind is not always within our power, for it is something that "comes to us" . . . and is "presented" to the mind.' *Ad Simplicianus* q. II.21–2; cf. *De libero arbitrio* III.25, 74. Cf. TeSelle, 287: 'Therefore when he says that the consenting or not consenting is man's own, he cannot mean that man himself decides the issue with what the scholastics would call "freedom of exercise", the freedom to act or not to act, for the act of the will is evoked by the persuasive quality of the call, and this is something that does not lie in man's power.'

[32] Geisler, however, considers Augustine's view to be one of compulsion of the will, based on *Epistola* 185 *ad Bonifacium de correctione Donatistarum* 6.22–4. PL 33.802–4. Geisler, ed., 176–7. At completely the other end of the spectrum, Portalié notes that early in his career, Augustine

God *prepared* people for faith through his prevenient grace. Then he *caused* people to have faith through his operative grace. Subsequently, he *aided* people in willing and doing the good through cooperative grace. So when faith arose in an individual, it was the work of God.[33] Moreover, when faith arose, then the will was freed to will the good. From that point on, the individual could will to do good works, and God would supply cooperative grace to help the believer pursue a progressively more righteous life. Augustine summarized, 'But unless the will is liberated by grace from its bondage to sin [i.e. *given* faith] and is helped to overcome its vices, mortals cannot lead pious and righteous lives. And unless the divine grace by which the will is freed preceded the act of the will, it would not be grace at all. It would be given in accordance with the will's merits, whereas grace is given freely.'[34] Kelly comments, 'From this point of view grace heals and restores [a man's] free will, not so much enlarging his area of choice as substituting a system of good choices for evil ones.'[35] Once a person received grace, that person's will was then freed to seek the good,[36] and with God's cooperating grace, the believer could live a progressively more righteous life, thus growing in internal righteousness toward the perfection that was the end goal of justification. Hence, 'Grace, far from *abolishing* man's free will, actually *establishes* it.'[37]

In summary, Augustine believed that people continued to have free will, even after the Fall, but that the range of free choices was restricted entirely to sin. Humans could not save themselves, or freely turn to God. While people had many free choices open to them, repenting and desiring the good was not one of those options. God had to act first, effectively giving people faith in Jesus, *causing* them to believe by means of a non-coercive providential involvement in their lives uniquely tailored to each chosen individual's situation. After the will had thus been changed to desire the good, then God cooperated with the individual's free choices to seek the good, with the result that the person could cooperate with God in seeking his salvation from that point onwards. In every case, though, with every human being, God had to act first and creatively cause her to have faith.

---

actually wrote that 'The call to faith is a gratuitous gift of God, but the acceptance of faith is an act of human liberty alone.' *De diversis quaestionibus LXXXIII* 68.3. PL 40.71. Cf. *Retractiones* I.26. PL 32.628.

[33] *De correptione et gratia ad Valentinum* 14.45. PL 44.943–4. Cf. Portalié 192–3.

[34] Trans. Williams, 127. *Retractiones* I.ix.4. PL 57.26.96–100.

[35] Kelly, 368. *De gratia et libero arbitrio ad Valentinum et cum illo monachos* 31. PL 44.899–900. *De spiritu et littera* 52. PL 44.233–4.

[36] Hence, as Geisler (p. 164) summarizes, only the redeemed are truly free. *De civitate Dei* XIV.11. *De nuptiis et concupiscentia* 1.8. PL 44.418–19. *Enchiridion* xxx. PL 40.246–7.

[37] McGrath, *Iustitia Dei*, 26. *De spiritu et littera* xxx.52. CSEL 60.208.16–27.

Of course, not everyone came to faith, and so Augustine's strongly theo-centric view of the first stages of a person's Christian conversion implied a doctrine of predestination. Augustine did, in fact, affirm such a doctrine.[38] In the *Retractiones*, he wrote, 'The grace of God [is that] by which he so predestines his chosen people that he himself prepares the wills of those who are already using their free choice.'[39] Kelly writes, 'Since grace takes the initiative and apart from it all men form a *massa damnata*, it is for God to determine which shall receive grace and which shall not. This He has done, Augustine believed on the basis of Scripture, from all eternity.'[40] This was a strong view of the sovereignty of God, and it meant that salvation was a gift, rather than something to be earned. To this end, Augustine frequently cited 1 Corinthians 4.7: 'What do you have that you did not receive? And if you received it, why do you boast as if it were not a gift?'[41] So because of God's predestination,[42] and because of humanity's Fall and corruption by original sin, humans, while possessing some measure of free will, were not the ultimate arbiters of their own salvation. The will was created free, but its range of choice was now limited by a bondage to sin, and it was only through the unilateral action of God that the wills of the elect were moved such that they would freely desire and choose to have faith in him, thus beginning a transformational process leading to salvation.

PETER LOMBARD: *1095–1160*

The next to adorn our chorus of the glad
was the great Peter, who, like the poor widow,
offered to Holy Church all that he had.

[38] *Ad Simplicianum de diversis quaestionibus* I.ii.6. CChr 44.30–1. PL 40.114–15. Much has been written on Augustine's doctrine of predestination. For one example, see James Wetzel, 'Predestination, Pelagianism, and Foreknowledge', in Eleonore Stump and Norman Kretzmann, eds., *The Cambridge Companion to Augustine* (Cambridge: Cambridge University Press, 2001), 49–58. TeSelle notes (on pp. 177–8) that Augustine's mature position on predestination began to surface following his detailed study of Romans 9–11 in AD 394–6.
[39] Trans. Williams, 125. *Retractiones* I.ix.2. PL 57.23–4.24–6.
[40] Kelly, 368. *De correptione et gratia ad eumdem Valentinum et cum illos monachos adrume-tinos* 12–16. PL 44.923–5. *Enchiridion* xcvii–xcix. PL 40.277–8.
[41] e.g. *De praedestinatione sanctorum* IV.8. See TeSelle, 180–1. When it came to 1 Timothy 2.4 ('God wills all to be saved'), Augustine interpreted Paul's words in a non-universalistic fashion: (1) No one is saved except through the will of God; and (2) God has elected *some* out of *all ranks* within human society. TeSelle, 319–20.
[42] *Ad Simplicianum de diversis quaestionibus* I.ii.14–16. CChr 44.38–42. PL 40.119–21. *De civitate Dei* XV.1; XXI.24. PL 41.437, 41.736–7. See also MacCulloch, *The Reformation*, 106.

So wrote Dante Alighieri, in his *Divine Comedy*, where he depicted Peter Lombard in the Heaven of the Sun, the heaven of the theologians.[43] Dante's praise mirrored the received wisdom on Peter Lombard for more than four hundred years, from the twelfth to the sixteenth century.[44] Probably the most influential theologian since Augustine, Peter Lombard was not known so much for his doctrinal originality, but rather for his synthesis and documentation of the existing theological tradition in the mid-twelfth century. While Peter did write glosses on the Psalms and on the Pauline epistles,[45] his most influential work was the *Sententiae in IV libris distinctae*, completed in 1158 and commonly called *The Sentences*.[46] This work was 'a systematic treatment of theology, dealing in an orderly fashion with the main themes of Christian theology'.[47] Here Peter presented 'the whole of Christian doctrine in one brief volume on the basis of Scripture, the Fathers, and the Doctors, with speculation held in firm control'.[48] Peter marked the turning-point in western theology from a monastic to a scholastic style,[49] and by the thirteenth century, praise of the Lombard had become a rote complimentary boiler-plate.[50] For the next four hundred years, *The Sentences* served as the master textbook for advanced theological training.[51] It was required reading for serious theologians, and 'all the great teachers of the thirteenth to the fifteenth centuries—and many others not so great—commented on *The Sentences* of Peter Lombard'.[52] Philipp Melanchthon would certainly have come across *The Sentences* during his theological training.[53]

---

[43] *Paradiso*, 10.106–8, trans. John Ciardi (New York: W. W. Norton, 1954), 453.

[44] After the sixteenth century, Protestants lost interest in Peter because they felt he represented erroneous scholastic thinking, while Roman Catholics began to favour Thomas Aquinas instead. See Justo L. González, *A History of Christian Thought*, vol. 2 (San Francisco: Harper & Row, 1984), 180; Marcia L. Colish, *Peter Lombard* (Leiden: E. J. Brill, 1994), 4–5. Colish presents an excellent in-depth study of the Lombard. A more introductory flavour may be found in Philipp W. Rosemann, *Peter Lombard* (Oxford: Oxford University Press, 2004).

[45] These can be found in PL 191.

[46] *Sententiae in IV libris distinctae*, 3rd edn., ed. Ignatius C. Brady, 2 vols. (Grottaferrata: Collegii S. Bonaventurae ad Claras Aquas, 1971–81). Unfortunately, *The Sentences* does not seem to be available in English translation, although the Franciscan Archive has one under way.

[47] González, 1.314.

[48] Ignatius C. Brady, 'Peter Lombard', in Berard L. Marthaler et al., eds., *New Catholic Encylopedia*, vol. 11, 2nd edn. (Detroit: Thomson Gale, 2003), 191.

[49] Marcia L. Colish, 'Peter Lombard', in *The Medieval Theologians: An Introduction to Theology in the Medieval Period*, ed. G. R. Evans (Oxford: Blackwell, 2001), 168.

[50] Colish, *Peter Lombard*, 31.

[51] See Martin Anton Schmidt, 'Das Sentenzenwerk des Petrus Lombardus und sein Aufstieg zum Muster- und Textbuch der theologischen Ausbildung', in *Handbuch der Dogmen- und Theologiegeschichte*, ed. Carl Andresen (Göttingen: Vandenhoeck & Ruprecht, 1988), 1.587–615.

[52] González, 2.178.

[53] Strangely, the literature on such an important figure as Peter Lombard is relatively sparse. Cf. Marcia Colish's complaint: 'Commentators have succeeded in marginalizing the most

It is fitting that our section on Peter Lombard immediately follows the section on Augustine, considering the great extent to which the Lombard relied on the bishop of Hippo.[54] McGrath calls *The Sentences* an 'Augustinian breviary', and he points out that the thousands of citations from Augustine in this work make up about four-fifths of the total book.[55] Peter, therefore, is significant both for his wide influence and for his role as preserver of the Augustinian theological tradition. Further, Peter Lombard did his work before the re-emergence of the influence of Aristotle in western theology, and this is one of the major differences between him and Thomas Aquinas. Peter represents the culmination of medieval, pre-Aristotelian, Augustinian theology.

To appreciate fully this influential man's thought on the will's role in conversion, we must first take a flying overview of his theological landscape, beginning with original righteousness and the Fall, and progressing to the problem of evil, the sovereignty of God, the nature of grace, and justification. We begin, naturally, with Adam.

Peter taught that Adam and Eve were born with a grace of creation. This grace meant that they were fully capable of rejecting evil (and hence had free will[56]), but they could not perfect themselves in good. Prelapsarian humanity still required cooperating grace from God in order to attain perfection.[57] This was indeed a limited kind of free will, for Peter was arguing that Adam and Eve had the genuine freedom to reject evil forever, but that they did not have the freedom to attain perfection in the good.[58]

---

central theologian of his time, and have created a modern Peter Lombard who is a caricature of his medieval reality, making it all but impossible to appreciate what his contemporaries found worthwhile in him.' *Peter Lombard*, 4.

[54] Within the literature on Peter Lombard, there is wide consensus on Augustine's influence on the author of *The Sentences*. For example, see Peter I. Kaufman, 'Charitas non est nisi a Spiritui Sancto: Augustine and Peter Lombard on Grace and Personal Righteousness', *Augustiniana* 30 (1980), 209, 220; Brady, 'Peter Lombard', 191; Jaroslav Pelikan, *The Christian Tradition: A History of the Development of Doctrine. The Growth of Medieval Theology (600–1300)* (Chicago: University of Chicago Press, 1978), 270, 275; Colish, *Peter Lombard*, 385; and Otto Baltzer, *Die Sentenzen des Petrus Lombardus: Ihre Quellen und ihre dogmengeschichtliche Bedeutung: Neudruck der Ausgabe Leipzig 1902* (Wiesbaden: Scientia Verlag Aalen, 1972), 32–4. For some moderation of this opinion, see Colish, *Peter Lombard*, 492; and Baltzer, *Die Sentenzen*, 61–7.

[55] McGrath, *Iustitia Dei*, 38.

[56] '[Peter] maintains . . . that free will is the natural rational capacity to choose either good or evil without restraint, and that the choice of good is assisted by grace, in Adam before the fall, just as it is in the case of angels'. Colish, *Peter Lombard*, 371.

[57] *Sent.* II, d. 24, c. 1–4. Colish, *Peter Lombard*, 371.

[58] *Sent.* II, d. 24, c. 1–2; d. 25, c. 1–d. 29, c. 2. Colish, *Peter Lombard*, 371.

With the Fall, mankind became guilty,[59] and the ability to reject evil forever became damaged.[60] That freedom of the will was seriously hampered,[61] so that fallen humanity now almost could not help but sin. Concupiscence, the tinder of sin, now resided in all.[62] For Peter, the greatest punishment for the Fall lay in the depression of the human will,[63] so that fallen humanity now tended much more readily toward the evil rather than the good. This indeed was a problem, and it led into the larger issue of the problem of evil and the sovereignty of God.

Was God the author of evil? No, said Peter Lombard, but he knew of it, without approving it.[64] God was not the author of evil, but he used evil to contribute to the whole—that is, God brought his good will to pass through (and despite) evil.[65] God indeed knew everything that would happen, for good or for ill. Past, present, and future all lay open and plain before him.[66] What God willed to happen could in no way be thwarted,[67] and while God did directly cause some things to happen, others he left open to free will and matters of contingency.[68] God foreknew all things, but his foreknowledge was not causative.[69]

What *was* causative, though, was God's predestination. The Lombard here essentially followed Augustine's teachings on the matter. From before all time, God chose a number of specific people to save, and within time, he granted to them the grace of preparation and perseverance in order to achieve his will of their salvation, and later, their glorification.[70] God's choice in this matter of salvation was final—it was impossible for any predestined person to be damned, and it was equally impossible for any reprobate person to be saved.[71]

---

[59] *Sent.* II, d. 30, c. 6.

[60] *Sent.* II, d. 30, c. 8.

[61] *Sent.* II, d. 25, c. 8; d. 30, c. 5. Colish, *Peter Lombard*, 394. See also Baltzer, 60–70.

[62] *Sent.* II, d. 30, c. 7.

[63] Colish, *Peter Lombard*, 383.

[64] *Sent.* I, d. 36, c. 2. Baltzer, *Die Sentenzen*, 30. See also *Sent.* I, d. 37.

[65] *Sent.* I, d. 46, c. 7, 9–10.

[66] *Sent.* I, d. 35, c. 1–6. Colish, *Peter Lombard*, 285.

[67] *Sent.* I, d. 46, c. 1.

[68] See Colish, 'Peter Lombard', 172–3; and Peter Lombard, 287.

[69] *Sent.* I, d. 38, c. 1–4. See also Baltzer, *Die Sentenzen*, 29–30.

[70] *Sent.* I, d. 39, c. 4. Cf. *Sent.* I, d. 35, c. 1; and *Sermo* 112 (PL 171.860C). For discussions in the secondary literature on the Lombard's views on predestination, see Colish, *Peter Lombard*, 288; Johann Schupp, *Die Gnadenlehre des Petrus Lombardus* (Freiburg im Breisgau: Herder, 1932), 105–15, 141–58, 204–6; Colish, 'Peter Lombard', 172–3; Baltzer, 29–34; McGrath, *Iustitia Dei*, 134.

[71] *Sent.* I, d. 40, c. 2–3. See also Baltzer, 32–3; and McGrath, *Iustitia Dei*, 134. For the Lombard's full discussion on predestination and reprobation, see *Sent.* I, d. 40–1. See also *Sent.* IV, d. 47, and Rosemann's commentary on it in *Peter Lombard*, 186–7 (who points out that the Lombard does refer to 'the reprobate' in this place).

All had sinned and earned a just damnation for themselves by their free evil actions, but God, in his mercy, predestined some to be saved, through no merit or cause in themselves.[72]

Those who were predestined, then, received God's grace—that is, the Holy Spirit took up residence in them.[73] Then, the Holy Spirit granted to the individual the desire to do good (operating grace), and then assistance in actually doing good (cooperating grace).[74] The function of grace was to free the will from its sinful bent in order to pursue and attain the good. The good will in and of itself was principally called 'grace'.[75] No human prerequisite disposition of the will was necessary—rather, God acted first (and unilaterally). God gently moved the will to a state of readiness for embarkation on the great journey of salvation.[76]

In his discussions on grace, Peter repeatedly cited Augustine, but he differed from the Bishop of Hippo in that he did not speak of 'irresistible grace'.[77] The effectiveness of grace was inferred from Peter's doctrine of predestination, but, in speaking of grace, the Lombard preserved a paradoxical tension in that he considered its effect to be to *strengthen* and *free* the individual human will, while yet allowing it the freedom to reject God.[78]

In sum, Peter's teaching on grace was that to those whom God predestined, God sent his Holy Spirit to work in their hearts both to will and to achieve a renewed life of good works. Peter Lombard was not overgenerous on the details of how this all worked. As Brady, writing in the *New Catholic Encyclopedia* states, 'Certain aspects of the Redemption and of the doctrine of grace in [*The Sentences*] leave much to be desired.'[79] As a result, due to the widespread use of *The Sentences,* as well as Peter's relatively undeveloped doctrine of grace, the ground lay fertile for future scholastics to develop and elaborate upon the Lombard's Augustinian views on grace.

---

[72] This is especially clear in the Lombard's comments on Romans 9.18 (PL 191.1462). In *Sent.* I, d. 46, c. 11–15, Lombard sets forth his teaching that the cause of man's worsening is not in God.

[73] *Sent.* I, d. 27, c. 2 and 6. Peter equated *gratia inhabitans* with the presence of the Holy Spirit himself. See Kaufman, 'Charitas', 209, 220.

[74] *Sent.* II, d. 26, c. 1, 8. Schmidt, 'Das Sentenzenwerk', 596. See also 597–8; Colish, *Peter Lombard,* 384, 491.

[75] *Sent.* II, d. 27, c. 5. See also *Sent.* II, d. 25, c. 16 (the freedom which comes from grace); *Sent.* II, d. 26, c. 4–7; and *Sent.* II, d. 27, c. 9 (on the differences between operating and cooperating grace).

[76] *Sent.* II, d. 26, c. 3–7; d. 27, c. 2–4. For further discussion, see Kaufman, 'Charitas', 211–18; Schmidt, 597; Colish, *Peter Lombard,* 490; and 'Peter Lombard', 172, 175, 212.

[77] Colish, *Peter Lombard,* 383–4.

[78] See Colish, *Peter Lombard,* 172.

[79] Brady, 'Peter Lombard', 191.

Ambiguity aside, it was clear, however, that Peter understood God's grace as essential for the justification of the fallen human being. Without grace, the human will tended more to evil than to good, but *with* God's grace, the human will inclined more to good than to evil.[80] God's grace revived and strengthened the will, which led to faith, a renewed passionate dedication to following God in all his ways, and, in the end, justification.[81]

This achievement of justification was neither solely the human's work, nor solely God's. It required God and the human working together in synergism. God predestined individuals for salvation and freed their will to pursue good works, and then human effort and choice were intimately involved in the process of striving toward righteousness.[82] God's grace was like rain falling on the earth of the human will, which, with the seed of a new inclination to the good, resulted in the fruit of virtue and righteousness.[83] God's grace enabled a free will to become a good will, and hence to embark on the journey towards salvation.

Salvation, for Peter, was a journey that each of us had to walk for ourselves. No one was going to do it for us. And this included Jesus! As important as he was, Jesus' death on the cross was no objective achievement of atonement once and for all, but was rather a subjective exhortation to the pious believer. Jesus' passion was an example for us all to emulate in our own journeys as we took up our crosses and followed him. Jesus was a model for pious living, and was not a sacrifice in and of himself. His passion took place in order to exhort believers to follow a similar path in exercising their free wills in pursuing their own salvations.[84] Jesus did not *achieve* salvation for the elect—instead, he just pointed it out; he showed them how it is done.

For Peter, justification was a process of working toward sinlessness—a goal that none attained in this life.[85] This process was made possible by God's grace, which freed the will,[86] but then the free application of the human will was required in order to gain merit and proceed down the road of salvation. The formal merit for human salvation came from the collaboration of God's grace with the application of the grace-empowered free human will. Grace

---

[80] This priority of grace before the free will is the position for both operating (*Wirkens*) and cooperating grace. Schmidt, 'Das Sentenzenwerk', 597.

[81] *Sent.* II, d. 27, c. 6.

[82] Kaufman, 'Charitas', 212. See *Collectanea in epist. D. Pauli*, PL 191.1361, PL 191.1460D–1461A, PL 192.245B. See also *Sent.* II, d. 27, c. 1 and 6; II, d. 24, c. 3; Schmidt, 'Das Sentenzenwerk', 597.

[83] *Sent.* II, d. 27, c. 1–c. 2.3.

[84] *Sent.* III, d. 19, c. 1.3–4.

[85] *Sent.* II, d. 25, c. 6. See also Schmidt, 'Das Sentenzenwerk', 597.

[86] *Sent.* II, d. 27, c. 3.

and free will together earned merit.[87] For Peter, without free will, there could be no merit.[88]

As a whole, Peter viewed the postlapsarian human will as inclined to evil; but, following God's grace, that will became more inclined to good. From thence, the free will, empowered by God's grace, worked with God to gain merit and strive to attain the reward of salvation and everlasting life.[89]

THOMAS AQUINAS: 1225–1274

From Peter Lombard, we move further into the realm of scholastic theology, beginning with Thomas Aquinas and John Duns Scotus. The teaching of both men influenced the ideas of the *moderni*, and managed to survive in their own right throughout the sixteenth century. Specifically, the Council of Trent was ample proof of the influence of these two men. Further, these high scholastic views would be the sorts of ideas that Melanchthon would often come across when he interacted with Catholic theologians of his own time. Consequently, a brief sketch of the teachings of Thomas and Scotus on free will is not without value.

The writings of Aristotle strongly influenced Thomas Aquinas, and so for him, free will occupied a necessary place in his soteriology. To see this in its full context, it will be useful to note the will's role in justification within the broader tapestry of Thomas's theological system.

Regarding original righteousness, Thomas taught that humans were not *naturally* capable of grace. Instead, at the moment of creation Adam was endowed with a special supernatural measure of grace, which was essentially alien to his nature.[90] Then with the Fall, this supernatural grace (*gratia gratum faciens*) was lost for all people, such that original sin could be defined as the privation of original righteousness.[91] Now, in their fallen state, human beings no longer had the ability to seek salvation, desire the good, or turn toward God (like Augustine, Thomas argued that human free will was weakened by sin).[92] Humans were lost, and they could neither save themselves, nor even

---

[87] *Sent.* II, d. 26, c. 3–8; d. 27 c. 3–d. 28 c. 4. See Colish, *Peter Lombard*, 385, 466, 491, and her 'Medieval Theologians', 177.

[88] *Sent.* II d. 27, c. 3.2.

[89] 'The tonality Peter gives to [the freedom of the will], despite his heavy dependence on Augustine is, finally, less typical of Augustine than it is of the theandric, synergistic relationship of grace and free will found in the Greek patrisitic tradition.' Colish, *Peter Lombard*, 385.

[90] ST Ia 97.1.

[91] McGrath, *Iustitia Dei*, 159. ST Ia2ae 109.3.

[92] ST Ia2ae 109.2.

turn themselves toward God to seek salvation from him. When it came to justification, human beings could not independently initiate their own salvation. Thomas agreed with Augustine on this matter. People desperately needed grace.

Thomas Aquinas spoke of grace in several different ways.[93] God's grace could come to a person immediately (that is, unmediated—apart from any intervening vehicle) or it could come to a person through the medium of another person. If grace came immediately to a person, it was called sanctifying grace (*gratia gratum faciens*), and this was the means by which people were united to God.[94] If grace came to a person through the medium of another person (say, through preaching), then it was called grace freely bestowed (*gratia gratis data*).[95] In any case, whether grace came to a person immediately or through the medium of another person, the first effect of grace upon a person was inevitably a changed disposition.

When grace first came to a person, it was the means by which God changed the interior disposition of the individual. God acted, and the human being was changed. This interior change of disposition was caused by operating grace (*gratia operans*). Following this changed internal disposition, the individual naturally began freely to will to do external actions that were commensurate with the newly changed internal disposition. In other words, the person sought to do good works from the moment of conversion onwards, and because the internal disposition had been changed to enable this phenomenon, and because God enabled such external actions to be performed, post-conversion grace was said to be cooperating grace (*gratia cooperans*). Further, the new will to do good works in the individual with whom God was cooperating by means of *gratia cooperans* was the will that he had worked in the individual through his *gratia operans* at the point of conversion. Hence, while the human will was involved, God was actually cooperating with his

---

[93] See Brian Davies's clear discussion on this topic in *The Thought of Thomas Aquinas* (Oxford: Clarendon, 1992), 266–73. The present discussion owes much to his work.

[94] ST Ia2ae 111.1.

[95] The English phrases 'sanctifying grace', and 'grace freely bestowed' come from the translation of Cornelius Ernst in ST. Thomas himself explained the difference between *gratia gratum faciens* and *gratia gratis data* as follows: 'The order of things consists in the fact that some things are brought back to God by others as Dionysius says. Since therefore grace is ordained to the bringing back of man to God, this takes place in a definite order, namely, the bringing back to God of some by others. Accordingly, grace is of two kinds. Firstly, there is grace by which people are united to God, and this is called *sanctifying grace*. Secondly, there is the grace by which one man cooperates with another so that he might be brought back to God. Now this kind of gift is called *freely bestowed grace*, because it is granted to man beyond the capacity of his nature and beyond his personal merit; it is not called *sanctifying*, however, because it is not given so that a man might himself be justified by it but rather so that he might cooperate in the justification of someone else.' ST Ia2ae 111.1.

own promptings in the achievement of post-conversion good works by the individual![96]

Grace was entirely the work of God, and therefore, in the matter of justification, human beings did not have the freedom to initiate their own salvation, but rather, God first changed the will of people such that they would freely choose to have faith of their own volition.[97] They could not, independent of God, turn to him in repentance and faith. Thomas wrote, 'And so it is only by way of God's converting him that man is turned to God. But to prepare oneself for grace is a kind of turning to God ... And so it is clear that man cannot prepare himself to receive the light of grace except by the gratuitous assistance of God moving him within.'[98] Again, 'man's will should be prepared by God through grace'.[99] Humans could do nothing to cause grace: 'The gift of grace surpasses every capacity of created nature, since it is nothing other than a certain participation in the divine nature, which surpasses every other nature. And so it is impossible that a creature should cause grace.'[100] The human will was involved in the decision-making process, but it was the grace of God (*gratia operans*) that drove the will.

Following conversion (which was the result of *gratia operans*), the individual sought to do good works, and God assisted this endeavour through cooperating grace (*gratia cooperans*). Then, if the individual persisted in doing good works, she would eventually attain glory, through the inner regeneration of her soul (the perfection of intrinsic righteousness). Davies summarizes Thomas's view of justification as follows: 'There are five effects of grace in us: firstly, the healing of the soul; secondly, willing the good; thirdly, the efficacious performance of the good willed; fourthly, perseverance in the good; fifthly, the attainment of glory.'[101] Grace was the motive force of

---

[96] ST Ia2ae 111.2.

[97] As Weisheipl writes, 'The part of Thomas's teaching most difficult to comprehend is his explanation of how God can move the human will, since it is a free agent.' James A. Weisheipl, *Friar Thomas D'Aquino* (Oxford: Basil Blackwell, 1975), 207. The conceptual difficulty involved in comprehending Thomas's doctrine of the will stems from the fact that he argued that God worked *through* the human will such that it remained free, and freely desired that which God *caused* it to desire. *De malo*, 6. Hence from a human perspective, the one who chose to have faith in God did so out of a free choice of the will, while from a divine and ontological perspective, the individual's exercise of the will in favour of God was entirely due to the effective operation of God's grace within that person.

[98] ST Ia2ae 109.6.

[99] ST Ia2ae 109.5 ad 1. Thomas here quoted 'Augustine' (actually Marius Mercator), from the *Hypognosticon* (PL 45.1623). See Ernst's n. 8 at ST Ia2ae 109.5 ad 1.

[100] ST Ia2ae.112.1.

[101] Davies, 272. ST Ia2ae 111.3. See also David Knowles, 'The Middle Ages 604–1350', in Hubert Cunliffe-Jones, ed., *A History of Christian Doctrine* (Edinburgh: T&T Clark, 1978), 272–4.

salvation, and grace was dispensed entirely at the volition of God. Humans ultimately had no say in whether they would receive grace or come to faith,[102] for Thomas had a strong view of the sovereignty of God, including a doctrine of predestination.

Thomas built his view of predestination on Romans, and Augustine's *De gratia et libero arbitrio*.[103] Davies writes, 'In the teaching of Aquinas... predestination means very much what it does for Augustine.'[104] McGrath concurs, noting that Thomas's view was in no way reminiscent of the Pelagian view (i.e. election being contingent on God's foreknowledge of free human choices): 'Thomas Aquinas taught that the divine decision in man's election was necessarily free and uncoerced, made without reference to man's foreseen merit or demerit.'[105] Thomas did indeed articulate a doctrine where before all time God chose those whom he would save and glorify.[106] He defined predestination as 'the planned sending of a rational creature to the end which is eternal life . . . , for to predestine is to send'.[107] For Thomas, predestination was integrally linked with the individual's inability to save himself, and it had everything to do with grace being entirely a work of God: 'How right it is that God should predestine human beings. We have seen that everything falls under his Providence, also that the function of providence is to arrange things to an end. Now the destiny to which creatures are ordained by God is twofold. One exceeds the proportion and ability of created nature, and this is eternal life which . . . consists in the vision of God and surpasses the nature of any creature. The other is proportionate to it, and can be reached by its own natural powers. Now when a thing cannot reach an end by its own natural power, then it has to be lifted up and sent there by another, as when an archer flights an arrow to the target. So a creature of intelligence, capable of eternal life, is brought there, properly speaking, as sent by God. The idea of this sending pre-exists in God, as does the idea of ordering the whole of things to their end, which we have called Providence.'[108] So because of the Fall, and because of the sovereignty of God (predestination), humans did not have the freedom independently to initiate their own salvation. God, by his grace, reoriented the hearts of the elect so that

---

[102] 'Since in assenting to the things of faith a person is raised above his own nature, he has this assent from a supernatural source influencing him; this source is God. The assent of faith, which is its principal act, therefore, has as its cause God, moving us inwardly through grace.' ST 2a2ae 6.1.

[103] PL 44.881–912.

[104] Davies, 167.

[105] McGrath, *Iustitia Dei*, 134.

[106] Davies (p. 167) notes that for Thomas, predestination was always discussed in the context of a predestination to life. Thomas did not speak of a predestination to damnation.

[107] ST Ia 23.1.

[108] ST Ia 23.1. Davies (pp. 168–9) misattributes this quotation to ST 3a 24.4.

they would freely choose to have faith in him. They did not choose God unless God chose them first, and this was essentially the same position on free will in justification as Augustine's.

Finally, it should be noted the modern scholars are divided on just how influential Thomas Aquinas was in his immediate historical context. Some speak of Ockham and Scotus destroying the Thomistic consensus balance of faith and reason.[109] Others posit that Thomas still languished in obscurity at this point, and that no such consensus existed.[110] Whatever the case, we move now to the Subtle Doctor.

DUNS SCOTUS: 1265–1308

Known as the 'Subtle Doctor' for his fine distinctions, John Duns Scotus taught in his short life at Oxford, Cambridge, and Paris. Scotus would begin a line of theological reasoning that would further be developed by the *moderni* Ockham and Biel. Scotus, therefore, represents the most obvious bridge between the thought of the *via antiqua* (as exemplified in Thomas Aquinas) and the thought of the *via moderna*.

Scotus insisted that God did not directly and unilaterally determine all things, and therefore humans had free will in their actions (the freedom of contingency). Wolter writes, 'Equally certain to Scotus was the experiential fact that we possess free will . . . and that contingency exists in the world around us. He considered the latter to be a "primary truth not demonstrable *a priori*".'[111] Contingent causation did exist,[112] and 'all contingent events are brought about by free will'.[113]

As for the Fall, it was indeed a tragedy, but it did not destroy human free will. Cross writes, 'Scotus's account of original sin, however, is in every respect weaker than the standard Augustinian one accepted by most of his

---

[109] e.g. A. Vos, 'William of Ockham', in Sinclair B. Ferguson and David F. Wright, eds., *New Dictionary of Theology* (Leicester: Inter-Varsity Press, 1988), 723.

[110] e.g. Marjorie O'Rourke Boyle, *Erasmus on Language and Method in Theology* (Toronto: University of Toronto Press, 1977), 64. For more on these issues, see Hamm, and Paul Vignaux, *Philosophy in the Middle Ages*, trans. E. C. Hall (London: Burns & Oates, 1961).

[111] John Duns Scotus, *Duns Scotus on the Will and Morality*, ed. and trans. Allan B. Wolter (Washington, DC: Catholic University of America Press, 1986), 9. See also Lee Sukjae, 'Scotus on the Will: The Rational Power and the Dual Affections', *Vivarium* 36 (1998), 40–54.

[112] Richard Cross, *Duns Scotus* (New York: Oxford University Press, 1999), 47. *Ordinatio* 1.2.1.1–2 n. 79 (Vatican 2.176 = PW 53–4). *De Primo Principio* 4.15 (p. 82).

[113] Cross, 48. *Ordinatio* 1.2.1.1–2 n. 81 (Vatican 2.177 = PW 54). *De Primo Principio* 4.15 (p. 82).

contemporaries. The supernatural gifts of unfallen humanity were minimal, and their loss has only the smallest effect on human existence.'[114] Sin resided in an *act*, and not in a *person*, and hence the Fall did not corrupt individuals such that their freedom of will became in any way constrained.[115]

For Scotus, the formal cause of justification was the extrinsic denomination of divine acceptation.[116] In other words, people were saved because from before all time God decided to save some of them. God predestined some people for salvation. Like Thomas, Scotus argued that the source of predestination lay within God's will. Predestination was based on God's free decision, rather than on his foreknowledge.[117] Knowles summarizes, 'Absolutely speaking God is free; the will of God and not his mind or law has the last word.'[118] Foreknowledge of course accompanied election, but it was never the basis for it.[119] The result was that 'the *processus praedestinationis* was ... such that eternal life preceded merit in terms of its logical analysis, but is consequent to it in terms of its execution in time.'[120] God's will was the ultimate source of soteriological achievements.

Also like Thomas, Scotus refused to posit that God actively willed the reprobation of the non-elect. Scotus claimed that the reprobate were justly condemned on an intellectualist basis—that is, God foresaw their sins and justly condemned them for their faults (as opposed to the elect, whom he predestined *before* considering their works).[121] As McGrath points out,[122] this delicate footwork seemed to pose a serious contradiction within Scotus' thought, and perhaps helped to explain why the *moderni* like Ockham and Biel sought a slightly modified system.

If God's predestining will was the primary cause of salvation, then the secondary cause was the created habit of grace.[123] The means by which God

[114] Cross, 83. For more on the influence of Augustine upon Scotus, see Benedykt Huculak's 'De mature augustiniano opere Johannis Duns Scoti', *Antonianum* 76 (2001), 429–78.
[115] *Ordinatio* 4.14.1, n. 3 (Wadding, 9.7). *Ordinatio* 2.37.1, n. 6 (Wadding, 6.981). Cross, 95, explains this very well.
[116] McGrath, *Iustitia Dei*, 166.
[117] *Ordinatio* 1.41.un., n. 36 (Vatican 6.330–1). See also *Ordinatio* 1.41.un., n. 40 (Vatican 6.332). Cross, 101. See also Wolfhart Pannenberg, *Die Prädestinationslehre des Duns Scotus* (Göttingen: Vandenhoeck & Ruprecht, 1954).
[118] Knowles, 281.
[119] McGrath, *Iustitia Dei*, 134.
[120] Ibid., 135.
[121] *Ordinatio* 1.41.un., n. 42 (Vatican 6.332–3).
[122] McGrath, *Iustitia Dei*, 136. Cross, 102, also shows that a doctrine of reprobation is strongly implied by Scotus' system, but that Scotus refused to accept it. See Scotus on the damnation of Judas, *Ordinatio* 1.41.un., n. 44 (Vatican 6.333–4).
[123] *Quodlibetum* 17, n. 4 (Wadding 12.461 = AW 390 [n. 7.8]). See also *Ordinatio* 1.17.1.1–2, nn. 106, 129 (Vatican 5.192, 202–3). *Ordinatio* 2.37.2, n. 6 (Wadding 6.993). *Ordinatio* 3.27.un., n. 19 (Wadding 7.655). *Duns Scotus on the Will and Morality*, 443. Cross, 107–11.

saved those whom he had predestined was through good works aided by
God's grace, such that righteousness slowly grew within the individual, and
that eventually, such a person would attain eternal life and beatitude.[124] This
secondary cause of salvation incorporated the genuine application of the
human free will,[125] such that salvation might still be said to occur on a
practical level via a *meritum de congruo* arrangement. As Pannenberg notes,
for Scotus, God worked *with* creaturely acts of the will.[126]

For Scotus, the causal relationship between the exertion of the human will
and the reception of grace was entirely contingent on God's decree that it
should be so. The secondary means of justification were causally connected
purely because God had *ordained* that they should be so—*de potentia Dei
ordinata* (according to the ordained power of God).[127] Causation occurred *ex
pacto divino* (from a divine pact) rather than *ex natura rei* (from the nature of
things).[128] God had instituted a divine covenant that justification should
occur via congruous merit through the application of the will coupled with
the gradual reception of grace. This was the way in which those whom he had
predestined would be saved. He could have ordained something entirely
different,[129] but the fact remained that he had not. This covenant theology
would later play an important role in the soteriological systems of Ockham
and Biel.[130]

Just as soteriological causality was a result of God's ordination, so merit
flowed from God's will as well. God was voluntaristic in his assessment of
merit—that is, he accepted the merit of every action as exactly as valuable as
he wanted it to be.[131] God made the rules, and God gave value according to
his own pleasure and his own counsel. No standard existed above him to

---

[124]   *Ordinatio* 1.41.un., n. 41 (Vatican 6.332–3). Scotus insisted that this secondary means of
salvation created a *real* (not merely forensic) change in the sinner: *Ordinatio* 1.17.1.1–2,
nn. 114–18 (Vatican 5.195–7).

[125]   *Ordinatio* 1.17.1–2, n. 191 (Vatican 5.229–30).

[126]   Pannenberg, 120.

[127]   McGrath, *Iustitia Dei*, 149. For more on Scotus' covenant theology of de *potentia absoluta*
versus *de potentia ordinata*, see Werner Dettloff, *Die Lehre von der Acceptatio Divina bei Johannes
Duns Scotus mit besondere Berücksichtigung der Rechtfertigungslehre* (Werl: Dietrich Coelde-
Verlag, 1954), 73–4, 204–9. See also Heri Veldhuis, 'Ordained and Absolute Power in Scotus'
Ordinatio I 44', *Vivarium* 38 (2000), 222–30.

[128]   For a thorough investigation of this topic of scholastic *pactum* theology, see Berndt
Hamm, *Promissio, Pactum, Ordinatio: Freiheit und Selbstbindung Gottes in der scholastischen
Gnadenlehre* (Tübingen: J. C. B. Mohr (Paul Siebeck), 1977).

[129]   *Ordinatio* 1.17.1.1–2, n. 160 (Vatican 5.215). See also *Ordinatio* 1.17.1.1–2, n. 164
(Vatican 5.217). Quodlibetum 17, n. 13 (Wadding 12.472 = AW 397–8 [n. 17.33]). *Duns Scotus
on the Will and Morality*, 258–9. Dettloff, 73.

[130]   McGrath, *Iustitia Dei*, 150.

[131]   *Ordinatio* 1.17.1.1–2, n. 115 (Vatican 5.196).

which he had to conform in assigning merit. God was never forced to act. Thus God saved those whom he predestined to salvation by choosing to accept their grace-aided best efforts of will as meritorious.[132] Hence, two factors comprised God's choice of some but not others for salvation: the first was God's decision to save the sinner. The second was God's predetermined decision to accept the best efforts of that sinner as congruently meritorious.

To put it all together, Scotus' theology was a complex attempt to balance divine sovereignty and human free will. Scotus essentially adopted an understanding of justification where the individual gradually grew in grace and good works, and then he encased this paradigm in an outer shell of a voluntaristic predestination to salvation. While this outer shell might logically have implied that people did not have free will, Scotus hedged from this conclusion by affirming free will as part of the secondary means of justification. The result was that people had free will, but the exercise of it could not lead to salvation unless God had decided beforehand to accept the individual in question. As a result, Scotus affirmed a qualified free will—meaning that while the will was free, it might or might not do the individual any good, depending on God's prior election. Despite Scotus' careful formulations, his qualified free will seemed ultimately to leave salvation out of the hands of the individual. Scotus preserved free will in justification (even to the extent of saying that all people had the free ability to come to faith, *de potentia dei ordinata*), but it was a weak doctrine, for salvation ultimately and ontologically rested in God's decision from before all time, rather than in the human will.

WILLIAM OF OCKHAM: 1285–1347

Ockham held a love–hate relationship with Scotus' thought,[133] for while on many points he agreed with the Subtle Doctor, on others he sought to craft improvements. Free will was one area in particular where this was true. Noting the general sense of ontological futility that accompanied Scotus' advocacy of free will in combination with voluntaristic merit, Ockham strove to create a stronger foundation for the propagation of the doctrine of a genuinely free will. In the process, he arrived at an understanding of free will that was noticeably Scotistic, but with some important modifications. To understand these changes, it will be useful to note Ockham's positions on

---

[132] *Ordinatio* 1.41.un., n. 54 (Vatican 6.337–8).
[133] Knowles, 283.

original righteousness, the Fall, the formal cause of justification, predestination, causality, and merit.

Regarding original righteousness, the Fall, and the formal and secondary causes of justification, Ockham seemed to be in general agreement with Scotus. Ockham affirmed the doctrine of original sin,[134] but he insisted that humans possessed a natural grace that was not entirely eradicated by the Fall. As Wood writes, 'He shares with Pelagius, and most importantly with Aristotle, the view that created human nature functions properly for the most part.'[135] The formal and secondary causes of justification were the extrinsic denomination of divine acceptation and the created habit of grace.[136] However, when it came to understanding grace, Ockham was unique. He argued that the notion of a created habit in the soul was not absolutely necessary.[137] Instead, he posited that grace was ultimately an arbitrary relationship between God and humans.[138] This statement was a result of Ockham's view of justification as God's direct acceptance of the sinner—when God chose to accept a sinner, he would subsequently view that person's free actions as meritorious.[139] Thus saving merit could *appear* to be anthropologically generated, but in every case it was actually derived solely from God's external imputation.[140] Moreover, this direct acceptance was most apparent in predestination.[141]

Ockham followed in the line of Scotus' advocacy of predestination to life—damnation was still based on a quality in the individual, rather than an act of the divine will.[142] But in order to avoid the inconsistency present in Scotus' doctrine of a voluntaristic predestination to life coupled with an intellectualist punishment of foreseen sin in reprobation, Ockham instead argued for two types of predestination.[143] The first was general predestination, and the second was special predestination. General predestination could not truly be called 'pre'-destination at all. For Ockham, predestination always referred to a future event. His major premise was that 'a man who finally perseveres

---

[134] *In libros sententiarum* I.17.1. OTh 3.447.

[135] Rega Wood, 'Ockham's Repudiation of Pelagianism', in *The Cambridge Companion to Ockham*, ed. Paul Vincent Spade (Cambridge: Cambridge University Press, 1999), 352.

[136] *Ordinatio* I, d. 17, q. 1. OTh 3.452, 456, 466.

[137] *Ordinatio* I, d. 17, q. 1. OTh 3.445, 454–5.

[138] Knowles, 285.

[139] *Ordinatio* I, d. 14, q. 2. OTh 3.472–3. Cf. Adams, 1273–5.

[140] *In libros sententiarum* I.17.1, III.9. OTh 3.466, 7.213. Wood, 353.

[141] Wood, 360. *In libros sententiarum* I, d. 40, q. un. OTh 4.593.21–3. Cf. OTh 4.594, 596–7.

[142] McGrath, *Iustitia Dei*, 137.

[143] Gordon Leff, *William of Ockham: The Metamorphosis of Scholastic Discourse* (Manchester: Manchester University Press, 1975), 469. *Ordinatio* I, d. 41, q. un., G. OTh 4.609–10. See also *Ordinatio* I, d. 40, q. un. OTh 4.593–4.

will be predestined',[144] which meant that no one could be said to be pre-destined until the moment he or she actually became glorified. This was a sort of *de facto* predestination, where the term simply described the state of achieved glorification, which occurred through merit garnered through the free exercise of the will in combination with God's responsive and gracious *meritum de congruo* system of justification. Consequently, the difficult question of election turned into a non-issue as a result of a complex philosophical construct that made any discussion of predestination prior to glorification an impossibility.

While Ockham's theory of general predestination left intact the soteriological importance of the proper exercise of the free will, it failed to do justice to the incidents in the Bible where individuals such as Jacob or Paul were seen to be accepted by God even *despite* their manifestly improper and sinful exercise of the will. For these instances, Ockham argued that God employed a special predestination. All had free will and the ability to seek their own justification from God, but for some specific individuals, God overrode the misuse of their wills to ensure salvation.[145] Leff summarizes, 'the salvation of the second group seems to depend on nothing except God's will that they should be saved without any preceding merits'.[146] As a result, most people were left to their own devices, but here and there a few individuals had been specially chosen to receive unmerited salvation.

For Ockham, the ultimate cause of salvation was simply God's will. In fact, God could have completely bypassed the created habit of grace, for all that was *truly* necessary was that God disposed the viator towards eternal life.[147] However, he had not circumvented the created habit of grace. Rather, God had set up a system of salvation that employed secondary causes. Here Ockham expanded Scotus' notion of the two powers of God (*de potentia absoluta* (absolute power) and *de potentia ordinata* (ordained power)).[148]

The dichotomy of powers idea posited that there were two powers within God: his absolute power (*potentia Dei absoluta*), and his ordained power (*potentia Dei ordinata*). God's absolute power was that which he had before all time, before he created the cosmos. At that point God's power was

---

[144] McGrath, *Iustitia Dei*, 138.

[145] *Ordinatio* I, d. 41, q. un. OTh 4.606–7.

[146] Leff, *William of Ockham*, 469.

[147] McGrath, *Iustitia Dei*, 151. *Ordinatio* I, d. 17, q. 1. OTh 3.445, 454–5.

[148] For a detailed account of Ockham's doctrines of *potentia Dei absoluta* and *potentia Dei ordinata*, see Klaus Bannach, *Die Lehre von der doppelten Macht Gottes bei Wilhelm von Ockham: Problemgeschichtliche Voraussetzungen und Bedeutung* (Wiesbaden: Franz Steiner Verlag, 1975). He gives a history of the development of this doctrine from Augustine to Ockham on pp. 54–275.

completely without bound. Next, after God created the universe and established the present moral and soteriological order, he limited himself to the
confines of that which he had established. God did not change his mind, and
he would now ever be faithful to his own self-imposed decisions. As Adams
writes, 'With respect to His absolute power, God can accept someone or some
act without any infused charity or grace, and He can not-accept someone or
some act with such infused charity or grace, while, with respect to His
ordained power, God cannot accept anyone or any act without infused charity
or grace, and He cannot *not* accept anyone with it.'[149] In other words, God
was all-powerful in his original set of possibilities, but now his ordained
power consisted of the options left after his own self-abridgment achieved
through the actualization of one set of his original choices.

This dialectic of powers served the purpose of retaining both God's absolute power, and the inherent stability and trustworthiness of the present
soteriological order. Courtenay comments, 'The dialectic of the two powers
is particularly useful in soteriology because it grants freedom and omnipotence to God without undermining the operation or predictability of the
present order.'[150] The dichotomy of God's powers therefore explained how
Ockham held together both God's will as the ultimate source of soteriological
causality, and the necessity of the application of the human will to congruously attain grace and justification. Causality was not *ex natura rei* (from the
nature of the thing), but rather *ex pacto divino* (from the divine pact).[151]

According to the ordained power of God, merit had its origin in the
uncoerced volition of the moral agent. Those who sought to do the good of
their own free wills thereby disposed themselves for the reception of grace.[152]
This reward was earned congruously—the Holy Spirit would not be given to
anyone who lacked infused charity, which was acquired congruously through
the exercise of the free will.[153] This acquired merit was not necessarily
sufficient to earn eternal life,[154] but it acted as the starting-point in the long
transformational process of justification. This progression represented the
usual ordained process of justification, although in all cases 'God is absolutely

[149] Marilyn McCord Adams, *William Ockham*, 2 vols. (Notre Dame: University of Notre
Dame Press, 1987), 1296. *Ordinatio* I, d. 17, q. 1. OTh 3.451.
[150] William J. Courtenay, 'Nominalism and Late Medieval Religion', in *The Pursuit of Holiness
in Late Medieval and Renaissance Religion*, ed. Charles Trinkhaus and Heiko A. Oberman
(Leiden: E. J. Brill, 1974), 47. See also Adams, 1295.
[151] Adams, 1274. *Ordinatio* I, d. 17, q. 2. OTh 3.471–2. See also *In libros sententiarum* I.17.2.
OTh 3.471–2.
[152] *In libros sententiarum* I.41.1. OTh 4.600.
[153] *Quaestiones variae in libros Sententiarum*, q. 1. OTh 8.16, 23. Cf. Adams, 1277.
[154] Wood, 361.

free to reward whom he will without precedent merit. No preparation or disposition is needed for any grace or for final salvation.'[155] According to God's absolute power, the created habit of grace was not necessary for salvation, although *de potentia Dei ordinata* (according to God's ordained power), it was.[156]

In summary, Ockham's theology reflected Scotus' thought on the will, extended and clarified through a strong emphasis on the two powers of God (ordained and absolute). While insisting on the sovereignty of God and the primacy of God's will in determining causality and merit, Ockham created a substructure of God's ordained power, wherein a reliable mechanism of salvation was created where the application of the free will was necessary, *de potentia Dei ordinata*. However, Ockham's optimism regarding human abilities lay only in the *moral* realm—i.e. regarding the intrinsic (ordained) value of activities. McGrath summarizes, 'Ockham's theology of merit allows him to take a favourable view of man's moral capacities, while at the same time totally destroying the theological foundation upon which man's acts might be considered as capable of meriting grace or eternal life.'[157] So while the will was free to seek salvation, it was God who ultimately decided whether or not to grant it.[158]

GREGORY OF RIMINI: D. 1358

Gregory of Rimini is often grouped with Ockham and Biel as theologians of the *via moderna*, one of the new theologians (as opposed to the *via antiqua* of Thomas and Scotus) who followed a nominalist epistemology (rather than a realist one).[159] Sometimes a further division is made amongst the nominalists, reserving the label *via moderna* for some like Ockham and Biel, while others, like Hugolino of Orvieto and Gregory of Rimini, are called the *schola Augustiniana moderna* due to their renewed emphasis on Augustine's theology. In fact, Gregory has been called the father of the *schola Augustiniana*

---

[155] Knowles, 284.
[156] *Ordinatio* I, d. 17, q. 1, B–E. *In libros sententiarum* I.17.1. OTh 3.466. *In libros sententiarum* III.9. OTh 6.281, 312.
[157] McGrath, *Iustitia Dei*, 116.
[158] Adams, 1273. *Ordinatio* I, d. 17, q. 1. OTh 3.454–5.
[159] Epistemology is the theory of how we know things. A nominalist epistemology says that we merely give names to the phenomena we observe (this view is often associated with Aristotle). A realist epistemology says that the phenomena we observe are particular expressions of greater universal realities (this view is often associated with Plato).

moderna.[160] A consensus in the literature has not yet been reached on how to define the group *schola Augustiniana moderna*,[161] and so we focus on the individual, Gregory of Rimini, whose distinctiveness was not so much contingent on his being part of a new group or movement, but simply for his strong Augustinian theological emphasis, and how this distinguished him from the soteriology of Ockham.[162] Gregory's importance, furthermore, appears in the fact that 'according to the statutes of 1508, [Luther] was obligated to teach at Wittenberg according to the *via Gregorii*.'[163] Steinmetz adds that this *via Gregorii* was given a new direction by Luther, and went on to become the 'true theology' (*vera theologia*) of the theologians at the University of Wittenberg.[164]

Like all the theologians mentioned so far in this chapter, Gregory believed in the freedom of contingency. God permitted (rather than caused) sin,[165] and freedom in non-soteriological matters was so obvious that it barely excited the briefest of comments.[166] As for the Fall, though, 'Gregory... adopted a traditional and dogmatic view of man's fallen nature.'[167] The Fall resulted in two disabilities for human beings: first, it made them ignorant of

---

[160] Steinmetz, *Luther and Staupitz*, 23.

[161] For a summary of the difficulties involved in defining the *schola Augustiniana moderna*, see McGrath, *Iustitia Dei*, 172–9. Heiko Oberman, for example, claims Gregory as a member of the *via moderna*, rather than the *schola Augustiniana moderna*: 'It is incontestable that Gregory wears the garb of the *via moderna* with zest and conviction.' *The Harvest of Medieval Theology: Gabriel Biel and Late Medieval Nominalism* (Cambridge, MA: Harvard University Press, 1963), 202.

[162] For a survey of research on Gregory of Rimini completed up until 1978, see Willigis Eckermann, *Wort und Wirklichkeit: Das Sprachverständnis in der Theologie Gregors von Rimini und sein Weiterwirken in der Augustinerschule* (Würzburg: Augustinus-Verlag, 1978), 21–42. See also Manfred Schulze, '"Via Gregorii" in Forschung und Quellen', in *Gregor von Rimini: Werk und Wirkung bis zur Reformation* (Berlin: Walter de Gruyter, 1981), 1–126. Gordon Leff's book, *Gregory of Rimini: Tradition and Innovation in Fourteenth Century Thought* (Manchester: Manchester University Press, 1961), is the most significant work on Gregory in the English language, and the present section owes much to this work.

[163] Steinmetz, *Luther and Staupitz*, 17, 24. Steinmetz goes on to say, however, that there is no evidence that Luther read or was familiar with Gregory before 1519 (p. 17). Leif Grane supports this position, in 'Gregor von Rimini und Luthers Leipziger Disputation', *Studia Theologica* 22 (1968), 31. Conversely, Heiko Oberman *does* see at least circumstantial evidence that Luther *was* influenced by Gregory of Rimini before the Leipzig Disputation: *Werden und Wertung der Reformation: vom Wegestreit zum Glaubenskampf* (Tübingen: J. C. B., Mohr, 1977), 82–140.

[164] Steinmetz, *Luther and Staupitz*, 24. See also Oberman, 'Headwaters of the Reformation', in *Luther and the Dawn of the Modern Era*, ed. Heiko Oberman (Leiden: E. J. Brill, 1974), 88. However, Steinmetz (pp. 27–8) argues that Staupitz and Luther were influenced more by Augustine directly, rather than Augustine mediated through Gregory of Rimini, despite the mention of *via Gregorii* in the Wittenberg books.

[165] I *Sent.* d. 46–47, q. 1, a.1, 153A. GA 3.507–19.

[166] II *Sent.* d. 24 and 25, q. 1, 90K. GA 6.2.2–4.

[167] Leff, *Gregory of Rimini*, 168. II *Sent.*, d. 30–3, q. 1, a. 1, 111M. GA 6.176.

the good,[168] and second, even if the will *could* recognize the good, it would be able neither to desire nor to accomplish it, unless it received special help from God (*speciali auxilio dei*).[169]

Humanity's fallen nature had to be healed, and given special grace in order for the individual to be saved.[170] It was not possible simply to act apart from special help. Fallen man could not even *want* to obey God's law unless God, by his grace, first moved the sinner to do so.[171] As Leff writes, 'In every good action, he says, there is a two-fold process: first, God operates in us that we may want good, and, secondly, He co-operates with us that we may realize this desire.'[172] Any given human action was only meritorious when God added his grace to it.[173] Hence, all human merits were gifts from God.[174] Justification was emphatically *sola gratia*.[175]

With God's special help, sinners began to reform their lives, such that righteousness increased within them, and, one day, in the life to come, they would reach perfect righteousness and so attain salvation. Justification was achieved through the habit of infused charity, although, according to God's absolute power, he did not theoretically *have* to accept an individual possessing such a habit.[176] This view of the process of justification was the classic transformational model articulated by Augustine, and also, in slightly varying forms, by Peter, Thomas, Scotus, and Ockham—at least as the secondary means of salvation, or, the method of salvation *de potentia Dei ordinata*.

For Gregory, merit depended on God's decision to add his grace to human works and subsequently decide to view them as meritorious.[177] The reason for viewing any one individual's works as meritorious lay in God's prior decision to save that individual. God would assist with grace and view as meritorious only the works of those individuals whom he had predestined to salvation from before all time.[178] As Leff comments, 'It is God who gives His grace freely, deciding whom to endow and whom not, and in this sense only can He

---

[168] II *Sent.*, d. 29, q. 1, a. 2, 106H. GA 6.137.

[169] II *Sent.*, d. 29, q. 1, a. 2, 108N. GA 6.153–4.32, 1–5.

[170] II *Sent.*, d. 29, q. 1, a. 1, 105L. GA 6.131–2. For a more detailed discussion of 'special help', see C. P. Burger, 'Der Augustinerschüler gegen die modernen Pelagianer: Das "auxilium speciale dei" in der Gnadenlehre Gregors von Rimini', in *Gregor von Rimini: Werk und Wirkung bis zur Reformation*, ed. II. A. Oberman (Berlin: Walter de Gruyter, 1981), 195–240.

[171] II *Sent.*, d. 26, q. 1, a. 1, 95J. GA 6.45–6.30, 1–2. See also II *Sent.*, d. 26–8, q. 1, a. 1, 92J. GA 6.19–20. Gregory also, naturally enough, rejected Pelagian-style works-righteousness. II *Sent.*, d. 26, q. 1, a. 1, 93E. GA 6.26.

[172] Leff, *Gregory of Rimini*, 195. II *Sent.*, d. 26–8, q. 1, a. 3, 99G. GA 6.78.4–5.

[173] II *Sent.*, d. 26, q. 1, a. 1, 93Q. GA 6.32.1–2.

[174] I *Sent.*, d. 17, q. 1, a. 2, 87Q. GA 2.234–5.

[175] Steinmetz, *Luther and Staupitz*, 23. See also Oberman, 'Headwaters', 84.

[176] I *Sent.*, d. 14–16, q. 1, a. 1, 83Q–84A. GA 2.201–2.

[177] II Sent., d. 26, q. 1, a. 1, 93Q. GA 6.31.

[178] For an extended work on Gregory's view of predestination and free will, see M. Schüler, *Prädestination, Sünde und Freiheit bei Gregor von Rimini* (Stuttgart, 1934).

be said to accept individuals.'[179] It was solely by God's mercy that anyone was predestined.[180] Further, Gregory affirmed a full doctrine of double predestination by also arguing that those whom God did not predestine were, in fact, chosen by him for reprobation.[181] Oberman states, '[Gregory's] ... position is marked by his outspoken defence of a predestination *ante praevisa merita* which we found to be the position of Scotus. He goes beyond Scotus, however, in also holding to reprobation *ante praevisa demerita*.'[182] God chose who would be saved, and who would be damned. He based his decision solely on his own inscrutable will,[183] and not on anything individual people did or would do.[184]

As a result of the helplessness of humans following the Fall, and owing to God's predestining will (which trumped all other considerations), salvation ultimately rested on God's choice of the individual, rather than the individual's choice of God. Nevertheless, like Augustine, Gregory's position was that the way in which God granted salvation to one of the elect was to change that person's will so that she would freely choose to have faith in God. So God first chose the individual, then inclined her will so that her free decision would be to have faith in Him. As Leff neatly summarizes, 'The order [of salvation] therefore is an invariable one from God's will to the effects of His willing upon His creatures.'[185]

GABRIEL BIEL: *c.*1415–1495

Gabriel Biel's theology was very similar to Ockham's,[186] and, like virtually all the scholastics, he affirmed the everyday freedom of contingency.[187] In those places where differences between Ockham and Biel emerged, Biel's statements usually seemed to represent a development or extension of Ockham's paradigms, rather than a refutation of them. In consequence of this similarity, Biel's views on free will may be noted with some brevity.

---

[179] Leff, *Gregory of Rimini*, 184. II *Sent.*, d. 26, q. 1, a. 3, 98K–L. GA 6.79–80.
[180] I *Sent.*, d. 40 and 41, q. 1, a. 2, 158B. GA 3.326.23–4.
[181] I *Sent.*, d. 40 and 41, q. 1, a. 1, 157M. GA 3.323.1–3.
[182] Oberman, *Harvest*, 204–5. I *Sent.*, d. 40–1 q. 1, a. 2, 160B. GA 3.343.1–3.
[183] I *Sent.*, d. 40 and 41, q. 1, a. 3, 161F. GA 3.353.11–12.
[184] I *Sent.*, d. 40 and 41, q. 1, a. 1, 157 N. GA 3.323.
[185] Leff, *Gregory of Rimini*, 198.
[186] McSorley, *Luther*, 199. Oberman, *Harvest*, 169–78.
[187] Wilhelm Ernst, *Gott und Mensch am Vorabend der Reformation: Eine Untersuchung zur Moralphilosophie und -theologie bei Gabriel Biel* (Leipzig: St Benno-Verlag, 1972), 288.

Biel's doctrine of justification relied heavily on the dichotomy of God's powers. According to Biel, God supplied prevenient grace in the form of the *pactum* (or an agreement he had made with himself to order reality in a specific way).[188] In this *pactum*, God declared that people were saved through congruous merit by doing good works of their own free will. In a sermon marking the circumcision of Jesus, Biel alluded to the grace inherent in the *pactum* soteriology when he declared of God, 'In truth *He has already saved His people by preparing medicine*.'[189] For Biel, it was by means of the *pactum* that God's grace was retained.

Biel's idea of grace through the *pactum* did not abnegate the freedom of the will.[190] Rather, as McSorley notes, 'In the order of salvation generously willed by God . . . nothing more is necessary for the sinner to begin his journey toward God than the proper use of his own fallen intellect and his own fallen will.'[191] This was the case because 'The impact of original sin and its consequences leaves the freedom of the will intact.'[192] Further, Biel writes, 'By his own natural powers man can do something morally right and dispose himself for grace, avoid sins and fulfil commandments.'[193] According to God's ordained power, he was obliged to give his grace to everyone who did their best—who did what lay within them (*quod in se est*).[194] For Biel, the human free will was quite powerful, and the exercise of the will was the first step towards salvation.

An illustration Biel used was illuminating of both his stance on free will and his theory of justification. Biel conjectured that sinful humanity was like a bird unable to fly due to a large stone tied to its feet. According to Biel, rather than removing the stone, salvation was like the strengthening of the bird's wings, by which the impediment of the stone became no impediment at all.[195] Biel then made his point explicit, in words reminiscent of Peter Lombard: 'Grace weakens the remaining power of sin, not—as many doctors say— because it forgives or wipes out sins, but because it strengthens human power.'[196] Free human power had to be exerted in order to merit the infusion

---

[188] See the discussion on Scotus above for further explanation.

[189] Gabriel Biel, 'The Circumcision of the Lord', in Heiko A. Oberman, ed. and trans., *Forerunners of the Reformation: The Shape of Late Medieval Thought Illustrated by Key Documents* (Philadelphia: Fortress Press, 1966), 166.

[190] Oberman goes so far as to describe Biel's view of the will as 'the inalienable freedom of the will'. *Harvest*, 131–2.

[191] McSorley, *Luther*, 204.

[192] Oberman, *Harvest*, 131.

[193] McSorley, *Luther*, 200. II *Sent.*, d. 28, q. un., art. 3 and dub. 2 (M).

[194] II *Sent.* d. 27, q. 1, art. 2, concl. 4. See Ernst, 320–4.

[195] Oberman, *Forerunners*, 171–2.

[196] Ibid., 171.

of special grace, which would empower the human to live an increasingly righteous life, and so eventually to attain unto salvation.

While this position was very similar to Ockham's (Biel viewed predestination in terms of divine foreknowledge of free human actions), Biel's writings were much less redolent with the voluntarism and sovereignty of God that constantly flavoured Ockham's theological formulations.[197] In fact, Biel tended to emphasize often the necessity and possibility of 'doing one's best', or doing what lay within one (*quod in se est*), and thus being justified through congruous merit. This heavy practical emphasis on the *use* of the will lent Biel's doctrine of free will a stronger subjective force than Ockham's.

JOHANN VON STAUPITZ: 1460–1524

Johann von Staupitz served as vicar general of the Augustinian Observant monks, and later, as Benedictine abbot in Salzburg. He was a friend of humanists, an academic city preacher, a man concerned for the reform of the religious orders, and, above all, a pastor. Through his Augustinian theology, his own unique doctrinal emphases, and his application of these ideas to the pastoral counsel he supplied to a particularly troubled young monk, Staupitz has no doubt had a significant impact on the development of Protestant Christianity. Luther, in a letter to Elector John Frederick on 27 March 1545, wrote, 'Doctor Staupitz is first of all my father in this doctrine and he has given birth to me in Christ.'[198]

Staupitz has long been considered a forerunner of the Reformation, and in recent years, his reputation has even increased beyond this: 'If Luther is to be believed, then Staupitz is not merely a forerunner but the Father of the Protestant Reformation.'[199] Franz Posset calls Staupitz 'the front-runner', rather than 'a forerunner' of the Reformation.[200] Indeed, although he himself did not actively support the Reformation,[201] his theology was, in retrospect,

---

[197] See Oberman's chapter on Biel's view of predestination in *Harvest*, 185–242.
[198] Quoted in Franz Posset, *The Front-Runner of the Catholic Reformation: The Life and Works of Johann von Staupitz* (Aldershot: Ashgate, 2003), xiii. WABr 11.
[199] Steinmetz, *Luther and Staupitz*, 4, 144.
[200] Posset, 1.
[201] Staupitz never broke with the Roman Catholic Church. He fought for Augustinian theology and a reform of church piety, but he remained within the monastic system, and did not concur with Luther and Melanchthon in proclaiming a strictly forensic mechanism of justification, as will be explained below. His theology was similar to Luther's (or, more properly, Luther's was similar to his), but Staupitz remained just 'orthodox' enough to stay in the good graces of the Roman Catholic hierarchy—at least during his lifetime.

deemed to smack too much of Lutheranism, and so, at the Council of Trent, Staupitz's writings were added to the papal *Index of Forbidden Books*.[202] Philipp Melanchthon, without question, was influenced by the teachings of Staupitz—if not directly, then surely through Staupitz's protégé, that troubled young monk, Martin Luther.

In order to grasp Staupitz's understanding of the will's role in justification, it will be useful to explore first his attitude toward Scripture, followed by his own influences. Next, we will briefly scan his views on free will at creation, and the will's capabilities following the Fall. Tied to these doctrines will be his views on predestination, grace, and merit. Altogether, this examination should afford an adequate summary of Staupitz's thoughts on the freedom of the will.

Staupitz believed that Scripture was the highest authority,[203] and as his career progressed, this conviction became increasingly pronounced.[204] He believed that everyone needed the life-giving Word,[205] and that both preaching[206] and religious reform[207] should be Bible-based. His contemporary, Christoph Scheurl, once called him 'the voice of Paul'.[208] Influenced by biblical humanism,[209] Staupitz believed in the authority of *sola scriptura*,[210] and helped instil that ethos at the university he played a key role in founding—the University of Wittenberg.[211]

Second only to Scripture, Staupitz valued the authority of the church fathers,[212] especially Augustine.[213] Perhaps through Staupitz's influence, the patron saint of the University of Wittenberg ended up being Augustine. Likewise, Staupitz also favoured Peter Lombard,[214] which is not surprising, considering the extent to which Peter modelled his own theology on

---

[202] Posset, xiii, 209, 369. Some of Staupitz's writings can be found in Johann von Staupitz, *Sämtliche Schriften, Abhandlungen, Predigten, Zeugnisse: Tübinger Predigten*, ed. Lothar Graf zu Dohna and Richard Wetzel (Berlin: De Gruyter, 1979–), vols. 1, 2, and 5 seem to be currently available. Another modern critical edition is Johann von Staupitz, *Salzburger Predigten 1512: Eine textkritische Edition*, ed. Wolfram Schneider-Lastin (Tübingen, 1990).

[203] Johann von Staupitz, in 'Nuremberg Table Talk', Kn. 43.

[204] Posset, 157.

[205] *Salzburger Predigten 1512: Eine textkritische Edition*, 94.

[206] Posset, 96.

[207] Ibid., 87.

[208] Christoph Scheurl, *Christoph Scheurls Briefbuch, ein Beitrag zur Geschichte der Reformation und ihrer Zeit, Erster Band: Briefe von 1505–1516; Zweiter Band: Briefe von 1517–1540*, ed. Franz Freiherr Von Soden and Joachim Karl Friedrich Knaake (Potsdam, 1867–72; reprinted Aalen, 1962), No. 114. See also Posset, 157.

[209] Posset, 42, 76.

[210] Ibid., 1.

[211] Ibid., 74, 79.

[212] Ibid., 47, 57.

[213] Ibid., 50, 100, 159, 175.

[214] Posset, 40, notes that Staupitz studied Peter Lombard and lectured on *The Sentences*, but preferred the Bible. See also Steinmetz, *Misericordia Dei: The Theology of Johann von Staupitz in its Late Medieval Setting* (Leiden: E. J. Brill, 1968), 73.

Augustine's.[215] Similarly, Staupitz also appreciated much of Scotus' thought.[216] As for Thomas, Staupitz favoured some things he wrote, and disparaged others.[217] The Thomist Egidio da Roma, further, was a respected friend of Staupitz (and also the teaching authority of the Augustinian Order) who perhaps had some small measure of influence upon his thinking.[218] Finally, Staupitz held a deep appreciation for much of the teaching of Jean Gerson.[219] Some have speculated that Staupitz may have also been influenced by Gregory of Rimini, but recent scholarship has found no evidence to support that purported link.[220] On the other side of the coin, Staupitz had little time for Aristotle,[221] Alexander of Hales,[222] parts of Thomas, or Ockham.[223] Gabriel Biel's theology, especially, differed from Staupitz's.[224] Johann von Staupitz was most certainly not an adherent of the *via moderna* school of thought.[225]

The writings of various theologians influenced Staupitz to one degree or another, but these played a secondary role for him to the authority of Scripture. Starting with Scripture, then, it makes sense to begin with Genesis and Creation. Staupitz taught that humanity was originally created with free

---

[215] It is unclear whether or not Staupitz had come across the writings of another famous Augustinian, Gregory of Rimini. Manfred Schulze and Heiko Oberman have written on this topic: Schulze, 'Via Gregorii', 1–126. Oberman, 'Headwaters', 41–88. Both Schulze and Oberman argue that Staupitz was a member of the *via Gregorii*, bringing the theology of Gregory of Rimini to Luther. Posset disagrees, 177 n. 166, 369–70.

[216] Posset, 40–1, 75, 100–1, 370. But it is worth noting that Staupitz rarely quoted Scotus, and that he did not follow Scotus' doctrine on the human ability to love God by natural capacity. Posset, 100.

[217] Ernst Wolf, writing in 1927, characterized Staupitz as a Thomist (*Staupitz und Luther: ein beitrag zur theologie des Johannes von Staupitz und deren bedeutung für Luthers theologishchen werdegang* (New York: Johnson, 1971 (reprinted)). Cf. Steinmetz, *Luther and Staupitz*, 10. However, Steinmetz argues, in *Misericordia Dei*, 92, that Staupitz was not a disciple of Thomas, based on the doctrines of election and grace. Posset concurs, arguing that Staupitz's thought was more Scotist (Franciscan) than Thomistic (370).

[218] Posset, 48.

[219] Ibid., 16–17, 101.

[220] Steinmetz, *Luther and Staupitz*, 17.

[221] Ibid., 40, 176.

[222] Steinmetz, *Misericordia Dei*, 79.

[223] Posset, 370.

[224] Steinmetz, *Luther and Staupitz*, 74, 80; Steinmetz, *Misericordia Dei*, 119. Posset, 101, 175, 179, and 370. Manfred Schulze agrees in his 'Tübinger Gegensätze: Gabriel Biel und Johannes von Staupitz: von spätmittelalterlicher Reform zu Luthers Reformation', *Tübinger Blätter* 72 (1985), 54–9. As different as Staupitz and Biel's theological teachings were, it is difficult to ascertain whether or not Staupitz actually read Biel.

[225] Further, in light of the inconclusive evidence regarding Staupitz's familiarity with Gregory of Rimini, it is appropriate to concur with Posset, when he writes, 'Staupitz cannot be claimed for any definite late medieval school at all', 177, and, 'One should not force Staupitz into a scholastic mould', 179.

will. God gave Adam and Eve the threefold gifts of nature, grace, and glory.[226] In the beginning, Adam and Eve had the ability to be conformed to Christ.[227] They also, however, had the freedom to apostatize from the purpose for which God created them.[228] One day, they exercised that freedom, and so, they fell.

When Adam and Eve fell, their whole beings became corrupted by sin, which, like systemic rot, made human beings utterly infirm.[229] The intellect, too, was not exempted from this corruption.[230] As a result, the human will became bound and enslaved to sin.[231] This situation could not be remedied through any amount of human exertion—the situation was absolute.[232] Human beings were not only helpless to save themselves,[233] but they even required God's grace just to perform even the most insignificant of good works.[234] This was the objective reality of the human condition: our wills lay prostrate, enslaved, wounded, and impotent.[235]

Despite the objective bondage of the fallen human will, humans yet retained a subjective psychological freedom. Our *experience* was one of free decisions. It was just that because of the corruption of our wills through sin, people freely and joyfully made destructive choices. They were not coerced into transgressing. Sinning was what people *wanted* to do. After the Fall, human beings retained free will, but the choices from which they chose were now a subset of sinful options, with the desire to choose moral perfection no

[226] *Hiob*, 24.194.16–24. Cf. Steinmetz, *Misericordia Dei*, 60–1. Staupitz, *Nachfolgung* (1515) in Kn. 52.

[227] Steinmetz, *Misericordia Dei*, 62, 187.

[228] Ibid., 59.

[229] *Hiob*, 12.104.14–18. Steinmetz, *Luther and Staupitz*, 75.

[230] *Libellus*, 48. Steinmetz, *Misericordia Dei*, 69. Hence, due to the fallen intellect's inherent corruption, it made sense for Staupitz to posit the subordination of the authority of intellectual systems to the witness of the Scriptures themselves.

[231] Staupitz called the will *ligata voluntas*. Staupitz II, 134. See also Posset, 187. Cf. *Hiob*, 11.92.9. See also *Libellus*, 48; and *Hiob*, 27.213.9–15.

[232] *Nachfolgung*, Kn. 56. Steinmetz, *Luther and Staupitz*, 75. See also *Nachfolgung*, Kn. 54.

[233] *Nachfolgung*, Kn. 78. Cf. Steinmetz, *Luther and Staupitz*, 86. In a sermon in 1520, Staupitz taught that the free will is enfeebled by original sin such that people do not have the ability to rise up from sin and to march on. Only God's grace can help. R. K. Markwald, ed. and trans., *A Mystic's Passion: The Spirituality of Johannes von Staupitz in his 1520 Lenten Sermons: Translation and Commentary* (New York, 1990), 56. See also Posset, 306. Further, human efforts not only fail to save, but instead increase the sinner's damnation! *Nachfolgung*, Kn. 54. *Lieb gottes*, Kn. 113. Cf. Steinmetz, *Misericordia Dei*, 70, 119. Luther, in his *Table Talk*, recalled that Staupitz taught that one cannot fulfil the Law through free will. WATr 2.665.28–666, No. 2797a.

[234] The righteousness of humans is impure. *Nachfolgung*, Kn. 69. Cf. Steinmetz, *Misericordia Dei*, 109. Prior to the infusion of *gratia gratum faciens*, the sinner can neither turn from evil nor praise God with his good works, words, and thoughts. *Hiob*, 1.3.8–10. Steinmetz, *Misericordia Dei*, 114.

[235] *Libellus*, 16. Steinmetz, *Misericordia Dei*, 70. Cf. ibid., 80. Posset (p. 1) writes that Staupitz's motto was, 'I am yours, save me.'

longer available to them. Simply put, the entire mass of humanity was continually busy finding all sorts of creative and unique ways to go to hell. The will, then, in light of the Fall, was objectively enslaved to sin, although it yet presented itself as subjectively free to human experience.[236]

All, then, in their own free, creative ways, were on the road to eternal damnation and were therefore helpless to save themselves.[237] But God, in his great mercy, unilaterally decided to save a remnant from out of this fallen mass of humanity. God predestined his elect for redemption and eternal life.[238] This indeed was his prerogative, because he alone was God. Sinners did not set the terms of mercy—God did.[239] God was Lord and the ultimate cause of all things[240] (except sin and evil, which he merely permitted in order to bring about a greater good).[241] God's rule was absolute, and his will immutable.[242] Consequently, *God* caused the election of specific human beings. People were incapable of meriting their own election.[243] Contrary to the teachings of Biel, Staupitz taught that predestination was not merited, but was entirely the free choice of God alone. Humans had nothing to do with it. God chose from before all time those whom he would save, and, in his death on the cross, the Lord Jesus effectively redeemed God's elect.[244]

Those who were elect, however, were not automatically and completely passively transferred directly from slavery to sin to exultation in glory. The elect had been chosen to enter into a *process*. Those who were predestined were given God's grace,[245] on account of which they repented of their sins and chose faith in Christ. This grace, accompanying the free efforts of the wills of the elect, transformed the chosen sinner[246] to be both conformed and united to Jesus Christ.[247] It was only at the end of this process that the perfected elect person entered into glory.

---

[236] *Libellus*, 32–3. Steinmetz, *Misericordia Dei*, 69–70, 113. See also *Hiob*, 15.134.41–135.3.

[237] *Libellus*, 48. Cf. *Hiob*, 11.92.9 and 27.213.9–15.

[238] *Hiob*, 11.92.6–22. Staupitz also has a chapter on the certainty of predestination in his, *Von dem heyligen rechten Christlichen glauben: Johannes Staubitz Nach seinem abschayden an tag kumen vnd außgangen* (Nuremberg: Jobst Gutknecht, 1525). See Posset, 346; Steinmetz, *Luther and Staupitz*, 72f., 79.

[239] Kn. 58. Steinmetz, *Luther and Staupitz*, 77, 123; *Misericodia Dei*, 80, 92f.

[240] Steinmetz, *Misericordia Dei*, 58.

[241] Ibid., 57.

[242] *Libellus*, 86.

[243] *Libellus*, 21. Steinmetz, *Misericordia Dei*, 79f., 114.

[244] *Libellus*, 84. For discussion, see Steinmetz, *Luther and Staupitz*, 104.

[245] Staupitz II, 96. See Posset, 369. See also *Libellus*, 22, 27; Kn. 142.

[246] Good works are not the presupposition of election, but its fruit. Steinmetz, *Misericordia Dei*, 79. *Libellus*, 52. Also *Libellus*, 45.

[247] *Libellus*, 20, 57. Steinmetz, *Misericordia Dei*, 89–91.

If God chose some to enter into an inexorable process leading to salvation, did it therefore follow that he actively selected the rest for damnation? No, Staupitz replied, not necessarily. The reprobate were simply those *not chosen* for election. They could hear the Word of the Lord, but they failed to act upon it. They then suffered damnation on account of their own freely chosen sins.[248] Staupitz refused to go so far as to advocate a predestination to death.[249]

Despite this strong view of the sovereignty of God, Staupitz argued that neither the reprobate nor the elect were deprived of the ability to make genuinely free choices.[250] The reprobate merely made free choices within their own limited subsets of sinful possibilities, and hence, no matter how they used their freedom, they ended up under the Lord's condemnation.[251] The elect, on the other hand, had *more* freedom than the reprobate. To the elect, God opened up possibilities for freedom of action additional to those choices available to the reprobate. To the elect, God allowed the freedom to select repentance, faith, and a transformed life. By artful application of continuous providential events in the lives of the elect, God presented the elect with repeated opportunities for conversion until the person freely decided to accept.[252] Predestination, therefore, for Staupitz, did not mean *less* freedom for people, but rather, *more!*[253]

Staupitz acknowledged that this doctrine of predestination was awesome and mysterious, and so he encouraged a large measure of intellectual humility. He advised that no person could know whether or not they were elect,[254] and he further stated that human beings could not know all of God's reasons for his actions. Therefore, no one should speculate about predestination, but merely contemplate the wounds of Christ and trust in the Lord.[255]

While no one could know for certain whether or not any particular person had been predestined, Staupitz argued that we do know that those who *were* predestined inevitably received the outpouring of God's justifying grace[256] (first infused at baptism[257]). Grace was necessary for salvation, and it was

---

[248] Steinmetz, *Misericordia Dei*, 73, 80, 92.

[249] Posset, 369.

[250] Staupitz II, 237. See Posset, 187.

[251] The reprobate are called to repent, but choose not to. *Libellus*, 24. Steinmetz, *Misericordia Dei*, 83.

[252] Posset, 197. Staupitz, *Sämmtliche Werke*, 115–16.

[253] *Libellus*, 170.

[254] Steinmetz, *Misericordia Dei*, 122–5.

[255] In *Table Talk*, Luther said of Staupitz: 'Staupitius: Si, inquiens, vis disputare de praedestinatione, incipe a vulneribus Christi . . .'. WATr 1.512.19–20, Nr. 1017. See also Posset, 307, 354.

[256] *Libellus*, 27. See also Steinmetz, *Misericordia Dei*, 79.

[257] *Hiob*, 23.189.23–6. The sacrament of penance then acts as a renewal of baptismal grace for those who fall into mortal sin. *Hiob*, 11.94.15–19. Steinmetz, *Misericordia Dei*, 97.

neither merited nor contingent upon any human choice or activity.[258] In a major break from those who came before him, Staupitz defined grace as simply God's mercy,[259] rather than metaphysical fuel for good works. Grace (divine mercy) was inevitably bestowed upon the elect, entirely at God's instigation.[260] Grace alone,[261] then, was the motive force in propelling the individual along toward salvation.

When God then began to grant his prevenient grace[262] to one of his elect, he effectively called that one to faith,[263] although in a non-coercive manner. *All* those who had been chosen would come to faith and reform their lives, although none were *forced* to do so.[264] God simply instilled humility in elect sinners by convincing them that they could not trust their own righteousness, but must trust in God alone.[265] God then instilled *gratia gratum faciens* into the person. However, here was a unique twist in Staupitz's thinking: *gratia gratum faciens* did not make the person pleasing to God, but rather, it made God pleasing to the person![266] Staupitz called this 'the sweetness of God', or sometimes, 'the heavenly sugar', or, 'the heavenly magnet'.[267] This was perhaps a development of Augustine's idea of God granting 'victorious delight' to the elect. In any case, Staupitz gave this idea new emphasis. At this point, the

---

[258] Grace as a gift: *Libellus*, 19, 33, 42. *Lieb gottes*, Kn. 113. See also Steinmetz, *Misericordia Dei*, 97.

[259] Posset, 46–7, notes that Staupitz makes no distinction between *gratia* and *misericordia*, thereby rendering them synonymous.

[260] Posset, 43, characterizes Staupitz as a 'sermonizer on the priority of God's mercy'.

[261] Posset, 1, 47, 159 n. 96. The primacy of grace is a major theme of Staupitz's sermons of 1512, which can be found in an accessible form in *Salzburger Predigten 1512*. See also *Nachfolgung*, Kn. 84; Sermon 1, Staupitz I, 49. This grace comes to us through Jesus Christ: 'Gratia dei per Iesum Christum dominum nostrum'. Sermon 27, Staupitz I, 399.

[262] Staupitz says that prevenient grace includes preaching (*Hiob*, 20.169.1–9), tribulation and temptation (*Hiob*, 12.108.7–12), a general call (*Libellus*, 24), and a special call within the believer's heart (Kn. 83, 106, 108–9). See Steinmetz, *Misericordia Dei*, 94.

[263] Quoted in Posset, 305. Folio 120r (Sermon 14). Cf. Adolar Zumkeller, *Johann von Staupitz und seine christliche Heilslehre* (Würzburg: Augustinus-Verlag, 1994), 157–8.

[264] Staupitz II, 237. See also *Libellus*, 90.

[265] *Hiob*, 1.3.5–24; 22.178.2–9; 23.187.5–8; 23.186.32–187.3. For Staupitz, humility is itself a fruit of predestination. *Hiob*, 11.91.27ff. and 11.92.30ff. See Steinmetz, *Luther and Staupitz*, 73 n. 53.

[266] Staupitz II, 116–17, no. 36 (ch. 6). See also *Libellus*, 40, 86, 131, and 152; Staupitz, *Sämmtliche Werke*, 28. Cf. Steinmetz, *Misericordia Dei*, 84 n. 3, 86, 97 n. 1; Posset, 178; Zumkeller, 199.

[267] To find Luther echoing this same language of 'the sweetness of God', see WA 8.379.2–21. '... [T]he Creator of nature is the mighty mover of a free-willed creation that the inexpressible loveliness of God as sensed in the heart lifts up, enkindles, melts, and joyously raptures the spirit full of jubilation. Does not the [magnet] draw the unmoved iron to itself? Then should the eternal heavenly Magnet [*adamant*] not draw the hardest and choked-up soul out of and above itself and guide it to Him?' Trans. Posset, 197. Staupitz, *Sämmtliche Werke*, 115–16.

sinner would freely choose to embrace this irresistibly attractive God, embarking on a new life of faith and good works.[268]

This inevitable free decision of the elect to have faith in Christ served as the cause of their salvation. Men and women were saved by faith alone.[269] But then, following the free gift of God's grace by which the decision of faith was made possible (and elicited), a Christian could *grow* in grace through the conscientious striving to do his best (*facere quod in se est*).[270] These works of the striving Christian were then deemed by God to be meritorious, even though such works were not *inherently* meritorious. God's prior decision to accept the individual was the basis upon which he decided to view that individual's grace-assisted strivings as meritorious.[271]

In conclusion, Staupitz's Augustinian bias and emphasis on salvation through Christ alone, grace alone, and faith alone provided a fertile seedbed for the emergence of Luther's own theological emphases, as we shall see. Further, while striving to preserve the dignity and importance of the human will in the decision to come to faith in Jesus Christ, Staupitz nevertheless insisted that only the elect could (and indeed, inevitably would) come to faith. So while attempting to preserve a role for the freedom of the will, Staupitz still subordinated the most significant human decisions to prior divine ones.

ERASMUS: *c.*1467–1536

At the beginning of the sixteenth century, no scholar was more influential than Desiderius Erasmus. He has been called the supreme humanist scholar, and he has jestingly been nominated as the patron saint of networkers, because of his enormous literary correspondence.[272] For both Luther and Melanchthon, Erasmus was a man who had to be taken seriously, and whose theological opinions *mattered*.

With the advent of the Reformation, Martin Luther caught Erasmus' attention when he published his *Assertio*,[273] in which he claimed that the

---

[268] While Staupitz appears to be unique in his use of the phrase 'the sweetness of God', this *does* sound quite similar to Augustine's 'victorious delight' (*victrix delectatio*). Staupitz may well have been inspired here by his reading of Augustine.

[269] Staupitz, fos. 181v–182r. Sermon 19, Zumkeller, 158. Quoted in Posset, 307. See also Staupitz's Lenten Sermon 5, Salzburg, 1520, in Markwald, *A Mystic's Passion*, 134.

[270] *Hiob*, 5.30.15–19; 5.32.1–9; 5.32.13–24; 20.168.39–169.1. See also Steinmetz, *Misericordia Dei*, 114–15.

[271] *Hiob*, 23.186.32–187.3; 23.189.23–6.

[272] MacCulloch, *The Reformation*, 94.

[273] *Assertio omnium articulorum M. Lutheri per bullam Leonis X. novissimam damnatorum*, December 1520. WA 7.94–151.

will was bound, and could do nothing but sin. In 1524, Erasmus took issue
with Luther on this doctrine, and wrote a major doctrinal work entitled *De
libero arbitrio (On Free Choice)*. There he defended his thesis on justification
that 'I think there to be a certain power of free choice'.[274] Within this work,
one could get a good grasp not only of Erasmus' views on the nature of the
will, but also on his entire soteriology.[275] Further, it was in reply to this work
that Luther would write his important *De servo arbitrio (On Bound Choice)*.

In *De libero arbitrio,* Erasmus employed his own unique theological methodology. A true humanist, Erasmus placed great importance on going back to
the original sources (*ad fontes*)—meaning the Scriptures. His work on producing a new scholarly edition of the Greek New Testament bore clear
testimony to this conviction. Further, because the Scriptures in their original
languages were so important, the faithful exegete had to master not only the
original tongues, but also the crucial disciplines of grammar and rhetoric. As
Marjorie O'Rourke Boyle points out, 'The theologian ought to be learned in
arts which might assist with the interpretation of the divine text.'[276] Or more
strongly, 'If the theologian is to be acute in the discernment of reality, he must
enter the path to knowledge with a grammar book in hand.'[277] For Erasmus,
rhetoric and grammar, were, in fact, more important subjects than the logic of
the schoolmen.[278] Regarding these scholastics, Erasmus wrote, 'They are more
stupid than any pig and lack common sense, they think they themselves
occupy the whole citadel of learning. They bring everyone to task; they
condemn; they pontificate; they are never in doubt; they have no hesitations;
they know everything. And yet few in number as they are, these people are
causing tremendous commotion.'[279] Rather, true doctrine came from the

---

[274] DLA I.a.5. LCC 17.37. 'Arbitror esse aliquam liberi arbitrii vim'. EAS 4.8.

[275] The strongly doctrinal nature of *De libero arbitrio* was a rare thing for Erasmus. He was
more wont to focus on simple piety rather than doctrine, and indeed, apart from the *Hyperaspistes* of 1526, Erasmus barely mentioned justification again. Luther complained about this
fact in 1532, saying, '[Erasmus] never has anything to say about the article of justification. He
mentions Christ for the sake of his stipends, but he doesn't care.' LW 54.136. '[Erasmus] nihil de
articulo iustificationis unquam loquitur. Nominat Christum propter praebendas, non curat.'
WATr 2.41.13–14. No. 1319.

[276] Marjorie O'Rourke Boyle, *Erasmus on Language and Method in Theology* (Toronto:
University of Toronto Press, 1977), 36. This is a major theme throughout this book, but see
also esp. pp. 37, 57, 119. For more on Erasmus' methodology, see also John F. Tinkler, 'Erasmus'
Conversation with Luther', *ARG* 82 (1991), 59–81.

[277] Ibid., 72.

[278] Ibid., 55, 96.

[279] Quoted in Boyle (quotation trans. Olin), *Erasmus on Language and Method in Theology*,
96. EE II.99 (No. 337.321–5). Erasmus also criticized the abuses of scholasticism (such as
profiteering, indulgences, and scaring people with hellfire if they did not do precisely what
the priors desired). e.g. DLA IV.15. LCC 17.95. EAS 4.186. Further, in a turn that puts the lie to
Erasmus' famous purported refinement, Euan Cameron points out that 'Erasmus could also

Scriptures, clearly understood and explained (with Christ the Word of God as their interpretive key) through the tools of grammar and rhetoric.

But despite Erasmus' emphasis on Scripture and his scorn for scholasticism, he nevertheless approached theology quite deferentially. Scripture was important, but so was church tradition. He declared, 'I everywhere willingly submit my personal feelings [to the decrees of the Church], whether I grasp what it prescribes or not.'[280] As McConica writes, 'He always stresses the corporate understanding of the community of the church and did not believe that a particular revelation could take precedence over the tested experience of the body of believers through the ages.'[281] Boyle, noting this tension in Erasmus between 'a bold transformation of the new philology into theological method, and a submissive appeal to Christian tradition', calls him 'a Janus in the history of theological methodology'.[282] Erasmus still felt that 'the old church, for all its faults, must remain the vessel of salvation, cleansed of its faults and abuses and opened to those who have fallen away'.[283] On salvation, the church continued to be correct, and with the doctrine of justification the church taught that free choice did in fact exist: 'There is a whole chorus of saints who support free choice.'[284] Moreover, Erasmus concurred with the church in denying Pelagius' view of free will, and he also rejected Luther's doctrine as being the opposite extreme. In the middle was Scotus, who, although a schoolman, had 'quite enough' free will.[285] Erasmus thus affirmed Scotus' doctrine of the will, which he then set out to defend against Luther in *De libero arbitrio.*

In approaching *De libero arbitrio*, Erasmus proceeded with an intentional rhetorical style. Assuming the role of instructor, with Luther as his pupil,[286]

---

descend to schoolyard insult: he repeatedly called Guillaume Farel "Phallicus". Cameron, 'Philipp Melanchthon: Image and Substance', *JEH* 48 (1997), 714.

[280] DLA I.a.4. LCC 17.37. EAS 4.6. See also DLA IV.17. LCC 17.97. EAS 4.194.

[281] OER 2.58. MacCulloch, *The Reformation*, 97.

[282] Boyle, *Erasmus on Language and Method in Theology*, 8. Janus was a Roman god customarily depicted with two faces, looking in opposite directions. See also Boyle, in *Rhetoric and Reform: Erasmus' Civil Dispute with Luther*, Harvard Historical Monographs 71 (Cambridge, MA: Harvard University Press, 1983), 22.

[283] J. Kelley Sowards, *Desiderius Erasmus* (Boston: Twayne, 1975), 130.

[284] DLA I.b.5. LCC 17.44–5. 'Totus sanctorum chorus, qui statuunt liberum arbitrium.' EAS 4.28.

[285] 'Pelagius has no doubt attributed too much to free choice, and Scotus quite enough (*Scotus tribuit affatim*), but Luther first mutilated it by cutting off its right arm; then not content with this he thoroughly cut the throat of free choice and dispatched it.' DLA IV.16. LCC 17.96. EAS 4.188. Erasmus also denied Pelagius at DLA IV.7. LCC 17.89. EAS 4.168.

[286] Boyle, *Rhetoric and Reform*, 5. While Boyle gives some insightful observations in this book on Erasmian rhetoric, she generally overemphasizes Luther and Erasmus' *style*, and underemphasizes the doctrinal *content* of their dispute.

Erasmus employed the Ciceronian rhetorical style known as *deliberative*. This was a style of speech normally utilized when speaking of the good of the commonwealth, and it employed the method of collecting and expressing opinions based on the balance of evidence, in order to obtain the most societally advantageous and morally upright result.[287] (Luther, in his reply, would use the much more assertive *judicial* rhetorical style—which seeks a definite answer, rather than a preponderance of opinion.) Hence, Erasmus, in the selection of even the rhetorical style of his diatribe, made a choice that highlighted the importance of personal moral endeavour. Erasmus, in fact, chose a formally moralizing structure for his book because such ethical striving was, for him, integral to the attainment of salvation. Luther, on the other hand, chose a judicial rhetorical style more fitting to his own forensic doctrine of justification by faith alone.[288]

In *De libero arbitrio*, Erasmus made a sustained argument in favour of free choice in justification, citing both church tradition and Scripture. He defined free choice as follows: 'By free choice ... we mean a power of the human will by which a man can apply himself to the things which lead to eternal salvation, or turn away from them.'[289] Erasmus did not immediately clarify what he meant by 'the things which lead to eternal salvation', but over the course of the book, he would explain that his view of salvation included grace (as metaphysical fuel for good works), human effort, and the traditional transformational model of justification—that is, with grace and human effort, people began to acquire their own righteousness within them, such that if they persevered, one day (perhaps after this life), they would become fully righteous and merit salvation from within themselves.[290]

An integral part of this transformational soteriological model included the doctrine of original sin. For Erasmus, the Fall was not the unmitigated disaster Luther made it out to be. Erasmus wrote, 'For although free choice

---

[287] Boyle, *Rhetoric and Reform*, 15. Boyle points out that Erasmus' use of the Ciceronian deliberative style explains Erasmus' famous remarks about being 'skeptical' (see pp. 17–19). Timothy Wengert, on the other hand, sees Erasmus' deliberative style as a *faux* neutrality: 'Erasmus maintains his neutrality in this matter, rather like the unfaithful spouse caught *flagrante delicto*, who when faced with his wife's angry assertions replies, "Let's talk about this like reasonable adults".' Wengert, 'Philip Melanchthon's Contribution to Luther's Debate with Erasmus Over the Bondage of the Will', in Joseph A. Burgess and Marc Kolden, eds., *By Faith Alone: Essays on Justification in Honor of Gerhard O. Forde* (Grand Rapids: Eerdmans, 2004), 111.

[288] Cf. Boyle, *Rhetoric and Reform*, 47. Boyle, while cleverly highlighting the two men's methodological tendencies, goes too far in labelling Erasmus as a sceptic and Luther as a stoic. Neither man fits quite so snugly into the labels of pagan antiquity.

[289] DLA I.b.10. LCC 17.47. EAS 4.36.

[290] This transformational model of justification would come to stand in contrast to Luther's and Melanchthon's doctrine of *imputed* rather than *intrinsic* righteousness.

is damaged by sin, it is nevertheless not extinguished by it.'[291] Original sin was not something intrinsically passed on to all human beings, but rather all human beings fell prey to it as a result of their own decisions to sin. Erasmus argued that 'No one failed to imitate the example of the first parent.'[292] Rabil explains, 'Erasmus refuses to make Adam responsible for the sin of all his descendants. We do indeed follow Adam, and there does seem to be a natural propensity in man to sin. But this propensity results more from imitation than it does from nature.'[293] Similarly, MacCulloch writes, 'We must note that Desiderius Erasmus did not share in the general stampede to praise Augustine. He had too much respect for creativity and dignity in human beings to feel that the human mind had been utterly corrupted in the Fall of Adam and Eve.'[294] Erasmus endorsed a weak view of original sin that left free will intact.[295]

Erasmus' mild view of original sin not only left intact the freedom of the will, but, as MacCulloch has already suggested, it also allowed for a higher estimation of reason than Luther and his followers were willing to admit. Erasmus maintained that 'Reason is obscured by sin, but not altogether extinguished.'[296] As a result, he had very little patience with the appearance of rational inconsistency (or paradox, or antinomy). He affirmed that Scripture could not be in conflict with itself,[297] and he wrote, 'But where axioms are put forward in the disputing of truth, I do not consider paradoxes of this kind should be used, for they are almost riddles, and in these matters it is moderation which pleases me at any rate.'[298] Elsewhere, he wrote, 'For . . . Luther's paradoxes I have not yet a mind to die.'[299] Bainton, putting a negative spin on Erasmus' position, writes, 'Erasmus would rather give up God's

---

[291] DLA II.a.8. LCC 17.51. 'Quamquam enim arbitrii libertas per peccatum vulnus accepit, non tamen exstincta est.' EAS 4.48.

[292] Trans. Albert Rabil, *Erasmus and the New Testament: The Mind of a Christian Humanist* (San Antonio: Trinity University Press, 1972), 147. LB 7.793b. Cf. LB 6.585b=590b.

[293] Rabil, 147.

[294] MacCulloch, 109.

[295] As for the view of original sin held by Luther and his followers, Erasmus said, 'they immeasurably exaggerate original sin'. DLA IV.13. LCC 17.93. 'Exaggerant in immensum peccatum originale'. EAS 4.182.

[296] DLA II.a.3. LCC 17.48. '[R]ationem dicere malis, per peccatum obscurata est, non exstincta.' EAS 4.40. Boyle shows that Erasmus believed God was impenetrable to human reason. *Erasmus on Language and Method*, 22.

[297] DLA I.b.10. LCC 17.47. EAS 4.36. DLA IV.1. LCC 17.85. EAS 4.156.

[298] DLA IV.16. LCC 17.96. 'Verum ubi in disquisitione proponuntur ἀξιώματα, non arbitror utendum huiusmodi paradoxis, quae non multum absunt ab aenigmatibus, mihi quidem in his placet moderatio.' EAS 4.188. For other passages against paradox, see DLA I.b.30. LCC 17.45. EAS 4.30. DLA IV.13. LCC 17.93. EAS 4.182. DLA IV.17. LCC 17.97. EAS 4.192.

[299] LB 10.1663A–B. Trans. in Marjorie O'Rourke Boyle, 'Stoic Luther: Paradoxical Sin and Necessity', *ARG* 73 (1982), 69.

absolute power than to make Him no longer amenable to the canons of human reason and moral sense.'[300] In other words, Erasmus was far readier to attempt rational explanations of difficult doctrines that others (such as Luther, with predestination and free will) were content to label a mystery, or a paradox. In the Fall, human reason was wounded, but not destroyed,[301] according to Erasmus.

Justification presented few mysteries, as far as Erasmus was concerned. Free choice and grace worked together,[302] and merit was the end product, by which salvation could be attained. It was necessary for the sinner to prepare his heart for grace,[303] and then, once received, grace was to be utilized in combination with free human effort to fulfil the Law and thus attain to righteousness. In Erasmus' words, 'Those who imitate and fulfil the law by their deeds and habits are considered righteous in God's judgment.'[304] Following the reception of grace, salvation was possible via good works, even as the Pelagians taught.[305] People were co-workers with grace in their salvation.[306] This was the method of justification that God had ordained, although by his absolute power he could surely operate outside the bounds of these parameters.[307] Thus Erasmus' overall view of justification fitted into the broad church tradition of justification as the slow growth of internal righteousness in the Christian. Yet, to understand precisely how Erasmus conceived of free will within this paradigm, a closer examination of his understanding of grace and merit is necessary.

---

[300] Roland H. Bainton, *Erasmus of Christendom* (London: Collins, 1969), 232. Cf. Boyle's more nuanced view in *Erasmus on Language and Method*, 138.

[301] See MacCulloch, *The Reformation*, 147.

[302] DLA III.a.17. LCC 17.74. EAS 4.120.

[303] DLA III.b.6. LCC 17.77. EAS 4.130.

[304] Trans. Rabil, 166. LB 7.783d. Cf. LB 7.787b–c; 801e.

[305] 'But, by the grace of God, when sin has been forgiven, the will is made free to the extent that, according to the views of the Pelagians, even apart from the help of new grace, it could attain eternal life, so that just as it could do homage for salvation received to God who created and restored free will, according to the orthodox, so it is possible for man, with the help of divine grace (which always accompanies human effort), to continue in the right, yet not without a tendency to sin, owing to the vestiges of original sin in him.' DLA II.a.3. LCC 17.49. The editors of LCC 17 comment that this Latin sentence 'is among the most obscure in the entire discourse': 'Sed per dei gratiam condonato peccato hactenus facta est libera, ut iuxta sententiam Pelagianorum absque praesidio novae gratiae posset adipisci vitam aeternam, sic tamen, ut salutem suam deo ferret acceptam, qui et condidit et restituit liberum arbitrium, secundum orthodoxos sic posset ope divinae gratiae semper adiuvantis conatum hominis perseverare in recto statu, ut tamen non careret proclivitate ad malum ex semel inoliti peccati vestigiis.' EAS 4.40.

[306] DLA IV.7. LCC 17.89–90. EAS 4.170. Here Erasmus used the word sunergein. See also DLA III.c.6–11. LCC 17.81–4. EAS 4.144–54.

[307] Erasmus spoke about the two powers of God in relation to justification at DLA III.a.8. LCC 17.67–8. EAS 4.100–2.

Erasmus taught that there were four types of grace: natural, peculiar, cooperating, and completing. Natural grace (*gratia naturalis*) was that grace available to all people by nature. It involved the freedom of contingency— freedom to do everyday tasks. Such freedom was vitiated, but not extinguished, by sin.[308] Peculiar grace (*gratia peculiaris*)[309] was that grace by which God urged people to repent of their sins. Such grace came in the form of preaching, for example. This was the grace 'where God, in his mercy, arouses the sinner wholly without merit to repent, yet without infusing that supreme grace which abolishes sin and makes him pleasing to God'.[310] Like natural grace, peculiar grace was common to all people,[311] and it was the means by which people were to prepare themselves for cooperating grace. Cooperating grace (*gratia ... quam cooperantem diximus*) was the grace by which God made the human will effective in its desire to seek the good.[312] This was the grace by which a person, through the efforts of her will, could become justified. Finally, completing grace (*gratia, quae perducit usque ad finem*) ensured that a person with cooperating grace persevered unto salvation.

With these four types of grace in mind, it became clear that when Erasmus argued that people had free choice, he assumed that all people possessed natural and peculiar grace (but not cooperating and completing grace). Having natural and peculiar grace was the default status for *all* people, and because people had that grace, they could 'apply themselves to the things which lead to salvation, or turn away from them'. In other words, when Erasmus said that justification took place through both grace and human free will, he meant that all people naturally possessed natural and peculiar grace, and therefore, they could, of their own free wills, decide whether or not they wanted to turn to God and receive cooperating and completing grace. This distinction made sense of all Erasmus' words on both grace and free

---

[308] DLA II.a.11. LCC 17.52. EAS 4.52. Further arguing for contingent freedom in the affairs of the world, Erasmus utilized the distinction between the necessity of the consequence and the necessity of the consequent. DLA III.a.8. LCC 17.68. EAS 4.100–4.

[309] Erasmus also referred to *gratia peculiaris* as *secunda gratia, quam diximus operantem* (EAS 4.54), or *gratia exstimulans* (EAS 4.56).

[310] DLA II.a.11. LCC 17.52–3. EAS 4.54.

[311] 'This grace, which we call the second grace, is, by the goodness of God, not denied to anyone, for the divine benevolence supplies sufficient opportunities to each in this life by which he may recover, if he will, the use of the free choice that remains to him and put his powers at the disposal of that divine will which invites but does not constrain him forcibly to higher things.' DLA II.a.11. LCC 17.53. EAS 4.54. This idea sounds strange to modern ears, for of course there are people who never hear about the Gospel during the course of their lives. Perhaps Erasmus did not allow his mind to range outside the scope of the Christian world.

[312] DLA II.a.11. LCC 17.53. EAS 4.56.

will.[313] Grace was the primary cause of salvation (because without natural and peculiar grace people could never effectively exercise their wills for salvation), and the use of the free will was the secondary cause of justification.[314]

According to Erasmus' conception of justification, equal opportunity for salvation was provided to all. Everyone had both natural and peculiar grace, and so everyone, if they so decided, could seek the things of God and accordingly receive cooperating grace. Rabil comments, 'The potential of those born to glory here on earth [must] be realized through their actions—or not at all. And contrariwise, the actions of those not born to glory can raise them to glory. This is the possibility which Christ has un-leashed in the world.'[315] Naturally, if salvation was equally open to all, then salvation rested in the free decisions of individuals, and not in God's pre-destining will. Accordingly, Erasmus taught that God foreknew all things, but that he did not determine events.[316] As for the word 'predestination' itself, Erasmus avoided it like the plague. He did, however, spend seventeen sections essentially interpreting Romans 9 in non-predestinarian terms.[317] Because humans had free choice, predestination could not be true.

To tie it all together, we have seen how closely Erasmus' advocacy of free will was incorporated into his traditional Roman Catholic doctrine of justifi-cation.[318] The transformational paradigm of justification where righteousness grew intrinsically within the Christian was a model (at least according to

---

[313] e.g. DLA III.a.4. LCC 17.66. EAS 4.96. In other words, humans were required to exercise their wills and give their best efforts, but their willing and their best efforts were only possible in the first place because they had the common natural and peculiar graces—apart from God such actions could never have been undertaken. Similar statements can be found scattered throughout DLA III.b.6–IV.10. LCC 17.77–91. EAS 4.130–76. See also DLA II.a.12. LCC 17.53: 'Those who . . . attribute most of all to grace and practically nothing to free choice, yet do not entirely remove it, for they deny that man can will the good without peculiar grace, they deny that he can make a beginning, they deny that he can progress, they deny he can reach his goal without the principal and perpetual aid of divine grace. Their view seems probable enough in that it leaves man to study and strive, but it does not leave aught for him to ascribe to his own powers.' EAS 4.56.

[314] 'Grace is the principal cause and the will secondary, which can do nothing apart from the principal cause, since the principal is sufficient in itself.' DLA IV.8. LCC 17.90. '[G]ratia sit causa principalis, voluntas secundaria, quae sine principali nihil possit, cum principalis sibi sufficiat.' EAS 4.172.

[315] Rabil, 154.

[316] DLA III.a.5. LCC 17.66. EAS 4.96.

[317] DLA III.a.1–17. LCC 17.64–74. EAS 4.90–120. Erasmus argued that the 'Esau have I hated' passage of Romans 9 referred only to temporal misfortunes, and not to salvation. Further, Erasmus interpreted the potter and clay illustration of the same chapter as an argument *for* free will.

[318] Nevertheless, at one point the Roman Inquisition sought to ban all of Erasmus' writings. MacCulloch, 101, 269.

secondary causes, if not primary) endorsed by Augustine,[319] Peter, Thomas, Scotus, Ockham, Gregory of Rimini, Biel, and even Staupitz. All these theologians viewed the created habit of grace as important. Erasmus viewed the exercise of the grace-aided free will as inherently necessary to this paradigm of justification. Further, free will eliminated the problem of the idea of reprobation, and it also provided the best motivation for doing good works—for, if one's very salvation rested upon doing good works (with the aid of cooperating grace), then surely, that was the strongest possible incentive to shape up and strive for righteousness.[320]

CONCLUSION

Having now surveyed some of the major historical positions on the freedom of the will that were present in the intellectual milieu of the early sixteenth century, we will be better placed to explore Melanchthon's views. It is interesting to note that in the progression from Augustine to Peter to Thomas to Scotus to Ockham to Biel to Erasmus, the doctrines of original sin presented grew gradually weaker, while the will's role for salvation grew gradually more significant. Scotus helped accelerate this transformative doctrinal process by affirming a distinction between God's absolute and ordained powers. Subsequent theologians (Ockham, Biel, and Erasmus) gradually shifted the emphasis from God's absolute power to God's ordained power, and in the process, the doctrine of predestination went by the wayside, to make more room for the activity of the will. At the same time, as we have seen above, at least two voices (Gregory of Rimini and Johann von Staupitz, probably independently of one another) reaffirmed many of the distinctives Augustine had originally laid out. *All* these theologians, however, described a cooperative, transformational model of justification.

Next, this background work of contextualization is not yet finished, for a thorough understanding of Melanchthon's theology is not possible apart from the weighty consideration of Martin Luther. We will devote now a chapter to Luther—his theology of the will, and his influence on Melanchthon.

---

[319] Interestingly, looking just at Augustine's views on free will apart from his transformational paradigm of justification, Erasmus said that he liked Augustine better *before* he had his controversy with the Pelagians: 'After his battle with Pelagius, Augustine became less just toward free choice than he had been before.' DLA IV.7. LCC 17.90. EAS 4.170.

[320] DLA IV.16. LCC 17.96. EAS 4.190.

3

Luther

The person who had the most profound effect on Melanchthon's theology was undoubtedly Martin Luther. Melanchthon arrived in Wittenberg on 25 August 1518, at the very beginning of the Reformation—ten months after Luther posted his theses, four months after the Heidelberg Disputation, and less than a month before Luther departed for Augsburg for his interview with Cajetan. Young Philipp was 21 years old. Upon his arrival to teach Greek at Wittenberg, Melanchthon began studying theology in earnest, under the direction of Luther, who was 32 at the time. To better understand the shape of Melanchthon's early theology, it is necessary to explore the nature of his relationship with Luther, the extent to which Luther influenced Melanchthon, and the content of Luther's doctrine of the will during this period.

THE RELATIONSHIP BETWEEN LUTHER AND MELANCHTHON

Personal Relationship

Melanchthon and Luther certainly respected each other as colleagues. As Steinmetz writes, '[Melanchthon] was the only humanist for whom Luther had an enduring, almost unexplainable respect.'[1] In evaluating his contemporaries, Luther once wrote on his table in chalk, 'Substance and words—Philip. Words without substance—Erasmus. Substance without words—Luther. Neither substance nor words—Karlstadt.' Melanchthon came into the room soon after, and seeing the writing, insisted that 'words' also be attributed to Luther.[2] Melanchthon and Luther did respect each other.

---

[1] D. C. Steinmetz, *Reformers in the Wings* (Philadelphia: Fortress Press, 1971), 49.
[2] LW 54.245, Nr. 3618. WATr 3.460–461.38–40, 1–3, Nr. 3619. 'Prima die Augusti a prandio sedebat in mensa, speculabatur et creta mensae scribebat: Res et verba Philippus, verba sine res Erasmus, res sine verbis Lutherus, nec res nec verba Carolostadius. Dum haec scripsisset, advenit casu Dominus Philippus cum Magistro Bailio, dicens in Erasmo et Carolostadio verum esse, sed sibi nimium tribui, et Luthero verba etiam tribuenda'.

However, in recent years there has been some discussion in the literature as to whether or not Luther and Melanchthon's mutual respect actually rose to the level of friendship. This issue has some bearing on the topic at hand, for friends are more likely to influence each other than acquaintances. Knowing Luther's forceful personality and tendency to alienate theological foes, if he and Melanchthon were true friends, then this would probably indicate substantial doctrinal unity between the two.

Lohse speaks carefully about a deep encounter between Luther and Melanchthon,[3] but Scheible and Wengert go beyond caution and overstate the case by claiming that the two were certainly not friends.[4] Wengert, in fact, claims that to call Luther and Melanchthon's relationship a 'friendship' is a mistake.[5] Based on evidence such as the fact that Melanchthon was not invited to Luther's wedding ceremony but only to the reception, Scheible writes, 'In conclusion, I understand the relation of Luther and Melanchthon to be less one of friendship than of friendly collegiality.'[6] This is a fine distinction, and Scheible's evidence is not overwhelming. His conclusion can only be supported by a very narrow definition of friendship.

In favour of the idea of friendship, in 1520, Melanchthon himself said that he would rather die than leave Luther.[7] When Luther fell ill in 1532, he summoned Melanchthon to his bedside for comfort.[8] In the same year, he

---

[3] Bernhard Lohse, 'Philipp Melanchthon in seinen Beziehungen zu Luther', in *Leben und Werk Martin Luthers von 1526 bis 1546*, ed. Helmar Junghans (Göttingen: Vandenhoeck & Ruprecht, 1983), 403.

[4] Heinz Scheible, 'Luther and Melanchthon', *Lutheran Quarterly* 4 (1990), 317–39. Wengert, *Human Freedom*, 70. Wengert cites Scheible's article and indicates his agreement with it ('[Here] the myth of Luther and Melanchthon's friendship is destroyed') without presenting evidence or arguments of his own, although he does make his case at some length elsewhere in 'Melanchthon and Luther/Luther and Melanchthon', *Lutherjahrbuch* 66 (1999), 54–88. Euan Cameron takes a similar tack when he makes a case that 'It would seem wrong to regard Luther and Melanchthon as close friends.' 'Philipp Melanchthon: Image and Substance', *JEH* 48 (1997), 721–2.

[5] Wengert, 'Melanchthon and Luther/Luther and Melanchthon', 56 n. 6. Despite this overstatement, Wengert's article is an overall good in-depth study of Luther and Melanchthon's relationship. For another strenuous denunciation of the category of friendship, see Wengert's essay, 'Philip Melanchthon's Contribution to Luther's Debate with Erasmus over the Bondage of the Will', in Joseph A. Burgess and Marc Kolden, eds., *By Faith Alone: Essays on Justification in Honor of Gerhard O. Forde* (Grand Rapids: Eerdmans, 2004), 113 n.14: 'The notion of friendship [is] completely unhelpful to this discussion. . . . This kind of psychologizing has plagued Melanchthon studies for years.'

[6] Scheible, 'Luther and Melanchthon', 332, 338. On the issue of Luther's wedding, MacCulloch writes, 'Melanchthon was hurt and furious at not being invited to the wedding or even told about it.' *The Reformation*, 139. See also E. Cameron, 'Philipp Melanchthon: Image and Substance', *JEH* 48 (1997), 705–22, esp. 721–2.

[7] CR 1.52.

[8] LW 54.23–4, Nr. 157. WATr 1.74–5, Nr. 157.

said, 'Philip lifts up my spirit with a mere word.'[9] This sounds like a description of a friend rather than of a mere colleague. Again, when Luther was stricken in 1537, Melanchthon came, and looking on him, dissolved into tears.[10] When Melanchthon himself fell dangerously ill in 1540, Luther came to his bedside and prayed until Melanchthon began to recover.[11] In more normal circumstances, Melanchthon at times had supper at Luther's house.[12] These intimate social interactions, both in sickness and health, speak more of friendship than the formality of a relationship restricted to the professional level. Perhaps Muelhaupt overstates the case when he portrays Luther and Melanchthon's relationship as 'love at first sight',[13] but Schneider is surely correct to say that Luther and Melanchthon 'remained friends for life, despite some differences between them'.[14] Nevertheless, whether or not Melanchthon and Luther were the closest of friends, or merely friendly colleagues, Estes (with Wengert and Scheible) is right to paint the relationship between Luther and Melanchthon as one of harmonious collaboration between two quite different men who engaged in 'theology through conversation' (Wengert's phrase), and did not take too seriously their divergences from one another.[15] Perhaps Wilhelm Pauck comes closest to the reality when he describes Luther and Melanchthon's relationship as a 'strong, comradely friendship'.[16]

As a result of Luther and Melanchthon's sustained friendship (or friendly collegiality, if one prefers), it is more likely that they influenced each other on doctrine, and in fact felt themselves to be in agreement. In Melanchthon's early years in Wittenberg, he had no prior formal training in theology, so his friendship with Luther in these years showed that Melanchthon was learning and accepting Luther's emerging Reformation theology. The extent of Luther's theological influence on young Melanchthon is of significance for understanding Melanchthon's doctrine of the will.

---

[9] LW 54.54, Nr. 360. 'Philippus me uno verbo erigit.' WATr 1.150–152.13–14, Nr. 360.

[10] LW 54.225, Nr. 3543A. WATr 3.387–388.22–3, 1, Nr. 3543A.

[11] LW 54.453–4, Nr. 5565. WATr 5.244–6, Nr. 5565. Cf. WABr 9.170–1. See Manschreck, *The Quiet Reformer*, 267–8.

[12] LW 54.257, Nr. 3692. WATr 3.537, Nr. 3692. LW 54.290, Nr. 3900. WATr 3.694, Nr. 3900.

[13] Erwin Muelhaupt, 'Luther und Melanchthon: Die Geschichte einer Freundschaft', in *Luther im 20. Jahrhundert* (Göttingen: Vandenhoeck & Ruprecht, 1982), 122.

[14] Schneider, *Oratio sacra*, 66.

[15] James M. Estes, *Peace, Order and the Glory of God: Secular Authority and the Church in the Thought of Luther and Melanchthon, 1518–1559* (Leiden: Brill, 2005), 180 n. 2. See also Estes' article, in which he makes a sustained case for the use of the term 'collaborator': 'The Role of Godly Magistrates in the Church: Melanchthon as Luther's Interpreter and Collaborator', *Church History* 67 (1998), 463–83.

[16] Wilhelm Pauck, 'Luther und Melanchthon', in Vilmos Vajta, ed., *Luther and Melanchthon in the History and Theology of the Reformation* (Philadelphia: Muhlenberg Press, 1961), 22.

Luther's Influence on the Young Melanchthon's Theology

By all accounts Luther exercised a profound influence on Melanchthon, especially in the early years of Melanchthon's career at Wittenberg. Mac-Culloch speaks of Melanchthon's deep admiration for his older colleague.[17] In 1521, Melanchthon himself wrote, '[Some] captious souls...think that Luther has changed everything, when he has done nothing else than to call us back to Scripture and also to the fathers who came closest to the meaning of Scripture.'[18] Later in life, in 1551, Melanchthon compared Luther to John the Baptist pointing out the Lamb of God.[19] Wilhelm Pauck declares that Luther and Melanchthon together are the fathers of Lutheranism, and that they help explain one another.[20] Consequently, due to this strong influence on Melanchthon, Luther and his thought are worth scrutiny, for therein lie some of the possible tensions that would become significant for Melanchthon's later shift on the freedom and role of the will in justification.

While Luther's influence on Melanchthon is well-known, the extent of that influence has been open to some debate. Stupperich and Maurer depict Melanchthon as heavily dependent on Luther. For Stupperich, Luther was the immovable pillar that gave Melanchthon strength, for Melanchthon 'never became free of a feeling of insecurity in theological work'.[21] Similarly, Maurer states that the main thrust of all Melanchthon's arguments against free will came from Luther's *Assertio* of 1520,[22] and that Melanchthon moved away from his transformational view of justification of 1519 largely because of discussions with Luther.[23] Similarly, Greschat sees Luther and Melanchthon's theological relationship as 'a polar unity'.[24]

On the other hand, Schneider, Green, Schäfer, Keen, Estes, Cameron, and Brüls speak for Melanchthon's substantial independence. Green and Schäfer both even argue that Luther learned the Reformation view of grace as favour

---

[17] *The Reformation*, 135. But MacCulloch also notes (p. 221) Melanchthon taking variant positions from Luther in the 1530s, particularly regarding the eucharist. MacCulloch also speaks of Melanchthon's 'independent mind' (p. 338).
[18] Trans. Charles Leander Hill, in Elmer Ellsworth Flack and Lowell J. Satre, eds., *Melanch-thon: Selected Writings* (Minneapolis: Augsburg, 1962), 74. *Widder das wuetende urteyl der Pariser Theologisten. Schutzred Phil. Melanchthon fuer Doctor Mart. Luther* (1521), WA 8.300.
[19] Melanchthon, *Confessio Saxonica*, 1551. MSA 6.95. The reference is to John 1.29.
[20] Pauck, 11.
[21] Stupperich, *Melanchthon*, 38.
[22] Maurer, *Der junge Melanchthon*, 2.271.
[23] Ibid., 2.235.
[24] Martin Greschat, *Melanchthon neben Luther: Studien zur Gestalt der Rechtfertigungslehre zwischen 1528 und 1537* (Witten: Luther-Verlag, 1965), 249.

from Melanchthon, rather than the other way around.[25] Similarly, Derk
Visser cites a second-hand report that Luther revered Melanchthon as his
Praeceptor.[26] Schneider maintains that when Melanchthon came to Wittenberg, he did not have a sudden conversion to Luther's point of view, but that
he was already leaning in that direction as a result of his own unique brand of
Christian humanism developed over his years at Tübingen.[27] Schneider comments that when one re-examines Melanchthon's beginnings, one begins to
see the 'unknown Melanchthon' (a reference to Stupperich's *Der unbekannte
Melanchthon*[28]), 'a figure of measurably greater vision, accomplishment and
stature than he has generally been given credit for in the histories'.[29] Likewise,
Euan Cameron says, 'Surely his works show that Philipp Melanchthon had a
religious agenda of his own; and that this agenda grew more, rather than less
distinct from Luther's as the years passed. . . . Melanchthon should never again
be reduced to merely an unreliable mouthpiece for Lutheran religious teaching.'[30] On the same theme, Brüls insists that Melanchthon is indeed unique,
when compared to Luther on theology.[31] Estes adds that Melanchthon interpreted Luther's theological thought with a considerable degree of intellectual
freedom.[32] Keen writes that Melanchthon was 'an independent thinker alongside Luther, not a mere follower'.[33] While these defenders of Melanchthon are
right to seek to counterbalance an entirely dependent view of Melanchthon,
they run the risk of establishing Melanchthon's independence from Luther in
terms that are too strong. In the end, Melanchthon did strive to be an
independent thinker, as his diverging thought on free will clearly illustrates.
He was not a *blind* follower of Luther.

[25] Lowell C. Green, *How Melanchthon Helped Luther Discover the Gospel: The Doctrine of
Justification in the Reformation* (Fallbrook, CA: Verdict, 1980), xx, 159. Rolf Schäfer, 'Melanch-
thon's Interpretation of Romans 5:15: His Departure from the Augustinian Concept of Grace
Compared to Luther's', in *Philip Melanchthon (1497–1560) and the Commentary*, ed. Timothy J.
Wengert and M. Patrick Graham (Sheffield: Sheffield Academic Press, 1997), 79–104.
[26] Derk Visser, *Niets menselijks is mij vreemd: leven en werk van Philippus Melanchthon*
(Kampen: de Groot Goudrian, 1995), 38, 190 n. 56. This is all cited by Estes, in 'The Role of
Godly Magistrates', 465 n. 6.
[27] John R. Schneider, 'Melanchthon's Rhetoric as a Context for Understanding His Theology',
in *Melanchthon in Europe: His Work and Influence Beyond Wittenberg*, ed. Karin Maag (Grand
Rapids: Baker/Paternoster, 1999), 145–6.
[28] See Robert Stupperich, *Der unbekannte Melanchthon: Wirken und Denken des Praeceptor
Germaniae in neuer Sicht* (Stuttgart: W. Kohlhammer, 1961).
[29] Schneider, 'Melanchthon's Rhetoric', 146.
[30] Cameron, Euan, 'Philipp Melanchthon: Image and Substance', *JEH* 48 (1997), 712.
[31] Brüls, 31–3.
[32] Estes, 'The Role of Godly Magistrates in the Church', 465.
[33] Ralph Keen, 'Introduction', in Keen, ed. and trans., *A Melanchthon Reader* (New York:
Peter Lang, 1988), 5.

Yet, Melanchthon clearly *was* a follower of Luther, even if he came to disagree with him in time (interestingly, it was not until well after Luther's death that Melanchthon explicitly said that Luther had been wrong on free will in the early 1520s). When Melanchthon first began writing about theology in 1519, he held to a traditional transformational view of justification (i.e. grace was divine aid in regeneration, rather than Melanchthon's later understanding of it as *favor Dei*—justification took place through the slow development of righteousness *within* the Christian, rather than being imputed to her from outside of herself).[34] Later in that same year, though, after studying with Luther, Melanchthon began to defend the idea of imputed (rather than intrinsic) righteousness in his *Baccalaureatsthesen*.[35] When Melanchthon became deathly ill in 1540 and expected to die, looking back on this time he gave thanks for Luther, saying that he learned the Gospel from him.[36] Later, in 1546, at Luther's funeral, Melanchthon said that Luther was greater than Caesar Augustus, and included him in the same company with Isaiah, John the Baptist, and Augustine.[37] 'Such a man we mourn for our own sakes. For we are very much like orphans deprived of a fine and faithful father.'[38] Clearly, even if Melanchthon thought for himself and evolved in his theology over time, he started out being heavily influenced by Luther. Throughout his life, Luther exerted a strong pull on Melanchthon's thought, much like a canoeist, whose direction would be influenced by a brisk river current.

LUTHER'S DOCTRINE OF THE WILL IN THE 1520s

Luther strongly opposed the idea of free will in justification. As part of the theocentric soteriology, salvation had to be entirely a work of God, and in no

[34] *Pauli ad Romanos epistolae summa*, CR 21.56. See also Melanchthon's definition of grace in *Theologica Institutio Philippi Melanchthonis in Epistolam Pauli ad Romanos*, where grace is not defined as favour, but as an indwelling of the Holy Spirit that causes regeneration: 'GRATIA, quam et spiritum vocat Paulus, *est spiritus, quo illustramur, purgamur, impellimur ad bona.*' CR 21.53.

[35] '10. Omnis iustitia nostra est gratuita dei imputatio'. MSA 1.24.

[36] CR 3.827, Nr. 1873. *Testamentum Melanthonis.* 1540. 'Ago autem gratias Reverendo D. Doctori *Martino Luthero*, primum, quia ab ipso Evangelium didici.'

[37] 'Solon, Themistocles, Scipio, Augustus and the like were clearly great men, who either established or ruled great empires; but still they are far inferior to those leaders of ours, Isaiah, John the Baptist, Paul, Augustine, Luther'. *Eulogy for Luther*, 1546. Keen, 91. 'Fuerint sane magni viri Solon, Themistocles, Scipio, Augustus, et similes, qui magna imperia vel constituerunt, vel rexerunt: tamen longe inferiores sunt his nostris ducibus Iesaia, Baptista, Paulo, Augustino, Luthero'. CR 11.728.

[38] Ibid. Keen, 93. '...nostra causa merito dolemus. Sumus enim simillimi orphanis praestanti et fideli patre orbati'. CR 11.731.

way a work of human beings. Hence, free choice was an unadulterated lie,[39] and it was 'nothing else but the supreme enemy of righteousness and man's salvation'.[40] Of the Catholic teaching on free will, Luther wrote, 'In other matters the frivolity and blindness of the pope could be tolerated, but when it comes to this chief article of the faith it is a pity that they are so senseless. Here they completely ruin everything God has given us through Christ'.[41] Indeed, 'This error about "free will" is a special doctrine of Antichrist',[42] for it deprived God of the glory he was due for *entirely* saving humans himself. Only God had true freedom: 'Free choice is plainly a divine term, and can be properly applied to none but the Divine Majesty alone; for he alone can do and does . . . whatever he pleases in heaven and on earth. If this is attributed to men, it is no more rightly attributed than if divinity itself also were attributed to them, which would be the greatest possible sacrilege'.[43] Again, 'Free choice is a divine term and signifies a divine power'.[44] Humans were entirely passive recipients of salvation: 'Thus the human will is placed between the two like a beast of burden. If God rides it, it wills and goes where God wills . . . If Satan rides it, it wills and goes where Satan wills; nor can it choose to run to either of the two riders or to seek him out, but the riders themselves contend for the possession and control of it'.[45] God was in control, humans were passive, and

[39] 'Free choice is a pure fiction.' DSA. LW 33.18. 'Liberum arbitrium esse merum mendacium.' WA 18.602.

[40] DSA. LW 33.250. WA 18.759.15–16. 'Simul certum est, Liberum arbitrium esse nihil aliud quam summum hostem iustitiae et salutis humanae.'

[41] *Grund und Ursach aller Artikel D. Martin Luthers so durch römische Bulle unrechtlich verdammt sind*, 1521. LW 32.93. WA 7.449.5–8. 'Und zwar des Papsts unnd der seinen leichtfertickeyt unnd blintheit were zu dulden ynn andernn stucken, aber ynn diszem hewbt Artikel ists zurbarmen, das sie szo unsynnig sein, denn damit vortilgen sie doch allis gantz, was wir von got durch Christum haben.' *Grund und Ursach* is Luther's fourth and clearest response to the papal bull of excommunication (see Forell's comments in LW 32.5). Citing Luther's arguments against free will in the three earlier essays, as well as in *Grund und Ursach*, would be merely repetitive. Luther wrote the three earlier essays in 1520, which were (in chronological order), *Adversus execrabilem Antichristi bullam* (WA 6.595–612), *Wider die Bulle des Endchrists* (WA 6.613–29), and *Assertio omnium articulorum M. Lutheri per bullam Leonis X. novissimam damnatorum* (WA 7.91–151).

[42] *Grund und Ursach*. LW 32.94. WA 7.451.3–4. 'Dieszer yrthum von freyen willen ist eyn eygen Artickel des Endchrist.'

[43] DSA. LW 33.68. WA 18.636.26–32. 'Liberum arbitrium esse plane divinum nomen, nec ulli posse competere quam soli divinae maiestati. Ea enim potest et facit . . . Omnia quae vult in coelo et in terra. Quod si hominibus tribuitur, nihilo rectius tribuitur, quam si divinitas quoque ipsa eis tribueretur, quo sacrilegio nullum esse maius possit.'

[44] DSA. LW 33.107. WA 18.664.15–16. 'Liberum arbitrium esse divinum nomen ac divinum virtutem significare.'

[45] DSA. LW 33.65. WA 18.635.17–22. 'Sic humana voluntas in medio posita est, ceu iumentum, si insederit Deus, vult et vadit, quo vult Deus. . . . Si insederit Satan, vult et vadit, quo vult Satan, nec est in eius arbitrio ad utrum sessorem currere aut eum quaerere, sed ipsi sessores certant ob ipsum obtinendum et possidendum.'

this meant everything for Luther on the topic of salvation. At the end of *De servo arbitrio*, Luther emphasized this point when he praised Erasmus for choosing the topic of free will: 'You and you alone have seen the question on which everything hinges, and have aimed at the vital spot; for which I sincerely thank you.'[46]

The Fall

Luther's Scripture-based theocentric soteriology represented the general framework in which he denied free will, and in which he put the specific arguments predicated on the Fall and the sovereignty of God. As for the Fall itself, Luther taught that 'since the fall of Adam, or after actual sin, free will exists only in name, and when it does what it can (*facit quod in se est*—Gabriel Biel's phrase), it commits [mortal] sin.'[47] The Fall resulted in humanity's total corruption and bondage to sin, even in reason.

Enslavement

Luther was adamant on the primary function of original sin regarding the will: enslavement. 'For all men are slaves of sin, because all commit sin, if not in outward works, yet in their concupiscence and inclination.'[48] Humans were unable to exercise the will to do good or seek salvation because they were rotten and twisted through and through—they were turned in on themselves (*incurvatus in se*).[49] 'Sin, in the Scripture, means not only the outward works of the body but also all the activities that move men to do these works, namely, the inmost heart, with all its powers.'[50] Further, 'Original sin itself,

---

[46] DSA. LW 33.294. WA 18.786.30–1. 'Unus tu et solus cardinem rerum vidisti et ipsum iugulum petisti, pro quo ex animo tibi gratias ago.'

[47] LW 32.92. The revised English Jacobs translation in LW leaves out the word 'mortal' (*todlich*), but it is clearly present in the WA. This was originally the thirteenth thesis from the *Disputatio Heidelbergae habita* of 1518: 'Liberum arbitrium post peccatum res est de solo titulo, et dum facit quod in se est, peccat mortaliter.' LW 31.40. WA 1.354.5–6. Luther here defended it in 1521 as the thirty-sixth article of *Grund und Ursach*: 'Der sechs und dreyssigt. Der frey wille nach dem fal Ade odder nach der gethanen sund ist eyn eytteler name, und wenn er thut das seine, szo sundigt er todlich.' WA 7.445.30–3.

[48] *Divi Pauli ad Romanos epistola. Die Scholien.* 1516. LW 25.357. 'Quia omnes sunt serui peccati, Quia omnes faciunt peccatum, si non opere, tamen concupiscentia et pronitate.' WA 56.367.28–30.

[49] *Divi Pauli ad Romanos epistola. Die Scholien.* 1516. LW 25.345. 'Et hoc consonat Scripture, Que hominem describit incuruatum in se adeo, vt non tantum corporalia, Sed et spiritualia bona sibi inflectat et se in omnibus querat.' WA 56.356.4–6.

[50] *Vorrede auff die Epistel S. Pauli an die Römer.* 1546 (1522). LW 35.369. 'Sunde heisset in der Schrifft, nicht allein das eusserliche werck am Leibe, Sondern alle das Gescheffte das sich mit reget vnd weget zu dem eusserlichen werck, nemlich, des hertzen grund mit allen krefften.'

therefore, leaves free choice with no capacity to do anything but sin and be damned.'[51] Consequently, postlapsarian humanity had freedom only within the scope of its now evil predisposition (as Augustine had taught), and freedom only to do evil was no freedom at all.[52] Luther scornfully declared, 'My opponents' position [i.e. free will] suggests that when nobody can control a wild and ravenous beast with chains, you let it go free and it will chain itself and go into captivity of its own accord.'[53] The downward bent of original sin made the upward movement of the will towards God a stark impossibility. The perversity of the heart as a result of the Fall kept the will in chains in regard to God.

Reason

With the advent of the Fall, the entirety of human beings became permeated with sin, including human reason. As a result, Luther had very little confidence in reason exercised apart from Scripture for the purpose of discerning the divine will. Natural human reason, fallen as it was, invariably came to the wrong conclusion about justification—namely, that people were saved through their *works*, and not by faith.[54]

Luther's primary definition of reason was simply a faculty of the human mind,[55] yet most often when he spoke of reason he meant the specific misuse of it that espoused the practice of good works as the road toward a justly merited salvation.[56] It was this particular soteriological theory stemming from fallen reason that stirred up Luther's anger and caused him to denounce reason (when applied to justification) as the devil's bride and a gorgeous

---

WADB 7.7.27–9. See also Lohse's chapter on Luther's view of sin (pp. 248–57), in Bernhard Lohse, *Martin Luther's Theology: Its Systematic Development*, ed. and trans. Roy A. Harrisville (Edinburgh: T&T Clark, 1999).

[51] DSA. LW 33.272. WA 18.773.17–18. 'Igitur ipsum originale peccatum liberum arbitrium prorsus nihil sinit posse nisi peccare et damnari.'

[52] *Grund und Ursach.* LW 32.92. 'Where, then, is this freedom, if of its own power it cannot do anything but sin?' WA 7.445.36. 'Wo ist denn die freiheit, szo sie nit mehr denn sundigen kan von yhr selb?'

[53] *Grund und Ursach.* LW 32.93. WA 7.447.36–8. 'Das were eben, alsz wen yemant sprech: Ein wilt wuttend thier mag niemant mit banden zeemen, aber wenn es losz ist, zeimet sichs selb und geht willig ynn die band.'

[54] See Karl Holl, 'Was verstand Luther unter Religion?' in *Gesammelte Aufsätze zur Kirchengeschichte* (Tübingen: Mohr, 1928), 37. Philip S. Watson, *Let God Be God! An Interpretation of the Theology of Martin Luther* (London: Epworth Press, 1947), 88. Alister E. McGrath, *Luther's Theology of the Cross: Martin Luther's Theological Breakthrough* (Oxford: Blackwell, 1985), 139.

[55] B. A. Gerrish, *Grace and Reason: A Study in the Theology of Luther* (Oxford: Oxford University Press, 1962), 67.

[56] Ibid., 169.

whore.[57] Luther wrote, 'The costliest and most sublime vices, such as idolatry and heresy... are not only in the flesh but also in reason.'[58] As a result, 'all human reason is sheer error and blindness'.[59] Fallen reason was an unreliable tool for seeking out divine truths all on its own.

Because of the Fall, reason (as a faculty of the human mind) had limitations. Reason could not comprehend the mysteries of God and salvation on its own, but required the direction of revelation (Scripture), for reason always expected the wrong thing (justification by works). Luther declared, 'Who can understand anything about these things by means of reason?'[60] Again, 'Do not think that you can interpret Scripture with your own reason and wisdom.'[61] The faculties of the mind required help in understanding the Bible because 'the Holy Spirit Himself must expound Scripture. Otherwise it must remain unexpounded.'[62] With this help of the Holy Spirit, the Scriptures should be easily understandable, for they were clear.[63] Yet, between understanding the Bible and coming to faith lay a large gap—one that reason was powerless to cross. As Gerrish notes, reason could not understand the concept of forgiveness,[64] and as Luther explained, 'Our faith transcends all reason and is solely a power of God.'[65] In regard to time, Luther again showed a limitation on reason when he wrote, 'For God does not see time longitudinally; He sees it transversely, as if you were looking transversely at a tall tree lying before you. Then you can see both ends at the same time. This you cannot do if you look at it longitudinally. With our reason we cannot look at time in any other way than longitudinally.'[66] Reason was unequal to the task of theology apart from revelation and the aid of the Spirit.

[57] 'Aber des Teuffels Braut Ratio, die schöne Metze... Es ist die höchste Hure die der Teuffel hat.' 17 January 1546. *Predigt am 2. Sonntag nach Epiphaniä.* WA 51.126.29, 31–2.
[58] *Epistel S. Petri gepredigt und ausgelegt. Erste Bearbeitung.* 1523. (Hereafter, this work will be abbrivated as I Pet.) LW 30.119. WA 12.373.28–30. '...sondern auch die hohisten und kostlichsten laster, als abgotterey und ketzerey wilche nicht alleyn ym fleysch, sondern ynn der vernunfft sind'.
[59] *Der ander Epistel S. Petri und eine S. Judas gepredigt und ausgelegt.* 1523/24. LW 30.165. WA 14.29.29–30. 'Aller menschen vernunfft ist eytel yrthumb und blindheyt.'
[60] LW 54.378. Nr. 5015. WATr 4.614.4–5, Nr. 5015. 'At quis potest ratione de eis aliquid intelligere?'
[61] II Pet. LW 30.166. WA 14.31.4–5. 'Da richtet euch nach und dencket nicht, das yhr die schrifft auslegen werdet durch eygene vernunfft und klugheit.'
[62] II Pet. LW 30.166. WA 14.31.9. 'Der heylig geyst sol es selbs auslegen odder sol unausgelegt bleyben.'
[63] *Rationis Latomianae confutatio.* 1521. LW 32.222. WA 8.102–3.
[64] Gerrish, *Grace and Reason*, 90.
[65] I Pet. LW 30.107. WA 12.361.16–17. '...unser glawb ubir alle vernunfft und alleyn Gottis krafft ist'.
[66] II Pet. LW 30.196. WA 14.70–71.30, 8–11. 'Denn Gott sihet nicht die zeyt nach der lenge, sonder nach der quer, als wenn du eynen langen baum, der fur dyr ligt, uber quer ansihest, so kanstu beyde ort und ecken zu gleich yns gesicht fassen, das kanstu nicht thun, wenn du yhn nach der lenge ansihest. Wyr kunnen durch unsere vernunfft die zeyt nicht anders ansehen, denn nach der leng.'

When Luther discussed reason, he often included philosophy as well, and when he mentioned philosophy, he almost always meant Aristotle in particular.[67] Luther's view of philosophy (and Aristotle) was similar to his view of reason in that philosophy was fine so long as it stuck to worldly matters. Luther in fact held some fondness for some of Aristotle's methodological disciplines.[68] So long as philosophy contented itself with temporal matters, there were no contradictions between it and theology.[69] But, when philosophy infiltrated theological matters (as had been the case with Thomas, Scotus, Ockham, and Biel), then it became evil and wrong, for Aristotle's ethics (i.e. that one became good by *doing* the good) embodied the worst folly of fallen reason—justification by works, rather than faith. It was in this sense that Luther heatedly wrote of 'that twice accursed Aristotle',[70] calling him 'the destroyer of godly doctrine'.[71]

According to Luther's thought, reason did have a place and a proper function. Luther divided reality into two realms. He posited, 'These are two [realms]: the temporal, which governs with the sword and is visible; and the spiritual, which governs solely with grace and the forgiveness of sins.'[72] Reason most properly belonged in the temporal realm, and so when Luther occasionally praised reason, he usually meant reason properly used within its rightful worldly sphere.[73] In fact, Luther spoke of reason in three different areas.[74] First, he praised natural reason ruling in its proper domain (the temporal realm). Second, he blasted the arrogant natural reason that would trespass on the domain of faith. Third, the reason of the regenerate had a role to play in humbly serving God, and being in obedience to Scripture. If used in its proper place, reason became a benefit and a blessing.

Luther only rejected reason in the spiritual realm. McGrath comments, 'Luther's rejection of *ratio* [reason] relates to his soteriology, particularly to the definition of *iustitia Dei* [the righteousness of God], which is of central importance to his theology as a whole.'[75] Watson maintains much the same

[67] McGrath, *Luther's Theology of the Cross*, 1.
[68] Ibid., 37.
[69] Ibid., 53.
[70] *Rationis Latomianae confutatio*. LW 32.217. WA 8.99.1. '...bis sacerrimo Aristoteli...'.
[71] Ibid. LW 32.258. WA 8.127.20. '...Aristotelis, vastatoris piae doctrinae'.
[72] *Eyn Unterrichtung wie sich die Christen ynn Mosen sollen schicken*. 1525. LW 35.164. WA 16.371.8–9. 'Das sind zwei reych: weltlich, das mit dem schwerd regirt und wird gesehen, das geystlich regirt allein mit gnaden und vergebung der sunden.' I have chosen to translate *reych* as 'realm' here, rather than the LW's 'kingdom'. This is to maintain consistency with my presentation of Luther's various dualities in reality, as seen in the next chapter, below.
[73] Gerrish, *Grace and Reason*, 169.
[74] Ibid., 26.
[75] McGrath, *Luther's Theology of the Cross*, 139.

when he writes, 'Outside the sphere of religion, he has nothing derogatory to say of reason, but quite the reverse; and within that sphere he criticizes it only as it is used to maintain doctrines and practices that from his theocentric standpoint must be condemned as idolatrous. Luther is no irrationalist except to those who either have not grasped, or refuse to share, his fundamental point of view.'[76] Reason could and should be used in earthly human endeavours (such as government and science), but it must not be used in matters of religion on its own, and it could only be used in theology after it had been enlightened by the Holy Spirit and informed by the Scriptures.

The Sovereignty of God

In addition to the Fall (which enslaved the will and deceived reason), Luther also argued against free will on the basis of God's sovereignty. Through predestination, God decided before all time whom he would save and whom he would damn. Moreover, God was in absolute control of everything that happened, and this was the basis of the reliability of God's promises: 'For if you doubt or disdain to know that God foreknows all things, not contingently, but necessarily and immutably, how can you believe his promises and place a sure trust and reliance on them?'[77] God alone commanded, and he alone fulfilled the commandments.[78] Consequently, according to divine necessity it was foolish to speak of any sort of human free will in *anything*.

Predestination

Luther mentioned predestination from time to time in a matter-of-fact fashion. For example, he wrote, 'The election and God's eternal foreordination is firm enough in itself and requires no confirmation.'[79] Again, 'The best and infallible preparation for grace and the sole disposition toward grace is

---

[76] Watson, 88. See also Gerrish, *Grace and Reason*—an entire volume devoted to this question.

[77] DSA. LW 33.42. WA 18.619.1–3. 'Si enim dubitas aut contemnis nosse, quod Deus omnia non contingenter sed necessario et immutabiliter praesciat et velit, quomodo poteris eius promissionibus credere, certo fidere et niti?'

[78] *Tractatus de libertate christiana*. 1520. LW 31.349. 'Thus the promises of God give what the commandments of God demand and fulfil what the law prescribes so that all things may be God's alone, both the commandments and the fulfilling of the commandments. He alone commands, he alone fulfils.' WA 7.53.11–13. 'Sic promissa dei hoc donant, quod praecepta exigunt, et implent quod lex iubet, ut sint omnia solius dei, tam pracepta et plenitudo eorum. Ipse solus praecipit, solus quoque implet.'

[79] II Pet. LW 30.158. WA 14.22.13–14. 'Die erwelung und ewige verfehrung Gottes ist zwar fur sich selb fest gnug, das man sie nicht feste darff machen.'

the eternal election and predestination of God.'[80] Further, Luther argued that predestination was as obvious to all people as was God's very existence: 'The knowledge of God's predestination and foreknowledge remained with the common people no less than the awareness of his existence itself.'[81] For Luther, predestination was integrally tied to the bondage of the will, 'For we shall not be able to bring ourselves to heaven or to create faith in ourselves. God will not admit all men to heaven; He will count His own very exactly. Now the human doctrine of free will and of our own powers no longer amounts to anything. Our will is unimportant; God's will and choosing are decisive.'[82] Moreover, 'We are so weak and uncertain that if it depended on us, not even a single person would be saved; the devil would surely overpower us all. But since God is dependable—his predestination cannot fail, and no one can withstand him—we still have hope in the face of sin.'[83] Because God chose who would be saved, humans could have no say independent of God's will.

Luther acknowledged that the doctrine of predestination could be a difficult one to accept, especially in its full double form (i.e. having both an elect and a reprobate). Writing about the idea of God damning people to hell from before all time, Luther wrote, 'And who would not be offended? I myself was offended more than once, and brought to the very depth and abyss of despair, so that I wished I had never been created a man, before I realized how salutary that despair was, and how near to grace.'[84] Luther's answer to the difficulties of reprobation involved trust in God, even when one failed to understand him: 'This is the highest degree of faith, to believe him merciful when he saves so few and damns so many, and to believe him righteous when by his own will he makes us necessarily damnable, so that he seems, according to Erasmus, to

---

[80] *Disputatio contra scholasticam theologiam.* 1517. LW 31.11. WA 1.225.27–8. '29. Optima et infallibilis ad gratiam praeparatio et unica dispositio est aeterna dei electio et praedestinatio.'

[81] DSA. LW 33.41. WA 18.618.13–15. 'In vulgo non minus relictam esse scientiam praedestinationis et praescientiae Dei quam ipsam notitiam divinitatis.'

[82] I Pet. LW 30.6. WA 12.262.8–13. 'Denn wyr werden uns selber nicht kunnen zum hymmel bringen odder den glauben ynn uns machen, Got wirt nicht alle menschen ynn hymmel lassen, die seynen wirtt er gar genaw zelen. Da gilt nu nichts mehr menschen lere vom freyen willen und untzern krefften. Es ligt nicht an untzerm willen, sondernn an Gottis willen und erwelung.'

[83] *Vorrede auff die Epistel S. Pauli an die Römer.* 1546 (1522). LW 35.378. WADB 7.23.30–4. 'Den wir sind so schwach vnd vngewis, das, wenn es bey vnd stünde, würde freilich nicht ein Mensch selig, der Teufel würde sie gewislich alle vberweldigen. Aber nu Gott gewis ist, das jm sein versehen nicht feilet, noch jemand jm weren kan, haben wir noch hoffnung wider die Sünde.'

[84] DSA. LW 33.190. WA 18.719.9–12. 'Et quis non offenderetur? Ego ipse non semel offensus sum usque ad profundum et abyssum desperationis, ut optarem nunquam esse me creatum hominem, antequam scirem, quam salutaris illa esset desperatio et quam gratiae propinqua.'

delight in the torments of the wretched and to be worthy of hatred rather than of love.'[85]

Along with continued trust in God, Luther also advocated staying away from speculating about God's hidden will. Staupitz, too, had warned against speculation. Humans were to focus on God's revealed will as found in the Bible, and not upon his secret will, whereby he may actually wish the death and damnation of some sinners. In relation to Ezekiel 18.23, 32,[86] Luther explained, 'For [Ezekiel] is here speaking of the preached and offered mercy of God, not of that hidden and awful will of God whereby he ordains by his own counsel which and what sort of persons he wills to be recipients and partakers of his preached and offered mercy.'[87] Again, 'To the extent, therefore, that God hides himself and wills to be unknown to us, it is no business of ours.'[88] Luther acknowledged that there were difficulties inherent in clinging to a full view of predestination both to heaven and to hell, but he argued that one must maintain such a view, and trust that God was still good and knew what he was doing. Furthermore, because of predestination, there could be no free will in justification. Melanchthon, as we shall see, could not bring himself to stick with Luther's advice on dealing with the difficulties of this issue of predestination.

Divine Determination: The Necessitarian Argument

Luther was concerned to affirm that God determined *everything*, and this meant that there could be no free will. Luther made a blanket statement about contingency in order to bolster his position on free will in relation to salvation. To this end, Luther argued, 'For if we believe it to be true that God foreknows and predestines all things, that he can neither be mistaken in his foreknowledge nor hindered in his predestination, and that nothing takes place but as he wills it (as reason itself is forced to admit), then on the

---

[85] DSA. LW 33.62–3. WA 18.633.15–19. 'Hic est fidei summus gradus, credere illum esse clementem, qui tam paucos salvat, tam multos damnat, credere iustum, qui sua voluntate nos necessario damnabiles facit, ut videatur, referente Erasmo, delectari cruciatibus miserorum et odio potius quam amore dignus.'

[86] 'Have I any pleasure in the death of the wicked, says the Lord God, and not rather that they should turn from their ways and live? ... For I have no pleasure in the death of anyone, says the Lord God. Turn, then, and live.' NRSV.

[87] DSA. LW 33.139. WA 18.684.34–37. '... Ezechiele, qui de praedicata et oblata misericordia Dei loquitur, non de occulta illa et metuenda voluntate Dei ordinantis suo consilio, quos et quales praedicatae et oblatae misericordiae capaces et participes esse velit.'

[88] DSA. LW 33.139. WA 18.685.5–6. 'Quatenus igitur Deus sese abscondit et ignorari a nobis vult, nihil ad nos.'

testimony of reason itself there cannot be any free choice in man or angel or any creature.[89] God did all in all.

In *De servo arbitrio*, in addition to the arguments for the bound will predicated on the Fall, Luther put forth his necessitarian argument, which hinged on the human creaturely subjection to the omnipotent God.[90] He added caveats to this blanket claim of determinism, but he maintained it nonetheless. The main negative consequence of this determinism was to make God appear responsible for sin and evil. Rupp summarizes, 'Thus God moves the whole course of history and gives life and breath to all things, superintending and working out his own purposes through good and evil. Luther believed that this is the view of the Bible.'[91] Luther did not see God's determination in terms of direct coercion or force, and he did not believe that God was directly responsible for evil: 'Since, then, God moves and actuates all in all, he necessarily moves and acts also in Satan and ungodly man.... It is like a horseman riding a horse that is lame in one or two of its feet; his riding corresponds to the condition of the horse, that is to say, the horse goes badly.'[92] God animated and energized all things, and when he used instruments which had evil wills, evil was the result—and it was the fault of the instrument rather than the Lord. Luther explained, 'Here you see that when God works in and through evil men, evil things are done, and yet God cannot act evilly although he does evil through evil men, because one who is himself good cannot act evilly; yet he uses evil instruments that cannot escape the sway and motion of his omnipotence. It is the fault, therefore, of the instruments, which God does not allow to be idle, that evil things are done, with God himself setting them in motion. It is just as if a carpenter were cutting badly with a chipped and jagged axe. Hence it comes about that the ungodly man cannot but continually err and sin, because he is caught up in the movement of the divine power and not allowed to be idle, but wills, desires, and acts according to the kind of person he himself

---

[89] DSA. LW 33.293. WA 18.786.3–7. 'Si enim credimus verum esse, quod Deus praescit et praeordinat omnia, tum neque falli neque impediri potest sua praescientia et praedestinatione, Deinde nihil fieri, nisi ipso volente, id quod ipsa ratio cogitur concedere; simul ipsa ratione teste nullum potest esse liberum arbitrium in homine vel angelo aut ulla creatura.'

[90] McSorley, *Luther*, 332. For a more recent treatment of the debate between Luther and Erasmus, see Gerhard O. Forde's *The Captivation of the Will: Luther vs. Erasmus on Freedom and Bondage* (Grand Rapids: Eerdmans, 2005).

[91] E. Gordon Rupp, *The Righteousness of God* (London: Hodder & Stoughton, 1953), 280.

[92] DSA. LW 33.176. WA 18.709.21–2, 24–6. 'Quando ergo Deus omnia movet et agit, necessario movet etiam et agit in Satana et impio.... tanquam si eques agat equum tripedem vel bipedem, agit quidem taliter, qualis equus est, hoc est equus male incedit.'

is.'[93] God thus determined all things, but without being responsible for sin and evil. While Luther could live with this distinction, Melanchthon would find it difficult to maintain.

For Luther, the main reason why he could live with 'rough edges' in his doctrine of God was that he had a very high view both of divine righteousness[94] and of the divine authorship of salvation. God had to be at the centre of salvation, and Luther could brook no compromise on that issue: 'Luther believes that to speak of a man as free in this realm of the Spirit, to be able to apply or not to apply himself to salvation, to embrace or not to embrace the Gospel, is in the end to make the universe irresponsible and to make salvation turn not upon God's loving will and saving initiative but on the changes and chances of unpredictable spontaneity. Thus his thought upon Free Will is bound up with his doctrine of Providence.'[95] Luther's determinism was directly tied to his theocentric soteriology.

In his deterministic view of predestination, Luther's main concerns about the nature of God interlocked with his concerns from the human perspective of salvation. If God was all-powerful and at the centre of salvation, then that salvation was secure. Rupp writes, 'Luther has a horror of a universe where the loving purposes and promises of God can be frustrated or mocked by chance, contingency or accident.'[96] Luther seized upon the security of salvation as the chief benefit of the doctrine of predestination. In this sense he made the doctrine of predestination subordinate to the doctrine of justification,[97] for if one could be assured of salvation, then one could safely leave to God the problem of the origins of sin and evil. To acknowledge holes in his knowledge of the nature and mysteries of God was for Luther by far preferable to making salvation even partially dependent on the free will of the individual.

With the security of the individual's salvation in mind, and with the conviction that that security could only be found in the hands of the all-determining God, Luther set forth to destroy the scholastic distinction that Erasmus levelled against him: the distinction between *necessitas consequentiae* (God foresees freely occurring events) and *necessitas consequentis* (*because*

---

[93] DSA. LW 33.176. WA 18.708.28–36. 'Hic vides Deum, cum in malis et per malos operatur, mala quidem fieri, Deum tamen non posse male facere, licet mala per malos faciat, quia ipse bonus male facere non potest, malis tamen instrumentis utitur, quae raptum et motum potentiae suae non possunt evadere. Vitium ergo est in instrumentis, quae ociosa Deus esse non sinit, quod mala fiunt, movente ipso Deo. Non aliter quam si faber securi serrata et dentata male secaret. Hinc fit, quod impius non possit non semper errare et peccare, quod raptu divinae potentiae motus ociari non sinitur, sed velit, cupiat, faciat taliter, qualis ipse est.'
[94] James MacKinnon, *Luther and the Reformation*, 4 vols. (London: Longmans, 1929), 3.250.
[95] Rupp, 278.
[96] Ibid. See also MacKinnon, 3.255.
[97] Rupp, 283.

God foresees events, they necessarily occur as a by-product of his will). Luther insisted on the latter position. In rejecting the necessity of consequence, Luther wrote, 'If God wills anything, it is necessary for that thing to come to pass, but it is not necessary that the thing which comes to pass should exist; for God alone exists necessarily, and it is possible for everything else not to exist if God wills.'[98] Luther then concluded that all this proved was that the event in question had no necessary existence and thus was not God. In Luther's mind, the necessity of consequence was just an absurdity that only proved that everything except God was not God. The premise that drove Luther's thinking in rejecting the necessity of consequence involved the idea that God's foreknowledge was an aspect of his will. What God foreknew he powerfully forewilled as well: 'God foreknows nothing contingently, but that he foresees and purposes and does all things by his immutable, eternal, and infallible will. Here is the thunderbolt by which free choice is completely prostrated and shattered.'[99] Luther continued, 'From this it follows irrefutably that everything we do, everything that happens, even if it seems to us to happen mutably and contingently, happens in fact nonetheless necessarily and immutably, if you have regard to the will of God.'[100] In other words, humans had absolutely no free will in anything.

Bayer finds Luther's argument profound: 'The traditional distinction between *necessitas consequentiae* and the *necessitas consequentis* only serves, as Luther astutely observes, to carve out a space for that tiny bit of human freedom.'[101] At its heart, Luther's position embraced the notion of the creaturely subjection to the omnipotent God.[102] This position ruled out the tendency of medieval philosophers to insist on a genuine contingency in events (though without explaining how God could have foreknowledge of genuinely contingent events).[103] However, McSorley insists that this very medieval position was what Luther *really* meant.[104] McSorley points out that apparent contradiction existed in Luther's statements of both divine

---

[98] DSA. LW 33.40. WA 18.617.3–5. 'Si Deus aliquid vult, necesse est ut ipsum fiat, sed non est necesse, ut id sit, quod fit. Solus Deus enim necessario est, omnia alia possunt non esse, si Deus velit'.

[99] DSA. LW 33.37. WA 18.615.13–15. 'Deus nihil praescit contingenter, sed quod omnia incommutabili et aeterna infallibilique voluntate et praevidet et proponit et facit. Hoc fulmine sternitur et conteritur penitus liberum arbitrium.'

[100] DSA. LW 33.37–8. WA 18.615.31–3. 'Ex quo sequitur irrefragabiliter, omnia quae facimus, omnia quae fiunt, etsi nobis videntur mutabiliter et contingenter fieri, revera tamen fiunt necessario et immutabiliter, si Dei voluntatem spectes.'

[101] Bayer, 'Freedom?', 381.

[102] McSorley, *Luther*, 307.

[103] Rupp, 279.

[104] McSorley, *Luther*, 331.

control and human choice, and that the only way this situation could be explained was through a genuine contingency of events, over which God nonetheless overruled providentially. McSorley concludes that Luther's true position actually embraced *necessitas consequentiae*. Nevertheless, the evidence does not lend itself to this conclusion. Luther explicitly condemned *necessitas consequentiae*,[105] and he insisted when he did speak of freedom and contingency, that such only *appeared* to be the case to human beings on a subjective level, while objectively, God determined all things, even if such did not *seem* to be the case to human cognition. Staupitz, too, had spoken of the subjective psychological *appearance* of freedom.

Overall, in his necessitarian argument Luther made it clear that all things happened by divine determination, but that God's direction of events came through the shaping of wills, while all individuals were left to freely follow their wills, making genuine choices as seemed best to them. Luther, while sounding at first almost fatalistic, instead posited a sophisticated providential divine rule amongst human events that from the earthly perspective happened freely. The only reason humans knew that God's guiding hand worked among the events of history was because God had revealed that that was the case, and the reason for this particular revelation embodied assurance for the elect. So that those who had faith might be confident, God revealed his electing and sustaining hand. Luther's concern, from first to last, remained entirely soteriological, and hence his disdain for the 'speculative' problems of the origins of sin and evil in a world entirely controlled by God. Whatever appearances might have been, God controlled and determined all events, and therefore there could be no objective free will in justification.

FREEDOM BELOW: LUTHER AND THE APPEARANCE OF RATIONAL INCONSISTENCY

While Luther taught that all things occurred as a result of divine determinism, he also sometimes spoke about a measure of freedom in non-soteriological matters. Luther's main concern was to deny free will in the matter of salvation and the things of God, but in some situations he was willing to speak of freedom in things not related to salvation. He conceded, 'You might perhaps rightly attribute some measure of choice to man, but to attribute free choice

---

[105] DSA. LW 33.37–41. WA 18.614–18.

to him in relation to divine things is too much.'[106] Humans were created to
have mastery over creation, and though people had been corrupted by sin
(which removed humanity's freedom in relation to God), freedom over
creation remained.[107] Luther wrote, 'We are not disputing about nature but
about grace, and we are not asking what we are on earth, but what we are in
heaven before God. We know that man has been constituted lord over the
lower creatures, and in relation to them he has authority and free choice, so
that they obey him and do what he wills and thinks.'[108] Rupp comments,
'Luther does not deny at all what most people nowadays mean when they
speak about Free Will. . . . He is not concerned with whether we are free when
we choose marmalade instead of jam for breakfast, with why we walk down a
road instead of up another, with why we choose our wives, or run our
businesses. These are great and important areas of human life in which he
concedes human freedom.'[109] Luther maintained, 'We know there are things
free choice does by nature, such as eating, drinking, begetting, [and] ruling.'[110] Again, 'I grant that Free Will can by its own endeavours move itself in
some directions, we will say unto good works, or unto the righteousness of
the civil or moral law, yet it is not moved unto the Righteousness of God.'[111]
Luther was willing to posit some measure of free will in the temporal realm,
but never in the spiritual realm (especially regarding justification).

At first glance this admission of some freedom in non-soteriological events
appeared to contradict Luther's assertion of divine necessity in *all* things.
However, Luther explained the problem by insisting on paradox, and he
scorned any attempt by humans to use logic to simplify things that properly
belonged to the mystery of God. As MacCulloch writes, Luther had 'a
theology full of paradoxes',[112] and, 'paradoxes . . . were always to characterize
his thought'.[113] Luther upbraided Erasmus, saying, 'My dear Erasmus, let me
too say in turn: If you think these paradoxes are inventions of men, what are
you contending about? Why are you so roused? Against whom are you

---

[106] DSA. LW 33.103. WA 18.662.5–6. 'Arbitrium fortassis homini aliquod recte tribueris, sed
liberum tribuere in rebus divinis nimium est.'

[107] Rupp, 275.

[108] DSA. LW 33.284–5. WA 18.781.6–10. 'Nos non de natura, sed de gratia disputamus, nec
quales simus super terram, sed quales simus in coelo coram Deo, quaerimus. Scimus, quod
homo dominus est inferioribus se constitutus, in quae habet ius et liberum arbitrium, ut illa
obedient et faciant, quae ipse vult et cogitat.'

[109] Rupp, 274–5.

[110] DSA. LW 33.240. WA 18.752.7–8. 'Scimus liberum arbitrium natura aliquid facere, ut
comedere, bibere, gignere, regere . . .'.

[111] Trans. Rupp, 274–5. WA 18.767.40.

[112] MacCulloch, *The Reformation*, 112, 126, 129, 147, and 174.

[113] Ibid., 121.

speaking? Is there anyone in the world today who has more vigorously attacked the dogmas of men than Luther? Therefore, your admonition has nothing to do with me. But if you think these paradoxes are words of God, how can you keep your countenance, where is your shame . . . ?'[114] Divine necessity and human freedom in the temporal realm (matters 'below') represented a paradox that Luther was willing to uphold. He summarized this paradoxical tension when he argued, 'But if we are unwilling to let this term [i.e. free choice] go altogether—though that would be the safest and most God-fearing thing to do—let us at least teach men to use it honestly, so that free choice is allowed man only with respect to what is beneath him and not what is above him (*arbitrium liberum non respectu superioris, sed tantum inferioris*). That is to say, a man should know that with regard to his faculties and possessions he has the right to use, to do, or to leave undone, according to his own free choice, though even this is controlled by the free choice of God alone, who acts in whatever way he pleases. On the other hand, in relation to God, or in matters pertaining to salvation or damnation, a man has no free choice, but is a captive, subject and slave either of the will of God or of the will of Satan.'[115] God determined all things, yet some things remained free.

---

[114] DSA. LW 33.59. WA 18.630–631.29–32, 1. 'Mi Erasme, Iterum et ego dico, si haec paradoxa ducis hominum esse inventa, quod contendis? quid aestuas? contra quem dicis? an est ullus in orbe hodie, qui vehementius hominum dogmata sit insectatus quam Lutherus? Igitur nihil ad nos ist monitio. Si autem Dei verba esse credis ea paradoxa, ubi est frons tua? ubi pudor?' Marjorie O'Rourke Boyle has written, 'Paradox, paradoxical, paradoxically. Hardly any vocabulary recurs more frequently in modern study of Luther, or more wrongly'. 'Stoic Luther: Paradoxical Sin and Necessity', ARG 73 (1982), 69. She argues that Luther embraced not so much paradox, but a thorough-going classical stoicism. However, Luther's repeated use of the word 'paradox' to describe his own thought (as seen in the present quotation) is evidence to the contrary. Further, Boyle further accuses Luther of 'embracing another pagan whore' by utilizing reason in his theology via a use of the dredged-up paradoxes of antique stoicism. However, Luther used paradox to express God's *supra*-rationality, rather than sub- or anthropo-rationality.

[115] DSA. LW 33.70. WA 18.638.4–11. 'Quod si omnino vocem eam omittere nolumus, quod esset tutissimum et religiosissimum, bona fide tamen eatenus uti doceamus, ut homini arbitrium liberum non respectu superioris, sed tantum inferioris se rei concedatur, hoc est, ut sciat sese in suis facultatibus et possessionibus habere ius utendi, faciendi, omittendi pro libero arbitrio, licet et idipsum regatur solius Dei libero arbitrio, quocunque illi placuerit. Caeterum erga Deum, vel in rebus, quae pertinent ad salutem vel damnationem, non habet liberum arbitrium, sed captivus, subiectus et servus est vel voluntatis Dei vel voluntatis Satanae.' Some scholars vary on the proper terminology for Luther's paradoxes. Boyle sometimes calls them 'antitheses', and Fredrik Brosché prefers the term 'antinomy'. I have already criticized Boyle's basic position on Luther's use of paradox above, but antinomy is a workable concept that I will explore further in Melanchthon's writings below. See Fredrik Brosché's densely scholarly book, *Luther on Predestination: The Antinomy and the Unity Between Love and Wrath in Luther's Concept of God* (Stockholm: Almqvist & Wiksell, 1978). (J. I. Packer gives a modern definition of antinomy as 'the apparent incompatibility between two apparent truths'. *Evangelism and the Sovereignty of God* (London: Inter-Varsity Fellowship, 1961), 18.)

Nevertheless, the realm of things that remained paradoxically both free and determined did not extend to justification—here, and here alone, God acted entirely unilaterally, with no concurrent or paradoxical free choice on the part of the individual.

CONCLUSION

Luther and Melanchthon were colleagues and friends, and the young Melanchthon learned the bulk of his theology from Luther. Luther's doctrine of the bound will was a vital part of the central theme of his theology—namely, that it was God, first and last, who saved people. God was at the centre of it all, and humans could in no way earn their salvation, even through the smallest exercise of their wills to turn toward God. Luther backed up his position by citing the helplessness of fallen humans, both in their ability to do good and seek God, and in their capability of thinking coherently and accurately about him. Fallen reason was not a reliable tool—God's revelation (Scripture) had to be trusted, and, on occasion, one had to accept paradox. If things God had revealed seemed to be rationally inconsistent, the fault lay with the weakness of human reason, rather than in the integrity of the doctrines God had laid out.

Luther also argued against free will on the basis of the sovereignty of God, whereby the Lord predestined those whom he wanted to save and damn, and he also providentially determined all things. As we shall see in the following chapter, the young Melanchthon utilized all these arguments in his earliest theological writings, with only a couple of omissions: Melanchthon rarely mentioned the reprobate, and he always steered clear of the appearance of rational inconsistency—especially in matters of determinism or the hidden will of God.

Part II

The Bound Will

4

1519–1522: Advent

INTRODUCTION

By 1519 Melanchthon had begun to settle into Wittenberg, and the theological instruction he received from Luther was thoroughly Reformational.[1] Melanchthon viewed Luther's theology as essentially that of Augustine,[2] of whom he certainly approved. Melanchthon called Augustine 'a man of both singular genius and great experience in sacred matters'.[3] Simultaneously, he castigated scholasticism and metaphysical philosophy, declaring, 'The dregs of philosophers, the scholastic theologians of our age, think that the minds of men are excited [by the Law] to the pursuit of virtue. What dreams! . . . Philosophy is in error; our minds are not equal to divine laws.'[4] Additionally, 'There is a common statement to the effect that a drink of water is not to be found in water which has been rendered turbid with filth. Just so, no faithful man has ever satisfied his mind with scholastic theology which has become polluted by so many human arguments, nonsense, tricks, and

[1] The arguments of Vogelsang, Boehmer, Hirsch, Bizer, Saarnivaara, and McGrath concerning the date of Luther's theological breakthrough need not detain us here. Even according to Bizer and Saarnivaara's view that Luther did not make his breakthrough until 1519, it is safe to assume that from this date onwards he utilized a definition of *iustitia Dei* meaning that God justifies sinners, rather than God punishes and rewards people *quid pro quo*. See also Scheible, *Melanchthon: Eine Biographie*, 57. Luther most likely guided Melanchthon in his work on his *Baccalaureatsthesen*, published in 1519.

[2] 'Is not Luther's view on free will and grace the whole view of Augustine, if you rightly judge the matter? And besides, Luther follows him throughout in his commentary on Galatians.' Trans. Hill, 74. *Widder das wuetende urteyl der Pariser Theologisten. Schutzred Phil. Melanchthon fuer Doctor Mart. Luther* (1521), WA 8.299.36–9: 'Ist nit Luthers meinung von dem freien willen, vond der gande, tzo imant die sach recht achtet, gantz S. Augustintz? Denn dem selben hat er aller dinge gefolgt ihm comment ad Galatas.'

[3] Trans. Hill, 43. 'Divus Augustinus, vir et ingenio singulari et magno sacrarum rerum usu . . .' *Declamatiuncula in Divi Pauli doctrinam. Epistola ad Johannem Hessum Theologum* (1520). MSA 1.40.2–3.

[4] Trans. Hill, 40. '. . . virtutis, hoc est lex, qua erigi hominum animos ad virtutis studium et philosophi et philosophorum faeces, scholae theologicae huius aetatis censent. O somnia! . . . Error est Philosophia, legibus divinis animi nostri non sunt pares.' *Declamatiuncula*. MSA I.36.14–17; 37.1–2.

trifling traditions.'[5] Elsewhere, he derided Bonaventure, Thomas, Scotus, and Ockham by name.[6] He also demonstrated a passion for *sola scriptura*, saying, 'What madness is it, therefore, what blindness, since the Scriptures alone point out a succinct way of salvation, if you seek the beauty and structure of virtue from the clever thoughts of philosophers when they are obsolete!'[7]

While Melanchthon enthusiastically accepted most of Luther's doctrines, he nevertheless thought for himself, and on a few issues differed slightly from his colleague. While the differences in these early years of the Reformation were not immediately noticeable, some of the variations in tone and emphasis between the two in the early 1520s would be a foreshadowing of a more serious later divergence of opinions regarding soteriology. Meanwhile, Melanchthon lent great energy to the movement for reformation in these early years, and, whether reluctantly or not, his teaching and writings were eagerly seized upon to aid in the push to publish quickly both theological tracts and substantive biblical commentaries embodying the new evangelical theology. In the first half of the 1520s, Melanchthon produced more theological titles than during any other period of his life.

Melanchthon's most important writing during this time was the *Loci communes* or *The Commonplaces* of 1521. It was an attempt to gather evangelical doctrine together in one convenient, concise book.[8] In addition

[5] Trans. Hill, 42, in *Declamatiuncula*. 'Vulgo dici solet, potum non inveniri ex aqua coeno turbata. Ita nec in scholastica Theologia animo satisfecerit pius quispiam, tot hominum argutiis, nugis, technis et traditiunculis conspurcata.' MSA 1.38.38–39.3.

[6] In 1521, when he wrote to the theologians of the Sorbonne, Melanchthon accused, 'But what do you do? Anything other than let the minds of Christians become great in the formalities of Scotus and in the connotations of Ockham rather than in Christ?' Trans. Hill, 74. *Widder das wuetende urteyl der Pariser Theologisten*, WA 8.300.19–22: 'Aber ihr, was thut ihr? Ists nit war, das ihr nichts anders thut, denn das die Christlichen hertzen mehr inn den formaliteten Scoti und connotaten Occam, denn inn Christo gross werden?' See also 'On Correcting the Studies of Youth' (1518), where Melanchthon indulged in a little further name-calling, not only of Scotus and Ockham, but also of Thomas and Bonaventure: 'Gradually the better disciplines were neglected, we left Greek learning behind, and everywhere bad things began to be taught as if they were good. From this proceeded Thomases, Scotuses, seraphic doctors [Bonaventure], cherubic doctors [joke], and the rest of their followers, more numerous than the offspring of Cadmus.' Keen, 49. 'Sensim neglectae meliores disciplinae, eruditione Graeca excidimus, omnino pro bonis non bona doceri coepta. Hinc prodiere Thomae, Scoti, Durandi, Seraphici, Cherubici, et reliqui proles numerosior Cadmea sobole.' MSA 3.32.23–7.

[7] Trans. Hill, 38, in *Declamatiuncula*. 'Proinde quis furor est, quae caecitas, cum iter compendiarium ad salutem solae Christianae literae indicent, iis exauctoratis, aliunde ex Philosophorum scitis virtutis formam ac ὑποτύπωσιν petere?' MSA 1.34.21–5.

[8] Melanchthon's *Loci communes* served as a kind of gathering place for evangelical theology, early in the Reformation. Similarly, one modern scholar has employed these Latin words to describe the cosy confines of the Gryffindor common room at Harry Potter's famous Hogwarts school. 'Postmeridiano tempore Harrius et Vislii beate vivebant inter se pugna furenti globorum

to this major document, Melanchthon's first drafts and notes leading up to the *Loci* shed additional light on his developing theology. As he began studying Romans in 1519,[9] he started to view theology as revolving around a series of key 'commonplaces', or *loci*. Melanchthon began summarizing these *loci* in his writing of 1519, the *Theologica Institutio*,[10] which was followed by the *Summa*.[11] Later that year, Melanchthon wrote a more expanded set of notes, known as the *Capita*.[12] These three documents represented Melanchthon's developing thoughts as he prepared to write the *Loci*.[13] Additionally, in 1522, for the seventh printing of the *Loci*, Melanchthon substantially rewrote his section on free will, which illustrated the further development of his thought.[14] Finally, Melanchthon also commented on several books of the Bible, with his annotations on Matthew[15] (c.1519–20, published by his students in 1523 from lecture notes), John[16] (1523), and Romans[17] (1522) being most important. The

nivalium in campo certantes. Tum frigidi, madentes, anhelantes ad ignem *loci communis* Gryffindorensis redierunt.' J. K. Rowling, trans. Peter Needham, *Harrius Potter et Philosophi Lapis* (New York: Bloomsbury, 1997), 164.

[9] Definitively dating many of Melanchthon's writings from 1519–22 is a matter of some debate. For more information on this topic, see Bizer's editorial introductions in *Texte aus der Anfangszeit Melanchthons* (Neukirchen-Vluyn: Neukirchener Verlag, 1966). See also Barton and Maurer's articles: P. F. Barton, 'Die exegetische Arbeit des jungen Melanchthon 1518/19 bis 1528/29: Probleme und Ansätze', *ARG* 54 (1963), 52–89. Wilhelm Maurer, 'Zur Komposition der Loci Melanchthons von 1521: Ein Beitrag zur Frage Melanchthon und Luther', *Lutherjahrbuch* 25 (1958), 146–80.

[10] *Theologica Institutio Philippi Melanchthonis in Epistolam Pauli ad Romanos.* c.1519. CR 21.49–60.

[11] *Summa.* c.1519. CR 21.56–60.

[12] *Rerum theologicarum capita seu Loci fere sunt.* c.1519–20. The CR editors also place this work under the heading of *Lucubratiuncula Philippi Mel.* CR 21.11–46.

[13] For an in-depth analysis of the chronology of these early works, see Rolf Schäfer, 'Melanchthon's Interpretation of Romans 5.15: His Departure from the Augustinian Conception of Grace Compared to Luther's', in Timothy J. Wengert and M. Patrick Graham, eds., *Philip Melanchthon (1497–1560) and the Commentary* (Sheffield: Sheffield Academic Press, 1997), 88–90.

[14] This work will be covered in greater detail in the following chapter.

[15] *Breves Commentarii in Matthaeum.* c.1519–20. CR 14.543–1042.

[16] *In Evangelium Ioannis Annotationes.* 1523. CR 14.1047–1220. For detailed information on the printings of Melanchthon's lectures on Matthew and John (among others), see appendices 2 and 3 in Timothy Wengert, *Philip Melanchthon's Annotations in Johannem in Relation to Its Predecessors and Contemporaries* (Geneva: Droz, 1987), 255–63.

[17] To the best of my knowledge, this commentary has not been reprinted in any modern work. For the purposes of the present study, citations will be taken from a printing from 1523, stored at the Bodleian Library of the University of Oxford. ANNO || TATIONES PHILIPPI || Melanchthonis in Epistolä Pau || li ad Romanos unam, Et ad || Corintios duas. || ARGENTOR-ATI APVD || Iohannem Heruagium. Anno || M.D.XXIII || Woodcut opposite title page, on title page, and on various pages. 144 leaves.

commentary on Romans dealt extensively with the question of free will, and merits closer examination than the other two.[18]

Overall, in the early 1520s, Melanchthon staunchly denied any freedom of the will. His justification for this stance rested on two main arguments: (1) the Fall (with the uncontrollability of the affections), and (2) predestination.

LOCI COMMUNES, FIRST EDITION[19]: 1519–1522

Melanchthon was clear at this stage of his career that the will possessed no freedom. This doctrine ranked uppermost in his thoughts in 1519, especially following the Leipzig Disputation, where he had witnessed Eck and Karlstadt debate this very issue. In a letter to Oecolampadius that year, Melanchthon attempted to summarize what had happened at Leipzig (concerning both Eck and Karlstadt's debate, and Luther's arguments with Eck regarding the authority of the pope).[20] The letter subsequently fell into Eck's hands, and he wrote a heated reply.[21] Melanchthon, clearly goaded, wrote a sharp defence[22] in which he claimed that no one who had heard Karlstadt's arguments would be so stupid as to accept Eck's solutions.[23] Further, Eck abused words by creating nonscriptural terms such as 'the plainly fictitious phrase "free choice", which comes from Ockham'.[24] In 1519, Melanchthon viewed the absence of free will as a key doctrine distinguishing evangelical theology

---

[18] For detailed information on Melanchthon's various lectures on Romans, and the emergence of the successive editions of his commentaries on Romans, see Timothy Wengert, 'The Biblical Commentaries of Philip Melanchthon', in Timothy J. Wengert and M. Patrick Graham, eds., *Philip Melanchthon (1497–1560) and the Commentary* (Sheffield: Sheffield Academic Press, 1997), 133–9.

[19] This section will also include some references taken from the *Loci* of 1522, where the quotations support the same substantial points as those made in 1521. For a deeper analysis of the development of these early documents through the *Loci*, see G. L. Plitt and T. Kolde, *Die Loci communes Philipp Melanchthonis in ihrer Urgestalt*, 4th edn. (Leipzig: Deichert, 1925)—especially the first section, titled, 'Melanchthons Theologische Entwicklung bis zur Herausgabe der Loci communes'.

[20] *Epistola de Lipsica disputatione.* Melanchthon (in Wittenberg), to Oecolampadius (in Augsburg), 21 July 1519. MSA 1.4–11. MBW 1.59. T1.59.

[21] *Excusatio Eckii ad ea, quae falso sibi philippus Melanchthon grammaticus Vvitembergensis super Theologica disputatione Lipsica adscripsit.* 1519. Suppl. Mel. 6.1.71.

[22] *Defensio Phil. Melanchthonis contra Joh. Eckium.* 1519. MSA 1.11–22.

[23] 'Quod lectorum ad suam conclusionem relegat, nemo tam stupidus est, qui putet Carolostadium Eckianam conclusionem defendendam suscepisse.' MSA 1.16.

[24] 'Porro, quid necesse erat novis glossematis et plane fictitiis asserere vim liberi arbitrii, qua bonum efficiat, cum receptissimum sit et apud scholasticos vel summae notae, nempe Occamicos, quosdam voluntatis actus tantum recipi.' MSA 1.17.

from scholasticism, and it was therefore not surprising that both the *Capita* (1519–20) and the following *Loci* of 1521 began with a discussion of the nature of the will, intentionally set out 'unmediated by the fog of scholastic thought'.[25] This discussion centred on the themes of the Fall (which affected both reason and the affections) and predestination.

The Fall

In these early writings (all of which were essentially commentaries on Romans), Melanchthon's doctrine of the will was a direct product of his soteriology. He embraced Pauline soteriology, and it was because of the strong view of human sin in Paul (especially in Romans 1–8) that Melanchthon said that people did not have free will. They could not overcome their sinful affections. Günther is correct when he writes that the Pauline doctrine of original sin left Melanchthon no room for free will, and further, all of Melanchthon's doctrine of the will was predicated on his doctrine of sin, which was the entry point to his soteriology.[26] The Fall was highly significant for Melanchthon's doctrine of the will, and its connection to human powers merits closer examination.

Melanchthon posited that in all people two powers existed: the first was the power of cognition (*vis cognoscendi*), and the second was the power in which the affections were born (*vis in qua affectus nascuntur*).[27] The works of cognition were to feel, see, hear, reason, and think; and the works of the affections were to love, hate, fear, and mourn.[28] Melanchthon went on to point out that while those without theological expertise tended to think of free will almost entirely in terms of the power of cognition (or reason), he was primarily concerned with the affections, which he felt were what Paul was talking about in Romans when he used the categories of law, sin, and grace.[29] Nevertheless, both powers of humans were corrupted by the Fall, so that all were sinners (even Paul).[30] Moreover, the entirety of each individual was

---

[25] Keen, 'Introduction', 6.

[26] Günther, 26–7.

[27] *Capita.* CR 21.13–14. Melanchthon was not consistent in his use of the phrase *vis cognoscendi.* Sometimes he replaced this phrase with *intellectus* or with *ratio.* Consequently, within the English narrative of the main text above, 'cognitive capacity', 'intellect', and 'reason' will be used fairly interchangeably.

[28] 'Opera cognitionis sunt Sentire videre Audire raciocinari intelligere. Opera affectus sunt Auersari persequi amare odire metuere dolere.' *Capita.* CR 21.13–14.

[29] *Capita.* CR 21.13–14. 'A dvim [Ad vim] affectuum virtus: vitium: peccatum: gratia. Quod discrimen accurate obseruandum est Quia vis cognoscendi in plura vulgatur quam vis affectuum.'

[30] 'Tantas vires esse peccato, Ut etiam in se ipso Paulo.' *Summa.* CR 21.58.

brimming with sin—for just as a fire shoots up, so it was with original sin.[31] All who were born of the flesh (i.e. of the old birth—not born again) were damned.[32] Thus, according to the power both of cognition and of the affections, due to the Fall, the idea of free will was false.

Cognition and Choice

With the Fall, the entire person became corrupted—both the cognitive capacity (reason), and the affections. Melanchthon followed Luther's *totus homo* theme, and spoke of the corruption of the cognitive capacity due to its taint from the Fall. As Maurer states, Melanchthon used Luther's concept of *totus homo* in opposition to the scholastics, the mystics, and the Christian humanists.[33] Human beings were entirely corrupted, in all facets of their being, both in their affections and in their reason (cognitive capacity). Melanchthon shared Luther's deep suspicion of human reason.

Further, in an argument that echoed Augustine, Melanchthon put forward that within humans the affections ruled over reason, and as a result of the Fall, those affections were twisted and evil. Consequently, a primary cause of the intellect's inability to change the heart lay in the fact that the intellect was ruled by the deeper will of the affections,[34] rather than the opposite. 'For the will in man corresponds to the place of a despot in a republic. Just as the senate is subject to the despot, so is knowledge to the will.'[35] Cognition was a natural ability, much like strength or constitution, which served the affections. Free choice in one's affections through the dictates of one's reason did not truly exist, for if one were to act or think contrary to what one felt in the heart, the heart would still yearn for its own desires, thus showing that the evil bent of the will could not be negated by reason.[36] The affections represented the emotional and motivational well of the soul, for, 'although knowledge gives good warning, the will casts knowledge out and is borne along by its own affection'.[37]

---

[31] 'Sicut in igne raptus est, quo sursum fertur: ita in homine ad peccatum.' *Theologica Institutio.* CR 21.51.

[32] '... damnat in totum veterem nativitatem.' *In Evangelium Ioannis Annotationes.* CR 14.1061.

[33] Maurer, *Der junge Melanchthon*, 2.233.

[34] 'Et quae de intellectu scripsi, eadem de voluntate sentio.' *Loci*, 1522. CR 21.94.

[35] *Loci*, 1521. LCC 19.24. 'Nam perinde, ut in republica tyrannus, ita in homine voluntas est.' MSA 2/1.9.24–5.

[36] *Loci*, 1522. 'Sed cum deligitur opus externum contra adfectum, fere fit, ut infirmior adfectus potiore vincatur, ut negari non potest...' CR 21.95.

[37] *Loci*, 1521. LCC 19.24. 'Quamquam bona moneat cognitio, respuat tamen eam voluntas feraturque affectu suo.' MSA 2/1.9.27–8.

Reason, or the human cognitive capacity, served the affections, and following the Fall, the affections were centred on the self.[38] This orientation of the affections toward the self rather than God represented the very definition of sin for Melanchthon.[39] As a result, the unrestrained horse of the affections could not be held in check by reason, and the cart crashed down into the abyss.[40] Reason was subject to the affections, and because the affections were corrupt, reason was doubly so—both weakened in its own right by the Fall, and enslaved to the selfish desires of fallen affections. As a result, the human intellect could only operate within the assumptions of carnal categories.[41] That is, it did not discriminate or sift good from bad, except according to carnal measures. By these standards bad was denoted by death, poverty, want, and ignominy; good was measured by life, wealth, power, and glory.[42] This carnal intellect could not understand God's anger and mercy,[43] and lived in ignorance of him. According to Melanchthon, people were profoundly blind,[44] and their capacities were indeed imbecilic.[45] Consequently, it may have *appeared* to frail human intellects that there was freedom of choice in external actions, but here the judgement of reason had to be overruled, Melanchthon insisted.[46] In this, Melanchthon echoed Staupitz and Luther. The weak intellect *perceived* contingency, but Scripture taught that all things happened by necessity.[47]

---

[38] 'Therefore, the dominant affection of man's nature is love of self.' *Loci*, 1521. LCC 19.31. 'Primus itaque affectus et summus naturae hominis est amor sui.' MSA 2/1.18–19.38–1.

[39] 'Sin is a depraved affection, a depraved activity of the heart against the law of God.' *Loci*, 1521. LCC 19.31. 'Pravus affectus pravusque cordis motus est contra legem dei, peccatum.' MSA 2/1.18.7–8. This argument was consonant with Augustine. In the *Loci* of 1521, Augustine was mentioned prominently and in an approving manner. In Melanchthon's very first sentence in the section on free will, he wrote, 'Augustine and Bernard wrote on free will, and the former revised his ideas extensively in the books that he later wrote against the Pelagians. Bernard is not consistent.' LCC 19.22. MSA 2/1.8.12–15. Again, 'In several volumes, Augustine brilliantly tore [the Pelagians'] teaching to bits.' LCC 19.32. 'Esse vero peccatum originale Pelagiani negasse feruntur, quorum dogma revellit Augustinus aliquot voluminibus erudite.' MSA 2/1.19.11–13.

[40] Maurer, *Der junge Melanchthon*, 2.261.

[41] 'Primum ergo sic censemus, intellectum humanum pro natura sua nihil intelligere, nisi carnalia.' *Loci*, 1522. CR 21.93.

[42] 'Mala esse iudicat mortem, inopiam, ignominiam. Bona, vitam, opes, gloriam.' *Loci*, 1522. CR 21.93.

[43] 'Esse deum, misericordiam, iram dei neutiquam intelligit.' *Loci*, 1522. CR 21.93–4.

[44] 'Profunda caecitas humana est.' *Loci*, 1522. CR 21.94.

[45] 'Item humanus captus imbecillior est.' *Capita*. CR 21.37–8.

[46] 'Quod si voluntatis humanae vim pro naturae captu aestimes, negari non potest iuxta rationem humanum, quin sit in ea libertas quaedem externorum operum, ut ipse experiris in potestate tua esse, salutare hominem aut non salutare, indui hoc veste vel non indui, vesci carnibus aut non vesci.' *Loci*, 1521. MSA 2/1.12.31–13.2. Here Melanchthon seemed to be enunciating a theme that Luther would extol in *De servo arbitrio*, namely, the (at least apparent) freedom of action in things not relating to salvation.

[47] 'Omnia necessario evenire scripturae docent. Esto, videatur tibi esse in rebus humanis contingentia, iudicio rationis hic imperandum est.' *Loci*, 1521. MSA 2/1.11.19–21.

The Implications of Reason's Weakness for Philosophy

As a result of the Fall, the intellect could not accurately perceive reality. It followed that the intellectual constructs stemming from metaphysical philosophy were as flawed and corrupt as the minds of those who created them. Melanchthon declared that 'the Scriptures everywhere contradicted the judgment of reason',[48] for reason tended towards a false belief in free choice.[49] All philosophers' opinions on justification were then to be considered as lies and darkness.[50] This was especially true of the scholastics (even those who did not argue that the location of grace lay in doing good works[51]), whose works-oriented philosophy was not effective for changing the heart or renewing the affections.[52] No external works would ever suffice to cleanse the spirit.[53]

The scholastics with their philosophy erred, because philosophy utilized a broken tool—reason. Consequently, it was prone to arriving at incorrect conclusions, and it was incapable of repairing the depraved affections. For this reason, Melanchthon (like Luther) tried to push aside philosophy's generally optimistic anthropology.[54] In 1520, Melanchthon had begun to move away from his previously positive appraisal of philosophy,[55] and in the *Loci communes* of 1521 he was positively scathing. Scheible notes that in the locus on anthropology, Melanchthon placed Christian doctrine in direct

---

[48] *Loci*, 1521. LCC 19.23. '... rationis iudicio viderent ubique refragari scripturas.' MSA 2/1.8.25–6.

[49] 'Although Christian doctrine on this topic [i.e. free will] differs altogether from philosophy and human reason, philosophy has gradually crept into Christianity. The godless doctrine about free [choice] (*arbitrium*) was taken over and the benefits of Christ were obscured through that profane and earthly wisdom of our reason.' *Loci*, 1521. LCC 19.23. 'Et in hoc quidem loco, cum prorsus christiana doctrina a philosophia et humana ratione dissentiat, tamen sensim irrepsit philosophia in christianismum, et receptum est impium de libero arbitrio dogma et obscurata Christi beneficentia per profanam illam et animalem rationis nostrae sapientiam.' MSA 2/1.8.26–32.

[50] 'Tenebras et mendacia esse universam philosophiam.' *Theologica Institutio.* CR 21.49.

[51] 'Et sunt in scholasticis, qui in bono opere gratiae locum non relinquant.' *Theologica Institutio.* CR 21.53.

[52] 'Ut praeteream, rem ipsam satis coarguere, τὴν διάλεξιν φιλοσόφου inefficacem esse ad immutanda hominum pectora, ad instaurandos hominum affectus.' *Theologica Institutio.* CR 21.49. Again, 'Verum *nulla eiusmodi sunt opera, tamque efficacia, quo intimam pectorum nostrorum propensionem mutare queant*' (Melanchthon's emphasis). CR 21.51.

[53] '*Ita nullis externis operibus animus purgatur*' (Melanchthon's emphasis). Theologica Institutio. CR 21.51.

[54] Heinrich Bornkamm, 'Melanchthons Menschenbild', in *Philipp Melanchthon: Forschungsbeiträge zur vierhundertsen Wiederkehr seines Todestages dargeboten in Wittenberg 1960*, ed. Walter Elliger (Göttingen: Vandenhoeck & Ruprecht, 1961), 81.

[55] This shift was clearly evident in a comparison of the *Elogion de Luthero et Erasmo* (1522, CR 20.699–704) with Melanchthon's inaugural speech in Wittenberg, titled *De corrigendis adolescentiae studiis* (1518, MSA 3.29–42).

opposition to philosophy and human reason.[56] For Melanchthon, everything in the existing commentaries reeked of philosophy.[57] The false doctrine of free will had come into the church through philosophy (that is, theological speculation apart from revelation). In the *Loci*, Melanchthon could not say enough bad things about reason in religion. Fallen reason always tended toward free will, and so reason-based philosophical metaphysics had to be kept strictly separate from the clear teaching of Scripture, which denied freedom to the will in justification following the Fall.

Enslaved Affections

In the *Loci* of 1521, Melanchthon expended a significant amount of effort to construct an argument (apart from Scripture) proving the inherent uncontrollability of the affections. Sperl counts Melanchthon's affections argument as a major component of his Reformation breakthrough (*Durchbruch*),[58] which could primarily be viewed as a psychological analysis of the human condition.[59] Maurer agrees, drawing a link between Melanchthon's views on the affections and his understanding of grace.[60] The substance of Melanchthon's affections argument included the assertion that the emotions, or the affections, were uncontrollable, and that any external variance in behaviour from the internal affections was merely a pretence that in no way changed the attitude of the heart.[61] The affections ruled the will,[62] as well as reason. The uncontrollability of the affections served as a major argument for Melanchthon in buttressing the doctrines of both predestination and the bound will.

Turning to Melanchthon's biblical interpretation of the affections, he maintained that God was not interested in external works so much as internal motivations of the heart, and here Scripture taught that there was no

---

[56] Heinz Scheible, 'Melanchthon zwischen Luther und Erasmus', in *Melanchthon und die Reformation: Forschungsbeiträge*, ed. Heinz Scheible (Mainz: Verlag Philipp von Zabern, 1996), 185.

[57] 'In general, whatever has been handed down in the commentaries reeks with philosophy.' *Loci*, 1521. LCC 19.23. 'Redolet philosophiam, quidquid omnino commentariis proditum est.' MSA 2/1.9.3–4.

[58] Sperl, 101. Sperl sees Melanchthon as having a Reformation *Durchbruch* in 1519, which consisted primarily of the realization that the affections were uncontrollable (which, in turn, implied the theocentric soteriology and bound-will position of Luther's theology).

[59] Ibid., 100.

[60] Maurer, *Der junge Melanchthon*, 2.246.

[61] Günther agrees with this summation, p. 36.

[62] Bayer ('Freedom', 379) claims that it was not clear whether the affections guided the will or the will guided the affections in Melanchthon's thought. While this may perhaps be true for the later Melanchthon, at this early stage (1519–22), it is certain that Melanchthon argued for the rule of the affections over the will.

freedom.[63] Melanchthon wrote, 'For it is not within our power to drive away from their own kingdom the passions of sin which occupy an abode deep within the soul like some impregnable fortress where they exercise their tyranny over all our members. . . . Some of the ancients thought that reason is conquered by passion. Holding the reins in vain, the charioteer is borne on by the horses. Nor does the team heed curb. Rather the passions shake off reason in the same way that the horses of the sun's chariot did Phaethon. This power of sin is conquered by the grace of Christ alone.'[64] The Bible spoke of law, sin, and grace in relation to the internal affections rather than to external works. Melanchthon acknowledged that some external affections (like hunger) might be conquered (for example, when a dog gets so engrossed in play that it forgets to eat).[65] However, the internal affections were unconquerable. So why boast of freedom in external acts when God required purity of heart?[66] Because humans could not attain purity of heart by their own efforts, this showed that the will was not free.

The affections were not only unconquerable, but they were also twisted in the wrong direction as a result of the Fall. Reprising the *totus homo* view of the Fall, Melanchthon argued that the affections as well as the cognitive capacity were corrupted. Just as the intellect discerned nothing but the carnal, so it was with the affections.[67] By nature the cognitive capacity might have had the freedom to choose both good and bad thoughts, but the affections were overwhelmingly corrupt[68] and lacking in such objectivity. Human affections loved the self more than anything else, including God.[69] Thus the carnal will (comprised of both the cognitive capacity and the affections) neither loved

---

[63] 'Verum quia deus externa opera non respicit, est enim καρδιογνώστης, sed internos cordis motus, ideo scriptura nihili facit hanc libertatem.' *Loci*, 1522. CR 21.94.

[64] 'Paul and the Scholastics' (1520), trans. Hill, 39. *Declamatiuncula*, MSA I.35.30–36.6: 'Neque enim in arbitrio nostro est, exturbare regno suo adfectus peccati, qui penitam animi sedem ceu inexpugnabilem arcem tenent, in omnia membra nostra tyrannidem falsa. . . . Ex veteribus quidam in homine rationem aurigae vice fungi censuerunt, equos vocarunt adfectus. Sed vincitur adfectu ratio. Et frustra retinacula tendens fertur equis auriga, neque audit currus habenas; immo non aliter atque Phaethonem solis equi rationem affectus excutiunt. Quae peccati vis solius Christi beneficio superatur.'

[65] Here Melanchthon made his point in a mix of German and Latin: 'Vincuntur tandem externae vires affectu. Exemplum. Der hundt wen er hungrigh ist vnd zu langk mit ym spilt fso leufft er zum äsge. Sic homo commotus. erumpunt affectus.' *Capita*. CR 21.17–18.

[66] 'Praeterea, quid attinet iactare externorum operum libertatem, cum cordis puritatem deus requirat?' *Loci*, 1521. MSA 2/1.16.8–10.

[67] 'Sicut enim nihil cernit intellectus, nisi carnalia, spirtualium prorsus ignorans, ita nihil adfectat voluntas, praeter carnalia . . .' *Loci*, 1522. CR 21.94.

[68] 'Natura enim bona et mala cognoscimus, tantum mala affectamus.' *Capita*. CR 21.13–14.

[69] This idea was expressed in Melanchthon's *Baccalaureatsthesen* of 1519, numbers 1 and 2:
1. 'Natura humana diligit sese propter seipsam maxime.'
2. 'Deum propter seipsum diligere nequit.' MSA 1.24.

nor feared God,[70] and through the sinful bent of both affections and cognitive capacity, the will had no freedom to do otherwise. This position ran counter to Scotus, Ockham, Biel, and Erasmus, who had a weaker view of original sin and who argued that people could prepare themselves for grace, seeking God with nothing more than natural grace.

In sum, Melanchthon denied that the internal affections were under human control.[71] This powerlessness existed because the heart had no power to stand against itself.[72] The scholastics (Scotus, Ockham, and Biel) falsely posited that humans could control the affections, but as already stated, the cognitive capacity served the will and not the other way around. So, for example, it followed that reason had no power to change the affection of envy.[73] Accordingly, if the affections and the cognitive capacities were carnal and alienated from God, and if humans had no power to change themselves, then it became evident that the reception of salvation required a motive force external to humans. As Melanchthon taught in 1520, '... there is need for some other teacher of souls, obviously the heavenly Spirit, to seize the innermost hearts of men, to renew, inspire, take possession of, enkindle, and transform them'.[74] This action was *God's* initiative.

A Limited Validation of Philosophy

The affections argument could not be considered unique to Melanchthon. The initial emphasis on the affections began with Aristotle, Cicero, and the Stoics (although Melanchthon did not have much time for the Stoics). Quintilian distinguished between strong and weak affections. Augustine spoke of loving God as the highest affection. Marsilio Ficino from the Florentine school wrote about the rhetorical uses of the affections, and he also began to bring religion into the matter.[75] Gerson (1363–1429) discussed the affections from the psychological angle in his *De theologica mystica*.[76] Erasmus, influenced by the

---

[70] 'Deum nec amat, nec metuit.' Here Melanchthon used the Greek word φρόνημα for the will. *Loci*, 1522. CR 21.94–5.

[71] 'Fateor in externo rerum delectu esse quandam libertatem, internos vero affectus prorsus nego in potestate nostra esse.' *Loci*, 1521. MSA 2/1.16.1–3.

[72] 'Nam adversus seipsum non potest cor statuere.' *Loci*, 1522. CR 21.95.

[73] 'Voluntas inuidens non potest deponere affectum inuidentiae cum ratio ponit illum.' *Capita*. CR 21.17–18.

[74] 'Paul and the Scholastics', trans. Hill, 38. *Declamatiuncula*, MSA 1.35.2–5: 'Quare alio quodam animorum magistro opus est, nempe, coelesti spiritu, qui intima hominum pectora occupet, instauret, inspiret, rapiat, inflammet atque transformet.'

[75] Maurer, *Der junge Melanchthon*, 2.255–6.

[76] See Jean Gerson, *De theologia mystica*, ed. Palémon Glorieux, vol. 3: *Œuvres completés* (Paris: Desclée, 1960–), 250ff.

devotio moderna, then took this a step further by speaking about the importance of the affections for morality and the Christian life.[77] Luther picked up on
Gerson's framework, and gave it an overtly religious understanding in his
lectures on the Psalms of 1519. Melanchthon, in turn, gave an increased
emphasis on the overriding importance of the internal disposition.[78]

Noting the fact that one may trace a long philosophical pedigree for the idea
of the importance of the affections and their uncontrollability, some scholars
have opined that Melanchthon began with rational presuppositions and only
secondarily used the Bible to back up his position. Gerhards makes a statement
in this vein when he differentiates Melanchthon's doctrine of the will from
Luther's by saying that Melanchthon's doctrine was not only theologically
grounded, but also *philosophically* grounded.[79] Neuser picks up the same
emphasis when he relates Melanchthon's affections argument purely to humanist thought.[80] Sperl, however, is correct to say that Neuser's statement shows
little appreciation for the Reformation *Affektenlehre,*[81] and Bornkamm accurately maintains that Melanchthon's psychological arguments were not the
primary discovery, but they were instead the arguments and explanations
given in *support* of the doctrines to which the holy Scripture gave rise.[82] For
Melanchthon, Scripture was the primary source of doctrine, and rational
arguments could secondarily be utilized to support points already made in
the Word. Thus, Melanchthon's affections argument affirmed what he drew
from Scripture even though he made his argument without explicitly *citing* it.
Herein lay Melanchthon's early partial validation of philosophy. He first found
the bound will in Scripture, and then used the affections argument of his *Loci* of
1521 to illustrate that point. In a letter to Spalatin in the beginning of
September 1521, Melanchthon replied to Spalatin's enquiry regarding his
teachings on the affections in the *Loci* by saying that his *Affektenlehre* was to
be read with reference to the section on 'Sin'.[83] Melanchthon accounted the

---

[77] For a discussion of Erasmus' use of the affections in his *Enchiridion militis christiani* of
1516, see Günther, 12–13.
[78] Maurer, *Der junge Melanchthon,* 2.255–6 (much of the present paragraph is a summation
of this passage). For a more detailed discussion of the sources of Melanchthon's affections
argument, see Maurer, *Der junge Melanchthon,* 2.255–61. See also Karl Heinz zur Mühlen,
'Melanchthons Auffassung vom Affekt in den Loci communes von 1521', in *Humanismus und
Wittenberger Reformation: Festgabe anlässlich des 500. Geburtstages des Praeceptor Germaniae,
Philipp Melanchthon, am 16. Februar 1997, Helmar Junghans gewidmet,* ed. Michael Beyer et al.
(Leipzig: Evangelische Verlagsanstalt, 1997), 331.
[79] Gerhards, 30–1.
[80] Neuser, *Der Ansatz,* 46.
[81] Sperl, 101 n. 5.
[82] Bornkamm, 'Melanchthon's Menschenbild', 81.
[83] 'De discrimine adfectuum habes, quid possint adfectus aut quales sint ii qui naturae
nostrae congeniti sunt, in mea Methodo, ubi de peccato disputo.' Melanchthon (in Wittenberg),

affections argument as valid because it reached the same conclusion as Scripture, and so for him those identical conclusions legitimated the affections argument. Once thus legitimated, Melanchthon felt comfortable making the affections argument a starting-point for his anti-free will argumentation, as in the *Loci* of 1521. The true origins of the affections argument hence lay in Scripture first, and philosophical tradition second, in a supporting role.

Looking more broadly at Melanchthon's use of philosophy in theology in these early years,[84] it is apparent that Melanchthon did not oppose philosophy in and of itself. The very fact that he used rhetorical thought forms as a hermeneutic for interpreting Scripture[85] showed that he found a significant positive use for philosophy. Schneider writes, 'Careful examination reveals that even his most severe criticisms of philosophy were not as exclusionary as they might sound. . . . In other words (in undertone) [philosophers] had the right questions and larger sense of purpose.'[86] Philosophers were heading in the right general direction for true religion, and yet they remained fundamentally misguided, so that 'Philosophical ethics [Melanchthon] could characterize as the worst enemy of grace.'[87] According to Stupperich, 'In Aristotle he found only dreams, whereas the truth was offered exclusively by Paul.'[88] In 1520, Melanchthon said, 'With what great damage the schools of theology have neglected Paul up to now, I shudder to say. For after having condemned the doctrine of Paul, they embraced Aristotle [beginning with Thomas Aquinas], and scarcely is the name of Christ left.'[89] Melanchthon opposed philosophy when it churned out the wrong answers—that is, whenever it attempted to think about religion apart from the guidance of Scripture. The correct answers were only to be found in the Bible, and only those philosophical constructs that matched up with biblical conclusions were valid. The Bible presented a way in which to check one's philosophical work, thereby showing up the good philosophy from the bad, at least where matters of religion and especially justification and the will were concerned.

---

to Spalatin (in Lochau), early September 1521. MBW 1.163. T1.163.3–5. CR 1.451 Nr. 130. MSA 7/1.131.4–6 Nr. 50. Suppl. Mel. 6.1.155 Nr. 170.

[84] While this topic may seem to be of slight relevance at present, the issue will re-emerge in later chapters as a significant influence in Melanchthon's shifting thought on free will, such that the time spent now laying a foundation for that later enquiry will prove not to have been ill-spent.

[85] Schneider, 'Melanchthon's Rhetoric', 155.

[86] Ibid., 157.

[87] Stupperich, *Melanchthon*, 37.

[88] Ibid., 43.

[89] 'Paul and the Scholastics', trans. Hill, 41. *Declamatiuncula*, MSA 1.37.19–23: 'Et hactenus quanta iactura scholae Theologicae Paulum neglexerint, horreo dicere. Postquam enim contempta huius doctrina Aristotelem complexae sunt, vix Christi nomen reliquum est . . .'

The logic of Melanchthon's thought flowed as follows: purely philosophical positions (that is, constructs derived from an epistemology of empiricism) were invalid as theological statements. Theological arguments had to be based on an epistemology of authority—the Bible. If independent philosophical and theological concepts had identical conclusions, then the philosophical proposition became valid through the authority of the theological case. That is, because the empirically-derived philosophical position arrived at the same conclusion as the biblically-derived theological concept, then the philosophical argument (or at least its conclusion) must have been true as well. Further, because the philosophical statement was now known to be true, it could be discussed on its own apart from Scripture. Melanchthon approved of *this* type of philosophical argumentation, as evidenced by his use of the affections argument in the *Loci* of 1521.

By contrast, Luther argued that philosophical positions were always invalid in theological matters. In the same situation as above (where an empirical philosophical construct led to the same conclusion as a biblical theological statement) Luther made no further connection at all. The theological case was valid through the authority of the Bible. Luther wrote, 'One passage or one text from the Bible is worth more than the glosses of four writers who aren't reliable and thorough.'[90] The philosophical concept was entirely irrelevant (except perhaps for a passing comment), but for Luther, all theological arguments were to be discussed in relation to the Bible at all times. To create a parallel philosophical argument rather than relying entirely on the biblical text was an unnecessary distancing from Scripture.

Melanchthon's validation of certain aspects of philosophy in theology represented a slight interpenetration of reason and revelation. Melanchthon here mixed together the epistemologies of authority (the Bible) and empiricism (observation of the ways of the nature), a mixture of theocentric condescension with anthropocentric ascension of the mind. Bornkamm claims that Melanchthon was increasingly unconcerned with the border between reason and revelation, but rather their interpermeation (*Durchdringung*).[91] Maurer argues that Melanchthon had an unclear mixing of philosophy and theology as early as the *Capita* of 1520.[92] Bornkamm goes even further—he points out how over the following decades Melanchthon attached more and more importance to the natural knowledge of God, and saw in revelation (the Bible) the necessary completion and perfection of that

---

[90] LW 54.352–3, Nr. 4567. WATr 4.380.29–30, Nr. 4567. 'Dan ein locus und text bibliae gilt mehr dan vier scribenten glossae, quae non sunt firmae et rotundae.'

[91] Bornkamm, 'Melanchthon's Menschenbild', 87.

[92] Maurer, *Der junge Melanchthon*, 2.264.

natural knowledge. This trend, Bornkamm states, necessarily ended (despite Melanchthon's best efforts) with an assertion of free will and a fine synergism.[93] Bornkamm's claim must be left until a later point in this work to be tested, but in the meantime, in the year 1522, Melanchthon began to have reason-based concerns relating to the idea of the bound will, primarily as a result of the notion of divine determination. But despite the questions that were beginning to surface in Melanchthon's mind by 1522, in the years 1519–22, Melanchthon made an enthusiastic case for the divine determination of all events, and the consequent lack of freedom afforded to the human will.

Predestination

Because of the Fall, both the affections and the cognitive capacity were corrupted. Even if the latter had remained untainted, it had no power to change the affections, and according to the Bible, the affections were precisely the thing that mattered most. As a result, a motive force external to human beings was required in order to transform the affections, and that external motive force could only come from God. Contrary to the notion of free choice, no one could come to Christ unless drawn by the Father.[94] This statement embraced the concept of predestination, which was also the idea underlying Melanchthon's argument that to the fallen cognitive capacity it only *appeared* that people possessed freedom in external acts. The notion of free will was indeed false, for in the light of predestination, the will was in no way free.[95] Everything that happened was necessary according to divine predestination, and so the human will could not possibly be free.[96] Predestination was the all-embracing assumption (*allumspannender Voraussetzung*) in Melanchthon's theology at this point.[97] God did all in all, and so human free will did not exist, in anything.

For Melanchthon, the doctrine of predestination was synonymous with divine determination in all things. In the *Loci* of 1521, Melanchthon wrote,

[93] Bornkamm, 'Melanchthon's Menschenbild', 89.

[94] 'Contra liberum arbitrium nihil potuit aptius dici, quod illi tantum ad Christum veniant, quos dat ei pater, seu quos trahit pater, sicut postea dicit, seu quos docet pater.' In *Evangelium Ioannis Annotationes*. CR 14.1102.

[95] 'Voluntas potest comparari vel ad praedestinationem, sic nullo modo et libera.' *Theologica Institutio*. CR 21.52.

[96] *Loci*, 1521. 'Quandoquidem omnia quae eveniunt, necessario iuxta divinam praedestinationem eveniunt, nulla est voluntatis nostrae libertas.' MSA 2/1.10.11–13.

[97] Paul Schwarzenau, *Der Wandel im theologischen Ansatz bei Melanchthon von 1525–1535* (Gütersloh: Carl Bertelsmann Verlag, 1956), 13.

'And what else does Paul do in Rom 9.11 but refer all things that happen to divine determination?'[98] Even external works were predetermined,[99] as well as all the 'liberty' of our wills.[100] God did all in all (*omnia in omnibus efficere deum*).[101] Predestination functioned as a cornerstone of Melanchthon's opposition to free will. The argument from the affections merely showed from observable signs what was revealed in the Bible in the doctrines of original sin and predestination. Divine determination was a mystery that meant that there was no free will in *anything*,[102] and so of course both the human cognitive and affective abilities were utterly helpless.[103]

Melanchthon acknowledged that some might find it difficult to grasp the doctrine of predestination.[104] Nevertheless, he taught that because predestination was in the Bible, it should be believed. It should be accepted as a mystery and a secret of God, and it was to be embraced so that through believing in God people might be saved.[105] Humans should not speculate about this topic, for to know the will of God regarding election or rejection, one was to look nowhere but the Word.[106] Melanchthon warned, 'We do better to adore the mysteries of Deity than to investigate them. What is more, these matters cannot be probed without great danger, and even holy men have

---

[98] LCC 19.25. 'Et quid aliud in nono capite et XI. ad Romanos Paulus agit, quam ut omnia, quae fiunt, in destinationem divinam referat?' MSA 2/1.11.1–4.

[99] 'Eveniunt enim omnia iuxta divinam praedestionationem, cum externa opera, tum internae cogitationes, in omnibus creaturis.' *Loci*, 1522. CR 21.96.

[100] 'Tollit itaque omnem libertatem voluntatis nostrae praedestinatio divina.' *Loci*, 1522. CR 21.96.

[101] 'Neque fidem, neque metum dei doceri posse iudico, nisi persuasum nobis sit, omnia in omnibus efficere deum.' *Loci*, 1522. CR 21.96.

[102] Melanchthon here cited Rom. 9.18; 1 Kings 10.26 (Saul); and 3 Kings [1 Chron.] 12.15 (Jeroboam) to argue that all events were determined by God. 'Ergo non est in potestate nostra quidquam Nec affectus internus nec externum opus. Si compares nostra cum praedestinatione. *Eueniuntque omnia ut consilio diuino destinata sunt*. Atque huius mysterii sublimior est ratio quam ut assequi eam humana imbecillitas possit, et in contemplacione eius admonearis benignitatis diuinae esse Quod apud sese est rerum omnium summa et imperium' (emphasis added). *Capita*. CR 21.15–16.

[103] 'Voluntas comparata cum praedestinacione non est libera Neque in bonis, neque in malis, Neque in externis operibus neque internis affectibus.' *Capita*. CR 21.13–14.

[104] *Capita*. CR 21.15–16. 'Quia locus praedestinationis sublimior est humano captu Simpliciter contuenda est natura voluntatis humanae Vtrum possit sese ad quamcumque rem applicare: aut a quacunque re auocare quocies consulit intellectus.'

[105] '... sciunt secreta Dei non dabere fare, sed credi debere, et sciunt se credentes salvari.' *In Evangelium Ioannis Annotationes*. CR 14.1106.

[106] 'Haec scire de voluntate Dei et de electione vel reiectione satis est, nec aliam voluntatem quaerito, sed iuxta hoc verbum iudicato, quod vere est lucerna sanctorum.' *Breves Commentarii in Matthaeum*. CR 14.952.

experienced this.'[107] God did what he pleased (*Dominus est enim, facit quod placet*[108]), and all were to accept that fact.

But, Melanchthon argued, according to the Bible, predestination also played an important role in comforting Christians. If the changed affections of Christians that allowed them to believe in God were not their own doing, then that meant that their perseverance in faith was also not their own doing. Because they had faith, this was a sign that God had changed their affections because he had predestined them to salvation, and so the one who changed the affections in the first place would cause believers to persevere in faith.[109] Believers could further take comfort by finding confirmation of their election through God's universal promises. Those who believed God's promises were the elect.[110]

In total, Melanchthon denied free will based on both the Fall and divine determination.[111] In his *Annotations on Romans* of 1522, Melanchthon would continue to state forcefully his position of divine determination. At the same time, here more than before, Melanchthon began to give voice to some serious questions about the implications of divine determination.

ANNOTATIONS ON ROMANS: 1522

Circumstances of Composition, and Significance

In the early 1520s, the Wittenberg theologians were engaged in a great effort to disseminate Reformation theology throughout Europe by means of printed commentaries, tracts, and other writings. Luther and Melanchthon turned out a large volume of biblical commentary in these years, and naturally, one of the most important would have been a commentary on Romans. But even though Melanchthon was lecturing on Romans in 1520 and 1521, he was not eager to publish his thoughts in the form of a commentary. Nevertheless, seeing the importance of such a work at this crucial stage in the Reformation,

---

[107] LCC 19.21. 'Mysteria divinitatis rectius adoraverimus quam vestigaverimus. Immo sine magno periculo tentari non possunt, id quod non raro sancti viri etiam sunt experti.' *Loci*, 1521. MSA 2/1.6.16–19.

[108] *Capita.* CR 21.15–16.

[109] Ibid.

[110] *Breves Commentarii in Matthaeum.* CR 14.952.

[111] Of course, divine determination as Melanchthon articulated it here in the early 1520s would naturally imply the absence of freedom for human beings even *before* the Fall. He did not go so far as to draw this out explicitly, but it had to be in his mind, especially as he began to think about the causes of evil, sin, and the Fall.

some of Melanchthon's students brought their lecture notes to Luther, who published them without Melanchthon's consent. At the beginning of the work, Luther provided an open letter in which he apologized to Melanchthon for going behind his back, but he also chided his colleague for not publishing this important work.[112] Luther described Jerome and Origen's commentaries on Romans as foolish and inept in comparison with Melanchthon's,[113] which was a better piece of work than Luther himself could have hoped to produce.[114] Indeed, Melanchthon's *Annotations on Romans* represented the heart of Luther's and Melanchthon's thought in the years 1522–4, and Wengert is right to state, 'The [*Annotations on Romans*] formed the cornerstone for the Wittenberg theologians' commentary on the entire New Testament from 1522 to 1524.'[115]

The central point Melanchthon discovered in Paul's letter to the Romans (which was also the central point of the Reformation), was that justification occurred by faith alone, and resulted in imputed righteousness for the believer.[116] Melanchthon saw Romans divided into three main themes— grace, law, and sin—and he observed Paul making his central point about justification by faith alone through the means of the clear application of the classical laws of rhetoric.[117] Throughout Melanchthon's career, this application of the classical rules of rhetoric to the exposition of Scripture would play a significant role in shaping his doctrine. This is a topic to which we shall return. In the meantime, it is enough merely to take in Melanchthon's strong and repeated declarations of the absence of free will for humans in justification.

---

[112] Ann. Rom., 1b. The date on this letter is 9 July 1522.

[113] 'Hieronymi et Originis commentaria esse meras nugas et ineptias, situis Annotationibus comparentur.' Ann. Rom., 2a.

[114] '... tuis annotationibus, labor est ante me ...'. Ann. Rom., 2a.

[115] Timothy J. Wengert, 'Philip Melanchthon's 1522 Annotations on Romans and the Lutheran Origins of Rhetorical Criticism', in *Biblical Interpretations in the Era of the Reformation: Essays Presented to David C. Steinmetz in Honor of his Sixtieth Birthday*, ed. Richard A. Müller and John L. Thompson (Grand Rapids: Eerdmans, 1996), 123.

[116] Melanchthon made this point in his introduction, on the central teaching of chapters 1–8: 'Status causae iustificari nos fide, quae sententia probatur multis argumentis, Tum Lex et Peccatum, cum gratia conferunter. . . . Nihil humanorum operum bonum esse, nihil humanarum virum aliquid posse. Sed quia Christus sit donatus, propter hunc si credas delicto ignosci, confidasque; te saluum fore, eam fidem reputari a Deo . . .', Ann. Rom., 3b. Additionally, Melanchthon stressed justification by faith in his comments on Rom. 1.17 and 1.18. On 1.17: 'Iustitia Dei revelatur, quae non est ex operibus, sed ex fide in fidem.' Ann. Rom., 8a. On 1.18: 'Summa narrationis. Propositio & status huius disputationis est, solem Fidem in Christum reputari pro iusticia.' Ann. Rom., 9a.

[117] 'Secundum, prior pars epistolae octo capitum, Gratia, Legem, Peccatum tractat. Idque; aptis simo ordine, & plane Rhetorica methodo.' Ann. Rom., 3b.

Arguments Against Free Will

Declarations against Free Will

More than in any other work, in the *Annotations on Romans*, Melanchthon repeatedly and definitely denied the freedom of the human will in justification. On Rom. 8.6,[118] Melanchthon declared, 'You will observe in this place how definitely those who assert free choice are refuted.'[119] Further, it was certain that the flesh did not possess the ability to accept God, as Thomas argued.[120] Additionally, there were no half-measures—people did *not* have the ability to cooperate with the Holy Spirit: 'And this is to say that for those whom the Holy Spirit leads, free choice is entirely driven out. Here Paul attributes all action to the Holy Spirit, and none to the will. The will is part of that which is mortified, and hence has no power to cooperate with the Holy Spirit.'[121] Arguments in favour of free choice were ridiculous, for the will was in no way free, but had to be impelled by God.[122] Human wills were not free to convert themselves to the good by their own free choice, and they were saved by no merit of their own, but solely according to God's mercy.[123] Throughout this work, Melanchthon repeatedly denied human free will in conversion.

Affections Argument?

In light of the fact that the affections argument played such a distinct role in Melanchthon's *Loci* of 1521, it would be reasonable to expect some vestige of it to survive in the *Annotations on Romans* of 1522. However, the reason-based argumentation of the affections argument did not appear in this work. As Wengert points out, here Melanchthon did not even mention the psychological side of his doctrine of free will—that is, he completely left out the

---

[118] 'To set the mind on the flesh is death, but to set the mind on the Spirit is life and peace.'

[119] 'Observabis autem hoc loco vel maxime refutari liberi arbitrij assertores, cum palam hic dicitur.' Ann. Rom., 43a.

[120] 'Vbi certe caro non potest modo Thomistico accipi.' Ann. Rom., 43a.

[121] On Rom. 8.13: 'Et diserte ait, qui spiritu Dei ducuntur, ut adimat omnem uim liberari arbitrij. . . . Hic vero Pau. tribuit omnem actionem spiritui, et nihil voluntati. Imo uoluntas ea pars est, quae proprie mortificatur, ergo non potest cum spiritu sancto cooperari.' Ann. Rom., 45a.

[122] 'Consequitur itaque; ridiculum commentum esse liberum arbitrium. . . . Quia voluntas nostra adeo non est libera, ut eo tantum feratur, quorsum a deo impellitur.' Ann. Rom., 50a.

[123] 'Adeo voluntas nostra non est libera, ut se ad bona conuertere possit, suo libero arbitrio, adeo nulla sunt plane merita nostra, & solius Dei misericordiae tribuendum est, quod salvamur.' Ann. Rom., 50b.

affections argument.[124] The term 'affections' itself appeared infrequently, and when it did appear, it was usually used in reference to original sin. For example, on Rom. 8.6, Melanchthon wrote, 'The affections of the flesh are death',[125] and later, in reference to Rom. 8.15,[126] Melanchthon argued that the affections were held captive, and that one could not naturally fear God.[127] Apart from oblique comments such as these, the affections argument against free will made no appearance. This fact illustrates the secondary importance Melanchthon afforded to it. The affections argument was originally only valid because it paralleled the teachings of the Bible. When faced with the task of commenting on the biblical text itself, Melanchthon felt no impulsion to import extra-biblical philosophical arguments. In Melanchthon's mind, the Bible was authority enough in its own right, and when immersed in the text of the Bible, one needed to bring in no outside references.

Divine Determination

Instead of dwelling on the affections argument, when he wrote against free will, Melanchthon drew on the strongest possible reason for denying human freedom—the divine determination of all events. Melanchthon felt that this conclusion was inevitable upon a close reading of Romans. In the introduction to his commentary on Romans 9–11, Melanchthon taught bluntly that everything that happened was necessary: *Necessario omnia eveniunt in omnibus creaturis.*[128] He followed up this assertion with nine proof texts, five drawn from the Old Testament, and four drawn from the New.[129] Clearly, Melanchthon believed that divine determination was taught not only in

---

[124] Wengert, 'Philip Melanchthon's 1522 Annotations on Romans . . .', 36.

[125] 'Affectus carnis est mors.' Ann. Rom., 43a.

[126] 'For you did not receive a spirit of slavery to fall back into fear, but you have received a spirit of adoption. When we cry, "Abba! Father!"'

[127] 'Horum est spiritus servitutis, Id est, affectus servi captivi, erga dominum, non filij erga patrem. Porro, non aliud potest natura, nisi metuere, & odisse Deum.' Ann. Rom., 45b.

[128] Ann. Rom., 49a.

[129] Rom. 11.36 (*For from him and through him and to him are all things*); Isa. 66.1 (*The heaven is my throne, and the earth is my footstool*); Pss. 113.11 [115.3] (*Our God is in the heavens, he does whatever he pleases*); Prov. 16.4 (*The Lord has made everything for its purpose, even the wicked for the day of trouble*); Isa. 45.7 (*I form light and create darkness, I make weal and create woe; I the Lord do all these things*); Eph. 1.11 (. . . *having been destined according to the purpose of him who accomplishes all things according to his counsel and will* . . .); Jer. 10.23 (*I know, O Lord, that the way of human beings is not in their control, that mortals as they walk cannot direct their steps*). Interestingly, while Melanchthon here interpreted this text from Jeremiah in terms of divine determination, he would specifically refute such an interpretation of the same verse in his *Loci* of 1535. 1 Cor. 12.6 (. . . *there are varieties of activities, but it is the same God who activates all of them in everyone*); Matt. 10.29–31 (*Sparrows* . . . *not one of them will fall to the ground apart from your Father.* . . . *Hairs of your heads are numbered* . . .) Ann. Rom., 49a–b.

Romans, but throughout the entire corpus of the Bible. Additionally, Melanchthon made it clear that God did not merely *permit* events to happen, but he instead impelled the occurrence of all things.[130] God did all things, not passively, but potently, as Augustine taught.[131] Obviously, if God determined all events, then there could be no free will, in anything.

Predestination to both Heaven and Hell

If God determined all things, then it naturally fell into place also that he predestined who would be saved, and also chose ahead of time who would be damned. Here Melanchthon did not simply state this doctrine as a logical corollary to divine determination, but found texts in Romans that he felt independently validated the teaching that God predetermined both those whom he would elect and those whom he would reject.

In his introduction, Melanchthon taught that the second part of Romans (chapters 9–11) dealt specifically with the doctrine of predestination and the calling of the Gentiles.[132] This was interesting, especially in light of the fact that in later commentaries on Romans (in 1529, 1532, 1540, and 1556), Melanchthon would relegate predestination to a subheading under the doctrine of justification. In the present work, by contrast, predestination enjoyed a more prominent role, and Melanchthon even devoted a special section to it (titled *De Praedestinatione*), beginning at Rom. 8.28.[133] In this section, Melanchthon spoke favourably about the necessity of predestination (*praedestinationis necessitas*), and cited John 6 in support.[134] He continued by teaching that God elected people apart from merit,[135] and that it was blasphemy to

---

[130] 'Nos uero dicemus, non solum permittere deum creaturis ut operentur, sed ipsum oīa [omnia] proprie agere . . .' Ann. Rom., 50a.

[131] 'Deum oīa facere, n pmißiue, sed potter, ut Aug. uerbo utamur [Deum omnia facere, non permissive, sed potenter, ut Augustinus verbo utamur].' Ann. Rom., 50a.

[132] 'Posterior pars epistolae praedestinationem & vocationem gentium tractat.' Ann. Rom., 3b.

[133] Ann. Rom., 48b–52b. Rom. 8.28–9 reads, 'We know that all things work together for good for those who love God, who are called according to his purpose. For those whom he foreknew he also predestined to be conformed to the image of his Son, in order that he might be the firstborn within a large family.' It was telling that in Melanchthon's commentaries on Romans from 1529, 1532, 1540, and 1556, he would skip over completely Rom. 8.28f. without any comment at all.

[134] Ann. Rom., 48b–49a.

[135] 'Quod deus, quos elegit, sine ullis meritis elegit.' Ann. Rom., 50b. Again, Melanchthon cited John 6.44–5 as a proof text: 'No one can come to me unless drawn by the Father who sent me; and I will raise that person up on the last day. It is written in the prophets, "And they shall all be taught by God." Everyone who has heard and learned from the Father comes to me.'

deny or to examine predestination, which was with God.[136] God immutably chose people, and this was to be a comfort.[137] Finally, Melanchthon declared that it was the work of God to make both the elect and the reprobate,[138] and he went on to pose the question, 'Why does God choose (*elegit*) some and reject (*reprobat*) others, when all are born sinners?'[139] Leaving Melanchthon's difficult question aside for the moment, it is enough to note that he affirmed God's dual predestination of individuals to either election or rejection, which inevitably supported his previously declared antipathy to any sort of free role for the will in justification.

Questions of Rational Consistency and the Pastoral Effects of Doctrine

Melanchthon's question about why some were elect and some were reprobate indicated a level of concern with the pastoral effects of his theological system on the hearts and minds of believers. Although the Bible seemed to make clear statements about divine determination, predestination, and the concomitant doctrine of the bondage of the will, these doctrines led to certain difficulties when followed to their furthermost logical consequences. The *effect* of these doctrines was not always salutary upon the mind and heart of the believer. With divine determination and predestination, the division of all of humanity into reprobate and elect seemed arbitrary, there appeared to be little rationale for the responsibility of people for their own actions, and the problem of the origins of sin and evil became entirely manifest. Melanchthon provided answers for these questions in his *Annotations on Romans* of 1522, but apparently he did not find these answers very satisfying, for in future theological writings he moved away from the positions he advanced in this work. Bearing this in mind, we turn now to Melanchthon's formulation of the problems already mentioned, and examine his answers to these difficult conundrums initiated by a strong view of the total governance of God.

Melanchthon acknowledged the qualms reason had with a robust view of the predestination of God, but he nevertheless maintained his affirmation for

[136] 'Praedestinationem igitur negare, quam apud Deum esse, breviter probavimus, immanis blasphemia est.' Ann. Rom., 51b.
[137] '...quia voluntas Dei qui elegit immutabilis est. Ergo nos consolemur...' Ann. Rom., 48b.
[138] 'Praeterea quid aliud sunt biblicae hystoriae, quam operum dei commemoratio, quae per electos & reprobos facit.' Ann. Rom., 49b.
[139] 'Cur Deus alios elegit, alios reprobat, cum tamen omnes iuxta peccatores nascamus?' Ann. Rom., 52b.

divine determination here in 1522. He argued that although it appeared plainly so to the flesh (i.e. human reason), events were *not* contingent but necessitated according to the determination of God.[140] Things only *appeared* to be contingent, but were in fact necessitated.[141] This was much in line with Luther's teaching. When things appeared to be contingent, Melanchthon advised his readers to remember the sacred doctrine, and that Scripture should be used to mortify the (false) senses of the flesh. As a result, it was ridiculous to talk about free choice.[142] Moreover, as for divine election, rejection, and the fairness of reprobation, Melanchthon put forward that such was attributable to the glory of God,[143] and he echoed the words of Paul when he wrote, 'O man, who are you to talk back to God?'[144]

Melanchthon gave a similar answer for the problem of evil. First, he acknowledged that God had a hand in evil. In one of his proof texts for divine determination (Isa. 45.7), Melanchthon attributed this Latin phrase to God: *Ego… creans malum*—'I create evil'. Later, in reference to 1 Kings 12.15,[145] Melanchthon argued that everything became as it was through God, as much good as evil.[146] In other words, God's total rule extended over both good and evil events. God, in a certain sense, was actually responsible for evil. But how could this be? Melanchthon replied that God used the wicked for his own glory, just as it was with Pharaoh, whose heart he hardened.[147] But was God really the source of evil? Melanchthon replied, 'Just adore his incomprehensible majesty!'[148] Again, if God did all things, both good and evil, why did he punish the wicked? Melanchthon responded with an answer that seemed to apply for all the qualms reason held with a

---

[140] 'In his palam apparet, quod quanquam ita carni videatur, tamen non sit rerum contingentia, sed necessitas quaedam, iuxta destinationem dei.' Ann. Rom., 49b. See also 49a: 'Porro in hac disputatione nihil tam mirari humana ratio solet, quam cum omnia uideantur contingenter, ac non necessario fieri, necessario tamen ita destinata fiant.'

[141] 'Contingentia quaedam in rebus videntur, cum tamen sit necessitas.' Ann. Rom., 49a.

[142] 'Videri esse contingentiam rerum, memineris sacram doctrina, scripturam esse prodita ad mortificandum sensum carnis. Consequitur itaque; ridiculum commentum esse liberum arbitrium.' Ann. Rom., 50a.

[143] Ann. Rom., 52b, 53a.

[144] 'O homo, tu quis qui respondeas Deo?.' Ann. Rom., 52b.

[145] 'So the king did not listen to the people, because it was a turn of affairs brought about by the Lord that he might fulfil his word, which the Lord had spoken by Ahijah the Shilonite to Jeroboam son of Nebat.'

[146] 'Itaque; sit haec certa sentétia, a Deo fieri omnia, tam bona quam mala.' Ann. Rom., 49b.

[147] 'Iam & illa ipsa mala quae fiunt, ipse ordinat ad suam gloriam, sicut ait Pharaoni, In hoc ipsum excitaui te, ut ofendam in te potentiam meam, & ut annuncietur nomen meum in tota terra.' Ann. Rom., 50b.

[148] 'Praeterea stultũ carni videtur, deum omnia facere & in his tam multa frivola & mala. Sed hic humanis cogitationibus imperandum est, & adoranda illa incompraehensibilis maiestas.' Ann. Rom., 49a.

strong view of the determination of God—it was an inexplicable mystery. Melanchthon did not know the answer. *Est autem hoc loco mysterium inexplicabile.*[149]

CONCLUSION

Despite Melanchthon's positive treatment of predestination as comfort, some doubts could be detected in his words as well. His references to predestination in these early years were usually brusque, and blunt. A short declarative sentence often seemed to require little or no elaboration. Melanchthon's vigorous espousal of predestination in 1519 was not propounded quite so vigorously by 1522. At this time, Melanchthon's formulations began to include some consideration of several pastoral questions related to the implications of such a strong view of the governance of God. He began to explore issues like reprobation, human responsibility for our own actions, and the origins of sin. These were probably questions that were occurring to Melanchthon himself, but no doubt he was also hearing them from his students in his daily teaching.

One aspect of predestination that gave Melanchthon particular concern related to the reprobate—those selected for damnation. Melanchthon insisted that God's promises were truly universal (i.e. they were for every single human individual), and that there was no contradiction in God's will: '*In Deo non sunt contradictoriae voluntates. Promissiones sunt universales.*'[150] Thus, if God really did wish for the salvation of every individual, then was not the idea of reprobation rationally inconsistent? Luther tried to resolve this tension in his own theology by resorting to a construct of God's hidden and revealed wills. But Melanchthon never took this path. Additionally, he probed further when he asked who was really responsible for the plight of the lost. Melanchthon settled on an answer in his commentary on Matt. 23.37.[151]

---

[149] 'Altera quaestio est. Si & mala & bona Dei uoluntate fiunt, quare accusat, & punit malos? Hanc quaestionem mouet, cum ait. Dices ergo mihi, quid adhuc conqueritur, Id est, quid accusat Deus, quandoquidem pro sua voluntate omnis eueniunt, cui resistere nemo potest. Neque; ad hanc quaestionem respondetur. Est autem hoc loco mysterium inexplicabile.' Ann. Rom., 53b–54a.

[150] *Breves Commentarii in Matthaeum.* CR 14.952.

[151] '... How often have I desired to gather your children together as a hen gathers her brood under her wings, and you were not willing!'

There Melanchthon wrote that those who rejected God did so not out of God's will, but out of Satan's will.[152]

Meanwhile, during this period Luther stood up for his writings at the Diet of Worms, and fell under the condemnation of the Holy Roman Emperor, Charles V. Elector Frederick, in order to protect the star professor of his University at Wittenberg, staged Luther's kidnapping by 'bandits' in the forest, and hurried him away in secret to the Wartburg Castle. Melanchthon, separated from Luther, now faced a situation in Wittenberg in which some wild characters emerged proclaiming more and more radical reformation. Riots broke out—and in the midst of it all, Melanchthon continued to teach and write about Christian doctrine.

---

[152] 'Voluntas in impiis libere adversatur verbo Dei, non cogitur a Deo, sed ipsa per se et incitata a Diabolo, est causa damnationis.' *Breves Commentarii in Matthaeum.* CR 14.980.

5

1522–1526: Unrest

INTRODUCTION

Between the years 1522 and 1526, the language of predestination and determinism began to disappear from Melanchthon's writings. New emphases appeared stressing the responsibility of humans for their own actions, and the possibility of a real contingency—that is, God might perhaps not determine *all* things after all. In these years, Melanchthon began to temper his thought on the determinism of God, and while he continued explicitly to deny free will in justification, his theology was becoming increasingly conducive to a greater degree of human freedom. This continuing development in Philipp's thought occurred in the midst of the Wittenberg disturbances of 1521–2, and in the revisions of the *Loci communes* undertaken in 1522. It could also be seen in the way Luther's emerging political theology (1522–3) impacted Melanchthon's own doctrines, as well as in Philipp's relationship to the debate on free choice between Luther and Erasmus (1524–6).

THE WITTENBERG UNREST: 1521–1522

In late 1521, a new strand in Melanchthon's theology began to surface: an increased emphasis on the responsibility of human beings for their own actions. Obviously this was a concept that fitted hand-in-glove with emerging questions about predestination and divine determinism, but it only truly came to light in Melanchthon's writings as a result of the real-world experience of the Wittenberg disturbances of 1521–2.

Melanchthon Before the Unrest: 1520–1521

In the Introduction, I mentioned three types of free will: contingency, justification, and good works. The focus of this book is on the second type of free will—that is, free will in justification, or the origins of a saving faith in Jesus. However, in the previous chapter it became necessary to mention Melanchthon's early thoughts on contingency, and now we will look briefly at Melanchthon's view of free will in good works, as a result of the Wittenberg disturbances. The doctrines of free will in contingency and free will in good works affected each other, and the Wittenberg disturbances would represent a catalyst to moderate change for both in Melanchthon's thought. Ultimately, Melanchthon's views on contingency and good works would together represent a logical force for change in his understanding of free will in justification.

Before the Wittenberg unrest, Melanchthon and Luther both strongly emphasized justification by faith alone apart from works as the means of salvation. They viewed this as an important correction to the faulty theology being taught in much of the church at the time. Good works played a *part* in the soteriological process, but they did not cause it. Melanchthon believed that the human will was impotent to change itself, and the only hope for moral regeneration came through God,[1] who always justified before he brought ethical renewal.[2] In 1520, Melanchthon rejected philosophical ethics, arguing that the ethics of the ancients was spoiled by self-love.[3] In the *Loci* of 1521, Melanchthon wrote, 'The philosophical virtues and all efforts of free [choice] are plainly "flesh".'[4] Following justification, moral renovation came automatically,[5] as individuals expressed thankfulness to God[6] and found themselves reoriented by the Holy Spirit toward a life of service and good works. As Luther also taught, good works for the redeemed were to be a *sign* of faith, and its natural fruit. They did not justify, but they naturally occurred in the justified.[7]

Meanwhile, as Luther remained hidden in the Wartburg Castle, Karlstadt and Zwilling stepped in at Wittenberg and pushed change onwards at a blistering rate. The Zwickau prophets (with whom Melanchthon was initially

---

[1] Sperl, 103. See also P. Joachimsen, who says that in this position against free will Melanchthon ruined the entire ethical world of humanism. 'Loci communes: Eine Untersuchung zur Geistesgeschichte des Humanismus und der Reformation', *Jahrbuch der Luthergesellschaft* 8 (1926), 78. See Chapter 4 above, where Melanchthon's teachings on the affections embodied the same principle.

[2] Maurer, *Der junge Melanchthon*, 2.240.

[3] Ibid., 270. Additionally, in the *Loci* of 1521, Melanchthon called philosophy, 'the chaos of carnal dreams.' LCC 19.99. '. . . illud carnalium somniorum, philosophia.' MSA 2/1.100.21–2.

[4] LCC 19.131. 'Pleneque caro sunt virtutes philosophicae et conatus liberi arbitrii qualescunque.' MSA 2/1.137.30–1.

[5] Maurer, *Der junge Melanchthon*, 2.365.

[6] Ibid., 382.

[7] For a summary of Luther's take on faith and works, see Lohse, *Martin Luther's Theology*, 264–6.

impressed) appeared, claiming direct revelation and arguing for the slaughter of the ungodly.[8] On 3 December 1521, 'Some students and townsmen, armed with knives, invaded the parish church, intimidated the priests, stoned some of those saying masses, and hacked the mass books.'[9] Then, on Christmas Eve, 1521, mobs rioted in the streets and converged on the parish church. The riots and iconoclasm were ostensibly about producing evangelical change—i.e. being faithful to biblically mandated practices. But in Melanchthon's mind, the problem here was undoubtedly maintaining public order, with the issues of the forms of worship thereby becoming secondary concerns. Another worry for Melanchthon included Karlstadt's new argument at this time that all education ought to be abolished, seeing as Christ and the apostles were, in all likelihood, not educated.[10] Civil order was breaking down, and the masses were listening to the vigorous preaching of Karlstadt and Zwilling. The situation deteriorated, and Melanchthon become distressed about the lack of order in Wittenberg.

Luther commented to Spalatin regarding this situation, 'I see that they do not need me anymore [in Wittenberg], except Philipp; he gives in too easily to his moods, and bears the cross more impatiently than is fitting for a disciple, especially such a great teacher of teachers.'[11] It appeared that the freedom being preached in the Reformation movement in Wittenberg in 1521–2 had sparked civil disorder characterized by a marked lack of ethical restraint.[12] Change was required. People needed to be taught to control themselves.

Melanchthon After the Unrest: 1522–1524

Luther, beginning in 1522, began to articulate two uses for the law.[13] The law's theological (or spiritual) use was to convict one of sin (and increase it), thus driving one away from self-reliance towards trust in God's promises in Christ. More pertinent for the maintenance of civil order, Luther also spoke of the political, or civil, use of the law. Lohse summarizes: 'By means of the political use, external order on earth is to be maintained, and peace and the securing of justice preserved. The law has also the task of inculcating the divine

---

[8] Roland H. Bainton, *Here I Stand: A Life of Martin Luther* (New York: Mentor, 1950), 161.

[9] Manschreck, *The Quiet Reformer*, 75. Cf. Melanchthon (in Wittenberg), letter to Elector Frederick of Saxony (in Lochau), 27 December 1521. MBW 1.192. T1.192. CR 1.513–14. MSA 7/1.158–61 Nr. 64.

[10] Manschreck, *The Quiet Reformer*, 75–6.

[11] 15 July 1521. LW 48.269. '[I]am nihil me opus eos habere intelligam, nisi quod philippus nimio indulgens affectibus crucem impatientius fert, quam deceat vel discipulum, nedum tantum tantorum Magistrum.' WABr 2.364.10–13.

[12] Maurer, *Der junge Melanchthon*, 2.221.

[13] See Lohse, *Martin Luther's Theology*, 270–3.

commandments and of instructing consciences. It also is to furnish the needed means by which to punish evildoers. The order established by the political use of the law is effected through the offices of the temporal authorities, of parents, of teachers, and of judges, instituted by God for that purpose. If the law in its political sense is obeyed, then an "external", "civic" righteousness is achieved, to which Luther assigned highest value.[14] The church ought to preach both uses of the law, for while the law's theological use held soteriological benefits, the law's civic use (though not salvific) served God's will by promoting peace and external righteousness in the land.

Following the unrest, Melanchthon came to a position similar to Luther's regarding the civic use of the law. By contrast, though, his emphasis was less on *preaching* the revealed law (although that, too, was important) and more on *teaching* the innate (or natural) law. During the unrest, Melanchthon started to focus more and more on natural law and an innate ethical spark in all people, even as expressed in the writings of ancient philosophers. With this thought in mind, and in light of the unrest at Wittenberg, Melanchthon began to advocate education as a way to build up and fortify the innate ethical knowledge of the populace. This emphasis on ethics would, in fact, become such a strong theme in Melanchthon that one modern scholar has dubbed him 'the Ethicist of the Reformation'.[15] In a letter to Christoph Hacke, in March 1523, Melanchthon praised the connection between education and piety,[16] and in *The Difference between Temporal and Christian Piety* of 1522, Melanchthon argued that all children should be taught the law.[17] At the opening of a new school in Nuremberg in 1526, Melanchthon declared, 'When youth are brought up properly . . . it will be a defence for the country: for no bulwark or city walls are stronger than citizens endowed with learning, prudence, and the other virtues.'[18]

---

[14] Ibid., 271.

[15] Wolfgang Trillhouse, 'Philipp Melanchthon, der Ethiker der Reformation', *Evangelische Theologie* 6 (1946/7), 389–403.

[16] Melanchthon (in Wittenberg), to Christoph Hacke (in Erfurt), 29 March 1523. MBW 1.274. T 2.274. CR 3.483–4 Nr. 1647.

[17] *Unterschidt zwischen weltlicher und Christlicher Fromkeyt*. '[Gott] wolle Kinder machen, die Gott lehre.' CR 1.525. 'Er well kinder machen, die Gott lere.' MSA 1.173.31–2. See also CR 1.526; MSA 1.174.13–22. This writing is occasionally dated to 1521 rather than 1522. This affirmation of a universal innate sense of right and wrong would be a lifelong theme for Melanchthon. In a letter to Michael Meienburg in 1549, Melanchthon argued that the whole world showed that God was creator and sustainer, and that while the knowledge of nature was admittedly imperfect, it did lead to God and virtue. 29 September 1549. MBW 5.5641. CR 7.474–7 Nr. 4603. See also Kolb, *Bound Choice*, 74: 'Public disorder . . . in the early days of the Reformation in Wittenberg in 1521 and 1522 . . . further strengthened [Melanchthon's] commitment to teaching the commandments of God for daily life.'

[18] 'In Praise of the New School', trans. Keen, 61. *In laudem novae scholae*, MSA 3.66.27–31: 'Cum . . . recte fuerit instituta iuventus, praesidio patriae erit: non enim ulla propugnacula aut moenia firmiora urbium monumenta sunt, quam eruditione, prudentia et aliis virtutibus praediti cives.'

Melanchthon's reaffirmation of ethics based on natural law from 1522 onwards is almost universally acknowledged in the literature. Bornkamm argues that Melanchthon returned more strongly than ever to his previous Ciceronian natural law background (which he never truly gave up in the first place), and that Melanchthon viewed natural insights (for example, an innate sense of right and wrong) as clear expressions of the will of God.[19] The innate ethical law was therefore a sign of human dignity.[20] Kusukawa maintains that Melanchthon began to stress God's providential design in the world, and that 'Motivated by the desire to check civil disobedience and promote Lutheran orthodoxy, he created a natural philosophy based on Aristotle, Galen and Plato, incorporating contemporary findings of Copernicus and Vesalius.'[21] Again, 'Melanchthon restored the teaching of classical moral philosophy as part of the Divine Law.'[22] Gerhards, Schwarzenau, Neuser, and Brüls make similar points.[23] For Melanchthon, human reason (as represented by ancient philosophy) and revelation (the Bible) came together in one single point: the law.[24] Here again lay Melanchthon's limited validation of philosophy.

Melanchthon's approval of natural law and an innate ethical consciousness in all people signified the first step in a reaffirmation of biblical humanism and philosophical ethics on the matter of civil righteousness. Bornkamm states that for Melanchthon, following the Wittenberg unrest, it was a *philosophical* teaching that people recognized and served God's will in the law.[25] Maurer maintains that in Melanchthon's critique of the excesses of Karlstadt and the Zwickau prophets, he found biblical humanism reawakening within himself, and that this led to a conscious distancing from Luther.[26] It was probably not *'einer gewissen Distanzierung gegenüber Luther',* but Melanchthon's strong focus on ethical education (as compared to Luther's related stress on preaching the civic use of the law) which represented an emphasis unique to him. Melanchthon felt that the key to making a genuine impact on people's ethical behaviour involved giving them a good education pertaining to rights

[19] Bornkamm, 'Melanchthon's Menschenbild', 84–5.

[20] Ibid., 85.

[21] Sachiko Kusukawa, *The Transformation of Natural Philosophy: The Case of Philip Melanchthon* (Cambridge: Cambridge University Press, 1995), i (abstract).

[22] Ibid., 74.

[23] Gerhards, 39. Gerhards is correct in saying that Melanchthon began to emphasize natural law, but his comment that Melanchthon's formulation of it is unscriptural is debatable. Schwarzenau, 13. Neuser, *Der Ansatz*, 34. Brüls, 29.

[24] Siegfried Wiedenhofer, *Formalstrukturen humanistischer und reformatorischer Theologie bei Philipp Melanchthon*, 2 vols. (Bern: Herbert Lang, 1976), 189.

[25] Bornkamm, 'Melanchthon's Menschenbild', 85.

[26] Maurer, *Der junge Melanchthon*, 2.203. See also p. 207, where Maurer sees Melanchthon placing the foundations of the Christian's new life on a humanistic footing.

and wrongs. In this sense, Melanchthon nudged his anthropology in a more positive direction than he had previously espoused, for it remedied civil disorder with indoctrination into natural law ethics, based on the assumption, no doubt, that to know the good would be to do the good—or at least, do not quite as much evil. Further, this ethical improvement required human *effort*[27] (though of course, one could say the same about Luther's preaching of the civic use of the law). This emphasis on teaching natural law ethics was a slightly different approach from Luther's emphasis on preaching the Bible alone. While Luther insisted on preaching alone (in addition to the enforcement of the laws of the land by the political prince) as the method of getting people to do good works and live ordered lives, Melanchthon had come to endorse basic education (even employing ancient pagan writings) as the means to fortifying all people's innate sense of right and wrong and thereby encouraging them to take responsibility for their own actions. Following the Wittenberg disturbances, therefore, Melanchthon chose to emphasize genuine civil (or external) freedom and human responsibility. As Green observes, 'Ever after the Wittenberg disturbances of 1521, Melanchthon assigned more and more responsibility to the individual and more and more power to the will.'[28]

THE *LOCI COMMUNES* REVISED: 1522

Within the *Loci communes* of 1522, Melanchthon made only two changes from the edition of 1521—he rewrote the sections on free will and Christian freedom.[29] In late 1521, Melanchthon wrote to Spalatin that he was changing his formulation of the affections argument in the *Loci* of 1521,[30] and indeed, within the *Loci* of 1522, Melanchthon expanded the affections argument.[31] In a further difference, at the end of the sections on free will of both the *Loci* of 1521 and the *Loci* of 1522, Melanchthon included a three-point summary of

---

[27] 'Everyone admires virtue tremendously, but thinks it can be cultivated without effort.' Melanchthon, 'In Praise of the New School', 1526. Keen, 61. *In laudem novae scholae*. MSA 3.65.38–9: 'Quotus quisque enim tantopere virtutem miratur, ut gratis eam colendam esse ducat.'

[28] Green, *How Melanchthon Helped Luther Discover the Gospel*, 195.

[29] Melanchthon (from Wittenberg) asserted that this was the case in a letter to Georg Spalatin (in Lochau), written on 10 June 1522. MBW 1.228. T 1.228. CR 1.572–3 Nr. 213. Suppl. Mel. 6/1.187–9 Nr. 253.

[30] Melanchthon (from Wittenberg), to Spalatin (in Lochau), early September 1521. MBW 1.163. T 1.163. CR 1.450–1. Suppl. Mel. 6/1.155 Nr. 170. MSA 7/1.131–2 Nr. 50.

[31] For the text of the section on free will from 1522, see CR 21.93–6. See also CR 21.66 for more information about the edition from 1522 as well as Plitt and Kolde.

his main arguments. In the conclusion of Melanchthon's section on free will from 1521, the argument from predestination came first.[32] It was telling, though, that in the rewrite of the free-will section in 1522, Melanchthon changed his summary so that the argument from the affections came first, predestination second, and the weakness of reason (which had in 1521 functioned as a corollary of the predestination argument) had now been replaced by a statement of the falsity of scholastic positions advocating free choice.[33] For an expert in rhetoric, this reordering of his summary on the bound will was significant. Melanchthon was beginning to let predestination slide away from prominence. This made sense if one were to take into account Melanchthon's questions about predestination and determinism in the *Annotations on Romans* from about this time. It also made sense in light of his move toward an emphasis on natural law, philosophical ethics, and an implied actual contingency in human affairs as a result of the Wittenberg disturbances of 1521–2.[34] Divine determinism was proving problematic, and Melanchthon was slowly de-emphasizing it in the early 1520s. In the meantime, the focus of his bound-will stance began to shift from predestination to the more immediately intuitive affections argument, which was ultimately based on a strong view of original sin.

As Melanchthon began to encourage civic order through education in natural law and philosophical ethics, he continued to deny the freedom of the will in justification, based increasingly on an argument from original sin, and less and less on an argument predicated on predestination or divine

---

[32] 'SUMMA

Si ad praedestinationem referas humanem voluntatem, nec in externis nec in internis operibus ulla est libertas, sed eveniunt omnia iuxta destinationem divinam.

Si ad opera externa referens voluntatem, quaedam videtur esse iudicio naturae libertas.

Si ad affectus referas voluntatem, nulla plane libertas est, etiam naturae iudicio.' MSA 2/1.17.1–10.

[33] 'SUMMA

Etiam iuxta naturae iudicium in adfectibus nulla libertas est.

Nulla item libertas est, si voluntatem humaam ad praedestinationem conferas.

Quare nihil commentum est, dogma scholasticum de libero arbitrio, de praeparandis nobis ad gratiam de merito congrui, de quibus infra suo loco dicemus.' CR 21.96. Noting this, Kolb comments, 'In 1522, the relationship of reason and will changes with the abandonment of [Melanchthon's] clear subordination of reason to will that had been present in his earlier comment.' *Bound Will*, 78.

[34] Both Gerhards and Neuser argue that the Wittenberg disturbances of 1521–2 had a direct bearing on Melanchthon's rewrite of the section on free will in the *Loci* of 1522. Gerhards, 48. Neuser, *Der Ansatz*, 76.

determinism. So Melanchthon continued to affirm the bound will in soterio-logical matters, but when it came to civil righteousness, he gradually began to open up to the possibility of the genuine responsibility of people for their actions—meaning real freedom, and at least some measure of contingency. Whereas just a year or two previously, he had been using divine determinism as a primary argument against *both* free will in contingency *and* justification, Melanchthon now advocated genuine free will in one's civil actions, along with a bound will in justification.[35]

Meanwhile, the emergence of Luther's distinctive political theology at this time would have an influence on Melanchthon.[36] It would become a convenient paradigm for arguing for free will in one area of life and a bound will in the other. We turn now to Luther's emerging political theology in 1522–3 in order to examine how it impacted Melanchthon, and how he utilized its themes in his own theology, especially in relation to the question of free will in justification.

LUTHER'S POLITICAL THEOLOGY: 1522–1523

Taming the Thicket

Luther's political theology is a vast and challenging subject. Essentially, 'The key to Luther's mature political and social thought lies in the complex of doctrines referred to by modern German scholars as his *Zwei-Reiche-* [two kingdoms] and *Zwei-Regimente-Lehre* [two governments doctrine].'[37] Unfortunately, '*Zwei-Reiche-Lehre*' has two meanings in modern German scholarship—the spiritual vs. temporal realms, and God's kingdom vs. Satan's kingdom.[38] '*Zwei-Reiche-Lehre*' can mean either the two realms that God has instituted for mankind, *or* the two opposing kingdoms of God and the devil.[39]

---

[35] For Gerhards' view on this doctrinal formulation, see his p. 90.

[36] Schwarzenau notes Melanchthon's separation of spiritual and corporal regiments begin-ning in 1523, and he puts it down to Melanchthon's strong view of predestination from 1522, coupled with his new ideas on Christian freedom. Schwarzenau, 15. However, while Schwarze-nau is on the right track, it is too much to place so much emphasis on Melanchthon's views of predestination in 1522, because even within 1522 they were beginning to be mitigated and to disappear from his writings. Rather, Melanchthon's insistence on the bound will in the spiritual realm would remain as a result of the affections argument (original sin), and the freedom in the temporal realm would remain as a result of the sheer necessity of positing a cause and accountability within people for their own actions.

[37] W. D. J. Cargill Thompson's *The Political Thought of Martin Luther*, ed. Philip Broadhead (Brighton: Harvester, 1984), 11.

[38] Ibid., 50–1.

[39] Ibid., 56.

As Thompson makes clear, the two (or four!) *Reiche* and the two governments
are concepts that are so closely enmeshed in Luther's theology that they
cannot be treated separately.[40] So treated, though, they have indeed been!
The literature on Luther's political theology is expansive, and the ideas
discussed therein are much in debate.[41] For example, even the title of 'two
kingdoms doctrine' is not universally accepted. As Bernard Lohse writes, 'The
summarizing of Luther's ideas under the concept of "the two-kingdoms
doctrine" is problematic. The term was evidently first used by Karl Barth in
1922. It is scarcely suitable for describing Luther's ideas, since it assumes a
system and consistency in application that simply cannot be documented.'[42]
James Estes voices agreement to this statement,[43] as does Per Frostin.[44]

Luther's own imprecision in his use of vocabulary in his political theology
poses a significant challenge to his readers. As Thompson comments,
'Luther's language is unclear: he uses the same terms in a wide variety of
different ways.'[45] For example, Luther's use of 'two governments' and 'two
kingdoms' frequently overlapped, and he sometimes used the differing
phrases synonymously.[46] This makes interpreting his doctrine a sometimes
frustrating, though not impossible, procedure. While we can, therefore, make
distinctions about his paradigms, we must view these distinctions as general,
or provisional, rather than absolute. Luther himself may not have drawn
precise distinctions in his own mind.[47] Of course, his political theology also
evolved over time, demonstrating different emphases in different historical
contexts.

Obviously, then, doing justice to the subject of Luther's political theology
in a mere section of a chapter is patently untenable. Despite limited space here
available, despite Luther's inconsistent vocabulary, and despite his systematic
imprecision and morphing ideas, some overarching themes in his political
thought can still be discerned. Some of these themes will prove illuminating in
understanding Melanchthon's developing thought on free will. Accordingly, in
the present section, I will attempt to describe the general outlines of Luther's
newly emerging political theology in 1522–3, using his own writings from this
period, along with the insights of modern scholars (many of whom, admittedly, are writing from the fuller perspective of Luther's political theology as

---

[40] W. D. J. Cargill Thompson's *The Political Thoughts of Martin Luther*, 57.
[41] Ibid., 36.
[42] *Martin Luther's Theology*, 154–5.
[43] Estes, *Peace, Order and the Glory of God*, 172, 334–36.
[44] *Luther's Two Kingdoms Doctrine: A Critical Study* (Lund: Lund University Press, 1994), ii.
[45] Thompson, 37, 40.
[46] Ibid., 42.
[47] Ibid.

developed over the full course of his career).[48] Following this, it will be useful to consider briefly how these themes affected Luther's (and then Melanchthon's) thought on the freedom of the human will, the governance of God, and the paradox (or rational inconsistency, or antinomy) of an all-controlling God operating through secondary free agents.

To begin with, though, a few words are in order regarding nomenclature. As discussed above, the phrase 'Luther's two kingdoms theology' is imprecise. Rather, Thompson's comment is apt: 'Luther is working with two sets of dualisms which, so to speak, cut across one another.'[49] Thompson then goes on to show *three* sets of dualisms in Luther's political theology, in addition to one in his anthropology. A more fitting title, then, especially considering the themes of Luther's broader theology, would be 'dualities in reality'. We will find these dualities reflected in Melanchthon's theology as well, and as his thought on free will developed in the coming years, it would follow the contours of these very dualities here laid out, starting as early as 1521, just before the Wittenberg disturbances.

Context: The *Invocavit* Sermons

Luther was distressed by the disturbances at Wittenberg, and seeing that Melanchthon was unable to restore order by clarifying and communicating the theological errors of the rioters, Luther returned in early March. In 1521, even before the Wittenberg disturbances, Luther and Melanchthon had conversed on the subject of temporal authority.[50] With that preliminary thinking in mind, Luther now (probably in collaboration with Melanchthon[51]) began to contemplate how best to preach in such a way as to advocate civil restraint. Whereas Melanchthon had sought solutions in general education in philosophical ethics (i.e. natural law), Luther felt that antinomianism at any time, and during the Wittenberg unrest in particular, was to be overcome through the preaching of the pure Gospel. The cure for antinomianism did not come from ethical education, but only from the living Word. The Gospel alone was the ground for changing people.[52] Luther's remedy embraced preaching the Bible, and as he did so here in 1522, his political theology began to take shape.[53]

[48] Thompson's book is the best English-language work known to this author at present, and the following discussion owes much to his work.
[49] Thompson, 39.
[50] Luther (at the Wartburg), letter to Melanchthon (in Wittenberg), 13 July 1521. MBW 1.151. T 1.151 (see esp. lines 30ff.). WABr 2.356. See also Lohse, *Martin Luther's Theology*, 149.
[51] Estes, 'The Role of Godly Magistrates', 470–1.
[52] Bornkamm, 'Melanchthon's Menschenbild', 84.
[53] Thompson, 12, 37.

On his first Sunday back in Wittenberg, Luther climbed the pulpit to put his theory into practice. He would preach every day for the next week. Luther sought to restore order in Wittenberg with his eight *Invocavit* sermons of 9–16 March 1522,[54] and his main points included letting love rule one's actions, looking out for the weak, giving way, and never forcing matters. In making these points and in trying to counteract the stringency that had permeated Wittenberg for the preceding few months, Luther emphasized free choice in unessential matters, and further introduced a distinction by associating 'unessential things' with temporal matters, and 'essential things' with spiritual matters. Luther argued that in unessential things (such as entering into marriage and choosing a monastic life), free choice was to be allowed. He declared, 'Now follow the things which are not necessary, but are left to our free choice by God and which we may keep or not, such as whether a person should marry or not, or whether monks and nuns should leave the cloisters.'[55] Further, he taught that outward things did no harm to faith,[56] and that the kingdom of God did not exist in outward things (*eüsserlichen dingen*).[57] In external practices like private confession, Luther would not force people into things they did not want to do, but would rather leave it as a matter of free decision.[58] What really mattered was faith, and faith was an internal, spiritual matter.[59] Hence, Luther spoke of two realms in reality: the (essential) spiritual, and the (non-essential) temporal. The spiritual realm was *internal* to the individual, and the temporal realm was *external*.

Following these *Invocavit* sermons, Luther's political theology of dualities continued to take shape in 1522 and 1523,[60] especially as seen in *On Temporal*

---

[54] LW 51.67–100. WA 10(iii).1–64.

[55] Third sermon. 11 March 1522. 'Nun volgen die ding, die unnöttig sein, sonder frei gelassen von gotte, die mann halten mag oder nit, als Eelich zu werden oder nitt, Münnich und Nonnen auß den klöstern geen.' WA 10(iii).18.

[56] '...Die eüsserlichen dinge dem glaüben kennen schaden züfügen mügen. Alleyne das hertze muß nicht daran hangen und sich nit darauff wogen. Sollichs müssen wir predigen und sagen....' Third sermon. 11 March 1522. WA 10(iii).29–30.

[57] Fifth sermon. 13 March 1522. 'Neyn, lieben freünde: Das reych gottes stehet nit in eüsserlichen dingen, das mann greyffen oder empfinden kan, sonder im glaüben.' WA 10(iii).43.

[58] Eighth sermon. 16 March 1522. Regarding private confession: 'Aber ich wil niemants darvon gezwungen haben sonder eim jeden frey heym gestelt haben.' WA 10(iii).63.

[59] Sixth sermon. 14 March 1522. 'Der glaüb müß da sein und di empfahunge geschickt machen und angenem vor got, sonst ist es ein laütter spiegel sechten und ein eüsserlich wesen in welchen die Christenheit nit steet, sonder alleyn im glaüben, daran kein eüsserlich werck wil gebunden sein.' WA 10(iii).49.

[60] Another important source in which one can see Luther's emerging dualities theology was his two sermons at Weimar, from 19 October 1522. LW 51.101–17. WA 10(iii).341–52.

Authority.[61] Luther did not stop his preaching on this subject on 16 March, for in a letter dated 3 November 1522, Melanchthon told George Spalatin that Luther was preaching every day on faith, works, and the two swords (*de duplici gladio*).[62] Again, in 1523, Luther elaborated, 'Here we must divide the children of Adam and all mankind into two classes, the first belonging to the kingdom of God (*reych Gottis*), the second to the kingdom of the world (*reych der welt*).'[63] Similarly, God had also ordained two governments (*regimente*), one spiritual (*geystliche*) and one temporal (*welltliche*).[64]

Having now at least alluded to Luther's three themes of the dual kingdoms (God's and the devil's), governments (spiritual and temporal), and realms (spiritual and temporal), it will be useful to sketch these ideas in greater detail.

Content: Dualities in Reality

As we have seen from the previous section, Luther's political theology emerged in response to successive crises. He did not set out to present his ideas in nicely delineated didactic morsels. The writer who dares to dissect and label Luther's thought here in overly-neat categories runs the risk of misrepresenting this famous Reformer. Even so, it is possible to tease out a few persistent themes in his political theology—themes that will be found to resonate closely with Melanchthon's thought as well.

Dual Kingdoms (Das Reich Gottes, Das Reich Teufels)

Luther taught that all of reality is divided between two kingdoms: the kingdom of God, and the kingdom of the devil.[65] This distinction represented a clear echo of Augustine's *City of God*, but Luther would, in the end, go

---

[61] LW 45.75–129. WA 11.(229), 245–80.

[62] 'Cum Wimariam redissent principes, auditus est quotidie Martinus dixitque ille cum communia illa de fide et operibus, tum etiam locum de duplici gladio seu administratione tractavit.' MBW 1.240. T 1.240.47–9. CR 1.580. Suppl. Mel. 6/1.196–8 Nr. 264.

[63] *Von welltlicher Uberkeytt, wie weyt man yhr gehorsam schuldig sey.* LW 45.88. 'Hie müssen wyr Adams kinder und alle menschen teylen ynn zwey teyll: die ersten zum reych Gottis, die andern zum reych der welt.' WA 11.249.24–5.

[64] *Von welltlicher Uberkeytt.* WA 11.251.15–18. LW 45.91.

[65] Luther referred to this kingdom of God with numerous phrases, including: *Reich Gottes, Reich Christi, regnum dei,* and *regnum christi.* Likewise, the kingdom of the devil could be indicated by *Teufels Reich, Reich der Welt, regnum diaboli,* and *regnum mundi.* Cf. Thompson, 38.

beyond the bishop of Hippo.[66] Luther defined 'the kingdom of God' (*das Reich gottes*) as all people who belonged to God through genuine, heartfelt faith in Jesus Christ. He defined 'the kingdom of the devil' (*das Reich teufels*) as all people who did *not* (and would never) have a saving faith in Jesus— including all who *professed* faith, but did not *actually* believe. At its core, the kingdom of God meant the elect, and the kingdom of the devil meant everyone else. All of humanity—both the living and the dead—were thus divided up between the kingdom of God and the kingdom of the devil. A person could be a member of only one kingdom (*Reich*),[67] for the two were mutually exclusive.

The kingdom of God was a kingdom of love devoted to God. The kingdom of the devil was a kingdom of lust, devoted to sin.[68] While ontologically the two kingdoms were polar opposites, superficially they remained often indistinguishable to human observation. One could not merely look at a person and know to which kingdom she belonged. But, even though individual membership could be uncertain to the human observer, the cumulative *effects* of humanity's divided loyalties were clearly evident. Throughout history, the devil worked in and through the people under his sway in order to seek to attack and overthrow the kingdom of God.[69] The devil's attacks included seeking to undermine both *governments* (*regimente*) instituted by the Lord.

Dual Governments (Das Geistliche Regiment, Das Weltliche Regiment)

For Luther, God was a God of order, and he had instituted two types of government (*regiment*) as expressions of his sole rule over all people.[70] *Both* types of government served God, yet each retained a separate (though complementary) function. Luther wrote, 'God has ordained two governments: the spiritual, by which the Holy Spirit produces Christians and righteous people under Christ; and the temporal, which restrains the un-Christian and wicked so that—no thanks to them—they are obliged to keep still and to maintain an outward peace.'[71] The spiritual government represented God's rule over Christians by means of his Word and Spirit. It was God's inward means by

[66] See Thompson, 2–3, 35.
[67] 'The words *Reich* and *regnum* are used not in the sense of government, but in the sense of the *people* over whom God and the Devil rule.' Ibid., 51 (emphasis added).
[68] Ibid., 51.
[69] Ibid., 52–3.
[70] Sometimes these dual governments are referred to as the two regiments, or the two orders.
[71] *Von welltlicher Uberkeytt.* LW 45.91. 'Darumb hatt Gott die zwey regiment verordnet, das geystliche, wilchs Christen und frum leutt macht durch den heyligen geyst unter Christo, und

which to bring people to salvation, and to unite and develop them in Christ. The temporal government functioned as God's rule over non-Christians by means of laws and the sword (that is, the coercive power of civil government). Its purpose was to restrain externally those unregenerate whose hearts had no internal constraints. The spiritual government was an internal regulation of the human heart resulting in external effects. The temporal government was solely an *external* regulation of human *behaviour*, with ostensibly no internal effects. As Thompson summarizes: 'The temporal [government] exists to maintain peace on earth, to enforce law and order and to prevent men from tearing one another to pieces like wild beasts.'[72]

God remained active, though often hidden, in both governments. He preferred the use of secondary means, acting *through* nature, and not in ways contrary to nature.[73] Using both governments, God not only ruled the world, but also actively opposed the disruptive work of the devil. Satan, on the other hand, continually sought to infiltrate and undermine *both* of God's two governments.[74]

While non-Christians rejected God's spiritual government and hence fell subject only to the temporal government, believers (that is, members of the kingdom of God[75]) were subject to *both* governments (*regimente*).[76] They were naturally subject to the Holy Spirit, who ruled and taught them the path of true righteousness according to the Word, and they also were to be subject to the temporal authorities (though they did not need to be) out of love. Luther taught, 'At one and the same time you satisfy God's kingdom inwardly, and the world outwardly.'[77] That is, those in the kingdom of God (*reych Gottis*) naturally satisfied the requirements of the temporal government (*regiment der wellt*), whereas non-Christians did not, and consequently required the rather sterner measures of the temporal authorities.

Notice here the duality in reality implied by Luther's dual governments—God had instituted two orders of government for two realms of

---

das welltliche, wilchs den unchristen und bößen weret, daß sie eußerlich müssen frid hallten und still seyn on ihren danck.' WA 11.251.15–18.

[72] Thompson, 47. See also his wider discussion on pp. 47–8.

[73] Ibid., 49.

[74] Ibid., 54–5.

[75] 'Wer is aber das reich gottes? Das ist das Christlich glaubig volck Christi.' 24 October 1522. *Der dritt predigt Martini Lutheris der selbigen vor genannten Wochen am Freittag uff dem schlos gethan.* WA 10(iii).371.

[76] See Thompson's discussion on pp. 57 and 61.

[77] *Von welltlicher Uberkeytt.* LW 45.96. '[D]u zu gleych Gottis reych und der wellt reich gnug thuest, eußerlich und ynnerlich.' WA 11.255.12–13. This falls in line with Galatians 5.22–23, 'The fruit of the Spirit is love, joy, peace, patience, kindness, generosity, faithfulness, gentleness, and self-control. There is no law against such things.'

existence.[78] The temporal government related to *external* things, and the
spiritual government related to *internal* things. Luther commented, 'Temporal obedience and authority, you see, apply only externally (*eusserlich*) to
taxes, revenue, honour, and respect.'[79] The idea of dual governments led to
the notion of dual realms, with which also appeared the paradigm of the
dual person.

Dual Realms (Das Geistliche Reich, Das Weltliche Reich)

Because the idea of the dual realms was so closely related to the idea of the
dual governments, Luther often used the terms *weltiches Reich* and *weltliches
Regiment* as well as *geistliches Reich* and *geistliches Regiment* synonymously.[80]
Here again, the caveat must be borne in mind that although the dual realms
and governments can be neatly distinguished (as has been done here in
separate sections), in practice, the lines of demarcation were often blurred
in Luther's writings. Nevertheless, the dual realms could be discerned as a
doctrine separate from (though related to) the dual governments. Moreover,
because the dual realms came to provide a framework for Melanchthon's
developing thoughts on free will, it is important to treat them distinctly.

Distinct treatment requires clearly defined words, and before describing
Luther's doctrine of the two realms, it will be helpful to consider Luther's use
of the word *die Welt* along with *weltlich*. The alert reader[81] will have noticed
the footnote above showing that when speaking of the kingdom of the devil,
Luther sometimes referred to it as the kingdom of the world (*Reich der Welt*).
Also, when referring to temporal government, Luther usually called it *das
weltliche Regiment*. Now, in reference to the temporal realm, Luther used the
phrase *das weltliche Reich*. To distinguish these differing uses of *die Welt* and
weltlich, one must recognize the two main connotations Luther attached to
these words. First, Luther tended to use *die Welt* in the same way that Jesus did
in John's Gospel.[82] That is, 'the world' referred to all those under Satan's
sway—i.e. the kingdom of the devil. Thus, 'the kingdom of the world', read in
light of John's Gospel, meant 'the kingdom of the devil'. Second, when Luther
used the word *weltlich*, he usually meant the natural or temporal order,[83]
which God had instituted as something good. As a result, *das weltliche*

---

[78] Thompson, 42.
[79] *Von welltlicher Uberkeytt.* LW 45.110. 'Sihe da, welltlich gehorsam und gewallt gehet nur
uber schos, zoll, ehre, furcht eußerlich.' WA 11.266.5–6.
[80] Thompson, 38.
[81] Apologies to humour writer Dave Barry for the use of this phrase.
[82] e.g. John 16.8ff.
[83] See Thompson, 41, 53.

Regiment meant 'the temporal government', and *das weltliche Reich* meant 'the temporal realm'.[84] With these definitions in mind, we can now proceed to the doctrine of the dual realms.

The idea of the dual realms flowed straightforwardly from the dual governments. If the spiritual government represented God's rule over the inner life of people, and the temporal government regulated external, physical life, then it obviously followed that people's existence could be divided into spiritual and temporal (or internal and external) realms. Thompson writes, 'Luther thinks in terms of two separate but parallel realms, the temporal and the spiritual, in which the Christian exists simultaneously in this life.'[85] Another way of putting it is that Luther differentiated between the natural (or material) world, and the spiritual world. These were parallel, and not hierarchical, realms.[86]

This division of reality into dual realms held both political and soteriological implications. For Luther, the temporal realm represented the order of creation, and the spiritual realm represented the order of salvation. Accordingly, two types of peace might prevail. One peace would be an external peace in the temporal realm, created through force in the maintenance of public law and order. The other peace would be an internal peace of the soul, derived through union with Christ.[87] Further, as Thompson writes, 'As the spiritual order exists to meet man's spiritual needs, so the temporal order exists to meet his physical, bodily needs.'[88] The realms were separate—nothing a person did in the temporal realm contributed to one's position in the spiritual realm.[89] The spiritual realm was where God ruled exclusively,[90] and, in 1525, Luther made it clear that the kingdom of God was a spiritual, and not a temporal, kingdom.[91] Hence, for Luther, the external matters of the temporal realm were transient and non-essential, while the internal things of the spiritual realm were permanent and

[84] To put it in its most linguistically pernicious form, *das weltliche Reich* indicated the temporal realm, and *das Reich der Welt* denoted the kingdom of the devil. The two ought not to be confused (but probably will be).
[85] Ibid., 25.
[86] Ibid., 44.
[87] Ibid., 46.
[88] Ibid., 43.
[89] Ibid., 44.
[90] Sermon, 24 October 1522. 'Das geistlich reich mus gott regirn und kein anderer.' WA 10 (iii).372.
[91] 'Denn eyn leybeygener kan wol Christen seyn und Christlich freyheit haben, gleich wie eyn gefangener odder krancker Christen ist, und doch nich frey ist, Es will dißer artickel alle Menschen gleich machen, und aus dem geystlichen reich Christs eyn welltlich eusserlich reich machen, wilchs unmuglich ist.' *Ermahnung zum Frieden auf die zwolf Artikel der Bauernschaft in Schwaben*, WA 18.327.

essential. That is why he could speak about the importance of internal things and the ultimate indifference of external things.

Shorthand Definitions
Kingdom of God = the elect
Kingdom of the devil = everyone else
Spiritual government = the Word
Temporal government = the sword
Spiritual realm = internal (to the individual)
Temporal (or civil) realm = external (to the individual)

The Dual Person

If reality was divided into a duality between the temporal and the spiritual, then it would also follow that individual human beings could be said to have both temporal and spiritual sides to them. In other words, the idea of the dual realms conformed nicely with the doctrine of a dual *person*. Thompson rightly states, 'For Luther . . . the inseparable corollary of the doctrine of the *Zwei-Reiche* and *Zwei-Regimente* is that of the Christian's *Zwei Personen*. He has two persons, and the key to all ethical and ultimately political behavior lies in the ability to distinguish correctly between them.'[92] A person could practise external righteousness while simultaneously remaining utterly incapable of spiritual righteousness. In other words, the human will could possess limited external freedom in the temporal realm (*das weltliche Reich*) and internal bondage in the spiritual realm (*das geistliche Reich*).

Antinomy: Dualities, Yet All Under God's Sole Rule

Before returning to Melanchthon's thought, it must again be pointed out that Luther's distinctions between these various dualities were not always clear-cut: 'As always, Luther distinguishes between the hidden and the revealed God.'[93] In a sermon on 25 October 1522, Luther taught that the Holy Spirit in fact ruled over *both* governments,[94] and that the temporal government was

---

[92] Thompson, 61.

[93] Paul Althaus, *The Ethics of Martin Luther*, trans. Robert C. Schultz (Philadelphia: Fortress, 1972), 45. Note, too, that Luther constantly refined and reformulated his theology, as the press of contemporary events demanded. See, for example, MacCulloch, *The Reformation*, 205, where he describes a change in Luther's expression of the two-kingdoms theology between 1531 and 1536, such that this shift 'hopelessly blurred the boundaries between ecclesiastical and civil power, but the times seemed to demand it'.

[94] 'Gestern habt ir gehörtt was das reich gottes sey, worinnen das stett, und das sölchs niemants anders regirn kan dan got durch seinen geyligen geist, Das in dem auch söllen geistlich und weltlich regiment regirtt werden an alles unser zu thun, an alle unsere werck und freyen

the means *through* which God ruled in this world.[95] Here Luther returned to his necessitarian paradox—while freedom existed in the temporal realm and the temporal government's job was to rein in the misuse of that freedom by sinful people, God nevertheless ruled necessarily over all events, both temporal and spiritual. God alone ruled in the kingdom of God, and he ruled simultaneously within human institutions in the temporal realm. Melanchthon, on the other hand, chose not to grasp this paradox (or antinomy, an apparent rational inconsistency), but instead to show God's rule absolutely in the kingdom of God, with genuine human freedom in the temporal realm, without God determining all events. This position will become more clearly apparent with an examination of Melanchthon's thought in the mid- to late 1520s. Meanwhile, within Melanchthon's writings in the early to mid-1520s, the influence of Luther's political theology of dualities could clearly be seen.

Dualities in Melanchthon's Writings

Melanchthon's formulation of such dualities can be found in his writings as early as the *Themes for the Sixth Holiday*, of 25 July 1522,[96] as well as in the previously mentioned *The Difference between Temporal and Christian Piety* of the same year.[97] In these works he distinguished between the spiritual government (*regimen spirituale*) and the temporal government (*regimen corporale*),[98] and he argued that the temporal government was constituted for external matters (i.e. non-spiritual affairs).[99] He also contrasted the

---

willen, dan got mus das regirn und niemants anders.' 25 October 1522. *Predigt in der Schloßkirche zu Weimar. (Sonnabend nach 18. Sonntag n. Trin.) Die vierde predigt Martini uff nach—folgenden Sonnabentt genannter wochen uff dem Schloß gethan.* WA 10(iii).379.

[95] 'Söllen wir den nun ein Regimentt ader schwertt haben, so müssen wir auch mit zu sehen, das die fürsten aus gott regirn, dan es ist ein ampt, das man wol regiren mus.' Ibid., WA 10 (iii).381.

[96] *Themata ad sextam ferieam discutienda.* CR 1.595–6. MSA 1.168–70. An English translation can be found in Hill, 89–91. See also Estes' discussion, on pp. 61–8 of *Peace, Order, and the Glory of God.*

[97] *Unterschidt zwischen weltlicher und Christlicher Fromkeyt.* CR 1.523–8. MSA 1.171–5.

[98] *Themata ad sextam feriam discutienda.* '1. Duplex est regimen, spirituale et corporale.' MSA 1.168.1. Melanchthon wrote something similar in the opening lines of the *Unterschidt zwischen weltlicher und Christlicher Fromkeyt:* 'Es ist zweierlei Fromkeit, da von geschrieben stehet, eine heißt göttlich, die ander weltliche.' CR 1.523. 'Es ist zweyerley Fromkeyt, davon geschriben steht, eyne heyst götlich, die ander Weltliche.' MSA 1.171.1–2.

[99] *Themata ad sextam feriam discutienda.* '2. Corporale regimen de externo rerum usu constituit.' MSA 1.168.2–3.

righteousness of the flesh against the righteousness of the spirit.[100] It was not surprising that the emphases of Luther's dualities should begin to show up so quickly in Melanchthon's work—Luther's preaching had worked, and order was restored in Wittenberg. Schwarzenau is correct to argue that Melanchthon's formulations of these dualities were not an independent endeavour, but were put forward in cooperation and as a co-worker with Luther.[101]

In December 1523, Melanchthon even devoted a work specifically to the subject of the dual governments.[102] Here he began with the straightforward statement, 'There are two governments: a spiritual, and a corporal',[103] and he explained that the corporal (or temporal) government (*regimen*) had to do with the use of external things.[104] The purpose of the temporal government was to coerce non-Christians (those without the Spirit of God) into obeying the laws of the land.[105] Here then was a development from his first inclinations in 1521 to concentrate largely on widespread education of the masses in the basics of natural law as they were to be found in philosophical ethics. Additionally, the wisdom of the two governments stood largely in contrast to one another, for the righteousness of temporal existence stood in ignorance and contempt of God (thereby showing that its righteousness was not life),[106] and the spiritual government was ruled solely by the Word of God (not human power).[107] Also, preaching the righteousness of the spirit had nothing to do with external things.[108]

---

[100] *Themata ad sextam feriam discutienda.* '9. Haec enim externa administratio iustitia carnis est.' MSA 1.169.1–2. Also, '21. Spiritualiter regitur, solo verbo dei, non humana potentia.' MSA 1.169.29–30. Further, the carnal righteousness of the world could never result in spiritual righteousness: '29. Misere falluntur, qui iustitiam spiritus nihil aliud esse iudicant, quam illam carnalem iustitiam mundi.' MSA 1.170.8–10. In the *Unterschidt zwischen weltlicher und Christlicher Fromkeyt*, Melanchthon wrote, 'Aeußerliche Ordnungen zergehen mit dem Fleisch, und haben kein Leben, darum können sie auch nicht Leben oder Fromkeit geben, Koloss. am andern. Wo auch solche äußerliche Fromkeit allein ist, ist nur Heuchelei.' CR 1.526. MSA 1.173–174.37–4 (with minor spelling variations from the CR).

[101] Schwarzenau, 52. Cf. MacCulloch, *The Reformation*, 152.

[102] *Themata Philippi Melanthonis de duplici iustitia; regimineue corporali et spirituali.* CR 21.227–30.

[103] *De duplici iustitia.* 'Duplex est regimen, spirituale, et corporale.' CR 21.227.

[104] 'Corporale regimen, de externo rerum usu constituit.' CR 21.227.

[105] 'Itaque corporale regimen institutum est ad cohercenda corpora eorum, qui carent spiritu Dei.' CR 21.230.

[106] 'Cum iustitia mundi stare potest ignoratio et contemptus Dei, quare ea iustitia non est vita.' CR 21.230.

[107] 'Spiritualiter regitur, solo verbo Dei, non humana potentia.' CR 21.229.

[108] 'Quod quia praedicat iustitiam spiritus, nihil constituit de externo rerum usu.' CR 21.230.

At this point, Melanchthon's theology was almost identical to Luther's,[109] but later change would be built, in part, on the ideas of the two realms. Melanchthon's new-found doctrine of dual governments, like Luther's theology, implied two separate but related realms within reality. These dual realms would represent a natural fault-line along which one could articulate differing paradigms for the governance of God. Melanchthon could argue for a real measure of contingency and human responsibility in the temporal realm while continuing to affirm humanity's bondage to sin and helplessness in the spiritual realm. As we shall presently discover, Melanchthon would begin to explore this theme in the mid- to late 1520s, thereby preparing the ground for a later shift on the role of free will in justification.

In the meantime, in the mid-1520s, Melanchthon's production of theological writing (as enumerated by the number of titles) trailed off in comparison with his earlier output, and the great theological debate between Luther and Erasmus on free will in justification filled the air from 1524 until 1526. Having already surveyed the ideas of Erasmus and Luther in Chapters 2 and 3 above, we turn now to look at just how that debate impacted Melanchthon and his views of free will at this time.

MELANCHTHON'S RELATIONSHIP TO THE DISPUTE BETWEEN LUTHER AND ERASMUS: 1524–1526

In any examination of Melanchthon's views on free will, it would be natural to compare his views with those of Luther and Erasmus, and then to place Melanchthon on one side or the other, or to describe his thought as moving from one view to the other, or even holding some sort of middle ground and attempting to bring the two sides together. However, this approach falls short, for it tends to view Luther and Erasmus as immovable objects with Melanchthon choosing one to which to attach himself. Instead, Melanchthon's views were his own, and were no mere mimicry or interpolation of the ideas of the other two men. Melanchthon represented his own pole in this debate, though his views were more similar to Luther's than to Erasmus'.

It has occasionally been put forth that Melanchthon's praise of Erasmus indicated friendship and agreement with the Rotterdam scholar on the

---

[109] James Estes, *Peace, Order and the Glory of God*, xi. The main point Estes makes in this work is that Luther and Melanchthon, throughout their careers, were in essential agreement in their political theology (especially regarding the role of the civil magistrate). See, for example, p. 212. See also Estes' earlier article, 'The Role of Godly Magistrates', 463–83.

doctrine of free will. For example, Stupperich sees Melanchthon and Erasmus as essentially agreed on viewing religion as a 'Christian philosophy'.[110] Bainton tends in a similar direction when he writes, 'The fact that to the end Melanchthon preserved the unbroken friendship of Erasmus would not of itself be particularly significant were it not that he was ever ready to place upon Luther's teaching an alien nuance.'[111] Certainly in 1519, Melanchthon was under the impression that Erasmus was a part of the Reformation movement. In early January of that year, he wrote an apologetic and indignant letter to Erasmus denying the report that he had criticized Erasmus' paraphrase of Romans.[112] In this letter, he was also attempting to bring Erasmus to Wittenberg's defence. Later that spring, he wrote another letter to George Spalatin, in which he argued that Erasmus' book, *Ratio seu compendium verae theologiae*, appeared to be in agreement with Luther.[113] Again, in that same month, Melanchthon wrote a foreword to Luther's *Operationes in Psalmos* in which he decried 400 years under the rule of the scholastics, and praised the genuine theologians who were now bringing light—Luther, Reuchlin, Capito, Oecolampadius, Karlstadt, and Erasmus.[114]

Luther, on the other hand, knew as early as 1516 that he differed from Erasmus on theology,[115] and he surely must have communicated this fact to

[110] Stupperich, *Melanchthon*, 34.

[111] Bainton, *Here I Stand*, 99. Bainton's claim of Melanchthon's 'unbroken' friendship with Erasmus is only possible under a loose definition of 'unbroken', with a possible reference to internal disposition rather than sustained contact. During the dispute between Luther and Erasmus over free will, tensions became strained between Erasmus and Melanchthon, as evidenced by a lack of communication between the two men from 10 December 1524, until 5 February 1528. Further, Erasmus (from Basel) wrote both the letter of 10 December 1524, immediately preceding the gap (MBW 1.360. T 2.360. CR 1.688–94 Nr. 302. EE 5.1523. Suppl. Mel. 6/1.266–8 Nr. 374), *and* the letter (from Basel) of 5 February 1528, which broke the silence (MBW 1.654. T 3.654. CR 2.844 Nr. 1255. Suppl. Mel. 6/1.414 Nr. 640. EE 7.1944). Hence, for a period of more than three years, during which the acrimonious debate on free will between Luther and Erasmus took place, Melanchthon made no effort to stay in touch with Erasmus at all (unless, of course, there *was* correspondence, but it is now simply lost to us). This apparent silence was hardly the epitome of an 'unbroken friendship'.

[112] Melanchthon (in Leipzig), to Erasmus (in Löwen), 9 January 1519. MBW 1.38. T 1.38. CR 1.59–60 Nr. 30. EE 3.910. MSA 7/1.55–7 Nr. 13.

[113] Melanchthon (in Wittenberg), to Spalatin (in Altenburg?), 13 March 1519. MBW 1.46. T 1.46. CR 1.74–6 Nr. 38. Suppl. Mel. 6/1.60 Nr. 57. MSA 7/1.63–4 Nr. 18.

[114] *Circa* 27 March 1519. MBW 1.47. T 1.47. CR 1.70–3 Nr. 36. WA 5.24–5. Suppl. Mel. 6/1.61–2 Nr. 59. Ironically, over time Melanchthon would find himself separated theologically in one way or another from all these men, even Luther, if the present book proves its point.

[115] 'I am reading our Erasmus but daily I dislike him more and more. . . . I am afraid . . . that he does not advance the cause of Christ and the grace of God sufficiently; here he knows even less than Stapulensis. Human things weigh more with him than the divine.' Letter to John Lang, 1 March 1517. LW 48.40. 'Erasmum nostrum lego, et indies decrescit mihi animus erga eum; placet quidem, quod tam religiosos quam sacerdotes non minus constanter quam erudite arguit et damnat inveteratae huius et veternosae inscitiae; sed timeo, ne Christum et gratiam Dei non

Melanchthon in 1519. Philipp 'burned with the enthusiasm of youth',[116] and was still learning theology from Luther at this time. Following 1519, Melanchthon's praise of Erasmus became restricted to his humanistic skills rather than his theology.[117] In fact, in 1522, Melanchthon wrote a work titled, *Elogion de Luthero et Erasmo*[118] in which he vigorously attacked Erasmus' theology. As Hoffmann summarizes, 'Luther preaches scriptural righteousness of the heart followed by good works, whereas Erasmus and the pagan philosophers teach the righteousness of good behaviour and civility. What have Christ and the philosophers in common?'[119] Luther preached the Gospel which the world could not understand, and Erasmus preached human righteousness, in the tradition of heathen philosophy.[120] Obviously, Melanchthon did not endorse Erasmus' soteriology. Two years later, in a letter to John Memmingen, Melanchthon wrote that Erasmus did not correctly teach justification or what the righteousness of God meant.[121] Günther rightly concludes that it was clear that even in the main area of Christian faith, agreement between Melanchthon and Erasmus was not possible.[122] Melanchthon continued to respect Erasmus as a humanist and as a human being, but not as a theologian.[123]

---

satis promoveat, in qua multo est quam Stapulensis ignorantior: humana praevalent in eo plus quam divina.' WABr 1.90.15–20. See also Luther's letter to George Spalatin on 19 October 1516, in which he criticized Erasmus for valuing Jerome over Augustine, and for being partial to Aristotelian ethics. LW 48.23–6. WABr 1.70–1.

[116] '[Melanchthon] burns with the enthusiasm of youth and wants to become and do all things for all men at the same time.' Letter to Erasmus, 28 March 1519. LW 48.119. '[Philippus Melanchthon] ardet pro aetatis calore omnia omnibus simul fieri et facere.' WABr 1.362.40–1.

[117] Wengert, *Human Freedom*, 7. On the other hand, Melanchthon did share Erasmus' aversion to paradox. Bainton, *Erasmus*, 234–5. For more on Melanchthon's view of paradox, see below.

[118] CR 20.699–708.

[119] Manfred Hoffmann, 'Rhetoric and Dialectic in Erasmus's and Melanchthon's Interpretation of John's Gospel', in *Philip Melanchthon (1497–1560) and the Commentary*, ed. Timothy J. Wengert and M. Patrick Graham (Sheffield: Sheffield Academic Press, 1997), 76.

[120] Günther, 56.

[121] Melanchthon (in Wittenberg), to Johannes Memmingen (in Torgau), c. 8 July 1524. MBW 1.332. T2.332.46ff. Suppl. 6/1.246–49 Nr. 350. See also Günther, 56.

[122] Günther, 56. Further, the criticism between Melanchthon and Erasmus went both ways. In 1532, Melanchthon wrote a commentary on Romans (and it is here, incidentally, that some argue that Melanchthon first exhibited a doctrine of the will in line with Erasmus). Erasmus read the commentary, and in a letter to Jacob Sadoleto on 31 October 1534, he described Melanchthon's commentary as miserable, saying that even though he claimed to state things simply, Melanchthon twisted Scripture. This was definitely not an endorsement. 'Miseram Commentarios Melanchthonis, non vt illos imitareris (nec enim alibi magis torquet scripturam, vtcumque miram professus simplicitatem), sed quum illic commemorantur variae multorum opiniones, sciebam tuam prudentiam illinc excerpturam quod ad mentis Paulinae faceret cognitionem.' EE 11.2971.21–25.

[123] Just before Erasmus' death in 1536, Melanchthon wrote to him to assure Erasmus of his veneration for him as well as to distance himself from the stridency of the anti-Erasmian

In the actual debate between Luther and Erasmus, comprised of Erasmus'
De libero arbitrio (*On Free Choice*, 1524), Luther's *De servo arbitrio* (*On Bound
Choice*, 1525), and Erasmus' *Hyperaspistes* (1526), some have claimed that
Melanchthon moved to the side of Erasmus. One of the earliest was Nikolaus
Gallus, a student of Melanchthon's who would make that charge in the 1550s
(which we will address in due course). Williams, Bayer, Stupperich, Maurer,
and Preus have already been mentioned in the Introduction. Additionally,
Green argues that by 1525 Melanchthon found himself in sympathy with
Erasmus.[124] But to the contrary, in his two works, Erasmus attacked Melanchthon, primarily for his sections on free choice in the *Loci communes* of
1521 and 1522. In true humanist fashion, of course, Erasmus' attacks did
not mention Melanchthon by name.[125] But the fact that Erasmus was still
attacking Melanchthon in the *Hyperaspistes* of 1526 makes it implausible that
Melanchthon had come around to Erasmus' viewpoint by that time.

If Melanchthon did not fully take on board the heart of Erasmus' position
on free choice, then some have argued that he tried to mediate between Luther
and Erasmus in an attempt to draw them together to a mutually acceptable
doctrine. Maurer believes that this was what Melanchthon was trying
to accomplish in his *Scholia in Epistolam Pauli ad Colossenses* of 1527.[126]
Keen sees Melanchthon's doctrine of the will as initially a compromise
between Luther and Erasmus.[127] Similarly, Bornkamm places Melanchthon
in the middle between Luther and Erasmus.[128] To some extent, Bornkamm is
correct—Melanchthon really was in the middle between Luther and Erasmus,
if not theologically, then at least diplomatically. Erasmus communicated with
Luther through Melanchthon, for in Erasmus' eyes, Melanchthon was the
safer and more restrained representative of Wittenberg. Immediately after he
published *De libero arbitrio*, Erasmus wrote to Melanchthon (rather than
Luther) in order to explain why he had written this work (it was for the
good of the people, he insisted).[129] Melanchthon wrote back with Luther's

writings appearing in Wittenberg at the time from Amsdorf, Luther, and Antonius Corvinus.
May 12, 1536. MBW 2.1735. T7.1735. CR 3.68–70 Nr. 1421. EE 11.3120.

[124] Green, *How Melanchthon Helped Luther Discover the Gospel*, 214.
[125] Scheible, 'Melanchthon zwischen Luther und Erasmus', 186.
[126] Maurer, 'Melanchthons Anteil', 137–62.
[127] Keen, 8. Keen does, however, see Melanchthon eventually going over to Luther's side.
[128] Bornkamm, 'Melanchthon's Menschenbild', 84.
[129] Erasmus (in Basel), to Melanchthon (in Wittenberg), 6 September 1524. MBW 1.341.
T 2.341. CR 1.667–73 Nr. 286. EE 5.1496. Suppl. Mel. 6/1.254–5 Nr. 358. No doubt Erasmus did
feel that his work was written primarily for the good of the people. However, it also served the
purpose of distancing himself from the Lutheran camp and placing him more on the side of the
Roman Catholics—which is something the Catholic theologians had been encouraging him to
do for some time.

greetings to say that while Luther and Erasmus were agreed on ceremonies, they held genuinely divergent opinions on free will. Nevertheless, Melanchthon assured Erasmus that Luther's response to *De libero arbitrio* would be just as moderate in tone as Erasmus' work (in any event, the promised moderation on the part of Luther never fully materialized).[130] Additionally, after Luther's *De servo arbitrio* was published, word came to Melanchthon that Erasmus viewed him as a collaborator in the work.[131] Melanchthon denied this rumour and distanced himself from *De servo arbitrio*.[132] But did Melanchthon actually try to find middle ground in this debate, if not in 1524–6, then in the couple of years following?[133] The evidence suggests otherwise, for from beginning to end, Melanchthon expressed his support for Luther's bound-will position, even if he had occasion to object to Luther's immoderate tone and style of argumentation.

Melanchthon strongly agreed with Luther's basic position that humans had no ability to seek God on their own power. He saw Luther's arguments in *De servo arbitrio* as supporting his own early affections argument,[134] and he commented that Erasmus' formulation of the doctrine of free choice was

[130] Melanchthon (in Wittenberg), to Erasmus (in Basel), 30 September 1524. MBW 1.344. T 2.344. CR 1.674–6 Nr. 289. EE 5.1500. Suppl. Mel. 6/1.256–7 Nr. 360. MSA 7/1.204–9 Nr. 91. See also the following letter: Erasmus (in Basel), to Melanchthon (in Wittenberg), 10 December 1524. MBW 1.360. T 2.360. CR 1.688–94 Nr. 302. EE 5.1523. Suppl. Mel. 6/1.266–8 Nr. 374. Regarding Luther's bellicose style in *De servo arbitrio*, Bainton makes an interesting point suggesting that Erasmus was no less belligerent, but merely differed in subtlety of style: 'If one is to be demolished, does it so much matter whether one is bludgeoned with a club or punctured by a rapier? In some respects Luther's technique was less galling. If he said to an opponent *Du Schwein* (you hog), the other could reply *Du Esel* (you ass), and they could have a merry bout with the same weapons. But when Erasmus lodged an oblique shaft of irony the victim might prefer to writhe in silence than by a retort to reveal how deeply he was touched and hurt.' Bainton, *Erasmus*, 336.
[131] Melanchthon (in Wittenberg), letter to Joachim Camerarius (in Bamberg), 11 April 1526. MBW 1.459. T 2.459. CR 1.793–4 Nr. 377. Suppl. Mel. 6/1.317 Nr. 465. MSA 7/1.253–5 Nr. 110.
[132] Melanchthon (in Wittenberg), letter to Sigismund Gelenius (in Basel), 4 July 1526. MBW 1.474. T 2.474. CR 1.806–7 Nr. 393. Suppl. Mel. 6/1.324 Nr. 480. As will become evident in the next paragraph, Melanchthon was distancing himself from the belligerent tone of Luther's writing, rather than from its actual theological content.
[133] Gerhards (p. 74) argues that Melanchthon was indeed influenced by Erasmus, if not on the doctrine of the will itself, then at least in the area of divine determinism, and specifically regarding the scholastic distinction between *necessitas consequentiae* and *necessitas consequentis*. However, we have already seen that Melanchthon was having second thoughts about determinism as early as 1522, so Erasmus' arguments against divine determinism in 1524 could only supplement the process in Melanchthon's mind that had been ongoing for the previous two years. Additionally, Calvin, too, affirmed the *necessitas* distinction, as shown by A. N. S. Lane in, 'Did Calvin Believe in Freewill?' *Vox Evangelica* 12 (1981), 72–90.
[134] Melanchthon (in Wittenberg), letter to Joachim Camerarius (in Bamberg), 4 April 1525. MBW 1.387. T 2.387. CR 1.734–6 Nr. 328. Suppl. 6/1.287–8 Nr. 404.

'over-subtle'.[135] Further, when Luther stated that 'free choice is allowed man only with respect to what is beneath him and not what is above him',[136] that sounded much like Melanchthon's own position of freedom in the temporal realm combined with bondage in the spiritual realm. He told Erasmus that it was not possible for him to condemn Luther's theology on this.[137] He again wrote to Erasmus in 1528 to distance himself from Luther's tone in *De servo arbitrio*, but not from the content. He endorsed Luther on the doctrine of the will, but he continued supporting Erasmus in the area of his humanistic goals (i.e. goals related to style, language, and education, rather than theology).[138] Finally, and most convincingly, Melanchthon wrote a letter to Caspar Aquila in October 1527, in which he wrote that he was greatly saddened by Erasmus' most cunning writing on free choice, but that he would nevertheless not be snatched away from the true meaning of the matter.[139] Thus, Wengert is indeed correct to say that Melanchthon was more a participant in this debate (on Luther's side), rather than someone caught in the middle.[140] Kolb similarly states, 'Melanchthon gave Luther his unmitigated, though not completely uncritical, support.'[141] Pauli agrees that Melanchthon clearly stood with Luther on the issue of the will, on the grounds of the simple inability of the sinful person to attain to holiness.[142] Scheible also sees Melanchthon as standing on Luther's side, and that if he was trying to mediate between the two disputants at all, it was to bring Erasmus over to Luther's side.[143] Boyle concurs.[144] As Cameron declares,

---

[135] Melanchthon (in Jena(?)), letter to George Spalatin (in Auerbach), 15 October 1527. MBW 1.603. T 3.603. CR 1.895–6 Nr. 468. Suppl. Mel. 6/1.390 Nr. 586. 'Erasmi scriptum de libero arbitrio est argutissimum.' T3.603.15–16. CR 1.896.

[136] *De servo arbitrio.* LW 33.70. '[H]omini arbitrium liberum non respectu superioris, sed tantum inferioris se rei concedatur.' WA 18.638.5–6.

[137] Melanchthon (in Wittenberg), letter to Erasmus, 30 September 1524. MBW 1.344. T 2.344.34–5. CR 1.674–6 Nr. 289. Suppl. Mel. 6/1.256–7 Nr. 360. MSA 7/1.204–9 Nr. 91. 'Ego integra conscientia dogmata Lutheri non possum damnare.' EE 5.1500.37.

[138] Melanchthon (in Jena), letter to Erasmus (in Basel), 23 March 1528. MBW 1.664. T 3.664. CR 1.945–7 Nr. 514. Suppl. Mel. 6/1.419 Nr. 650. EE 7.1981. MSA 7/2.45–8 Nr. 123.

[139] Melanchthon (in Jena), letter to Caspar Aquila (in Saalfeld), end of October 1527. MBW 1.616. T 3.616. CR 4.963–4 Nr. 484b. Suppl. Mel. 6/1.392 Nr. 590. 'Erasmus scripsit argutissime de libero arbitrio, et quidem his diebus propter id scriptum graviter contristatus sum. Neque tamen eripiet mihi veram sententiam.' T3.616.12–14. CR 4.963–4.

[140] Wengert, *Human Freedom*, 73. See also Wengert, 'Melanchthon and Luther/Luther and Melanchthon', 58. Additionally valuable is Wengert, 'Philip Melanchthon's Contribution', 110–24.

[141] Kolb, *Bound Will*, 71.

[142] Frank Pauli, *Philippus: Ein Lehrer fur Deutschland; Spuren und Wirkungen Philipp Melanchthons* (Berlin: Wichern-Verlag, 1996), 43.

[143] Scheible, 'Melanchthon zwischen Luther und Erasmus', 193.

[144] Boyle, *Rhetoric and Reform*, 38.

'It is plainly absurd to describe Melanchthon as a "follower" of Erasmus.'[145] In the end, Melanchthon clearly placed himself on Luther's side in supporting a doctrine of the bound will rather than Erasmus' doctrine of the free will.

Melanchthon's support for Luther's strong view of the bound will was not lost on at least one Roman Catholic theologian: Johannes Cochlaeus. Basing his critique primarily on Melanchthon's views as seen in the *Loci communes*, he wrote an entire book accusing Melanchthon of making human beings into senseless objects.[146] Many of Melanchthon's formulations in the following years would be specifically addressed to these concerns.

CONCLUSION

In the mid-1520s, Melanchthon continued formally to agree with Luther on the bondage of the will when it came to the decision to trust in Jesus for one's salvation. But as a result of the Wittenberg disturbances and the influence of Luther's political theology, Melanchthon now spoke of this bondage of the will solely in relation to the spiritual realm. In the temporal realm, he taught that the will was genuinely free and responsible for its decisions—whereas just a few years earlier, Melanchthon had taught the will was bound in *all* realms of human existence—both spiritual and temporal. Along with this shift toward temporal freedom (the freedom of contingency) came the elimination of determinism, the fading of predestination, and a diminishing role for the affections argument.

Meanwhile, many scholars conclude that beginning in around 1526, Melanchthon's shifting thought on free will could be traced to a re-emergence of philosophical metaphysics in his theological formulations. Consequently, we move now to a consideration of the role of philosophy in Melanchthon's theological thought, and then proceed from there to examine his writings on Colossians in 1527–8. These writings will shed further light both on his relationship to the debate between Luther and Erasmus, and on his understanding of the proper role and limitations of philosophy.

---

[145] Cameron, 'Philipp Melanchthon: Image and Substance', 714.

[146] Kolb, *Bound Will*, 75. Johannes Cochlaeus, *De libero arbitrio hominis adversus locos communes Philippi Melanchthonis, libri duo* (Tübingen: Morhart, 1525). See also Wengert, *Human Freedom*, 80–6.

6

———

1526–1528: Philosophy

INTRODUCTION

As a young man, Melanchthon was strongly influenced by the scholarship of Erasmus. Then, upon his arrival at Wittenberg, he fell under the sway of Luther's theology, and vigorously supported Martin's basic teachings. Many modern scholars, though, view the influence of Erasmus reasserting itself in Melanchthon's mind in the mid- to late 1520s, as exemplified by new studies of Aristotle, a recommitment to the principles of humanism, and a resulting admixture of philosophical metaphysics into his theology. This was the cause, some suggest, of Melanchthon's shifting formulations on the freedom of the will. However, this theory is unsupported by the facts, as I intend to demonstrate below. Still, the story is complicated, and it will remain important to notice how Melanchthon emphasized rational consistency in the formulation of doctrine at the expense of paradox (or antinomy). Although this consideration of the role of humanism and philosophy in Melanchthon's thought will necessitate some slight divergence from our chronological narrative, it will be a helpful foundation to establish before returning to Melanchthon's writings in 1527 and 1528.

A RESURGENT PHILOSOPHICAL HUMANISM?

In the introduction to this thesis we noted that within the literature relevant to Melanchthon's doctrinal journey on the origins of faith, several scholars have argued that the primary reason Melanchthon's theology changed over time involved the re-emergence of humanist and philosophical preconceptions held before he arrived in Wittenberg.[1] In other words, Melanchthon

---

[1] Those who make this argument include Sperl, Neuser, Schneider, Gerhards, Meijering, Hägglund, Günther, and Brüls. Focusing more on a re-emergence of scholastic theology in Melanchthon's thought, Engelland and Noryskiewicz make arguments similar to the aforementioned authors.

incorporated philosophy (that is, rationally based extra-biblical arguments and Aristotelian metaphysics) into his theology, and as a result, moved away from a bound-will position and (eventually) ended up with a measure of free will in justification. Those who make this argument tend to place the re-emergence of Melanchthon's humanism in the mid- to late 1520s. As a result, it is appropriate to consider this hypothesis at the present juncture in our narrative. We will begin by looking at how Melanchthon viewed the relationship between philosophy and theology, and then proceed to an examination of the particular question of how Melanchthon conducted his biblical exegesis.

Melanchthon's Separation of Philosophy and Theology

In the *Loci* of 1521, Melanchthon made extraordinarily clear his opposition to the mixing of philosophy with theology.[2] However, as we have seen in the Introduction, within the secondary literature the idea that in the 1520s Melanchthon reverted to a prior incorporation of philosophy into his theology has found some acceptance. According to this argument, it was the influence of philosophy acting upon Melanchthon's theology that led to his later shift from his strict bound-will position of the early 1520s.[3] Steinmetz, Gerhards, and Günther note that Melanchthon began writing on Aristotle's *Nichomachean Ethics* in 1527,[4] and they take this as proof of Melanchthon's return to philosophy.[5] Euan Cameron states, 'With no less zeal than an Aquinas, or the later sixteenth-century Spanish neo-Thomists, Philipp Melanchthon produced a university Aristotelianism which meshed precisely with

---

[2] See the following two letters from around the same time in which Melanchthon warned of the futility of philosophy, he mourned over its continuing influence in the theology of the time, and he spoke against the errors of Aristotelian theology (as well as the errors of Origen). Melanchthon (in Wittenberg), to Nikolaus von Amsdorf (in Wittenberg), after April 1520. MBW 1.89. T 1.89. CR 1.273–5 Nr. 96. Suppl. Mel. 6/1.122 Nr. 126. Melanchthon (in Wittenberg), to Tilemann Plettener (in Wittenberg), March 1521. MBW 1.132. T 1.132. CR 1.510–12 Nr. 168. CR 21.81–4. Suppl. Mel. 1.1.3–5; 6.1.134–5 Nr. 141. MSA 2/1.3–5.

[3] Gerhards' thesis is probably the most comprehensive study of the relationship between philosophy and theology in Melanchthon's thought and the resulting effect of this relationship upon Melanchthon's doctrine of the will. Gerhards' thesis statement: 'Es ist die Aufgabe dieser Arbeit, den philosophiegeschichtlichen Standort Melanchthons in der Frage der Willensfreiheit aufzuzeigen und in diesem Punkte des Verhältnis von Theologie und Philosophie zu klären', p. 9.

[4] *Enarrationes aliquot librorum ethicorum Aristotelis*. CR 16.277–416. This work first appeared in print in 1529. In 1530, Melanchthon also published *Commentarii in aliquot politicos libros Aristotelis*. CR 16.417–52. Later works on Aristotle include *De vita Aristotelis* of 1537 (MSA 3.96–104), the *Oratio de Aristotele* of 1544 (MSA 3.122–34), and the various editions of *De anima* (e.g. the 1553 edition, which can be found in MSA 3.305–72. Cf. also CR 13.5–178. For an English translation, see Keen, 239–89.) See below for more on this edition of *De anima* (*On the Soul*).

[5] Steinmetz, *Reformers in the Wings*, 51. Gerhards, 74–5. Günther, 80.

his Protestant theology.'[6] Schwarzenau also chimes in that Melanchthon dropped his anti-philosophy polemic in 1524,[7] but cautions that the shifts in Melanchthon's theology in the late 1520s probably had more to do with Melanchthon's use of the two-kingdoms theology than philosophy.[8] To have a look at just how Melanchthon did view the relationship between philosophy and theology, it would be helpful first to make a distinction about the definition of philosophy, which will aid us in divesting the notion of 'philosophy' of unnecessary ambiguity.

Green makes a very helpful point when he writes, 'It becomes apparent that we are here dealing with two uses of the word philosophy: first, philosophy as synonymous with the liberal arts (grammar, rhetoric, and dialectic) applied to theology, without altering theological content, a practice which Melanchthon approved, and second, philosophy as metaphysics applied to theology, a practice which corrupted its content and which he rejected. In the first instance, we are dealing with philosophy and theology in conjunction; in the latter case, with philosophy and theology in disjunction.'[9] For Melanchthon, metaphysical philosophy could never be normative for theology, and in fact, it was best to keep such philosophy and theology entirely separate. As for philosophical tools such as grammar, rhetoric, and dialectics—they were entirely appropriate means by which to read and understand the Bible, and hence interpret and construct evangelical theology. In sum, one could say that Melanchthon approved of 'philosophy' in the humanist sense, and rejected it in the scholastic sense.

Melanchthon always protested against any sort of mingling between philosophical metaphysics and theology. In the *Loci* of 1521 he made this point clear, and decades later in 1543 he continued to argue that theology informed philosophy, and not the other way around.[10] Again, in 1544, Melanchthon was still stressing the differences between law, Gospel, and philosophy.[11] In 1545, he argued specifically that philosophy was to be kept separate from the Gospel, though he admitted that Aristotle's writings at times approximated natural law.[12] For Melanchthon, theology had to be based on the Bible, and

---

[6] Cameron, 'Philipp Melanchthon: Image and Substance', 709.

[7] Schwarzenau, 19.

[8] Ibid., 52–3.

[9] Lowell C. Green, 'Melanchthon's Relation to Scholasticism', in *Protestant Scholasticism: Essays in Reassessment*, ed. Carl R. Trueman and R. S. Clark (Carlisle: Paternoster, 1999), 277.

[10] Melanchthon (in Wittenberg), letter to Balthasar Käuffelin (in Tübingen), 8 February 1543. MBW 3.3160. CR 5.33–5 Nr. 2634.

[11] Melanchthon (in Wittenberg), letter to George Helt (in Wittenberg or with Fürst George von Anhalt), April 1544. MBW 4.3546. CR 5.560–3 Nr. 3103.

[12] Melanchthon (in Wittenberg), letter to Arnold Burenius (in Rostock), February 1545. MBW 4.3825. CR 2.849–54 Nr. 1260. CR 16.5–10.

the Bible alone, and metaphysical philosophy had no right to enter into the realm of theology as it related to salvation.

However, in some cases, for Melanchthon metaphysical philosophy approximated universal truths that were to be found in natural law. Philosophy could at times reflect the teachings of the law, and it was useful worldly wisdom for the practice of civil order. Yet, while metaphysical philosophy could occasionally dimly reflect the law, it could never even begin to approach the truths of the Gospel.

Philosophical Metaphysics and the Mosaic Law

When Melanchthon spoke about philosophical metaphysics, he most often meant ancient Greek philosophy—particularly Aristotle (as well as all the writers subsequent to him who utilized his ideas). Aristotle had no place in *theology*, but as for worldly wisdom, he could be studied.[13] The ethics of Aristotle and his general teachings on virtue (i.e. his moral philosophy) was only a shadow of godly wisdom, comparable to a fig leaf, but it was nevertheless necessary for external culture.[14] Hence, Melanchthon approved Greek learning regarding the universal laws of nature, and, in 1518, he called Aristotle's *Moralia* and Plato's *Laws* especially strong.[15] In other words, the best of ancient Greek philosophy reflected some semblance of natural law, and could perhaps be equated to the aspects of external behaviour required by the law (i.e. civil righteousness). As Melanchthon wrote in 1532, 'Philosophy is neither gospel nor any part of it, but it is a part of divine law.'[16] Of course, Aristotle's ethics focused on external actions, whereas the law of the Bible went further and demanded purity of internal disposition to go along with the external actions. Thus, in going back to Melanchthon's terminology of the dual realms, Aristotle could be seen as being useful in the realm of civil

---

[13] Heinz Scheible, 'Aristoteles und die Wittenberger Universitätsreform: Zum Quellenwert von Lutherbriefen', in *Humanismus und Wittenberger Reformation: Festgabe anlässlich des 500. Geburtstages des Praeceptor Germaniae Philipp Melanchthon am 16. Februar 1997: Helmar Junghans gewidmet*, ed. Michael Beyer and Günter Wartenberg (Leipzig: Evangelische Verlagsanstalt, 1996), 142.

[14] Melanchthon (in Wittenberg), letter to Peter Medmann (in Emdem), before 1 May 1551. MBW 6.6071. CR 7.769–75 Nr. 4884. See also Melanchthon (in Jena), letter to Leonhard von Eck (in Munich), 18 October 1535. MBW 2.1647. T 6.1647. CR 2.956–8 Nr. 1345. In this letter Melanchthon again spoke about his understanding of the significance of Aristotle.

[15] Melanchthon, 'On Correcting the Studies of Youth'. Keen, 54. *De corrigendis adolescentiae studiis*. MSA 3.39.9: 'Plurimum valent Aristotelis Moralia, Leges Platonis . . .'.

[16] Melanchthon continued, 'For philosophy, properly speaking, is nothing other than the explanation of the law of nature.' Keen, 204.

righteousness and public order (that is, the temporal realm), but not in the spiritual realm.[17]

The Necessary Separation of the Gospel and Philosophical Metaphysics

Philosophical metaphysics might occasionally reflect the law, and it was eminently useful for teaching civil righteousness in the temporal realm. However, when it came to the Gospel, the philosophical metaphysics of Aristotle and all his adherents had no place whatsoever. Green writes, '[Melanchthon's] opposition to medieval scholasticism revolved around the intrusion of metaphysical philosophy into theology.'[18] In this sense, Melanchthon repeatedly condemned Aristotle, Origen, and Thomas Aquinas.[19] Reason could not know or recognize the divine will.[20] When it came to salvation, reason and revelation had to be kept separate.[21] Salvation (the Gospel) had to be based entirely on the Bible, and *not* Aristotle.[22] In 1520, Melanchthon said, 'Philosophy teaches that virtue comes by practice and habit, but with natural feelings opposing, do we still not see that nothing is accomplished by practice? For just as an ape is always an ape, even though clothed in purple, by the same token one will not conquer sickness of the soul by any counsel or any art.'[23] In 1521, Melanchthon stormed, 'For what is that to us, what that dirty man has contrived? We should not make Aristotle more than Christ, should we?'[24]

---

[17] Melanchthon's approval of Aristotle for use in the realm of civil righteousness (but not in matters of spiritual righteousness) explains his oft-cited renewal of interest and endeavour in Aristotle in 1527. Melanchthon found Aristotle's thought to be useful for teaching civic virtue and also to be a good example of some of the best of the world's wisdom. This did not mean, however, that Melanchthon was mixing Aristotelian ideas into his soteriological formulations.

[18] Green, 'Melanchthon's Relation to Scholasticism', 277.

[19] Melanchthon (in Wittenberg), letter to Thomas Cranmer, Archbishop of Canterbury, 1 January 1553. MBW 7.6696. CR 8.8–11 Nr. 5305. See also Melanchthon (in Wittenberg), letter to Veit Amerbach (in Wittenberg), April 1542. MBW 3.2949. CR 5.231–3 Nr. 2802. Both of these letters are from the latter part of Melanchthon's theological career. Regarding the beginning, see Wengert, 'Philip Melanchthon's 1522 Annotations on Romans', 140.

[20] Wiedenhofer, 187.

[21] Ibid.

[22] As zur Mühlen (p. 330) points out, Melanchthon drew more on Neoplatonism, Augustine, and the Bible, than on Aristotle. Zur Mühlen's statement is accurate for the *Loci* of 1521, but the same is true for Melanchthon throughout his theological career.

[23] 'Paul and the Scholastics', trans. Hill, 38. 'Docet Philosophia virtutem usu et assuetudine comparari, sed repugnantibus naturae affectibus nondum videmus usu quam nihil profectum sit? Nam ut simia semper est simia, etiamsi purpuram induta, ita nullo consilio, nulla arte, animi morbum viceris.' *Declamatiuncula in Divi Pauli doctrinam: Epistola ad Johannem Hessum Theologum.* MSA 1.34.28–33.

[24] 'Luther and the Paris Theologians' (1521), trans. Hill, 75. *Widder das wuetende urteyl der Pariser Theologisten. Schutzred Phil. Melanchthon fuer Doctor Mart. Luther.* WA 8.301.10–11:

Philosophical scholastic notions did not lead to Christian righteousness, and the Word of God in its source needed no interpretation. It would ever bring light from God.[25] For the Gospel, it was the Bible, and not philosophical metaphysics that was required.

In fact, philosophical metaphysics and the Bible were to be kept in strict separation. In 1538, Melanchthon asked rhetorically, 'What has philosophy to do with the Gospel?'[26] Two years earlier we find him saying, 'Theology and philosophy are to be differentiated; they may not be mixed together like broth in the kitchen.'[27] In 1521, Melanchthon wrote, 'Philosophy prostitutes, I repeat, it prostitutes the church, and we would contend that it does so with the unnatural appetites of Sodom.'[28] As Wiedenhofer notes, it was Melanchthon's view that when a false philosophy was uncritically mixed with revelation, the Gospel and Christ were darkened.[29] The Gospel was to be derived entirely from the Bible, apart from any and all influences associated with philosophical metaphysics, and Melanchthon consistently held this position throughout his life.

Philosophy (When Defined as Tools of Textual Analysis and Interpretation) Approved for Theology

The Gospel had to be based entirely on the Bible, apart from any sort of interference from outside philosophical metaphysical constructs. This being said, the Bible had to be read and understood. To that end, Melanchthon insisted on the importance of grammar, rhetoric, and dialectics[30] for the

'Was geht uns an, was der selb unsawber mensch gemacht hatt? Solten wir Aristotelem hoher denn Christum halten?' As early as 1518, Melanchthon was already pointing out that Aristotelian theologians were error prone. 'On Correcting the Studies of Youth', Keen, 53. *De corrigendis adolescentiae studiis.* MSA 3.37–8.

[25] Melanchthon, foreword to *Augustini Hipponensis Episcopi liber de spiritu et litera* (Wittenberg: Josef Klug, July 1545). MBW 4.3973. CR 5.803–10 Nr. 3235.

[26] 'Quid interest inter Philosophiam et Evangelium?' This is a heading for a small section in *Philosophiae moralis epitomes*, 1538. CR 16.21–3. Gerhards cites this quotation, and comments, 'Zeigt Melanchthon, daß die Botschaft des Evangeliums mit den Erkenntnismitteln der Philosophy nicht erfaßt werden kann', p. 88.

[27] 'Nec ego ignoro aliud doctrinae genus esse Philosophiam, aliud Theologiam. Nec ego illa ita misceri volo, ut confundit multa iura coquus, sed adiuvari Theologum volo in oeconomia methodi.' *Declamatione de philosophia*, 1536. CR 11.282 The English translation in the main text above comes from Engelland, 'Introduction', xxxii.

[28] 'Prostituit, inquam, prostituit Ecclesiam philosophia, ut cum infandis etiam Sodomae libidinibus certemus.' *Didymi Faventini adversus Thomam Placentinum pro Martino Luthero theologo oratio*, 1521. CR 1.313. MSA 1.87.1–3. The English translation in the main text above is Green's, from 'Melanchthon's Relation to Scholasticism', 281.

[29] Wiedenhofer, 188.

[30] In 1518, Melanchthon defined dialectics as follows: 'Dialectic is a certain short method for all inquiries, both managerial and judgmental: in which consists the order and judgment of each

proper comprehension of the Scriptures. As Keen explains, 'This is not, however, to reduce theology to subservience to philosophy: it is to make it comprehensible with the natural abilities that God has implanted in us.'[31] Estes writes that Melanchthon believed 'that humanist rhetoric and dialectic were the indispensable tools for the fruitful analysis of texts in their original languages'.[32] Green argues that both Melanchthon and Luther approved the use of rhetoric and dialectics as tools for understanding the Bible,[33] but, as for dialectics, Luther's words said otherwise: 'Honestly, I do not see how dialectic would not be rather harmful for a true theologian. Maybe it could be play and exercise useful for the minds of youngsters, but in Bible study, where only faith and enlightenment from above are desired, all syllogism has to be left behind' (admittedly, this was not necessarily Luther's view for the entire course of his career).[34] In any event, Steinmetz writes, 'Melanchthon took up the tools of philosophy to ground, clarify, and order the biblical theology of Luther.'[35] As Wartenberg points out, 'Against all resistance, even from his own camp, [Melanchthon] insisted that a completed course at the arts or philosophy faculty remain a prerequisite for entering the theology faculty, and that experience gained in language and logic would help prevent error, division, and inconsistency.'[36] He said, 'For I am clearly persuaded of the

matter to be treated, so that we may also see what, how much, of what kind, why, how, if something is simple; but if it is complex, whether it be true or false.' 'On Correcting the Studies of Youth', trans. Keen, 51. *De corrigendis adolescentiae studiis*. 'Primum dialectica, ut dixi, methodus quaedam est omnium quaestionum compendiaria, διοικητική, τε και διακριτική: qua constat ordo et iudicium cuiusque rei tractandae, ut in quoque videamus, quid, quantum, quale, cur, quomodo, si simplex sit; sin complexum, verum ne an falsum.' MSA 3.4–9.

[31] Keen, 36.

[32] *Peace, Order, and the Glory of God*, 87.

[33] Green, 'Melanchthon's Relation to Scholasticism', 281. In contrast, Neuser argues that one of the key *differences* between Luther and Melanchthon was that Luther was no humanist, while Melanchthon kept some of the trappings of humanist argumentation—i.e. classical rhetoric and dialectics. *Der Ansatz*, 33.

[34] LW 48.56–7. 'Ego sane non video, Quomodo non sit noxia potius Dialectice vere Theologo. Esto quod sit forte utilis Iuvenilium ingeniorum lusus vel exercitatio, Sed in sacris literis, ubi mera fides & superna expectatur illustratio, foris relinquendus universus syllogismus.' WABr 1.149.10–13. Of course, Luther made this comment in 1518, and it belies the fact that he cheerily used dialectics in his own work in subsequent years.

[35] Steinmetz, *Reformers in the Wings*, 53. Steinmetz goes on to argue that Melanchthon engaged in a kind of 'philosophical theology' that Luther did not, but as we have seen, Melanchthon assiduously separated philosophical metaphysics from theology. However, if one were to interpret Steinmetz's statement as saying that Melanchthon placed greater emphasis on rhetoric and dialectics than Luther, then this is surely a valid assertion. See also Estes, *Peace, Order, and the Glory of God*, 81–2, 152. Cf. Nicole Kuropka, *Philipp Melanchthon: Wissenschaft und Gesellschaft: Ein Gelehrter im Dienst der Kirche (1526–1532)* (Tübingen: Mohr Siebeck, 2002).

[36] Günter Wartenberg, 'Philip Melanchthon, the Wittenberg Reformer Alongside Luther', *Lutheran Quarterly* 12 (1998), 375.

view, as one who likes things that are distinguished, that the mind must previously be exercised prudently and sufficiently by the human disciplines (for such I call philosophy) in order to excel, whether it be in sacred things or the marketplace.'[37] Further, 'With the Spirit as leader, and the cult of our arts as ally, we may approach the holy.'[38] Consequently, 'philosophy', when defined as grammar, rhetoric, and dialectics, was absolutely essential to the successful practice of theology, and Melanchthon required it of all his students.

While Melanchthon denigrated Aristotle's *metaphysical* philosophy, he then turned around and embraced him in the subject of *linguistic* philosophy—rhetoric and dialectics. In 1536, Melanchthon declared, 'I am calling for a learned theology, not for cavils which have no real substance. For that reason I have said that one class of philosophy is to be taught, which has the least possible sophistry and retains the right method: that is the teaching of Aristotle.'[39] Melanchthon maintained that in this area, Aristotle was the master, and that through his teachings, scholars could ably seek one simple and minimally sophistic doctrine.[40] 'How useful it is to be at home in Aristotelian reason and method. For I would say that without it there can never be any craftsmen in any genre.'[41] Melanchthon emphatically stated, 'I feel strongly that a great confusion of doctrines would follow if Aristotle, who is the one and only creator of method, were neglected. By no other plan can anyone learn method except by regular practice in the genre of Aristotelian philosophy.'[42] Concluding the same speech, Melanchthon went on (rather flamboyantly) to compare Aristotelian method to the Promethean fire: 'Wherefore I urge you, not only for yourselves, but for all posterity, to cultivate and preserve that best form of doctrine. Plato said that the fire

---

[37] 'On Correcting the Studies of Youth' (1518), Keen, 54. *De corrigendis adolescentiae studiis.* 'Nam in ea sum plane sententia, ut qui velit insigne aliquid, vel in sacris, vel foro conari, parum effecturum, ni animum antea humanis disciplinis (sic enim philosophiam voco) prudenter et quantum satis est, exercuerit.' MSA 3.38.36–39.2.

[38] Ibid., Keen, 55. 'Duce Spiritu, comite artium nostrarum cultu, ad sacra venire licet.' MSA 3.40.5–6.

[39] Keen, 68. *Declamatione de philosophia* (1536). 'Eruditam philosophiam requiro, non illas cavillationes, quibus nullae res subsunt. Ideo dixi unum quoddam philosophiae genus eligendum esse, quod quam minimum habeat Sophistices, et iustam methodum retineat: talis est Aristotelis doctrina.' MSA 3.93.17–22.

[40] Ibid., Keen, 69. MSA 3.93–4.

[41] Melanchthon, *De vita Aristotelis* (1537). Keen, 72. '... quantum prosit ad Aristotelicam rationem ac methodum assuefactum esse. Ita enim statuo sine hoc neminem umquam fore artificem methodi ullo in genere'. MSA 3.98.9–12.

[42] Keen, 77. *De vita Aristotelis* (1537). '... planeque ita sentio magnam doctrinarum confusionem secuturam esse, si Aristoteles neglectus fuerit, qui unus ac solus est methodi artifex. Nec alia ratione ad methodum assuefieri quisquam potest, nisi in hoc genere philosophiae Aristotelicae mediocriter exerceatur.' MSA 3.104.25–9.

that had been taken by Prometheus from the sky was method.[43] But if that little fire is lost, men will be transformed back into beasts; for indeed if the true plan of teaching is removed, nothing will separate man from beasts. So then let us hold onto that fire, that type of doctrine that Aristotle handed down, and preserve it with the greatest zeal. I have spoken.'[44] Similarly, in 1544, Melanchthon concluded another oration with the following: 'Then let us love philosophy and know that it is to be used by the church to her great benefit, if it is used rightly. The minds of the pious would be thoroughly shocked if among the sacred things they saw the altars smeared with the sordid and filthy. It is no less evil to rush upon heavenly teaching barbarically, with inadequate knowledge of languages, history and arts, than it would be to desecrate sacred altars. Then let us cultivate the studies of literature, languages and honourable subjects, and give our work to the glory of God; and if we do that, it will be in God's care, and will not lack rewards. I have spoken.'[45]

Noting Melanchthon's limited, linguistically related endorsement of Aristotle's teachings, Engelland states, 'Philosophy thus becomes the helpmate of theology.'[46] Scheible reinforces this point when he comments that Melanchthon taught that theology could not be understood by means of philosophy, but rather through language—which meant dialectics.[47] Melanchthon insisted on the necessity of dialectics for theology,[48] and his numerous writings on rhetoric and dialectics bear witness to the importance he afforded these disciplines. Dialectics, rhetoric, and grammar—the tools of philosophy—

---

[43] Keen here cites *Philebus* 16c5–6.

[44] Keen, 77. *De vita Aristotelis* (1537). 'Quare vos hortor, non solum vestra causa, sed etiam propter universam posteritatem, ut hoc optimum doctrinae genus diligenter colatis et conservetis. Plato ait igniculum illum a Prometheo de caelo allatum methodum esse. At hoc igniculo amisso, rursus homines transformarentur in beluas; profecto enim sublata vera docendi ratione, nihil distant homines a beluis. Ut igitur hunc igniculum retineamus, hoc doctrinae genus, quod tradidit Aristotelis summo studio conservandum est. Dixi.' MSA 3.104.29–38.

[45] Keen, 87. *Oratio de Aristotele* (1544). This was an oration written by Melanchthon, and delivered by Erasmus Floch. 'Amemus igitur philosophiam, et sciamus eam magno ornamento atque usui esse ecclesiae, si dextre tractetur. Perhorrescerent animi piorum, si inter pia sacra viderent aras sordibus ac caeno conspurcari. Non minus autem mali est doctrinam caelestem obruere barbarie, deleta linguarum, historiarum et artium cognitione, quam aras inter ipsa sacra polluere. Colamus ergo litterarum, linguarum et honestarum artium studia, et hunc laborem nostrum ad gloriam Dei referamus, quod si faciemus, Deo curae erit, ne desint praemia. Dixi.' MSA 3.134.7–16.

[46] Engelland, 'Introduction', xxxii. He cites CR 11.282 in support of his statement.

[47] Scheible, 'Aristoteles und die Wittenberger Universitätsreform', 139. I would add to Scheible's statement the clarification that when he says 'philosophy', he means philosophical metaphysics, and not rhetoric and dialectics.

[48] For example: 'Quanquam autem sacrae literae non sumant res a philosophia, tamen, quia sermonem a publica consuetudine mutuantur, sine dialectica et cognatis artibus compositio sermonis cognosci non potest.' *Oratio de dialectica*, 1528. CR 11.162.

were ever necessary for theology, but, of course, metaphysical philosophical speculation could never be mixed with theology. Melanchthon was consistent on this view of the relationship between philosophy and theology throughout his theological career.

Scriptural Exegesis

Scripture Alone: Divine Rhetoric

Melanchthon saw the Bible as the source of theology. He valued the opinions of the church Fathers throughout the ages as well, but their writings were of a distinctly secondary importance in relation to Scripture.[49] In fact, it seems that Melanchthon did not use the Fathers as independent authorities, but he instead only cited those whose ideas matched his own interpretation of Scripture.[50] With the possible exception of Augustine, Melanchthon tended to use the Fathers merely as additional support for his own Bible-based arguments. The Bible was absolutely central.

Scripture was the key to all theology, and it had to be read and understood. Here Melanchthon always used the rhetorical methods of the humanists.[51] Rhetoric and dialectics were bound together,[52] and dialectics (even the dialectics of Aristotle) was to be utilized for theology.[53] In 1547, Melanchthon wrote, 'I, on the other hand, profess the true uncorrupted and original dialectic, which we have received from Aristotle as well as from some of his reliable commentators.... I declare that it is very useful, not only in the forum and in trials, but also in the Church.'[54] In fact, it was impossible to

---

[49] Fraenkel, 17–18. See also Meijering, 138.

[50] Meijering, 139. Cf. Timothy Wengert, who rejects Meijering's view in '"Qui vigilantissimis oculis veterum omnium commentarios excusserit": Philip Melanchthon's Patristic Exegesis', in David C. Steinmetz, ed., *Die Patristik in der Bibelexegese des 16. Jahrhunderts* (Wiesbaden: Harrassowitz, 1999), 115–34.

[51] Gerhards, 25–6.

[52] Oswald Bayer, *Theologie, Handbuch systematischer Theologie*, vol. 1 (Gütersloh: Gütersloh Verlagshaus, 1994), 141. See also Schneider, *Oratio sacra*, 68: 'Melanchthon proposed that dialectic and rhetoric were two elements of the same substantive procedure rather than discrete disciplines, and that differences between them were strategic and secondary.' In Melanchthon's own words, this point can be found in his letter to Johannes Schwertfeger (in Wittenberg), dated March 1520. MBW 1.78. T 1.78. CR 1.152–4 Nr. 67. Suppl. Mel. 6.1.90 Nr. 88.

[53] 'Melanchthon stellt ... die aristotelische Rhetorick und Dialektik in den Dienst der Theologie.' Gerhards, 77.

[54] 'Ego veram, incorruptam, nativam Dialecticen, qualem et ab *Aristotele*, et aliquot eius non insulsis interpretibus.... Hanc affirmo non modo in foro et in iudiciis, aut in philosophia, sed etiam in Ecclesia valde utilem esse.' Melanchthon (in Wittenberg), letter to Johannes Camerarius (in Königsberg), 1 September 1547. MBW 5.4696. CR 6.655. This

do theology without dialectics, for doctrine could only be formed through it.[55] Moreover, as part of his rhetorical-dialectical focus, doctrine had to be presented with eloquence[56] and consistency.[57] This was all possible, finally, because Scripture itself (especially Paul's letters) adhered to the rules of rhetoric and dialectics.[58] In his *Scholia in Epistolam Pauli ad Colossenses* of 1527, Melanchthon wrote, 'It may perhaps seem inept of me to relate Paul's prose to rhetorical conventions. But it is my opinion that the Pauline style of writing can be better understood if the *series* and *dispositio* of each section is taken into consideration.'[59] Neuser aptly comments that humanistic dialectics and Pauline thought were closely bound together for Melanchthon,[60] because Scripture *was* rhetoric. It was, in the words of Schneider, 'sacred oration'.[61] As a result, Melanchthon said that an unlearned theology was evil[62]—meaning, a right understanding of the Word of the Lord required skill in rhetoric and dialectics.

document was also the dedicatory letter to Melanchthon's *Erotemata Dialectices* of 1547. The English translation in the main text above is Kusukawa's. Sachiko Kusukawa, ed., *Philip Melanchthon: Orations on Philosophy and Education* (Cambridge: Cambridge University Press, 1999), 86.

[55] Melanchthon, in an unused foreword (although, in some editions, it *was* used) to *Melanchthon, Opera*, dated 27 July 1541, wrote that in the *Loci* and in his commentaries on Romans he was bringing together Reformation doctrine in a dialectical method. MBW 3.2780. T 10.2780. CR 4.715–22 Nr. 2418. See Engelland, 'Introduction', xxxii. See also Wiedenhofer, 382.

[56] Stupperich (MSA 3.43), Introduction to *Encomium eloquentiae* (1523).

[57] 'There are nevertheless two of the highest effects of the art which not even clever men can achieve without knowledge or erudition. The first is to see the causes of certitude, that is, why the beliefs we embrace are fixed, and why what we construct needs to be consistent. . . . What we construct needs to be consistent . . .' Trans. Kusukawa, *Orations on Philosophy*, 84. 'Tamen due sunt summa artis opera, quae ne ingeniosi quidem sine doctrina et sine literis efficere possunt: quorum prius est videre causas certitudinis, cur firmae sint sententiae, quas amplectimur, et cur necesse sit cohaerere ea. . . . [D]educaturque ad extremum ad normas certitudinis . . .' Melanchthon (in Wittenberg), letter to Johannes Camerarius (in Königsberg), 1 September 1547. MBW 5.4696. CR 6.654.

[58] Schneider, *Oratio sacra*, 119.

[59] Trans. Parker, 32. [Col. 1.3]. 'Videar fortassis ineptus, si Pauli sermonem ad rhetorica praecepta conferam. Ego tamen sic existimo intelligi melius posse orationem Paulinam, si series et dispositio omnium partium consideretur'. MSA 4.214–15.32–34, 1.

[60] Neuser, *Der Ansatz*, 33.

[61] Schneider, *Oratio sacra*, 157. See also Kenneth Hagen's argument to the same effect on pp. 10 and 38 in *Luther's Approach to Scripture as seen in his 'Commentaries' on Galatians, 1519–1538* (Tübingen: Mohr, 1993).

[62] Keen, 67. *Declamatione de philosophia* (1536). '. . . tantum habeat mali inerudita theologia . . .' MSA 3.91.6.

Exegesis: The Importance of Rational Consistency

Melanchthon wrote influential textbooks on dialectics and rhetoric.[63] He defined dialectics as the art or the way of correct, exact and clear teaching, right definition and division, connecting true arguments, and annulling and refuting false or badly coherent arguments.[64] Melanchthon's use of dialectics so overshadowed his entire theological method that Ernst Troeltsch called Melanchthon's early theology a 'theology of definitions'.[65] Wengert elaborates that, 'What Luther solved through paradox, Melanchthon explained with definitions.'[66] Schneider argues that this focus on definitions 'was hardly that of "Luther's lexicon", but was rather a dialectical and rhetorical notion with immense implications for human life. Properly formed "definitions" tapped into the greatest cosmic powers in the universe, and they unleashed those powers in the most perfect and humanly momentous manner possible.'[67] Perhaps Schneider overstates the case, but Melanchthon himself called dialectics 'the art of arts, the science of sciences'.[68] Luther himself praised Melanchthon's work in dialectics, declaring, 'Philipp has done in dialectics what nobody else has done in a thousand years. I knew dialectics before, but Philipp taught me to apply dialectics to the concrete. Nobody can repay Philipp for his work.'[69] Dialectics was the spade by which Melanchthon dug for theological gold.

Rhetoric went hand in hand with dialectics because an unconvincing presentation of truth spoiled whatever dialectical efforts had led to the discovery.[70] For Melanchthon rhetoric and dialectics were inextricably intertwined.

---

[63] *De rhetorica* (1519, not available in a modern edition), *Compendiaria dialectices ratio* (1520, CR 20.748–50), *Institutiones rhetoricae* (1521, not available in a modern edition), *De dialectica* (1528, CR 11.159–63), and *Elementorum rhetorices* (1531 (and revised in 1542), CR 13.413–506).

[64] 'Dialectica est ars seu via, recte, ordine, et perspicue docendi, quod fit recte definiendo, dividendo, argumenta vera connectendo, et male cohaerentia seu false retexendo et refutando.' *Erotemata Dialectices.* CR 13.513. See also Melanchthon (in Wittenberg), letter to Johannes Camerarius (in Königsberg), 1 September 1547. MBW 5.4875. CR 6.653–8 Nr. 3992.

[65] Ernst Troeltsch, *Vernunft und Offenbarung bei Johann Gerhard und Melanchthon* (Göttingen, 1891), 59.

[66] Wengert, *Human Freedom*, 146.

[67] Schneider, *Oratio sacra*, 159.

[68] 'Dialectica est ars artium, scientia scientiarum, ad omnium methodorum principia viam habens.' CR 13.515. *Erotemata Dialectices.* 1547.

[69] *Tischrede.* 20 May 1532, LW 54.156. 'Philippus fecit, quod nullus fecit in mille annis in dialectica. Dialecticam hab ich gewust, aber Philippus hatt michs lernen appliciren ad rem. Philippo khan sein arbeit niemant bezalen.' WATr 2.127.23–6.

[70] On the importance of rhetoric, see Melanchthon (in Wittenberg), letter to Leonhard Crispinius (in Homberk [Bezirk Kassel]), 1 August 1538. MBW 2.2072. T 8.2072. CR 3.563 Nr. 1706.

Schneider put forth that 'what would distinguish Melanchthon's rhetoric from all other models in his time (and perhaps in any time) is the thoroughly systematic integration of dialectics into it'.[71] The two belonged together, and both placed a high value on the use of reason. In fact, Melanchthon saw the aggregate of rhetoric and dialectics as the height of reason, and (following Agricola), as philosophy in its most concentrated form.[72] This was a significant point, for it meant that Melanchthon (who heartily approved of rhetoric and dialectics) did in fact approve of philosophy in *this* capacity, as we have already seen.

When it came to the actual exegesis of Scripture, Melanchthon rigorously applied the principles of rhetoric and dialectics—and vital to these were order, consistency, and the absence of contradiction. Doctrine had to be rational.[73] Melanchthon was known as the first Protestant systematizer for a reason. Stupperich states that Melanchthon drew conclusions from Scripture with greater consistency than Luther.[74] According to Buzogany, one of Melanchthon's favourite maxims came from Xenophon's *Oeconomicus*: 'If something lacks order, it is not worthy of respect, and is useless.'[75] Maurer points out that Melanchthon had an aversion to paradox, and in that sense was more strongly traditional than Luther.[76] Schneider views Melanchthon as focused on the logical operations of the intellect, seeking perfect logical coherence, and believing in the literal unity of Scripture.[77] Kolb, too, notes 'the greater inclination [than Luther] on Melanchthon's part to try out formulations that resolved the tension of the paradox of God's and human responsibilities'.[78] Engelland criticizes Melanchthon for his aversion to paradox and his attempts to bring God down to the level of human understanding. Engelland even goes

[71] Schneider, *Oratio sacra*, 149. See also Schneider's 'The Hermeneutics of Commentary: Origins of Melanchthon's Integration of Dialectic into Rhetoric', in *Philip Melanchthon (1497–1560) and the Commentary*, ed. Timothy J. Wengert and M. Patrick Graham (Sheffield: Sheffield Academic Press, 1997), 20–47. Melanchthon's rhetoric also differed from the rhetoric of Erasmus. See Manfred Hoffman, 72–3.

[72] Schneider, 'Melanchthon's Rhetoric as a Context for Understanding His Theology', 150. Melanchthon stated this opinion before his arrival at Wittenberg, and in his inaugural address there (MSA 3.35–7). I concur with Schneider against Neuser that Melanchthon maintained this rhetorical theory throughout his life.

[73] Brüls, 31.

[74] Stupperich, *Melanchthon*, 39.

[75] Deszo Buzogany, 'Melanchthon as a Humanist and a Reformer', in *Melanchthon in Europe: His Work and Influence Beyond Wittenberg*, ed. Karin Maag (Grand Rapids: Baker/Paternoster, 1999), 91. Buzogany does not, however, cite his source for this assertion. For more on Melanchthon's method of 'finding order in chaos', see Wiedenhofer, 369.

[76] Maurer, *Der junge Melanchthon*, 2.237.

[77] *Oratio Sacra*, 30, 70, and 103.

[78] Kolb, *Bound Will*, 95.

on to suggest that the later movement of Melanchthon's theology in a Pelagian direction was at least partly the result of this very aversion to paradox.[79]

In Melanchthon's own words, his many writings on rhetoric and dialectics stressed definition, order, and rational consistency. In 1536, Melanchthon wrote, 'We may expect perfect doctrine from the greatest efforts of minds, from which some usefulness may accrue to the state and the church.'[80] The purpose of dialectics was to 'judge whether in teaching everything is consonant with everything else'.[81] In 1546, Melanchthon favourably referenced Aristotle, noting that he had censured absurdity and emptiness in words. Melanchthon also endorsed a teaching of Euripides that 'the clear is good', and 'clarity is the sign of a generous mind'.[82] He lauded the logical consistency of Cicero,[83] and decried 'absurd and inane studied subtleties' of Politan and Pliny.[84] Melanchthon concluded, 'Thus let us flee from the hiding places of words and let us love clarity, especially in teaching.'[85]

Regarding paradox in particular, Melanchthon mentioned his disapproval a number of times in 1536. Two of Melanchthon's specifically anti-paradox statements came in his final letter to Erasmus, dated 12 May 1536. In Greek, he wrote, 'For I do not like, nor will I tolerate, irrational words and vulgar

---

[79] Engelland, *Glauben und Handeln*, 509–14.

[80] *Declamatione de philosophia* (1536). Keen, 66. '... summa contentione animorum expetamus perfectam doctrinam, ex qua ad rempublicam et ad ecclesiam utilitas aliqua pervenire possit'. MSA 3.89.28–31.

[81] Trans. Mary Joan La Fontaine, 'A Critical Translation of Philip Melanchthon's "Elementorum Rhetorices Libri Duo" (Latin Text)', unpublished dissertation (Ann Arbor: University of Michigan, 1968), 80. 'Ut autem dialecticae finis est, iudicare, Utrum in docendo apte consentiant omnia.' Melanchthon, *Elementorum rhetorices libri duo* (1543), CR 13.419.

[82] *Commentary on Aristotle's Ethics, Book I*, 1546. Keen, 190. *Enarrationes aliquot librorum ethicorum Aristotelis.* '... et non sit nimia obscuritas, dogmata sint perspicua, et proprie dicta, et ἐσθλὸν τὸ σαφές, inquit Euripides, id est, perspicuitas est generosi animi indicium'. CR 16.294.

[83] 'Others [than Cicero] join very different ideas and have a great many thoughts mangled, so to speak, and sometimes add foreign ideas. But Cicero aptly includes all things which pertain to a subject and he connects them so that the parts are as consistent as the proofs of a logician.' Trans. La Fontaine, 322. 'Alii coacervant sententias longius inter se distantes, et plaerasque relinquunt quasi truncatas, et nonnunquam admiscent alienas. At Cicero apte complectitur omnia quae ad rem pertinent, eaque ita connectit, ut inter se membra proxime cohaereant, velut dialecticae probationes.' CR 13.498.

[84] 'But in serious affairs nothing is more absurd [and inept] than these studied subtleties. What have we gained in reading them?' (of Politan and Pliny). Trans. La Fontaine, 339. '... sed in seriis negociis nihil est ineptius atque inanius illis affectatis argutiis. Quid autem assecuti sumus horum lectione?' CR 13.503.

[85] *Commentary on Aristotle's Ethics, Book I*. Keen, 190. *Enarrationes aliquot librorum ethicorum Aristotelis.* 'Quare fugiamus verborum latebras et amemus perspicuitatem praesertim in docendo.' CR 16.294.

paradoxes.'[86] He went on later in that same letter to assure Erasmus that he was neither the author nor the supporter of new dogmas, but that he had collected the common doctrines of religion, as simply as possible, without defending paradoxes.[87] These statements clearly demonstrate that while Luther had no problems with paradox, Melanchthon did. Melanchthon's entire exegetical method favoured order, precision, and the absence of rational contradictions—even paradox, if it could be adequately interpreted through other Scripture passages. Melanchthon sought to move beyond paradox to arrive at 'perfect doctrine'.

Before moving forward, however, it is important to clarify our definitions, for what Melanchthon understood by the word 'paradox' was often, in fact, something different from what the modern Anglophone reader would understand by the same word. In modern English, *The Oxford American Dictionary* defines 'paradox' as 'a statement etc. that seems to contradict itself or to conflict with common sense but which contains a truth (as "more haste, less speed")'.[88] Melanchthon, though, defined 'paradox' according to a much earlier Greek usage. He defined it, not as apparent contradiction, but simply as something unexpected. He wrote, 'The paradox, or the unexpected, is well known, as: "Never did I believe, Judges, that anything would find favour for the defendant Scaurus in this trial of his". And there are many forms of this time. For there is wonderment, as, "I wonder how I came to be suspected by you."'[89] Indeed, Melanchthon's usage here is standard for the ancient world. Both classical and New Testament Greek dictionaries define paradox as 'unexpected; incredible, marvellous; strange, wonderful, startling, astonishing.'[90] New Testament usage bears out this definition, as seen in Luke 5.26. After

---

[86] *Οὐ γὰρ ἥδομαι οὐδε ατέργω ἀκυρολογίας καὶ φορτικωτέροις παραδόξοις.* Melanchthon (in Leipzig), letter to Erasmus (in Basel), 12 May 1536. MBW 2.1735. T 7.1735.11–14. CR 3.68–70 Nr. 1421. EE 11.3120. By *vulgar* paradoxes, I take Melanchthon to mean that he does not tolerate the appearance of contradiction. However, his quotation here can be interpreted in more than one way.

[87] 'Deinde toties profiteor me nec autorem novorum dogmatum nec suffragatorem esse, sed collegi communem doctrinam religionis, quam potui simplicissime, ne nostrorum quidem paradoxa defendens.' T 7.1735.30–2. Günther also mentions this quotation on pp. 111–12 of his thesis.

[88] Eugene Ehrlich et al., eds., *The Oxford American Dictionary* (New York: Oxford University Press, 1980).

[89] Trans. La Fontaine, 255. 'Cognatum est *paradoxon* [παράδοξαν] seu inopinatum, ut: Nunquam credidi fore iudices, ut reo Scauro, ne quid in eius iudicio gratia valeret. Ac formae multae sunt huius generis. Est enim admiratio, ut miror, quomodo tibi in suspicionem venerim.' *Elementorum rhetorices.* CR 13.477.

[90] See, for example, Karl Feyerabend, ed., *Langenscheidt's Pocket Greek Dictionary: Classical Greek–English* (Berlin: Langenscheidt, n.d.): παράδοξος, and *The Analytical Greek Lexicon* (Grand Rapids: Zondervan, 1967): παράδοξος: (παράδοξαν, beside expectation).

digging a hole in the roof, some men lowered a paralysed man on a stretcher down in front of Jesus. Jesus first forgave the man's sins, and then, to prove that he had the authority to do so, also healed the man's body, commanding him to get up, take his mat, and go home. Verse 26 describes the response of the crowd (NRSV): 'Amazement seized all of them, and they glorified God and were filled with awe, saying, "We have seen strange things (παράδοξα) today."' With this in mind, if we want to speak about Melanchthon's views on the use of apparent contradictions in theology, we should probably not use the word 'paradox' with its present-day connotations, but instead, use the word that Melanchthon usually did: antinomy (*anti-nomos*—opposed laws).[91]

Melanchthon defined antinomy in *On the Elements of Rhetoric* (1543): 'The status of opposing laws occurs when contradictory laws give rise to possible dispute, as quite often happens. The Greeks call this state antinomies. [For example:] It is better to marry than to be consumed by passion. And the canon: Priests are not permitted to marry.'[92] Melanchthon proceeded to teach that antinomies could not be allowed to stand as presented. They had to be smoothed out through ordered reasoning.[93] This was especially true in civil legal reasoning, and here, Melanchthon laid out a method for resolving such antinomies: 'Confirmations and refutations are drawn from efficient causes. For a law gets its authority from an efficient cause. Here there are governing formulas. A lesser law gives way to a higher one. A special law restricts a general law. The laws of man yield to the laws of God. Old laws are emended or cancelled out by new ones. Confirmations and refutations are drawn also from the intrinsic material, that is, from *the laws themselves if they agree with reasoning or conflict with reasoning*, if the circumstances under which they were enacted are considered, and if they are properly adapted to these cases. And by such procedures very many controversial aspects of the laws are ironed out' (emphasis added).[94] Notice that the conflicted laws *had to agree*

---

[91] Please note, however, that I will continue periodically to use the word 'paradox' or 'paradoxical', in its modern sense. To say 'antinomian' would lead to great confusion, considering the rich theological heritage already attached to that word!

[92] Trans. La Fontaine, 155. 'Contrariarum legum status est, cum faciunt controversiam contrariae leges, quemadmodum saepe accidit, Graeci vocant hunc statum *antinomias* [] ut, *antinomiai* [ἀντινομιαι] sunt: Melius est nubere quam uri. Et Canon: Non liceat sacerdotibus uxores ducere'. CR 13.441.

[93] La Fontaine, 155. CR 13.441.

[94] Trans. La Fontaine, 156. 'Confirmationes et confutationes ducuntur ex causis efficientibus. Lex enim habet autoritatem ab efficiente causa. Hinc sunt regulae. Lex inferior cedit superiori. Lex specialis derogat generali. Lex humana cedit divinae. Leges veteres corriguntur aut abrogantur novis. Ducuntur etiam confirmationes aut confutationes ex materia, hoc est, ex ipsis legibus, si cum ratione consentiant, aut pugnent cum ratione, si circumstantiae expendantur, quibus latae sint, et an ad hos casus recte detorquentur etc. Et ex talibus regulis dirimuntur pleraeque legum controversiae'. CR 13.441.

with reasoning. This idea would have significance for Melanchthon in sorting through the antinomy of a doctrine of predestination held in tension with the idea of human free will (or genuine responsibility for reprobation). However, in the example just mentioned, Melanchthon was speaking of civil legal reasoning. Did the same rules apply for him in ecclesiastical (theological) thinking? If one remembers that Melanchthon was the originator of the phrase 'forensic [legal] justification' the answer should be obvious.

He wrote, 'Now ecclesiastical disputes have in large part a certain resemblance to forensic debates. They expound laws, refute antinomies, that is, rules that seem to contradict each other; clear up ambiguities, argue at times *de jure*, at times *de facto*; and seek an understanding of the facts.'[95] Antinomies, or apparent contradictions, were to be resolved—*even in church affairs, that is, in theology.* Melanchthon elaborated, 'Confirmations and confutations in ecclesiastical affairs are drawn from the clearer testimony of the Scripture. Sometimes, however, dialectics is to be called upon because we often are compelled to infer something from the definition or from the cases that are in Scripture. But here it must be seen to that things which do not belong together in an *anacholoutha* (lack of connection) are not connected, or, as the dialecticians say, that *illogical constructions are not stitched together'* (emphasis added).[96] Illogical constructions were not to be stitched together! Melanchthon therefore had an aversion to antinomy (or an aversion to paradox, if one simply *must* use the modern English word). For Melanchthon, theology had to be rationally consistent. This emphasis on the rational consistency of doctrine would turn out to play at least an important ancillary role in the evolution of Melanchthon's thought on the freedom of the will, for it was part of the thinking that led him to resolve the apparent tension between predestination and free will.

Moreover, Melanchthon's aversion to the appearance of rational inconsistency in doctrine was no mere rhetorical-dialectical convention. It was not the fussy rigour of an obsessive grammarian. Melanchthon saw that theological doctrinal coherence was important for calming the worries of mortal men and women facing their eternal destinies. Pastoral comfort could only come from the reassurance of the *truth*, and the truth about the Good News of Jesus Christ

[95] Trans. La Fontaine, 114. 'Nam disputationes ecclesiasticae, magna ex parte similitudinem quandam habent forensium certaminum. Interpretantur enim leges dissolvunt *antinomias* [ἀντινομίας], videlicet sententia[s], quae in speciem pugnare videntur, explicant ambigua, interdum de iure, interdum de facto disputant, quaerunt factorum consilia.' CR 13.429.

[96] Trans. La Fontaine, 160–1. 'Confirmationes et confutationes in ecclesiasticis negociis ducuntur ex testimoniis scripturae clarioribus. Interim tamen ex dialectica adhibenda est, quia saepe ex definitione, aut ex causis, quae sunt in scriptura, ratiocinari aliquid cogimur. Sed hic videndum est, ne connectantur male coherentia seu *anacholoutha* [ἀναχολουθα], seu ut dialectici loquuntur, ne malae consequentiae consuantur.' CR 13.443.

had to make sense. As a theologian and a teacher of pastors, Melanchthon had to teach the Word of God coherently and clearly or else risk hurting the faith of the people. To put it more technically, he was concerned about the *effect* of doctrine. In 1536, in an address to new master's graduates, Melanchthon emphasized this point. He began by quoting Horace, and then added his own thoughts: '"If a painter wished to join a human head to a horse's neck, and set multicoloured feathers about . . ." Nothing in that coheres; not the beginnings, nor the middles, nor the ends can be discerned. Such a doctrine cannot help but engender infinite errors, unending dissipation, and misunderstandings occur on account of the great confusions that arise. Meanwhile hesitant consciences depart. And because no furies torture the spirit more vehemently than doubts about religion, so the universal religion is maliciously discarded, and minds become profane and Epicurean.'[97] Doctrine had to be *consistent*, and for a scripturally-based Christianity, therefore, theology had to be subordinate to the rules of rhetoric.[98] Luther, noting this tendency in Melanchthon, would later comment to Brück in 1536 that Melanchthon was a very learned man, but that 'reason occasionally caused him trouble—he would have to be on his guard lest he end up at the same point where Erasmus came out.'[99] Melanchthon's view of reason, in the end, did *not* lead to the same point where Erasmus came out, but did, in fact, contribute to an evolving soteriology that turned out to be something altogether new, as we will see.

The Consistency of Melanchthon's Views on Humanism and Philosophy

Melanchthon's view of the relationship between philosophy and theology was complex, but it remained consistent from the earliest days of his theological career all the way until his death in 1560. Melanchthon's changing thought on

---

[97] Keen, 66–7. *Declamatione de philosophia.* '*Humano capiti cervicem pictor equinam / Iungere si velit, et varias inducere plumas.* Nihil in ea cohaeret, non initia, non progressiones, non exitus cerni possunt. Talis doctrina non potest non gignere infinitos errores, infinitam dissipationem, quia in tanta confusione alius aliud intelligit, et dum suum quisque somnium defendit, existunt certamina et dissensiones. Interim conscientiae relinquuntur ambigentes. Et quia nullae Erynnes vehemtius cruciant animum, quam haec dubitatio de religione, tandem odio quodam abiicitur universa religio, et fiunt mentes prphanae et Epicureae.' MSA 3.90.32–91.5.

[98] Quirinus Breen, 'The Subordination of Philosophy to Rhetoric in Melanchthon: A Study of His Reply to G. Pico della Mirandola', *ARG* 43 (1952), 13–28.

[99] Trans. Wengert, 'Melanchthon and Luther/Luther and Melanchthon', *Lutherjahrbuch* 66 (1999), 88. 'Es wäre ein teurer gelehrten Mann, sprach Martinus, aber die Vernunft plagte ihn darneben; er müßte sich wohl vorsehen, daß es ihm endlich nicht dahin geriete, wie mit dem Erasmo . . .' WABr 7.412 Nr. 3022.

the governance of God and human free will in justification cannot be traced to any sort of resurgence of humanist or philosophical thought on Melanchthon's part. Melanchthon *always* kept a strict separation between theology and metaphysical philosophy. While Philipp did believe that metaphysical philosophy could be helpful for maintaining civil order in the temporal realm, he nevertheless afforded it no soteriological significance in the spiritual realm whatsoever. Thus, Melanchthon's renewed study of Aristotle in the late 1520s had no bearing on his doctrine of justification or the operation of the human will therein. Rather, he studied Aristotle for his *methodological*, not metaphysical, contributions. As Keen observes, Melanchthon felt that by teaching the classics, he could prepare young theologians *linguistically* for pursuing theology in a civilized manner.[100] Melanchthon allowed no mixing of theology with metaphysical philosophy, and therefore those who argue that Melanchthon's thought on free will in justification changed as a result of a 'return to philosophy' in the late 1520s are in error.

Melanchthon experienced no 'resurgent humanism' or 'return to philosophy' in the mid- to late 1520s. He studied philosophical writings at this time, but he also studied astrology, mathematics, and medicine. All of these were subjects worth studying (except perhaps astrology), but had little bearing on theology. Melanchthon viewed philosophy in a similar light.

This being said, another aspect of Melanchthon's thought that remained consistent, from the beginning of his theological career until the end, involved his methods of exegesis. Here, at least tangentially, philosophy might have had some bearing on Melanchthon's thought on free will in justification. While Melanchthon disdained mixing theology with philosophical metaphysics, he enthusiastically endorsed the use of grammar, rhetoric, and dialectics as tools of scriptural exegesis. One could argue that Melanchthon mixed theology and philosophy only if one were to define 'philosophy' solely as the aggregate of grammar, rhetoric, and dialectics. Further, a strict adherence to rhetoric and dialectics resulted in a unique spin on biblical exegesis. Because of the focus on precision of definition, order, and rational consistency that embodied Melanchthon's teachings on rhetoric and dialectics, it made sense that he would explicitly denigrate the concept of antinomy (the appearance of contradiction). Luther ever felt comfortable expressing antinomies, and hence he could balance divine determination and human responsibility in counterintuitive competing statements. Melanchthon, because of his aversion to the appearance of rational inconsistency, experienced more difficulty in making these statements than did Luther. This phenomenon of a reluctance to affirm

---

[100] Keen, 7.

antinomy (which was a part of Melanchthon's thought throughout his life) will become increasingly evident through further examination of some of Melanchthon's theological writings in the second half of the 1520s, beginning with his writings on Colossians.

COLOSSIANS: 1527–1528

In the years immediately following Luther's and Erasmus' dispute over the freedom of the will, Melanchthon reasserted his commitment to the bound will. His work on Colossians in particular encompassed his reply to Erasmus on free will, and it also showed some of the shifting bases of his argumentation for the bound will. In refuting the ideas of Erasmus, Melanchthon also added his own twists and nuances to Luther's position, which meant leaving out divine determinism. Here, he began to argue for the bound will almost entirely on the basis of the fallen human nature, while all talk of predestination and determinism fell by the wayside.

The *Scholia in Epistolam Pauli ad Colossenses*[101] was one of Melanchthon's most significant theological writings. He had begun lecturing on this letter in 1526, and the first publication in 1527 was most likely a student's set of lecture notes sent to the printer without Melanchthon's permission. This document was *Philippi Melanchthonis in locum ad Colossenses: Videte ne quis vos decipiat per philosopham inanem, dissertatio* (henceforth referred to as the *Dissertatio*).[102] Melanchthon himself issued the second and most important publication of 1527, the *Scholia*. Melanchthon devoted a significant amount of space in this work to the issue of free will, and it is clear that in so doing he was registering his own response to the Luther–Erasmus debate.[103] That is, he was presenting his own arguments for the bound will in opposition to Erasmus.[104] In the expanded edition of 1528, Melanchthon elaborated his arguments even further.

---

[101] MSA 4.209–303. See also Philipp Melanchthon, *Paul's Letter to the Colossians*, trans. D. C. Parker (Sheffield: Almond, 1989). For a detailed, monograph-length examination of Melanchthon's doctrine of the will as it appeared in all of his writings on Colossians, see Wengert, *Human Freedom*.

[102] CR 12.691–6.

[103] Günther (p. 58) rightly argues that Melanchthon used his *Scholia* of 1527 to reply to Erasmus' *Hyperaspistes*.

[104] Melanchthon said as much in a letter to Luther dated 2 October 1527 (Melanchthon was in Jena at the time). He wrote that in his lectures on Colossians (soon to be published as the *Scholia*), he had dealt at length with Erasmus' points on free will, and that hence there was no need for Luther to write another reply along the lines of *De servo arbitrio*. MBW 1.597. T 3.597. CR 1.893–4 Nr. 466. WABr 4.256–7 Nr. 1152. MSA 7/2.26–7 Nr. 118.

Dissertatio

In the *Dissertatio*, Melanchthon focused on Colossians 2.8, where Paul warned against being deceived by philosophy.[105] Melanchthon used this verse as a jumping-off point to discuss the dichotomy between the temporal realm and the spiritual realm as well as the use and limits of philosophy. He affirmed a certain freedom in civil (external) actions in the temporal realm[106] as well as the bondage of the will in relation to justification in the spiritual realm.

In this document Melanchthon continued to speak of the dichotomy between civil and spiritual righteousness. In the temporal realm (that is, regarding external actions undertaken either in alignment with or in contradiction to the desires of the heart), people had freedom. Through natural law they were responsible to do external good works and to be obedient to the earthly authorities.[107] People had freedom and jurisdiction from God over the natural practices of the temporal realm—things such as counting, measuring, building, and medicine.[108] Philosophy, when defined as all non-theological disciplines, held tremendous sway over the affairs of the temporal realm. However, philosophy belonged *only* in this area and in matters concerning the bodily life. It had no right or ability to discern the divine will on its own.[109] If it tried to discern the divine will, then worthless dreams (*inania somnia*) were the only result.[110] Paul warned against the *misuse* of philosophy. Like wine, philosophy taken in moderation and appropriately was fine.[111] Philosophy had its uses, but it also had its limits—it was best suited for the temporal realm and the temporal government.

Melanchthon viewed philosophy as dangerous when it over-extended its limits. This was the case wherever philosophy intruded into the spiritual realm or spiritual government apart from Scripture. Philosophy could be

[105] 'See to it that no one takes you captive through philosophy and empty deceit, according to human tradition, according to the elemental spirits of the universe, and not according to Christ.'
[106] Of course, to affirm genuine civil freedom was to deny divine determinism.
[107] 'Est enim ipsum iudicium rationis, quod in rebus naturalibus et civilibus moribus Deus dedit humanae naturae, verum et certum, quia dicit Paulus Rom. 2.: Gentes habet legem Dei scriptam in cordibus, id est, habent iudicium, quo iudicare possunt, neminem laedendum esse, gratiam pro benefactis habendam esse, magistratibus obsequendum esse, et similia.' CR 12.692.
[108] 'Habent ergo homines verum ac certum iudicium a Deo de civilibus moribus: Item habent de rebus naturalibus de numberando, de mensuris, de aedificando, de remediis morborum.' CR 12.692.
[109] 'Sic igitur philosophia seu iudicium rationis de divina voluntate nihil certi adfirmare potest, sed de natura rerum deque civilibus moribus recte iudicare potest.' CR 12.694.
[110] 'Non est enim philosophia, cum de divina voluntate ex ratione iudicamus, sed sunt inania somnia.' CR 12.695.
[111] 'Ita Paulus non ait, philosophiam esse malum, sed sic ait: videte ne quis vos decipia per philosophiam, ut si dicat: vide, ne te decipiat vinum.' CR 12.695.

used as a tool to help in the understanding of Scripture (i.e. through grammar, rhetoric, and dialectics—the temporal containers of spiritual truth), but
it could never stand on its own apart from the Word nor explain justification.
When philosophy thus overstepped its bounds, three prime errors occurred. It
happened that Melanchthon's discussion of these three errors added up to a
refutation of Erasmus' free-will position as well as a corrective to the determinism of Luther's bound-will position. Here Melanchthon put forth his own
view of free will, which, while compatible with Luther's, also contained some
important differences.

In the first error of reason, Melanchthon wrote that philosophy erred
because it failed to see God's governance of the world. Philosophy, noting
the evil in the world, posited that God must not be involved, that he must be
like a shipbuilder who once having constructed the vessel, set it adrift and left
it to its own devices.[112] Philosophy therefore erred in failing to see God's hand
at work in the world.

This repudiation of the complete freedom of the events of the world spoke as
much in what it did not say as in what it did say. Notice that Melanchthon no
longer taught in terms of determinism, or predestination. He spoke of God's
governance (*gubernatio*), which was quite different from determinism (*determinatio*). Divine 'governance' allowed significantly more freedom on the
human end of things. The primary meaning of *guberno* was to guide the course
of, or to steer, a ship. God may have been at the tiller of history, but he was not
necessarily determining every movement of every person throughout the ship.
Consequently, in the softening of his language from *determinatio* to *gubernatio*,
Melanchthon backed away from complete determinism, thus opening the door
to some measure of contingency in non-soteriological events (that is, in the
temporal realm).[113] In distinction from Luther, humans had real (not just
imagined, or paradoxical) free will in their outward actions. Thus the devil
and humans, not God, were responsible for sin and evil in the world. This had
been one of Erasmus' chief objections to Luther's doctrine of necessity.

In the second error of philosophy intruding into spiritual matters,
Melanchthon warned that free action in the temporal realm never had

[112] 'Nam etiamsi permittat, quod Deus condiderit res, tamen offensa ratio, quia in mundo
tam multa iniuste fiunt, negat a Deo res gubernari, sed somniat, quod Deus nunc ocium habeat,
et sinat suo quodam impetu naturam ferri, sicut faber, qui navem fecit, ubi absolvit, discedit ab
ea et committit eam fluctibus et non gubernat eam. Hic Christiana doctrina diversum docet, et
monet nos, ne per philosophiam decipiamur.' CR 12.693.
[113] It should be noted that the use of the word *gubernatio*, on its own, is not necessarily
incompatible with a strong view of God's rule. For example, in *Institutes* I.xvi–xviii, Calvin used
this word numerous times, to make similar points, and no one has accused him of softening his
views of God's rule.

anything to do with justification in the sight of God. Righteousness in the face of God (*coram Deo*) was only through faith in Christ.[114] Here Melanchthon was beginning to move from a discussion of God's general governance to a strong statement of the bound will in justification. The connection between the two concepts was made possible by Melanchthon's use of the dual realms. Freedom in the temporal realm eliminated the negative implications of absolute determinism. Bondage in the spiritual realm maintained the key doctrine of justification by grace alone and faith alone. To confuse civil (temporal) freedom with the ability to generate any amount of merit in the face of God was foolish, for while humans could control their external actions, they had corrupt, fallen hearts and could not earn or make any contribution toward their own salvation. Scotus, Ockham, Biel, and Erasmus were therefore all in error on this point.

In his description of the third error of philosophy, Melanchthon stressed the bondage of the will. The third error of philosophy came with the belief that people had power to combat vice and rule themselves apart from the Holy Spirit, culminating in purity.[115] Instead, the heart was filled with concupiscence, and the devil tempted humans.[116] Only through the Holy Spirit, not the human will, could the heart be changed. The final result of this position was that sin kept human beings in bondage, and that even though people might have had some genuine freedom in external actions (that is, in the temporal realm), they could never change their own hearts (in the spiritual realm), and so free will in justification remained a fiction.

By maintaining the bondage of the human will to sin, Melanchthon came out solidly in support of Luther in this document. Nevertheless, by rejecting Luther's necessitarian argument in favour of the looser term of God's 'steering' (*gubernatio*) of the world, Melanchthon had embraced a shift in his understanding of the rule of God. Due to Melanchthon's unwillingness to endorse antinomy, his freedom in the temporal realm was *true* freedom, which was not simultaneously determined by the Lord. This went contrary to Luther. Melanchthon here began to say that God 'steered', or 'administered' the world, though he did not determine every action. This spoke of a dynamic

---

[114] 'Secundo errat philosophia de iustificatione, si statuat, coram Deo satis esse civilem iusticiam. At christiana doctrina docet, iusticiam coram Deo fidem esse in Christum.' CR 12.693. Melanchthon thus rejected the idea of the free procuration of *meritum de congruo* from God, in opposition to Scotus, Ockham, and Biel.

[115] 'Tertio fallitur, si putat rationem satis habere virum ex sua natura contra vicia, nec videt opus esse spiritu sancto, qui et corda reddat puriora, et regat nos, ne vel ab infirmitate naturae vel Diabolo praecipitemur in manifesta flagicia.' CR 12.694.

[116] 'Sed Evangelium docet, cor esse impurum et ardere concupiscentia: Item, diabolum nobis ita insidiari, ut etiam in manifesta flagitia pertrahit.' CR 12.694.

interactive relationship between creation and Creator, which, importantly, added something to Melanchthon's theology that Luther lacked: *reactivity* on the part of God. Here Melanchthon introduced the significant aspect of God *reacting* to events in the world (in the civil, or temporal realm), though still governing in such a way as to bring about his will in the end. Luther, on the other hand, argued that God always directly acted *upon* creation (or vicariously acted through the hardening of the hearts of evil-doers to carry out his judgements, though with wrong and sinful motives on their part). Melanchthon used the concept of the dual realms as a tool to temper the absolute determinism of God, and in so doing introduced a new reactive, or at least cooperative, aspect to his doctrine of God in all human and natural events not pertaining to salvation.

First Edition of the *Scholia*: 1527

In the *Scholia* of 1527, Melanchthon amplified many of the arguments he made in the *Dissertatio*. His style of commentary involved looking for important theological *loci*, and then using those verses as jumping-off points for longer essays in which he attempted to draw together the wider biblical doctrine to which the verse in question referred. In this manner, Melanchthon used Colossians 1.15[117] as the location for an essay on the freedom of the will, and 2.8 (on which the *Dissertatio* was based) as the springboard for a discussion about philosophy. The treatment of Colossians 2.8 was even printed separately as a pamphlet following the publication of the *Scholia* of 1527.

One of Melanchthon's main achievements in the *Scholia* of 1527 was his definition of the benefits and limits of philosophy. This definition had a close bearing on the formulation of his doctrine of the human will. Melanchthon used this understanding of philosophy throughout this work as he clearly demonstrated his opposition to Erasmus' view of the will (though without ever mentioning the Rotterdam scholar by name). Additionally, Melanchthon's criticism did not extend to Erasmus alone. Melanchthon also sought to temper Luther's views by gently denigrating the idea of complete divine determinism. So, by surveying Melanchthon's views on philosophy, his opposition to Erasmus, and his tempering of Luther in this work, we shall be able to observe Melanchthon's continuing doctrinal journey on the origins of faith.

---

[117] 'He is the image of the invisible God, the firstborn of all creation.'

Philosophy

As in the *Dissertatio*, Melanchthon here defined philosophy as all non-theological disciplines. Wengert notes that the largest addition to the *Scholia* in
comparison with the *Dissertatio* came not in the attack on philosophy, but in
its defence.[118] Philosophy was a great tool and benefit to mankind—it was a
gift from God. Melanchthon wrote, 'It is a genuine and good creature of God.
It is that genuine and reliable judgment of the mind in natural and social
affairs, which God has given to human nature.'[119] Philosophy represented an
entirely valid instrument for use in understanding and mastering the natural
world (that is, in the temporal realm and government), and those who
rejected it were in error: 'Those people also err, who reject the capacity of
philosophy to form opinion about natural reality. This is to condemn God's
gift.'[120] Paul did not warn about philosophy itself in Colossians 2.8, but rather
the *misuse* of philosophy.[121]

Melanchthon limited the proper use of philosophy to the temporal realm.
Philosophy was not to trample unaided into the spiritual realm or spiritual
government. As he said in the *Dissertatio* and now repeated, reason in the
spiritual realm and in spiritual government led to three errors: reason failed to
see God's governance (or steering) of the world,[122] it dreamed that it could
achieve righteousness through works,[123] and it also thought it could change
the human heart by its own power.[124] Philosophy and reason failed in the
spiritual realm because they were unable to make any judgement about God's
will.[125] This had ever been Luther's chief point in his criticism of reason.

---

[118] Wengert, *Human Freedom*, 92.
[119] Trans. Parker, 46. [Col. 2.8] 'Est vera et bona creatura Dei, est enim ipsum iudicium
rationis, quod in rebus naturalibus et civilibus Deus dedit humanae naturae verum et certum.'
MSA 4.230.
[120] Trans. Parker, 55. [Col. 2.8] 'Rursus etiam errant ii, qui aspernantur philosophiam
iudicantem de naturalibus rebus. Nam id est contemnere Dei donum.' MSA 4.240.27–9.
[121] Trans. Parker, 55. [Col. 2.8] 'Ideo Paulus non ait philosophiam malam esse, sed sic ait:
"Videte, ne quis vos decipiat per philosophiam".' MSA 4.241.5–7.
[122] 'Although it [reason] admits that God created reality, yet it cannot accept that reality is
governed [not determined!] by God.' Trans. Parker, 53. [Col. 2.8] 'Primo enim errat ratio de
rerum gubernatione. Nam etiamsi permittat, quod Deus condiderit res, tamen offensa ratio,
quia in mundo tam multa iniuste fiunt, non potest statuere a Deo res gubernari.' MSA
4.238.8–11. Note especially Melanchthon's use of *gubernatione* and *gubernari* rather than
determinatio, or *necessitas*.
[123] Trans. Parker, 37. [Col. 1.13] 'Tertio nescit ratio, quae sit iustitia coram Deo, somniat
enim placari Deum nostris operibus.' MSA 4.221.1–2.
[124] 'It is true that reason, or free will, accomplishes human righteousness; but it neither
changes nor sanctifies the heart.' Trans. Parker, 58. [Col. 2.10a] 'Humanum vero iustitiam efficit
ratio seu liberum arbitrium, quae tamen cor non mutat aut sanctificat.' MSA 4.244.31–3.
[125] Trans. Parker, 46. [Col. 2.4] 'Humana ratione non possit iudicare de Dei voluntate.' MSA
4.230.2.

Melanchthon wrote, 'Thus philosophy, or the formation of judgments according to reason, cannot make reliable statements about the divine will. It can only form correct judgments about the nature of reality and about social morals. Consequently those people err who form decisions about Christian doctrine from the standpoint of reason or philosophy.'[126] Just as two kinds of seed were not to be planted in the same field [Lev. 19.19], so the doctrines of the Gospel were not to be mingled with philosophy.[127] To make judgements about Christian doctrine on the basis of philosophy was as insane as basing them on the principles of cobbling.[128]

Contra Erasmus: No Free Will

Melanchthon's section on Colossians 1.15 made his opposition to Erasmus' free-will position crystal clear. He wrote, 'What we must hold is, that a man's nature cannot bring forth out of its natural abilities, true fear of God, or true trust in God, or any of the other spiritual dispositions and movements.'[129] The question of free choice only mattered in relation to justification,[130] and there the servitude to sin that was the result of the Fall resulted in the absence of free will. The Fall removed humanity's free will in relation to justification:

---

[126] Trans. Parker, 55. [Col. 2.8] 'Sic igitur philosophia seu iudicium rationis de divina voluntate nihil certi affirmare potest, sed de natura rerum deque civilibus moribus recte iudicare potest. Quare errant, qui ex ratione aut philosophia iudicant de doctrina Christiana.' MSA 4.240.19–23.

[127] Trans. Parker, 55–6. [Col. 2.8] 'Et sicut in lege praeceptum est, ne quis dissimile semen serat in eodem agro, cavendum est, ne commisceantur evangelii doctrina et philosophia.' MSA 4.241.27–30.

[128] Trans. Parker, 55. [Col. 2.8] 'Et sicut insania esset dicere, quod ex artis sutoriae praeceptis sit iudicandum de Christiana doctrina, ita desipiunt, qui ex philosophia iudicant de doctrina Christiana.' MSA 4.240.31–4.

[129] Trans. Parker, 39. [Col 1.15] 'Hoc itaque tenendum est naturam hominis naturalibus viribus non posse efficere verum timorem Dei et veram fiduciam erga Deum et reliquos affectus et motus spirituales.' MSA 4.223.1–4.

[130] 'When the question is raised as to the faculty and powers of [free choice], one should not ask whether it resides in our power to eat, drink, walk, see, hear, and perform similar *psychika* [natural] actions. The question is, whether we are able to fear God, to believe in God, to love the cross, and so forth, without the Holy Spirit. To put it another way, the question is not concerning the created order, as to the way in which God is the mover of all creatures, of trees, beasts and men. But it is to do with justification and sanctification, with those actions which do not fall within the sphere of a man's natural life that is imparted by God to good and bad alike.' Trans. Parker, 39. [Col. 1.15] 'Cum de liberi arbitrii facultate ac viribus quaeritur, non hoc quaeritur, an in potestate nostra sit edere, bibere, ire, videre, audire, et similia ψυχικὰ opera facere, sed quaeritur, an sine Spiritu sancto possimus Deum timere ac credere Deo et crucem amare etc. Seu ut aliis verbis dicam: non quaeritur de creatione, quomodo agitet Deus omnes creaturas, arbores, bestias, homines, Sed quaeritur de iustificatione et sanctificatione, deque his actionibus, quae non cadunt in hominem quamquam naturali vita viventem, quam iuxta Deus impertit bonus et malis.' MSA 222–223.27–36, 1.

'Therefore, it is not hard for anyone who looks at what is lost to human nature to understand that the human will has no freedom.'[131] Unaided human reason was not strong enough to resist the devil,[132] and so the Holy Spirit had to work in human hearts.[133] Melanchthon declared, 'What need would there be for the Holy Spirit if the human will could by its own abilities fear God, trust God, put down concupiscence, love the cross? In a word, what is it but pure arrogance not to seek the Holy Spirit's help, when Christ promised, indeed commanded it, and instead to seek help in our own abilities? This, then, is what reason cannot effect by itself.'[134] Humans, wounded by the Fall, had no ability to change their own hearts or seek the good. They were bound from within themselves.

Melanchthon's opposition to free will rested entirely on the notion of the corruption spawned by the Fall. He did not speak of divine determinism, and nowhere in this document did he even once mention the word 'predestination'. This silence on determinism indicated Melanchthon's discomfort with it, for otherwise he surely would have mentioned it as a reason for the bound will as he did in 1519 in the *Theologica Institutio*, in 1520 in the *Capita*, in the *Loci* of 1521, and in the *Annotations on Romans* of 1522. Melanchthon's silence on predestination could be viewed as a criticism of the extremity of Luther's anti-free-will stance. Erasmus' chief complaint about Luther's bound-will position was the doctrine of necessity, and Melanchthon also sought to offer a milder view of that doctrine.

Tempering Luther: Silence on Predestination

In the *Scholia* of 1527, Melanchthon continued the theme that he had begun in the *Dissertatio* of God governing, or steering, the world. He used the shipbuilder image again[135] and reiterated the dual-realms theme of freedom

---

[131] Trans. Parker, 40. [Col. 1.15]. 'Itaque non difficile intellectu est humanam voluntatem non habere libertatem, si quis huc respexerit adimi naturae hominis.' MSA 4.223.17–19.

[132] 'For the powers of human reason are in no way strong enough against the devil.' Trans. Parker, 95. [Col. 3.11] '[R]ationis humanae vires nullo modo satis roboris habent adversus diabolum.' MSA 4.287.17–19.

[133] Trans. Parker, 89–90. [Col. 3.1] MSA 4.280–281.26–33, 1–33.

[134] Trans. Parker, 40. [Col. 1.15] 'Quid enim opus est Spiritu sancto, si humana voluntas suis viribus potest timere Deum, fidere Deo, deponere concupiscentiam, amare crucem? Denique quae est ista arrogantia non petere auxilium Spiritus sancti, cum promiserit eum Christus, sed magis iubere, ut a viribus nostris auxilium petamus? Habes igitur, quae non possit efficere ratio per sese.' MSA 4.223.23–9.

[135] 'He [God] is not like a carpenter who hands the ship he has built over to the crew and goes away. In my opinion, this knowledge is useful for the nourishing of fear and faith.' Trans. Parker, 38. [Col. 1.15] 'Nec somniare debemus Deum a conditis rebus discessisse, sicut fabrum a

in the temporal realm coupled with bondage in the spiritual realm. Although God governed generally, he allowed human freedom under his rule in temporal matters. Melanchthon wrote, 'The general action or motion with which God moves nature is of such a kind as belongs to each part of nature. He moves trees in one way, beasts in another, and men in yet another. In this way he grants to men a certain reason and power of choice. God does not take away this power to choose. He imparts life and motion, while we choose and do, showing the truth of the saying "In him we have our being and live and move" [Acts 17.28].'[136] People had genuine freedom in external (that is, temporal) acts: 'The human will has freedom in loving those things which are *psychika*, like choosing this or that kind of food, wearing these clothes or those, going this way or that. It can also perform fleshly and social righteousness: a man can withhold his hand from murder and theft, and he can keep himself away from his neighbour's wife. To that extent, a man's reason can govern him.'[137] Again, as in the *Dissertatio*, Melanchthon said nothing to indicate that this external freedom of the temporal realm was just a misapprehension of the fallen reason. While Melanchthon may have made such an argument in 1521, at this point in 1527 he clearly saw human freedom in external acts to be entirely real. The only things that hindered (though did not eliminate) human freedom in civil actions were the weakness of the flesh (original sin) and the devil.[138]

Melanchthon's affirmation of a genuine human freedom, even if tempered by sin and God at the world's tiller, allowed him to escape from the darker implications of absolute divine determinism. Due to Melanchthon's reluctance to embrace antinomy, the problem of evil could only be solved either by allowing freedom somewhere, or by making God responsible for evil. Finding

navi facta discedere videmus eamque aliis tradere gubernandam. Atque haec cognoscere ad timorem, ad fidem alendam utile esse existimo.' MSA 4.3–6.

[136] Trans. Parker, 41. [Col. 1.15] 'Sic igitur agitat Deus naturam hac generali actione seu motione, ut talem agitet, qualis est unaquaeque naturae pars, aliter arbores, aliter pecudes, aliter homines movet, rationem quandam et electionem tribuit homini. Eam electionem non adimit, sed vitam et motum impertit, dum eligimus, agimus, ut verum sit, quod scriptum est: "In ipso sumus, vivimus, et movemur".' MSA 4.224.29–35.

[137] Trans. Parker, 40. [Col. 1.15] 'Habet libertatem voluntas humana in diligendis his quae ψυχικά sunt, ut hoc aut illud cibi genus eligere, hoc aut illo genere vestitus uti, huc aut illuc ire, habet et vim carnalis et civilis iustitiae efficienda, continere manus potest a caede, a furto, abstinere ab alterius uxore. Eatenus ita potest hominum ratio gubernare.' MSA 4.223–224.32–34, 1–4. This was the theme of Melanchthon's theology in the late 1520s—people had true freedom in matters of civil righteousness. '[H]abet et vim carnalis et civilis iustitiae efficiendae...'

[138] 'Although Holy Scripture grants to the human will a certain freedom in social activities, yet it teaches that this freedom is double hindered. First, by the weakness of the flesh, by original sin.... Second, the devil obstructs our freedom.' Trans. Parker, 41. [Col. 1.15] 'Et quamquam tribuunt sacrae litterae quandam libertatem humanae voluntati in civilibus actionibus, tamen eandem docent impediri dupliciter. Primo infirmitate carnis seu peccato originali.... Secundo impedit libertatem diabolus.' MSA 4.225.6–11.

the latter scenario reprehensible, Melanchthon embraced the former. Thus he could safely relegate blame for evil to the freely acting devil and humanity. Consequently, 'I do not make God out to be the author of sin. Rather, he is the one who preserves nature, and who imparts life and motion: a life and motion which the devil and godless people do not use aright.'[139] Again, 'it is Satan who drives godless people on to perpetrate all kinds of wickedness.'[140] Wengert comments, 'Of course Melanchthon had not so much answered the question [of the problem of evil] as placed two sets of biblical texts in opposition to one another. He did not simply assume some free sphere of human activity and then fit God into what remained. Instead, he began with the activity of God, described in broad terms, and then wedged diabolic activity into it.'[141] Melanchthon made God the general director and sustainer of the universe, but he refused to view God in terms of absolute determinism.

The refusal to argue for the bound will on the basis of divine necessity represented a significant divergence from Luther. While both continued to argue against the bound will, some of the foundations of their arguments were beginning to diverge. Melanchthon's arguments for the bound will in 1527 were not as theoretically overwhelming as Luther's. Luther's arguments rested on a radical dichotomy between divine action and human passivity. God was absolute, and in total control of all things. Melanchthon, on the other hand, argued for the bound will solely from the position of bondage to sin. Melanchthon endorsed a *situational* (i.e. post-Fall) foundation for the bound will, while Luther's position was intrinsic to the structure of reality itself. For Melanchthon, our fallen humanity held us back. For Luther, our humanity in and of itself held us back.[142]

Second Edition of the *Scholia*: 1528

After reading *Hyperaspistes*, Erasmus' lengthy and vigorous reply to Luther's *De servo arbitrio*, Melanchthon revised and altered the *Scholia* of 1527, resulting in the *Scholia* of 1528[143] (and Justas Jonas' loose German translation

---

[139] Trans. Parker, 39. [Col. 1.15] '[N]on faciam Deum auctorem peccati, sed naturam conservantem et vitam et motum impertientem, qua vita et motu diabolus aut impii non recte utuntur.' MSA 4.222.16–19.

[140] Trans. Parker, 38. [Col 1.13] 'Nam impios impellit satan ad omnis generis flagitia perpetranda.' MSA 4.221.5–7.

[141] Wengert, *Human Freedom*, 89.

[142] For a detailed account of Luther's position (with citations), see Chapter 3 above.

[143] Melanchthon, *Scholia in Epistolam Pauli ad Colossenses, recognita ab autore* (Wittenberg: Joseph Klug, 1528). See the bibliography for full manuscript details. It is a shame that this document does not appear in any scholarly edition of Melanchthon's works, let alone in English translation.

of 1529).[144] With a sharpened tone (although still without mentioning Erasmus by name[145]), Melanchthon bolstered and reformulated some of his arguments, showing both a response to Erasmus and the ongoing development of his own thought.

Philosophy

As in the 1527 edition, Melanchthon's main excursus on philosophy in 1528 came in his discussion of Colossians 2.8.[146] With his comments nearly doubled in length, he did not alter his earlier arguments against the errors of philosophy. Instead, he gave an expanded discussion on rhetoric and dialectics[147] in which he first defended their use in the temporal realm. For things such as lawmaking, Melanchthon said that rhetoric and dialectics were of obvious use—otherwise Christians would end up hanging around with nothing to say, much like silent characters in a Greek comedy.[148] Building on this, Melanchthon then made a case for the use of rhetoric and dialectics in the interpretation of Scripture, as aided by the Holy Spirit. He wrote, 'And nevertheless, since the Holy Spirit teaches us through the Word, the nature of speech (*sermo*) must be known.'[149] The Holy Spirit taught *through* the Word, and not apart from it. In his German translation, Justas Jonas framed Melanchthon's point even more strongly, making an explicit case for the use of rhetoric and dialectics in addressing the question of the will's role in justification.[150]

Overall, Melanchthon's discussion of philosophy fitted the pattern already discussed above. Namely, Melanchthon continued steadfastly to reject philosophical metaphysics due to the fallenness of human reason. In this sense, philosophy and the Gospel were to be kept separate.[151] While people had some limited freedom in the temporal realm, this civil righteousness would not justify before God.[152] In contrast, Melanchthon did approve of the use of 'philosophy' when defined as the tools of textual analysis, interpretation, and explication. In this sense, philosophy was the gift of God.[153] Rhetoric and

---

[144] Melanchthon, *Die Epistel S. Pauli zun Colossern* (Michael Lotter, 1529). See the bibliography for full manuscript details.

[145] Wengert points out that although Melanchthon did not mention Erasmus by name, he *did* identify John Fabri, Erasmus' patron, as a target of attack. *Human Freedom*, 100.

[146] *Scholia* 1528, 23°v–38°r. *Die Epistel* 1529, 22°v–35°r.

[147] Wengert, *Human Freedom*, 99. See also Kolb, *Bound Will*, 80.

[148] *Scholia* 1528, 27°v–28°r. Wengert, *Human Freedom*, 99.

[149] Trans. Wengert, *Human Freedom*, 99. 'Et tamen, quoniam spiritus sanctus docet nos per uerbum, sermonis natura cognoscenda est.' *Scholia* 1528, 29°v.

[150] *Die Epistel* 1529, 22°v–35°r. Wengert, *Human Freedom*, 103.

[151] 'Discrimine Euangelij ac Philosophiae.' *Scholia* 1528, 34°r.

[152] 'Iustitia civilis non iustificat coram Deo.' *Scolia* 1528, 36°r.

[153] 'Philosophia Dei donum.' *Scholia* 1528, 33°r.

dialectic were tools to be used—even in the analysis of Scripture, which came already packaged in human language with all its grammatical, rhetorical, and dialectical components. Of course, such a use would include the resolution of antinomy. The elimination of apparent rational inconsistency would be a fundamental principle of scriptural explication and doctrinal formulation—leading Melanchthon (as at least an ancillary reason) to seek to resolve the tension between the ideas of predestination and human free will. This was, indeed, what he did, in time.

Contra Erasmus: No Freedom of the Will

At its heart, Melanchthon's rejection of free will was an affirmation of justification by *faith*, rather than works. He was rejecting Erasmus' transformational model of justification where struggling sinner and divine grace worked together to grow intrinsic righteousness in that person until one day, perhaps post-purgatory, that individual might attain to worthiness for entry to heaven. No, salvation was *God's* work, not ours. Unaided reason could not even assent to the promises of God by itself. '[Hypocrites] teach that faith is effected in us by the powers of the free [choice] (*liberum arbitrium*). For reason is not able to assent to God's promises.'[154] Hezekiah was helped by faith, not reason, when surrounded by Sennacherib's army.[155] As Wengert summarizes, '. . . the theological grounds of Melanchthon's rejection of Erasmus: the certainty of faith. Erasmus wanted to encourage anyone who tried. Melanchthon tried to comfort everyone in the midst of distress and failure. In such anxiety only the certainty of God's Word, not the vagaries of reason or free choice, provided help.'[156] Melanchthon was especially concerned about the *effect* of the doctrine: justification by faith was a comfort to a struggling sinner. The Roman Catholic justification by faith *and* works was a terror.

As in the 1527 edition, in 1528 Melanchthon chose to address the issue of the freedom of the will primarily in his discussion of Colossians 1.15.[157] He rewrote the section, sharpening the tone and changing some of the content. In the end, it was only a page longer than the 1527 edition. In the first part of the section, Melanchthon essentially reproduced what he had already laid out in 1527—the denial of God's responsibility for evil, the way in which he governed the world and its creatures, and an explicit repudiation of the freedom

---

[154] Trans. Wengert, *Human Freedom*, 96. *Scholia* 1528, 19°r: 'qui docent uiribus liberi arbitrij fidem effici in nobis. Ratio enim non potest assentiri promissionibus Dei.' See also 14°r: '. . . ratio humana non possit efficere iusticiam Christianam . . .'

[155] *Scholia* 1528, 19°v. Wengert, *Human Freedom*, 96–7.

[156] Wengert, *Human Freedom*, 97.

[157] *Scholia* 1528, 10°v–15°v. *Die Epistel* 1529, 11°v–14°r.

of the will in justification. Human beings were capable of producing some civil righteousness (through freedom in the temporal realm), but even here we needed God's help.[158] What did change, however, was that Melanchthon enlarged his teaching on the role of the Holy Spirit in the lives of believers. 'The Spirit renewed hearts; brought forth in believers new movement, life, light, and knowledge; and through the Word worked fear and faith in their hearts.'[159] The work of the Holy Spirit was necessary for anyone to be saved, for otherwise, fallen reason was no match for the lure of sin and the wiles of the devil: 'They are completely in error who think the power of [free choice] (*liberum arbitrium*) suffices for changing concupiscence. Much more do they err who dream they can be defended against the devil by the powers of free [choice] (*liberum arbitrium*).'[160] Hence, in 1528, Melanchthon strengthened his emphasis on original sin, the weakness of fallen reason, and the consequent necessity of God's gracious initiative through the work of the Holy Spirit. As in 1527, he remained silent on the issues of determination and predestination—but otherwise supported Luther's cause in rejecting Erasmus' conception of human free choice in justification.

Meanwhile, during the same period in which Melanchthon was working on the various editions of the *Scholia*, he was also putting theory into practice. He and Luther were diligently involved with the visitation of parish churches, and the attempt to help pastors preach the pure Gospel. This project, too, provides a window into Melanchthon's ongoing consideration of scriptural teaching regarding the will's role in justification.

THE VISITATION ARTICLES[161]: 1527–1528

On 16 June 1527, the prince elector, John Frederick, ordered visitations of schools and churches in his domains. Because his instructions were not sufficiently detailed, the Wittenberg theologians, along with the councillors

---

[158] 'Discamus igitur … ne quidem ciuilem iusticiam praestare possimus sine auxilio Dei.' *Scholia* 1528, 14°v.

[159] Ibid. See also Kolb, *Bound Will*, 80.

[160] Trans. Wengert, *Human Freedom*, 97. The rewritten material begins after MSA 4.223.17: 'Longe errant qui existimant ad concupiscentiam mutandam liberi arbitrij vires sufficere. Multo magis errant, qui somniant se uiribus liberi arbitrij aduersus diabolum defendi posse.' *Scholia* 1528, 11°v–12°r.

[161] *Articuli de quibus egerunt per Visitatores in regione Saxoniae.* 1527. CR 26.7–28. *Vnterricht der Visitatorn an die Pfarhern ym Kurfurstenthum zu Sachssen.* 1528. CR 26.49–96. MSA 1.215–71. Another, even more recent, scholarly edition can be found in volume 3 of Hans-Ulrich Delius, ed., *Martin Luther: Studienausgabe* (Berlin: Evangelische Verlagsanstalt, 1979–99), pp. 402–62.

of the electorate, drafted the *Visitors' Instruction to the Pastors in the Electorate of Saxony*. This document, also known as the *Visitation Articles*, was drafted in model form first by Melanchthon, in Latin, in 1527. The subsequent German-language edition, which appeared in 1528, while largely formulated by Melanchthon, also had contributions by Luther, Johannes Bugenhagen, Georg Spalatin, and the councillors of the electorate.[162] Using these articles as a guide, the visitors to the various evangelical churches in Saxony were to examine doctrine and morals, and each local pastor was to be given a copy of the document. This endeavour was accomplished at the request of the Elector John, and it was done primarily to keep the evangelical churches in agreement regarding doctrine as well as to guard against any rising Anabaptist sentiments.

The first edition of the *Visitation Articles*, written by Melanchthon and published in 1527, consisted entirely of doctrine. The second edition, published in 1528 with the contributions of others, was written in German, and it included both doctrine and ritual. It was much longer than the Latin edition. In a preface to the German edition, Luther railed against the poor state of the churches, noted that the bishops were doing nothing, and called for the churches to be set straight with good doctrine.[163] Obviously, this represented a ringing endorsement of the theology that Melanchthon put forth in the edition of 1527 of the *Visitation Articles*, including his section on free will. However, we shall see that Melanchthon's formulation of his bound-will argument continued on the trajectory he took in his Colossians writings, though with a much narrower rationale for the bound will than Luther had taken.

In the *Visitation Articles* of 1527, Melanchthon saw himself filling the role of a prophet like Jeremiah or Ezekiel, commanded to speak.[164] He was sure of himself, as well as conscious of the task of explaining as simply as possible the essentials of evangelical doctrine. As a result of this didactic effort, the changing structure of his thought on free will that had emerged piecemeal

---

[162] Helmar Junghans, 'Augsburg Confession', in OER 1.93–4. This seems to me to be the best explanation for the authorship of the *Visitation Articles*. Experts, however, adhere to a variety of opinions on the subject. MacCulloch, for example, says Luther was the author (*The Reformation*, 558). Wengert, on the other hand, attributes it to Melanchthon: 'Melanchthon and Luther/ Luther and Melanchthon', *Lutherjahrbuch* 66 (1999), 70–1. Keen, too, says that Melanchthon wrote it (Keen, 9). Estes says that Luther wrote the preface, and Melanchthon the main body of the text. 'The Role of Godly Magistrates', 472. In any event, it is clear that Melanchthon and Luther both played a role in this project, and that, at this early stage in the Reformation, they retained a substantial agreement on the doctrines here espoused. (See also Delius' introduction in *Martin Luther: Studienausgabe*, 3.402–5).

[163] Delius, 3.407ff. CR 26.43–4.

[164] CR 26.9.

in his Colossians writings was here presented with greater clarity and suc-
cinctness. Interestingly, the section on free choice was the second-to-last of
seventeen topics, whereas it had been first in the *Loci* of 1521. In this section
on free choice, Melanchthon began by commenting on the necessity of his
own teaching in light of the false teaching circulating at the time.[165] This
phrase probably referred to Erasmus' *De libero arbitrio*, and *Hyperaspistes*.
Next, it was clear from the start that Melanchthon's appropriation of Luther's
paradigm of the dual realms had continued to be a significant theme in his
thought.

Free will existed in the civil (temporal) realm, but not in the spiritual realm.
Citing Romans 2 for natural law, Melanchthon insisted that humans had free
will in acts of civil righteousness.[166] The flesh of man had within its power a
righteousness to flee evil and do good works.[167] Humans were perfectly
capable of going through all the external motions demanded by the law. On
the other hand, this civil (external) freedom was not completely unfettered,
but was restricted by Satan and evil human desires, although prayer could be
of help.[168] Nevertheless, Satan and human corruption merely made the
exercise of civil freedom more difficult, not impossible. Freedom, though
hampered, was no illusion in the temporal realm.

Reason, however, was corrupt, and looked at the outward physical mimicry
of the works of the law as the path to justification. Humans could not change
their own hearts.[169] In the German edition of 1528, the point bore repetition:
'*kan der mensch aus eigener krafft das hertz nicht reinigen*'.[170] As much as God

---

[165] (Latin edition, 1527). CR 26.26–7.

[166] 'Voluntas humana est vis libera, ut facere possit iustitiam carnis seu iustitiam civilem, ubi
lege et vi cogitur, ut non furari, non occidere, non moechari' (1527). CR 26.27. In the German
edition of 1528, the passage read: 'Der mensch hat aus eigener krafft ein freyen willen,
eusserliche werck zu thun odder zu lassen, durchs gesetz vnd straffe getrieben, Derhalben
vermag er auch weltliche frümickeit vnd gute werck zu thun aus eigener krafft, von Gott dazu
gegeben vnd erhalten, Denn Paulus nennets gerechtickeit des fleischs, Das ist, die das fleisch
odder der mensch aus eigener krafft thut.' Delius, 3.444.14–18. CR 26.78.

[167] 'Wirckt nu der mensch aus eigenen krefften eine gerechtickeit, so hat er ia eine walh
vnd freyheit, böses zu fliehen, vnd guts zu thun' (1528). Delius, 3.444.18–20. CR 26.78.

[168] (Latin, 1527). CR 26.10. 'Doch wird diese freyheit verhindert durch den teuffel. Denn
wenn der mensch durch Gott nicht würde beschüzt vnd regirt, so treibt yhn der teuffel zu
sunden, das er auch eusserliche frümickeit nicht hellt. Solchs ist not zu wissen, das die leute
lernen, wie ein schwach elend mensch ist, der nicht hülffe bey Gott sucht, Solchs sollen wir
erkennen, vnd Gott vmb hülffe bitten, das er dem teuffel were, vnd vns behüte, vnd vns rechte
Göttliche gaben gebe' (1528). Delius, 3.444.30–445.2. CR 26.79.

[169] (1528). 'Dem gerechten ist kein gesetz geben, sondern dem vngerechten, vnd vngehorsa-
men, den Gottlosen vnd sundern, Als wolt, Sanct Paul sprechen, Wir können das hertz aus eigener
krafft nicht endern, aber eusserlich vbertrettung mügen wir verhüten.' Delius, 3.444.23–6. CR
26.78–9.

[170] (1528). Delius, 3.445.3. CR 26.79.

encouraged civil righteousness, such was not the path to justification. True Christian righteousness could only be found in the divine acceptance,[171] and divine acceptance came only with the secret work of the Holy Spirit within, in the spiritual realm.[172] The work of the Holy Spirit was necessary, for, as Melanchthon repeatedly insisted in his Colossians writings, the human heart could not change itself. While civil (temporal) free will existed, spiritual free will did not: '*Voluntas humana non est libera, si respicias opera spiritualia, ut veram fidem habere erga Deum, deponere concupiscentiam, sui amorem, castum cor.*'[173] Reason had no spiritual power.[174] On account of this, the intervention of the Holy Spirit was necessary, by which people received the freedom of the Christian: remission of sins and rescue from the devil.[175]

For Melanchthon, external civil freedom stood side by side with internal spiritual bondage, and of the two, the spiritual bondage was what really mattered. This emphasis on the spiritual was necessary for Melanchthon, for in his rejection of determinism, he found himself constrained to preserve true freedom in the temporal realm of existence. The doctrine of the dual realms provided a convenient structure that Melanchthon could use to describe his evolving thought on the freedom of the will in justification, and it made for an interesting picture.

With temporal freedom and spiritual bondage, Melanchthon had effectually split and partially limited the rule of God. In the temporal realm, God steered the course of the flow of history, though he did not control every detail. He allowed some measure of actual freedom, thus limiting his governance and making himself at least in part *reactive* in relation to humanity. On the other hand, in the spiritual realm, Melanchthon maintained God's complete determination. No one could be saved unless God acted to change their hearts. Thus God's rule over the temporal realm was partial, while his rule over the spiritual realm was total. God was in complete control in one area, while not entirely so in another. This served as an intermediate step in the evolution of Melanchthon's doctrine of God's rule: he began in 1519–21 with God's total rule in both temporal and spiritual realms, he shifted in the 1520s

---

[171] (1527). 'Atque hoc est demum, veram Christianam iustitiam divinitus accipiendam esse, Civilis iustitia non est satis coram Deo, quamvis etiam Deus exigit eam.' CR 26.28.

[172] (1527). 'De peccato, quod non credat Deo, quod non possunt a ratione iudicari. Ratio enim tantum externa peccata iudicat, ut furtum, caedam, ebrietatem, adulterium et huismodo. Sed Spiritus sanctus etiam occulta et proprie latentia in corde arguit, ut contemptum Dei, vacare metu iudicii Dei, Deo diffidere, desperare de Dei benignitate et misericordia.' CR 26.17–18.

[173] (1527). CR 26.27.

[174] (1527). 'Vera illa spiritualia non potest efficere ratio, scilicet timorem Dei, castum cor, gaudium in cruce.' CR 26.28.

[175] (1527). 'Libertas Christiana primum haec est, habere remissionem peccatorum per Christum et consequi Spiritum sanctum, per quem liberemur a potestate diaboli.' CR 26.25.

to God's partial rule in the temporal realm along with his continued total rule in the spiritual realm, and he would end up in the next decade with God's partial rule in *both* temporal and spiritual realms.

1519–21	Temporal realm	*God's total rule. No human freedom.*
	Spiritual realm	*God's total rule. No human freedom.*
1522–31	Temporal realm	*God's partial rule. Some human freedom.*
	Spiritual realm	*God's total rule. No human freedom.*
1532–60	Temporal realm	*God's partial rule. Some human freedom.*
	Spiritual realm	*God's partial rule. Some human freedom.*

CONCLUSION: THE DIVIDED RULE OF GOD

In 1522, Melanchthon began to cease making affirmations about divine determinism and predestination. These ideas were downgraded in their significance in the section on free choice of the *Loci* of 1522, and disappeared entirely shortly thereafter. Throughout the 1520s, Melanchthon's affirmation of the bondage of the will in justification did not change, but his basis of argumentation shifted from resting primarily on the total determination of God to being based entirely on the postlapsarian bondage of the human will to sin. Why the shift in the basis of his argumentation? Metaphysical philosophy certainly did not make a reappearance in Melanchthon's theology, and an examination of the evidence shows that Melanchthon clearly saw himself as being on Luther's side in his debate with Erasmus over free choice. The most likely explanation of the shift involves the simple theological implications of a strong view of the total governance of God. First of all, if God determined all things in the temporal realm, then that could allow people to make excuses for unlawful behaviour. Case in point: the Wittenberg disturbances of 1522. This civil unrest illustrated to Melanchthon the dangers of such a strong view of the rule of God—people might not take responsibility for their own unruly civil behaviour. So to teach human responsibility for temporal behaviour, Melanchthon backed away from the total rule of God in the temporal realm.

In the spiritual realm, too, a strong view of God's governance held serious implications. If God determined *all* things, and predestined both the elect and the reprobate, then that made God directly responsible for sin, evil, and the lost. This was an uncomfortably negative effect of the doctrine, and the gradual disappearance of such language from Melanchthon's formulations on the freedom of the will shows that this is precisely how he was thinking about the matter.

In addition to these pastoral effects of doctrine, Melanchthon's shifting ideas were also aided by an interpretive framework that denigrated antinomy. For example, Luther affirmed a strong view of the governance of God *without* holding him responsible for the negative implications of such a view—he felt no qualms about affirming even what appeared to be rationally inconsistent so long as that was what Scripture said. He simply chalked it up as a mystery of God beyond the grasp of reason. Melanchthon, on the other hand, viewed Scripture as sacred oration. For him, the formation of doctrine through biblical exegesis required the application of the classical tools of Aristotelian rhetoric and dialectics, including an emphasis on rational consistency. So while Luther could tolerate the appearance of rational inconsistency in doctrine, Melanchthon was much less likely to do so. As Wengert writes, 'What Luther solved through paradox, Melanchthon explained with definitions.'[176]

Throughout the 1520s, Melanchthon's doctrine of the will was undergoing slow, steady change as a result primarily of processing the negative pastoral implications of his formerly deterministic view of the rule of God in all areas of existence, and as aided by an interpretive framework that favoured rationally-consistent doctrine rather than the presence of antinomy. This gradual transformation would continue, even in the midst of the great events leading up to the dramatic Diet of Augsburg, in 1530.

---

[176] Wengert, *Human Freedom*, 146.

7

1529–1531: Augsburg

INTRODUCTION

So far this study has traced Melanchthon's thought from 1519 to 1528. During this period, it has become clear that the changes in Melanchthon's formulations on free will in justification stemmed from the internal dynamics of his presuppositions.[1] These presuppositions worked themselves out within the framework of Luther's theology, which Melanchthon held in 1519. This process of change was hastened and fomented (though not necessarily caused) by historical events. Some modern scholarship maintains that Melanchthon's change began with the Luther–Erasmus controversy in the mid-1520s,[2] but in fact, the process of change was well under way by then, having begun in 1519.[3]

Now, in the years 1529 to 1531, Melanchthon continued formally to teach that the will was bound in the area of justification. Likewise, he still maintained his now-established position on the rule of God, which allowed some freedom in the temporal realm, but none in the spiritual realm. During these years, as historical forces began to put pressure on the Wittenberg Reformation, Melanchthon and Luther felt compelled systematically to confess and defend their theology, against both the Catholics and the Anabaptists. Because

---

[1] Gerhards, 75.

[2] Wilhelm Maurer, *Historical Commentary on the Augsburg Confession*, trans. H. George Anderson (Philadelphia: Fortress Press, 1986), 274.

[3] It has been occasionally argued in the literature (e.g. Maurer, *Historical Commentary*, 278) that Melanchthon's examination of free will took place primarily in the mid-1520s during the Luther–Erasmus dispute, and that he came down on the side of Erasmus. In previous chapters in this study, I have shown that Melanchthon decisively took Luther's side on the issue of free will, and if there were any lingering doubts about it, Melanchthon's letter on 24 July 1529 should put such questions to rest. In this letter to Camerarius (in Nürnberg), Melanchthon (from Wittenberg) asked his friend not to write to Erasmus any more in order to avoid his harmful influence on theology. Melanchthon even specifically mentioned Erasmus' view of justification as something of which to be especially dubious. MBW 1.807. T 3.807 (esp. lines 28–39). CR 1.1082–4 Nr. 624. MSA 7/2 92–8 Nr. 133. This hardly suggested theological agreement!

Luther was under the imperial ban,[4] it often fell to Melanchthon to travel and officially represent the Lutheran position, resulting in a number of public documents from his pen.

By examining Melanchthon's works during this significant period in the history of the Reformation, the continued slow, structural evolution of his theology will come to light. In 1529, Melanchthon wrote a new commentary on Romans, attended the Second Diet of Speyer, penned the *Schwabach Articles*, and was present at the Marburg Colloquy. In 1530, Melanchthon attended the Diet of Augsburg, and authored the *Augsburg Confession*. Finally, in 1531, Melanchthon defended that theology in the weighty *Apology to the Augsburg Confession*.

ROMANS: SPRING 1529

With the Anabaptists on one side and the Catholics on the other, the Wittenberg Lutherans began to be pressed. Roman Catholics thought the Reformation had gone too far. Anabaptists protested that it had not gone far enough. Politically and theologically, the position of Luther and Melanchthon came under renewed attack. Perhaps in reaction to this pressure, Melanchthon moved from commenting on Colossians to a commentary on Romans, which he took to be the key to understanding all of Scripture.[5]

Melanchthon wrote the *Dispositio orationis in Epistola Pauli ad Romanos* in 1529. It first appeared during the Second Diet of Speyer (1529), and was published in its final form in 1530. Melanchthon drew heavily on this document during the composition of the *Augsburg Confession* in that same year.

In the *Dispositio*, the evolving shape of Melanchthon's theology continued to emerge. With Luther, Melanchthon affirmed that the doctrine of justification by faith alone lay not only at the centre of Romans, but at the heart of the entire Church. It was the chief doctrine of Christianity (*caput et summa est universae doctrinae Christianae*).[6] Further, Melanchthon began to use forensic language to describe justification. Contrary to human notions of works-righteousness,

---

[4] Luther and his teaching had been condemned by Charles V at the Diet of Worms in 1521. Luther was now subject to arrest if he travelled abroad, although the Elector of Saxony protected him so long as he remained within his own domains.

[5] Melanchthon (in Speyer), letter to Count Hermann von Neuenahr (in Speyer), March/April 1529. MBW 1.767. T 3.767. CR 1.1043–5 Nr. 594. This letter also served as the foreword to the *Dispositio orationis in epistola Pauli ad Romanos*. CR 15.443–92.

[6] CR 15.445. Also, 'Tota doctrina Christiana versatur circa hunc locum, quomodo coram Deo iustificemur, seu quid sit iusticia Christiana. Haec definitio caput et summa est universae

God reputed people to be just on account of Christ.[7] The use of forensic language indicated Melanchthon's continuing desire to express his theology as clearly and succinctly as possible. With his humanist background, he sought elegance and clarity of expression. This also applied to the dichotomy between spiritual righteousness and civil righteousness.

Based on the idea of freedom in the temporal realm and bondage in the spiritual realm, Melanchthon taught that while civil (or temporal) righteousness was possible, spiritual righteousness was not. He had not yet coined a short phrase to describe this dichotomy, but had instead described it at length in each of his most important writings of the late 1520s. But here, in the very first sentence of the commentary on Romans, Melanchthon coined a new term for it: twofold righteousness (*duplex iustitia*). He wrote that in all of Scripture, it came through quite strongly that righteousness was double.[8]

Melanchthon next used this paradigm of a twofold righteousness as a means of denying the freedom of the will in justification in opposition to Erasmus. As Wengert notes, 'By 1529 a yawning gulf had opened between Erasmus and Melanchthon on the question of free will.'[9] On 24 July of that year, Melanchthon wrote to Camerarius, 'Where in all of [Erasmus'] books is there one word worthy of a Christian concerning justification . . . ? I require a proper treatment of [this matter] from great men.'[10] This separation between Melanchthon and Erasmus was further evidenced in the *Dispositio* in chapter 8. Here Melanchthon argued that the whole chapter had been contaminated in the recent literature by Origen (one of Erasmus' favourite theologians[11]) and others (meaning Erasmus) who defended his philosophy. Cuttingly, the

---

doctrinae Christianae, quare hanc definitionem patefaciendam et illustrandam suscepit. Haec satis sit hoc loco de consilio Pauli, et de argumento Epistolae dixisse.' CR 15.445.

[7] 'Iusticia Dei est credere, quod propter Christum recipiamur in gratiam patris, sine nostris meritis, etc. Vocat autem sua phrasi iusticiam Dei hanc, qua *Deus reputat nos iustos, seu qua nos sumus iusti coram Deo,* opponitur enim carnali seu humanae iusticiae, quae sic appellatur ab efficiente causa, qua caro se iustificat, aut iustam efficit' (emphasis added). CR 15.445.

[8] 'Valde prodest in universae scripturae lectione observare, quod duplex sit iustitia.' CR 15.443. *Duplex iustitia* was an interesting phrase to use, for over the next decade and a half, Martin Bucer and the Catholic theologians John Gropper and Cardinal Gasparo Contarini would use the same phrase. Together with them, Melanchthon had a hand in crafting Article V on justification of the Regensburg Colloquy (1541) which embraced *duplex iustitia*, though with a different understanding of the term from that Melanchthon here employed in 1529.

[9] Wengert, *Human Freedom,* 141.

[10] 'Quae litera in illis libris est digna viro christiano de iustificatione, de iure magistratum? Horum locorum perfectam tractationem a magnis viris requiro.' MSA 7/2.95 Nr. 113. CR 1.1084 Nr. 624. MBW 1.807. T 3.807.36–9. See Estes, *Peace, Order, and the Glory of God,* 56.

[11] Boyle, *Erasmus on Language and Method in Theology,* 24. 'Origenis operum bonam partem euolui; quo praeceptore mihi videor non nullum fecisse operaeprecium. Aperit enim quasi fontes quosdam et rationes indicat artis theologicae.' Erasmus, letter to John Colet, EE I.405 (No. 181.38–41).

word 'defend' was rendered in the Greek as ὑπερασπίζουσι, a clear swipe at Erasmus' *Hyperaspistes*. These philosophers (not theologians!), maintained Melanchthon, wrongly attributed justification to human reason and civil works.[12] Melanchthon stated his opposition to the doctrine of free will in justification, a doctrine only supported by philosophers (like Erasmus) who intruded human reason and philosophical metaphysics into the divine doctrine of justification.

A couple of years earlier, in his writings on Colossians and in the *Visitation Articles*, Melanchthon had both denied the total rule of God in relation to determinism on the one hand, and remained quiet on predestination on the other. In the *Dispositio*, he continued to remain silent on these topics. However, in chapter 9 of Romans, Melanchthon ran into the problem that Paul himself explicitly discussed predestination. Melanchthon, despite his reservations about the doctrine, sought to explain the text and used Romans 9 as a *locus* in which to mention election. Melanchthon posed the question of why God chose some for salvation and not others. He argued that the children of God were chosen by election, not by nature or merit.[13] God's choice of some was mercy, not debt.[14] Why God chose some but not others belonged to the will of God, and humans were not to debate with God or accuse him.

It was a measure of Melanchthon's integrity that, although he evidently felt uncomfortable with the doctrine of election because of its non-inclusion in his other theological writings of the mid- to late 1520s, he did not try to explain away the clear meaning of the text in Romans 9. On the other hand, he did not elaborate upon it either. His 'explanation' of the text provided little more than a rephrasing of the words of Paul. For the verses dealing with predestination, Melanchthon slipped from commentary to summary. Also, he resisted making any inferences about reprobation at verse 9.22 as well as in the rest of the section. Melanchthon carefully used the language of the election of some but not others (*cur eligit Deos alios, alios non eligit*)[15] throughout this section.[16]

---

[12] 'Nam hoc totum caput Pauli sceleste contaminatum est ab Origene et aliis, cui tanquam iurati in verba Origenis ὑπερασπίζουσι τῆς φιλοσοφίας: sed horum intempestiva philosophia, dum tribuunt iustificationem viribus rationis, inde oritur, quod nihil requiri putant in homine, nisi civilia opera.' CR 15.468.

[13] '[Conclusio] est autem haec sententia propositionis: Filii Dei fiunt electione, non natura, aut mieritis nostris.' CR 15.473.

[14] '[E]ligere est misericordiae, non est debitum.' CR 15.474.

[15] CR 15.472.

[16] Later generations of theologians would use the label 'single predestination' for this formulation, but it might be anachronistic to do so here.

When Melanchthon summarized the main points of Romans 9, election only came into the picture obliquely. First, humans did not save themselves by their own merit, but were saved by God. Second, God only saved humans through his pure mercy. Third, no one was to debate with God as to why not everyone was saved, but rather to focus instead on the universal promises of Christ.[17] The first point warned against works righteousness and instead insisted on salvation by grace through faith. The second point illustrated the fact that humans could not change their own hearts. The third point advised focusing on the personal reception of the Gospel (the universal promises of Christ through faith), keeping silent on the subject of predestination. Melanchthon was more than happy to keep such silence. This summary of Romans 9, therefore, left intact Melanchthon's system of a twofold righteousness. It also left hanging a conceptual loose end. If Melanchthon insisted on using the language of God choosing some but not others, that meant that he was unwilling to make God responsible for choosing the lost to be destroyed, as would be the case in the fuller doctrine of God choosing some for life and *also choosing some for death*.[18] If God was not responsible for the damned, then who was?

THE SECOND DIET OF SPEYER: APRIL 1529

As Melanchthon's commentary on Romans first went to press, the Second Diet of Speyer opened in April of 1529. The first Diet of Speyer, in 1526, had ended with a somewhat ambiguous pronouncement requiring the German princes to promise to carry out the Edict of Worms (which banned Lutheran theology) according to their own consciences. Effectively, this meant that princes who supported Luther merely declined to enforce the Edict of Worms. In this second diet at Speyer, Charles V sought to make a stronger statement.

The purpose of the Second Diet of Speyer was both political and theological. Several Catholic bishops, the non-Catholic princes (including those of lower Germany, upper Germany, and the Swiss city-states), and the Lutheran theologians (including Melanchthon, though not Luther) all attended. As the diet began, Melanchthon was not at all happy with how things were shaping up. Melanchthon observed that the bishops attended in large numbers and were openly hostile to the Reformation (as was Charles V, who breathed out

---

[17] CR 15.475–6.

[18] Again, later generations of theologians might term this idea 'double predestination', but it would no doubt be anachronistic to employ it here.

threats against the Lutherans and the invading Turks in equal measure).[19] Melanchthon's fears were justified when the diet decreed that the traditional religion was to be restored, non-Catholic teaching on the sacraments was to be suppressed, and all the Anabaptists were to be outlawed. The Edict of Worms, which condemned Luther and his teaching, was to be enforced. The Lutheran princes swiftly lodged their famous formal Protest (from which came the title 'Protestant'), arguing that in matters of God's honour and one's salvation, every man had to stand before God and give an account of himself. Melanchthon rued this development, writing to Camerarius how terrible it was to now have two sharply defined parties in the empire.[20] At this point, the Protestant princes began to talk about a military self-defence league united around a common confession of faith. Protestant theology would certainly require further defence, and Melanchthon would be one of the principal authors of the forthcoming documents. These writings would further illustrate Melanchthon's slowly evolving theology, beginning with the *Schwabach Articles* a few months later.

THE SCHWABACH ARTICLES: SEPTEMBER 1529

Following Speyer, the Protestant princes felt very much inclined to form a military league for mutual protection against the Catholic princes as well as the emperor. Landgrave Philip of Hesse, in concert with the government of elector-al Saxony and several south German cities (especially Ulm, Strassburg, and Nuremberg), began to organize that alliance. Margrave Georg of Brandenburg-Ansbach-Kulnbach, along with Elector John of Saxony, stressed that such a league would be most firmly established if it were based on doctrinal agree-ment.[21] In fact, Luther and Melanchthon opposed any military league that was *not* founded on a common confession of faith.

In order to craft a common confessional standard, Elector John ordered the Wittenberg theologians to meet in Torgau in mid-September 1529. They drafted seventeen articles at that meeting. These articles were approved by Schleiz, Saxony, and Brandenburg-Ansbach in the first week of October. Finally, on 16 October, the articles were approved in Schwabach by represen-tatives from Nuremberg, and so came to be called the *Schwabach Articles*.

---

[19] Melanchthon (in Speyer), letter to Camerarius (in Nürnburg), 15 March 1529. MBW 1.760. T 3.760. CR 1.1039–40 Nr. 589.

[20] Melanchthon (in Speyer), letter to Camerarius (in Nuremberg), 20 April 1529. MBW 1.772. T 3.772. CR 1.1059 Nr. 602.

[21] See Krodel's historical summary in LW 49.237 n. 14.

Melanchthon worked with Luther and other colleagues on the *Schwabach Articles*. They were not his exclusive work, yet they also did not represent doctrines to which he was *opposed*. Due to the cooperative nature of this venture, one cannot read the *Schwabach Articles* as a definitive and personal expression of Melanchthon's theological views. However, his agreement with the articles and his role in helping draft them makes them useful to consult for the present study in the evolution of his views on free will. Moreover, because Melanchthon took these articles into account as he drafted the *Augsburg Confession*, they are worthy of attention.

The *Schwabach Articles*[22] were based on Luther's confession of faith of 1528.[23] Luther wrote this confession because he feared that he might die soon, and that once he had died, the Anabaptists would completely distort his writings to try to support their positions. Luther found this idea intolerable, so in the third part of his *Vom Abendmahl Christi: Bekenntnis* (1528), he systematically set forth his beliefs.[24] One of those beliefs included a vigorous denial of human free will as a means of achieving righteousness.

Of the seventeen *Schwabach Articles*, though, the authors put forward no special article devoted to free will.[25] Nor did they explicitly discuss original sin. For Melanchthon, the most important doctrine was justification; while for Luther, free will was most important *precisely because* of its intrinsic link with justification. The doctrine of the will did not receive heavy emphasis in the *Schwabach Articles*, but it could still be found in Articles V and VI, concerning justification and the nature of faith. On justification, the Wittenberg theologians wrote that it was impossible for people, out of their own powers or through good works, to become righteous and pure.[26] Regarding the nature of faith, the authors argued that holy faith was not a human work, nor was it possible out of human powers, but that it was a work of God who gave the Holy Spirit through Christ.[27]

---

[22] *Articuli XVII Suobacenses. Artickel vom Churchfürst von Sachssen des glawuns halb.* WA 30/3.81–91 (here titled more simply as *Schwabacher Artikel*). CR 26.151–60. WA 30/3.81–91. The *Schwabach Articles* may also be found in English translation, in William R. Russel, trans. 'The Schwabach Articles', in Robert Kolb and James A. Nestingen, eds., *Sources and Contexts of the Book of Concord* (Minneapolis: Fortress Press, 2001), 83–7.

[23] Maurer, *Historical Commentary*, 23.

[24] LW 37.360–72. WA 26.499–509.

[25] See Maurer's discussion in *Historical Commentary*, 23–6.

[26] Art. V. '... ists unmuglich, das sich ein Mensch aus seinen crefften oder durch seine gute werck heraus würcke, damit er wider gerecht und frumm werde.' WA 30/3.87.34–88.1. CR 26.154. Trans. Russell, 85.

[27] Art. VI. 'Das solicher glaub nit sei ein menschlich werck noch aus unsern krefften muglich, Sonder es ist ain gotts werck und gabe, die der heilig gaist durch Christum gegeben.' WA 30/3.88.15–17. CR 26.155. Trans. Russell, 85.

Electoral Saxony and Brandenburg-Ansbach came to a full agreement on the *Schwabach Articles*, but the more Zwinglian south German cities rejected them. Consequently the *Schwabach Articles* failed to serve as the basis for a Protestant league, though they did form a firm foundation for the later drafting of the *Augsburg Confession*. Yet before Augsburg, another meeting with the Zwinglians would produce a new set of articles, written this time in the town of Marburg.

THE MARBURG ARTICLES: OCTOBER 1529

After the failure of the *Schwabach Articles* to serve as the basis for a Protestant league, Philip of Hesse was not ready to give up.[28] Young, militant, and politically resourceful (some might say dangerously so, in relation to the Pack Affair of 1528), Philip sought one more time to gather a Protestant doctrinal agreement for the purpose of unifying a military alliance. With the knowledge that the Zwinglian Swiss and south German cities were the main stumbling-block to Protestant unity, Philip of Hesse conspired to bring their main theologians together with the Wittenbergers. However, at this time Luther was embittered toward the Zwinglians over the subject of the Lord's Supper. Melanchthon expressed every bit as much passion about the Zwinglians as Luther, as was evident from the young professor's correspondence in June and July 1529 (nearly every letter contained warnings and condemnations in relation to Zwinglian theology). Undeterred, Philip of Hesse pressed the issue, telling Luther and Melanchthon that only Oecolampadius, Melanchthon's old friend, would be there. Melanchthon and Luther believed the young prince, and reluctantly agreed to attend,[29] only to be surprised to find Zwingli present as well.[30] Nevertheless, they sat down to the task of seeking evangelical unity, with the primary sticking-point being the Lord's Supper.

The *Marburg Articles*[31] closely followed the *Schwabach Articles*. Luther authored the document, but Melanchthon was no doubt influential in its

---

[28] For another introduction to the *Marburg Articles*, see Kolb and Nestingen, eds., p. 88.

[29] For evidence that Philip of Hesse only mentioned Oecolampadius, see Melanchthon's letter to the prince on 22 June 1529. MBW 1.802. T 3.802. CR 1.1077 Nr. 619. MSA 7/2.87–9 Nr. 131a. See also Luther and Melanchthon's joint letter to him on 8 July. MBW 1.806. T 3.806. CR 1.1080 Nr. 621.

[30] In addition to Luther, Melanchthon, Zwingli, and Oecolampadius, those present included Jonas, Osiander, Stephen Agricola, Brenz, Bucer, and Hedio.

[31] *Articuli XV Marpurgenses*. WA 30/3.160–71 (there titled, *Die Marburger Artikel*). CR 26.121–8. For an English translation, see Russell, trans. (in Kolb and Nestingen), 88–92.

formulation. But seeing that Philipp was a signatory to the completed work, and because he later utilized this document as a source in the composition of the *Augsburg Confession*, it is worth consideration.

Fourteen of the seventeen articles from Schwabach found their way into the *Marburg Articles*. Again, the colloquy put forth no specific article on free will, though the same phrases used in the *Schwabach Articles* relating to justification and faith reappeared here. Article VI, on conversion, asserted that faith was a gift of the Holy Spirit, given through the hearing of the Scriptures.[32] This document retained the same low profile for the doctrine of free will as appeared in the *Schwabach Articles*. The denial of free will implicit in both the *Schwabach Articles* and the *Marburg Articles* was fully compatible with Melanchthon's divided rule of God between temporal and spiritual realms, because in the spiritual realm the sinful nature still fatally impaired the free operation of the human will. But, the truly telling sign was the absence in both of these documents of any mention at all of predestination, the question left hanging at the end of Melanchthon's commentary on Romans 9 earlier in the year. Meanwhile, another imperial diet loomed.

THE DIET OF AUGSBURG: MAY–AUGUST 1530

Convening the Diet

During the middle 1520s, Emperor Charles V of the Holy Roman Empire was in no position to give his full attention to the domestic matters of religious controversies within his domains. Instead, he was forced to deal with a number of extremely pressing matters of state: war with the papal states, war with France, and a desperate endeavour to stave off the persistent Muslim invasions of the Ottoman Turks. The Ottomans besieged Vienna, and if they had taken that city, the German heartland would have lain open before them. In the summer of 1529, things began to go the emperor's way. The emperor and Pope Clement VII came to a peace agreement in the Treaty of Barcelona. On 5 August, the emperor concluded the Treaty of Cambrai with King Francis I of France. Even better, by mid-October, the West saw some success against the Muslim armies when the Turks were forced to give up their siege of Vienna

---

[32] Art. VI. 'Zum Sechsten, das solcher glaube, sei ein gabe gottes, den wir, mit keinen vorgehenden Wercken oder verdienst erwerben, noch aus eigener Craft machen konnen, Sondern der heillig gaist gibt und schaft, wo er wil, denselbigen jn unsere hertzen, wen wir das Euangelion oder wort Christi horen.' WA 30/3.163.7–10. CR 26.124. Trans. Russell, 89.

and withdraw to Hungary. With these foreign matters now improving, Charles had the opportunity to turn his attention to putting to rest the religious controversies that were causing such trouble in his empire. In so doing, he hoped to unite Europe (in order to pursue the ongoing conflict against the Turks) and to consolidate his power in Germany (at the cost of the independent territorial princes). Beyond geo-political concerns, Charles also held a genuine personal interest in the life of the church; he wanted to further real moral and institutional reform, and he thoroughly despised Luther's doctrinal reformation—and therefore wanted to put an end to it.

At Augsburg on 11 March 1530, Emperor Charles V called for an imperial diet to meet, in which he demanded an explanation as to why the princes allied with Luther were failing to enforce the Edict of Worms of 1521. This meeting represented the closest Charles would come to trying to call a church council on his own authority. The Protestants welcomed the opportunity to discuss their faith and doctrine, but their hope for reconciliation would come to naught, for Charles's 'intention had been clear at least since the Barcelona treaty, and this intention was to lead the Protestants back into obedience to the Roman church by all means possible, perhaps by some concessions in matters of ecclesiastical practice, or by force if necessary'.[33] By setting the Protestants in line, Charles could satisfy the dictates of his own Catholic faith, honour his geo-political commitments to regional Catholic political powers, and create a pan-European unity to face the invading Turkish armies. While the Protestants would get a chance to articulate their faith, there was little chance of that faith being accepted by the emperor, let alone the Catholic theologians who were already well dug-in in their hostility to the Reformation.

Nevertheless, following the failure to reach Protestant concord with the *Schwabach Articles* and *Marburg Articles*, and in light of the forthcoming diet, Elector John of Saxony decided to have one more try at drafting a unifying set of doctrine. He ordered Luther, Melanchthon, Bugenhagen, and Jonas to Torgau.[34] There the four did produce a few fragmentary articles denouncing church abuses,[35] but they had little to say touching on the doctrine of the will, except for a routine denunciation of works-righteousness.[36] These were

[33] Krodel, LW 49.281 n. 5.

[34] Elector John of Saxony (in Torgau), letter to Luther, Jonas, Bugenhagen, and Melanchthon (in Wittenberg), 21 March 1530. MBW 1.879. T 4/1.879. CR 2.33 Nr. 675.

[35] *Articuli Torgavienses.* CR 26.171–200. See also Melanchthon's report to Elector John on the outcome of the work at Torgau, MBW 1.883. T 4/1.883 (this letter is of significant length, at 400 lines long in the *Texte*). CR 4.985–99 Nr. 678a. CR 26.171–82.

[36] *Articuli Torgavienses (B).* CR 26.182–5. What we call 'the Torgau Articles' were, in all likelihood, merely the drafts and notes these men put together in preparation for Augsburg. A certain measure of scholarly uncertainty still swirls around them today. See the introduction in Kolb and Nestingen, p. 93.

mostly rough drafts. Meanwhile, in Innsbruck in early May 1530, Hans von Dolzig submitted the *Visitation Articles* and the *Schwabach Articles* to the emperor, who reluctantly received them.

As the date for the diet approached, Elector John refused to allow Luther to travel to Augsburg out of fear that it would be too dangerous for him to be there. Instead, he had Luther stay in the castle of Coburg. It then fell to Melanchthon to be the leader of the Lutheran delegation at Augsburg, and as a primary author of the previous sets of Lutheran articles at Schwabach and Marburg, it was only natural that he should take the lead as the author of the *Augsburg Confession*. While others collaborated with Melanchthon, the *Augsburg Confession* was definitely his work.[37] Further, he used his own theological formulations without feeling compelled to adhere exactly to Luther's manner of teaching.[38] This was especially true of Article XVIII on free will.

Melanchthon viewed the entire endeavour at Augsburg as an attempt at peace, for he feared that if no reconciliation could take place at Augsburg, then the military leagues beginning to form on both sides would inevitably come to war. At this point, Erasmus of Rotterdam felt the same way, and out of the interests of seeking political peace in Europe, he wrote to Melanchthon. While Melanchthon and Erasmus did renew a generally friendly correspondence, this did not in any way indicate theological rapprochement on the doctrine of the will, or indeed on any other theological doctrine on which the two differed. Instead, their communications stuck rigidly to the issues surrounding the establishment of peace in Europe. Although the two maintained their theological differences, in the pursuit of peace they were of one heart.[39] Melanchthon sought such peace with all of his being, but he also sought accurately and completely to set forth the Gospel as he understood it.

---

[37] Stupperich contends that out of concern for Protestant unity, Melanchthon did not present his own opinions in the *Confessio Augustana. Melanchthon*, 85. However, while Melanchthon might have used diplomatic language, he never would have 'confessed' to doctrines he believed were in error.

[38] Stupperich agrees with this point (*Melanchthon*, 85). MacCulloch, however, notes that Melanchthon used the fourteen articles of Marburg as the foundation for this confession. *The Reformation*, 169.

[39] See Melanchthon and Erasmus' correspondence of July and August 1530. Erasmus (in Freiburg), letter to Melanchthon (in Augsburg), 7 July 1530. MBW 1.956. T 4/1.956. EE 8.2343. Melanchthon (in Augsburg), letter to Erasmus (in Freiburg), 1 August 1530. MBW 1.1004. T 4/2.1004. CR 2.232–3 Nr. 807. MSA 7/2.243–5 Nr. 198. Erasmus (in Freiburg), letter to Melanchthon (in Augsburg), 2 August 1530. MBW 1.1007. T 4/2.1007. CR 2.244–5 Nr. 817. Erasmus (in Freiburg), letter to Melanchthon (in Augsburg), 12 August 1530. MBW 1.1019. T 4/2.1019. CR 2.268 Nr. 834. Erasmus (in Freiburg), letter to Melanchthon (in Augsburg), 17 August 1530. MBW 1.1028. T 4/2.1028. CR 2.288–9 Nr. 847. See also Melanchthon's letter to Luther (in the Coburg) on 27 July. MBW 1.991. T 4/1.991. CR 2.229–30 Nr. 804. WABr 5.507–9 Nr. 1663. MSA 7/2.229–33 Nr. 190.

John Eck's *Four Hundred Four Articles*: May 1530

Melanchthon and Justas Jonas accompanied Elector John to Augsburg. On the way there, Melanchthon was probably already at work drafting a written defence of the evangelical theology. Then, a mere two days after the arrival of Elector John's delegation, John Eck's *Four Hundred Four Articles for the Imperial Diet at Augsburg* appeared.[40] Eck was one of the brightest and most capable of Roman Catholic theologians in Germany at the time. A professor from Ingolstadt, Eck had, in 1519, made Luther admit that he sided with John Huss. Now, in 1530, Eck's *Four Hundred Four Articles* was an assault on everything he considered to be heresy. Eck covered much more than the Wittenberg theologians, seeing fit to attack various Anabaptist doctrines as well. This broadside doctrinal attack upped the ante for the Diet of Augsburg. Now, instead of defending a limited number of issues of reform, the Protestants would have to defend the catholicity and orthodoxy of their entire doctrinal system. Eck's work made the impending Protestant *Augsburg Confession* all the more important.

Regarding the will's role in justification, Eck cited as heresy Melanchthon's teachings from his *Loci* of 1521. In Eck's words, Melanchthon's heresy was: '171 [172]: All things happen according to divine predestination. Thus our will has no freedom. For according to his predestination, all things happen to all creatures by necessity. Melanchthon.'[41] Eck also attacked as heretical Luther's words from his *Assertio* of 1520: '331 [332]: This term "free will" came from Satan's teaching for seducing people away from God's way. In fact, this is a mere fantasy because the will contributes nothing toward its willing, and it is wrong [to say] that it is active in good works. Luther. Carlstadt. Rhegius.'[42] These critiques guaranteed that the issues of the will and predestination would be addressed in the *Augsburg Confession*.

---

[40] Joannes, Eck, *Sub Domini Ihesu et Mariae Patrocinio. Articulos 404 partim ad disputationes Lipsicam, Baden, & Bernen attinentes, partim vero ex scriptis pacem ecclesiae perturbantium extractos, Coram divo Caesare Carolo V. Ro. Imp. semp Augu. etc. ac proceribus Imperii, Ioan Eckius minimus ecclesiae minister, offert se disputurum, ut in scheda latius explicatur Augustae Vindelicorum* (Ingolstadt, 1530). The *Four Hundred Four Articles* can be found in English translation in "John Eck's Four Hundred Four Articles for the Imperial Diet at Augsburg", trans. Robert Rosin, in eds. Robert Kolb and James A. Nestingen, *Sources and Contexts of the Book of Concord* (Minneapolis: Fortress Press, 2001), 31–82.

[41] Eck, trans. Rosin, 53. Eck was referring to Loci 24: CR 21.87–8.

[42] Eck, trans. Rosin, 73. Eck was referring to Luther's *Assertio*, Article 36: WA 7.145.

The Augsburg Confession: 25 June 1530

Within the *Augsburg Confession*,[43] Melanchthon's view of the divided govern-ance of God in the dual realms, which had evolved over the course of the late 1520s, began to prove less stable than he might have hoped. The question of the absolute determinism of God (in matters both temporal and spiritual) was not addressed within the confession. It was no longer an issue for him. But, in order to stress the Protestant position that justification took place by grace alone through faith alone, accomplished through God's instigation and the conversion of bound wills, Melanchthon found himself forced to explore something of the rule of God in the spiritual realm. In framing articles and arguments around God's rule in the spiritual realm, Melanchthon continued to assert the bound will, but cracks began to appear in his argument. Although he did his best to avoid discussing predestination (as he had successfully done throughout most of the 1520s), he found it necessary to mention it in an at least oblique fashion. In thus alluding to predestination, Melanchthon began to pick his words with extreme care, like a man treading on a floating log ever afraid that his footing was about to spin out from under him.[44] Melanchthon restricted himself to the vocabulary of God's election of some but not others, thereby weakening his position on the complete rule of God in the spiritual

---

[43] *Confessio Augustana.* BSLK 33–137 (this has the German and Latin in parallel columns). Another source for the Latin text is CR 26.263–336. In German, the title is *Confessio odder Bekanntnus des Glaubens etlicher Fürsten und Stedte: Uberantwort Keiserlicher Maiestat zu Augspurg*, and it can be found (in addition to BSLK) in CR 26.537–688. In modern English translation, see BoC 27–105 (Tapp. 23–96). See also TRE 4.616–28.

[44] Melanchthon evidently succeeded in his balancing act, for Luther read and heartily approved the *Confessio Augustana*. On 15 May he wrote to the Elector John, 'I have read through Master Philipp's *Apologia* [that is, the *Augsburg Confession*], which pleases me very much; I know nothing to improve or change it, nor would this be appropriate, since I cannot step so softly and quietly. May Christ, our Lord, help [this *Apologia*] to bear much and great fruit, as we hope and pray. Amen.' LW 49.297–8. (The editors of LW, on p. 297, n. 12, make it clear that Luther is referring to the draft of the *Augsburg Confession*, and not the later *Apology to the Augsburg Confession*). 'Ich hab M. Philipsen Apologia vberlesen, die gefellet mir fast wol, vnd weis nichts dran zu bessern noch endern, Wurde sich auch nicht schicken, Denn ich so sansst vnd leise nicht tretten kan. Christus unser herr helffe, das sie viel vnd grosse frucht schaffe, wie wir hoffen vnd bitten, Amen.' WABr 5.319.5–9. While some scholars have viewed Luther's *leise treten* comment as a criticism of Melanchthon, it is more likely just an observation on the differences in tone and style between Luther and Melanchthon. (Other contemporaries accused Melanchthon of writing too strongly and sharply. See Melanchthon's June 26 letter to Camera-rius. MBW 1.939. T 4/1.939. CR 2.140. MSA 7/2.188–9.) Luther gave his approval of the theology of the *Confessio Augustana* when he wrote to Melanchthon on 3 July, 'Yesterday I carefully reread your whole *Apologia*, and I am tremendously pleased with it.' LW 49.343. 'Relegi heri tuam Apologiam diligenter totam, et placent vehementer.' WABr 5.435.4–5. For even stronger praise (i.e. elevating the *Confessio Augustana* above Augustine and all the doctors of the church, for instance), see *Tischrede*, LW 54.34. 'Apologia Philippi praestat omnibus doctoribus ecclesiae, etiam ipso Augustino.' WATr 1.106.6–7 Nr. 252.

realm, and putting pressure on his bifurcated doctrine of God's governance, moving toward a uniform *limited* governance of God in *both* the temporal and spiritual realms.

Doctrines Related to Free Will

On issues related to free will and the rule of God, Melanchthon discussed original sin, the cause of sin, forensic justification, and the nature and place of good works within Christian theology. Article II asserted original sin, and condemned the Pelagians (*damnant Pelagianos*).[45] In Article XIX, he traced the cause of sin to the will to evil of the devil and the impious.[46] Melanchthon argued that although God created and sustained nature, he was not responsible for evil. This was the same argument he put forth in his Colossians writings of the late 1520s. Article IV dealt with justification, and forcefully maintained that humans did not have the power to justify themselves in the face of God (*homines non possint iustificari coram Deo proprijs viribus*). Instead, justification happened by Christ, through faith and grace. God imputed this faith as righteousness in his sight (*Hanc fidem imputat Deus pro iustitia coram ipso*).[47] Further, as Melanchthon taught in Article VI, good works did not justify before God (*coram Deo*), but arose out of faith, for believers would, *after* justification, seek to live in accordance with God's will.[48] Articles VII to XVI covered the church, sacraments, and the validity of the civil authorities. Article XVII discussed eschatology, and within this article Melanchthon made reference to predestination—a rare reference indeed.

The Last Day, and Predestination

Article XVII stated, 'that Christ will appear at the end of the world to judge, and the dead shall rise, the pious and elect will be given eternal life and perpetual joy, but the impious people and the devil will be condemned to be tortured eternally'.[49] The apposition of the 'pious and elect' who were saved with the 'impious and the devil' who were condemned was significant. Those who were saved were elect, while those who were condemned were impious.

---

[45] CA II. BSLK 53.3. CR 26.273–4.

[46] CA XIX. BSLK 75.1–11. CR 26.284, 573.

[47] CA IV. BSLK 56.9–10. CR 26.275.

[48] CA VI. BSLK 60. CR 26.276. See also Article XX, BSLK 75f. CR 26.283–4.

[49] 'Item docent, quod Christus apparebit in consummatione mundi ad iudicandum, et mortuos omnes resuscitabit; piis et electis dabit vitam aeternam et perpetua gaudia; impios autem homines ac diabolos condemnabit, ut sine fine crucientur.' CA XVII. BSLK 72.3–9. CR 26.282.

The apposition of dual nouns made for nice rhetorical symmetry—pious and elect versus impious and the devil—but a corresponding conceptual symmetry was absent. The first two adjectival nouns both applied to humans. Those who were saved were both pious and elect. The second two nouns, however, represented two different subjects, rather than being two adjectival nouns describing a single thing. Here, Melanchthon did not refer to two qualities of those who were lost, as he did for those who were saved. One would have expected him to say something like 'the impious and *the reprobate*'. Instead, he left out the idea of those predestined to damnation by God, and he filled in the gap by adding the condemnation of the devil with the impious. The elect were to receive eternal life, but the impious would get eternal punishment. Melanchthon attributed God's causation to those who were saved, but not to those who were condemned.

Melanchthon's choice of words was not accidental. Being a master grammarian, linguist, dialectician, and rhetorician, it was unlikely that his words were unexamined, or written in haste. The German version of the *Augsburg Confession* reflected the same formula of the elect being saved, while the impious, or godless, were condemned.[50] The only alternative text that could possibly be construed in terms of active reprobation was a German translation of a preliminary stage of the *Augsburg Confession*, sent to Nuremberg on 3 June 1530.[51] In this translation from an early Latin version of the text, the translator (somebody other than Melanchthon) wrote, 'the chosen [receive] eternal blessing, but the condemned people (*verdamten menschen*), together with the devil, will never become released from eternal torture'.[52] Even this phrasing was somewhat ambiguous, and easily conducive to Melanchthon's own clearer expression.

Apart from the phrasing of articles which appeared in the final form of the *Augsburg Confession*, the early German translation here and there revealed sections that made it into the *Confession* during the early stages of formulation, but which were later purged. One such section can be found in the early German translation of Article XVII. Here, apart from the different phrasing of the sentence we have just observed, one finds an explicit denunciation of

---

[50] 'Auch wird gelehret, daß unser Herr Jesus Christus am junsten Tag kummen wird, zu richten, und alle Toten auferwecken, den Glaubigen und Auserwählten ewigs Leben und ewige Freude geben, die gottlosen Menschen aber und die Teufel in die Helle und ewige Straf verdammen.' BSLK 72.1–9. CR 26.569.

[51] Theodore Kolde, ed., *Die älteste Redaktion der Augsburger Konfession mit Melanchthons Einleitung* (Gütersloh, 1906).

[52] 'darunter die auserwelten ewicklich selig, aber die verdamten menschen sambt den teufel aus hellischer pein nimer in ewickeit erlost werden.' Ed. Kolde, 15. (In this document, this is article XVI rather than XVII.)

Origen following the words about those saved and those condemned.[53]
Melanchthon, while affirming that God chose some but not others, sought
to affirm God's saving role for those who were saved over and against the
free-will position of Origen. Erasmus made a great deal of Origen and
actively endorsed his free-will position.[54] Hence, Melanchthon's condemnation of Origen was an implicit condemnation of Erasmus, and he thereby
reaffirmed his opposition to Erasmus on the question of the free will. The
foundations of Melanchthon's bound-will position may have been eroding
away, but he as yet maintained it in 1530. The condemnation of Origen did
not make it into the final draft of the *Augsburg Confession*, but Melanchthon's
thoughts were clear from the early German translation. The Origen section
disappeared, no doubt in the interests of sparing offence to the Catholics and
to Erasmus, who at this time was just renewing his correspondence with
Melanchthon. Nevertheless, Melanchthon's continued support of the bound
will was evident from the very next article, devoted entirely to the question of
the freedom of the will.

Free Will

The Latin text of Article XVIII on free will began with the assertion,
'Concerning free [choice (*de libero arbitrio*)], our churches teach that the
human will has some freedom (*humana voluntas habeat aliquam libertatem*)
for producing civil righteousness and for choosing things subject to reason.'[55]
Note that this was not merely the subjective perception of liberty, as Luther
asserted in *De servo arbitrio*, but rather *actual*, ontological liberty in the
temporal realm. One might object that Melanchthon used the subjunctive
mood of 'to have' (*habeat*), and hence a more accurate translation would read,
'the human will *may* have some freedom'. Such a rendering would allow
Luther to read his own meaning into the text while also allowing others to
read into the text their own views that free will in civil righteousness was
genuine. Whatever the case, the sense of the passage was to affirm free will in
the civil or temporal realm, and this was stated in the unflinching indicative
in the German version of the *Confession*: 'Concerning free will, it is taught that
a human being has some measure of free will (*der Mensch etlichermass ein
freien Willen hat*), so as to live an externally honourable life and to choose

---

[53] Ed. Kolde, 15.
[54] For example, see *De libero arbitrio*, LCC 17.65, EAS 4.98, where Erasmus cited Origen
approvingly. See also André Godin, *Érasme, lecteur d'Origéne* (Geneva: Droz, 1982).
[55] CA XVIII. The English translation is from BoC 51.1–2 (Tapp. 39.1). 'De libero arbitrio
docent, quod humana voluntas habeat aliquam libertatem ad efficiendam civilem iustitiam et
deligendas res rationi subiectas.' BSLK 73.2–5. CR 26.282–3.

among the things reason comprehends.'[56] Free will genuinely existed in the area of civil righteousness within the temporal realm even though it may have been hindered to some extent by sin and the devil.

According to Melanchthon's conception of the divided governance of God, the Lord's direction concerning temporal matters was self-limited, while his control over spiritual matters was absolute. As a result, civil freedom was balanced by spiritual helplessness, or bondage. Such was the case in the present article on free will, which turned immediately from speaking of external or civil freedom to pondering the righteousness of God. Melanchthon wrote, 'However, [the will] does not have the power to produce the righteousness of God or spiritual righteousness (*iustitiae spiritualis*) without the Holy Spirit because "those who are natural do not receive the gifts God's Holy Spirit" [1 Cor. 2.14)]. But this righteousness is worked in the heart when the Holy Spirit is received through the Word.'[57] Spiritually, the will was helpless.[58]

Melanchthon next supplied a quotation from Book III of (pseudo-) Augustine's *Hypognosticon* to support his position: 'Augustine says this in just so many words: "We confess that all human beings have [free choice] that possesses the judgment of reason. It does not enable them, without God, to begin—much less complete—anything that pertains to God, but only to perform the good or evil deeds of this life."'[59] A list then followed of both good and evil free external acts. Melanchthon here again affirmed his basic

---

[56] CA XVIII. BoC 50.1 (Tapp. 39.1). 'Vom freien Willen wird also gelehrt, daβ der Mensch etlichermaβ ein freien Willen hat, aüβerlich ehrbar zu leben und zu wählen unter denen Dingen, so die Vernunft begreift.' BSLK 73.2–5. CR 26.570.

[57] CA XVIII. BoC 51.2–3 (Tapp. 39.2). 'Sed non habet vim sine spiritu sancto efficiendae iustitiae Dei seu iustitiae spiritualis, quia animalis homo non percipit ea, quae sunt spiritus Dei; sed haec fit in cordibus, cum per verbum spiritus sanctus concipitur.' BSLK 73.5–11. CR 26.283.

[58] The German text said essentially the same thing, but substituted the phrase 'becoming pleasing to God' for 'the righteousness of God' and 'spiritual righteousness'. This sentence included such concepts as warmly fearing God, loving, and believing—all of which were impossible apart from the Holy Spirit. These were also the same concepts included in Melanchthon's affections argument of 1521 against free will. CA XVIII. 'Aber ohn Gnad, Hilfe und Wirkung des heiligen Geists vermag der Mensch nicht Gott gefällig zu werden, Gott hertzlich zu fürchten, oder zu glauben, oder die angeborene böse Lüste aus dem Hertzen zu werfen. Sondern solchs geschieht durch den heiligen Geist, welcher durch Gotts Wort geben wird. Dann Paulus spricht. 1. Korinth. 2.: "Der natürlich Mensch vernimmt nichts vom Geist Gottes."' BSLK 73.6–15. CR 26.570.

[59] CA XVIII. BoC 51.4 (Tapp. 39.4). 'Haec totidem verbis dicit Augustinus lib. III. Hypognosticon: "Esse fatemur liberum arbitrium omnibus hominibus, habens quidem iudicium rationis, non per quod sit idoneum in his, quae ad Deum pertinent, sine Deo aut inchoare aut certe peragere, sed tantum in operibus vitae praesentis tam bonis quam etiam malis."' BSLK 73.11–19. CR 26.283. The German text here reads, 'in *external* acts of this life': 'sonder allein in äuβerlichen Werken dieses Lebens' (underlining added). BSLK 74.5–6. CR 26.571. Apart from this extra word, the German text does not significantly vary from the Latin.

position of the limited rule of God in the temporal realm, in contrast with the determinism of God in the spiritual realm. People had free choice in external, civil matters; but not in internal, spiritual ones.

After condemning the Pelagians, Melanchthon summed up the whole article on free will in one sentence which vividly brought out the dichotomy between temporal freedom and spiritual bondage: 'Although nature can in some measure produce external works (*externa opera*)—for it can keep the hands from committing theft and murder—nevertheless it cannot produce internal movements (*interiores motus*), such as fear of God, trust in God, patience, etc.'[60]

The *Confutation of the Augsburg Confession*: 3 August 1530

After Melanchthon completed the *Augsburg Confession*, the Protestant princes submitted it to the emperor and it was read out on 25 June. Charles gave it to the Catholic theologians to study, and with Eck and Bishop Johannes Fabri of Vienna taking the lead,[61] they soon drafted a *Confutation* to refute the Protestant position. Eck's *Four Hundred Four Articles* naturally was an important source document in the process. Once the new document was completed, the imperial counsellors demanded that the Protestants submit to it without having heard it, and to promise not to make any public response to it. Unsurprisingly, the evangelicals declined.[62]

On 3 August, Alexander Schweiss, the imperial secretary, read out the German version of the *Confutation*.[63] The Roman Catholic theologians

---

[60] CA XVIII. BoC 53.9 (Tapp. 40.9). 'Quamquam enim externa opera aliquo modo efficere natura possit,—potest enim continere manus a furto, a caede—tamen interiores motus non potest efficere, ut timorem Dei, fiduciam erga Deum, patienciam etc.' BSLK 74, in the apparatus linked to line 11. CR 26.283. (This Latin text was added in the *editio princeps* in 1531.) Tappert translates *interiores motus* as 'inward affections', rather than 'internal movements'. The German text is not substantially different. CR 26.572. This is the same language that Melanchthon used in his affections argument of 1521 (*interiores motus*), but without the philosophical argumentation that accompanied such words at that time.

[61] Melanchthon (in Augsburg), letter to Friedrich Myconius (in Gotha), 8 August 1530. MBW 1.1018. T 4/2.1018. CR 2.260–1 Nr. 830. MSA 7/2.257–8 Nr. 205. Other notable theologians included Johannes Cochleaus, Konrad Wimpina, Johann Dietenberger, and Julius Pflug. The papal legate Cardinal Lorenzo Campeggio assisted the committee.

[62] See Robert Kolb and James A. Nestingen, 'The Confutation of the Augsburg Confession: Introduction', in *Sources and Contexts of the Book of Concord* (Minneapolis: Fortress Press, 2001), 105–6. See also TRE 4.628–32.

[63] The *Responsio Pontifica seu Confutatio Confessionis Augustanae* can be found in CR 27.82–183. To read it in English, see Mark D. Tranvik, trans., 'The Confutation of the Augsburg Confession', in Robert Kolb and James A. Nestingen, eds., *Sources and Contexts of the Book of Concord* (Minneapolis: Fortress Press, 2001), 106–39. See also Herbert Immenkötter, ed., *Die Confutatio der Confessio Augustana vom 3. August 1530* (Münster: Aschendorff, 1979).

sought to employ a moderate tone in this document, gladly highlighting articles of agreement with the Protestants, but also vigorously demarcating issues of divergence. (This document was actually the second edition of the *Confutation*—the first one had been much more hostile in its tone.) Significantly, in Article IV on justification, the Catholics opposed the Protestants by affirming a role for human merit in salvation: 'To reject human merit, which is acquired through the assistance of divine grace, is to agree with the Manicheans and not the catholic church.'[64] Further, 'All Catholics admit that our works of themselves have no merit but God's grace makes them worthy to earn eternal life.'[65] Building on this, in Article VI, the Catholic theologians continued, 'However, in the same article [the Protestants] attribute to justification by faith alone that which is wholly opposed to evangelical truth. The Gospel does not exclude good works.'[66] 'Thus, no matter how much a person believes, if that person does not do good works, then he or she is not a friend of God.'[67] Hence, 'Nor is their teaching on justification approved by Christ. . . . For faith and good works are gifts of God, to which eternal life is given through God's mercy.'[68]

All of this led to the Catholic *agreement* with what Melanchthon had written in Article XVIII on free will—albeit, with different assumptions in mind: 'In the eighteenth article, they confess that the free will has the power to effect civil righteousness but that it lacks the power, apart from the Holy Spirit, to produce the righteousness of God. This confession is received and approved.'[69] The Catholics agreed with Melanchthon and the Protestants on the human *external* freedom, or the freedom of civil righteousness in the temporal realm, and they further agreed that the exercise of such freedom could not lead to justification. One *needed* the grace of God in order to move toward salvation. For Melanchthon this 'grace' meant the *favour* of God, but for the Catholics it meant the *aid* of God. For the Protestants, God's favour

---

[64] Trans. Tranvik, 108. 'Nam si quis intenderet improbare merita hominum, quae per assistentiam gratiae divinae fiunt; plus assentiret Manichaeis, quam ecclesiae catholicae.' CR 27.93.

[65] Trans. Tranvik, 109. 'Attamen omnes catholici fatentur, opera nostra ex se nullius esse meriti; sed gratia Dei facit, illa digna esse vita aeterna.' CR 27.95.

[66] Trans. Tranvik, 109–10. 'Quod vero in eodem articulo iustificationem soli fidei tribuunt, ex diametro pugnat cum evangelica veritate, opera non excludente.' CR 27.99.

[67] Trans. Tranvik, 110. 'Unde, quantumcunque quis crediderit, si non operetur bonum, non est amicus Dei.' CR 27.100.

[68] Trans. Tranvik, 110. 'Neque suffragatur eis verbum Christi . . . Nam fides et bona opera sunt dona Dei, quibus per misericordiam Dei datur vita aeterna.' CR 27.101.

[69] Trans. Tranvik, 116. 'Articulo decimo octavo confitentur liberi arbitrii potestatem, quod habeat potestatem ad efficiendam civilem iustitiam, sed non habeat vim sine Spiritu sancto efficiendae iustitia Dei: quae confessio acceptatur et approbatur.' CR 27.118.

came in the choice of faith in Jesus, resulting in salvation via imputed righteousness. For the Catholics, God's *aid* came in his help to live a life of good works, which resulted in salvation via cooperatively-cultivated intrinsic righteousness. In sum, Melanchthon and the Catholics agreed that the human will was incapable of saving itself, and that it needed help from God. They just differed on what that help was. For Melanchthon, if you believed in Jesus, then his merit was yours, meaning you were saved. For the Catholics, if you believed in Jesus, then God would begin to strengthen you to do good works, and in doing them, he would add some of his merits to your own so that, in time, you could attain sufficient merit for your salvation. That is why the Catholic theologians concluded their discussion of Article XVIII by saying, 'On this issue Catholics pursue a middle way, siding neither with the Pelagians, who ascribe too much to free will, nor with the godless Manicheans, who take away all liberty. Both these groups are in error. As Augustine says: "We firmly teach and preach that there is a free will in human beings."'[70] These two views (the Protestant view of justification by faith alone, and the Catholic view of justification by faith *and* works) represented the difference between an *evangelical* soteriology and a *Roman Catholic* soteriology.

After hearing the reading of the *Confutation*, Melanchthon now wrote to Luther that matters did not look good for peace.[71] Melanchthon's observation turned out to be prescient, for the emperor now considered the Protestants to be refuted, and he flatly demanded that they recant. The Edict of Worms was to be enforced, and the Lutheran governments were to return to Roman obedience by 15 April 1531. The Protestants, though, did not by any means feel that they had been refuted, and they requested a copy of the *Confutation* so that they could study it and give their own reply. The emperor denied this request, so the Protestants scraped together all the notes they had hastily taken during the reading of the *Confutation* (some of which actually turned out to be very accurate and complete stenographic transcripts) and gave them to Melanchthon. Almost immediately Melanchthon began working on a confutation of the *Confutation*, but the emperor would not recognize any further writings from the Protestants. In his mind, they had been decisively refuted, and recantation remained the only path open to them. Meanwhile, the Catholic and Protestant theologians formed committees in the hope that a smaller group could iron out

---

[70] Trans. Tranvik, 116. 'Nam sic catholicos convenit media via incedere, ne nimium tribuant libero arbitrio cum Pelagianis, neque omnem eit libertatem adimant cum impiis Manichaeis: nam utrumque non caret vitio. Sic Augustinus inquit: Liberum arbitrium inesse hominibus, certe fide credimus et praedicamus indubitanter.' CR 27.118–19.

[71] Letter from Melanchthon (in Augsburg) to Luca Bonfio (in Augsburg), 4 August 1530. MBW 1.1010. T 4/2.1010. CR 2.248–9 Nr. 820. MSA 7/2.245–8 Nr. 199.

the differences between the two parties. The two sides instituted a committee of fourteen participants in the first instance, and then reduced it to six a few weeks later. These meetings stretched into the beginning of November when the diet at Augsburg finally dispersed with no agreement.

The End of the Diet of Augsburg: August 1530

After Augsburg, the Protestants felt that their only hope for remedying the breach in the church was for somebody to call a general council. The pope refused to do so, and Charles's gathering at Augsburg had failed to reunite western Christendom. In a final effort, the Protestant princes had Melanchthon draft two almost identical letters, both dated 16 February 1531.[72] In those two letters, the collective Protestant princes explained that Charles V had rejected the *Augsburg Confession*, and that to reject the *Augsburg Confession* was to deviate from Scripture. In the first letter, addressed to Francis I, king of France, the Protestant princes noted that their theology was in line with the thought of Jean Gerson, and they called on Francis to convene a general council of the church. In the second letter, addressed to Henry VIII, king of England, the Protestant princes noted how their theology was in line with the thought of John Colet, and they petitioned Henry to convene a general council of the church. These petitions fell on deaf ears, and so Melanchthon worked all the harder on his *Apology to the Augsburg Confession* over which he had laboured continuously ever since the reading of the *Confutation* in August of 1530.

THE APOLOGY TO THE AUGSBURG CONFESSION: APRIL 1531[73]

In the *Apology*,[74] Melanchthon reinforced and reiterated the doctrines of the *Augsburg Confession*. In the foreword, he complained about the emperor's

---

[72] Letter drafted by Melanchthon, from the Protestant princes, to King Francis I of France. MBW 2.1127. T 5.1127. CR 2.472–7 Nr. 958. The second letter was to King Henry VIII of England. MBW 2.1128. T 5.1128. CR 2.477–8 Nr. 959.

[73] The first edition (quarto edition) of the *Apology* appeared in April or early May 1531. Melanchthon then asked for feedback from trusted theologians, and the second edition, the octavo, appeared in September 1531. It was this second edition that Melanchthon preferred.

[74] While the *Apologiae confessionis Augustanae* can be found in CR 27 and 28, the newer edition in BSLK 139–404 is better. This source prints the Latin and German texts in parallel columns, with the result that a citation for the Latin text will also lead the reader to the German text. Citations will be given exclusively for BSLK. For a relatively recent study of the *Apology*, see

unfair treatment of the Protestants in not giving them a copy of the *Confutation*, and he explained that the sharp tone he used was entirely the fault of his opponents.[75] Within the *Apology*, Melanchthon gave special attention to Article IV, the doctrine of justification. This article dominated the *Apology*.[76] Throughout the *Apology*, Melanchthon's shifting foundation for his position on the freedom of the will continued to become more evident, and his implicit understanding of the divided governance of God continued to be in evidence.

Throughout the various articles of the *Apology*, Melanchthon made a cohesive argument regarding free will. Melanchthon's main concern centred around the doctrine of justification, which he saw to be the most significant error of Catholic theology. In seeking to rectify that error, Melanchthon militated against mixing the ideas of the temporal and spiritual realms, and he thereby reaffirmed the ideas of a divided governance of God.

Temporal Freedom (Non-soteriological)

Throughout the *Apology*, Melanchthon continued to affirm civil (or temporal) freedom.[77] Regarding the law, he referred to 'outward civil works that reason can produce to some extent'.[78] More explicitly, 'To a certain extent, reason can produce this righteousness by its own powers, although it is often shackled by its natural weakness and by the devil, who drives it to shameful acts. Moreover, we willingly give this righteousness of reason the praises it deserves, for our corrupt nature has no greater good than this, as Aristotle rightly said: "Neither the evening star nor the morning star is more beautiful

---

Christian Peters, *Apologia Confessionis Augustanae: Untersuchungen zur Textgeschichte einer lutherischen Bekenntnisschrift (1530–1584)* (Stuttgart: Calwer Verlag, 1997).

[75] *Vorrede zu: Apologia Confessionis*. April 1531. MBW 2.1148. T 5.1148. CR 2.495–7 Nr. 979. See also TRE 4.632–9.

[76] Melanchthon remained deeply concerned with the formulation of Article IV well into 1533. His letters from 1531–3 showed an emphasis on it that bordered on obsession. For example, see MBW 2 (and T 5).1132, 1151–2, 1164, 1193, 1209, 1250, 1299, 1300, 1351, and 1370.

[77] This freedom was by no means absolute. It was impeded by sin and the devil, and God was also in overall guidance of history, although he did not micromanage all the details. God providentially took care of people, and men were not born and did not die by chance. Ap. IV. BoC 141.135 (Tapp. 125.135). BSLK 187.5–9. However, while God established and preserved everything that existed, the cause of sin was the will of the devil and people turning away from God. Ap. XIX. BoC 235.1 (Tapp. 226.1). BSLK 313.10–17. God was involved in the world, but he did not determine all things.

[78] Ap. IV. BoC 121.8 (Tapp. 108.8). '...externa opera civilia, quae ratio utcunque efficere potest'. BSLK 160.16–18.

than righteousness." God even honours it with temporal rewards.'[79] In the section on free will itself, Melanchthon made a statement very similar to the passage on free will in the *Augsburg Confession*, although here explicitly stressing that this freedom humans had was restricted to the temporal realm:

Nor indeed do we deny that the human will has freedom. The human will possesses freedom regarding works and matters that reason can comprehend by itself. It can to some extent produce civil righteousness or the righteousness of works. It can talk about God and offer God acts of worship with external works; it can obey rulers and parents. By choosing an external work it can keep back the hand from murder, adultery, and theft. Because human nature still retains reason and judgment concerning things subject to the senses, it also retains the ability to choose in such matters, as well as the freedom and ability to achieve civil righteousness. For Scripture calls this the righteousness of the flesh, which carnal nature (that is, reason) produces by itself apart from the Holy Spirit.[80]

Melanchthon continued by adding an important caveat—this temporal freedom did exist, but it was impeded by sin and the devil, such that achieving civil righteousness, while possible, was extremely difficult.[81]

After affirming the genuine presence of temporal freedom, Melanchthon moved swiftly to argue against adding a false interpretation to this freedom. For Melanchthon, the temporal and spiritual realms never, ever, mixed when it came to the issue of salvation. This, in Melanchthon's opinion, was the chief

---

[79] Ap. IV. BoC 124.23–4 (Tapp. 110.23–4). 'Et potest hanc iustitiam utcunque ratio suis viribus efficere, quamquam saepe vincitur imbecillitate naturali et impellente diabolo ad manifesta flagitia. Quamquam autem huic iustitiae rationis libenter tribuimus suas laudes; nullum enim maius bonum habet haec natura corrupta, et recte inquit Aristoteles: Neque hesperum neque luciferum formosiorem esse iustitia, ac Deus etiam ornat eam corporalibus praemiis.' BSLK 164–165.46–56, 1.

[80] Ap. XVIII. BoC 233.4 (Tapp. 225.4). 'Neque vero adimimus humanae voluntati libertatem [.] Habet humana voluntas libertatem in operibus et rebus deligendis, quas ratio per se comprehendit. Potest aliquo modo efficere iustitiam civilem seu iustitiam operum potest loqui de Deo, exhibere Deo cerum cultum externo opere, obedire magistratibus, parentibus, in opere externo eligendo potest continere manus a caede, ab adulterio, a furto. Cum reliqua sit in natura hominis ratio et iudicium de rebus sensui subiectis, reliquus est etiam delectus earum rerum et libertas et facultas efficiendae iustitiae civilis. Id enim vocat scriptura iustitiam carnis, quam natura carnalis, hoc est, ratio per sese efficit sine spiritu sancto.' BSLK 311.22–39.

[81] 'To be sure, the power of concupiscence is such that people more often obey their evil impulses than sound judgment. Moreover, the devil, who is at work in the ungodly as Paul says [Eph. 2.2], never stops inciting this feeble nature to various offenses. For these reasons even civil righteousness is rare among human beings. We see that not even the philosophers, who seemed to have aspired after this righteousness, attained it.' Ap. XVIII. BoC 234.5 (Tapp. 225.5). 'Quamquam tanta est vis concupiscentiae, ut malis affectibus saepius obtemperent homines quum recto iudicio. Et diabolus, qui est efficax in impiis, ut ait Paulus, non desinit incitare hanc imbecillem naturam ad varia delicta. Haec causae sunt, quare et civilis iustitia rara sit inter homines, sicut videmus ne ipsos quidem philosophos eam consecuios esse, qui videntur eam expetivisse.' BSLK 311.40–9.

error of Catholic doctrine. The Catholics assumed that God would honour the proper exercise of civil freedom with the gift of salvation. No, for Melanchthon, salvation was a *spiritual* issue, and could only be achieved by spiritual means within the individual by God himself, acting unilaterally. Free civil actions *never* translated into spiritual rewards because the external actions, apart from the proper internal disposition (which only God could provide), held no spiritual value at all.

Melanchthon also warned against mixing civil and spiritual righteousness elsewhere in the *Apology*. In the article on original sin, Melanchthon argued, 'Now the scholastics mingled Christian teaching with philosophical views about the perfection of nature and attributed more than was proper to [free choice] and to "elicited acts" by teaching that human beings are justified before God by philosophical or civil righteousness (which we also admit are subject to human reason and are somehow within our ability). As a result they failed to see the inner impurity of human nature.'[82] For Melanchthon, civil (temporal) and philosophical righteousness were the same thing. He again cautioned, 'So if we accept the opponents' doctrine that we merit the forgiveness of sins and justification by the works of reason, there will indeed be no difference between philosophical—or at least Pharisaic—righteousness and Christian righteousness.'[83] By mixing the ideas of civil righteousness with spiritual righteousness, the Catholics became Pelagians despite their distinctions between merit of congruity and merit of condignity.[84] Melanchthon stated this point most powerfully in the section on free will where he grew irate at the Catholic confusion of temporal freedom with spiritual righteousness: 'But what is the difference between the Pelagians and our opponents? Both hold that apart from the Holy Spirit people can love God and keep the commandments of God "according to the substance of the act"[85] and can merit grace and justification by works that reason can produce by itself. How many absurdities follow from these Pelagian opinions that are taught in the

---

[82] Ap. II. BoC 114.12 (Tapp. 102.12). Notice here that Melanchthon was denigrating philosophical metaphysics (that is, philosophical speculation), and not philosophy as defined as grammar, rhetoric, or dialectics. 'Sed postquam scholastici admiscuerunt doctrinae christianae philosophiam de perfectione naturae, et plus, quam satis erat, libero arbitrio et actibus elicitis tribuerunt, et homines philosophica seu civili iustitia, quam et nos fatemur rationi subiectam esse et aliquo modo in potestate nostra esse, iustificari coram Deo, docuerunt: non potuerunt videre interiorem immunditiam naturae hominum.' BSLK 149.31–42.

[83] Ap. IV. BoC 122.16 (Tapp. 109.16). 'Itaque si recipimus hic adversariorum doctrinam, quod mereamur operibus rationis remissionem peccatorum et iustificationem, nihil iam intererit inter iustitiam philosophicam, aut certe pharisaicam, et christianam.' BSLK 162.8–13.

[84] Ap. IV. BoC 122–124.17–21 (Tapp. 109–110.17–21). BSLK 162.29–164.36.

[85] 'Quoad substantiam actuum' (see the following note). This is a technical phrase quoted pejoratively from Biel and Ockham.

schools with great authority!'[86] Temporal freedom did in fact exist, but under no circumstances could it ever lead to salvation.

Spiritual Bondage (Soteriological)

Salvation never occurred through the exercise of civil freedom—it came from God, through the work of the Holy Spirit.[87] The Holy Spirit, not the human will, achieved justification. Melanchthon wrote, 'Even though we concede to free [choice] the freedom and power to perform external works of the law, nevertheless we do not ascribe to free [choice] those spiritual capacities, namely, true fear of God, true faith in God, and the conviction and knowledge that God cares for us, hears us, and forgives us, etc. These are the real works of the first table [of the Ten Commandments], which the human heart cannot produce without the Holy Spirit.'[88] Again, 'Apart from the Holy Spirit human hearts lack the fear of God and trust in God. They do not believe that God hears their prayers, forgives them, or helps and preserves them.'[89] The Holy Spirit gave rise to faith.

The Holy Spirit gave rise to faith, but the Holy Spirit only came where faith was already present. Melanchthon declared, 'We receive . . . the Holy Spirit by faith alone.'[90] In another place, he stated, 'Faith truly brings the Holy Spirit.'[91] This may at first appear to be a rational inconsistency, but the apparent tension between the inception of faith and the reception of the Holy Spirit could be resolved through noting that the Spirit had a twofold function for

---

[86] Ap. XVIII. BoC 233.2–3 (Tapp. 225.2–3). 'Praeclare sane; sed quid interest inter Pelagianos et adversarios nostros, cum utrique sentiant homines sine spiritu sancto posse Deum diligere et praecepta Dei facere quoad substantiam actuum, mereri gratiam ac justificationem operibus, quae ratio per se efficit sine Spiritu Sancto? Quam multa absurda sequuntur ex his Pelagianis opinionibus, quae in scholis magna auctoritate docentur!' BSLK 311.9–19.

[87] 'We are speaking about the kind of faith that is not an idle thought, but which frees us from death, produces new life in our hearts, and is a work of the Holy Spirit.' Ap. IV. BoC 131.64 (Tapp. 116.64). 'Cum autem de tali fide loquamur, quae non est otiosa cogitatio, sed quae a morte liberat, et novam vitam in cordibus parit, et est opus spiritus sancti.' BSLK 173.9–12.

[88] Ap. XVIII. BoC 234.7 (Tapp. 225.6.7). 'Igitur etiamsi concedimus libero arbitrio libertatem et facultatem externa opera legis efficiendi, tamen illa spiritualia non tribuimus libero arbitrio, scilicet vere timere Deum, vere credere Deo, vere statuere ac sentire, quod Deus nos respiciat, exaudiat, ignoscat nobis etc. Haec sunt vera opera primae tabulae, quae non potest humanum cor efficere sine spiritu sancto.' BSLK 312.10–19.

[89] Ap. XVIII. BoC 234.6 (Tapp. 225.6). 'Nam humana corda sine spiritu sancto sunt sine timore Dei, sine fiducia erga Deum, non credunt se exaudiri, sibi ignosci, se iuvari et servari a Deo.' BSLK 311–312.54–56, 1–2.

[90] Ap. IV. Tapp. 119.86. (BoC 135.86 does not have this precise quotation in the main body of its text because the phrase 'Holy Spirit', while present in the first edition (the quarto edition), was not present in the second edition of the *Apology* (the octavo edition). 'Cum autem sola fide accipiamus remissionem peccatorum et spiritum sanctum.' BSLK 178.27–9.

[91] Ap. IV. BoC 140.125 (Tapp. 124.125). '[V]ero fides affert spiritum sanctum.' BSLK 185.23.

Melanchthon. First, the Holy Spirit elicited faith in the individual. Then, as a result of that faith, the power of the Holy Spirit for sanctification would be wrought in the heart of the believer.

The Holy Spirit called forth faith, through which the sanctifying power of the Holy Spirit was received, so that true good works could be done. Outward good works could become inward good works (that is, true good works) only if the Holy Spirit had set the affections in order. Melanchthon maintained, 'Although it is somewhat possible to do civil works, that is, the outward works of the law, without Christ and the Holy Spirit, still the impulses of the heart toward God, belonging to the essence of the divine law, are impossible without the Holy Spirit.'[92] The Holy Spirit brought new life: 'We are justified for this very purpose, that, being righteous, we might begin to do good works and obey God's law. For this purpose we are reborn and receive the Holy Spirit, that this new life might have new works and new impulses.'[93] True good works followed salvation. They could never precede it. While the will was free in temporal matters, no external human action could lead to salvation. Spiritually (where it really mattered), the will remained utterly helpless and dependent on God's good pleasure.

This vigorous view of the control of God in the spiritual realm implied predestination, but on that topic the *Apology* was silent. After referring to it tangentially in Article XVII of the *Augsburg Confession*, Melanchthon here reverted to his normal silence. But, outside of the *Apology*, in an extant letter, Melanchthon explained why he did not mention predestination in the *Apology*.[94] That letter is worthy of a closer look.

In an epistle of 30 September to Johannes Brenz, Melanchthon first acknowledged that he fled from 'the inexplicable disputation' of predestination throughout the entire *Apology*.[95] Melanchthon agreed with Brenz that it was

[92] Ap. IV. Tapp. 125.130. This passage can be found in a more literal translation in BoC 141.130. However, the translation in Tappert is more succinct and gets the central point of the text across with more force than BoC. As a result, in this instance, I have deviated from my normal practice of supplying BoC English quotations, and have, in this particular case, used Tapp. in the main body of the text above. 'Quamquam igitur civilia opera, hoc est, externa opera legis sine Christo et sine spiritu sancto aliqua ex parte fieri possint, tamen apparet ex his, quae diximus: illa, quae sunt proprie legis divinae, hoc est, affectus cordis erga Deum, qui praecipiuntur in prima tabula, non posse fieri sine spiritu sancto.' BSLK 186.8–15.

[93] Ap. IV. Tapp. 160.348–9. This passage was not included in BoC, even though it can be found in the first edition (quarto edition) of the Ap. The editors of the BoC based their translation on the second edition of the Ap. (the so-called octavo edition, which lacked the passage at hand). 'Ideo iustificamur, ut iust bene operari et obedire legi Dei incipiamus. Ideo regeneramur et spiritum sanctum accipimus, ut nova vita habeat nova opera, novos affectus.' BSLK 227.4–6.

[94] Melanchthon (in Wittenberg), letter to Johannes Brenz (in Schwäbisch Hall), 30 September 1531. MBW 2.1193. T 5.1193. CR 2.547 Nr. 1010.

[95] 'Tu subtiliter et procul ex praedestinatione colligis cuilibet suum gradum distributum esse, et recte raciocinaris. Sed ego in tota Apologia fugi illam longam et inexplicabilem disputacionem de praedestinatione.' T 5.1193.6–9. CR 2.547.

best to stay away from the doctrine because of its unhelpful (i.e. discomforting) effect upon people. He also admitted that people everywhere said that predestination followed the Protestant view of faith and works. But, Melanchthon maintained, he did not want to perturb consciences with this 'inexplicable labyrinth'.[96] For him, justification was of first significance, and it was easy to understand.[97] Thus Melanchthon the teacher, the *Preceptor Germaniae*, avoided discussing predestination because it confused people. The *effect* of the doctrine was unhelpful. Instead, he sought to focus almost exclusively on the doctrine of justification, which was simple and could easily be grasped. Melanchthon was pastorally concerned to steer people to the immediate practicalities of justification, rather than allowing them to be confused by doctrines of predestination, reprobation, and the mysteries of God.

However, there was more to Melanchthon's non-inclusion of predestination than simply didactic and pastoral concern (i.e. concern over the effects of doctrine). This reason for avoiding predestination was the same argument that Erasmus employed in *De libero arbitrio*. He said that predestination and free will should not be discussed in public for fear of harming and confusing simple Christians.[98] Luther reacted with scorn to this idea saying that everything in the Bible needed to be preached to all people.[99] Melanchthon took Luther's side in that dispute, so was he changing his mind here? No, Melanchthon staunchly affirmed the bound will in justification, but he probably knew that if he examined predestination too closely, it might disrupt his orderly theological system. Ignoring this doctrine was not a long-term solution to its perceived negative effects on the mind and heart of everyday believers.

CONCLUSION

In Melanchthon's life, the years 1529 to 1531 included the writing of a commentary on Romans, the *Augsburg Confession* and its *Apology*, and attendance

---

[96] 'Ubique sic loquor, quasi praedestinatio sequatur nostram fidem et opera. Ac facio hoc certo consilio. Non enim volo conscientias perturbare illis inexplicabilibus labyrinthis.' T 5.1193.9–11. CR 2.547. Calvin, too, wrote of a fear of theological labyrinths, but he resolved the tension between predestination and free will by coming down on the side of predestination (as opposed to Melanchthon's eventual position of evangelical free will).

[97] 'Iusticia autem, hoc est acceptacio simul habet vitam aeternam. Quare fides sola vivificat, cum pacificat cor. Haec sunt plana et facilia intellectu. Quae utrum tibi satisfaciant, velim te quam primum mihi significare.' T 5.1193.13–165. CR 2.547.

[98] LCC 17.40–1. EAS 4.14–16.

[99] LW 33.44–58. WA 18.620–30.

at several confessional meetings. Over these years, Melanchthon's theology of the freedom of the will in justification remained constant. The only thing different was that during this period he began clearly to express what in the late 1520s could only be drawn from a close reading of his texts. In 1531, in the section of the *Apology* on free will, he clearly summarized the paradigm for free will that his position of the divided governance of God implied: 'Therefore, it is helpful to distinguish between civil righteousness, which is ascribed to [free choice], and spiritual righteousness, which is ascribed to the operation of the Holy Spirit in the regenerate.'[100] The Roman Catholic mistake was to say that the exercise of free choice in civil righteousness allowed one to bridge the gap to spiritual righteousness through the procuration of *meritum de congruo*. Instead, for Melanchthon, spiritual righteousness came only through God, and never through human will or effort. In the spiritual realm, God was in absolute control. In the temporal realm, humans had a measure of independent input.

While from 1529 to 1531 Melanchthon continued to sharpen the clarity of his dichotomy between temporal freedom and spiritual bondage, he did his best to avoid predestination. If he had to mention it, he did so briefly. He effectively recoiled from the issue. But he did think about it—his letter to Brenz of September 1531, showed that. And as he mulled it over, all the while trying to avoid a public pronouncement, predestination must surely have aggravated him, like a burr inside his clothing. In 1532, he would deal with that burr.

---

[100] Ap. XVIII. BoC 234.9 (Tapp. 226.9). 'Prodest igitur ista distributio, in qua tribuitur libero arbitrio iustitia civilis, et iustitia spiritualis gubernationi spiritus sancti in renatus.' BSLK 312.37–40. Stated slightly differently, 'Darum ists gut, daß man dieses klar unterscheidet, nämlich, daß die Vernunft und frei Wille vermag, etlichermaß äußerlich ehrbar zu leben, aber new geboren werden, inwendig ander Herz, Sinn und Mut kriegen, das wirket allein der heilge Geist.' BSLK 312.37–42.

Part III

Evangelical Free Will

8

1532–1535: Conversion

INTRODUCTION

In 1532, Melanchthon's gradually evolving doctrine of the will's role in justification finally reached a tipping-point. In *The Summary of Ethics*, he was almost there. In the *Commentary on Romans*, he *was* there, and in the *Loci* of 1533–5, he strengthened his position. A subtle change had taken place in Melanchthon's thinking, marking a transition from a bound-will position to one of evangelical free will. It was no sudden breakthrough, but rather, the next logical step in a long doctrinal journey on the origins of faith. This was not a change brought from the outside via the influence of Erasmus or metaphysical philosophy. Rather, it came from within, from the internal dynamic of Melanchthon's own theological system, examined with a sympathetic eye toward the effects of doctrine upon the faith and assurance of regular Christians. Secondarily, Melanchthon's emphasis on rational consistency as an interpretive rule for the exegesis of Scripture made it less likely that he would maintain the apparent contradiction of divine predestination *and* human free choice. Ultimately, it could not be both.

THE SUMMARY OF ETHICS: 1532

In 1532, Melanchthon wrote a work called the *Epitome ethices*, or *The Summary of Ethics*.[1] Here Melanchthon once again explored the issue of free will. His discussion is important because it demonstrated that he continued to speak of external freedom in the temporal realm while also now remaining silent on the issue of the internal bondage of the will in the spiritual realm. This represents a dramatic, though incremental, step toward a consistent understanding of the will that would, however limited, be both externally *and* internally free.

---

[1] *Epitome ethices*, ed. Heineck. This work can be found translated into English in Keen, 203–38.

In the *Summary of Ethics*, Melanchthon's teachings on the will were similar to what he had said in the preceding few years. However, in discussing human external freedom, Melanchthon developed his doctrine, pushing the realm of freedom forward to now include external actions that had internal effects—namely, the acquisition of skills. Furthermore, Melanchthon also now spoke strongly *against* the ideas of necessity and divine determinism, ideas that he himself had advocated in 1519–21. In conclusion, Melanchthon finished this writing with some caveats enumerating limitations on human freedom.

It is indeed notable here that Melanchthon did *not* speak of bondage to sin in the spiritual realm. Perhaps one may account for this fact by noting that such an omission would be entirely to be expected in an essay on *ethics* (as opposed to theology). However, I believe it is equally likely that Melanchthon's reticence here to teach the bondage of the will in the spiritual realm indicated that he no longer had full confidence in this doctrine's total veracity. In other words, just as Melanchthon went silent on predestination when he began to have concerns about it, so he here went silent on the bondage of the will in justification.

External Freedom: Action

In the affirmation of external (temporal) freedom, Melanchthon was as clear as ever here: 'The human will is free to a certain extent in taking up external actions; that is, the human will can obey the judgment of reason seeking or fleeing things before it, or commanding the lower members and the powers in external actions to obey the judgment of reason.'[2] People were free, at least externally, to carry out their responsibilities under the law.[3] Melanchthon believed that this was clear from Scripture.[4] This idea of external, temporal freedom was the same teaching that Melanchthon had been advocating for about the last decade. But in this document, Melanchthon developed this doctrine a step further.

---

[2] Keen, 214. 'Voluntas humana est aliquo modo libera in externis actionibus suscipiendis; hoc est, voluntas humana potest obtemperare iudicio rationis expetens aut fugiens res oblatas aut imperans inferioribus membris ac viribus in externis actionis ut obsequantur iudicio rationis.' Ed. Heineck, 16.
[3] Ibid.   [4] Ibid.

External Freedom with Internal Effects:
Growth in Skills and Virtue

Melanchthon stated, 'Also it is clear that men can apply their zeal to various arts and become practiced in different skills.'[5] This was an interesting statement because it represented an extension of freedom from merely the external movements of the members of the human body to the use of the body to acquire and develop skills. In other words, freedom in the temporal realm now extended to physical actions that resulted in *internal* effects. The lines differentiating between internal and external areas of human existence were becoming blurred, and the freedom that Melanchthon had attributed to human external actions was now invading the previously inviolate realm of the *internal* life. This change became even more pronounced when Melanchthon did not stop at declaring freedom in developing *skills*, but then moved on to assert that the same pattern held with getting good at acts of virtue, which rather obviously hinted at matters of the spiritual realm![6] Melanchthon went on to write that some freedom of the human will in the acquisition of skills and virtue was obvious from experience.[7]

Against the Necessitatarian Argument and Divine Determinism

Next, Melanchthon commented, 'Some people, lacking due thought to our nature, look at divine governance and teach that all things which are ruled by divine plan happen by necessity. And with this reasoning they detract from the will.'[8] He continued, 'For however much the theologian needs wisdom in this matter, let him not remove liberty on grounds of divine governance, since scripture testifies that there is some freedom in nature.'[9] In this way, Melanchthon here ruled out necessitarianism and divine determinism. He posited at least some measure of genuine human freedom while declining to advocate complete passivity on the part of the Lord. Melanchthon retained God's providential involvement in the world when he concluded, 'But God governs

---

[5] Keen, 214. 'Item manifestum est homines posse animos ad varias artes applicare et adsuefieri in variis artibus.' Ed. Heineck, 16.

[6] Ibid.

[7] Ibid.

[8] Keen, 214. 'Quidam omissa naturae nostrae consideratione respiciunt ad divinam gubernationem ac docent necessario fieri omnia quae regantur dei consilio. Et hac ratione detrahunt libertatem voluntati.' Ed. Heineck, 16.

[9] Keen, 214. 'Quamquam enim theologo adhibenda est prudentia in hoc loco ne tollat libertatem propter divinam gubernationem, cum scriptura testatur aliquam in natura libertatem esse.' Ed. Heineck, 16–17.

nature according to their own conditioning, and moves rational natures in one way, brutes in another.'[10] Yet, this divine activity did not preclude independent human volition.

Caveats: Limitations on Human Freedom

Melanchthon next proceeded to discuss the weak, sinful nature of human beings. He did concede that the sinful nature mitigated the freedom of the human will, for he wrote, 'Another reason for removing freedom is the very weakness of human nature. For our nature is so vitiated by original sin that it is full of bad emotions.'[11] Another check on human freedom involved the hostile endeavours of the devil: 'For because of the weakness of nature it often happens that men obey false emotions more than right reason. For often the devil impels men to outward shameful deeds, for he holds the impious in his power.'[12] Honing his point, Melanchthon went on to maintain that although sin and the devil *impeded* human free will, they did not negate it: 'Even if it were true that the will by itself is not able to get rid of all bad emotions, nevertheless we are able to control and do our honest outer deed by ourselves, even if in some way freedom is held back by man, either by the weakness of nature or even the devil.'[13]

Conclusion: Teetering Towards Free Will

In the *Epitome ethics*, Melanchthon's distinction between external (temporal) freedom and the internal (spiritual) bondage of the will became blurred. Melanchthon continued to insist on temporal freedom, which he

---

[10] Keen, 214. 'Sed deus gubernat naturas pro ipsarum conditione, aliter movet rationales aliter brutas.' Ed. Heineck, 17.

[11] Keen, 214. 'Altera ratio est tollendae libertatis ipsa naturae humanae imbecillitas. Ita enim vitiata est natura peccato originis, ut plena sit malorum affectuum.' Ed. Heineck, 17.

[12] Keen, 215. 'Nam propter imbecillitatem naturae saepe fit ut obtemperent homines magis vitiosis affectibus quam rectae rationi. Saepe etiam diabolus impellit homines ad externa flagitia, habet enim impios in potestate.' Ed. Heineck, 17.

[13] Keen, 215. 'Etsi autem verum est, quod voluntas per sese non potest abiicere omnes vitiosos affectus, tamen externas actiones honestas imperare nobis et facere possumus, etsi aliquo modo retardatur homini libertas tum imbeccillitate naturae tum etiam a diabolo.' Ed. Heineck, 17. In relation to natural human weakness (sin), Melanchthon also wrote, 'It remains that some liberty still remains in men for choosing honest external acts, even if it is not without difficulty that natural weakness is conquered.' Keen, 215. 'Reliquum est igitur quod tamen aliqua libertas manet in hominibus deligendi externas actiones honestas, etsi non sine difficultate naturalis imbecillitas vincitur.' Ed. Heineck, 17.

sometimes described as freedom in civil virtue, freedom in moral virtue, or liberty or choice in the same. However, he did not speak of the spiritual bondage of the will. Perhaps this omission was due to fidelity to the narrow topic of ethics, but it seems to me to be more likely that Melanchthon's convictions regarding the total spiritual bondage of the will were now wavering. Further, it is interesting to note how in this document Melanchthon expanded the range of human freedom from simply the external ordering of the bodily members to include the use of the body to make *internal* (that is, intellectual, or spiritual) changes. Humans now had not only the freedom to act, but also the freedom to grow in skills and moral virtue. This was but a small step away from embracing human free will in the choice to have faith in Jesus Christ. This was a step that Melanchthon was just about to take.

THE SHIFT: THE *COMMENTARY ON ROMANS*: 1532

Melanchthon's shift from a bound will to a unique position of free will in justification can be seen within the writing of the *Commentary on Romans* of 1532.[14] Engelland calls the new formulation in this writing a 'shaking change',[15] but as we have seen, Melanchthon's slow, steady, doctrinal journey on the origins of faith began in 1519, and had been steadily building up to this moment. This shift in 1532 was merely the next logical step in a gradual evolution. This was certainly no sudden *Turmerlebnis.*[16]

Neither, though, was the new commentary of 1532 inconsequential. Throughout his life, Melanchthon rewrote successive editions of some of his most important works, with *Romans* and the *Loci communes* being two of the most obvious and significant examples. Each rewrite suggested that Melanchthon had been thinking things over and had new, different, or expanded things to say. In 1543, when explaining the various editions of the *Loci*, Melanchthon said, 'Not for ambition, not for the desire to be right, not from rivalry, and not to sow the seeds of discord have I established and collected these things, but primarily to teach myself, and then so that I might help the honest and pious

---

[14] *Commentarii in Epistolam Pauli ad Romanos.* MSA 5.25–371.

[15] Engelland, 'Introduction', xxxvi.

[16] For a discussion of the term *Turmerlebnis* ('tower experience') in relation to Luther's Reformation discovery of justification by faith, see McGrath, *Luther's Theology of the Cross*, 141–2. See also W. D. J. Cargill Thompson, 'The Problem of Luther's "Tower Experience" and Its Place in His Intellectual Development', in *Studies in the Reformation: Luther to Hooker*, ed. C. W. Dugmore (London: Athlone Press, 1980), 60–80.

studies of those who read here.'[17] The internal dynamic of his own thought, in light of his interpretive rhetorical-dialectical framework, and in concert with his concern for the pastoral encouragement of simple Christians, drove the evolution of Melanchthon's theological development. 'I place the testimony of my conscience before the accusations of Eck, Cochlaeus, Alfonsus and all those who applaud them.'[18] Melanchthon wanted to understand for himself what God's Word said, and then communicate that to the pastors and people in the pews, for their eternal well-being. It was too important a subject to leave alone, and so Melanchthon continued to apply himself to understanding and teaching theology in the midst of the ongoing events of the Reformation.

Following the *Augsburg Confession,* and with the writing of the *Apology,* Melanchthon became very concerned about correctly understanding and teaching the doctrine of justification. Article IV (Justification) dominated the *Apology,* and Melanchthon's correspondence showed him enquiring of many friends and colleagues about their opinions on this subject. Now, in late May of 1532, Melanchthon wrote to Antonius Corvinus (in Witzenhausen) that he would further seek to clarify the doctrine of justification in his new *Commentary on Romans.*[19] Significantly, Melanchthon made it quite clear that this commentary of 1532 would replace his *Annotations on Romans* of 1522.[20] Melanchthon here effectively disavowed what he had previously taught in that work—namely, both divine determinism and the idea that God actively predestined elect and reprobate alike.

In the early chapters of the *Commentary on Romans* of 1532, Melanchthon's theological formulations remained conducive to a doctrine of a bound will in justification, while the force of his argument implied a measure of free will. Realizing the incongruity of his syntax with the developing shape of his thought, Melanchthon altered his soteriological formulation in chapters 8 and 9 to admit the use of the human will in justification, as we shall explore below. He did it quietly and without fanfare. He did not construct a dedicated

---

[17] Keen, 137. *Philippus Melanchthon Pio Lectori S. D.* (1543). 'Non ambitione, non φιλονεικίᾳ non aemulatione, non ut sererum rixas, haec et institui et collegi, sed primum ut me ipsum erudirem, deinde ut aliquorum, qui haec legebant, honesta et pia studia adiuvarem.' MSA 2/1.165.15–19.

[18] Keen, 137. *Philippus Melanchthon Pio Lectori S. D.* (1543). '. . . meae conscientiae testimonium antefero criminationibus Eccii, Cochlei, Alfonsi et multorum, qui illis applaudunt.' MSA 2/1.165.20–2.

[19] MBW 2.1250. T 5.1250. CR 2.567–8 Nr. 1032.

[20] Melanchthon (in Wittenberg), letter to Archbishop Albrecht of Mainz, August 1532. (This letter also served as the foreword to the *Commentarii*). MBW 2.1276. T 5.1276. CR 2.611–14 Nr. 1076; 3.128 and 20.786–7. MSA 5.25–9. 'Nam ante aliquot annos edita est sylvula quaedam commentariorum in Romanos et Corinthios meo nomine, quam ego plane non agnosco. Hanc ut opprimerem, paravi enarrationem locupletiorem in Romanos.' T 5.1276.19–22. MSA 5.26.5–8.

argument for the use of the will. Instead, he assumed the operation of the free will and included it almost casually within the framework of his prime concern in this commentary, which was salvation through God's mercy, not by human works.

The emergence of free will within the Romans commentary marked the culmination of the evolutionary theological processes that had begun within Melanchthon's thought in 1519. Here, in 1532, Melanchthon finally faced up to predestination in a fully dialectical-logical fashion. He made manifest what had been implicit from the force of his wider theology. That is, he now limited the rule of God within the spiritual realm to make it parallel to God's self-limited governance within the temporal realm. As Schwarzenau comments, this commentary on Romans closed the gap opened by Melanchthon's theology of the two governments.[21] Melanchthon achieved this unification of the divided governance of God by tempering predestination to make it simply a metaphor for justification by grace rather than works. Concurrently, if reprobation was not to be attributed to the will of God, then the cause of damnation had to reside within the human will. Melanchthon affirmed this conclusion by saying that although salvation occurred because of God's grace rather than human works, sinners had to deliberately accept that grace. Justification happened when the Word and the Holy Spirit worked together, and at the same time the free human will actively decided to assent to the promises of God.

Tempering Predestination

Melanchthon made it clear throughout this commentary on Romans that he sought to temper predestination. That is, he desired to give it the minimum possible attention, and he excoriated any and all speculation about it. He was even capable of expressing disapproval of the word itself, as used in a specific context. In relation to Romans 1.4, he took issue with the Vulgate translation, which called Jesus 'the predestined Son of God with power according to the Spirit of holiness by resurrection from the dead, Jesus Christ our Lord'.[22] Melanchthon argued that 'declared' was a better word than 'predestined' because 'this word [i.e. predestination] gives birth to multiple inept disputations'.[23] Even when Melanchthon did use a word like 'elect', he did not define

---

[21] Schwarzenau, 96. From the context of this passage, Schwarzenau is thinking specifically of Melanchthon's *Scholia in Epistolam Pauli ad Colossenses* of 1527.

[22] '...qui praedestinatus est Filius Dei in virtute secundum Spiritum sanctificationis ex resurrectione mortuorum Iesu Christi Domini nostri.'

[23] 'Deinde addit: "Qui declaratus est esse filius Dei". Vetus translatio incommode vertit: "Qui praedestinatus est". Et id vocabulum peperit multas ineptas disputationes, quomodo Christus

it,[24] and indeed, 'elect' seemed to mean for Melanchthon those who have faith in Christ, and not necessarily a finite number of individuals preordained for salvation. Throughout this book Melanchthon maintained consistent scorn for 'Epicureans' and 'Stoics' whom he associated with the doctrine of predestination. Additionally, when he came to Romans 8.29 (which explicitly mentioned predestination) and 9.22 (the text most conducive to an argument for reprobation), Melanchthon had not a single word of commentary. This silence stood in stark contrast to the *Annotations on Romans* of 1522, where at this point Melanchthon offered a lengthy and detailed passage on election, reprobation, and divine determinism. When Melanchthon did offer commentary on other passages, he put forth two clear points in relation to predestination: first, the Bible was to be taken at face value, without speculation; and second, in a point connected to the first, the promises of the Gospel were genuinely universal.

The Bible Is to Be Taken at Face Value

Melanchthon repeatedly insisted that the teachings of the Bible were simply to be accepted without speculation about effects beyond the scope of the literal meaning of the words. In relation to Romans 9 he wrote, 'It is impious to question the will of God without (and against) the Word of God, for God neither wants to be, nor can be, known except through his Word.'[25] On Romans 11.33 Melanchthon asserted that Paul was teaching that humans were not to enquire into arcana, but rather to obey the Word of God.[26] That is, people were not to probe beneath the surface of the clear meaning of biblical texts. Specifically, Melanchthon's concerns in stating this principle related to predestination and the promises of the Gospel. The promises were not to be read in combination with the idea of predestination so that one might be drawn to the conclusion that the promises were only truly for

fuerit praedestinatus. His disputationibus hoc loco nihil opus est.' MSA 5.59.8–12. The original Greek phrase is τοῦ ὁπισθέντος υἱοῦ θεοῦ, with the key word being ὁρίζω, as put into the participial form as an aorist passive genitive masculine singular. ὁρίζω means decide, determine; appoint, designate. Most English translations (e.g. NRSV, NIV, KJV, NKJV) go along with Melanchthon and translate this phrase as 'declared to be Son of God'.

[24] For example, at Romans 4.13, Melanchthon wrote, 'Indeed, all [in the world] is put together for Christ and the elect.' MSA 5.151.12–13. 'Omnia enim propter Christum et electos condita sunt.'

[25] 'Primum, hoc sciendum est, quod quaerere de voluntate Dei sine verbo Dei et contra verbum Dei impium est, quia Deus neque vult neque potest cognosci nisi per verbum ab ipso propositum, sicut ubique nos docet scriptura.' MSA 5.251.30–3.

[26] 'Significat enim apostolus non esse quaerendas causas horum arcanorum, sed verbo Dei oboediendum.' MSA 5.280–281.35, 1–2.

the elect. On Romans 9.6, Melanchthon forcefully drew attention to the promises and cautioned against enquiring into the arcane counsel of predestination.[27] At all costs, Melanchthon refused to countenance the possibility of divine reprobation for anybody. That would have made God responsible for evil.[28] The promises *had* to be genuinely universal, and Melanchthon spent a good deal of effort making that point clear.

The Gospel Promises Are Genuinely Universal

Throughout the *Commentary on Romans* of 1532, Melanchthon took great care to affirm the genuine universality of the Gospel promises, because to say that the promises only applied to the elect would make God responsible for reprobation. Melanchthon could not abide that thought. So, on Romans 5.3–5, he taught, 'Because the sentence is universal "That all may receive mercy", on that account it is opposed to dangerous imaginations regarding predestination, lest we dispute that mercy was promised to others but not to us. Such imaginations are false and impious to indicate that these promises are deceitful and misleading, because to all much mercy is promised and required, in order that all believe. In such a universal sentence we are also included. And similar universal testimonies are available for consideration.'[29] The promises were truly universal, and they were the actual (not just a sham) will of God;[30] for just as according to the one sin of Adam, death spread to all, so according to the righteousness of Christ, life was now offered to all.[31]

---

[27] 'Vide autem, quomodo revocat eos ad promissionem! Iubet hanc apprehendere; non iubet arcanum consilium praedestinationis inquerere.' MSA 5.259.24–6.

[28] 'Cum autem promissio sit universalis, quid aliud est quaerere de electione quam promissionem in dubium vocare? Id autem vere est abrogare evangelium et Deum accusare mendacii. Tantum mali habet haec curiositas: scrutatur Deum sine verbo, postea vocat in dubium promissionem divinam, ita et abicit evangelium et accusat Deum mendacii.' On Romans 9. MSA 5.252.16–22.

[29] 'Est et hoc observandum, quod sententia est universalis "ut omnium misereatur", ideoque opponenda est periculosis imaginationibus de praedestinatione, ne disputemus aliis promitti misericordiam, nobis non promitti. Tales imaginationes falsae sunt et impiae, quia calumniantur et corrumpunt has promissiones, quae omnibus pollicentur misericordiam et requirunt, et credant omnes. In eiusmodi universales sententias nos quoque includamus. Ac prodest similia testimonia universalia habere in conspectu.' MSA 5.161–162.36, 1–8.

[30] 'In summa, certum est in evangelio omnibus offerri remissionem peccatorum, et gratis offerri. In hanc universalem singuli nos includamus et ab hoc verbo ordiamur, cum quaerimus de Dei voluntate, ac vere statuamus evangelium ad nos quoque pertinere.' On Rom. 9. MSA 5.253.15–19.

[31] 'Itaque sicut propter unius Adae delictum mors irrogata est omnibus, ita propter unius Christi iustitiam offertur vita omnibus. Haec sunt satis plana et perspicua.' On Rom. 5.19. MSA 5.190.12–15.

Righteousness was *offered* to all (*iustitiam offertur vita omnibus*). Offering implied a measure of passivity, for once offered, something could be either accepted or rejected. Melanchthon's thought here implied that if it was not the will of God that any should reject the Gospel (and indeed it was not, for God did not will the damnation of any), then the cause for such rejection must have lain within the individual human being. Melanchthon acknowledged this conclusion by saying that salvation was *offered* to all, and that humans were accepted so long as they *held onto* the promises of God in trust.[32] The sinner played a genuine role in first accepting and then holding onto God's promises. Following the offer of the promises, God then became passive as he awaited the individual's choice.

On occasion, Luther, too, affirmed things like the idea that humans were accepted so long as they *held onto* the promises of God in trust. Luther was not averse to active language such as this that Melanchthon here used. However, Melanchthon's use of active language in the decision of faith was different from Luther's use of active language. Luther made enthusiastic use of antinomy—he could speak of the requirement that people make an active choice to believe in Christ, but for him, that did not therefore rule out (as it did for a Melanchthon) a paradoxical strong affirmation of the full determination of God. Thus, active language for Melanchthon—with his grammatical expertise, dialectical methods, and aversion to the appearance of rational inconsistency—meant something different for his theology from a similar use of such language by Luther. Melanchthon and Luther simply had different ways of doing theology, thus indicating the breadth of theological options available in Wittenberg in the 1530s.

Conversion

After tempering predestination to eliminate reprobation, Melanchthon's doctrine of conversion could not remain unchanged. If God did not will reprobation, then damnation had to be the fault of human beings who failed to accept grace through faith. Therefore faith, the acceptation of the universal Gospel promises, had to be a human choice—or at least, human choice had to be involved.

Melanchthon argued that faith was necessary for salvation, and that it had to take the form of a genuine desire of the will to accept God's promises.[33] But

---

[32] 'Nec opus est hic disputatione de praedestinatione. Tantisper enim vincimus, dum hanc dilectionem Dei agnoscimus et opponimus peccati terroribus; *tantisper, dum fiduciam hanc tenemus*, quod propter Christum accepti simus patri, Deus diligit ac servat nos.' Emphasis added. On Rom. 8.32. MSA 5.247–248.35, 1–4.

[33] 'Et tamen hanc misericordiam fide accipi oportet. Et est fides non solum notitia, sed in voluntate velle et accipere promissionem.' In the *Argumentum* to Romans. MSA 5.53.35–7.

faith did not spring up on its own. It arose in the company of the Word and the Holy Spirit. The Spirit and the Word moved the heart towards faith[34]— they proclaimed the promises of God and encouraged a response.[35] Moreover, to describe faith, Melanchthon employed active language such as 'we raise ourselves up by faith'.[36] In fact, he went so far as to say, 'The mercy of God is the true cause of election, but nevertheless to some degree there is some cause in the one accepting, insofar as one does not refuse the offer of the promise due to the evil that is within us'.[37] Election represented God's mercy or grace which came to us in the form of the promises in the Word illumined by the Spirit. The human will, also, had a real role in justification. As Manschreck rightly observes, 'Ethical responsibility would not allow [Melanchthon] to admit that man had nothing whatever to do with election'.[38] As a result, conversion required three interrelated things: the Word, the Holy Spirit, and the human free will.[39] Melanchthon had now effectively shifted his theology from the bound will to the free will in relation to the specific decision of whether or not to accept God's gift of salvation. The shift to free will in justification had been made.

LOCI COMMUNES, SECOND EDITION: 1533–1535

Having given free will a role in justification in 1532, Melanchthon subsequently began to settle into his revised soteriology. In the second edition of the *Loci communes* (written between 1533 and 1535[40]), Melanchthon more

---

[34] 'Et concipitur, cum assentimur promissioni Dei, qua, cum erigimur, spiritus sanctus simul per verbum movet corda ad credendum.' In the *Argumentum* to Romans. MSA 5.53–54.37, 1–2. Also, 'Sed neque accipi promissio misericordiae neque concipi fiducia potest nisi spiritu sancto per verbum movente corda iuxta illud: "Nemo venit ad me, nisi quem pater traxerit".' On Rom. 9. MSA 5.254.12–15.

[35] 'Per spiritum sanctum agnoscamus Deum et vere invocemus.' On Rom. 8.16. MSA 5.236.24–5.

[36] 'Sed cum fide erigimus nos.' On Rom. 5.15. MSA 5.185.22.

[37] 'Misericordiam Dei vere causam electionis esse, sed tamen eatenus aliquam causam in accipiente esse, quatenus promissionem oblatam non repudiat, quia malum ex nobis est.' On Rom. 9. MSA 5.254.8–12.

[38] Manschreck, *The Quiet Reformer*, 295. See also Schwarzenau, 110.

[39] Rogness, on p. 128 of *Melanchthon: Reformer Without Honor*, describes this teaching of Melanchthon in a letter of his of February 1557 to Duke Albert of Magedeburg (CR 9.100f.). Rogness, however, seeing that the Word and Spirit are prerequisites for faith, considers Melanchthon's position to be therefore compatible with Luther's, where God chooses the elect. However, Rogness does not highlight the fact that for Melanchthon, the grace of Word and Spirit is general, universal, and resistible. This then, is a *different* soteriology from either Luther's, or the early Melanchthon's.

[40] Melanchthon lectured on the *Loci communes* in 1533, and students copied down his lectures and published them. These notes can be found in CR 21.253–332, and in most cases

emphatically made his case for contingency, and he continued to clarify his positions on predestination and free choice in justification. Contingency showed Melanchthon's dedication to the self-limited rule of God in the temporal realm, while his positions on predestination and free will showed his commitment to the self-limited rule of God in the spiritual realm. However, at this point, the distinction between the temporal and spiritual realms started to fade as Melanchthon incorporated the uniform limited governance of God into his overall system of theology. As a result, the second edition of the *Loci communes* (1533–5) revealed a stronger and clearer advocacy of free will in justification than was to be found in the *Commentary on Romans* of 1532.

Emphatic Contingency

In this second edition of the *Loci*, Melanchthon emphatically insisted upon contingency.[41] He utterly rejected the notion of divine determinism, which he had argued in previous years, saying that determinism would make God responsible for evil and sin,[42] an unconscionable position. This was his main reason for insisting on contingency.[43] Rather than determining all things at all times, God created and sustained the world, but the will of the devil and humans was the cause of sin.[44] Further, in a new layer of complexity that emerged between 1533 and 1535, Melanchthon asserted that God could determine individual events if he so chose, but that it was within God's ability to foresee and determine contingently without taking away the mode of the will's activity or its ordering.[45] In relation to the texts in Exodus about God

are nearly identical to the 1535 edition of the *Loci* that Melanchthon himself published, which can be found in CR 21.347–558. The present section refers to both works, citing the earlier notes whenever possible, and in all cases listing the date of the reference before its place in the CR.

[41] See 'De Causa Mali et Contingentia' in 1533, CR 21.271–4. Cf. 'De Causa Peccati et de Contingentia' in 1535, CR 21.371–3.

[42] 'Si enim natura non potest agere nisi Deus eam assiduo agitet, sequi videtur, deum autorem esse peccati.' 1533. CR 21.271.

[43] 'Ideo defendenda est contingentia, ne Deum faciamus autorem seu causam peccati.' 1535. CR 21.372.

[44] 'Itaque etsi Deus conservat naturam et suppeditat ei vitam et vires, tamen voluntas diaboli aut hominis deficiens in agendo, et resistens in obiecto prohibito a Deo, est causa peccati.' 1533. CR 21.272.

[45] 'Quare etiamsi praevidet Deus et determinat contingentia, tamen ita determinat, ne modum agendi voluntatis seu ordinationem suam tollat.' 1535. CR 21.372. This statement was not so much an assertion of paradox as it was an affirmation that the goals of God's general governance of history would still be met by a deity who could take into account free human actions.

hardening Pharaoh's heart, Melanchthon maintained that 'hardening the heart' was a Hebrew phrase signifying permission rather than a direct shaping of the will.[46] God did not impel Pharaoh to act the way he did but he merely permitted Pharaoh to act in the manner he naturally desired—or so Melanchthon argued, even if the grammatical points to which he alluded did not entirely prove his case.[47]

In a larger sense, even though Melanchthon later complained that 'scholastic baggage' was a burden to him,[48] he here explicitly embraced the scholastic distinction between *necessitate consequentiae* and *necessitate consequentis* (or absolute necessity).[49] Events were not necessary because of complete divine determinism (*necessitate consequentis*), but they were necessary (*necessitate consequentiae*) only in that they were the natural result of preceding events (or because perhaps God had stepped into history and made a specific event necessary through the force of his will, as in miracles). Thus Melanchthon rejected divine determinism, or 'the delirium of Stoic fate',[50] and spoke of liberty as the gift of God.[51] In this way also Melanchthon rejected his own position of 1521 on divine determinism as well as Luther's advocacy of divine determinism in *De servo arbitrio*, a cornerstone of his bound-will position. In fact, Erasmus' main concern with Luther's *De servo arbitrio* involved his insistence on the absolute determinism of God. In counterpoint, Erasmus affirmed this same distinction between *necessitate consequentiae* and *necessitate consequentis* as Melanchthon here maintained. Regarding determinism, therefore, Melanchthon accepted Erasmus' critique of Luther. Hence, Melanchthon once again affirmed the self-limited rule of God.

[46] 'Certum est enim, Ebraica phrasi significare eas permissionem, non voluntatem efficacem.' 1535. CR 21.371.

[47] Melanchthon's exegesis is difficult to reconcile with the Hebrew grammar of Exodus. For example, when the LORD said of Pharaoh, 'I will harden his heart', in Exodus 4.21, the verb used was a Piel imperfect, which is an intensive active (or resultative) verb: וַאֲנִי אֲחַזֵּק אֶת־לִבּוֹ This was not the grammar of permission, and this same Piel verb form was used in Exodus 10.20, 10.27, 11.10, 14.4, 14.8, and 14.17. Further, in Exodus 7.3, when the LORD said, 'But I will harden Pharaoh's heart', the verb used was a Hiphil imperfect, which was a causative active verb even stronger than the Piel in affirming that the action was being done *by* the LORD to the heart of Pharaoh: וַאֲנִי אַקְשֶׁה אֶת־לֵב פַּרְעֹה Another Hiphil verb was used in Exodus 10.1 when the LORD said 'I have hardened [Pharaoh's] heart': אֲנִי הִכְבַּדְתִּי אֶת־לִבּוֹ When Melanchthon argued that the Hebrew grammar indicated permission rather than direct divine action, it appears that he was trying too hard to make the Scriptures say what he desired that they *should* say.

[48] 'Preface to *The Corpus of Christian Doctrine* (1560)', Keen, 141. '... hanc scholasticam sarcinam Deus mihi imposuerit...' *Praefatio Philippi Melanthonis*. MSA 6.9.8–9.

[49] 1533. CR 21.274. 1535. CR 21.372–3.

[50] 'Deliramenta de Stoico fato.' 1535. CR 21.372–3.

[51] 'Et libertas donum Dei est, seu ordinatio Dei in voluntate.' 1535. CR 21.372.

Predestination

Melanchthon defended contingency in order to preserve genuine freedom in the temporal realm. Such freedom in civil events allowed God to be freed from the charges of authorship of sin and evil. Taking this idea a step further, in 1535 Melanchthon started to connect contingency with predestination as well. The last sentence in his section on predestination of the *Loci* reads, 'On the cause of evil and contingency, I have already spoken.'[52] In other words, by providing a cross-reference within his section on predestination to the section on contingency, Melanchthon demonstrated that it would be natural to discuss contingency under the heading of predestination. Previously Melanchthon had kept predestination and contingency strictly separate, for predestination involved God's absolute control in the spiritual realm, whereas contingency concerned God's self-limited involvement in the temporal realm. But now, with God's governance self-limited in both areas, it became possible to draw connections between the temporal and spiritual realms. Melanchthon was beginning to apply a systematic uniformity to his thought, and with no more divided governance of God, greater coherence and interconnectedness within his theology was now both possible and desirable.

Regarding the doctrine of predestination as it stood by itself, in the second edition of the *Loci*, Melanchthon continued with the basic ideas of the *Commentary on Romans* from 1532, though with bolder strokes. He discussed the authority of Scripture, the universality of the promise of the Gospel, justification by grace rather than works, and predestination *a posteriore*.

Scripture Alone, Without Speculation

For predestination, Melanchthon insisted that one had to look at the Word alone, taken at face value. It would be useless to dwell on things that disturbed consciences and detracted from the Gospel[53] (i.e. speculation about predestination apart from the literal meaning of the text). People would be lost if they enquired about election apart from God's Word.[54] If people began to worry about their own possible reprobation rather than focusing on the promises of the Gospel, then this could only be harmful. Out of pastoral concern for ordinary Christians (that is, concern for the *effects* of doctrine), Melanchthon directed them exclusively to the clear promises to be found in the Scriptures.

---

[52] 'De caussa mali, item de contingentia supra dictum est.' CR 21.453.

[53] 'Nec moror etiam si quis hic alia quaedam obscuriora velit quaerere; quae etiamsi quid habent perturbant conscientias, et abducunt eas a conspectu Evangelii.' 1535. CR 21.452.

[54] 1535. CR 21.452.

God's will could not be judged outside of his Word.[55] Neither reason nor the law taught about predestination, but only through the filter of the Gospel could one make sense of it.[56] Justification and predestination held together would make everything simple,[57] and it was not possible to avoid error if anyone searched beyond the Gospel for the cause of election.[58]

By sticking closely to the biblical text, Melanchthon sought to head off any talk of reprobation. As in 1529, Melanchthon still had no desire to countenance that idea in 1533. Also as in 1529, Melanchthon continued to affirm the genuine universality of the promises of the Gospel.

Universal Promise

Cameron correctly writes, 'There is no doubt that Melanchthon moved steadily away from his earlier "Lutheran" positions, while still remaining within the Protestant mainstream. He became progressively more convinced that the discussion of predestination had no place in the reformed teaching of justification. It was better to say that the promises of Christ applied to everyone'[59]—and this is precisely what Melanchthon did in the 1533–5 edition of the *Loci communes*. Here, Melanchthon repeatedly emphasized the universality of the promise: *Promissio est universalis.*[60] *Promissionem vere universalem esse.*[61] *Promissio et gratuita universalis est.*[62] If the promise was not universal, that would indicate the existence of a reprobate group of people. Many would agonize over whether they were one of that unfortunate number, and their faith would be uncertain.[63] This was a pastorally untenable

---

[55] 'De voluntate dei non est iudicandum extra verbum et sine verbo.' 1533. CR 21.332.

[56] 'Neque ex ratione, neque ex lege, sed ex Evangelio iudicandum est de praedestinatione.' 1533. CR 21.330.

[57] 'Deinde non alia causa praedestinationis quam iustificationis quaerenda est, si quis haec constituerit initio facile se ex multis quaestionibus explicabit, Nam si tantum ex Evangelio iudicandum est, si praedestinatio cum iustificatione conferenda est, una et simplex via erit.' 1533. CR 21.330.

[58] 'Si quis extra Evangelium causam quaerit electionis, is non potest non errare.' 1533. CR 21.331–2.

[59] Cameron, 'Philipp Melanchthon: Image and Substance', 719.

[60] 1533. CR 21.331.

[61] 1533. CR 21.332.

[62] 1535. CR 21.452. See also Melanchthon (in Jena), letter to Friedrich Myconius (in Gotha), 31 October 1535. MBW 2.1654. T 6.1654. CR 3.439–40 Nr. 1625. In this letter Melanchthon discussed the universal offer of salvation, and 1 Tim. 2.4.

[63] 'Cum igitur promissio sit gratuita, recte statuimus misericordiam esse causam electionis, deinde cum promissio sit universalis, si quis ex universali particularem velit efficere is reddet simpliciter incertam promissionem et tollet fidem.' 1533. CR 21.332.

outcome. The promise had to be universal, and all human beings were included in it.[64]

Predestination and Justification

More than anything else, predestination illustrated that justification occurred by God's grace, not by human works. In the second edition of the *Loci*, Melanchthon continued to emphasize this theme. The scholastic doctors erred because they thought about predestination in terms of human merit or dignity.[65] Instead, mercy was the cause of election.[66] Nothing humans did could earn merit. God's mercy was the cause of election, and God's mercy was expressed through the universal promise. Salvation came when humans accepted the universal promise through faith. That promise became effective through the drawing of the Holy Spirit (as in John 6.44). However, the effectiveness of the Word and the Spirit only occurred when humans apprehended, or took hold of, the Word. Melanchthon envisaged a simultaneous operation of the human will with the calling of God through the Word: *Itaque cum verbum apprehendimus, simul Deus est efficax per verbum.*[67] Though God was at work in justification, the elect were those who cooperated with God and freely, of their own wills, chose to accept his promises.

Predestination a Posteriore

Melanchthon's view of predestination developed most significantly here, from 1532 to 1533, in his description of predestination *a posteriore*. Melanchthon now plainly stated what he had first ventured in 1532: 'We can judge election afterwards, never doubting that one is elect who apprehends mercy.'[68] Those who 'apprehended' (an active verb) mercy were the elect.[69] Again, 'Afterwards (*a posteriore*) in justification we say there is some cause in the one accepting,

[64] 'Ideo neque dignitatem nostram respicere debemus, neque ex universali promissione particularem efficere. Sed singuli nos in illam universalem includamus.' 1533. CR 21.331. Note again the use of the subjunctive, *includamus.* This suggested the possibility of inclusion, provided that faith (which depended on the use of the free will) was present.

[65] 1533. CR 21.331.

[66] 'Misericordiam causam esse electionis.' 1535. CR 21.453.

[67] 1535. CR 21.452.

[68] 'Ita et de electione a posteriore iudicemus, videlicet haud dubie electos esse eos qui misericordiam apprehendunt, nec abiiciunt eam fidciam ad extremum.' 1533. CR 21.332.

[69] Melanchthon argued that according to Rom 8.30, the sanctified ones could be certain that they were among the elect of the church. 1535. CR 21.453. That is, they had grasped God's graceful and merciful universal promises, and through their faith they had received the imputation of Christ's merit, thus ensuring their salvation.

of course not in worthiness, but because of apprehending the promise, with which the Holy Spirit acts.'[70] Those who chose to have faith in cooperation with the Holy Spirit were in fact the predestined. Here Melanchthon was using a technical theological term ('*a posteriori*'), meaning 'from the latter', which was 'a description of inductive reasoning that moves from effect to cause, from the specific instance to the general principle'.[71] Those who chose to have faith (the effect) were, therefore, the elect (the cause). One was not to begin with the cause and speculate as to its present and future effects, but rather, one should only look at the effect (faith) and reason back from it to the cause (predestination). In other words, one should focus on the decision of faith without going into mental contortions speculating about predestination.

Free Choice

While the section on free choice from the second edition *Loci* bore much resemblance to Melanchthon's thought on free will as espoused in the course of his *Commentary on Romans* of 1532, it is precisely because of this resemblance that it bears recounting. As with the above section on predestination, the similarities between Melanchthon's doctrines of 1532 and 1533–5 showed that what he had begun to articulate in 1532 was no mere aberration, but was the beginning of a new formulation of theology that he would continue to develop and hone for the rest of his life. Further, in noting the continuing trend of Melanchthon's revised soteriology incorporating free human choices, it is worth noting how his arguments gained force and clarity over their initial disparate structure in the *Commentary on Romans*.

As in 1532, in 1533–5 Melanchthon's continuing commitment to justification by grace rather than works formed the centrepiece of his soteriology and intimately influenced how he formulated his doctrine of the will. He took great care to refute any notions of Pelagian free will as well as scholastic, Roman Catholic free will. After refuting these two errors, Melanchthon turned to his own original formulation of free will in justification. In fact, Melanchthon was the first major proponent of a decidedly *evangelical* free will.[72]

---

[70] 'A posteriore in iustificatione dicimus aliquam in accipiente causam esse, videlicet non dignitatem, sed quia promissionem apprehendit, cum qua spiritus sanctus est efficax.' 1533. CR 21.332.

[71] '*A posteriori*', in Richard A. Müller, *Dictionary of Latin and Greek Theological Terms, Drawn Principally from Protestant Scholastic Theology* (Grand Rapids: Baker, 1985), 17.

[72] One or more of the early radicals may well have enunciated a position of free will in justification in the decade prior to the emergence of Melanchthon's distinctive doctrine. However, these early radicals had little immediate influence, and they did not teach a doctrine of forensic justification (which I view as one of the key features of Melanchthon's position).

Contingency and Free Choice in Justification?

Before expressing his opposition to Pelagianism and scholasticism, and before articulating his doctrine of evangelical free will, Melanchthon began his section on free choice with a few words about contingency. Contingency, he sternly stated, had nothing to do with the abilities of the will.[73] He warned, 'One does not inquire into the arcane councils of God governing all; one does not inquire about predestination, nor chase after the contingency of all things. On that note, the prudent reader takes disputations about contingency and predestination and lays them aside, and removes himself far away from this subject.'[74] Again, 'Our work is not to walk in the air and by the heavens scrutinize the manner of the divine governance or predestination.'[75] Instead, free choice in justification had nothing to do with necessity, determinism, or contingency.[76]

However, Melanchthon's own words in the *Loci* of 1533–5 offered at least a tenuous link between contingency and free will. As we have already seen above, Melanchthon associated contingency with predestination by cross-referencing the reader from his section on predestination to his section on contingency. Additionally, we have already explored how closely Melanchthon held together predestination and free will in justification. Contingency was at least notionally tied to predestination, and predestination was definitely tied to free will in justification. Therefore contingency had at least an indirect bearing on free will in justification.

Melanchthon did not want to make this connection, as was obvious from his several strong explicit rebuffs of the link, yet his thought nevertheless

Regarding the word 'evangelical', this was one of Melanchthon's favourite terms in reference to biblical theology throughout the whole reforming movement. For example, even as early as 1518, he wrote, 'I feel that there is absolutely nothing more important than what is approved by the decrees of the Evangelical church...' 'On Correcting the Studies of Youth', in Keen, 55–6. *De corrigendis adolescentiae studiis.* 'Sentio autem omnino aliud nihil, quam quod Evangelicae veritati ecclesiae decretis probatur...' MSA 3.41.10–11.

[73] 'Sed aliena est disputatio de contingentia ab hoc loco de viribus humanis.' 1535. CR 21.373.

[74] 'Non quaeritur de arcano Dei consilio gubernantis omnia; non quaeritur de praedesti-naione; non agitur de omnibus contingentibus. Ideo prudens lector disputationes de contingentia, item de praedestinatione hic seponat et procul ab hoc loco seiungat.' 1535. CR 21.373. Notice again how Melanchthon here notionally linked contingency and predestination. With no more divided governance of God, the two ideas naturally went together as an expression of God's self-limited rule in both the temporal and spiritual realms of reality.

[75] 'Non est opus ἀεροβατειν et caelestia scrutari de modo gubernationis divinae, aut de praedestinatione.' 1535. CR 21.373.

[76] 'Ideo cum de libero arbitrio quaeritur, non sunt infartiendae disputationes de necessitate, nec ideo tollendum est lib. arbitrium quia videantur omnia necessario fieri eo quod deus determinet omnia contingentia.' 1533. CR 21.275.

tended in that direction. In 1521, Melanchthon's unified total governance of God allowed for an easy crossover between determinism and the bound will. Divine determinism was one of his principal arguments against free choice in justification at that time. In the same way, Melanchthon's unified limited rule of God in the early 1530s allowed for an easy crossover between contingency and free will, if only he would let it happen.

No Pelagian Free Will

But Melanchthon was not about to discuss a direct link between contingency and free will in justification in 1533–5. What concerned him most was justification by grace, and to that end he virulently opposed Pelagian[77] free will—that is, the idea that people had the innate ability to fulfil the total law of God and thus earn salvation by their own merits.

According to the Pelagian idea of free will, humans could earn their salvation through works. Melanchthon's primary objection to this idea centred on original sin. Because of innate human corruption, fulfilment of the law had become impossible. Melanchthon wrote, 'Moreover, [people] are full of many contrary natural affections which militate against the law of God',[78] and, 'It is not possible for this corrupt nature to stand in obedience to the conditions God requires.'[79] The Gospel taught the futility of trying to fulfil the law out of human strength,[80] for the law required a renewal of the internal affections,[81] impossible without the Holy Spirit.[82] Works righteousness, achieved through the free will, was simply out of the question, and this was one of the most important reasons for exploring the extent of the freedom of

---

[77] Melanchthon did not mention Pelagius by name, but he clearly attacked Pelagian ideas.

[78] 'Praeterea plena est natura multorum aliorum affectuum qui cum lege dei pugnant.' 1533. CR 21.276. Again, here was the affections argument from 1521, but shorn of its philosophical trappings and stated simply in the context of original sin.

[79] 'Haec corrupta natùra non potest praestare obedientiam ad quam eramus conditi et quam requirit Deus.' 1533. CR 21.275. Also, 'Homines non posse legi Dei satisfacere.' 1535. CR 21.375. Again, 'Facile videbis quod homo non potest praestare integram obedientiam dei.' 1533. CR 21.277. Just in case the alert reader had still not yet picked up on his drift, Melanchthon declared once more, 'Paulus ubique contendit homines non posse iustificati lege.' 1533. CR 21.281.

[80] 'Secundo: Evangelium docet in natura horribilem corruptionem esse, quae repugnat legi Dei, hoc est, facit, ne praestare integram obedientiam possimus.' 1535. CR 21.374.

[81] 'Nam Lex divina requirit non tantum externa facta, sed interiorem mundiciem, timorem, fiduciam, dilectionem Dei summam, denique perfectam obedientiam in hac corrupta natura non praestare.' 1535. CR 21.375.

[82] 'Et hanc corruptionem non potest humana voluntas per sese ex natura tollere.' 1535. CR 21.374. Additionally, 'Voluntas humana non potest sine Spiritu sancto efficere spirituales affectus.' 1535. CR 21.375.

the will in the first place.[83] To say that the freedom of the will reached so far as to allow works righteousness would have been to abnegate the necessity of a grace-based soteriology. For the sake of preserving forensic justification (justification by faith alone), the Pelagian notion of the freedom of the will had to be firmly rejected.

No Scholastic Free Will

Additionally, for the sake of preserving forensic justification, all scholastic notions of free will had to be rejected. Thomas, Scotus, Ockham, and Biel were wrong to advocate any sort of free will whereby human effort became transformed into intrinsic merit, no matter whether this happened by *meritum de condigno, de congruo,* or both. God alone supplied *all* merit, independent of human exertions, through his Son Jesus Christ. True, some civil freedom did exist for doing external works. Melanchthon began his condemnation of the scholastics by acknowledging this. However, he proceeded to argue that the scholastics erred by thinking that civil works of piety could somehow form a bridge towards justification.

As he had done since 1526, Melanchthon readily admitted the existence of freedom in external actions or civil works in the temporal realm. He wrote, 'There remains nevertheless some sort of natural free will in people, some sort of power of the human will apart from the Holy Spirit, such that, without his renovation, external works of the law may be done.'[84] The ability to do civil works remained after the Fall,[85] and this was the sort of free will philosophy spoke about.[86] Such philosophical (civil) free will was impeded by both the devil[87] and innate human corruption.[88] In illustration, Melanchthon quoted

---

[83] 'Quorsum opus est sic discernere quid natura hominis possit quid non possit? Maxime opus est, Primum enim oportet scire quod homines non possint satisfacere legi dei. Nisi enim id teneamus, non poterit intelligi hoc quod Evangelium praecipue praedicat. homines propter Christum iustos pronunciari, non propter nostram impletionem legis.' 1533. CR 21.279.

[84] 'Manet tamen aliqua voluntatis humanae libertas in natura hominis. potest enim humana voluntas aliquo modo sine spiritu sancto i.e. sine illa renovatione facere externa opera legis.' 1533. CR 21.278.

[85] 'Cum in natura hominis reliquum sit iudicium et delectus quidam rerum, quae sunt subiectae rationi aut sensui; relinquiis est etiam delectus externorum operum civilium.' 1535. CR 21.374.

[86] 'Haec est libertas voluntatis, quam Philosophi recte tribuunt homini.' 1535. CR 21.374. Melanchthon also noted that Erasmus called it the free will of philosophy. 'Erasmus haec est libertas voluntatis de qua philosophi loquuntur.' 1533. CR 21.279.

[87] 'Nunc illud tantum addam: hanc ipsam libertatem efficiendae civilis iustitiae saepe vinci naturali imbecillitate, saepe impedire a Diabolo.' 1535. CR 21.374.

[88] 'Nam cum natura sit plena malorum affectuum, saepe obtemperant homines pravis cupiditatibus, non recto iudicio.' 1535. CR 21.374.

the poet describing Medea, who ruefully admitted, 'I see and approve the good, but I follow the bad.'[89] Nevertheless, even with these difficulties of the devil and human corruption, some vestiges of liberty to perform acts of civil righteousness remained.[90]

However, freedom to achieve civil works could in no way lead, or even begin to lead, to salvation. While humans could freely do works externally, inside them the affections and sensual appetites rebelled against those external actions.[91] In other words, the external semblance of piety was a façade, a sham portrait, at best, of what people might like to be but deep at heart were not. Further, as he argued in opposition to Pelagian free will, without the Holy Spirit the human will was unable to achieve the *motus interiores* required by the law. Out of their own wills and apart from the Holy Spirit, people could not truly get rid of doubts about God, nor genuinely fear him, nor take hold of God's mercy in true faith, nor obey him in light of death and other afflictions.[92] People could perform civil works without the Holy Spirit, but they could not even take the first step toward salvation. Yet the scholastics taught that civil works *were* the first step toward salvation, that they indicated a proper preparation of the heart. As the *moderni* might have said, they represented God's precondition for salvation—that one do what lies within him or her (*quod in se est*). Melanchthon wrote, 'The scholastic doctors teach that the Law of God can be satisfied through civil mores. In this they err regarding sin and the Law of God.'[93] The scholastics were simply wrong.[94]

---

[89] 'Sicut inquit apud Poetam Medea: Video meliora proboque, deteriora sequor.' 1535. CR 21.374. Melanchthon would again quote this passage later in 1558, in his *Responsiones scriptae a Philippo Melanthone ad impios articulos Bavaricae inquisitionis*, MSA 6.311.14–15. (See below for a full analysis of that work.)

[90] 'Sed tamen inter has difficultates, utcunque reliqua est aliqua libertas efficiendae iustitiae civilis.' 1535. CR 21.374.

[91] 'Sed voluntas potest nobis externum et simulatum opus imperare, etiam contra suam et sensuum appetitionem.' 1533. CR 21.275.

[92] 'Voluntas non potest sine spiritu sancto abiicere dubitationem de deo, vere timere deum, veram fiduciam misericordiae dei concipere, veram obedientiam in morte et aliis afflictionibus praestare, et habere similes motus interiores iuxta legem dei.' 1533. CR 21.277.

[93] 'Scholastici doctores putant legi dei satisfieri per civiles mores. Hic errant de peccato et de lege Dei.' 1533. CR 21.280.

[94] See also Melanchthon (in Wittenberg), report to Ulrich Geiger (for Guillaume du Bellay), 1 August 1534. MBW 2.1467. T 6.1467. CR 2.741–5 Nr. 1205. Additionally, in a reprint of the *Loci communes*, printed in September 1541, Melanchthon denounced the errors of the 'new learning' (the *via moderna*) as being the same as the errors of Thomas Aquinas (though as we have seen from Chapter 2, this would be an oversimplification—except in their common acceptance of a transformational (rather than forensic) model of justification). MBW 3.2799. T 10.2799. CR 21.341–8. Melanchthon's harsh opinion of scholastic theology (both new and old) would not change over time. Even as late as 1 January 1553, in a letter to Archbishop of Canterbury Thomas Cranmer, Melanchthon argued that Origen, Thomas Aquinas, and the scholastic monks held to false paradigms of justification. MBW 7.6696. CR 8.8–11 Nr. 5305.

Melanchthon criticized the scholastics not so much because of their position on civil free will (he agreed with them about civil works), but because of what they affixed to this sort of freedom—salvation. Melanchthon maintained, 'Therefore the scholastics are reprehensible, not so much regarding free choice, as regarding other impious dogmas which they had affixed to it, such as when they put forth their teaching that people were able to fulfil and satisfy the law of God through free choice, and be pronounced just according to human effort.'[95] Clearly, by 'the scholastics', Melanchthon meant primarily the doctrines of the *via moderna*, by theologians such as Gabriel Biel. The 'scholastics' made civil free will the first step toward salvation. They made philosophical free will a bridge from external works to internal renewal. Such an idea of doing good to become good found its source in Aristotle's ethics. In the *Summary of Ethics* of 1532, Melanchthon had said that external actions could have internal effects even in the establishment of some degree of moral virtue. However, he *never* said that such a crossover between the temporal and spiritual realms would be sufficient to garner (or even *begin* to garner) salvation. This was clear from the Bible. Yet the 'scholastics' argued that freely-achieved external good works acted as a minimal precondition for the infusion of God's vivifying and enabling grace. For Melanchthon, the key issue at stake here was justification by grace, that is, God's mercy or favour. God's favour had to be accepted through faith, following which the total merit for salvation was imputed to the sinner in a forensic fashion, from outside. Any idea of humans earning their own merit, no matter how little, violated Melanchthon's soteriology of forensic justification and therefore could not stand. Scholastic (or *via moderna*) free will had to be opposed because it misconstrued genuine temporal free will as meritorious towards salvation.

Evangelical[96] Free Will

Having refuted both Pelagian and scholastic paradigms of free will in justification, Melanchthon moved on to establish his own position. In previous years, at this point in his composition, Melanchthon would have described the bound will. However, in 1532, having switched to a soteriology utilizing the free will, Melanchthon now attempted to give voice with greater clarity to his new ideas about the nature of the will.

[95] 'Proinde reprehendendi sunt scholastici non tam de libero arb. quam de aliis impiis dogmatibus quae affinxerunt, cum putarent illam disciplinam, quam potest praestare liberum arb. legi dei satisfacere, et propter eam homines pronunciari iustos.' 1533. CR 21.280.

[96] The word 'evangelical' was used very early in the Reformation, even before 'Protestant', and to this day continues to be a useful word for Bible-believing Christians with a Reformation heritage. See MacCulloch, *The Reformation*, 343.

Melanchthon's advocacy of free will within the realm of justification hinged upon the ability of the will to hear and accept God's universal promises of salvation. The first area in soteriology where free will held any place was at the moment of conversion.[97] The will never allowed one to do works and earn merit, but it did allow one to choose to accept God's free gift of merit through Jesus Christ. Justification required three things: the Word, the Holy Spirit working through the Word,[98] and the human will, which chose to believe the Spirit-enlightened promises of the Word. Melanchthon cited Romans 8.26 in support of this position: 'Likewise the Spirit helps us in our weakness; for we do not know how to pray as we ought, but that very Spirit intercedes with sighs too deep for words.' He commented, 'In this example we see that these causes are connected: the Word, the Holy Spirit, and the will, not indifferently, by all means, but resisting our infirmity.'[99] Melanchthon sought both to amplify the aid of the Holy Spirit and to sharpen the care and diligence of human wills.[100] In so doing, he crafted a careful balance between promoting the priority of the Word and Spirit while simultaneously allowing for the human will's free, uncoerced, reaction to that very Word.

To that end, the Spirit's work in the heart of the hearer of the Word was not automatically effective, according to Melanchthon. He made this quite clear by citing Ecclesiasticus 15.14 (one of Erasmus' favourite texts): 'It was [God] who created humankind in the beginning, and he left them in the power of their own free choice.'[101]

For two reasons, it is interesting and rather odd that Melanchthon cited this text: First, it came from the Apocrypha. Second, verse 15 seemed to directly contradict all of Melanchthon's arguments against any human ability to fulfil the law. Verse 15: 'If you choose, you can keep the commandments, and to act faithfully is a matter of your own choice.' Perhaps Melanchthon understood this verse as referring to civil works, yet he himself defined the true import of the commandments as referring to the internal affections over which humans had no control. Hence, by citing Ecclus. 15.14, Melanchthon was most likely stretching for a verse that would most directly aid his argument, even if it had

---

[97] Schwarzenau (p. 119) argues that through the Word and Holy Spirit, a new Being is created—one who has free will. This theory sounds somewhat like Thomas Aquinas, but in light of Melanchthon's frequent explicit denunciations of Thomas as well as the scant evidence in Melanchthon's texts to support Schwarzenau's idea, I find his thought unsustainable.

[98] The Holy Spirit worked through the Word. 'Et Spiritus sanctus ibi efficax est per verbum.' 1535. CR 21.376.

[99] 'In hoc exemplo videmus coniungi has causas, Verbum, Spiritum sanctum, et voluntatem, non sane otiosam, sed repugnantem infirmitati suae.' 1535. CR 21.376.

[100] 'Imo et amplificat Spiritus sancti auxilium, et acuit curam ac diligentiam nostrae volutatis.' 1535. CR 21.377.

[101] 1535. CR 21.377.

to be taken out of context (especially in relation to verse 15). This awkward-
ness showed that Melanchthon was not yet comfortable in his new-found
arguments for free will.

In any case, building on this quotation, Melanchthon added the comment,
'I say that the will is not indifferent in pious actions, but nevertheless is helped
by the Holy Spirit. Thus it has true freedom.'[102] Again, 'I do not approve the
deliriums of the Manicheans who attribute absolutely no action to the will,
nor help from the Holy Spirit. They act as if they have no interest at all about
the standing of the will.'[103] For Melanchthon, the will played a genuine role in
justification.

Melanchthon advocated the simultaneous action of the will with the
Spirit. The will had to assent to the Spirit, or forensic justification could
not occur. This was a unique doctrine, for previous advocates of free will
(Pelagius and the various scholastics) had utilized the operation of the will
as the beginnings of human-earned merit. Further, this was not Erasmus'
doctrine of free will, for Erasmus connected the free operation of the will to
scholastic conceptions of intrinsic righteousness and a gradual transformational conception of justification. Keen writes, 'The difference between
Melanchthonian and Erasmian conceptions of righteousness is so complete
that one must see Erasmus' indifference to the alien elements of the gospel as
profoundly opposed to Melanchthon's thought.'[104] Melanchthon, in contrast, restricted the will to conversion and ascribed absolutely no merit to it
whatsoever. In this sense he was the first to argue for *evangelical* free will—
that is, free choice in conversion combined with a soteriology of forensic
justification. The free operation of the human will in choosing to have faith
in God was *instrumental* rather than *causative* for salvation. It was the
passive means by which salvation was *received* rather than the active
means by which it was *earned*. For Melanchthon, this doctrine had to be
the truth, for it both preserved justification by grace rather than works, and
it also allowed people to be responsible for their own damnation if they
failed to accept God's promises.

---

[102] 'Dico voluntatem in piis actionibus et conatibus non esse otiosam, sed tamen adiuvan-
dam esse a Spiritu sancto: ita fit verius libera.' 1535. CR 21.377.

[103] 'Non probo deliramenta Manichaeorum, qui prorsus nullam voluntati actionem tribue-
bant, ne quidem adiuvante Spiritu sancto; quasi nihil interesset inter statuam et voluntatem.'
1535. CR 21.377.

[104] Ralph Keen, 'Melanchthon and His Roman Catholic Opponents', *Lutheran Quarterly* 12
(1998), 422. Günther (pp. 108–9), makes a similar point when he notes that while Erasmus used
the scholastics, Melanchthon did not. Further, Melanchthon kept a stronger doctrine of original
sin than Erasmus did.

CONCLUSION

In 1532–5, Melanchthon began to articulate his own unique doctrine of evangelical free will. While yet retaining the Reformation soteriology of forensic justification by faith alone, Melanchthon now began to teach that in the decision of faith, in the context of hearing the Spirit-inspired Word, the individual will was free to either accept or reject the gift of salvation in Jesus Christ.

Theological colleagues would soon note this revision to Melanchthon's theology, and they would begin to challenge him on it. Meanwhile, the great events of the Reformation swept on, and as Melanchthon both taught and represented the Protestant cause on the wider western European stage, he continued to hone this new evangelical understanding of the will's role in justification.

9

1536–1547: Tremors

INTRODUCTION

By the mid-1530s Melanchthon's views on the role of the human will in choosing faith in Jesus had changed. It was no longer solely the work of the Lord, but was now a free human choice that was enabled by God through the means of Word and Spirit, yet was neither predetermined nor coerced. From this point onwards, Melanchthon proceeded to consolidate his theological system in light of his new convictions. Meanwhile, other theologians noticed Melanchthon's new ideas. 'For years before his own death in 1560, he was himself the object of grave suspicion from self-appointed guardians of Luther's legacy, who denounced aspects of his teaching they regarded as treacherous and labelled Philippism.'[1] Some, like Camerarius, politely sought further information.[2] Others immediately pounced. The first of these was Conrad Cordatus.

THE CORDATUS CONTROVERSY: 1536–1537

Cordatus, a student of Melanchthon's from the early 1520s, noticed the change in Melanchthon's doctrine of justification and promptly challenged him on it beginning in the middle of 1536.[3] On 6 December 1536, Cordatus drafted a direct challenge to Melanchthon, but, for whatever reason, he did not send it to him.[4] On 14 April 1537, however, Cordatus wrote another challenge to

[1] MacCulloch, *The Reformation*, 245 (see also 338–40).
[2] See Melanchthon's reply to Camerarius, written on 22 December 1535 (from Schmalkald), to Camerarius (in Tübingen). MBW 2.1678. T 6.1678. CR 2.1027–8 Nr. 1381.
[3] For more information on this controversy, see Scheible, 'Luther and Melanchthon', 333–4; and Stupperich, *Melanchthon*, 97–8. Jakob Schenk, a preacher from Freiburg and another of Melanchthon's former students, also attacked him on justification.
[4] MBW 2.1819. T 7.1819. CR 3.202–4 Nr. 1496.

Melanchthon, and this time he actually did send it.[5] In this document he criticized Melanchthon for departing from Luther on Pauline doctrine, especially with reference to justification. Cordatus, in contrast, defended the soteriology Melanchthon had taught fourteen years earlier (in 1519–21). Cordatus had obviously noticed the way in which Melanchthon had limited the spiritual determination of God and had inserted a measure of free will into justification. He further attacked Melanchthon on his doctrine of good works.[6]

Melanchthon's reply to this challenge was most illuminating—his essential argument was that he had *not* deviated from Luther, and that, in fact, he and Luther were in complete agreement on justification and the doctrine of the will. Melanchthon wrote, 'As you know, I formulate some things less harshly [*minus horride*] concerning predestination, the assent of the will [to grace], the necessity of our obedience [after justification], and mortal sin. I know that on all these issues Luther is in fact of the same opinion. But the uneducated people love his coarse formulations too much, because they do not perceive what context they belong in.'[7] In essence, Melanchthon was not denying that his theology was somewhat at odds with Luther's earlier formulations (including *De servo arbitrio*), but Melanchthon maintained that Luther tended to exaggerate in his stronger statements, and that if he had thought things through carefully (e.g. on the full implications of divine determinism on the terrified conscience), then Luther would not really have said those things. In other words, Luther and Melanchthon seemed to differ in their theology, but they were actually in agreement, for Luther did not really mean what he had said earlier.[8] Further, stepping back from Melanchthon's own analysis of

---

[5] Conrad Cordatus (in Niemegk), to Melanchthon (in Wittenberg). MBW 2.1887. T 7.1887. CR 3.341–2 Nr. 1558.

[6] From April 1537, until August of the same year, Cordatus' attacks shifted from free will and justification to an emphasis on Melanchthon's doctrine of good works. Cordatus (in Niemegk), letter to Melanchthon (in Wittenberg), 17 April 1537. MBW 2.1892. T 7.1892. CR 3.351 Nr. 1561B. Melanchthon (in Leipzig), letter to Martin Bucer (in Strassburg), 23 April 1537. MBW 2.1895. T 7.1895. CR 3.356 Nr. 1566. Melanchthon (in Wittenberg), letter to George Scarabaeus (in Hanover), 2 June 1537. MBW 2.1910. T 7.1910. CR 5.753–4 Nr. 3185.

[7] Translated into English by Scheible, in 'Luther and Melanchthon', 334. 'Scis me quedam minus horride dicere de praedestinatione, de assensu voluntatis, de necessitate obedientiae nostrae, de peccato mortali. De his omnibus scio re ipsa Lutherum sentire eadem, sed ineruditi quaedam eius φορτικώτερα dicta, cum non videant quo pertineant, nimium amant.' Melanchthon (in Wittenberg), letter to Veit Dietrich (in Nuremberg), 22 June 1537. MBW 2.1914. T 7.1914.12–15. CR 3.383 Nr. 1588.

[8] Stupperich picks up on this point in *Melanchthon*, 97. However, Melanchthon's argument that he and Luther were in agreement in opposing parts of DSA was seriously compromised by Luther's letter of 9 July 1537, to Wolfgang Capito. There Luther wrote, 'Regarding [the plan] to collect my writings in volumes, I am quite cool and not at all eager about it because, roused by a Saturnian hunger, I would rather see them all devoured. For I acknowledge none of them to be really a book of mine, except perhaps the one *On the Bondage of the Will* and the *Catechism*.' LW

the situation, we can see why Melanchthon and Luther continued to feel that they remained in agreement on justification: they both advocated justification by faith rather than works, with faith being instrumental (and non-meritorious) rather than causative for salvation.

In his letters, Melanchthon repeatedly defended himself against Cordatus' attacks, arguing again and again that he and Luther were agreed on justification and free will.[9] On 15 April 1537, Melanchthon responded to Cordatus himself with a carefully worded missive saying that he had never mocked Luther's teaching, but that one had to be cautious in formulating theological doctrine, especially with justification. One had to formulate theology so that it would be useful to people. (Here was Melanchthon's pastoral concern again—that is, care for the effects of doctrine.) Melanchthon suggested that he could easily dispose of Cordatus' theological objections.[10]

Melanchthon tried to downplay the fact that his theology had changed. He sought at all costs to maintain unity with Luther, and he vehemently denied that he had deviated from the older man's doctrine. As we have seen in tracing his theology carefully through his progressive theological writings, however, Melanchthon's theology in 1536 was without a doubt different from his theology in 1519, particularly in the area of the determination of God and the role of the will in justification. Scholars other than Cordatus began to challenge Melanchthon on these changes. For example, Nikolaus von Amsdorf published pieces in 1536 and 1541 attacking Melanchthon's altered views on necessity. By contrast, he sought to defend Luther's strong assertions from *De servo arbitrio*.[11] Melanchthon's dispute with Cordatus was at an end by

50.172–3. WABr 8.99–100. That Luther would name DSA as one of his two best works out of all his writings does not lend much credence to Melanchthon's claim that Luther had moved on from what he had written therein. On the other hand, in defence of Melanchthon, some might argue that Luther viewed DSA as a defence of justification by faith alone, and that he approved of it for that purpose without necessarily continuing to endorse the passages with which Melanchthon took issue.

[9] Melanchthon was especially preoccupied with this issue in November 1536. See Melanchthon (in Wittenberg), letter to Martin Luther, Justas Jonas, Johannes Bugenhagen, and Caspar Cruciger (in Wittenberg), 1 November 1536. MBW 2.1802. T 7.1802. CR 3.179–81 Nr. 1480. WABr 7.579–83 Nr. 3099. Melanchthon, letter to Veit Dietrich (in Nuremberg), 5 November 1536. MBW 2.1808. T 7.1808. CR 3.185–6 Nr. 1483. Melanchthon, letter to Veit Dietrich, 16 November 1536. MBW 2.1810. T 7.1810. CR 3.187–8 Nr. 1486. Melanchthon, letter to Joachim Camerarius (in Tübingen), 29 November 1536. MBW 2.1815. T 7.1815. CR 3.193–4 Nr. 1492.

[10] Melanchthon (in Wittenberg), letter to Conrad Cordatus (in Niemegk), 15 April 1537. MBW 2.1889. T 7.1889. CR 3.341–2 Nr. 1558.

[11] Nikolaus von Amsdorf, *De contingentia. Disputatione prima pars* (Dresden: Sächsische Landesbibliothek, Ms. Dres. A180, 1536), 752–70. Nikolaus von Amsdorf, *Annotationes quibus indicatur paucis quae in locis communibus Philippi Melanchthonis displicent per N.A.* (Weimar: Goethe-Schiller Archiv der Nationale Forschungs- und Gedenkstätten der klassischen deutschen Literatur: Ehemalige Thüringische Landesbibliothek folio Band XL, 1541), 301–9. For secondary

July 1537,[12] but in October of that year, he was still communicating to Brenz that he thought his work had been treated disrespectfully.[13] Meanwhile, a more famous figure began to take note of Melanchthon's changed thought on the will.

CALVIN'S CONCERNS: 1538–1539

John Calvin quickly noticed Melanchthon's shift in his doctrine of the will, especially as it connected to predestination. As Cameron notes, Melanchthon was 'willing to incur Calvin's wrath over predestination'[14] despite the fact that early on the two considered themselves to be allies.[15] Calvin sustained a long and generally friendly correspondence with Melanchthon between 1538 and 1558,[16] and in some of these letters, Calvin took the opportunity to respectfully enquire into the way in which Melanchthon's theology of predestination and the will had evolved.[17]

In the late 1530s, the thirty-year-old Calvin noted Melanchthon's recent silence on predestination when he wrote in the epistolary dedication to his 1539 *Commentary on Romans*, 'Philipp Melanchthon, who, by his singular learning and industry, and by that readiness in all kinds of knowledge, in

literature, see Kolb, *Bound Will*, 95–7, and Kolb, 'Nikolaus von Amsdorf on Vessels of Wrath and Vessels of Mercy: A Lutheran's Doctrine of Double Predestination', *Harvard Theological Review* 69 (1976), 325–43. Reprinted as chapter 2 in Kolb, *Luther's Heirs Define His Legacy: Studies on Lutheran Confessionalization* (Aldershot: Variorum, 1996).

[12] Melanchthon (in Wittenberg), letter to Veit Dietrich (in Nuremberg), 13 July 1537. MBW 2.1920. T 7.1920. CR 3.387–8 Nr. 1590. See also another letter to Dietrich, dated 23 July. MBW 2.1922. T 7.1922. CR 3.392 Nr. 1594.

[13] In 1537, in a letter to Brenz he complained that Cordatus had trod the *Loci* with his feet. 12 October 1537. MBW 2.1952. T 7.1952. CR 3.390–1 Nr. 1592.

[14] Cameron, 'Philipp Melanchthon: Image and Substance', 719.

[15] Keen, 1.

[16] According to the listings in MBW, 24 letters between the two men remain extant: MBW 2.2103 (T 8.2103), 3.3157, 3.3169, 3.3245, 3.3273, 4.3531, 4.3803, 4.3884, 4.3885, 4.3886, 4.3928, 6.5830, 6.6576, 6.6655, 7.7273, 7.7306, 7.7424, 7.7489, 7.7562, 7.7957, 8.8293, 8.8331, 8.8384, and 8.8782. Of these, one was a draft that was never sent (4.3884 was a draft of 4.3885), and of the remaining 23, 15 were from Calvin to Melanchthon, and only eight were from Melanchthon to Calvin. Melanchthon was a reluctant correspondent with Calvin if the ratio of letters found in MBW is accurate.

[17] For more on Calvin and Melanchthon's correspondence, see Timothy Wengert, '"We Will Feast Together in Heaven Forever": The Epistolary Friendship of John Calvin and Philip Melanchthon', in *Melanchthon in Europe: His Work and Influence Beyond Wittenberg*, ed. Karin Maag (Grand Rapids: Baker, 1999), 19–44. See also J. T. Hickman, 'The Friendship of Melanchthon and Calvin', *Westminster Theological Journal* 38 (1975–6), 152–65.

which he excels, has introduced more light than those who had preceded him. But as it seems to have been his object to examine only those things which are mainly worthy of attention, he dwelt at large on these, and designedly passed by many things which common minds find to be difficult.'[18] Again, Calvin put it charitably: 'Philipp attained his object by illustrating the principal points: being occupied with these primary things, he passed by many things which deserve attention; and it was not his purpose to prevent others to examine them.'[19] Calvin graciously said that Melanchthon's omissions (e.g. on predestination, especially in his *Commentary on Romans* of 1532) allowed Calvin to write his own commentary.[20]

THE AUGSBURG CONFESSION *VARIATA*: 1540

The attacks by Cordatus may have left Melanchthon embittered, but they did not cause him to waver in affirming his new theology. In 1540, within a revised edition of the *Augsburg Confession*, Melanchthon continued to express his revised theology of the will's role in justification. He made one relatively minor change to his language about the last judgement in Article XVII, and then inserted his new doctrine of conversion into the middle of Article XVIII on free choice. Finally, he added an entirely new unnumbered section simply titled, *De Fide*, from which several of the following quotations are taken. Throughout the *Variata*, Melanchthon firmly advocated evangelical free will.

In 1530, Melanchthon's Article XVII stated, 'that Christ will appear at the end of the world to judge, and the dead shall rise, the pious and elect will be given eternal life and perpetual joy, but the impious people and the devil will be condemned to be tortured eternally'.[21] This article in 1540 was exactly the same, except that the words *et electis* had been dropped.[22] In 1530 Melanchthon had been comfortable using the language of election to salvation (but note that he said only that the 'impious' would go to hell, and he avoided

[18] John Calvin, *Commentaries on the Epistle of Paul the Apostle to the Romans*, ed. and trans. John Owen, in *Calvin's Commentaries* (Grand Rapids: Baker, 1979), vol. 19, p. xxv.

[19] Ibid., xxvi.

[20] Ibid., xxvi.

[21] 'Item docent, quod Christus apparebit in consumatione mundi ad iudicandum, et mortuos omnes resuscitabit, pijs *et electis* dabit vitam aeternam et perpetua gaudia, impios autem homines ac diabolos condemnabit, ut sine fine crucientur' (emphasis added). CR 26.282.

[22] 'Item docent, quod Christus apparebit in consumatione mundi ad iudicandum, et mortuos omnes resuscitabit, pijs dabit vitam aeternam et perpetua gaudia, impios autem homines ac diabolos condemnabit, ut sine fine crucientur.' CR 26. 361.

using the word 'reprobate'[23]). Yet, by 1540 Melanchthon no longer felt it necessary to mention that word 'election' unless it came in a biblical text that used the word explicitly. Melanchthon felt that the word 'election' upset people, leading them to question their salvation, thinking that maybe they were reprobate. Pastorally, this was unhelpful, to say the least. Predestination was not to be pondered upon, but instead people were to give their attention to the universal promises of the Gospel,[24] realizing that because salvation came through grace and faith, there was now certainty and comfort for the terrified conscience.[25] Certainty and comfort, of course, so long as one maintained faith.

Faith, or full assent to (and trust in) God's promises, was necessary for salvation. In Article XVIII on free choice, Melanchthon added the new sentences, 'But spiritual righteousness is effected in us when we are helped by the Holy Spirit. Furthermore, we receive the Holy Spirit when we assent to the Word of God, in order that we might be consoled in our terrors by faith. As Paul taught [in Galatians 3.14], you receive the spiritual promise through faith.'[26] The Holy Spirit helped, but salvation only occurred when one received (or assented to) the Word of God (*cum verbo Dei assentimur*). Again, 'It is necessary to accept by faith the merciful promises of Christ.'[27] It was *necessary* to accept (*oportet fide accipi*). This faith, this saving acceptance of God's promises, required a choice of the will, which, even if assisted, was never coerced by the Holy Spirit. Salvation depended on the free human choice to believe God's promises.

THE COMMENTARY ON ROMANS: 1540

In the same year that the *Variata* appeared, Melanchthon wrote yet another commentary on Romans.[28] In this new edition, he continued to affirm that

---

[23] Melanchthon continued to teach the reality of hell throughout his career. In his *De anima* of 1553, Melanchthon said, 'Just as without doubt we are sure that twice four is eight, so it must be stated that God will...subject the impious to eternal punishments.' Keen, 266. 'Ut sine dubitatione asseveramus, bis 4 esse 8: ita statuendum est Deum excitaturum esse homines mortuos, et ecclesiam ornaturum aeterna gloria, et impios abiecturum in aeternas poenas.' MSA 3.341.39–342.2.

[24] 'Non est hic opus disputationibus de predestinatione aut similibus. Nam promissio est vniuersalis...' CR 26.365.

[25] CR 26.365–6.

[26] 'Efficitur autem spiritualis iusticia in nobis, cum adiuuamur a spiritu sancto. Porro Spiritum sanctum concipimus, cum verbo Dei assentimur, vt nos fide in terroribus consolemur, Sic ut Paulus docet ait, Vt promissionem spiritus accipiatis per fidem.' CR 26.362.

[27] 'Sed hanc misericordiam promissam propter Christum, oportet fide accipi.' CR 26.367.

[28] *Commentarii in Epistolam Pauli ad Romanos*, 1540. CR 15.495–796. For an English translation, see Philipp Melanchthon, *Commentary on Romans*, trans. Fred Kramer (St Louis:

the exercise of the will in choosing to believe God's promises was necessary for salvation. This requirement of the free operation of the will, here expressed more decidedly than ever, continued to be held in place by his unique view of predestination.

A Predestined Church[29]

In Melanchthon's *Commentary on Romans* of 1540, he reiterated several previous points in relation to predestination—namely, the necessity of accepting the Bible without speculating beyond its bounds,[30] the genuine universality of the Gospel promises,[31] and the cause of election being God's mercy.[32] Further, Melanchthon strongly and repeatedly affirmed that the cause of reprobation was not God, but the free will of individuals in resisting Him.[33] Finally, in this work Melanchthon began to advocate something new—'election' referred to the *church*, rather than individuals. Kolb writes, '[Melanchthon] shifted his definition of the chief concern of [Romans 9] from the doctrine of election, a subdivision of the doctrine of justification, to the doctrine of the church, a shift that parallels the shift in the treatment of the doctrine of election itself—from an emphasis on its connection with justification to a focus on its significance for ecclesiology—in his *Loci communes theologici*.'[34] Reprobation was the fault of the individual will in resisting

Concordia, 1992). Unless otherwise indicated, Kramer's translation will be used for English translations.

[29] It should be acknowledged that the phrase 'predestined church' has precedent in Augustine. See *City of God*, xx.8.

[30] 'We need to make pronouncements about our deeds and about the will and judgment of God according to the express Word of God.' Trans. Kramer, 48. 'Nos de nostris factis, et de voluntate ac iudicio Dei, iuxta verbum Dei expressum pronunciare debemus.' CR 15.535.

[31] 'The promises are universal. Since this is so, God commands and teaches that all should believe that they are equally loved and accounted righteous.' Trans. Kramer, 120. On Rom. 4.23–5. 'Promissiones sint universales. Hoc cum ita sit, Deus postulat ac praecipit, ut omnes credant se pariter diligi et iustos reputari.' CR 15.610.

[32] 'The mercy of God is the cause of election, as Paul clearly teaches here and elsewhere.' Trans. Kramer, 187. On Rom. 9. 'Misericordia Dei sit causa electionis, sicut Paulus clare docet, hoc loco, et alibi.' CR 15.679.

[33] 'But not all attain the benefits because many resist the Word. And it is evident that resistance is an act of the human will, because God is not a cause of sin.' Trans. Kramer, 187. On Rom. 9. 'Sed non omnes consequuntur beneficia, quia perique repugnant verbo. Et manifestum est, quod repugnare sit voluntatis humanae, quia Deus non est causa peccati.' CR 15.680. Again, 'Here [Paul] expressly sets down the cause of reprobation, namely, because they fight against the gospel.' Trans. Kramer, 192. On Rom. 9.18–24. 'Hic expresse ponit causam reprobationis, scilicet, quia repugnent Evangelio.' CR 15.685.

[34] Robert Kolb, 'Melanchthon's Influence on the Exegesis of his Students: The Case of Romans 9', in *Philip Melanchthon (1497–1560) and the Commentary*, ed. Timothy J. Wengert

God, and salvation also was dependent on the human will in assenting to God. Obviously, election could not refer to God's choice of individuals for salvation or damnation because such things were dependent on the wills of individuals. Election had to refer to the church, or to the means of grace. Melanchthon wrote, 'We must declare that the church has been elected not on account of worthiness and human merit, not on account of righteousness of the Law, not on account of human authority.'[35] Elsewhere, he stated, '[Paul] is speaking of the effect of the election, that the true church has been elected through mercy.'[36] Finally, and most clearly, 'Therefore, the church is by election, not by natural gifts or merits.'[37] Individual human wills, by their assent or resistance to God, determined their own salvations. Election, therefore, referred to the church in a *corporate* sense. One could begin to discern this idea in Melanchthon's *Commentary on Romans* of 1532, but he expressed it more vigorously here in 1540.

Avoiding Fatalism

In 1540, Melanchthon furthered his argument for the universal application of the promises of the Gospel. Demonstrating once again his pastoral concerns, he put forward that if anyone said that the promises were not universal, then one could easily fall into one of two errors—works righteousness, or speculations about election. He wrote, 'One must know that this gospel promise is universal. The godly must be reminded of this because uneasy minds argue most of all about these two questions: worthiness and election.'[38] Predestination of individuals to salvation would also imply the reprobation of individuals to damnation, an evil and untenable position in Melanchthon's eyes. Melanchthon derided such a doctrine of

and M. Patrick Graham (Sheffield: Sheffield Academic Press, 1997), 206. Kolb sees Melanchthon's reorientation of election towards the church rather than individuals as early as the *Commentary on Romans* of 1532. However, the most convincing texts he cites in support are from the *Commentary on Romans* of 1540 (e.g. p. 199). If this new thought is indeed to be found in the *Commentary on Romans* of 1532, it emerges much more vigorously in 1540.

[35] Trans. Kramer, 182. On Rom. 8.30. 'Necesse est enim nos statuere, quod sit Ecclesia electa, non propter iusticiam legis non propter autoritatem humanam, non propter praerogativam successionis.' CR 15.675.

[36] Trans. Kramer, 186. On Rom. 9. 'Loquitur igitur de electionis effectu, quod sit vera Ecclesia electa per misericordiam.' CR 15.679.

[37] Trans. Kramer, 189. On Rom. 9.6b. 'Ergo fit Ecclesia electione, non donis naturalibus aut meritis.' CR 15.682.

[38] Trans. Kramer, 20. 'Sciendum est autem hanc evangelicam promissionem universalem esse, quod eo necesse est admoneri pios, quia pavidae mentes de his duabus quaestionibus maxime disputant, videlicet de dignitate et de electione.' CR 15.505.

predestination as a metaphysical philosophical (i.e. Stoic) intrusion into theology, and he maintained that the universal nature of God's promises clearly refuted such a fatalistic notion of salvation. He wrote, 'For also the philosophers agree that God favours a certain few, namely, heroic men, and that he governs their fate, but they believe that the rest of men are neglected by God. Precisely in this way the mind thinks about predestination, as they call it. However, the heavenly voice criticizes this human opinion. This distinguishes the gospel from philosophical opinions and from the Law, for it shows that the will of God is otherwise. It shows that God truly wants to accept also the unworthy, and that he offers grace to all, asking only that they believe the promise.'[39] Salvation did not hinge upon God's choice of individuals (which would be fatalism), but upon the individual's choice of God at the moment when he heard the Spirit-illumined Word.

The Necessity of 'the Impulse'

Once a person's eyes were opened through the Word and the Spirit, salvation depended upon the individual's free decision to have faith in God. Melanchthon declared, 'But it is necessary that mention be made of faith because it is necessary that there be some impulse by which we accept the gift and apply it to ourselves.'[40] 'Some impulse' (*aliquem motum*) was necessary, naturally flowing from the free will. This impulse would cause the will to 'accept the gift and apply it to ourselves'. While this impulse would come in the company of the ever-Spirit-illumined Word, neither the Word nor the Spirit working through it directly caused this impulse. Certainly, the impulse could not have been caused by God, for then the fact that some received the impulse and others did not would be a return to the type of predestination Melanchthon identified with a heretical non-Christian fatalism. Hence, the origins of the mysterious impulse to grasp salvation in faith had to be traced back to a choice of the will—free will.

---

[39] Trans. Kramer, 20. 'Nam et Philosophi adsentiuntur, Deum paucis quibusdam, videlicet heroicis viris favere, et eorum eventus gubernare, sed reliquos homines negligi a Deo cogitant. Prorsus hoc modo cogitat mens de praedestinatione, ut vocant. Sed hanc humanam opinionem taxat vox coelestis. Hoc differt Evangelium a philosophicis opinionibus et a lege, quia aliter monstrat Dei voluntatem, ostendit Deum vere et indignos velle recipere, et omnibus offerre gratiam, modo ut credant promissioni.' CR 15.505.

[40] Trans. Kramer, 29. 'Sed necesse est fidei mentionem fieri, quia oportet aliquem motum esse, quo accipimus munus, et nobis applicamus.' CR 15.515.

THE REGENSBURG COLLOQUY: 1541

In 1541, the will's role in justification was a major issue at the Colloquy of Regensburg, the last major attempt by the Protestants and Roman Catholics to find common ground on the doctrine of justification.[41] The Protestant party included Melanchthon, Bucer, and Pistorius, while the Catholic party was comprised of Eck, Gropper, and Julius Pfug (with Cardinal Contarini acting as a powerful force in the background). Melanchthon, Bucer, Gropper, and Contarini turned out to be the major players in this colloquy, and their most important formulations relating to the will involved Articles II (on free choice)[42] and V (on justification).[43]

At first glance, Article II on free choice might appear useful for understanding Melanchthon's developing thought on free will. However, closer examination of this article reveals it to be a straightforward denial of Pelagianism and an endorsement of the necessity of grace in justification. In one way or another, almost all Roman Catholic and Protestant theologians would have been able to support such a broad general statement, so it is not particularly useful in getting a better understanding of Melanchthon's thought in particular.

Similarly, Article V on justification used the hazy language of theological compromise. It contributes little to our understanding of Melanchthon's thought on free will in 1541 with the notable exception of section 8 of Article V. In this section, the phrase *libero arbitrio tanquam partiali agente* appears. In a letter to Camerarius, Melanchthon acknowledged that Luther would not have approved of this stance on free choice, but that he himself would not reject it *cum sit verum* ('because it was true').[44] Hence, even within the diplomatic theology of Regensburg, some hint of Melanchthon's position on free will could be discerned.

---

[41] For more information on Regensburg and a good bibliography on the topic, see Vinzenz Pfnür, 'Colloquies', in OER 1.375–83. Regarding ecumenical effectiveness, MacCulloch calls Regensburg a fiasco (*The Reformation*, 262).

[42] CR 4.191–3.

[43] Three drafts of Article V may be found in ARC 6. The first draft can be found in ARC 6.30–44, the second draft in ARC 6.44–52, and the third in ARC 6.52–4 (as well as in CR 4.198–201). The copy of the *Liber Ratisbonensis* that can be found in CR 4.190–238 is dated 27 April 1541, and represents the finished agreement of the colloquy rather than the initial version of the *Liber Ratisbonensis* presented to the delegates at the beginning of the gathering. Additionally, a fragmentary document bearing Melanchthon's autograph also contains the final draft of the article on justification from Regensburg: *Fragm. de iustificatione.* CR 10.112–15 Nr. 7106.

[44] Melanchthon (in Regensburg), letter to Joachim Camerarius (in Tübingen), 21 June 1541. MBW 3.2732. T 10.2732. CR 4.407 Nr. 2272.

The Regensburg Colloquy was a highly significant event in its own right and deserves a great deal of space. Melanchthon was a notable participant in this event, but his dealings here in his role of diplomatic theological ambassador shed little light on his personal views on the will's role in the decision of faith. Therefore, I must leave a full treatment of Regensburg to others and turn instead to the writings that flowed indisputably from Melanchthon's pen. To that end, we turn now to the 1543 edition of Melanchthon's textbook, *The Elements of Rhetoric*. At first blush it might seem odd to look for theology in a text on rhetoric, but there we will find that Melanchthon took a particular digression to lay out explicitly his understanding of the origins of faith and how the will was involved.

THE ELEMENTS OF RHETORIC: 1543

In his textbook of 1543, Melanchthon explicitly advocated the use of classical rhetoric as a tool for understanding Scripture and theology.[45] To illustrate his method, he gave an extended example of how to apply the categories of rhetoric to theological analysis. In a move highly convenient for the present work, Melanchthon chose for his case study the issue of faith—what it is, what its parts are, what causes it, what its effects are, and what things are related and opposed to it.[46] He wrote, 'These principles [*loci*—places, topics] should be consulted when we wish to teach men. And minds must be trained in such a way that immediately there will come to mind those principles that will tell them where to look and how to select things from the great store of material and in what order it should be set out.'[47] In following his discussion, we can

---

[45] *Elementorum rhetorices libri duo.* CR 13.413–506. The text can also be found both in the original Latin, and in parallel English translation, in Sister Mary Joan La Fontaine's useful unpublished dissertation, 'A Critical Translation of Philip Melanchthon's "Elementorum Rhetorices Libri Duo" (Latin Text)' (Ann Arbor: University of Michigan, 1968).

[46] 'Loci simplicis quaestionis sunt.
'Quid sit.
'Quae sint partes vel species.
'Quae causae.
'Qui effectus.
'Quae cognata et pugnantia.' CR 13.424. The section on faith begins under the heading of 'Another example' (*aliud exemplum*), CR 13.426, and continues to CR 13.428. (This corresponds with La Fontaine, 106–11.)

[47] Trans. La Fontaine, 99. 'Hi loci consulendi sunt, cum docere de aliqua re homines volumus. Et assuefaciendi sunt animi, ut quaecunque res proposita fuerit, stat[im] in hos locos intueantur, qui admonent, ubi quaerenda sit materia, aut certe quid ex magno acervo eligendum, e[t] quo ordine distribuendum sit.' CR 13.424. The items in brackets are text included in the CR but excluded in La Fontaine's transcription of the Latin.

see both his views on the role of the will in the origins of faith and how rhetorical method helped shape Melanchthon's theological thinking.

What Is Faith?

Melanchthon began, 'What is faith? First, let me consider the meaning of the word faith. Sometimes faith simply signifies an acknowledgement of the historical story of Christ. But elsewhere in the writings of the prophets and apostles, faith means faithfulness, by which we give assent to the promises of God as in St Paul to the Romans. For here he openly affirms when speaking about faith that we give assent to a promise. He says: "For through faith is the promise truly made strong" [Rom. 4.16].'[48] As Melanchthon had asserted before, he here defined faith as not only intellectual comprehension, but also personal application: 'It is faith therefore by which we give assent to the promise of God that Christ would be a sacrifice (propitiation) for us. This faith embraces two things: the acknowledgement of history and faithfully assenting to a promise to which that history refers.'[49]

What Are the Parts or Species of Faith?

'Now what are the parts? Just as the movement of the eyes cannot be divided into parts, so also neither the movement of the mind or the will can be divided, and yet faith brings together the acknowledgement (of Christ) in both the intellect and will and leads it to accept the proffered blessing, namely, assent to promise.'[50] Interestingly, here Melanchthon gave neither mind nor will precedence in the decision-making process, but described them as operating simultaneously and cooperatively. In 1521, in the *Loci communes*, Melanchthon wrote that the will took precedence, and later, in 1553, in *De*

---

[48] Trans. La Fontaine, 106. La Fontaine's translation of Rom. 4.16a is shaky. Here is the NRSV: 'For this reason it depends on faith, in order that the promise may rest on grace...' 'Quid est Fides? Primum significatio vocabuli consideranda est. Interdum fides significat noticiam historiae de Christo. Sed alias in Prophetis et Apostolis, fides significat fiduciam, qua assentimur promissionibus Dei, sic Paulus Roma. 4. palam affirmat se de fide loqui, qua assentimur promissioni, cum ait: Ideo ex [f]ide[, gratis,] ut sit firma promissio.' CR 13.426.

[49] Trans. La Fontaine, 107. 'Est igitur fides assentiri promissioni, in qua Deus pollicetur se nobis propicium fore propter Christum. Complectitur ergo haec fides, noticiam historiae, et fiduciam assentientem promissioni, ad quam historiae referenda est.' CR 14.426.

[50] Trans. La Fontaine, 107. 'Quae partes? Sicut oculorum motus non potest secari in partes, sic nec mentis aut voluntatis motus secantur in partes, sed tamen fides complectitur noticiam in intellectu, et voluntatem, quae vult et accipit beneficium oblatum, id est, assentiri promissioni.' CR 13.426.

anima (*On the Soul*), he would write that the mind took precedence. Here in 1543, he was at the mid-point in this transformation of his views.

What Are the Causes of Faith?

In this section, Melanchthon employed precise categories, touching on the object of faith and then proceeding to its instrumental and efficient causes.[51] 'What are the causes? The object of faith is mercy promised through Christ, by which God pronounces us just people, not because of the law or our dignity or our good works, but because of Christ who willed to be our Saviour.'[52] In other words, the object of a person's faith was God's grace expressed through the work of Jesus Christ, in whom one received personal salvation. For faith to occur, however, the object of faith had to be presented to the individual, and this came about through the Bible, which was therefore the instrumental cause of faith: 'And this mercy is revealed to us through the Word, namely the Gospel or the promises, which are clearly revealed in the Gospel.'[53] Melanchthon continued, 'I have spoken concerning the object of faith, the instrument of faith that works in us is the Word itself.'[54] Next, with the individual having heard the Gospel, Melanchthon presented the efficient cause of the decision of faith. He described it as formally singular but effectively dual. He wrote, 'The efficient cause [*causa*—singular!] is the Holy Spirit which is effective [*impellit*] through the Word and work on the mind and will of man.'[55] Yet, despite positing the Holy Spirit as the single efficient cause of faith in a person, Melanchthon tacked on (with the little Latin word *et*) a second condition: 'And the will assents or does not struggle.'[56] Even though the

---

[51] Richard A. Müller provides some useful technical definitions here: '*causa instrumentalis*: instrumental cause; in the realm of *causa secundae* (q.v.), the means, or *medium*, used to bring about a desired effect, distinct from the material and formal causes . . . as a tool is distinct from both the material upon which it is used and from the form that determines what the material is or will be.' *Dictionary of Latin and Greek Theological Terms: Drawn Principally from Protestant Scholastic Theology* (Grand Rapids: Baker/Paternoster, 1985), 62. '. . . [T]he *causa efficiens*, the efficient cause, or productive, effective cause, which is the agent productive of the motion or mutation in any sequence of causes and effects.' Ibid., 61.

[52] Trans. La Fontaine, 108. 'Quae causae? Obiectum fidei est Misericordia promissa propter Christum, qua Deus nos pronunciat iustos, non propter legem aut dignitatem nostram aut opera nostra, sed propter Christum, quem voluit esse redemptorem nostrum.' CR 13.427.

[53] Trans. La Fontaine, 108. 'Et haec misericordia ostenditur nobis in Verbo, videlicet in Evangelio seu promissionibus, quae extant in Evangelio.' CR 13.427.

[54] Trans. La Fontaine, 108. 'Dixi de obiecto fidei, instrumentum quo fit in nobis, est ipsum Verbum.' CR 13.427.

[55] Trans. La Fontaine, 108–9. 'Causa efficiens, Spiritus sanctus, qui est efficax per Verbum, et impellit mentem et voluntatem hominis. Et voluntas adsentiens seu non repugnans.' CR 13.427.

[56] Trans. La Fontaine, 109. 'Et voluntas adsentiens seu non repugnans.' CR 13.427.

Holy Spirit impelled one toward faith, the final decision to accept or reject Christ lay with the individual's free choice. The tidy theological point here was that Melanchthon described the will as being *passive* in assent to the Holy Spirit (thereby giving God the glory), and *active* in dissent (thereby giving man the blame).

What Are the Effects of Faith?

'What are the effects? I call all those things effects which necessarily follow true faith.'[57] Melanchthon continued, 'Justification follows faith from the covenant of God, that is, reconciliation or the imputation of justice. This could be called the special characteristic of faith or a corollary (*correlativum*) to faith because it is something that necessarily comes from the covenant of God (*ex pacto Dei*), and once joined to faith, it shows that we can no longer assent to the promise except by faith.'[58] This definition made a clear distinction from the soteriology of Erasmus. The Rotterdam scholar, in arguing for free will, had tied faith to a transformational view of justification predicated on the slow growth of *intrinsic* righteousness throughout life and on into completion in the heat of purgatory. Melanchthon, by contrast, tied faith to *imputed* righteousness—instant forensic justification at the moment of faith, followed by a lifetime of sanctification, completed at death. Erasmus supported *Roman Catholic* free will. Melanchthon supported *evangelical* free will: 'The promised reconciliation comes about, not because of our works or our dignity or our virtue, but because of Christ. And nevertheless it ought to be something we accept as a blessing.'[59]

Melanchthon was keen, however, to prevent the acceptance of faith from being construed as any sort of meritorious action. Again, he described the acceptance of faith as passive (and non-meritorious), and the rejection of

---

[57] Trans. La Fontaine, 109. 'Qui effectus? Voco effectus omnia, quae necessario veram fidem sequuntur.' CR 13.427.

[58] Trans. La Fontaine, 109. 'Comitatur autem fidem *ex pacto Dei* iustificatio, id est, reconciliatio seu imputatio iusticiae. Haec potest dici proprium fidei seu correlativum, quia est quiddam quod necessario ex pacto Dei, fidem comitatur, quia non possumus aliter assentire promissioni, nisi fide' [emphasis added]. CR 13.427. Notice that Melanchthon used the phrase *ex pacto Dei*, which has echoes of the scholastic *ex pacto divino*. However, whereas the schoolmen meant a pact God had made with himself to honour a method of salvation that included faith *and* human works/merit, Melanchthon meant simply God's new covenant (new testament) to justify people by faith (alone).

[59] Trans. La Fontaine, 109. 'Contingit igitur promissa reconciliatio, non propter aliquod nostrum opus, aut nostram dignitatem aut nostras virtutes ullas, sed propter Christum, et tamen aliquid esse oportet, quo id beneficium accipi[a]mus.' CR 13.427.

faith as active (and therefore meritorious (as it were) of condemnation). Melanchthon employed further careful nuance: 'We accept it, therefore, by faith. And so justification, or reconciliation, is not the effect of faith, but proper [or, characteristic] to it or correlative (*correlativum*) to it. It is even the movement of faith [by which the Spirit is accepted].'[60] For Melanchthon, faith *correlated* with justification. As any statistician would point out, correlation is different from causation (it *may* include it, but the question is left up in the air). I believe Melanchthon deliberately used this word, 'correlation' to blunt possible objections that he was granting any merit to the human choice of faith in Jesus.

Along with justification, of course, came many benefits: 'The effects can truly be listed as tranquillity and joy of conscience; because by faith, fear and terror are overcome. Invocation (prayer) and delight follow this effect because we ask for that which we highly esteem. And because I list as effects all things that certainly follow, I include eternal life. Likewise, freedom as well as all events followed the faith of [Hezekiah].'[61]

What Things Are Related to Faith and What Things Are Opposed to It?

Melanchthon dealt with this category in just a few lines: 'What are the similarities? The hope of expecting freedom in the future, prayer, and love.'[62] 'The things against it: False faith, despair, and unholy fear.'[63]

Conclusion: Rhetoric as a Tool for Theological Discernment in Support of Evangelical Free Will

In concluding his case study on faith, Melanchthon wrote, 'When in this fashion all the subject matter is encompassed in the boundaries of the art, comprehension will be more sure. And the individual proofs supply a huge

---

[60] Trans. La Fontaine, 110. 'Fide igitur accipimus. Quare non effectus fidei, sed proprium seu correlativum est iustificatio, id est, reconciliatio. Est etiam fides motus, quo accipitur spiritus.' NB, La Fontaine did not translate the underlined phrase into the English, and indeed, one perhaps might make a case for a variant from my own. CR 13.427.

[61] Trans. La Fontaine, 110. 'Effectus vero numerari possunt tranquillitas et gaudium conscientiae, quia fide vincuntur terrores. Hunc effectum sequuntur invocatio et dilectio, quia invocamus et diligimus placatum. Et quia voco effectus, omnia certo sequentia, hic numero etiam vitam aeternam. Item omnes eventus, ut Ezechiae fidem sequitur liberatio.' CR 13.427.

[62] Trans. La Fontaine, 110. 'Quae cognata? [Spes] expectans futuram liberationem, Invocatio, Dilectio.' CR 13.427.

[63] Trans. La Fontaine, 110. 'Pugnantia. Simulatio fidei, Desperatio, Pavor impius.' CR 13.427.

body of matter in explanation.'[64] For Melanchthon, all subject matter, including theology, was to be 'encompassed in the boundaries of the art' of rhetoric. 'Therefore, this diligence is a great help both in making judgment about obscure matters and in explaining and illustrating them. There is no doubt but that in Plato these numerous places praising the method should commend to us this same practice of reviewing in accordance with these goals the questions we are going to treat.'[65]

Most significantly, Melanchthon employed the rules of rhetoric in his formulation of theological doctrines, including that of the will. La Fontaine comments that 'Melanchthon's methodology establishes intellectual content as paramount in his rhetorical method. His treatment of method has educational value in itself, and in respect to its implicational ideas on . . . theology.'[66] One of these rules of rhetoric with theological application included the principle of eliminating the appearance of rational inconsistency. In modern-day English we could say that Melanchthon was averse to paradox, which meant, in the vocabulary of the sixteenth century, that Melanchthon was opposed to antinomies (apparent logical contradictions). Because the simultaneity of divine control (predestination) and human responsibility (free will) could fall under this definition, Melanchthon's own commitment to a rigorous application of the rules of rhetoric would have at least contributed to the evolution of his doctrine of the freedom of the will. His resulting doctrine of evangelical free will, it is worth noting, could no longer be classed as an antinomy.

LOCI COMMUNES, THIRD EDITION: 1543

Besides a textbook on rhetoric, 1543 also marked the appearance of the Latin-language third edition of the *Loci communes*. This edition was reprinted nearly word-for-word in 1559 and so will not require separate treatment at that stage. Nevertheless, Melanchthon did produce a German edition in 1555, and this version did contain some significant changes. Consequently, I will give dedicated space to that edition once we reach that stage in the story. In

[64] Trans. La Fontaine, 110–11. 'Cum hoc modo res includuntur metis artis, certius comprehendi possunt. Et singuli loci suppeditant ingentem copiam rerum in explicando.' CR 13.427.

[65] Trans. La Fontaine, 111. 'Quare haec diligentia plurimum prodest, et ad iudicandas materias obscuras, et ad explicandas atque illustrandas. Nec dubium est, quin illa innumerabilia encomia methodi, quae sunt apud Platonem, hanc ipsam exercitationem nobis commendent, ad has metas revocandi quaestiones quas explicaturi sumus.' CR 13.428.

[66] La Fontaine, 67.

the meantime, we turn now to consider Melanchthon's views on the origins of justifying faith as seen in the *Loci communes* of 1543.

In this edition of the *Loci*, Melanchthon set out his concept of evangelical free will in the clearest and most uncompromising way possible. Here Melanchthon polished his formulation of the doctrine of contingency, explicitly linked predestination to free will in a manner conducive to a foreknowledgist position, and expanded the role of the free will beyond the moment of conversion.

Contingency

In the *Loci* of 1543, Melanchthon brought together all of his ideas and concerns about contingency from the previous twenty-four years, weaving them together into a nuanced, cohesive doctrine articulating the idea of the self-limited governance of God in the temporal realm. Melanchthon dealt with his concerns in order: (1) the problem of the origins of evil and sin, (2) retaining an imperative for doing good works, and (3) refraining from totally stripping away God's direct rule.

Melanchthon's first concern involved the origins of sin and evil, and here his doctrine remained the same as in the mid-1520s. God did not create or ordain evil or sin, but instead the blame lay entirely with the misused wills of the devil and human beings.[67] God did not determine all things, but instead allowed humans a measure of free will. Melanchthon summarized, 'Thus God is not the cause of sin. For although He does sustain human nature to an extent, yet the defects in the human mind are not produced by Him, and Eve's free will was properly and truly the cause for her action and she voluntarily turned herself away from God.'[68] Because God was not the

---

[67] Philipp Melanchthon, *Loci Communes 1543 Philip Melanchthon*, trans. Jacob Preus (St Louis: Concordia, 1992), 36. 'The substances of the devil and of man were created and sustained by God and yet the will of the devil and the will of man are the causes of sins. For the will could abuse its own liberty and turn itself from God.' The original Latin text for the *Loci communes* of 1543 may be found in CR 21.601–1106. The Latin text of the *Loci* of 1559, found in MSA 2/1–2/2, is identical with that of 1543 except for minor variations in punctuation, spelling, and capitalization. Citations shall be given for both the 1543 and 1559 editions in the following notes (the placement of commas, spelling, etc. follows the MSA standards for 1559). The Latin for the quotation at the beginning of this footnote is as follows: 'Substantiam a Deo conditam esse et sustentari et tamen voluntatem Diaboli et voluntatem hominis causas esse peccati, quia voluntas abuti libertate sua potuit seque a Deo avertere.' (1543) CR 21.645. (1559) MSA 2/1.226.4–7.

[68] (1543) Trans. Preus, 37. 'Nec propterea Deus est causa peccati. Etsi enim sustentat aliquantisper naturam, tamen defectus illi in mente non efficiuntur ab ipso, et voluntas libera Evae proprie et vere erat causa suae actionis ac sponte se avertit a Deo.' (1543) CR 21.647. (1559) MSA 2/1.228.33–7.

cause of evil, he could not be all-determining. Melanchthon argued, 'Sin occurs by contingency' and 'The contingency of our actions is the freedom of our will.'[69] Humans therefore had at least some measure of genuine freedom.

This requisite measure of genuine human freedom also ensured that a real imperative for doing good works could be articulated. As for divine determinism, 'The idea is harmful to good morals as is stated in the tragedies, "The guilt lies with fate, and let no one interfere with fate". For example, the servant of Zeno used to say that he was unjustly punished because fate forced him to do wrong. We must flee such talk and ideas.'[70] In opposition to divine determinism, Melanchthon maintained, 'This also must be granted, that apostolic Scripture attributes to man, even now after the Fall, a certain liberty of choosing those things which are subject to reason and of performing the external works commanded by the law of God. Thus the righteousness of the Law is called the righteousness of the flesh, Romans 10.3–5, because to some extent external obedience can be accomplished by the powers of this nature.'[71] Temporal freedom was necessary both for separating God from responsibility for evil and for ensuring that humans were responsible for civil order and their own outward behaviour. God therefore limited his own control within the temporal realm.

Within his letters in the 1540s and 1550s, Melanchthon strongly argued against divine determinism. In 1544, he declared that he did not believe in a fixed destiny as the Stoics did.[72] In 1547, he argued that a parent's love indicated the kind of love God had for people, and that this had nothing to

---

[69] (1543) Trans. Preus, 37. 'When this statement has been established, that God is not the cause of sin and that He does not will sin, it follows that sin occurs by contingency, that is, that not all things which happen take place by necessity. For since sin has arisen out of the will of the devil and of man and does not take place by the will of God, [human] wills were so constituted that they were able not to sin. Furthermore the cause of the contingency of our actions is the freedom of our will.' 'Constituta autem hac sententia, quod Deus non sit causa peccati nec velit peccatum, sequitur contingentiam esse, hoc est, non omnia, quae fiunt, necessario fieri. Quia enim peccatum ortum est a voluntate Diaboli et hominis nec factum est Deo volente, sic erant conditae voluntates, ut possent non peccare. Est autem causa contingentiae nostrarum actionum libertas voluntatis.' (1543) CR 21.647. (1559) MSA 2/1.228.38–229.7.

[70] (1543) Trans. Preus, 39. 'Deinde et moribus perniciosum et illud, quod in Tragoedia dicitur: Fati ista culpa est, nemo fit fato nocens. Sicut et Zenonis servus dicebat se iniuste plecti, quia fato coactus esset peccare. Tales igitur sermones et opiniones fugiamus.' (1543) CR 21.650. (1559) MSA 2/1.234.21–5.

[71] (1543) Trans. Preus, 37. 'Deinde concedendum et hoc est, quod scriptura Apostolica tribuat homini etiam nunc post lapsum libertatem aliquam deligendi ea, quae sunt subiecta rationi, et faciendi externa opera mandata Lege Dei. Ideo enim iustitia Legis dicitur iustitia carnis, quia viribus huius naturae externa illa disciplina utcunque praestari potest.' (1543) CR 21.647. (1559) MSA 2/1.229.10–16.

[72] Melanchthon (in Wittenberg), letter to Paul Eber (in Wittenberg), October 1544. MBW 4.3723. CR 6.301–2 Nr. 3642.

do with stoic fate.[73] In a letter to Archbishop Thomas Cranmer in March of 1548, Melanchthon distanced himself from the beginning of the German reformation with its 'stoic disputations on fate, which damaged discipline'.[74] Because some of the prime texts of the early German Reformation were Melanchthon's own, he was here effectively repudiating his early work. Melanchthon would no longer tolerate divine determinism—God's rule was self-limited.

In counterbalance to God's self-limited governance in the temporal realm, Melanchthon sought to emphasize that God's rule was only limited *to a certain extent.* He was not totally absent from this world. God could take direct control whenever he liked, thus directly determining events from time to time. (This was actually a point that Peter Lombard had made.) In this fashion God established and continued to guide his church in this world.[75] As a result, people should be consoled, for God was not absent from the world.[76] In support of this doctrine, Melanchthon moved on to discuss absolute necessity and the necessity of consequence (*necessitate consequentiae*). He denied absolute necessity because he viewed it as Stoicism,[77] but he retained the necessity of consequence, meaning that events were only necessary insofar as preceding events made them inevitable, or (in rare cases) an event was necessary because God directly determined that it was to happen. So God *could* unilaterally determine temporal events, but for the vast majority of time he chose not to. This doctrine preserved a faint echo of the scholastic distinction between *potentia Dei absoluta* and *potentia Dei ordinata* (God's absolute and ordained powers).[78] Melanchthon concluded, 'God is present with His work, not as a Stoic god but as a truly free agent who sustains His creation and governs many things.'[79]

---

[73] Melanchthon (in Zerbst), letter to Christoph Pannonius (in Frankfurt/Oder), 6 April 1547. MBW 5.4693. CR 6.468–9 Nr. 3817.

[74] 'Nimis horridae fuerunt initio *Stoicae* [italics in original] disputationes apud nostros de Fato, et disciplinae nocuerunt.' Melanchthon (in Wittenberg), to Archbishop of Canterbury Thomas Cranmer, before 26 March 1548. MBW 5.5103. CR 6.801 Nr. 4142. Cf. George Cornelius Gorham, ed., *Gleanings of a Few Scattered Ears, During the Period of the Reformation in England and of the Times Immediately Succeeding* (London: Bell and Daldy, 1857), vi. He dates this letter to 'about' 1 April 1548.

[75] (1543) Trans. Preus, 38–9. (1543) CR 21.649. (1559) MSA 2/1.232.21–7.

[76] Melanchthon, *Loci consolationis.* Before 8 April 1547. MBW 5.4696. CR 6.483–8 Nr. 3834.

[77] (1543) Trans. Preus, 39. 'The opinions of the Stoics must never be brought into the church. For how can the man pray to God when he holds that all things happen by necessity?' 'Nequaquam Stoicas opiniones in Ecclesiam invehendas esse. Quomodo enim invocabit Deum is, qui omnia necessario evenire statuit?' (1543) CR 21.650. (1559) MSA 2/1.234.18–21.

[78] For more on this topic, see McGrath, *Luther's Theology of the Cross*, 55–8, 167, 193.

[79] (1543) Trans. Preus, 40. 'Et in summa teneatur haec propositio: Adest Deus suo operi non ut Stoicus Deus, sed vere ut liberum agens, sustenans creaturam et multa moderans.' (1543) CR 21.652. (1559) MSA 2/1.236.21–4.

Note the limited rule of God espoused in Melanchthon's last phrase: God 'governs *many* things'—not all things. Melanchthon did not use *gubernatio* here, (as he did in the *Scholia in Epistolam Pauli ad Colossenses* in 1527) but rather, *moderor*, which, like *gubernatio*, could mean 'to govern', but, while generally synonymous with *guberno*, carried a stronger nuance of *passive* governance. According to the *Oxford Latin Dictionary*, *moderor* means 'to restrain, hold back, check'.[80] God did not maintain active control, but rather passive restraint. God set certain boundaries and then allowed free action within those limits. Melanchthon now taught that God merely retained oversight over a generally free world. From *determinatio* in 1521, to *gubernatio* in 1527, to *moderor* in 1543, Melanchthon's shifting language clearly showed his progressive limitation of God's rule in the temporal realm.

Predestination

Melanchthon's opposition to 'Stoicism' also carried over into his doctrine of predestination. His formulation in 1543 of the doctrine of election followed the same contours that had emerged over the previous ten years. He made the same arguments for accepting the Bible at face value without speculation,[81] the genuine universality of the Gospel promises,[82] the cause of election being God's mercy,[83] and 'predestination' only being a valid category for discussion

---

[80] The OLD lists this definition third. The first two definitions are (1) to direct the course or motion of, guide; and (2) to have control of, govern, rule. However, according to the context (in which Melanchthon contrasted *moderor* with the active control of 'Stoicism'), it is unlikely that he had either of these first two definitions in mind. The sense of the statement lends itself to a passive governance rather than an active governance, and indeed, other Latin dictionaries list the OLD's third definition ('to restrain, hold back, check') as the primary definition of *moderor* (e.g. Charlton T. Lewis and Charles Short, eds., *A Latin Dictionary* (Oxford: Clarendon Press, 1879), and S. A. Handford and Mary Herberg, eds., *Langenscheidt's Pocket Latin Dictionary* (Berlin: Langenscheidt KG, 1955)).

[81] 'We must look for a promise in which God has expressed His will, and we must understand that no other will is to be sought concerning His grace outside of His Word. The immutable will of God is that we are to hear His Son.' (1543) Trans. Preus, 173. 'Quaeramus ergo promissionem, in qua voluntatem suam expressit Deus, et sciamus non esse aliam voluntatem quaerundam de gratia extra verbum, sed mandatum Dei immutabile esse, ut adiamus Filium.' (1543) CR 21.914. (1559) MSA 2/2.594.30–3.

[82] 'He accuses the disobedience of all, He calls all to repentance, and again He offers mercy to all. . . . For since God is God, He treats all equally: He convicts us of sin, and yet He receives all who flee to the Son.' Trans. Preus, 173. 'Arguit omnium inobedientiam, omnes vocat ad poenitentiam, rursus etiam omnibus misericordiam offert.' (1543) CR 21.915. (1559) MSA 2/2.595.20–2.

[83] 'It is correct to say that the cause of our election is the merciful will of God, who does not will that the entire human race should perish, but for the sake of His Son He gathers and preserves His church.' Trans. Preus, 173. 'Econtra vero recte dicitur causam electionis esse

following justification—predestination *a posteriore*.[84] All in all, predestination was an illustration of justification by grace. What was new in 1543 was the force with which Melanchthon defended his total redefinition of election. For him, it was not permissible to view election as God's effective choice of individuals for salvation. Instead, he defined election as an individual's free choice of God. He realized that he had stood predestination on its head in the mid-1530s, and here he adamantly defended doing so. 'Predestination', or salvation, had to be contingent upon the correct operation of the human free will.

Melanchthon insisted that 'an elect' truly did exist,[85] but that those who might be termed 'elect' were simply those who received salvation. He affirmed that 'The entire human race has not been created for destruction and for the present miseries and for the things which befall our perishing condition, as is the case with plants and animals.'[86] Further, 'A church of the elect shall always remain, which God, in a miraculous manner—even in this life—shall preserve, defend, and govern.'[87] Additionally, all the predestined were elect on account of Christ, accepted through faith, 'For unless we hold to the knowledge of Christ, we cannot speak of election.'[88] Melanchthon simply meant by all this that some people would grasp salvation through faith in Christ. Christ made salvation (or 'election') possible, but it was up to humans to believe him, and hence *become* elect, that is, part of the elect *Church*. As Kolb argues, in the *Loci* of 1543, predestination's 'content had been substantially reworked

---

misericordiam in voluntate Dei, qui non vult perire totum genus humanum, sed propter Filium colligit et servat Ecclesiam.' (1543) CR 21.915. (1559) MSA 2/2.596.26–9.

[84] 'So also regarding our election, we must judge from the effects (*a posteriori*), that is, there is absolutely no doubt that the elect are those who in faith take hold of God's mercy, which has been promised for the sake of Christ, and who never give up this confidence.' (1543) Trans. Preus, 173. 'Ita de electione a posteriore iudicamus, videlicet haud dubie electos esse eos, qui misericordiam propter Christum promissam fide apprehendunt nec abiiciunt eam fiduciam ad extremum.' (1543) CR 21.916. (1559) MSA 2/2.597.8–12.

[85] 'First, He has demonstrated with manifest miracles that there certainly is a definite gathering of people which he loves, cares for, and will adorn with eternal blessings' (1543) Trans. Preus, 172. '...ac primum esse aliquem coetum, quem diligat, curet et aeternis bonis ornaturus sit, ipse manifestis miraculis declaravit.' (1543) CR 21.913. (1559) MSA 2/2.592.32–4.

[86] (1543) Trans. Preus, 172. 'Nec totum genus humanum ad interitum et praesentes miserias ac vices materiae pereuntis conditum est, ut poma aut pecudes.' (1543) CR 21.913. (1559) MSA 2/2.593.7–9.

[87] (1543) Trans. Preus, 172. 'Mansura est igitur semper aliqua electorum Ecclesia, quam Deus mirabiliter etiam in hac vita servat, defendit et gubernat.' (1543) CR 21.913. (1559) MSA 2/2.593.35–7.

[88] (1543) Trans. Preus, 172. 'Altera est: Totus numerus salvandorum propter Christum electus est. Quare nisi complectamur agnitionem Christi, non potest de electione dici.' (1543) CR 21.914. (1559) MSA 2/2.594.18–20.

into an element of Melanchthon's ecclesiology'.[89] The elect were not some select group of individuals preordained for salvation (though of course God foreknew who would accept his promises), but they were merely those who did, in actual fact, *choose* salvation—and this salvation could only be grasped through faith, an active choice of a free will.[90]

Salvation and a redefined predestination became virtually interchangeable terms for Melanchthon, and the key to both was the free choice of the individual. Melanchthon made it clear that the only reason anybody was damned was because of a choice of their own will. All were reprobate on account of their fallen and sinful nature, and only those who rejected God out of a free choice of their will would stay reprobate and become damned for all eternity. He explained, 'It is certain that the cause of reprobation is the sin in men who do not hear or receive the gospel or who reject the faith, even before they have departed from it. In those people it is certain that the cause of their reprobation is their sin and their human will.'[91] Melanchthon illustrated his point with the example of Saul, who damned himself by the misuse of his own free will: 'Saul of his own free will drove out the Holy Spirit, and of his own free will he fought against the Holy Spirit when the Spirit tried to move him. These things certainly are the cause of his rejection or reprobation, for the promise requires faith.'[92] Reprobation depended on the choice of the will.

Salvation also depended on the choice of the will—grace had to be seized. Melanchthon maintained, 'In receiving there must be a grasping (*apprehensio*)',[93] and as to being saved, 'There is some cause or reason in the one who accepts.'[94] Through his Spirit and his Word, God helped people to understand the universal promises of the Gospel, but it was up to them to accept them: 'God begins and draws us by His Word and the Holy Spirit, but it is necessary for us to hear and learn, that is, to take hold of the promise and assent to it,

---

[89] Kolb, 'Melanchthon's Influence', 199.

[90] Melanchthon also stressed that the 'elect' could sin and lose the Holy Spirit. Salvation was not secure for the elect. Melanchthon, report for Herzog Albrecht von Preußen, 15 July 1545. MBW 4.3950. CR 5.792–3 Nr. 3221.

[91] (1543) Trans. Preus, 173. 'Causam igitur reprobationis certum est hanc esse, videlicet peccatum in hominibus, qui prorsus non audiunt nec accipiunt Evangelium, aut qui abiiciunt fidem, antequam hinc discedunt. In his certum est causam esse reprobationis peccatum ipsorum et humanam voluntatem.' (1543) CR 21.915. (1559) MSA 2/2.596.12–18.

[92] (1543) Trans. Preus, 173. 'Saul volens effudit Spiritum sanctum, volens moventi Spiritui sancto repugnavit. Haec de causa reiectionis seu reprobationis certa sunt. Promissio enim requi-[rit] fidem.' (1543) CR 21.915. This version is missing the letters in brackets. (1559) MSA 2/2.596.21–5.

[93] (1543) Trans. Preus, 173. '…in accipiente concurrere oportet apprehensionem…' (1543) CR 21.916. (1559) MSA 2/2.597.1–2.

[94] (1543) Trans. Preus, 173. 'Ergo ut in iustificatione diximus aliquam esse in accipiente causam.' (1543) CR 21.916. (1559) MSA 2/2.597.4–7.

not to fight against it or be hesitant and filled with doubt.'[95] Hence, being 'elect' did not depend on God's choice of us, but rather on our choice of God. 'Election' was the reward for giving in to the right choice, not the cause of the choice in the first place. Melanchthon concluded, 'Therefore He gives approval to and elects those who are obedient to His call.'[96] Those who were obedient—those who had faith born of their own free will—*became* elect thereby.

Free Choice

Having stated his support of free will so clearly in the sections on contingency and predestination, the section on free choice ran the risk of becoming redundant. Here Melanchthon added new material relating to contingency, the place of the affections in relation to the will, and a final summary of his doctrine of the will.

In the second edition of the *Loci* (1533–5), Melanchthon had nominally linked contingency with free choice, though he had quickly asserted that contingency really had nothing at all to do with justification or free will. But now, in the third edition of the *Loci* (1543), he dropped much of that reluctance. One of his opening sentences of Locus 4, 'Human Powers of Free Choice', reads, 'We must not import Stoic ideas into the church or uphold the fatalistic necessity of all things; but rather we must concede that there is some place for contingency.'[97] He swiftly hedged by mentioning that divine determination was not the same argument as free choice,[98] yet he left the connection between contingency and free choice intact. This connection indicated that his former separation between the temporal and spiritual realms had become less distinct since he realigned the divided governance of God in 1532

---

[95] (1543) Trans. Preus, 173. 'Orditur Deus et trahit verbo suo et Spiritu sancto, sed audire nos oportet et discere, id est, apprehendere promissionem et assentiri, non repugnare, non indulgere diffidentiae et dubitationi.' (1543) CR 21.916. (1559) MSA 2/2.597.15–19.

[96] (1543) Trans. Preus, 173. 'Approbat igitur ac eligit obtemperantes vocationi.' (1543) CR 21.917. (1559) MSA 2/2.599.24–5.

[97] (1543) Trans. Preus, 41. 'Supra non esse in Ecclesiam invehendas illas Stoicas opiniones nec defendendam esse necessitatem fatalem omnium, sed aliquam contingentiam concedendam.' (1543) CR 21.652. (1559) MSA 2/1.236.34–7.

[98] 'We must not confuse the argument concerning divine determinism with the question of free choice. For when we ask about the will of man and other human powers, the discussion revolves around only the matter of human weakness and not around all the powers in his complete nature.' (1543) Trans. Preus, 41. 'Nec miscenda est disputatio de determinatione divina quaestioni de libero arbitrio. Nam cum de voluntate hominis et de ceteris humanis viribus quaeritur, tantum de humana infirmitate disseritur, non de omnibus motibus in tota natura.' (1543) CR 21.652. (1559) MSA 2/1.237.1–5.

to make it a unified self-limited rule of God in both realms. With God's rule self-limited in the same fashion in both realms, carrying arguments from one to the other became less troublesome. Consequently, human free choice in civil works (argued in order to prevent God from being responsible for sin and evil, and to maintain a subjective moral imperative for works of civil righteousness) could sound quite similar to human free will in choosing to have faith (argued in order to prevent God from being responsible for reprobation). Melanchthon did not explicitly make this sort of argument, but his willingness to mention contingency in relation to free will here showed the progressive tightening and systematic integration of his overall theology. His theological writings now carried more of a tone of consolidation and a tying up of loose ends rather than searching for answers. Melanchthon was settled with his soteriology of evangelical free will, and he was not about to go back.

He would not, for example, return to his affections argument, which had played such a large role in his rejection of free will in 1521. There he had argued that the affections represented the *real* will of the individual, and while one could control external actions, the internal state of the affections could not be mastered. One could be nice to an enemy, but the hatred inside could not be changed. One could not just suddenly decide to stop being angry, or to *become* angry, for that matter. The affections were uncontrollable, and therefore so was the will. Now, in 1543, Melanchthon distinguished between the affections and the will, calling them two separate entities within the human being. He described three levels within the human being.[99] The mind (*mens*) came first, and here existed the ability to know and judge, accomplished through the intellect and reason. Second, underneath the mind, or subject to it, came the will (*voluntas*), which Melanchthon called the seeking part of the human. The will either obeyed or resisted the judgement of the mind. Third, the affections, or desires of the senses, came underneath the will. The affections sprang forth from the heart, which sometimes agreed with and sometimes contended against the will. Also at the level of the affections, and also underneath the will, came the locomotive part of man. Consequently, both the locomotive part of the human and the affections were separate from, and subject to, the will.[100]

---

[99] (1543) Trans. Preus, 41. 'In homine est pars cognoscens ac iudicans, quae vocatur mens vel intellectus vel ratio, in hac parte sunt notitiae. Altera pars appetens vocatur voluntas, quae vel obtemperat iudicio vel repugnat, et sub voluntate sunt appetitiones sensuum seu affectus, quorum subiectum et fons est cor, qui interdum congruunt, interdum pugnant cum voluntate. Est sub voluntate et locomotiva.' (1543) CR 21.653. (1559) MSA 2/1.237.17–24.

[100] However, in 1546, in his *Commentary on Aristotle's Ethics, Book I*, Melanchthon spoke again of a link between the affections and the will. Here he said that the affections *impeded* the will. This is a more nuanced position than either of his previous arguments (which were first

This philosophy of the three parts of a human represented a strong conceptual platform on which to rest a doctrine of free will.[101]

Melanchthon proceeded to define free choice according to the above paradigm when he wrote, 'It is called free choice when the mind and the will are joined together. Or free choice is the name given to the faculty or power of the will to choose and seek those things which have been shown to it, or to reject them.'[102] Following his definition of free choice, he unequivocally endorsed it using David as his example: 'Nor must we permit the Manichean ravings which argue that there is a certain number of men, whom they call materially minded and earthly, who cannot be converted. Nor does the conversion of David take place in the way that a stone might be turned into a fig. But the free choice did something in David. When he heard the rebuke and the promise, he willingly and freely made his confession. And his will did something when he comforted himself with [Nathan's] statement, "The Lord has taken away your sin".'[103] This was a clear distancing from Calvin's 'Stoic' position.

In conclusion, Melanchthon wrote: 'The free choice in man is the ability to apply oneself toward grace, that is, our free choice hears the promise, tries to assent to it and rejects the sins which are contrary to conscience.'[104] Free will in conversion was now a decisive part of Melanchthon's theology of

(1521) that the affections determine the will; and second (1543) that the affections did not affect the will at all): 'The will is indeed seized by diverse affections, so that there may not be the firm assent that there is with observable things, as we experience every day that true judgments are impeded by emotions.' Keen, 184. *Enarratio Libri I. Ethicorum Aristotelis.* 'Ideo rapitur voluntas diversis affectibus, ne tam firma sit assensio, sicut in speculabilibus, ut quotidie experimur, adfectibus impediri vera iudicia.' CR 16.287.

[101] Melanchthon would further develop this framework over the next few years, as seen in the 1553 edition of *De anima*.

[102] (1543) Trans. Preus, 41. 'Vocantur autem liberum arbitrium mens et voluntas coniunctae. Aut vocatur liberum arbitrium facultas voluntatis ad eligendum ac expetendum ea, quae monstrata sunt, et ad reiiciendum eadem.' (1543) CR 21.653. (1559) MSA 2/1.237.26–9.

[103] (1543) Trans. Preus, 43. 'Nec admittendi sunt Manichaeorum furores, qui fingunt aliquem esse numerum hominum, quos vocant ὑλικοὺς καὶ χοικοὺς qui converti non possint. Nec fit conversio in Davide, ut si lapis in ficum verteretur, sed agit aliquid liberum arbitrium in Davide, cum audivit obiurgationem et promissionem, volens iam et libere fatetur delictum. Et agit aliquid eius voluntas, cum se sustentat hac voce: "Dominus abstulit peccatum tuum".' (1543) CR 21.659. (1559) MSA 2/1.244.32–245.3.

[104] (1543) Trans. Preus, 44. 'Liberum arbitrium in homine facultatem esse applicandi se ad gratiam, id est, audit promissionem et assentiri conatur et abiicit peccata contra conscientiam.' (1543) CR 21.659. (1559) MSA 2/1.245.30–3. While this definition was very similar to Erasmus' definition of free will in DLA, it should be remembered that Melanchthon saw grace as divine favour, but Erasmus viewed grace as divine aid. Melanchthon endorsed free will to believe in Christ and hence instantly be justified through imputed merit, while Erasmus advocated free will to seek God's aid in doing good works and hence become justified gradually with intrinsic merit. For Melanchthon, it was free will to *receive* salvation, while for Erasmus it was free will to *earn* salvation.

justification. Meanwhile, six hundred miles to the south-west, a certain pastor and scholar could not quite believe what he was reading.

INTERACTIONS WITH CALVIN: 1543–1546

John Calvin's first *explicit* comment on Melanchthon's shifting thought on free will came following the publication of the *Loci communes* of 1543. Having noticed Melanchthon's changed doctrine, Calvin sought to draw him out. Albert Pighius had attacked Calvin on the doctrine of the will,[105] and in so doing, he had criticized Melanchthon for deviating from Luther (and Calvin). In 1543, Calvin responded with a full-fledged book: *Defensio sanae et orthodoxae doctrinae de servitute et liberatione humani arbitrii adversus calumnias Alberti Pighii Campensis.*[106] Calvin dedicated it to Melanchthon, whom he defended,[107] calling him 'a most famous man'. Calvin addressed the preface to Melanchthon, writing, 'I am dedicating to you a book which I know for certain will be doubly pleasing to you, both because of your love for me the author and because it contains a defence of the godly and sound teaching of which you are not only a most zealous supporter, but a distinguished and very brave champion.'[108] Calvin here was referring to Melanchthon's early writings on free will, and in so doing, he was taking a subtle dig at Melanchthon over his newly changed formulations.

Several months later, Melanchthon wrote back to Calvin, thanking him for the dedication and praising him for his simplicity of presentation and eloquence of style. However, he felt constrained to say that he supported the insolubility of the problem of providence and contingency, and that he felt God was the author of free will but not of original sin.[109] The context of this

---

[105] *De libero hominis arbitrio et divina gratia, Libri decem* (Cologne: Melchior Novesianus, 1542). Apparently no modern edition of this work exists.

[106] CO 6.229–404. This work can be found in English translation in John Calvin, *The Bondage and Liberation of the Will: A Defence of the Orthodox Doctrine of Human Choice against Pighius*, ed. A. N. S. Lane, trans. G. I. Davies (Grand Rapids: Baker, 1996).

[107] CO 6.250–1.

[108] Trans. G. I. Davies, 3. MBW 3.3157. CO 6.229.

[109] Melanchthon (in Bonn), letter to Calvin (in Geneva), 11 May 1543. MBW 3.3245. CR 5.107–9 Nr. 2702. CO 11.539–42 Nr. 467. Notice that although Melanchthon favoured the rational consistency of doctrine as an exegetical principle for the exegesis of the Scripture, he was not legalistic in insisting on it in every case. Nevertheless, here, even though he said that he supported the insolubility of the problem of providence and contingency (a possible antinomy), he still offered something of a rationally consistent solution when he said that God was the author of free will but not sin.

statement shows that Melanchthon was here speaking of free will in relation to contingency rather than in relation to justification. Justification, though, was the key question, and Melanchthon had completely side-stepped it in his reply to Calvin! Perhaps Melanchthon's conscience bothered him on this evasion, for a few months later, in July of 1543, Melanchthon again wrote to Calvin. This time he expressed himself more clearly on the question of free will in justification. He claimed to actually agree with what Calvin said about the will, but he rejected the doctrine of predestination.[110]

Melanchthon concurred with Calvin that people could not choose to have faith in God unless they heard the Spirit-illumined Word of God—that is, they could not choose to have faith unless God acted first. But the difference between the two was that Calvin drew a distinction between a general calling and a special calling in which the Holy Spirit *effectively* called the elect and gave them faith.[111] Melanchthon drew no such distinction, instead arguing that the Gospel promises were truly universal—i.e. Calvin's general calling (and not the special calling) was all that existed. All people, when they heard the Word of God (which was *always* illuminated by the Holy Spirit) had, at that moment, the free choice of whether or not to have faith in Christ. Predestination was not involved at all. The effectiveness of the Spirit's call was contingent upon the free response of the individual human will.

Melanchthon's doctrine of the will was not at all consonant with Calvin's. Nonetheless, Calvin did not choose to engage in a public dispute with Melanchthon at this time, although he did allude to their differences from time to time. In 1546, Calvin wrote a preface to the French edition of Melanchthon's *Loci communes*, and in it he mentioned Melanchthon's shift on free will.[112] Calvin discussed the fact of the discrepancy between his theology and Melanchthon's, but he did not press the issue, for, as Wengert argues, he and Melanchthon were eager to avoid a full-blown public dispute on the doctrine of predestination.[113] The German and Swiss parties of the Reformation were already having enough trouble coming to an agreement on the Lord's Supper. Additionally, Reformation unity was a prize to be sought, especially in light of the great Roman Catholic consolidation taking place in the various stages of the Council of Trent. The doctrinal formulations pro-mulgated at Trent were of enormous significance, both for Roman Catholi-cism and for Protestant theologians such as Melanchthon who had long

---

[110] Melanchthon (in Bonn), letter to Calvin (in Strassburg), 12 July 1543. MBW 3.3273. CO 11.594–5 Nr. 488.

[111] *Institutes* III.xxi.3. Here Calvin was criticizing Melanchthon, though without naming him. See Cameron, 'Philipp Melanchthon', 719 n. 68.

[112] CO 9.848–9.

[113] Wengert, 'We Will Feast Together in Heaven Forever', 32.

sought the reform and reconciliation of the old institutional church. As a result, it will be important to pause here and survey some of the key soterio-logical teachings of Trent, for these formulations informed nearly all of Melanchthon's subsequent theological writings.

THE COUNCIL OF TRENT: 1545–1547

A Transformational Model of Justification

At the Council of Trent,[114] the Roman Catholic leadership sought to pro-nounce on both doctrine and ecclesiastical reform, all with a special concern towards refuting the Protestant challenge. For the purposes of this study, the first phase (1545–7), dealing with justification, looms especially large, for it represented a counterpoint for much of Melanchthon's writings in the years following. Space limitations do not permit a full discussion of the Tridentine doctrine of justification, but a brief overview will provide a helpful context for Melanchthon's subsequent theological writings.

At Trent, justification was defined in the way that justification *and* sanctifi-cation *together* were defined by the Protestants.[115] The Catholics focused on the slow transformation of the entire person (faith *and* works), while the Protestants stressed the immediate imputation of total righteousness (faith alone). This fact on its own explains much about their divergent soteriologies.

The Tridentine teaching on original sin was that the Fall was so severe that people could no longer save themselves.[116] Baptism, however, removed the stain of original sin *ex opere operato* (that is, just from having done the sacrament). At baptism, the merits of Christ were applied, such that the baptized person subsequently only struggled with concupiscence—an inclin-ation to sin which was not sin itself.[117] Free will, though weakened by the Fall, remained,[118] even as Erasmus had maintained against Luther. This free will allowed for human merit in justification,[119] and absolved God of responsibil-ity for evil.[120]

---

[114] See Alberigo's good summary in OER 4.173ff.
[115] McGrath, *Iustitia Dei*, 259, 269.
[116] CT 21, 30, and 45 (Canon 23).
[117] CT 23.
[118] CT 30, 43 (Canon 5), and 45 (Canon 22).
[119] CT 43 (Canon 7).
[120] CT 43 (Canon 6).

Besides baptism, the first stage of justification included a call by means of God's grace,[121] the consequent human efforts to arrive at a suitable disposition to receive salvation,[122] and active faith.[123] All these things *began* with God's grace—so they were not works-righteousness.[124] But then, once faith emerged, it had to be accompanied by good works. Human faith and works, in cooperation with God's grace, together created congruous merit (*meritum de congruo*)—a key scholastic principle found in Scotus, among others. For the Catholics, salvation happened through a joint effort between God and the believer.[125] For Protestants, salvation was a unilateral action by God. It was something that happened *to* a person.

The Uncertainty of Salvation

The Tridentine view of justification had to do with the slow and uncertain growth of *intrinsic* righteousness, rather than the immediate and certain imputation of *extrinsic* righteousness (as Melanchthon argued). One stressed righteousness from *within* (that is, growing up within the person), and the other, righteousness from *without* (that is, coming from Jesus). According to Trent, salvation could not be received apart from the active merits and good works of the free individual.[126] Therefore, because human effort played a role in the Catholic understanding of salvation, one could never quite be certain whether or not one was within God's grace. Unlike the Protestants, the Catholic formulation advised continual fear and uncertainty about one's salvation. For example, Chapter IX of the decree was titled, 'Against the vain confidence of the heretics'.[127] Here the Protestant notion of the security of one's salvation was stiffly attacked with the following: 'Among heretics and schismatics this vain and ungodly confidence may be and in our troubled times indeed is found and preached with untiring fury against the Catholic Church.'[128] Instead of security, there ought to be fear, for justification partly depended on human effort: 'Each one, when he considers himself and his own weakness and indisposition, may have fear and apprehension concerning his own grace, since no one can know with the certainty of faith, which cannot be

---

[121] CT 31, and 42 (Canon 3).
[122] CT 31–2. See McGrath, *Iustitia Dei*, 269.
[123] CT 34–5.
[124] CT 35. See also CT 42 (Canon 1).
[125] CT 33, and 43 (Canon 12).
[126] CT 41.
[127] CT 35.
[128] CT 35.

subject to error, that he has obtained the grace of God.'[129] One could never be certain of attaining salvation, and for Melanchthon, this would turn out to be an entirely unacceptable doctrine, causing much undue terror on the part of believers.

According to Trent, predestination also came to be singled out as a false doctrine on which to base the certainty of one's salvation. Chapter XII warned that the 'rash presumption of predestination is to be avoided',[130] and that 'For except by special revelation, it cannot be known whom God has chosen for Himself.'[131] God did predestine individuals for salvation, but no one could know just who these individuals might be. Canons 15 and 16 expanded this point, arguing that believers could not know if they were elect (even in the presence of faith), and the uncertainty of one's perseverance in righteousness and grace until the end was maintained.[132] In fact, it proved very possible to fall away from grace. If salvation could be enhanced by freely chosen works, it could also be lost by works, hence requiring restoration through the sacrament of penance.

In Sum: Roman Catholic Free Will

The Tridentine understanding of justification was essentially synergistic. Salvation was the joint effort of people and God, though God's prevenient grace set the process in motion. Similarly, both church and God were necessary for salvation, for the church provided the essential justifying sacraments of baptism[133] and penance. In some sense, one could argue that the soteriological trinity in Tridentine thought was comprised of faith, works, and church. In the Catholic Church, justification remained an ever uncertain and tenuous business. While empowered by intrinsic righteousness to resist sin, failure to do so would result in the loss of salvation. Faith alone proved insufficient to save, for faith apart from grace and works was inadequate. Here the goal of creating a theological identity distinct from the Protestants was fulfilled, for the Tridentine ideas about justification were radically divergent from the Protestant ideas, and the Protestant security of salvation by the means of faith in Christ alone was anathema to the Roman Catholic Church.

In the end, at the Council of Trent, the Roman Catholic Church affirmed an uncertain, transformational model of justification that included a measure of free will. This was therefore a distinctively *Roman Catholic* free will. Melanchthon's doctrine, on the other hand, allowed for a measure of free will in

---

[129] CT 35.   [130] CT 38.   [131] CT 38.
[132] CT 44 (Canons 15, 16).   [133] CT 53 (Canon 4).

connection to a forensic doctrine of certain justification by faith alone. This differentiated his understanding of the will's role in justification from that of the Council of Trent, and is the reason why a better term for his formulation would be *evangelical* free will.

CONCLUSION

The latter half of the 1540s were a time of tremendous political upheaval in western Europe. The death of Luther and the advent of the Schmalkaldic War made all things uncertain, and during these turbulent years, a lacuna appeared in Melanchthon's otherwise steady production of theological writings. With the defeat of the Protestant forces, and the coming of a Bavarian inquisition, the 1550s would prove to be a tumultuous decade. In addition to these trials, Melanchthon would also face continued criticism from Protestants who took issue with the way his theology of the will's role in justification had transformed over the years. With pen in hand, Melanchthon resolutely set out to meet these challenges, but in so doing, he began to express a weariness with the ways of the world. Indeed, he would not be much longer for it.

10

1548–1553: Aftermath

INTRODUCTION

With the disastrous conclusion of the Schmalkaldic War and the imposition of the Leipzig Interim by Charles V, 1548 and 1549 were tumultuous years. Melanchthon was consulted by the new Catholic political leadership on this, and he did his best to use his influence to preserve what he considered to be the central tenets of evangelical theology, while being more flexible on the things he deemed to be of secondary importance—the *adiaphora*. When the demands of these events began to settle down somewhat, Melanchthon returned to a focus on theological teaching and writing.

The early 1550s marked a flurry of theological productivity from Melanchthon. While dealing with the attacks of Matthias Flacius Illyricus, Melanchthon prepared a major response to the Council of Trent—a substantive document known as *The Saxon Confession*. At about the same time, Melanchthon and Calvin finally began to have a real falling-out over the issue of the will's role in justification. Soon thereafter, Melanchthon prepared a German-language theological guide for the examination of ordinands. In the same year, Melanchthon issued the fourth edition of the *Loci communes*. In all these contexts Melanchthon continued to refine his teaching on the origins of a saving faith in Jesus Christ.

CRITICISM FROM MATTHIAS FLACIUS ILLYRICUS: 1549–1550

If Calvin had begun to notice Melanchthon's shift on free will in justification in 1538, other theologians noticed it in the 1550s. Matthias Flacius Illyricus was the most notable of these, and he launched strenuous attacks on Melanchthon's newly formed theology of justification.

Born in 1520, Matthias Flacius Illyricus[1] spent his adult life in Germany. As a young academic in Wittenberg, Luther had been kind to him, and Melanchthon had been a personal friend as well as his teacher. Listed as 'Mattheus Watzer' in the Wittenberg matriculation record, Flacius considered himself a friend of Melanchthon. At one point, Flacius offered to accompany Melanchthon on a dangerous journey to the Council of Trent. On a personal level, Melanchthon even helped Flacius find a wife.[2] In 1549, Flacius wrote to Melanchthon, 'I have honestly loved you more than any other.'[3] Melanchthon, in turn, wrote to Flacius, calling himself 'an old friend who truly loved you.'[4] Likewise, in another letter, he said, 'Between myself and Illyricus, there was sweet friendship and intimacy.'[5] This relationship began to change, however, in the aftermath of the Schmalkaldic War.

With the defeat of Elector Johann Friedrich of Saxony and Landgrave Philip of Hesse, Saxony came under Roman Catholic rule. In 1547–8, the emperor promulgated the Augsburg Interim, in which he sought to subject Protestants to Roman obedience. This was rejected by nearly everyone, including Melanchthon. Philipp, though, was committed to saving the University of Wittenberg, and so agreed to give his advice on a new interim document. Melanchthon did his best to preserve Protestant distinctives in helping to draft this new document, especially regarding justification. But many Protestants, including Flacius, Nikolaus von Amsdorf, and Nikolaus Gallus, were not satisfied. They believed that Melanchthon had conceded too much, and they termed this new document of 1548 the Leipzig Interim.[6]

---

[1] For articles on Flacius, see OER 2.110–11 and TRE 11.206–14. The classic biography of Flacius is Wilhelm Preger's *Matthias Flacius Illyricus und seine Zeit*, 2 vols. (Hildesheim: Georg Olms Verlag, 1859–61 (reprinted in 1964)). More recently, see also Lauri Haikola's *Gesetz und Evangelium bei Matthias Flacius Illyricus: Eine Untersuchung zur lutherischen Theologie vor der Konkordienformel* (Lund: CWK Gleerup, 1952), esp. pp. 266–78 on Flacius' views on the will's role in conversion. Most recent is Oliver K. Olson's admiring book, *Matthias Flacius and the Survival of Luther's Reform* (Wiesbaden: Harassowitz, 2002). In this book, Olson consistently portrays Melanchthon in an unflattering, even hysterical light—while he presents Flacius as gracious, calm, and reasonable. These are overly simplistic and often unwarranted characterizations.

[2] Olson, *Matthias Flacius*, 42.

[3] Trans. Olson, *Matthias Flacius*, 42. Olson cites as the primary source for this quotation Flacius' *Entschuldigung Matthiae Flacij Illyrici, geschrieben an die Universitet zu Wittemberg der Mittelding halben. Item sein brief an Philip. Melanthonem sampt etlichen andern schriften dieselbige sach belangend. Verdeudscht* (Magdeburg: Christian Rödinger, 1549). See also the summary version of Flacius' open letter (written in Magdeburg) to Melanchthon (in Wittenberg), dated 20 October 1549. MBW 5.5655.

[4] Trans. Olson, 42. '... veterem amicum, qui te vere dilexit...' CR 8.840 Nr. 6067. 5 September 1556. MBW 7.7947 (approximately).

[5] Trans. Olson, 42. 'Fuit mihi dulcis et amicitia et familiaritas com Illyrico...' CR 8.798 Nr. 6031. 15 July 1556. MBW 7.7892 (approximately).

[6] See Kolb, *Bound Will*, 103–6.

Specifically, the area of Melanchthon's alleged concession came with these words: 'Although God does not make human creatures righteous through the merit of their own work, which they perform, but through his mercy, freely, without our merit—so that we boast not of ourselves but of Christ, through whose merit alone we are redeemed from sin and made righteous—nonetheless, the merciful *God does not deal with human creatures as with a block of wood but draws them in such a manner that their will cooperates,* if they are of the age of reason. They do not receive Christ's benefits if the will and heart are not moved by prevenient grace, so that they stand in fear of God's wrath and detest sin.'[7] Philipp supported this formulation. Flacius and Gallus (later termed the 'Gnesio-Lutherans'[8]) did not. The 'block of wood' analogy seemed to them to mark a heterodox departure from Luther's doctrine of the bound will. Flacius, who was teaching at Wittenberg University at the time, quit his academic post to express his views freely at Magdeburg, which had become a stronghold for those resisting compliance with the victorious emperor, Charles V.[9]

Flacius maintained that the 'block of wood' language of the Leipzig Interim was an endorsement of Erasmus' view of free will in faith, leading to a Catholic transformational model of justification, rather than the forensic imputation of Christ's righteousness. Tied into this was a debate about the necessity of good works for salvation—which, for Flacius, was a harbinger of heresy. It suggested to him that people were meriting part of their own salvation, just like the old scholastic theology that Luther had been so vehement in refuting. In sum, Flacius feared that Melanchthon had abandoned the principle of justification by faith alone.[10]

Flacius quickly attacked Melanchthon on the Leipzig Interim, especially regarding his doctrine of the will. Melanchthon did not see this as valid

---

[7] Emphasis added. Trans. Kolb, in 'The Leipzig Interim', in *Sources and Contexts of the Book of Concord*, p. 185. 'Wiewohl Gott den Menschen nicht gerecht macht durch Verdienst eigner Werck, die der Mensch thut, sondern aus Barmherzigkeit umsonst, ohne unser Verdeinst, daß der Ruhm nicht unser sey sondern Christi, durch welches Verdienst allein werden wir von Sünden erlöst und gerecht gemacht: gleichwohl wircket der barmherzige Gott nicht also mit dem Menschen wie mit einem Block, sondern zeucht ihn also, daß sein Wille auch mitwircket, so er in verständigen Jahren ist. Denn ein solcher Mensch empfähet die Wohlthaten Christi nicht, without nicht durch vorgehende Gnade der Wille und das Herz bewegt wird, daß er für Gottes Zorn erschreckte, und ein Mißfallen habe an der Sünde.' CR 7.51. Cf. the nearly verbatim passage from the Augsburg Interim, *Sources and Contexts,* 152; and Joachim Mehlhausen, ed., *Das Augsburger Interim von 1548,* 2nd edn. (Neukirchen: Neukirchener Verlag, 1996), 48–9.
[8] This debate continued beyond Melanchthon's death. Later scholarship has termed those who supported Melanchthon as 'Philippists'.
[9] MacCulloch, *The Reformation*, 338–40. Kolb, *Bound Will*, 107.
[10] Olson, *Matthias Flacius*, 99–101. This is obviously Olson's own opinion as well, based on the fact that he titled this section 'Melanchthon Surrenders Justification by Faith Alone'.

Part III. Evangelical Free Will

criticism, but in a letter to Adam Cureus, he called Flacius (and those who agreed with him) foolish, especially in his thought about the freedom of the will.[11] In another letter to Albert Hardenberg, Melanchthon again had harsh words for Flacius' arguments about the will, and he called Flacius hateful.[12] A few months later it became clear to Melanchthon that Flacius' attack was specifically directed at his view of the will's role in conversion. By August of 1550, Melanchthon had come to the conclusion that he ought to reply to the arguments of Flacius.[13]

Clearly annoyed, in a letter to Prince Georg of Anhalt of 7 September 1550, Melanchthon vigorously denied that he had abandoned justification *sola fide*. He wrote, 'It is necessary for me to refute Flacius' lies. Never did I say, never did I write, never did I think, what he says I am saying—that this proposition that "We are justified by faith alone" is just parsing words and quibbling. I have written much proving this proposition. . . .'[14] Melanchthon went on to speak of the venom of vipers.[15] In another letter on the same day, Melanchthon expressed concern about the perceived hatred of Flacius towards him, and he further argued that it was a lie when Flacius called him 'over-subtle' on the doctrine of justification.[16] Yet, despite his obvious displeasure, Melanchthon did not see fit to write a direct reply to Flacius' accusations. Perhaps he was referring to Flacius, among others, when he occasionally denounced Stoics and fatalists.[17] In any case, Melanchthon's divisions with Flacius deepened over the next six years, and although he expressed a desire to meet with Flacius to work out their differences, the chasm between them now seemed so great that he thought it imprudent: 'I should like to discuss the whole system of doctrine with [Flacius]. But he has circulated things about me which I have never uttered, and which never entered into my thoughts. Therefore, I fear

---

[11] Melanchthon (in Wittenberg), letter to Adam Cureus (in Nordhausen), 11 April 1550. MBW 6.5769. CR 7.571–2 Nr. 4699.

[12] Melanchthon (in Wittenberg), letter to Albert Hardenberg (in Bremen), 30 April 1550. MBW 6.5781. CR 8.475 Nr. 5776.

[13] Melanchthon (in Wittenberg), letter to Caspar Hedio and Johannes Marbach (in Strassburg), 12 August 1550. MBW 6.5872. CR 7.643–4 Nr. 4771. Melanchthon (in Wittenberg), letter to Albert Hardenberg (in Bremen), 29 August 1550. MBW 6.5891. CR 7.650 Nr. 4780.

[14] This is my translation. 7 September 1550. 'Refutare me *Flacii* mendacia necesse est. Nunquam dixi, nunquam scripsi, nunquam cogitavi, quod ait me dicere ἀκριβολογίαν καὶ λεπτολογίαν esse, hanc propositionem, *Sola fide iustificamur*. Meis scriptis haec propositio declarata est . . .' CR 7.658 Nr. 4789. MBW 6.5898. See also Olson's (quoted) translation and discussion, in *Matthias Flacius*, 101.

[15] 'Ego exilia aut mortem facilius feram, quam haec viperarum venena, quae tamen potero, si ero alibi, et si vivam, depellere.' CR 7.658 Nr. 4789. MBW 6.5898.

[16] Melanchthon (in Wittenberg), letter to Kilian Goldstein (in Halle), 7 September 1550. MBW 6.5899.

[17] Kolb, *Bound Will*, 107.

treacherous intentions in all this. Oh! that he would act toward me with the same sincerity with which I should wish to approach him! But not one of my friends is willing to be present at such an interview and they are of the opinion that it is not safe for me to meet him alone.'[18]

For the time being, though, Melanchthon let his theological writings do the talking, beginning with the *Saxon Confession* in 1551.

THE SAXON CONFESSION[19]: 1551

Introduction

With an eye to influencing the proceedings set to resume in 1551, Melanchthon wrote the *Saxon Confession* in defence of Protestant theology and in response to the pronouncements of the Council of Trent (1545–7).[20] Melanchthon was seeking to reiterate the basic tenets of the *Augsburg Confession*,[21] writing on behalf of the entire evangelical movement as well as for himself. Elector Moritz had approached Melanchthon for this task, insisting that the document represent not the evangelical *states*, but the evangelical *theologians*. To work on this project in peace and quiet, Melanchthon went with Camerarius to Dessau to the Prince of Anhalt's estate. On 7 October 1551, the professors from Leipzig and all the Saxon superintendents met in Wittenberg and signed the document. This confession never had much theological or political effect, either at the Council of Trent, or otherwise. Nevertheless, it remains an important record of Lutheran theology in the 1550s, and of Melanchthon's thought in particular.[22]

Melanchthon began the confession by insisting that it was not the goal of the evangelical party to give rise to dissension, but rather to embrace Luther's theology and simply to repeat the doctrines of the *Augsburg Confession*.[23] His

---

[18] Trans. Olson, *Matthias Flacius*, 311. '...et cum [Illyrico] libenter colloquerer de toto corpore doctrinae. Sed sparsit antea, quae a me nec dicta nec cogitat fuerunt: quare nunc quoque insidias metuo. Utinam pari candore, quo ego libenter velim cum eo agere, ageret mecum. Sed nemo meorum amicorum vult interesse colloquio, et iudicant, mihi non esse tutum, solum cum eo colloqui.' CR 8.798 Nr. 6031. Melanchthon, letter to Hubert Languet. 15 July 1556. MBW 7.7890.

[19] Philipp Melanchthon, *Confessio Doctrinae Saxonicarum Ecclesiarum scripta Anno Domini MDLI ut Synodo Tridentinae exhiberetur*, MSA 6.80–167.

[20] MSA 6.166.

[21] MSA 6.165.14–17.

[22] This paragraph is condensed from the editors' introduction in MSA 6.80–1. See also Keen, 15.

[23] MSA 6.81–2.

next comments reflected a long engagement with theological critics (both Catholic and Protestant). He went on to say that it was easy to excerpt, mutilate, and cavil about words, and many now loved this game.[24] The devil himself liked to misquote and mischaracterize, and so the evangelicals would leave it to the pious and well-educated to make a level judgement. The main focus, however, would be on Jesus Christ, and on his death and resurrection.[25]

Next, as he moved into the main text, Melanchthon firmly contradicted the Tridentine soteriology of 1545–7. He asserted that one of the key doctrines of the Christian faith was the remission of sins through the acceptance of faith,[26] and he gave thanks to God for the Gospel through whose light God had converted many people to himself.[27] Here already were Melanchthon's key themes regarding the origins of faith: first, it required the acceptance of the will; second, that acceptance could only take place upon the hearing of the Gospel. Having now laid out his chief themes, Melanchthon proceeded to an aggressive refutation of the doctrines of the Roman church.[28]

In his subsequent section titled 'On Doctrine', Melanchthon spoke of the clarity of the evangelical doctrine, its origins in Scripture, and its support in the Apostles', Nicene, and Athanasian creeds.[29] Focusing especially on the Apostles' Creed, Melanchthon indicated that this *Saxon Confession* would centre on two main phrases of that ancient creed: 'I believe in the remission of sins,' and, 'I believe in the holy catholic church.'[30] As he moved to a consideration of the remission of sins, he began by discussing the Fall and its results.

The Fall

Original Righteousness and its Loss

In the beginning, when God created both angels and humans, he made them righteous, or upright.[31] This original righteousness on its own was not enough to make one acceptable before God, but it provided the person with enough mental illumination to be able to give a firm assent to the Word of

---

[24] 'Facile est excerpere mutilata dicta et ea cavillari, ac delectat nunc multos hic ludus.' MSA 6.82.

[25] MSA 6.82–3.

[26] '...de fide accipiente remissionem peccatorum...' MSA 6.84.15–16.

[27] '...et Deo gratias agere pro hoc immenso beneficio oportuit, quod reddita Evangelii luce, plures ad se convertit.' MSA 6.84.19–21.

[28] MSA 6.83–9.

[29] MSA 6.89.28–9.

[30] MSA 6.90.7–15. Melanchthon reiterated this focus on the remission of sins and the doctrine of the church later on, at MSA 6.93.24–7.

[31] '...diaboli et homines...amiserunt rectitudinem, in qua conditi erant.' MSA 6.91.7–10.

God. This assent resulted in the turning of the will to God and the genuine obedience from the heart of the individual in accord (*congruens*) with God's laws, which were already present in the person's mind.[32] In this state, it was possible to be righteous or to Fall. Unfortunately, some angels and all humanity Fell, but this was not God's doing. He neither wanted, approved, nor aided sin. Both categories of creatures misused their free wills, so losing their original righteousness as the direct result of their own folly.[33]

Original Sin

Melanchthon consciously affirmed the doctrine of Augustine against Pelagius.[34] Citing Romans 5, he wrote that after the Fall, all people born of the sexual union of a man and a woman carried original sin.[35] (Notice that with this definition, Jesus' virgin birth preserved him from the stain of original sin.) Melanchthon defined original sin as the loss of original righteousness.[36] In other words, all people, being subject to original sin, lacked the inner illumination of God, and consequently human wills held an aversion to God and a proud repugnance of the heart for the law of the mind.[37] Melanchthon deftly defined original sin using all parts of the human being: will (*voluntas*), heart (*cor*), and mind (*mens*). Hence, the entire human being was subject to original sin. Original sin was total depravity (*totalem depravationem*)—the complete loss of original righteousness.[38]

This complete loss of original righteousness made it impossible for a human to fulfil the law, and the failure to fulfil the law was sin. Original sin ought not to be extenuated. Even concupiscence itself was sin.[39] Fallen people,

---

[32] '...quia iusticia originalis non tantum fuit acceptatio generis humani coram Deo, sed etiam in ipsa natura hominum lux in mente, qua firmiter adsentiri verbo Dei poterat, et conversio voluntatis ad Deum, et obedientia cordis congruens cum iudicio legis Dei, quae menti insita erat.' MSA 6.92.9–14.

[33] 'Sed diaboli et homines libertate suae voluntatis abusi defecerunt a Deo, et hac inobedientia facti sunt rei irae Dei et amiserunt rectitudinem, in qua conditi erant. Itaque libera voluntas in diabolis et hominibus causa fuit eius lapsus, non voluntas Dei, qui nec vult peccatum, nec adprobat, nec adiuvat...' MSA 6.91.7–14.

[34] MSA 6.91.30–6.

[35] 'Ac dicimus omnes homines post lapsum primorum parentum, qui nascuntur ex commissione maris et feminae, nascentes secum afferre peccatum originis...' MSA 6.91.37–92.2.

[36] 'Nec nobis displicet definitio usitata dextre intellecta: Peccatum originis est carentia iusticiae originalis debitae inesse...' MSA 6.92.7–9.

[37] 'Et haec depravatio est carere iam luce Dei seu praesentia Dei, quae in nobis fulsisset, et est aversio voluntatis nostrae a Deo, et contumacia cordis repugnans legi mentis...' MSA 6.92.31–4.

[38] 'Hos defectus et hanc totalem depravationem dicimus esse peccatum...' MSA 6.93.1–2. 'Total depravity' sounds very much like a Reformed term, but I will leave it to more adventurous scholars than I to ascertain any connection between Melanchthon's use of the phrase and that of Calvin (or any other Reformed figure).

[39] MSA 6.93.24–7.

therefore, try how they might, could never make themselves acceptable in God's sight.

External Freedom

However, the inability of fallen human beings to justify themselves in God's sight did not in any way usher in determinism or eliminate the inherent freedom of contingency with which we were made. Melanchthon clearly affirmed this sort of external freedom in the temporal realm. After the Fall, human beings retained the liberty to control their outward members rationally and voluntarily, just as Achilles could either draw his sword or sheathe it and Scipio could coerce his outward members.[40] In this area of contingency, fallen human beings had free choice (*liberum arbitrium*).[41] Yet, returning to the key point, this external free choice of the temporal realm was powerless to achieve personal salvation. In fact, for our first parents, this external discipline of the members was no more than a fig leaf covering their nudity.[42] Instead, God himself had to intervene in human history in order for *anyone* to be saved.

God's Saving Intervention

Demonic Confusion and the Role of the Law

External, temporal freedom, though genuine, was not sufficient for salvation. But this idea of people's inability to earn their own salvation lay under demonic attack. Most people experienced confusion on this subject, erroneously supposing that the correct use of their external free choice would lead to salvation. Through this false understanding, the devil and demons sought to kill the church.[43] This demonic confusion surfaced after Moses, and it cropped up again after the Apostles.[44] It could be found in the writings of Pelagius and Origen, while in Augustine the truth shone forth.[45] But despite

[40] MSA 6.95.36–96.9.
[41] In the section titled, 'De Libero Arbitrio', Melanchthon wrote: 'Iam hic nota sit etiam doctrina de libero arbitrio. Semper in Ecclesia homines recte eruditi distinxerunt disciplinam et novitatem spiritus, quae est initium vitae aeterna, et docuerunt in homine libertatem voluntatis talem esse ad regendos externos motus membrorum, qua etiam non renati utcunque disciplinam, quae est externa obedientia iuxta legem, praestare possint.' MSA 6.106.1–10.
[42] '...haec disciplina est qualiscunque externa gubernatio, similis folio ficus, quo tegunt nuditatem suam primi parentes post lapsum.' MSA 6.96.26–8.
[43] MSA 6.94.11–15.   [44] MSA 6.94–5.   [45] MSA 6.95.

Augustine's witness, in time the rites of the church came to be thought of as the mechanism of salvation.[46]

God, in his mercy, had given the law through which the demonic confusion might be dispelled. Part of the purpose of the law was to give a clear understanding of just how high God's standards of righteousness are, and to demonstrate to the earnest person of piety the impossibility of her attainment of that holy standard. The law therefore demonstrated the insufficiency of external (temporal) free choice in achieving righteousness before God. It showed us our sin, revealed God's judgement, and prepared the way in human hearts for the reception of the promises of the Gospel.[47]

Consequently, Melanchthon declared, it was outrageous to say that any of our works merited the remission or propitiation of our sins.[48] Casting aside even the careful formulations of scholastic tradition, Melanchthon exclaimed, 'Therefore we clearly condemn those Pharisees and delirious Pelagians who pretend that external discipline can fulfil God's law and merit the remission of sins—either by *meritum de congruo* or *meritum de condigno*, and thus be accepted as righteous in God's sight (*coram Deo*).'[49]

The Gospel of Jesus Christ

Instead, the light of the Gospel shone as the free remission of sins through the Mediator, received through faith.[50] 'Whoever believes in the Son has eternal life. Whoever does not believe remains under the wrath of God.'[51] It was the works of *Jesus Christ* that saved, not the inadequate efforts of the individual. Jesus alone, by his obedience, did merit the placation of the wrath of God,[52] and it was totally through the mercy of God (rather than as a result of anything we had done) that he was given for us.[53]

---

[46] MSA 6.94.15–32.   [47] MSA 6.98.

[48] 'Et contumelia est filii Dei fingere ulla nostra opera merita esse, seu precium remissionis peccatorum et esse propiciationes pro peccato.' MSA 6.97.3–5.

[49] 'Ideo pharisaica illa et pelagiana deliramenta clare damnamus, quae fingunt disciplinam illam esse impletionem legis Dei, item mereri remissionem seu de congruo seu de condigno, vel esse iusticiam, qua homines coram Deo sint accepti.' MSA 6.97.6–10.

[50] '...luce Evangelii, in qua proponitur gratuita remissio propter mediatorem accipienda fide...' MSA 6.95.3–5.

[51] 'Qui credit in Filium, habet vitam aeternam. Qui non credit, manet ira Dei super eum.' MSA 6.95.29–30.

[52] MSA 6.97.11–16.

[53] 'Tanta misericordia, ut filius pro nobis datus sit.' MSA 6.97.29–30. See also MSA 6.106.17–21: 'Ac Deo gratias agimus pro hoc immenso beneficio, quod nobis propter filium et per eum dat Spiritum sanctum et nos suo spiritu regit, Et damnamus Pelagianos et Manicheos, ut haec suo loco copiosius explicamus.'

Imputed Righteousness by Faith Alone

Jesus Christ earned perfect righteousness through his good works, and fallen human beings received the gift of that righteousness. It was an imputed (rather than intrinsic) righteousness.[54] Intrinsic righteousness would later grow up in the believer as part of the process of sanctification, but this was not the basis on which the individual was saved.[55] Salvation came through the imputed righteousness of Jesus Christ, received by faith alone.[56] Faith, then, was the one necessary human precondition for salvation. The individual *had to accept* remission of his sins through faith.[57]

If it was so important, what then exactly *was* faith? Melanchthon described faith as more than historical knowledge—it was the firm embrace of God's promises for oneself. From the Apostles' Creed one said, '*I* believe in the remission of sins.'[58] In other words, a saving faith went beyond the mere assent of the mind to include also the acquiescence of the heart.[59] Further, faith was not the mere self-absorbed contrition of the heart,[60] but the turning of the heart to accept the gift of justification from *outside* of itself. The human Narcissus must look up from his own reflection to gaze upon Christ. Faith embodied the reliance of the entire self upon Jesus Christ.

The Origins of Faith

Because faith was so crucial to salvation, Melanchthon did not fail to mention his views on its origins. Here his formulations continued to be consistent with what he had been teaching for nearly the last two decades. The choice of faith in Jesus had three sources in combination: the Gospel, the Holy Spirit, and the human will.

Naturally, having already stressed the centrality of salvation by faith in Jesus Christ, it followed that one had to hear about Jesus before one could believe in him. Faith, therefore, required the hearing of the Gospel. This hearing,

---

[54] 'Hac fide cum erigitur, certum est donari remissionem peccatorum, reconciliationem et imputationem iusticiae propter ipsius Christi meritum...' MSA 6.98.35–99.2.

[55] MSA 6.100.

[56] 'Sola fide iustificamur.' MSA 6.100.26–7.

[57] '...de fide, qua accipi remissionem oportet...' MSA 6.94.6–7. '...et hanc [remissionem] fide accipiendam esse...' MSA 6.94.20–1.

[58] 'Sunt autem nota vocabula. Fides significat non tantum historiae noticiam... sed significat amplecti omnes articulos fidei et in his hunc articulum: Credo remissionem peccatorum.' MSA 6.99.13–18.

[59] '"Fide iustificamur", hoc est fiducia Filii Dei iustificamur, non propter nostram qualitatem, sed quia ipse est propiciator, in quo cor acquiescit fiducia...' MSA 6.100.17–19.

[60] MSA 6.100.

though, was no static or neutral thing. Wherever the Gospel was to be found, there also was the Holy Spirit, hard at work in the hearts of the hearers, endeavouring to excite them to accept God's promises.[61] Without the Gospel and the Spirit (and of course the reality of Christ's death and resurrection to which they pointed), no person could be saved. Then, upon hearing the always Spirit-illumined Gospel, the individual experienced, as it were, at least the partial restoration of original righteousness so far as it applied to having the freedom to either believe in the Lord or deny him. The Christian could have the consolation, then, of reflecting on the fact that her decision to accept the Son of God was a movement of assent from the Holy Spirit, who made her heart alive and liberated her from death.[62] The natural human being by no means had the ability to free himself from sin and death unto eternal life, but this liberation and conversion to God in Christ came through the Holy Spirit—and yet, the human will, in accepting the Spirit, was not idle.[63]

The Gospel and Spirit could point the way to salvation through faith in Christ, but then the human will still had the responsibility to make a free choice to either accept or reject that gift of forgiveness. The remission of sins had to be *apprehended* by faith.[64] The heart and spirit were not idle in this process.[65] Hence, the origins of the decision of faith were temporal rather than timeless. In other words, no individual was predestined from before all time to come to faith, but rather, people had the free opportunity within their lifetimes to hear the Gospel of Jesus Christ, and, upon hearing that Good News, to experience the inevitable tug of the Holy Spirit to which the addition of a free decision of acceptance by the person would seal the deal. The result of this faith would be salvation through the imputed righteousness of Christ. Faith therefore came from the Gospel, the Holy Spirit, and the newly freed human will all working in concert.

---

[61] '"Fide iustificamur", hoc est fiducia Filii Dei iustificamur, non propter nostram qualitatem, sed quia ipse est propiciator, in quo cor acquiescit fiducia ipse Spiritu suo sancto exuscitat, sicut inquit Paulus, "Accepistis Spiritum adoptionis filiorum, quo clamamus, Abba pater"'. MSA 6.100.17–22.

[62] 'Cum autem in hac ipsa consolatione fiducia, qua acquiescimus in filio Dei, vere sit motus accensus a Spiritu sancto, quo vivificatur cor et liberatur ex eterna morte, dicitur haec conversio, regeneratio Ioh. 3 "Nisi quis renatus fuerit ex aqua et Spiritu"'. MSA 6.104.30–4.

[63] 'Sed homo nequaquam potest se liberare a peccato et morte aeterna viribus naturalibus, sed haec liberatio et conversio hominis ad Deum et novitas spiritualis fit per filium Dei vivificantem nos Spiritu sancto, ut dictum est: "Si quis Spiritum Christi non habet, hic non est eius". Et voluntas accepto Spiritu sancto iam non est ociosa.' MSA 6.106.10–16.

[64] '. . . fide adprehendi oportet . . .' MSA 6.101.3.

[65] MSA 6.105, 106. See also MSA 6.120.18–20 (notice the active verbs): 'Deo gratias agimus et eum invocamus et petimus, accipimus et expectamus aeterna bona.'

The Assurance of Faith

We have seen through his writings that Melanchthon held a keen concern throughout his life for the pastoral consolation of wavering believers (that is, for the effects of doctrine). Whereas under a doctrine of individual predestination one could reassure believers by reminding them that the choice had ultimately been God's and not theirs (and hence not subject to revision), Melanchthon's own formulation required a different approach. If salvation depended in part on the will of the individual, then that might lead some to worry if they felt that they vacillated about the genuineness of their belief. Moreover, the recent pronouncements from the Council of Trent had strongly advocated the benefits of doubts about one's personal salvation. The argument had been that such doubts served as the greatest possible motivating impetus for strenuous efforts to live a transformational life of Christian piety.

Melanchthon strongly rejected the Tridentine advocacy of soteriological doubt, declaring instead that Christians should find *assurance* in their faith.[66] Melanchthon's pastoral solution here was to turn the attention of the fretting soul away from one's own inconstant human will and toward the unchanging promises of the divine will. God's offer of the remission of sins was a genuine, universal promise. Jesus had said, to all who would accept it, 'Come to me all who are weary and heavy-laden, and I will give you rest.'[67] Melanchthon stressed that every single individual was included in this promise. No one should distrust that promise, but rather work to assent to God's Word and yield to the Holy Spirit, asking, if necessary, for help. As it said in Luke 11.13, 'How much more will God give the Holy Spirit to those who ask!'[68]

This focus on the reality of God's promises and their universal application was a distinct rebuttal of standard predestinarian paradigms. Melanchthon did not assert any sort of 'hidden will' of God for some to accept the promises and others to reject them. Nor was there any sort of 'special call' of the Holy Spirit that some people received and others did not. Instead, God's promises were fairly and truly offered to all so that any who should choose to believe them would receive their benefits. Indeed, the *Saxon Confession* did not even contain a section on predestination, and in speaking of pastoral assurance, Melanchthon specifically made the point that predestination should *not* be

---

[66] MSA 6.104, esp. 13–15.

[67] 'Ita et promissio universalis est et omnibus offert remissionem peccatorum, iuxta illa dicta universalia, "Venite ad me omnes, qui laboratis et onerati estis, et ego reficiam vos".' MSA 6.105.20–4, citing Matthew 11.28.

[68] 'In hanc universalem promissionem singuli se includant, et non indulgeant diffidentiae, sed luctentur, ut adsentiantur verbo Dei et obsequantur Spiritui sancto et iuvari se petant, sicut dictum est, "Quanto magis dabit Spiritum sanctum petentibus".' MSA 6.105.28–33.

considered on the grounds that it was an unhelpful goad to unnecessary speculations. For Melanchthon, it was far more helpful to meditate upon the revealed promises of Scripture than to speculate about one's inclusion or exclusion in God's kingdom via the doctrines of predestination or election.[69]

Corporate Election

Continuing a theme that he had taken up for the last couple of decades, Melanchthon then proceeded to make the case that the biblical references to 'election' referred to the *church* as a body rather than to *individuals* as helpless pawns to be cast willy-nilly into hell or elevated to glory. People had neither been created by chance nor made for the purpose of eternal destruction. Rather, God's will was to gather them to himself via the Gospel, illuminated by the Holy Spirit, and agreed upon by the human will. These who had thus been gathered were the order of the people of the church to whom he would eternally communicate wisdom, goodness, and joy.[70] The true church was comprised of those who believed God's promises,[71] and these people together represented the elect.[72] The visible, worldly *institution* of the church did not represent the elect body, but rather, it was the true, invisible church made up of those who believed in Jesus.[73] The true church as a whole was predestined, but the individual constituent *members* of that group were not, and they could freely join or leave this elect *body*. This body was indeed the body of Christ, who drew this eternal church to himself by the voice of the Gospel[74] to which the human will must assent. Hence, upon hearing the Spirit-illumined Gospel, individuals would have a free choice as to whether or not they wanted to *become* part of the elect church or stay out of it.

Interestingly, however, while in the *Commentary on Romans* of 1540, Melanchthon had repeatedly referred to the 'elect church' (*Ecclesia electa*),

---

[69] MSA 6.105, esp. lines 11–18: 'Et quia conscientiis in poenitentia consolationem proponimus, non addimus hic questiones de praedestinatione seu de electione, sed deducimus omnes lectores ad verbum Dei et iubemus, ut voluntatem Dei ex verbo ipsius discant, sicut aeternus Pater expressa voca praecipit: "Hunc audite". Non quaerant alias speculationes.'

[70] 'Vult Deus intelligi genus humanum non casu nasci, sed a Deo conditum esse, et conditum non ad aeternum exitium, sed ut colligat sibi in genere humano Ecclesiam, cui in omni aeternitate communicet suam sapientiam, bonitatem et laetitiam.' MSA 6.119.19–23.

[71] MSA 6.120.13–18.

[72] 'In hoc coetu vocatorum certo scias aliquos electos esse, et ad hunc coetum te adiungito confessione et invocatione.' MSA 6.120.27–121.2.

[73] MSA 6.125.

[74] 'Commendamus autem et Ecclesiam et nos ipsos Filio Dei, Domino nostro Iesu Christo, quem scimus voce Evangelii colligere sibi aeternam Ecclesiam . . .' MSA 6.166.23–6.

this phrase had disappeared from the *Saxon Confession*. The same *principle* of corporate rather than individual election was present, but Melanchthon had backed away from the *language* of the 'elect church'.

Conclusion

For Melanchthon in the *Saxon Confession*, the key determinant in whether an individual went to heaven or hell lay in the free choice of the human will. This choice of faith in Jesus was not coerced by God, but neither could it happen without God. The free choice of the will could only take place when framed in the context of the hearing of the Gospel which was always illumined by the Holy Spirit. Furthermore, it was not the choice in and of itself that saved, as if it were a good work. Melanchthon had been attacked by Flacius on this point, and his clarification of the choice of faith as *non*-meritorious was no doubt a response to that critique. For Melanchthon, the choice to trust fully in Jesus was the *instrument* by which the individual passively received the salvation which was merited in full through the life, suffering, death, and resurrection of Jesus Christ. Faith then was the *active* assent of the will in order *passively* to receive imputed righteousness from Christ. As a result, one's eternal destination depended on the person's own (non-meritorious) choice rather than God's specific predestining will.

For Melanchthon, and for those to whom he wished to offer pastoral counsel, this construct removed the speculative terror of wondering if one might be among the reprobate. Yet, at the same time, Melanchthon realized that by making the reception of one's salvation contingent upon a free choice of the human will, he had removed the assurance that could be found in supposing oneself to be firmly saved as one of God's individual elect. Nevertheless, Melanchthon preserved an assurance of salvation by focusing on the reliability of God's promises in relation to all those who did choose to have faith in Christ. Assurance came not from *God's* choice (predestination), but from the *person's* choice (free will) as bolstered by *God's* promises in relation to that choice. These were careful distinctions, but John Calvin, for one, was not going to put up with them.

CALVIN'S FALLING OUT WITH MELANCHTHON: 1551–1552

In 1551, controversy over the doctrine of predestination arose in Geneva, and John Calvin found himself having to defend his position over and against

Melanchthon's, especially as articulated in the *Loci communes* of 1543. During the Bolsec controversy, Melanchthon's formulation of predestination from this document was used in opposition to Calvin's doctrine of predestination.[75] Word of this dispute found its way back to Melanchthon,[76] and Calvin prepared to defend himself.

In 1552, Calvin publicly distanced himself from Melanchthon on the doctrine of predestination.[77] He wrote a book titled, *De aeterna praedestinatione Dei* (*On the Eternal Predestination of God*).[78] This book acted both as a completion of his reply to Pighius and also as a refutation of Bolsec. It distinguished Calvin's position from Melanchthon's, though it did not mention him by name. Calvin wrote to Melanchthon on 28 November 1552, to confirm this development. He began the letter by reiterating his friendship with Melanchthon. Calvin then went on gently to separate himself from Melanchthon on the doctrines of free will and predestination, and he referred him to *De aeterna praedestinatione Dei*.[79] However much Calvin respected Melanchthon and desired evangelical unity, he simply could not go along with Melanchthon's new doctrine of free will and predestination.

Meanwhile, Philipp turned his attention back to his life's calling: preparing young seminary students for pastoral ministry, helping the church as a body discern just which individuals were doctrinally prepared to enter the local parish.

---

[75] For a detailed account of the Bolsec controversy, see P. Holtrop, *The Bolsec Controversy on Predestination from 1551 to 1555* (Lewiston, NY: Edwin Mellen, 1993). See also *Actes du Procès; Intenté par Calvin et les autres ministres de Genève a Jérome Bolsec de Paris*. 1551. CO 8.141–248.

[76] Rumours of this controversy reached Melanchthon in 1552 as evidenced by two of his letters: Melanchthon (in Nuremberg), letter to Joachim Camerarius (in Leipzig), 1 February 1552. MBW 6.6322. CR 7.930–1 Nr. 5038. Melanchthon (in Nuremberg), letter to Caspar Peucer (*en route* to Wittenberg), 1 February 1552. MBW 6.6324. CR 7.931–2 Nr. 5040.

[77] MacCulloch, *The Reformation*, 341.

[78] *De aeterna Dei praedestinatione, qua in salutem alios ex hominibus elegit, alios suo exitio reliquit: item de providentia qua res humanas gubernat, consensus pastorum Genevensis ecclesiae, a Io. Calvino expositus*. CO 8.249–366. This work can be found in a modern English translation in John Calvin, *Concerning the Eternal Predestination of God*, trans. J. K. S. Reid (Louisville, KY: Westminster John Knox, 1961).

[79] Cf. *Institutes* III.xxi.3, where Calvin criticized those who would 'bury predestination', though without naming Melanchthon. Over the next few years, Calvin and Melanchthon would stay in contact, but apart from some gentle prodding on the part of Calvin in one letter in 1555, the two would not speak on the topic of free will and predestination again. The letter from 1555: Calvin (in Geneva), letter to Melanchthon (in Wittenberg), 5 March 1555. MBW 7.7424. CO 15.488–9 Nr. 2139.

THE EXAMINATION OF ORDINANDS, GERMAN EDITION: 1552

Introduction

Melanchthon wrote the *Examen ordinandorum* as a tool for discerning readiness for ministry among those called to the pastorate. The great purpose of the document was to ensure the pure preaching of the Gospel through which Christ was seeking to gather an eternal church.[80] The first edition appeared in German in 1552. A later Latin edition appeared in 1554, but this work was no mere translation of the German text—it represented a substantial rewrite. Accordingly, it will be helpful first to examine the German edition of 1552 here and then to proceed to the Latin edition of 1554 in due course.[81]

In the *Examination of Ordinands*, Melanchthon crystallized his theological ideas, and his clearly expressed prose demonstrated an increasingly integrated doctrinal system. By the 1550s, Melanchthon was no longer silent about uncomfortable topics like election, but rather forthrightly laid out his own interpretation of this biblical language. Simultaneously, while it was evident that Melanchthon had come to a mature culmination of his theological development, he nevertheless here began to show a certain flexibility in his language in relation to election. While those familiar with the context of the evolution of Melanchthon's theology would probably discern his positions, the casual reader might well read Melanchthon's words and initially believe them to be in accord with Luther's much stronger view of the God who elected *individuals* for salvation rather than a corporate *body* of freely responding believers. In this capacity, Melanchthon may well have been demonstrating a consciousness of the theological scrutiny that was increasingly being directed upon him (from Calvin, in particular). Nevertheless, when it came to the Reformation doctrine of justification by faith, Melanchthon expressed himself with more assurance and clarity than ever. Before discussing justification and election, however, prudence demands beginning, once again, with creation and the fall.

---

[80] MSA 6.171.3–6.

[81] Rogness, 127–8, gives a few pages of discussion on the role of the will in the *Examen ordinandorum*, primarily as seen in the later Latin edition. His opinion is that, 'It would, of course, be quite "un-Lutheran" to say that the human will contributes to or is a cause of the first moment of conversion, but Melanchthon neither said nor intended to say that' (p. 128). Hopefully the present work has demonstrated, and will continue to demonstrate, that Rogness's evaluation is not accurate. Melanchthon *did* say that the human will contributes to the first moment of conversion (in that it must make a free choice for faith), but the free choice of the will does *not* contribute any instrinsic *merit* towards one's salvation.

Creation and the Fall

In themes that are by now familiar, Melanchthon strongly affirmed that at the beginning of time, all God's creatures, including mankind, were created good.[82] Humanity's highest good was in God, and Adam and Eve had wisdom, righteousness, and free will.[83] These gifts would have been passed on to their descendants.[84] But Adam and Eve were tempted by the devil, and out of their own free wills they were disobedient to God's law. Hence, they Fell into sin and death.[85] The Fall was therefore the fault of the devil for tempting and of Adam and Eve for choosing to give in to the temptation. The source of evil was the misapplication of free demonic and human wills and was in no way God's fault.[86]

As a result of the Fall, Adam and Eve's original grace was removed, so they could no longer fulfil God's law. Additionally, they lost their former higher gifts of wisdom, righteousness, and free will.[87] Now all those naturally born of human seed were subject to original sin, an innate blindness and evil inclination. Every individual now remained under God's condemnation. They would have remained thus in eternal death, if it had not been for the miraculous intercession of Jesus Christ.[88]

Salvation in Christ by Faith Alone

Melanchthon emphatically maintained that God justified sinners solely on account of his grace, received through faith alone in Jesus Christ. The merit for salvation entirely stemmed from Christ's work. It had no basis at all in

---

[82] 'Dieses ist gantz gewis und festiglich zu halten, das Gotte alle Creaturen gut erschaffen hat. . . . Und ist gewislich war, das der Mensch dazu erschaffen ist . . .' MSA 6.181.23–4, 25–6.

[83] 'Hat in darumb erstlich also erschaffen, das er ihn begabt hat mit den höhesten Gütern, die in Gott sind. Nemlich mit Weisheit, Gerechtigkeit und freiem willen, das er ein rein ebenbild Gottes were.' MSA 6.181.27–30.

[84] 'Und haben die ersten Menschen, Adam und Heva, diese güter sollen auff die Nachkomen erben, so sie im gehorsam bestendig geblieben were.' MSA 6.181.31–3.

[85] 'Aber Adam und Heva sind durch des Teufels anreitzung und durch ihren freien willen dem göttlichen Gebot ungehorsam worden und sind also ihn ungnad, sünd und tod gefallen . . .' MSA 6.181.34–7.

[86] 'Und ist nötig hie zu erinnern, das gewislich war ist und festiglich zu gleuben, Das Gott nich ursach ist der Sünden. Er wircket sie nicht, hilfft nicht dazu, wil sie nicht, Sonder zürnet grausamlich wider sie. Aber der Teufeln und menschen will selb ist ursach der Sünden.' MSA 6.182.10–14.

[87] 'Beraubt sind sie der gnaden, das sie nicht mehr Gott gefellig gewesen sind, und haben dau verloren die hohen gaben . . .' MSA 6.182.1–3.

[88] MSA 6.182.7–34.

human endeavour.[89] Consequently, the papal party, the Pharisees, the heathen, and the Turks (Muslims) were all wrong to teach that one could become righteous and please God through good works. Further, they erred in thinking that anyone could fulfil God's law in this life.[90] True Christian freedom was not the ability to fulfil or cooperate in fulfilling God's law, but rather, in being forgiven for one's sins and being made righteous on account of Christ, apart from one's own merit[91]—and this happened only through faith.

On Faith

God, through the Gospel, offered the gift of eternal life to all those who would believe in Jesus Christ. Faith, then, was the name given to the human act of grasping those promises for oneself. Faith was *active* (the person *grasped* the promise).[92] Moreover, faith was no mere intellectual acquiescence to the veracity of historical knowledge. Rather, faith was a personal, thoroughgoing trust of the entire person solely in Jesus Christ.[93] Melanchthon declared, 'This trust is as far from the devil's belief as heaven is from hell, and life from death.'[94]

Having now affirmed what faith *was*, Melanchthon went to great pains to show what faith was *not*—namely, faith was not a work, and hence held no intrinsic soteriological merit in and of itself. Christians were righteous solely for the sake of Christ.[95] Faith was the active decision *passively* to receive Christ's merit. Faith was *correlative* with righteousness[96] rather than *causative*.

---

[89] MSA 6.188.10–22. See also MSA 6.198. 'Diese rede, Allein durch glauben werden wir Gerech, Sola fide iustificamur, Ist eben diese rede Gratis iustificamur fide.' MSA 6.189.22–4.

[90] MSA 6.193–5. See also MSA 6.174.15–20.

[91] 'Was ist Christlicher freiheit? Antwort. Christliche freiheit ist erstlich diese hohe unaussprechliche gnad, das wir one unsere verdienst umb des Herrn Christi willen vergebung der Sünden haben und gerecht sind, das ist, Gott gefellig durch den glauben, ob gleich in diesem elenden Leben noch viel schwacheit und sünd an uns klebet.' MSA 6.231.15–19.

[92] 'Sondern allein umb des Herrn Christi willen empfahen wir vergebung der Sünden und sind Gerecht, das ist Gott gefellig, Und dieses kan anders nicht denn durch Glauben angenommen werden, *der die verheißung fasset*, wie S. Paulus spricht, Ideo ex fide, gratis, ut sit firma promissio.' Emphasis added. MSA 6.189.36–190.3. For another description of faith as active, see MSA 6.191.34–6: 'Und dieses geschihet allein durch glauben, damit das hertz die verheissung fasset und den Herrn Christum anschauet und annimpt.'

[93] MSA 6.190.5–20. Also, 'Und *[Glauben] ist also ein warhafftig hertzlich vertrauen* auf den Son Gottes Ihesum Christum den Mittler und versüner, das wir umb seinet willen und durch ihn haben vergebung der Sünd, gnad und seligkeit.' Emphasis added. MSA 6.190.30–3.

[94] 'Dieses vertrauen ist so fern von des Teufels glauben, als der Himel ist von der hell und Leben vom Tod.' MSA 6.190.34–5.

[95] MSA 6.191.23–192.3.

[96] 'Und ist nicht zu verstehen, das der Glaub gerecht mache, Darumb das er ein besonder hohes werck ist, sondern *correlative* sol diese rede verstanden werden, Durch den Son Gottes Jhesum Christum haben wir vergebung der Sünden und gnad, welchen wir mit glauben annemen.' Emphasis added. MSA 6.191.37–192.3.

Likewise, faith was no intrinsic virtue like some sort of facet of obedience to the law, but rather, being devoid of its own merit, faith served to receive Christ's merit—that is, the total forgiveness of sins, through *his* achievement alone.[97]

As to the question of the origins of this faith, Melanchthon revealed his thought more by implication than by direct explanation. Bear in mind that the *Examination of Ordinands* was a public document designed for use by the whole Lutheran Church. Therefore, it was in Melanchthon's interest to produce a theological tract that sounded as much like Luther's strongly theocentric views as possible. Consequently, Melanchthon did not emphasize the role of the free human will in the choice of faith, he held silence on the idea of individual predestination, he staunchly affirmed the genuine universality of God's promises of salvation,[98] and he described the decision of faith using the grammatically active language already noted above. Together these things strongly inferred that human beings have free choice as a contributing factor in the origins of their faith. Melanchthon would state this much more emphatically in the Latin edition of the *Examination of Ordinands* of 1554, as we will see below. Meanwhile, Melanchthon's doctrine of election in relation to the church made quite clear the role of the free human will in the decision of faith.

Election and the Eternal Church

While in previous years Melanchthon had been quite explicit in talking about an elect *church*,[99] he now used much more malleable language. In a nuanced shift, the talk of an elect church was replaced with talk of an *eternal* church (*ein ewige Kirche*)[100] which was comprised of the elect. Such a formulation held the distinct benefit of being able to be interpreted either per Melanchthon's previous discussions (i.e. election referred to the *church* as a body, which individuals could freely join or leave) or according to Luther's doctrine (i.e. election referred to the individuals who comprise the true church, and every elect individual would necessarily come to faith as God overcame their bound wills). Melanchthon's ability to craft ambiguous and subtle formulations combined with his passionate devotion to justification by faith alone

---

[97] MSA 6.192–3. Cf. MSA 6.189.36–190.3.

[98] On Christ: 'Und hat dabei seine eigne Lere gegeben, dadurch er die Menschen zur ewigen Seligkeit berufft, und wil allen Menschen, die durch das göttliche Wort zu ihm bekehret werden und in rechtem glauben und vertrauen auf den Heiland Christum vergebung der Sünden empfahen durch den Herrn Christum . . .' MSA 6.169.

[99] e.g. in his *Commentary on Romans*, of 1540: 'Ergo fit Ecclesia electione.' CR 15.682.

[100] MSA 6.169, and in numerous places throughout this work (e.g. MSA 6.174.10).

may well go a long way to explain why Melanchthon and Luther had remained on good terms, even when Melanchthon's doctrine of the will shifted away from Luther's. In any case, one could also describe Melanchthon's language about election as increasingly reflecting a more biblical usage (in accord with the humanistic principle of *ad fontes*) without necessarily going *beyond* biblical usage to explicate the underlying meaning.

As for the church, human beings were not created for transient misery, but God desired their ingathering amongst the generations into the eternal church.[101] God sought to gather this eternal church through the preaching of the Gospel.[102] The elect (*die Auserwählten*) were those who heard the Gospel and responded in faith.[103] Melanchthon did not elucidate for his readers the question of whether those who responded to the Gospel did so *because* they were elect, or rather that they *became* 'elect' *because* they had freely decided to believe in the Gospel. From the overall shape of his theology, it is clear that Melanchthon meant the latter, but a simple grammatical analysis of Melanchthon's statements on the elect (apart from their broader context) did not rule out a presumption of the former. In other words, in his statements about election, Melanchthon probably *meant* evangelical free will, but he could easily be misconstrued as articulating Luther's bound-will position from *De servo arbitrio*. It appeared that Melanchthon's use of flexible formulations (previously seen in ecumenical discussions with Roman Catholics, as at Regensburg), was now resurfacing as a tool for peace amongst contentious Lutherans.

Conclusion: No Doubts

While Melanchthon's formulations in the *Examination of Ordinands* of 1552 clearly implied evangelical free will, he did not make obvious his case for the role of the free human will in conversion. But what he did make obvious was

---

[101] '...dieses Arme, elende menschlich Geschlecht nicht zu diesem vergänglichen wesen erschaffen sei, sondern das er ihm eine ewige Kirche im menschlichen Geschlecht samlen wolle, welcher er seine Weisheit, Gerechtigkeit und Freude in Ewigkeit mitteilen wolle.' MSA 6.169.

[102] 'Und bitten wir den Son Gottes Ihesum Christum, der ihm selb krefftiglich ein ewige Kirche bei denen samlet, da das heilig Euangelium rein geprediget wird, er wolle gnediglich dieser Lande Kirchen regieren, bewaren und erhalten.' MSA 6.171.3–6.

[103] 'Denn da wircket Gott krefftiglich durch sein Euangelium, und sind in dieser Versammlung fur und fur etliche heilige und ausserwelte [Auserwählte], die selig werden. Wie der Herr Christus spricht: "Meine Schefflin hören meine Stimme".' MSA 6.174.26–31. Cf. also lines 31–6, where Melanchthon spoke of 'heilige und auserwelte Menschen'. See also MSA 6.212.23–9, where Melanchthon mentioned '... Eine versamlung, die das Euangelium in rechtem gleichen verstand helt, darin viel auserwelte sind zu ewiger Seligkeit...'.

his strong devotion to a forensic doctrine of justification by faith alone along with the assurance of salvation that such a doctrine provided. Melanchthon objected to the Roman Catholic insistence at Trent that Christians should be in doubt about their salvations. He called such a teaching cruel heathen blindness.[104] This statement demonstrated Melanchthon's pastoral concern for the troubled Christian conscience, and was the primary motivating force for his long-term shift from the bound will implicit in individual predestination to the evangelical free will of his uniquely non-predestinarian mature soteriology. As the 1550s went on, Melanchthon would express himself on these matters with increasing clarity, beginning with the fourth edition of the *Loci communes*, in 1553.

LOCI COMMUNES, FOURTH EDITION: 1553

Ostensibly, the fourth edition of the *Loci communes* was merely a German translation of the Latin version from 1543. However, Melanchthon revised the German in several places to reflect his responses to the Council of Trent, as well as to the controversy over some of the language from the Leipzig and Augsburg Interims regarding the will as being 'not like a block of wood'. Additionally, other sections reflected Melanchthon's ongoing theological development in matters touching on the role of the human will in the origins of a saving faith in Christ. Accordingly, this edition of the *Loci* will benefit from an analysis in its own right.

Melanchthon wrote this German edition of the *Loci communes* in 1553, and published it in 1555.[105] In it, he followed the same essential contours as the Latin edition of 1543. But while Melanchthon's teaching on the freedom of contingency remained virtually unchanged, his thoughts on predestination reflected the developments we have already seen in the *Saxon Confession* (1551) and the German edition of the *Examination of Ordinands* (1552).

---

[104] 'Pepstliche lere, das die Menschen in zweivel bleiben sollen, ist grausame, Heidnische blindheit.' MSA 6.195.20–1.

[105] For the German text of the *Loci* of 1553/5, citations will be given first in Manschreck's English translation (Philipp Melanchthon, *Melanchthon on Christian Doctrine: Loci Communes, 1555*, trans. Clyde L. Manschreck (New York: Oxford University Press, 1965)), and then in the original German from the CR. German citations will also be referenced to Melanchthon's 1553 draft of the *Loci* as presented in *Heubtartikel Christlicher Lere: Melanchthons deutsche Fassung seiner Loci Theologici, nach dem Autograph und dem Originaldruck von 1553*, ed. Ralf Jennett and Johannes Schilling (Leipzig: Evangelische Verlagsanstalt, 2002). The German of *Heubtartikel* usually varies from the CR only in minor variations of spelling, but as a newer scholarly edition, I recommend the *Heubtartikel* as a better resource.

He now spoke of 'the eternal church' rather than predestination. Moreover, in a new wrinkle, he began to grapple with some of the ideas related to reprobation in a new way. Finally, he continued to maintain a strong emphasis on a genuine, free human role in conversion—the choice to believe in Jesus Christ.

Contingency

As in the *Loci* of 1543, Melanchthon here treated (1) the problem of the origins of evil and sin, (2) retaining an imperative for doing good works, and (3) refraining from totally stripping away God's direct rule.

Melanchthon first spoke to the origins of sin and evil, and here his doctrine remained the same as it had for nearly thirty years. God was the Creator, though not of evil: 'The being of the spirits and the body and soul of men were created by God, and also are upheld by God; nevertheless, the disorder and the rent, or breach, in creation is not of God, but is of the free will of the devils and the first men.'[106] Again, Melanchthon wrote, 'Sin is a corruption, a breach, a disorder in the rational, very beautiful, good, and noble order of created things, spirits and men, and this disorder came first through the free will of the devils, and afterward through Adam and Eve, *who themselves freely* turned away from God.'[107] Because God was not the cause of evil, he could not be all-determining. Melanchthon enjoined, 'I beg all the pious to be forewarned, and for the sake of God's honor to maintain with firmness that God does not desire sin, that he effects nothing pertaining to sin, and that sinful deeds *do not of necessity* happen.'[108] To be clear, '*God is not the cause of sin; on the contrary he is definitely the enemy of sin.*'[109] Temporal events were not fatalistically determined, so people therefore had at least some measure of freedom.

---

[106] Trans. Manschreck, 46. 'Das Wesen der Geister, vnd Leib vnd Seele der Menschen von Gott erschaffen ist, vnd noch erhalten wird, Vnd das gleichwol die vnordnung vnd der Riss, oder Bruch darinne, nicht von Gott ist, sondern von dem Teuffel, vnd ersten Menschen freien willen.' CR 22.137–8. *Heubtartikel* 134.18–21.

[107] The emphasis is Manschreck's. Trans. Manschreck, 46. 'Sondern [die Sünde] ist eine verderbunge, bruch vnd vnordnung in den vernüfftigen, seer schönen, guten vnd edlen erschaffenen dingen, Geistern vnd Menschen, welche vnordnung erstlich durch den freien willen der Teuffel, vnd hernach Adams vnd Heua geschehen ist, Welche sich selbs freiwilliglich von Gott abgewandt haben.' CR 22.137. *Heubtartikel* 134.12–17.

[108] Trans. Manschreck, 48. 'Sondern [wil ich] alle gottfürchtigen, wie zuuor, trewlich gewarnet haben, vnd bitte, sie wöllen vmb göttlicher ehre willen, fest vber diesen Sprüchen halten vnd dabey bleiben, nemlich das Gott die Sünde nicht wölle, auch nichts darzu wircke, vnd das die sündigen werck nicht müssen geschehen.' CR 22.139. *Heubtartikel* 136.26–9.

[109] Manschreck's emphasis. Trans. Manschreck, 50. 'Gott sey nicht vrsacher der sünden, sondern sey warhafftiglich der sünden feind.' CR 22.142. *Heubtartikel* 138.29–30.

Such freedom made people genuinely responsible for their actions no matter how vitiated by the malevolent impulses of hostile demonic powers. 'The madness in Cain, Pharaoh, Saul, and Judas is from their own free wills, even though the devil drives them with it, as the text says, "Satan entered the heart of Judas" [Luke 22.3]. However, they were not forced, and this is not God's activity and doing.'[110] So while the devil could lead one's will astray, the will still had the freedom and responsibility to choose rightly. So, 'We must also admit, even as Scripture certifies, that after Adam's fall this freedom remains, so far as rational external activity is concerned. We are able to restrain external members, such as the hands and feet, the tongue and eyes, to keep discipline, and to refrain from doing external works of shame.'[111] Civil (temporal) freedom was necessary both for separating God from responsibility for evil and for ensuring that humans were responsible for civil order and their own outward behaviour. Thus, Melanchthon denied absolute necessity, saying, 'We should not insist that everything that happens must happen just so (as the Stoics have said of their fate), and that God and the wills of men are bound.'[112] God *was* at work in the world, but his actions took place amongst free creatures.[113] A freedom of contingency existed in the world, and along with it, human freedom, at least insofar as the general control of one's external actions was concerned.

An Eternal Church

Just as God was not the author of evil and sin, so too was he innocent of the blood of the damned. Whereas in 1543, Melanchthon had advised discussion of predestination only *a posteriori* (that is, inferring it as the 'cause' from the

---

[110] Trans. Manschreck, 50. 'In Cain, Pharao, Saul, vnd Juda, ist jr wüten von jrem Freiem willen, vnd treibet sie der Teuffel mit, wie der Text spricht, Der Satan ist in Judas hertz komen, Aber sie sind vngezwungen, vnd ist Gottes treiben vnd wirckunge nicht darbey.' CR 22.142. *Heubtartikel* 138.18–21.

[111] Trans. Manschreck, 46–7. 'So mus man auch bekennen, vnd ist gewisslich war vnd bezeuget durch göttliche Schrifft, das dem menschen nach Adams fall, diese Freiheit in vernünfftigen eusserlichen wercken bleibet, das er die eusserlichen Gliedmass, als Hende vnd Fusse, zungen vnd augen, vffhalten kan, das sie Zucht halten, vnd nicht eusserliche schendliche wercke thuen.' CR 22.138. *Heubtartikel* 134.28–32.

[112] Trans. Manschreck, 47. 'Es folget auch, Das man es nicht dafür halten sol, das alles, was geschiehet, müsse also geschehen, wie die Stoici von jrem Fato geredt haben, vnd Gott vnd menschlichen willen angebunden.' CR 22.138. *Heubtartikel* 135.19–21.

[113] 'God cares for the faithful, preserves them, and wishes to aid them against their enemies, the devils and tyrants. It does not follow that devils and tyrants must of necessity undertake their blasphemy, unchastity, and murder.' Trans. Manschreck, 48. 'Gott für die Gleubigen sorget, sie bewaren vnd jnen helffen wölle, wider die Feinde, Teuffel vnd Tyrannen, Aber daraus folget nicht, das Teuffel vnd Tyrannen müssen jre Gotteslesterung, vnzucht, vnd mord fürnemen vnd anfahen.' CR 22.140. *Heubtartikel* 137.8–11.

'effect' of the choice of faith), he now took his own advice and focused primarily on the importance of the decision of faith.

Melanchthon began by exhorting his readers to look to Scripture alone without speculating further: 'Despite contrary disputations, an unchangeable truth is that we should draw conclusions about God's nature and will from his Word, namely through his only begotten Son Jesus Christ revealed through the prophets and apostles, and outside of God's Word we should not invent a single thought about his nature and will.'[114] Adopting a pastoral tone, Melanchthon explained that within those Scriptures, God's promises, as always, were genuine and universal: 'Yes, one might say, the promise belongs to those whose names are written in God's book, David, Peter, and some others, but perhaps it does not belong to *me*? Is the promise offered to *all*? Here we should firmly conclude that preaching is *universales*, both the preaching of punishment and the preaching of grace; God is just; he is not a "respecter of persons". He has offered his promise to *all* who will turn to him and seek comfort in the Lord Christ.'[115] God's grace, then, was the ultimate source of election.[116]

Moreover, one should not speculate about the election or non-election of individuals, but rather view the church as an eternal elect institution which anyone could join through free acceptance of God's gracious, universal promises of salvation. 'Let our hearts firmly believe God's Word, and be reassured that God himself is gathering an eternal Church among men through the gospel.... To bring this about God revealed his promises and has had them preached throughout the world, and there have always been children of God, those who have received the promises in true faith.'[117] The

---

[114] Trans. Manscreck, 187. 'Wiewol nu mancherley Disputationes da von geschrieben sind, so ist doch dieses die vnwandelbare warheit, Wir sollen von Gottes wesen vnd willen dieses gewisslich schliessen, das er durch sein wort, nemlich, durch seinen eingebornen Son, Jhesum Christum, durch die Propheten vnd Aposteln geoffenbaret hat, vnd sollen nicht ausserhalb Gottes wort eigene gedancken tichten, von seinem wesen vnd willen.' CR 22.418. *Heubtartikel* 302.28–33.

[115] Trans. Manschreck, 189. 'Ja sprichstu, die Verheissung gehöret vff etliche die in Gottes Register angeschrieben sind, als vff David, Petrum etc. vieleicht gehöret sie nicht vff mich? Antwort wider die ander anfechtung, Ob die Verheissung allen angeboten sey? Hie soltu festiglich schliessen, das beide Predigten vniuersales sind, Straffpredigt, vnd Gnadepredigt, Gott ist gleich, vnd ist nicht bey jm acceptio Personarum, vnd hat seine Verheissung in gemein, allen menschen angeboten, die sich zu jm bekeren wöllen, vnd trost am Herrn Christo suchen.' CR 22.420. *Heubtartikel* 304.11–17.

[116] 'Only *God's mercy, for the sake of Christ,* is the source of being chosen to eternal salvation.' Trans. Manschreck, 188. 'Allein Gottes barmhertzigkeit vnd [*umb*, in *Heubtartikel*] des Herrn Christi willen vrsach ist, der erwehlung zu ewiger seligkeit.' CR 22.418. *Heubtartikel* 303.7–8.

[117] Trans. Manschreck, 187. 'Vnd Sollen vnsere hertzen Gottes wort festiglich gleuben, vnd wissen, das gewisslich Gott jm eine ewige Kirchen im menschlichen Geschlecht in diesem leben, durch das Euangelium samlet.... Dazu hat er auch als bald die Verheissungen geoffenbaret vnd offt erholet, vnd in aller Welt predigen lassen, vnd sind alle zeit diese Gottes kinder worden, die diese Verheissunge mit rechtem glauben angenommen haben.' CR 22.418. *Heubtartikel* 302.11–13, 20–2.

free offer of the Gospel was the mechanism by which God actively gathered his eternal church. God had not chosen *individuals*, but a *body* of believers, elected for the sake of Jesus Christ on the basis of faith, not works.[118]

Consequently, even though Melanchthon had at least mentioned the word 'reprobation' in 1543, here in 1555 he dropped mention of it completely, saying only, 'But those who did not or do not believe are condemned.' Damnation then was not due to a timeless decree of reprobation from God, but rather it happened as the result of the guilt of human sin which went unatoned in the face of a free human decision to deny Jesus Christ.[119] When faced with the Gospel, therefore, salvation depended on the choice of the will. Here, Melanchthon explicitly related justification and election, and he argued that the same method worked for both—one was justified by faith, and one also *became* predestined through faith: 'As we previously said about forgiveness of sins and righteousness, so we say now about election, namely that we have forgiveness of sins, the Holy Spirit, and eternal salvation for the sake of the Lord Jesus Christ, out of grace, through faith, and thus [or because] we are also predestined to eternal blessedness.'[120] Finally, in order to ward off criticism that he might have been implying some contribution of human merit to one's own salvation, Melanchthon dropped his assertion from 1543 that 'There is some cause or reason in the one who accepts.'[121]

Complications with Reprobation

Melanchthon clearly abhorred the idea of reprobation, or God's prior choice of a specific individual for damnation. But while denying the notion of reprobation, Melanchthon found that he could not entirely interpret the Bible in such a way as to eliminate unfairness in soteriological matters

---

[118] 'Election to eternal salvation is not on account of the law, but *for the sake of Christ through faith.*' [Manschreck's emphasis]. Trans. Manschreck, 188. 'Die erwehlung zu ewiger seligkeit, ist nicht von wegen des Gesetzes, sondern vmb des Herrn Christi willen, durch den glauben.' CR 22.419. *Heubtartikel* 303.28–9.

[119] Trans. Manschreck, 187. 'Wer aber nicht hat gleuben wollen, oder nicht gleubet, der ist verdampt.' CR 22.418. *Heubtartikel* 302.22–3.

[120] Trans. Manschreck, 188. 'Vnd wie wir zuuor von vergebung der sünden vnd gerechtigkeit geredt haben, also reden wir auch von der Erwehlung, nemlich, das du vergebunge der sünden, heiligen Geist vnd ewige seligkeit hast, vmb des Herrn Jhesu Christi willen, aus gnaden, durch den glauben, also bistu auch ausserwehlt zu ewiger seligkeit.' CR 22.419. *Heubtartikel* 303.30–3. One reviewer of this book suggested that Manschreck's translation could be improved (as seen in the bracketed text), thus producing a meaning more in line with predestination *a posteriori* rather than predestination as God's foreknowledge of a future decision of faith.

[121] (1543) trans. Preus, 173. 'Ergo ut in iustificatione diximus aliquam esse in accipiente causam.' (1543) CR 21.916. (1559) MSA 2/2.597.4–7.

altogether. God's grace was not distributed evenly throughout the world.[122] Melanchthon admitted this fact as early as the *Commentary on Romans* of 1540.[123] Some people had the opportunity to hear the Gospel, and hence they had the chance to employ their own free will as to whether or not they would believe the promises of the Gospel. Melanchthon wrote, 'Now we are called, and we should not despise the calling, but *thank God for placing us in this group*, where we can hear and acknowledge the Lord Jesus Christ.'[124] Other people in the world never had the chance to hear God's Word and so the Holy Spirit never illumined God's Word to them with the result that their wills were never enlightened to have a genuine free choice regarding the acceptation of God's promises. Some people ended up having a free choice regarding God's promises, while others never even had the opportunity to make a soteriological decision of any kind. These choice-deprived people, then, were effectively doomed to damnation. God may not have singled them out from before all time for damnation, but the result was the same: they never had a chance. They might as well have been reprobate. In fact, they were *effectively* reprobate, only without God's direct will.

This difficulty with reprobation represented a rough spot in Melanchthon's theology, and it was apparent that he did not consider it much until the 1550s, when he had already had many years to get used to his anthropocentric conception of 'predestination'. Further, Melanchthon only dealt with the issue briefly in the German edition of the *Loci* in 1553, and here his thinking was quite sketchy, as if he had only considered the question recently. On the topic of those people who had never heard God's Word (and despite what he had said previously), Melanchthon here also argued that all nations in the world *had* heard God's Word, and that those who did not have it now had in former times rejected God's Word of their own free wills.[125] Melanchthon

---

[122] Erasmus, on the other hand, had argued that God's grace (both natural and peculiar) *was* universally distributed.

[123] 'Deus non reddit paria paribus Esau et Iacob, Davidi et Sauli, quia Iacob et David eliguntur per misericordiam.' On Rom. 9.14–15. MSA 5.261.18–20.

[124] Trans. Manschreck, 190 (emphasis added). 'Nu bistu beruffen, vnd solt den Beruff nicht verachten, sondern Gott hertzlich dancken, das er dich in diesen hauffen setzet, da du das Euangelium hörest, vnd den Herrn Jhesum Christum erkennen kanst.' CR 22.421–2. *Heubtartikel* 306.18–21.

[125] 'It is not necessary for us to dispute why the heathen have been left so long in blindness, for God originally revealed his promises, established his Church, and made himself known among the heathen, in Egypt and in Babylon. Afterward he revealed himself through the apostles' preaching. God adorned his Church in Israel with Elijah and the other prophets. In all kingdoms it has been known. However, like the Jews, many have scorned God and have entirely lost the teaching of the gospel through their own evil and ingratitude. We should tremble before such examples of wrath, and earnestly learn the truth and live in fear of God and

especially had the Jews in mind here, and, according to his doctrine, their rejection was based on their own decision not to believe—which also meant that it was possible for them to be saved if they should ever make that choice of faith.

While Melanchthon primarily referred to the Jews here, the broader question of soteriological 'fairness' to people who had never heard the Gospel presented a challenge to Melanchthon's paradigm—for it seemed that the universal *application* of God's promises was not matched by the universal *communication* of those promises to the world. This being said, Philipp, in fact, did not take up this issue any further within his theological writings, thereby leaving this implication of his theological system unresolved.

Conversion: God Draws the Willing

Melanchthon was reluctant to write on free will because (as he stated in 1556, after suffering through no small measure of theological controversy on this matter) he believed that disputes over this doctrine undermined order and discipline[126] and thus were not pastorally beneficial. The effects of the doctrine were not acceptable. Nevertheless, here Melanchthon echoed his material from the *Loci* of 1543 by repeating himself on contingency, and then, most significantly, presenting a clear picture of the genuine freedom and responsible role of the human will in conversion.

First, Melanchthon laid out even more arguments for the reality of a freedom of contingency. He wrote, 'Some people introduce extraneous questions: Do all the natural effects in the air, in the water, and on the earth, all the good deeds and all the evil, happen of necessity? Does God's knowing in advance force the human will to act in a certain way? As was said previously, we should not be sidetracked by these questions. The Stoics should not be

---

in prayer.' Trans. Manschreck, 191. 'Ist dir nicht not zu disputiren, warumb die Heiden so lang in blindheit gelassen sind, Sie sind selbs vrsach jrer blindheit, denn Gott hat anfenglich seine Verheissunge geoffenbaret, vnd offt erholet, vnd für vnd für dir Kirchen vffgericht vnd bekandt gemacht vnter den Heiden, als in Egypten zu Babylon, vnd hernach durch der Apostel predigt, vnd hat Gott seine Kirchen in Israel also gezieret mit Elia vnd andern Propheten, das sie allen Konigreichen bekandt gewesen ist, Das aber viel in verachtunge Gottes blieben sind, vnd hernach die lere des Euangelij gantz verloren haben, ist vrsach jrer eigenen bossheit vnd undanckbarkeit, wie bey den Jüden, vnd sollen wir für solchen zornexempeln erschrecken, vnd erstlicher die warheit lernen, vnd in Gottes furcht vnd anruffung leben.' CR 22.422. *Heubtartikel* 306.24–34.

[126] Foreword to Arnold Burenius, *Causae cur scholae philosophicae praefecti in Academia Rostochiana in disciplina resarcienda elaborarint . . .* (Wittenberg: Peter Seitz Erben, 1556). MBW 7.7670. CR 8.628–32 Nr. 5892.

judges and masters in the Christian Church.'¹²⁷ The world was not determined as the Stoics thought, and yet, in transitioning to the will's role in
conversion, Melanchthon made it clear that the freedom of contingency was
a separate matter from the will's relative freedom in matters of salvation.
'When we speak of free will, we are simply talking about the deterioration
of human strength through sin, man's inability to free himself from sin
and death, and about the works that man is able to do in such a state of
weakness.'¹²⁸ More specifically, when applied to an individual, free will
meant the entirety of the decision-making process—including cognition,
emotions, and the will. 'When free will is mentioned, we mean understanding and will, heart and will; and they belong together, without hypocrisy.'¹²⁹
He seemed to be assuming here the paradigm for the will he had laid out in
On the Soul in 1553.

As to conversion itself, the choice of faith in Jesus, Melanchthon taught
that it had to begin with the hearing of the Gospel, following which the
human will had to give a free response. In an echo of the language of the
Augsburg and Leipzig Interims, Melanchthon wrote, 'We should not think
that a man is a piece of wood or a stone, but as we hear the Word of God, in
which punishment and comfort are put forth, we should neither despise
nor resist it. We should immediately rouse our hearts to earnest prayer, for
the Lord Christ says, "How much more will your heavenly Father give his
Holy Spirit to you if you ask him!"'¹³⁰ 'Again, Chrysostom says that God
draws man. However, he draws the one who is willing, not the one who
resists. (*Trahit Deus, sed volentem trahit.*) And Basil says that God comes

¹²⁷ Trans. Manschreck, 51. 'Etliche haben andere frembde Sachen mit vntergemenget, Ob alle
ding in allen natürlichen wirckungen, in lufft, wasser vnd vff Erden Jtem alles gutes vnd böses
müsse also geschehen? Jtem, ob Gottes wissen auch den menschlichen willen zwinge? Diese
Fragen sollen wir nicht mit einmengen, vnd ist zuuor dauon geredt, Die Stoici sollen nicht
Richter vnd Meister sein, in Christlicher Kirchen.' CR 22.146. *Heubtartikel* 139.5–10.
¹²⁸ Trans. Manschreck, 51. 'Sondern allein dauon ist hie zu reden, Wie menschliche kreffte
durch die sünde verderbet sind, vnd können sich selbs nicht von sünden vnd tode frey machen,
vnd welche werck ein mensch in dieser schwacheit zuthun vermag.' CR 22.146. *Heubtartikel*
139.10–13.
¹²⁹ Trans. Manschreck, 52. 'Also, wenn man den Freyen willen nennet, so begreiffet man
verstand vnd willen, vnd gehören zusamen beide, hertz vnd wille one heucheley.' CR 22.147.
Heubtartikel 140.8–10.
¹³⁰ Trans. Manschreck, 60. 'Du solt nicht gedencken, das ein Mensch ein holtz oder stein sey,
sondern so du Gottes wort hörest, darinne strasse vnd trost fürgetragen wird, soltu das selbige
nicht verachten, vnd solt jm nicht widerstreben, du solt auch zu gleich dein hertz zu ernstlichem
Gebet erwecken, Wie der Herr Christus spricht [Luc. 11, 13], Wie viel mehr wil euch der
himelische Vater seinen heiligen Geist geben, so jr jn darumb BITTET.' CR 22.157. *Heubtartikel*
149.24–9. The reference to the 'piece of wood' is in reference to a phrase that first appeared in
the Augsburg Interim, and it became an oft-repeated catchphrase in Melanchthon's discussions
with Gallus and Flacius.

first toward us, but nevertheless that we should also will that he come to us. And take the wonderful parable in which the son who had squandered and wasted his inheritance in riotous living comes home [the prodigal son, in Luke 15]. As soon as the father sees him from afar, he pities him, runs to him, falls on his neck, and kisses him. Here the son does not run back, does not scorn his father, but instead goes also toward him, acknowledges his sin, and begs for grace. From this illustration we should learn how this teaching is to be used and how this passage in Basil is to be taken. *Tantum velis, et Deus praeoccurrit.* We need only to will, and God has already come to us.'[131]

The choice of faith therefore required both the hearing of the Gospel and the application of the free human will. This hearing of the Gospel, though, was no impartial or static event. Upon the reading and explanation of the Gospel, the Holy Spirit was always at work in the human heart. 'Without this activity of the Holy Spirit in our hearts, there is not true faith ...'[132] Conversion, then, had three causes: it began with the hearing of the Gospel, it proceeded with the working of the Holy Spirit within the heart of the hearer, and it was concluded with the free response of the will to assent to the call of the Spirit. God took the initiative in offering salvation through the substitutionary death and resurrection of Christ, but it was up to the individual to choose freely whether or not he would receive that gift of eternal life. It was not the freedom to apply oneself to Spirit-aided good works as in Roman Catholic teaching, but it was simply the freedom to accept or reject forensic justification based exclusively on the merit of Jesus Christ. This was an *evangelical* free will.

---

[131] Trans. Manschreck, 60. 'Vnd also spricht Chrysostomus, Gott ziehet den Menschen, Er ziehet aber den, welches wille mit gehet, vnd nicht widerstrebet, Trahit Deus, sed uolentem trahit, Vnd Basilius spricht, Gott gehet dir zuuor entgegen, doch soltu auch wöllen, das Er zu dir komme, Vnd nimet diese rede aus der lieblichen Gleichnis, da der Son widerumb kommet, der sein Erbteil vbel [vmbbracht vnd] verschlemmet hatte, als balde jn der Vater von ferne sihet, erbarmet er sich sein, Lauffet jm entgegen, fellet jm vmb den hals, vnd küsset jn. Hie lauffet der Son nicht zurücke, bekennet seine sünde, vnd bittet vmb gnade. Aus diesem bilde können wir lernen, wie diese lere zu vben ist, vnd hat Basilius diesen Spruch daraus genomen, Tantum uelis, et Deus praeoccurrit.' CR 22.157–8. *Heubtartikel* 149.31–150.9. The words in brackets (*vmbbracht vnd*) do not appear in the text from 1553.

[132] Trans. Manschreck, 59. 'Und one dise wirkung des heiligen geists in den hertzen ist nicht rechter glaub ...' *Heubtartikel* 149.5–6. In CR 22.156, the *Heubtarikel* reading is given in a footnote, but the main text reads, 'Und without der Son Gottes nicht mit dem Euangelio liect vnd erkenntnis Gottes gibet, vnd nicht der heilige Geist trost vnd freude an Gott gibet, da ist nicht rechter glaube vnd liebe zu Gott.'

CONCLUSION

In the early 1550s, Melanchthon continued to teach evangelical free will. Salvation could be received by faith alone in Jesus Christ, resulting in the passive imputation of his righteousness to the believer. This was the evangelical forensic justification, rather than the Roman Catholic transformational model of justification. This saving faith originated from three sources working in concert: the Word, the Spirit, and the human free will.

Since Melanchthon had now articulated this doctrinal formulation for more than twenty years, many people had had the chance to read and understand what he was teaching. Many did not like what they were reading, and so they attacked. As a result, the last seven years of Melanchthon's life were characterized by a mostly defensive posture. Assailed by both Protestant and Catholic critics, Melanchthon had to explain himself repeatedly. This he continued to do for as long as his strength remained.

11

1554–1560: Twilight

INTRODUCTION

In the mid-1550s, Nikolaus Gallus joined Flacius and Calvin in bringing a concerted Protestant critique of Melanchthon's doctrine of the will. Gallus' attacks were persistent and intense, requiring a response. Meanwhile, Melanchthon produced a revised Latin edition of the *Examination of Ordinands* in 1554. Soon thereafter, the Bavarian Inquisition levelled serious charges, and Melanchthon found himself impelled to produce a rigorous defence. At around the same time, in 1558 and 1559, even the Elector began to ask Melanchthon for an explanation of his doctrine of the will's role in conversion. To the very end, Melanchthon maintained evangelical free will. Upon Philipp's death in 1560, Gallus was in the process of publishing more writings against him, and John Calvin had finally found it necessary for a brutal public denunciation. Melanchthon had begun his career as a controversialist in the Reformation, and now, despite a record that included many attempts at theological reconciliation with opponents, Philipp's career also ended with controversy. We turn now to trace his teachings on the origins of faith as expressed in the twilight of his life.

THE EXAMINATION OF ORDINANDS, LATIN EDITION: 1554

The Latin edition of the *Examen ordinandorum*,[1] far from being a simple translation of the German edition of 1552, turned out to be a further development. Here Melanchthon's ideas on the will's role in justification continued to be in accord with the German edition, but they were now

---

[1] The full title is, *Examen eorum qui audiuntur ante ritum publicae ordinationis, qua commendatur eis ministerium evangelii*, and it can be found in CR 23.1–88.

emerging into sharper focus—especially in his unprecedentedly specific section, titled, 'On Conversion'.

Original Sin and the Fall

Before discussing conversion, however, Melanchthon once again alluded to the problem for which all people required salvation: sin. Adam and Eve had been created with original righteousness which included the inherent illumination of their minds by the power of the Holy Spirit. But our first ancestors, on account of their own free, proud, wilful decision, turned away from God to evil. This choice was the original sin which resulted in the imputation of guilt to Adam and all his progeny. Along with this guilt came the removal of the divine light in the minds of humanity, such that their thoughts were darkened and error-prone, inclined now to follow only evil. Natural people now were practitioners of evil—enemies of God subject to his eternal damnation.[2]

External Freedom

Yet, neither the present human bent toward sin nor any biblical doctrine of God pointed to the determination of all things by a puppet-master deity. Melanchthon strongly rejected Stoic necessity, calling it delusional.[3] Despite the Fall, freedom existed in the temporal realm, and human beings, even though their hearts were wicked, could control themselves in the free exercise of external discipline. Therefore, people could at least superficially comply with the law of God in how they comported themselves. Melanchthon said, 'First, regarding external discipline, it is known that all people, even the unregenerate, have this freedom, that is, the faculty, in some manner, to control their movements, and make their external actions congruent with the Law of God.'[4] God allowed this sort of freedom to exist for two reasons:

---

[2] 'PECCATUM ORIGINALE est reatus propter Adae lapsum, et propter privationem lucis divinae, et firmae agnitionis Dei in mentibus hominum, et propter aversionem voluntatis a Deo, et propter contumaciam cordis, quae mala sequunta sunt lapsum Adae in natura hominum, et sunt inimicitiae adversus Deum, et damnata a Deo.' CR 23.12.

[3] 'Respondeo. Cum fit mentio Liberi arbitrii, non misceantur Stoica deliramenta de Necessitate omnium actionum in omnibus Elementis, in pecudibus et hominibus, bonis et malis.' CR 23.14.

[4] 'Primum igitur de disciplina externa hoc sciatur, omnes homines, etiam non renatos, habere hanc libertatem, id est, facultatem, ut aliquo modo possint regere locomotivam, et facere externa opera congruentia cum Lege Dei.' CR 23.14. See also, on the same page, where Melanchthon mentioned, '...gubernatio externorum operum iuxta Legem Dei'.

1. God wanted people to understand the distinction between what freedom they had and what freedom they effectively did *not* have. For example, by free observation, people could see that fire could do nothing other than burn (and by implication, people could do nothing other than sin).[5] 2. God had allowed external freedom so that the law might provide some use in civil government and instruction for peace in the temporal realm.[6] External freedom was weak, but useful nonetheless in that it pointed to a greater reality, and it served an immediate purpose in contributing to the peace of society.

The Righteousness of the Spirit

External freedom, though, did not mean that people could, of their own free wills, please God and gain righteousness in his sight. As he had stressed again and again over the course of his career, Melanchthon argued that one could not be saved through good works. Instead, Melanchthon drew a distinction between external discipline and the righteousness of the Spirit (*iustitiae Spiritualis*).[7] No one could fulfil the law.[8] Therefore, the Pelagians, Manichees, and the enthusiasts (including the Anabaptists and Schwenckfeldians) all deserved rich condemnation.[9] While an external approximation of the law was possible, it was impossible even to begin to achieve genuine internal obedience to the Lord, apart from the Gospel and the Holy Spirit. Even faith could not arise apart from Gospel and Spirit.[10] Both were necessary for

---

[5] 'Vult enim Deus hanc libertatem reliquam esse in homine, ut intelligatur discrimen inter agens liberum, et inter agentia non libere: Sicut ignis non potest non urere admota corpora.' CR 23.14.

[6] 'Item, ut sciamus ipsum Deum esse agens liberrimum. Item, ut possit in societate humana gubernatio aliqua esse externorum membrorum. Ac nequaquam vult Deus prorsus inutilem esse vocem Legum in civili gubernatione seu paedagogia. Ideo inquit Paulus: Lex paedagogus est, scilicet docens et cohercens membra.' CR 23.14.

[7] 'Sed tantum nos ipsos aspiciamus, et consideramus, quomodo Legi Dei obedire homines aut non obedire possint. Semper haec simplex et vera distinctio teneatur, disciplinae externae et iustitiae Spiritualis.' CR 23.14. See also CR 23.16, where he described it as the distinction between the righteousness of the flesh and the righteousness of faith: '... et discernatur Iustitia carnis a Iustitia fidei'.

[8] 'Nec posse hominem perfecte satisfacere Legi Dei.' CR 23.15.

[9] CR 23.15.

[10] 'Secundo sciendum est, homines sine Evangelio, et sine Spiritu sancto, nec posse inchoare interiorem obedientiam, praeceptam in Lege Dei, videlicet verum timorem Dei, veram fidem....' CR 23.14. 'Item: Si quis Spiritum Christi non habet, non est ipsius.' CR 23.14. 'Sit igitur notum discrimen inter externam disciplinam et inter motus interiores, qui fiunt, quotiescunque filius Dei voce Evangelii consolatur corda, et Spiritu sancto accendit fidem et invocationem Dei, et alios motus spirituales...' CR 23.14.

conversion, and both could be found in the preaching of the Word, for 'faith comes from hearing' (*fides ex auditu*—Rom. 10.17).[11] This was the means, then, by which God collected the eternal church.

The Eternal Church

In 1554, Melanchthon continued to use his new nomenclature of 'the eternal church' (*aeternam Ecclesiam*) rather than 'the elect church', as he had done in 1540 and 1551. Instead of explicitly describing the church as an elect institution, which people could join or leave according to their free decisions, Melanchthon stressed God's initiative and action in gathering people into his church. He said, '*God* collects an eternal church by the voice of the Gospel' (emphasis added).[12] Further, he also spoke of 'the elect unto life' being in the church.[13] However, one should not confuse Melanchthon's change in emphasis with a change in doctrine. His language here remained consistent with his views from 1540 on the elect church, but he rephrased his words in such a way as to leave room for a stronger view of election more in accord with the teachings of Luther (and Calvin). God did not irresistibly draw people to faith. Instead, he collected the church only insofar as he provided the mechanism by which people could freely accept or reject membership in the eternal church.

The Three Causes of Conversion: Word, Spirit, and Will

Part of this mechanism of conversion included the Law–Gospel dialectic. God used the law to convict people of sin, who would then, in fear, turn and run to accept the promises of God.[14] Melanchthon continued to stress that these promises were genuinely universal. They applied ontologically to all people, for God showed no partiality (Rom. 2.11).[15] In the hearing of those promises,

---

[11] 'Et consideremus ordinem a Deo sanctum: Fides ex auditu est, auditus per verbum Dei, etc.' CR 23.15.

[12] 'Colligit Deus aeternam Ecclesiam voce Evangelii.' CR 23.15. See also CR 23.2: 'Deus... colligat sibi in genere humano Ecclesiam propter Filium, et per eum...'.

[13] 'Sola autem illa congregatio, in qua agnoscitur filius Dei, Dominus noster Iesus Christus, crucifixus pro nobis et resuscitatus, est Ecclesia, in qua sunt multi vere placentes Deo, et recte invocantes eum, *et electi ad vitam aeternam*, iuxta haec dicta, Iohannis 5. Qui non honorat Filium, non honorat Patrem, qui misit eum' (emphasis added). CR 23.1.

[14] CR 23.14–15.

[15] 'Ac ne indulgeamus diffidentiae, considerandum est, utramque concionem universalem esse, concionem poenitentiae, et promissionem gratiae...' CR 23.15. 'Rursus et promissiones universalem in conspectu sint.' CR 23.16. 'Item: Apud Deum non est προσωπολη[μ]ποία

it was the Holy Spirit who sent faith into the heart.[16] Nevertheless, people could freely either accept or reject that guidance of the Spirit. Thus, the Lord wanted all people to hear and assent to these promises, and not to indulge in unbelief.[17] People ought to ask God to strengthen their faith, and they should not reject the leading of the Holy Spirit.[18] Melanchthon wrote, 'This saying is pertinent: God draws, but he draws the willing.'[19] Grace both preceded *and* accompanied the will.[20] That is, through Gospel and Spirit, God *invited* faith, but did not compel it. In the decision of faith, the Gospel, the Holy Spirit, and the free human will all worked together. 'Therefore, these causes of conversion coincide: the Word of God, the Holy Spirit (whom the Father and the Son send in order to illuminate our hearts), and the assent of our wills, which does not reject the Word of God.'[21]

Evangelical Free Will

I call Melanchthon's doctrine of the will's role in conversion 'evangelical free will' simply because it is unlike all the major teachings that came before. Melanchthon's doctrine was that of neither Augustine, Peter Lombard, Thomas Aquinas, Duns Scotus, William of Ockham, Gregory of Rimini, Gabriel Biel, Johann von Staupitz, Erasmus, nor Luther (or Calvin). Still, it was firmly grounded in Scripture, most centrally in the Gospel of Jesus Christ. For Melanchthon, the most important question that ought to be asked of every ordinand was, *Quidnam docebis?* ('What will you teach?'). The answer was clear: *Docebo Evangelium Domini nostri Iesu* ('I will teach the Gospel of our Lord Jesus Christ').[22] Melanchthon's limited doctrine of free will in conversion was, decidedly, an *evangelical* doctrine of free will. Even from

---

CR 23.16. See the more complete discussion in CR 23.15–16, where Melanchthon elaborated at some length on the universality of the promises.

[16] 'Spiritus sanctus. . . . Et nobis sic manifestata est, quot mittatur in corda credentium . . .' CR 23.4.

[17] 'Tradidit etiam promissionem gratiae, cui vult nos assentiri, et non indulgere diffidentiae.' CR 23.15.

[18] 'Item: Quanto magis Pater vester coelestis dabit Spiritum sanctum petentibus, quasi dicat, non repugnantibus.' CR 23.15. See also the lines before and after this quotation.

[19] 'Huc pertinent haec dicta: Trahit Deus, sed volentes trahit.' CR 23.15.

[20] 'Item: Gratia praeeunte, comitante voluntate.' CR 23.15.

[21] 'Concurrunt igitur in conversione hae causae, verbum Dei, Spiritus sanctus, quem Pater et Filius mittunt, ut accendat nostra corda, et nostra voluntas assentiens, et non repugnans verbo Dei.' CR 23.15.

[22] CR 23.1.

just within the *Examination of Ordinands* of 1554, seven main distinctives could be seen that characterized this evangelical free will.

Forensic Justification by Faith Alone

Justification could neither be earned outright (as Pelagius asserted) nor earned in cooperation with God through congruous merit (as in, for example, William of Ockham and Gabriel Biel). Justification was like being acquitted (or pronounced righteous) in a court of law.[23] Human beings contributed no merit towards their own salvation, but strictly and passively they simply received the imputed merit of Jesus Christ.[24] This differed, for instance, from Erasmus' transformational model of justification wherein Christ was more of an example to be emulated than a sacrifice to be substituted.

Salvation as God's Work at His Initiative

Salvation, then, for Melanchthon, was totally the work of God, at his own initiative. After the Fall, human beings had been lost with no hope of salvation. But God, in his grace (that is, out of his unmerited mercy[25]), decided to bring salvation to humanity. So he himself became incarnate in the Son, who was born supernaturally of the virgin, and was thus unblemished by original sin. He lived the perfect life no one else could, then suffered and died as the substitutionary atonement, the sacrifice for the sins of the world. On the third day, in vindication, he rose from the dead, later sent the Holy Spirit to his disciples, and commissioned them to bring the Gospel (*Evangelium*) to the whole world. God caused the promulgation of the Gospel; and, for all who would believe, at some point the Gospel came to them and they heard it. At that moment, the Holy Spirit worked in their hearts to invite faith—which was no mere historical knowledge, but the genuine reliance of the whole person on the promises of God, and through them, on the reality of their own personal salvation in Jesus Christ as their Lord and Saviour.[26]

---

[23] CR 23.1, 16–33. See also, more succinctly, Melanchthon's *Catechesis puerilis* of 1558: 'Iustificari significat forensi more iustum reputari seu pronuntiari.' CR 23.178.
[24] CR 23.16–33. Cf. CR 23.178.
[25] 'Gratia apud Paulum in hac doctrina significat Ebraea phrasi misericordiam gratuitam...' CR 23.19.
[26] CR 23.19.

Predestination as Corporate, not Individual

At this point, though, Melanchthon rejected the traditional idea of the predestination (and reprobation) of individuals to salvation (or damnation). This went against Augustine, Peter Lombard, Thomas Aquinas, Gregory of Rimini, Scotus, Ockham, Luther, and Calvin. Melanchthon neither resorted to a dialectic of powers (God's absolute versus ordained powers) as did Scotus and Ockham, nor did he view predestination as simply God's foreknowledge (as in Biel). Instead, the church itself was an elect body, and individuals could freely enter or leave that body. God gathered the church through the offer of the Gospel, but it was the people who were responsible to embrace the Gospel to be part of the church.[27] While Melanchthon explained this idea most clearly in 1540, it could still be detected in his writings in the 1550s, even though he had altered his language to sound a bit more like individual predestination (in deference to his critics).

God's Undivided Will to Save

Luther, in affirming a strong view of individual predestination, eventually had to speak about God's revealed will, meaning the universal promises of grace, and God's hidden will, meaning his secret will to cause some to respond to those promises and others to fail to do so. Melanchthon recoiled at such a thought, and he insisted, time and again, that God's promises were universal and true. Here, too, we see something of his continuing antipathy to the appearance of rational inconsistency. 'These true and most sweet consolations are always in sight, and there is in God no contradictory will.'[28] Again, 'God *wants* us to believe in the Son, and he promises grace to all who flee to the Son seeking his help, just as the Psalm [2.13] says, "Blessed are all who rely on him".'[29]

The Genuine Contribution of Human Assent (or Dissent)

By interpreting predestination as he did, Melanchthon absolved God of responsibility for the lost. Consequently, the decision for whether one went to heaven or hell was ultimately left up to the individual, who, after Christ had

---

[27] 'Ecclesia est populus Dei, in quo Deus vere colligit coetum,... homines amplectentes Evangelium...' CR 23.37.

[28] 'Hae verae et dulcissimae consolationes semper in conspectu sint, nec ponantur in Deo contradictoriae voluntates.' CR 23.16.

[29] 'Vult nos Deus credere Filio, et promittit gratiam omnibus confugientibus ad Filium, et petentibus auxilium, sicut Psalmus inquit: Beati omnes qui confidunt in eum.' CR 23.16.

already died for him, and after the Spirit-illumined Gospel had been presented to him, had the genuinely free choice of either accepting or rejecting that forensic justification. The only contribution people made to their own salvations was the decision of whether or not to allow themselves to *be* justified, passively.

Faith Was not a Work

For Melanchthon, faith was merely assent to *God's* work of salvation, and was in no way a work in and of itself. It was not meritorious. Faith was the *instrument* by which salvation was received. Conversion was a passive event of active acceptance of God's promises.[30] Faith was not *causative* of God's saving grace, but it was *correlative* with it.[31] As a result, Melanchthon's critics are not accurate to describe his doctrine as 'synergistic'. 'Synergistic' means 'working with', and for Melanchthon, faith was not a work, so people were not 'working with' God in their salvation. 'Synergistic' would be a better descriptor of the soteriologies of, say, Gabriel Biel or Erasmus.

Consolation in the Promises

While those Protestants who affirmed a strong view of individual predestination described it as a comfort in the assurance of salvation, Melanchthon saw that doctrine as primarily a vehicle for *discomfort* among people who questioned God's fairness in (apparently) arbitrarily picking some and not others, and who also feared that they themselves might in fact be helplessly reprobate. Melanchthon taught that comfort for the troubled conscience should come instead from the genuine, universal promises of God that were to be found in the Gospel. Faith alone in those promises brought consolation to the troubled heart.[32]

These seven distinctives together fleshed out Melanchthon's biblically constructed soteriology. It was unique to him, and could best be called evangelical free will.

Not everyone, though, accepted what Melanchthon was teaching. Throughout his life Melanchthon had been attacked by Catholics and Anabaptists, magisterial

---

[30] 'Homo in conversione, id est, in veris doloribus et pavoribus accipit remissionem peccatorum, propter Mediatorem Filium Dei, Dominum nostrum Iesum Christum, Deum et hominem, Gratis, sola fide, non propter propriam dignitatem, seu propter virtutues proprias, aut propria opera seu merita.' CR 23.20.

[31] 'Propositio haec, Fide sumus iusti, intelligitur correlative, videlicet per misericordiam sumus iusti propter Filium Dei, et id beneficium oportet fide accipi.' CR 23.22.

[32] CR 23.20–1, 33. See esp. CR 23.78–81.

Reformers, and former students. Now, one more former student emerged to challenge Melanchthon in print, arguing that this new teaching on the will's role in justification was an unscriptural error. His name was Nikolaus Gallus.

CONTROVERSY WITH GALLUS: 1556–1558

Not long after Flacius began his criticisms of Melanchthon on free will, Nikolaus Gallus of Regensburg also joined in.[33] He, too, was displeased by the apparent role of the will as set out in the compromise agreements with the new Catholic political government. Melanchthon had helped draft these agreements, known as the Leipzig and Augsburg Interims, and Gallus thought he had given away too much.

Nikolaus Gallus came to Wittenberg at the age of fourteen and studied there until 1540. His academic skills drew Melanchthon's praise.[34] He went on to become a deacon in Regensburg, and later came back to Wittenberg upon the application of the Augsburg Interim following the defeat of the Protestants in the Schmalkaldic War. By 1548, he was serving as a pastor in Magdeburg where he became a leader in the ministerium—the same circle in which Flacius and Amsdorf were influential.

The Leipzig Interim appeared in 1548, and in 1550, on behalf of the ministerium of Magdeburg, Gallus wrote a treatise that Kolb terms 'the programmatic declaration of independence from Melanchthon's school'.[35] Many later scholars consider this to be the beginning of the Gnesio-Lutheran movement. It was called the *Confession, Instruction, and Admonition of the Christian Church at Magdeburg*.[36] In it, Gallus rebuked Melanchthon's position on the will's role in justification, arguing instead that people could not call upon the Holy Spirit or choose faith with their own innate powers or free will.[37]

---

[33] See Kolb, 'Nikolaus Gallus' Critique of Philip Melanchthon's Teaching on the Freedom of the Will', *ARG* 91 (2000), 87–110.

[34] Kolb, *Bound Will*, 107. Melanchthon, letter to Geroge Sturz, 3 March 1538. MBW 2.2005. T 8.2005. CR 3.500–1 Nr. 1658.

[35] Kolb, *Bound Choice*, 107.

[36] Nikolaus Gallus, *Bekentnis Vnterricht vnd vermanung/der Pfarrhern vnd Prediger/der Christlichen Kirchen zu Mageburgk. Anno 1550. Den. 13. Aprils* (Magdeburg: Michael Lotther, 1550). In Latin: *Confessio et Apologia pastorum & reliquorum ministrorum Ecclesiae Magdeburgensis. Anno 1550. Idibus Aprilis* (Magdeburg: Michael Lotther, 1550).

[37] Gallus, *Bekentnis*, C2a–C3a, D3a–34a. *Confessio*, B1b–B2b, B4b–C1b. Kolb, *Bound Will*, 107–8. See also David Mark Whitford, *Tyranny and Resistance: The Magdeburg Confession and the Lutheran Tradition* (Saint Louis: Concordia, 2001).

In the following years, Gallus attacked Melanchthon for his section on free choice in the *Loci communes* of 1543 and 1555,[38] and he was offended by comments such as Melanchthon's famous 'block of wood' analogy,[39] taken from the Interims and repeated in the German *Loci*, published in 1555. In April 1556, word reached Melanchthon that Gallus was prepared to publish a book against him on the doctrine of the will.[40] Then, in May, word came that Gallus had actually published something.[41] In June, Melanchthon wrote to Mathesius that 'the pugnacious Gallus' had written that he, Melanchthon, did not approve of Luther's *De servo arbitrio*.[42]

Finally, in November, Gallus wrote directly to Melanchthon with his criticisms about Melanchthon's view of the will's role in justification. Gallus made it clear that he was concerned only with conversion and rebirth, and he criticized Melanchthon's definition of free will as it appeared in the later editions of the *Loci*, saying that it departed from Luther and resembled the teachings of Peter Lombard and Erasmus.[43] Kolb summarizes Gallus' concerns when he writes, 'Unstated, but shaping and determining their disagreement, was a difference in paradigm: Gallus defined the person in conversion as a child being brought to life, Melanchthon as an adult who accepts a gift.'[44] Again, Kolb succinctly sums up Gallus' position with the following statement: 'Newborn children do not play a role in their own conception; they are not responsible for their own birth.'[45]

Gallus' attack, when combined with Flacius' earlier ones, provided a sharp incentive to Melanchthon to articulate a defence of his theology of the will's role in justification. Yet Melanchthon, as with the challenge from Flacius, was not eager to reply immediately to Gallus. In fact, Melanchthon had never directly replied to Flacius in the early 1550s, choosing instead to address the criticism indirectly through other doctrinal writings such as the *Saxon Confession* and the Latin edition of the *Examination of Ordinands*. Melanchthon

---

[38] Kolb, 'Nikolaus Gallus' Critique', 96.

[39] 'Du solt nicht gedencken, das ein Mensch ein holtz oder stein sey, sondern so du Gottes wort hörest, darinne strasse vnd trost fürgetragen wird, soltu das selbide nicht verachten, vnd solt jm nicht widerstreben, du solt auch zu gleich dein hertz zu ernstlichem Gebet erwecken.' *Loci*, 1555. CR 22.157. See also Manschreck, *The Quiet Reformer*, 293.

[40] Melanchthon (in Wittenberg), letter to Albert Hardenberg (in Bremen), 23 April 1556. MBW 7.7793. CR 8.736 Nr. 5968.

[41] Melanchthon (in Leipzig), letter to Johannes Mathesius (in Joachimsthal), 1 May 1556. MBW 7.7807. CR 8.747 Nr. 5976.

[42] Melanchthon (in Wittenberg), letter to Johannes Mathesius (in Joachimsthal), 30 June 1556. MBW 7.7873. CR 8.789 Nr. 6022. Kolb, *Bound Choice*, 108.

[43] Gallus (in Regensburg), letter to Melanchthon (in Wittenberg), November 9, 1556. MBW 7.8017. CR 8.895–902 Nr. 6113.

[44] Kolb, 'Nikolaus Gallus' Critique', 100.

[45] Ibid., 105.

eventually did decide to write a response to these challenges from Flacius and Gallus, but it did not thrill him to do so.

Following Flacius' attacks in 1550, Melanchthon expressed his resolution not to get pulled into a new dispute on the freedom of the will.[46] In 1553, when questioned by Christoph Stathmion on his doctrine of the will, Melanchthon replied that he was too busy to answer in detail.[47] However, in May 1555, after rumours of Gallus' impending criticism, Melanchthon wrote that he was getting ready to defend himself.[48] He emphasized that he would pen a reply to Flacius if Gallus joined in the attack.[49] By early June, Melanchthon was commenting on the growing opposition he was receiving to his doctrine of the will.[50] Later that month, he insisted that if attacked, he would definitely defend himself.[51] When August arrived, Melanchthon continued stoutly to insist that he was still thinking about answering his critics on free will,[52] and six months later, in February of 1556 he let it be known that he continued seriously to mull the issue over.[53] When summer arrived, Melanchthon complained that his critics were continuing to attack him,[54] and he insisted that, truly, if he was attacked one more time on the freedom of the will, he really would have to reply.[55] Gallus did continue the attacks, and Melanchthon privately complained that Gallus sinned when he denied free will.[56] Finally, in December of 1556, after nearly seven years of pressure from Flacius and Gallus, Melanchthon at last answered his critics in the form of a direct letter to Gallus.

[46] Melanchthon (in Wittenberg), letter to Laurentius Camillus (in Stendal), 7 March 1550. MBW 6.5745. CR 7.555–6 Nr. 4683.

[47] Melanchthon (in Wittenberg), letter to Christoph Stathmion (in Coburg), 31 March 1553. MBW 7.6785. CR 9.1081 Nr. 6963.

[48] Melanchthon (in Wittenberg), letter to George Agricola (in Amberg), 20 May 1555. MBW 7.7493. CR 8.484–5 Nr. 5786.

[49] Melanchthon (in Wittenberg), letter to Johannes Mathesius (in Joachimsthal), 22 May 1555. MBW 7.7499. *ARG* 30 (1933), 40–1 Nr. 29 [H3404].

[50] Melanchthon (in Wittenberg), letter to Tilemann Heshusen (in Goslar), 1 June 1555. MBW 7.7511.

[51] Melanchthon (in Wittenberg), letter to Albert Hardenberg (in Bremen), 21 June 1555. MBW 7.7526. CR 8.504 Nr. 5808.

[52] Melanchthon (in Wittenberg), letter to Albert Hardenberg (in Bremen), 21 August 1555. MBW 7.7559. CR 8.524–5 Nr. 5828.

[53] Melanchthon (in Wittenberg), letter to Johannes Stigal (in Jena), 7 February 1556. MBW 7.7713. CR 9.89–90 Nr. 6195.

[54] Melanchthon (in Wittenberg), letter to Matthäus Collinus (in Prague), 17 June 1556. MBW 7.7861. CR 8.783 Nr. 6015.

[55] Melanchthon (in Wittenberg), letter to Abdias [Praetorius] (in Magdeburg), 7 July 1556. MBW 7.7886. CR 8.794 Nr. 6027.

[56] Melanchthon (in Wittenberg), letter to Martin Schalling (in Regensburg), 18 October 1556. MBW 7.7996. Bds 401 Nr. 417.

In his letter to Gallus of 1 December 1556, Melanchthon did not say anything that he had not said before. He denied that he had moved away from Luther's position in *De servo arbitrio,* and he reasserted his formulation of free will in justification that had appeared in the *Loci communes* of 1543 and 1555.[57] Melanchthon simply restated his case and hoped that that would be the end of it. But it would not be the end of it. About a month later, Gallus replied with a long letter.[58] He explained that he wanted to counter any tendency to allow humans some role in conversion. Gallus said that he was not talking about free will in contingency (the stoic accusation), nor was he referring to free will in doing good works post-conversion—but he was *only* speaking of the lack of free will in the choice of faith in Jesus at the time of *conversion.*[59] Four months later, Gallus again wrote to Melanchthon, and it was clear that he was still not in agreement with his former teacher on the will's role in conversion.[60] Nevertheless, Gallus refrained from public confrontation until two years later, following the publication of Melanchthon's *Response to the Bavarian Articles.*

A REPORT TO ELECTOR AUGUST: 4 MARCH 1558

Word of the criticisms of Melanchthon's doctrine of the will eventually found its way to Elector August of Saxony, who, in 1558, was in Frankfurt am Main. The Elector requested a report from Melanchthon on this issue. In his reply of 4 March 1558, Melanchthon reaffirmed the central tenets of his understanding of free will in justification—that is, he rejected stoic necessity, affirmed contingency, and said that in conversion the Holy Spirit was at work, but it was the human will that accepted faith.[61] Further, he argued that the believer should find consolation in the Word of God (meaning, the universal promises of the Gospel), and *not* in a doctrine of predestination. Predestination was to be left well alone. These were all themes that Melanchthon had stated before, but in the midst of all this familiar theology lay a new emphasis. Melanchthon

---

[57] Melanchthon (in Wittenberg), letter to Nikolaus Gallus (in Regensburg), 1 December 1556. MBW 7.8042. CR 8.915–17 Nr. 6127.

[58] Nikolaus Gallus (in Regensburg), to Melanchthon (in Wittenberg), 12 January 1557. CR 8.933–4 Nr. 6137 (where it is dated 25 December 1556). MBW 8.8089.

[59] Kolb, *Bound Choice,* 108.

[60] Nikolaus Gallus (in Regensburg), to Melanchthon (in Wittenberg), 19 April 1557. CR 9.142–3 Nr. 6232. MBW 8.8199.

[61] Melanchthon (in Wittenberg), report for Elector August of Saxony (in Frankfurt am Main), 4 March 1558. MBW 8.8543. CR 9.462–78 Nr. 6471.

said that although it was the decision of the believer to have faith, that decision to accept God was a *passive* decision. It was a passive *reception* of merit rather than an active cooperative work that earned merit. It was *not* synergism![62] This was an important emphasis, for in Melanchthon's previous works and writings on free will from 1532 until the *Examination of Ordinands* in 1554, he had not done much to clarify that the exercise of the human free will in choosing to have faith in God was anything but an *active* decision. Melanchthon was, in effect, nuancing his theology at this point in response to Gallus and Flacius, who had argued that Melanchthon made the free decision of the will into a meritorious action. Melanchthon specifically denied that there was any merit involved in the free choice of the will.[63]

Melanchthon affirmed that upon hearing the Spirit-illumined Word, people had a genuine free choice of whether or not to have faith in God. Melanchthon sought to show that this choice was freely and solely contingent upon the human will which could either reject or accept the offer from God. Further, upon the decision to accept, the individual was justified according to the imputed merit from Christ. Christ's merit, credited to the believer, comprised one hundred per cent of the merit required to justify that person. The free decision to accept Christ could not be meritorious in even the smallest way, for this would then be to say that Christ's merit was insufficient to save a sinner by itself. Hence, to remove even the faintest semblance of that free choice being a work of merit, however small, Melanchthon defined it as a *passive* decision by the will, rather than an active one. This was precisely the same doctrine of the will as Melanchthon had held before Gallus' attacks, but he now simply denied that the choice of the will to have faith in God was an active decision. A person still made a free and genuine decision, but the decision was now defined as passive rather than active. So, in assent to faith, the will merely passively gave-in to the pull of the Holy Spirit. In rejecting faith, the will had to actively struggle against the Spirit's tugging. Acceptance of faith was passive and non-meritorious, giving all the glory to God for one's salvation. Denial of faith was active and *non-* (*or de-*)*meritorious*, making the individual responsible for her own resultant damnation.

The free, passive decision of the will to believe the promises of the Gospel was a key distinguishing factor of Melanchthon's unique doctrine of evangelical free will, for it was both *passive* and *non-meritorious*. The use of the free will in

---

[62] '... [D]er menschliche Wille nur annimmt, ist nicht Mitwirker, hält sich pure passive.' CR 9.468.

[63] 'Consequentien nicht daraus, daß darum der Mensch Verdienst habe etc., wie Gallus zu Regensburg und Antonius zu Nordhausen cavilliren.' CR 9.468.

choosing to have faith was thereby *instrumental* rather than *causative* for salvation. Faith was the free, passive means by which salvation was *received* rather than *earned.*[64]

THE RESPONSE TO THE BAVARIAN ARTICLES[65]: AUTUMN 1558–SPRING 1559

Introduction

In 1556, Duke Albrecht of Bavaria allowed the Jesuits into Bavaria, and the Inquisition soon made itself at home (though the Jesuits themselves never served as actual Inquisitors). In September 1558, the Inquisitors drafted 31 theological articles, and if any evangelical were to fail to provide satisfactory responses to those articles, then they were to be punished or expelled from the land.[66] Melanchthon had the news of this development in hand by 10 September 1558,[67] and he set immediately to work on a response. In it, he would also address the criticisms of Gallus and Flacius regarding his teachings on the will's role in conversion. That this was his intention is clear from his comments in February 1560. In the preface to his *Corpus Doctrinae*, Melanchthon declared that the *Response to the Impious Bavarian Articles* had dealt with the calumnies woven together from his writings by 'the synagogue of Flacius and Gallus' band concerning [matters of necessity]'.[68] Melanchthon thus had more than one audience in mind when he wrote *The Response*.

---

[64] This passive reception of salvation by faith alone allowed Melanchthon to remain in general agreement with Luther, and it also distinguished him from Erasmus and all the scholastics, who saw the exercise of free will as meritorious and causative for salvation. For Erasmus and the scholastics, the use of the free will pertained to doing good works, which were meritorious congruently. For Melanchthon, on the other hand, the exercise of free will was in no way meritorious, but was restricted solely to the free acceptance of the gift of salvation through Christ.

[65] *Responsiones Scriptae a Philippo Melanthone ad impios articulos Bavaricae inquisitionis.* 1558. MSA 6.285–364.

[66] MSA 6.278. See the more thoroughgoing introduction given there, on which the present paragraph is largely based.

[67] CR 9.610 Nr. 6593. MBW 8.8700 (approximately).

[68] Keen, 141. '... my recent book about the Bavarian inquisition clearly reveals my views about many controversies at this time....The synagogue of Flacius and Gallus' band, struggling over necessary matters, have not failed to weave insults. ...' 'Cumque recens meum scriptumde Bavarica inquisitione de multis controversiis huius temporis perspicue meas sententias ostendat....Flacii συναγωγή et cohors Galli tanquam de necessariis rebus certantes, non desinunt calumnias texere...' MSA 6.10.11–19. See also Kolb, *Bound Choice*, 114. CR 9.1054 Nr. 6932. MBW 8.9236.

Melanchthon structured his response around the 31 'impious' articles posed by the Bavarian Inquisition. He began by listing all the articles, and then proceeded to give a thorough response to each. He completed his work within a couple of months of the appearance of the *Bavarian Articles*, and the first edition of his response (in Latin) appeared in print in early 1559. A second edition appeared shortly thereafter, to which Melanchthon added a foreword and conclusion.[69] Additionally, Philipp commissioned a German translation,[70] which also appeared in 1559. He obviously viewed his *Response to the Impious Bavarian Articles* to be an important work because he sought to include it in his *Corpus doctrinae* before his death.[71]

Additionally, the *Response to the Bavarian Articles* is of significance for the present study of his views on free will in the decision of faith, for Article 22 was both among his last essays on the subject, and it was one of his most extensive discussions on the topic to date. As a result, while ascertaining a full view of Melanchthon's thoughts on free will in previous writings usually required considering a number of disparate sections, in his *Response to the Bavarian Articles* he gathered so many strands of thought together under a single heading in Article 22 that we may focus our attention almost exclusively on that place.

Article 22: On Free Choice

The question posed to the evangelicals by the Inquisition was whether or not they believed that human beings had free choice.[72] Melanchthon developed a very thorough answer. He began by affirming some measure of external human freedom, and, building on that topic, affirmed the free contingency of events in the world. Next, he spoke of the limits of that freedom and to affirm the necessity of God's action in order for anyone to be saved. But lest any tender consciences be troubled by speculations about election, he concluded with a long and passionate pastoral (almost sermonic) exhortation to the believer to trust in God's promises, and there to find the assurance of salvation. Herein his thought on the will's role in conversion would be revealed. Not only would this approach ease the worries of the speculative thinker regarding election, but it also directly

---

[69] MSA 6.278.

[70] MSA 6.279. Translated by Jac. Eysenberg, it was publised in Wittenberg, and titled, *Anleitung Ph. Melanchthons, wie christlich zu antworten sey auf abgöttishcen Artickel in Baiern gestellt.*

[71] MSA 6.278–9: 'Volo confessionem meam esse Responsiones de Bavaricis articulis contra pontificios, Anabaptistas, Flacianos et similes.' CR 9.1099.

[72] 'XXII. Articulo. An credant in homine esse liberum arbitrium?' MSA 6.310–24.

contradicted the promulgated doctrine of the Council of Trent enjoining all Christians to remain in doubt about their salvation. Here at the end of his life, more than ever, Melanchthon showed great concern for the faith of the ordinary Christian. This is the same concern that had motivated so much of the evolution of his thought on free will throughout his professional life.

But first, before assuaging troubled consciences, Melanchthon got down to the business of giving the Inquisition its answer—beginning with external freedom.

External Freedom

'Even in unregnerate humanity, there is some freedom of the will, when it comes to doing external actions.'[73] Melanchthon accordingly affirmed the presence of an external (or locomotive) freedom in all human beings—believers and non-believers alike. This relative freedom had survived the Fall and existed even in our present corrupt human nature.[74] People therefore had the general ability to control their actions as they saw fit. Achilles and Alexander the Great, for example, had the ability either to act, or not to act.[75] This natural strength was now so strong in people that as soon as the thought occurred to them, they tended to give in to it.[76]

Yet, it was not always good to give in to every inclination. God had allowed this external free choice to remain in fallen humanity for two purposes: (1) that people might be aware of their freedom, and (2), that people could live according to a rule of discipline.[77] God wanted people to understand the difference between acting freely and not acting freely, thereby realizing that the freedom to act made one *responsible* for one's freely chosen actions. The awareness of freedom naturally led on to the conclusion that human freedom should be used *well*. This is a theme we have met before in Melanchthon, particularly following the Wittenberg disturbances back in 1522—and he continued to stress it here in 1558–9: external freedom allowed one to discriminate between justice and injustice.[78] It was a locomotive freedom by

---

[73] 'Etiam in homine non renato est aliqua libertas voluntatis, quod attinet ad externa opera facienda.' MSA 6.310.6–7.

[74] 'Hanc libertatem aliquo modo reliquam esse in hac corrupta natura manifestum est.' MSA 6.310.12–13.

[75] MSA 6.310.8–11.

[76] 'Quia nunc quoque talis est natura nervorum, ut, sicut cogitatione cientur, obtemperare possint.' MSA 6.310.13–15.

[77] 'Hanc libertatem vult Deus in omnibus hominibus reliquam esse, ut aliquo modo intelligant discrimen inter agens liberum et non liberum, et ut regi disciplina possit.' MSA 6.310.15–18.

[78] '... nomino eam libertatem regendae locomotivae...' MSA 6.310.20 (see also lines 20–35).

which one could *externally* obey the law in overt actions such as parricide, blasphemy, and the taking of the sword. This was freedom in the temporal realm.

This locomotive freedom, though, was in no way absolute, even when strictly limited to the realm of external action. In all people (and especially in the impious), two things horribly impeded external freedom: (1) human infirmity, and (2) diabolical impulsion.[79]

Due to the Fall, people were now morally infirm, intentionally doing evil even when they knew better. People were always submitting to their crooked affections, suppressing their consciences, and giving way to thoughts which stoked the impetuosity of their hearts and turned their external members to wicked works.[80] (Notice here that for Melanchthon, the affections, while quite important, were not all-determining, as they had appeared to be in the *Loci* of 1521.) He continued, 'As Medea says, "I see and approve the better way, but follow the worse one".'[81] People were self-centred from birth. Due to original sin, the light by which we took some notice of the law was small, while the huge bonfire of our evil affections emptied our hearts of the fear of God, of true faith in God, and, in fact, made the heart devoid of God. The affections burned with self-love, desiring forbidden things. They grieved, saddened, and angered God.[82] Human sin, therefore, seriously hampered external freedom.

As if that wasn't enough, external freedom was also frustrated by diabolical and demonic sin. Melanchthon did not develop this theme in great detail, but he did make it clear that he believed the devil and the demons acted malevolently upon people in order to pervert their wills to evil. As proof, he cited the biblical precedent of Satan entering into the heart of Judas[83] and, supplementally, mentioned Mohammed as a clear case of Satanic possession (along with innumerable other heretics).[84]

---

[79] 'Simul autem sciendum est, hanc libertatem regendae locomotivae etiam horribiliter impediri duabus rebus, praesertim in impiis, videlicet humana infirmitate et impulsionibus diabolorum.' MSA 6.311.7–10.

[80] 'Valde saepe cedunt homines pravis affectibus, qui rectum iudicium in mente reprimunt, et alias cogitationes accendunt, quae adiutae impetu cordis, cient externa membra ad turpia opera...' MSA 6.311.10–14.

[81] MSA 6. 311.14–15. See also the *Loci* of 1535, where Melanchthon quoted the same passage. CR 21.374.

[82] 'Quia utrunque nascentes afferimus, et exiguam lucem, quae est alia legis noticia, et ingens incendium malorum affectuum, quos gignit peccatum originis, quia corda vacua timore DEI et vera fiducia DEI, seu vacua DEO, ardent amore sui, appetunt res prohibitas, dolent, fremunt, oderunt DEUM...' MSA 6.311.21–6. He went on to cite Genesis 6.

[83] 'Satanas intravit in cor eius.' MSA 6.312.2–3. Cf. John 13.27; Luke 22.3.

[84] MSA 6.312.5.

Contingency and the Problem of Evil

The existence of human locomotive freedom naturally indicated the freedom of contingency in the world. In other words, God was not directly determining everything that happened in the universe. As was now habit with Melanchthon, he condemned (and detested!) both the Stoics and the Manichees.[85] Sounding a note once heard from Erasmus[86] (although only in reference to external freedom) Melanchthon argued that biblical exhortations implied an ability to obey: 'If all things are necessary, then there is no need for deliberation and diligence. As Paul says [in Ephesians 5.15], "Be careful how you walk, not in foolishness . . .".'[87]

This freedom of contingency, then, neatly absolved God of responsibility for sin and evil. Melanchthon emphatically declared that God did not will sin, impel created wills to sin, nor help or approve of sin. To the contrary, God was horribly angry at sin.[88] Melanchthon cited Psalm 5.4, 'For you are not a God who delights in wickedness.'[89] Instead, because God had (emphatically) nothing to do with sin, it followed that the wills of the devil and human beings were not coacted, but had freely turned themselves from God.[90] God was *not* the cause of sin.[91] Therefore, contingency was a reality and the contingency of our actions was the font of free will.[92]

The Soteriological Necessity of Divine Action

Of course, as I noted in Chapter 1 when defining free will, the freedom of contingency is different from freedom in conversion. This distinction was clearly reflected in Melanchthon's essay at this point when he made the transition from contingency to conversion. That is, while insisting on some

[85] 'Palam etiam reiicio et detestor Stoicos et Manichaeos furores, qui affirmant omnia necessario fieri, bonas et malas actiones . . .' MSA 6.312.11–13.
[86] In *De libero arbitrio, passim.*
[87] 'Nam si omnia necessario fiunt, nihil opus est deliberatione et diligentia, de qua Paulus dicit: "Accurate ambulate, non ut fatui".' MSA 6.312.16–18.
[88] 'Firmissima veritas est, Deum nec velle peccata, nec impellere voluntas ad peccandum, nec adiuvare nec approbare peccata, sed vere et horribiliter irasci peccatis.' MSA 6.312.25–8.
[89] MSA 6.312.28–9.
[90] 'Cum igitur non sit causa peccati Deus, nec velit peccatum, nec impellat voluntates ad peccandum, nec adiuvet, nec approbet peccatum, ed vere irascatur peccantibus, sequitur, voluntates in Diabolis et hominibus non coactas, sed sua libertate abutentes avertisse se a Deo.' MSA 6.312.33–313.1.
[91] 'Deum non esse causam peccati.' MSA 6.313.23.
[92] 'Est igitur contingentia, et contingentia nostrarum actionum fons est libertas voluntatis.' MSA 6.313.1–3.

measure of external (or locomotive) freedom,[93] Melanchthon went on to note
that this sort of freedom was not the same sort of thing that the Pelagians or
the monks taught that we had.[94] In other words, external freedom did not
equip people fully to obey God's law and thus earn their way to heaven
(Pelagianism), nor did it even allow people to do *enough* good works, with
God's help, to get there (either *iustificatio de congruo*, or what McSorley calls
'semi-Pelagianism'). Melanchthon rejected these 'pharisaic and monastic'
errors. These doctrines incorrectly denied original sin and improperly amplified free choice beyond its actual bounds.[95]

People's limited external free choice was insufficient to achieve salvation.
Human free choice could neither remove sin and death nor even make a start
at internal obedience to the Lord apart from his initiative. To that extent,
regarding salvation, *the human will had no freedom.*[96]

The Soteriological Necessity of a Free Response

God had to take the initiative through the incarnation, life, death, and
resurrection of Jesus Christ; then he also had to (providentially) take the
initiative in bringing the Spirit-illumined Gospel to the attention of people. It
was only there, when faced with the Gospel, that people had the freedom to
either accept or reject it for themselves. At this point, Melanchthon gave only
cursory and implicit affirmation of genuine freedom in the choice of conversion. In this section he elaborated on the external freedom of contingency,
spoke against any sort of works-based model of justification, and then leaped
over the question of conversion, moving straight on to the role of the will in

---

[93] 'Et aliquam esse libertatem regendae locomotivae.' MSA 6.313.23–4. Regarding this
section of Melanchthon's essay, Kolb says: '[Melanchthon] cited one of his instructors in
Tübingen forty years earlier, Franz Kircher of Stadion: "Both propositions must be believed:
there is divine determination, and there is contingency, and not every point of contradiction
between the two can be explained".' *Bound Choice,* 73. MSA 6.313.16–20. However, in the
following sentences, Melanchthon did not affirm this saying, but instead said that it was all
murky, and that all he knew was that we had to hold onto the fact that God was not the cause of
sin, and that we have some locomotive liberty. Kolb suggests that Melanchthon agreed with
Kircher's statement, but the context shows that he did not. The following sentences cast doubt
upon Kircher's assertion, and the context of the whole passage was to describe a genuine
freedom of contingency (which goes against determination!). If Melanchthon *had* affirmed,
paradoxically (or in an antinomy) both divine determination and contingency at this point, it
would have been a rather surprising departure from his teachings on the matter, both in the
months and years immediately preceding 1558 and in the months and two years following.

[94] MSA 6.314.1–2.

[95] MSA 6.314.2–15.

[96] 'Non possunt tolli peccatum et mors libero arbitrio hominum, nec potest voluntas
humana inchoare interiorem obedientiam sine filio Dei, sine Evangelio et sine Spiritu sancto.
Talis non est libertas humanae voluntatis.' MSA 6.314.25–9 (emphasis added).

good works that *followed* conversion. In this context, therefore, in Melanch-thon's writings in the years immediately before and after 1558, one can here extrapolate his views on evangelical free will in conversion in the *Response to the Bavarian Articles*. In analysing his discussion of the role of the Holy Spirit and the free human will in the process of sanctification, one can see principles at work similar to those in his doctrine of conversion, and further, more would be revealed in his pastoral advice on election. Nevertheless, no doubt in deference to his critics, Melanchthon only tangentially touched on the subject of the free decision of the will to trust in Jesus Christ for the gift of one's own salvation.

As in the life of good works, so, presumably, did the will also operate in the decision of a saving faith. In such free decisions, the Holy Spirit invited, but did not coerce, assent. As Melanchthon put it, the Holy Spirit utilized doctrine to approach the thoughts of the mind while also exciting emotion in the heart, of such a quality that the will would give way willingly, without being forced.[97] The Holy Spirit would lead, but the individual could ignore or repudiate the leading of the Spirit, much as David did when he chose adultery.[98]

Next, after granting just enough freedom to the human will to absolve God of responsibility for sin, evil, and the damnation of the lost, Melanchthon returned to a strongly theocentric emphasis. He stressed that one could only please God through faith alone in Christ.[99] More surprisingly, Melanchthon returned to Jeremiah 10.23, a verse he had used earlier in his career[100] to support the bondage of the will, even in conversion! The verse reads, 'I know, O LORD, that the way of human beings is not in their control.' Only now Melanchthon's explanation of the verse had nothing to do with the bondage of the will in an individual's conversion and everything to do with God's overall responsibility for gathering, governing, protecting, liberating, and serving the church as a body. More generally, Melanchthon interpreted this verse to mean that God still tenderly cared for us in every stage of life as he had promised in Isaiah 46.4, saying, 'I have made, and I will bear; I will carry and will save, even to your old age, I will carry you.'[101] So in 1522, Melanchthon

---

[97] 'Filius Dei accendens cogitationem in mente per doctrinam, et Spiritus sanctus excitans motus in corde, qualis ipse est, et voluntas obtemperat volans, non coacta.' MSA 6.315.15–18.

[98] MSA 6.315.18ff.

[99] MSA 6.316.

[100] 1522. Ann. Rom. 49a–b. See Chapter 4 above.

[101] 'Verissimum est, mirandis modis a Deo colligi, gubernari, protegi, liberari et servari Ecclesiam, et dari bonos eventus, ut dicitur Esaiae 46[:4], "Ego feci, ego gestabo, et salvabo, ego ipse etiam in senecta gestabo vos".' MSA 6.316.36–317.3.

interpreted Jeremiah 10.23 to rule out free will in conversion, but in 1558, he did not. Instead, he affirmed that the will does play some sort of role, *even in being born again.*[102]

Pastoral Counsel Relating to the Idea of Election

While Melanchthon did not directly address the issue of free will in conversion in this work, he moved next into a long and passionate pastoral treatment of how a Christian should approach the potentially troubling topic of election. This showed his continuing concern for the effects of doctrine. Whereas the Roman Church at Trent had decreed that doubt about one's salvation was beneficial, Melanchthon strenuously disagreed.[103] He thought Christians should be assured of their salvations, and because the doctrine of election caused many people much anxious doubt, Melanchthon sought to explain how one might overcome those fears and grow in the assurance of faith. In the midst of this discussion, Melanchthon's views on the will's role in conversion came to light.

Regarding the assurance of salvation, Melanchthon saw two main catalysts of doubt: human weakness and disputes about election.[104] By human weakness Melanchthon meant that believers in Christ had trouble changing their sinful ways, and thus began to doubt their salvation, wondering if they were, in fact, reprobate. Melanchthon recalled one particular case of a man who regularly came to church to hear words of consolation, but who nevertheless continued to lapse into adultery.[105] He also noted that in many who had been born again, their faith was languid—like a small spark in a dense fog. Their inchoate new life was a tiny drop in a vast ocean.[106] Additionally, disputes about election had led many to doubt. Interestingly here, although Melanchthon in recent years had tried to redefine election as corporate (in the

---

[102] '[E]tiam in renatis aliqua ex parte sunt voluntatis.' MSA 6.317.13–14. Of course, *renatis* could refer to regeneration instead of being born again (i.e. the decision of faith). Once again, this reflects Melanchthon's careful dance around the issue of free will in conversion that seems to characterize this particular document (but which most certainly does not extend to the 1559 edition of the *Examen ordinandorum* (see below)).

[103] MSA 6.318.34–319.12. See also MSA 6.320.25–6.

[104] 'Manifestum est, et varie oppugnari fidem in illis ipsis quoque, qui ad Deum conversi, renati et sancti sunt, cum aut aspiciunt suam infirmitatem, aut disputant de electione.' MSA 6.318.22–5.

[105] 'Et ego memini quendam, qui huc venit, ut consolationem audiret, ac fatebatur se saepe relapsum esse in adulteria.' MSA 6.319.16–19.

[106] 'Est autem et in plurimis renatis languida fides, et ut parva scintilla in magna caligine, et inchoata novitas est ut parva guttula collata ad amplitudinem Oceani.' MSA 6.320.3–6.

church),[107] he now acknowledged that most people still thought of it in *individual* terms. Indeed, in discoursing on the nature of the church, Melanchthon reverted to language more amenable to a traditional understanding of individual election,[108] but without developing (or even discussing) such a doctrine, for he knew of many like the Italian Francisco Spiera, who had died in desperation on account of disputes about election.[109] Hence, the *Bavarian Articles* does not contain a section on predestination or election.

In seeking to assuage the doubts of believers about their salvation, Melanchthon began with advice based on a strong view of original sin. Emphatically, he warned believers against rational speculation. People 'should not inquire of that which the Lord has not commanded that we inquire, as Sirach [3.22] said, "It is good to reflect upon what God has commanded".'[110] Further, in quoting the first half of Sirach 3.22, Melanchthon implied the second: '. . . for what is hidden is not your concern'. Likewise, the one who doubted the voice of God's promise saying, 'What kind of God is this for whom it is not possible to damn me?', was employing the faulty imagination of reason, against the Word of God.[111] Coming now to the heart of his remedy for doubt, Melanchthon rhetorically exclaimed, 'Why do you first want to know whether you are elect when you already believe the Gospel?'[112]

Leaving the fretful speculations of fallen reason behind, Melanchthon directed the doubting disciple to the Word of God, to his genuine, universal Gospel promises of salvation. The disputers would say that the Gospel applied only to the elect,[113] but to them Melanchthon would respond that the promise was universal, it was certain, and it pertained to all who

---

[107] Such a definition was still discernible in Melanchthon's thought at this point, seeing that he defined the church not as 'the elect' but as the gathering of those who embraced the Gospel and the right use of the sacraments: 'Ecclesia in hac vita est coetus amplectentium Evangelium et recte utentium Sacramentis . . .' MSA 6.285.12–13.

[108] For example, 'Et sunt in eo [i.e. in ecclesia] coetu multi *electi* et alii non sancti, sed tamen de vera doctrina consentienties' (emphasis added). MSA 6.285.16–18. See also MSA 6.285.22–3: '. . . vere filius Dei in ea [i.e. in ecclesia] regnat et multa sunt membra sanctificata Spiritu sancto et *electa*' (emphasis added). MSA 6.285.22–3.

[109] 'Et de multis extant historiae, qui desperatione oppressi sunt propter disputationem de electione seu de particularitate, ut ante paucos annos quidam nomine Spiera in Italia hoc modo periit.' MSA 6.319.13–16.

[110] '. . . nec inquirant ea, quae Deus non iussit inquiri, sicut Siracides inquit: "Quae praecepit tibi Deus, sancte cogita".' MSA 6.318.31–3. Melanchthon repeated this advice a few pages later: 'Iam in praesentibus doloribus cogitent, quid praeceperit Deus, videlicet ut audiant Evangelium, nec omisso Evangelio quaerant alia. Regulam igitur tenant: "Quae praecepit Deus, haec sancte cogita [Sirach 3.22a].' MSA 6.321.34–322.1.

[111] 'Tum ille spreta voce promissionis inquit: Qualis hic Deus esset, qui me non posset damnare? Haec est rationis imaginatio, discedentis a verbo Dei.' MSA 6.319.25–8.

[112] 'Cur prius scire vis, an sis electus, quam credis Evangelio?' MSA 6.322.3–4.

[113] 'Sed dicunt illi disputatores, Evangelium tantum ad electos pertinere.' MSA 6.322.5–6.

accept it.[114] Jesus really meant it when he said, 'Come to me all who are heavy-laden, and I will give you rest.' It was indeed true that 'the same Lord . . . is generous to all who call on him', and that 'God has imprisoned all in disobedience so that he might be merciful to all.' God wanted *all* people to be saved, and he showed no partiality.[115] 'It is, in fact, most manifestly clear that God's command for all to believe in the Son is universal and immutable.'[116] True consolation sprang not from the law, nor from the judgement of reason, but from the Gospel, because the Son of God had come forward from the very heart of the Father.[117]

These universal promises of the Gospel, then, consoled the fearful soul, not by pointing to some eternal decree of predestination, but by staunchly affirming the logic of justification by faith alone. All who believed in Jesus as their Lord and Saviour would be justified. Do not worry about predestination or being good enough to please God—just trust in Jesus, and you will be fine. That was Melanchthon's message.[118] Further, Melanchthon did not leave his readers merely with the exhortation to have faith. He laid out how to go about strengthening one's own faith, and in so doing he established the implicit contours of his thought on the will's role in conversion.

For Melanchthon, both conversion and the strengthening of faith happened through the same multifaceted process: a person had to be exposed to the Gospel, which in turn was always illuminated by the Holy Spirit, following which one's will had to freely decide to assent to these promises of God. Word, Spirit, and will all worked together.[119] Grace came first and was accompanied by the will.[120] Faith began with the hearing of the Word, in which the Spirit would draw (or invite—though not force!) the will, which would then need to

---

[114] 'Ad id respondeo . . . promissio est universalis, et certum est pertinere eam ad omnes, qui eam accipiunt.' MSA 6.6–9.

[115] Matthew 11.28; Romans 10.12; 11.32; 1 Timothy 2.4 (with a very different interpretation from Calvin's!); and Romans 2.11. MSA 6.322.9–16.

[116] 'Denique manifestissimum est, mandatum Dei universale et immuabile esse, ut omnes credant filio.' MSA 6.322.17–18. See also MSA 6.322.2–3, where Melanchthon referred to Mark 1.15, saying, 'Nota sunt autem praecepta immutabilia: "Agite poenitentiam, et credite Evangelio".' Cf. MSA 6.319.19–23.

[117] 'Sint igitur noti fontes verae consolationis, et sciamus non ex lege, nec ex ratione iudicandum esse, sed ex Evangelio, quod filius Dei ex sinu aeterni patris protulit.' MSA 6.319.31–4. 'Ex sinu aeterni patris protulit' is an allusion to John 1.18. See also MSA 6.323.20–7, 30–5.

[118] e.g. MSA 6.319.34–320.2; 6.324.19–22, and *passim.*

[119] 'Cumque disputant fidem Dei donum esse, sciant donari per verbum, et sustentatem se voce Evangelii vere trahi spiritu Sancto inchoante consolationem et accendente invocationem, qua assidue petendum est: "Converte me, Domine, et convertar" [Jeremiah 31.18].' MSA 6.322.26–30.

[120] 'Et congruunt haec ad vetera dicta: Praecedente Gratia, comitante voluntate.' MSA 6.322.35–7. Melanchthon went on to cite Gregory of Nazianzus for support. MSA 6.322–3.

offer free assent to the Gospel offer.[121] Faith came from hearing (*fides ex auditu est*—Romans 10.17).[122] One *came* to faith by hearing the Gospel, and one *grew* in faith by hearing the Gospel. The doubter could find consolation then by exposing himself to the Gospel. In hearing God's promises, illuminated by the Holy Spirit, he would find his faith growing and his doubts dissipating.[123] One could pray, as the anxious father did in Mark 9.24, 'I believe, Lord! Help my unbelief!' (But Melanchthon, who was never fond of antinomy, chose to render the Greek as 'I believe, Lord! Help my weakness!'[124])

Conclusion

Faith originated and grew through the interplay of Word, Spirit, and the assent of the free will.[125] Christians should find consolation through God's universal promises of an unmerited forensic justification, and not worry about predestination. Melanchthon asserted that this seemed to him to be the ancient belief taught in Scripture,[126] and if anyone should try to cite Augustine as an authority saying otherwise, then they were interpreting him too harshly and committing an injury against him.[127] Moreover, even Luther himself used to worry about election, but he, too, found (and gave) peace through meditating on God's genuine, universal Gospel promises. Here Melanchthon drew even on the name of Luther to defend his unique doctrine of evangelical free will![128]

---

[121] 'Orditur a verbo, vocari et trahi inquit voluntatem, quae non expectet coactionem, sed luctetur, ut assentiatur promissioni.' MSA 6.323.2–4.

[122] MSA 6.319.25–30. See also MSA 6.324.

[123] MSA 6.320–21.

[124] 'Credo, Domine, opem fer imbecillitati meae.' MSA 6.324.14. The Vulgate (for Mark 9.23) reads, 'Credo adiuva incredulitatem meam', and even Luther's translation has, 'Ich glaube; hilf meinem Unglauben!' Melanchthon had to stretch it a bit to translate ἀπιστία with 'imecillitati', rather than the directly paradoxical 'Credo . . . incredulitatem.' He did the same thing in the Latin *Examen ordinandorum* of 1554: CR 23.16.

[125] 'Habent autem conversi auxilium, quod non aspernentur, videlicet SPIRITUM SANCTUM, quem non contristent, et cogitatione verbi Dei et ardenti precatione excitent, sicut Pauls iubet Timotheum [2 Timothy 1.6] ἀναζωπυρεῖν donum Dei.' MSA 6.320.37–321.4.

[126] MSA 6.324.5–15.

[127] 'Et qui Augustinum durius interpretantur, iniuriam ei faciunt.' MSA 6.324.7–8.

[128] 'Hoc modo et in scriptis et coram Lutherus interrogantes consolatus est, ut multi norunt, qui adhuc vivunt.' MSA 6.322.33–5. 'Vidimus ipsum Lutherum in suo quodam agone ego et alii saepe repetentem hoc dictum: "Conclusit omnes sub peccatum, ut omnium misereatur".' MSA 6.323.35–324.1.

GALLUS' TRACTS: 1559–1560

Following the publication of the *Response to the Bavarian Articles*, 'Gallus remained suspicious of his preceptor's way of describing the action of the human being in conversion, fearing that he was leaving room for a contribution of the human will to this process apart from the Holy Spirit's irresistible causation. Therefore he finally rose to the challenge of *The Response* and engaged Melanchthon openly in print regarding the bondage of the will.'[129] In 1559–60, Gallus published a series of German-language popular-level tracts critiquing Melanchthon's theology of the will.[130] Simultaneously, he published two more technical treatises in Latin addressing the same issues.[131] At this time, he also reissued Luther's *De servo arbitrio*.[132]

By 1560, Gallus was attacking Melanchthon by name, arguing that Melanchthon's 'use of the language of the medieval theologians regarding the ability of the sinful heart to "make an effort in the direction of grace" was in direct opposition to Luther's refutation of that position in Erasmus, and was indeed a rejection of Melanchthon's own position in the Augsburg Confession and Apology.'[133] Gallus, along with Flacius, was convinced that Melanchthon had simply gone over to Erasmus' understanding of the freedom of the will, resulting in a synergistic 'working-with' the Holy Spirit to achieve one's own

[129] Kolb, *Bound Choice*, 114. This section is heavily dependent on Kolb's excellent research, as presented in *Bound Choice*, pp. 113–17.

[130] Nikolaus Gallus, *Erklerung der Religions streite/zu nottu[e]rfftigem vnterricht der Kirche/ vnd ablenung falscher Calumnien. Wider die verfelscher der waren Augspurgischen Confession* (Regensburg: Heinrich Geissler, 1559), Aij b–B b. *Wa[e]chterstimme/Nic. Galli. Wo vnd in was Stücken/vnter dem Namen Lutheri/der Augspurgischen Confession vnd H. Schrift/Wider Lutherum/wider die Augspur. Conf. H. Schrift jtzo gelehret wird* (Regensburg: Heinrich Geissler, n.d.), Aiija–Aiiija. *Religion streit vnd Einigkeit* (Regensburg: Heinrich Geissler, 1560), Aiija. *Tafel der verkerten/vnd gleich vmbgekerten etlicher Lere/bey der wahren Christlichen Augsp. Conf.* (Regensburg: Heinrich Geissler, 1560).

[131] Nikolaus Gallus, *Qvaestio libero arbitrio, qvatenvs illa qvibvsdam nunc disceptatur in Ecclesijs Augustanae Confessionis. Cvm adsertione ex perpetva propheticae et apostolicae scripturae sententia, & ex sententia Lutheri instaratoris doctrinae, authoris & interprecis Augustanae Confessionis* (Regensburg: Heinrich Geissler, 1559). *Erklerung vnd Consens vieler Christlichen Kirchen/der Augspurgischen Confession/auff die newe verfelschung der Lehre vom Freyen willen/wie die aus dem INTERIM von etlichen noch gefu[e]rt vnd verteidigt wird* (Regensburg: Heinrich Geissler, 1559).

[132] Martin Luther, *Das der freie Wille nichts sey/Antwort/D. Martini Lutheri/an Erasmum Roterodamum/Verdeudscht durch D. Justum Jonam/Zuuor niemals allein im Druck ausgangen* (Regensburg: Heinrich Geissler, 1559). Gallus also insisted that Luther had *not* abandoned his position from DSA! *Das der freie Wille nichts sey*, 1559, 2b–3a.

[133] Gallus, *Wa[e]chterstimme*, Aiij a–Aiiij b. *Religion streit*, Aiij a. *Tafel der verkerten Lere*, Aij a–Aiij a. Kolb, *Bound Choice*, 116.

salvation.[134] In opposition to this idea, Gallus insisted on the doctrine of predestination, and he affirmed that Luther had, in *De servo arbitrio*, already demonstrated that his doctrine of necessity was not that of the Stoics but rather that of the apostles and prophets.[135] Gallus said that 'the fallen human will should not be compared to a block of wood since it is active in rejecting God's Word until the Holy Spirit has changed it into a new creature.'[136] In sum, for Gallus, the human will was 'purely passive. Indeed, it functions but is dependent upon the assistance of the Holy Spirit, who enacts the changes in the human mind, will, and heart which bestow upon the repentant person a new way of thinking, willing, and acting.'[137] These were rigorous critiques of Melanchthon's position. Meanwhile, only a year after the first, Melanchthon submitted a second report to the Elector.

A SECOND REPORT TO ELECTOR AUGUST:
9 MARCH 1559

While the full weight of Gallus' barrage of tracts had yet to be felt, Melanchthon reiterated his position on free will in a second report to the Elector, dated 9 March 1559.[138] Here Melanchthon again systematically laid out his under-standing of the role of the human will in justification. A new addition was the outright denunciation of Luther's *De servo arbitrio*, which Melanchthon now argued was filled with Stoic and Manichean errors. Melanchthon went on to deny the doctrine of predestination which he equated with Schwenkfeldianism. This was a strong criticism indeed, for Melanchthon considered Schwenkfeld and all those doctrinally akin to him to be 'Anabaptist trash'.[139] He instead argued that he and Luther were actually in agreement on this issue, and that for both of them the most important thing was to focus on the universality of God's Gospel promises, and not to talk about election. Thus, the criticism from Flacius and Gallus in the 1550s eventually drove Melanchthon to restate his theology of the role of the human will in justification, and in so doing, he stated with new clarity his position of evangelical free will—that is, a forensic justification that included a genuine role for the human will in the decision of conversion.

---

[134] Gallus, *Das der freie Wille nichts sey*, 1559, 2a. Kolb, *Bound Choice*, 114.

[135] Gallus, *Das der freie Wille nichts sey*, 1559, A1a–b. Kolb, *Bound Choice*, 115.

[136] Gallus, Qvaestio, C b–Ciij a. (1559). Kolb, *Bound Choice*, 116.

[137] Kolb, *Bound Choice*, 117.

[138] Melanchthon (in Wittenberg), report for Elector August of Saxony (in Dresden), before 10 March 1559. MBW 8.8886. CR 9.763–75 Nr. 6705. See also Kolb, *Bound Choice*, 111–13.

[139] 'Preface to *The Corpus of Christian Doctrine*, 1560'. Keen, 140. *Praefatio Philippi Melanthonis*. '. . . a colluvie Anabaptistica et aliis erroribus . . .' MSA 6.7.24–5.

Melanchthon wrote, 'grace precedes, but the will goes along with it, and God draws, but he draws the person whose will is functioning.'[140] Needless to say, Flacius and Gallus were not impressed[141]—and neither was Calvin.

CALVIN'S CONCLUSION: 1560

On 19 April 1560, Philipp Melanchthon died. While he was no longer in a position to debate theology, this did not stop his critics from pronouncing a last word upon him. The chief of these was John Calvin, who now dropped his former restraint in order to serve the greater purpose of the public defence of the Gospel as he saw it. From the pulpit he condemned Melanchthon for his position on free will and predestination, calling him 'evil-disposed', a 'Rustic', a practitioner of 'villainous slander' (for equating a strong view of the determination of God with Stoicism), a 'Clown [who] babbleth of Free will', a man in error, a 'troublecoast', 'vile dog', 'villain', and 'troubler'.[142] Melanchthon's final formulation of his doctrine of the will in justification was intolerable for Calvin.

[140] Trans. Kolb, in *Bound Choice*, 113. 'Praecedente gratia, comitante voluntate, Deus trahit sed volentem trahit.' CR 9.769.

[141] Flacius and Gallus both continued to be critical of Melanchthon's doctrine of the will. Gallus (in Regensburg), letter to Melanchthon (in Wittenberg), 19 April 1557. MBW 8.8199. CR 9.142–3 Nr. 6232. Melanchthon (in Wittenberg), letter to David Chytraeus (in Rostock), 14 November 1558. MBW 8.8777. CR 9.9657 Nr. 6632. Melanchthon (in Wittenberg), letter to Abdias Praetorius (in Frankfurt an der Oder), 1 September 1559. MBW 8.9045. CR 9.906–7 Nr. 6808. In 1559, Gallus republished Luther's DSA with an attack on Melanchthon in the preface. Kolb, 'Nikolaus Gallus' Critique', 93. This work was titled, *Das der freye Wille nichts sey. Antwort / D. Martini Lutheri / an Erasmum Roterodamum / Verdeudscht durch D. Justum Jonam / Zuuor niemals allein im Druck ausgangen*, Regensberg, 1559. The debate within Lutheranism set into motion by Melanchthon's shift in doctrine, followed by the attacks by Flacius, Gallus, and others, continued through the *Formula of Concord* of 1577, which represented an important milestone in Lutheran theology by speaking against Melanchthon's doctrine. The debate, however, continued, as Irene Dingel has shown in *Concordia controversa: die öffentlichen Diskussionen um das lutherische Konkordienwerk am Ende des 16. Jahrhunderts* (Gütersloh: Gütersloher Verlagshaus, 1996).

[142] John Calvin, 'An Answer to certain slanders and blasphemies, wherewith certain evil disposed persons have gone about to bring the doctrine of God's everlasting Predestination into hatred', in *Sermons on Election and Reprobation*, ed. Ernie Springer, trans. Iohn Fielde (Audobon, NJ: Old Paths Publications, 1996), 305–17. The original text of this sermon may be found in John Calvin, *Traité de la prédestination éternelle de Dieu, par laquelle les uns sont éleuz à salut, les autres laissez en leur condemnation* (Geneva, 1560). This work was also republished in Geneva in 1562 as *Treze sermons traitans de l'élection gratuite de Dieu en Iacob, et de la réiection en Esau*.

CONCLUSION

The years 1554–60 represented the twilight of Melanchthon's career and life. He remained vigorously active in his work right up until his death. Although reluctantly, he took on his critics from several directions as he sought to refute the teachings of the Council of Trent, navigate the limitations imposed by Roman Catholic government in Saxony, and respond to the critiques of Flacius, Gallus, Calvin, and the Bavarian Inquisition. All the while, he still sought to produce helpful documents for the building up of the church, as evidenced by the *Examination of Ordinands*. Throughout it all, he continued to nuance his teaching of evangelical free will, but he never abandoned it. Melanchthon went to meet his Lord, convinced that on the question of the origins of faith, *this* is what the Bible taught.

12

Conclusion

On the origins of faith, Melanchthon began with predestinarian determinism, moved to temporal freedom coupled with spiritual bondage, and ended up with both temporal and spiritual freedom, however limited.[1] Throughout, he affirmed a strong view of the Fall, along with its deleterious effects on the operation of the will. This meant that God had to take the initiative in salvation, which he did both through the death and resurrection of Christ and in his providential sending of the preaching of the Gospel into all the world. When the Gospel was preached, the Holy Spirit always infused it such that the unconverted hearer would be drawn and invited to heartfelt repentance and a total trust in Jesus Christ. At that moment, the human will could freely and *passively* assent to that divine call, or freely and *actively* reject it. Assent was a passive and non-meritorious action, the result of which was forensic justification—the total imputation of the merits of Christ to the believer, resulting in salvation. Rejection of the Gospel was an active, effortful rebellion against God's call. It was therefore an evil work, and any who persisted in their active denial of Christ would eventually reap eternal damnation as a result. *All* the glory for salvation belonged to God, and *all* the blame for damnation belonged to the recalcitrant sinner.

Accordingly, God did not predestine individuals for salvation or damnation. Rather, God predestined an eternal, elect *church*, as a body, for salvation. This was corporate rather than individual predestination. The eternal fate of individuals was in their own hands at the moment when they heard the Spirit-illumined Gospel promises. Altogether, therefore, the choice for a saving faith in Jesus had three origins: the Word, the Spirit, and the individual free will.

Melanchthon's theological journey to this position was slow and systematic rather than sudden and isolated. He had no dramatic 'breakthrough', for the seeds of the change that would become obvious in 1532 were already in place

---

[1] For example, even well after his shift, Melanchthon continued to make statements like the following: 'The heart has wandering and errant impulses, and takes the will along with itself.' *Commentary on Aristotle's Ethics, Book I*, 1546. Keen, 201. *Enarratio Libri I. Ethicorum Aristotelis*. 'Cor habet vagos et errantes impetus, et rapit secum voluntatem.' CR 16.308.

in 1519. Ultimately, the evolution of Philipp Melanchthon's thought on free will was driven by a pastoral concern for the *effect* of doctrine. Quite simply, he wanted to comfort people worried about their salvation, and he wanted doctrine to make sense.

A strong doctrine of determinism and individual election produced doubt and fear among Christians—and these were the two things most antithetical to faith. 'You of little faith, why did you doubt?' Jesus demanded of his disciples.[2] Elsewhere, Christ said, 'Do not be afraid.'[3] Melanchthon sought to erase doubt and fear for everyday Christians, and to do so, he moved from the bound will in justification, to evangelical free will. This effectively put one's eternal destination in one's own hands, so long as one concentrated on the generous promises of the Gospel.

While a pastoral concern for the effects of doctrine was the primary motive for Melanchthon's doctrinal journey on the origins of faith, his embrace of the rules of classical rhetoric also provided some ancillary support. Melanchthon viewed Scripture as sacred oration, subject to the rules of Aristotelian rhetoric and dialectics. These disciplines required that in the interpretation of a passage, doctrine should avoid antinomy, or the appearance of rational inconsistency. So, to use the modern English phrasing, we could say that while Luther embraced paradox, Melanchthon did not. The application of rhetoric and dialectics to Christian doctrine therefore encouraged the elimination of the appearance of rational inconsistency, and it is significant that Melanchthon's final formulation of evangelical free will *was*, in fact, entirely rationally consistent. If it had to be *either* God choosing individuals *or* individuals choosing God, Melanchthon came down on the side of individuals choosing God.[4]

In the introduction to this book, I presented alternative interpretations prevalent in the literature for why Melanchthon changed his position on free will over time. The two main positions in opposition to my own were: (1) That Melanchthon's philosophical humanism influenced his theology in the 1520s and caused the change. In other words, he mixed philosophical

---

[2] Matthew 14.31.

[3] Matthew 28.10.

[4] 'I wanted nothing more splendid, and with pious effort as befits one in the catechism, than to propound useful things to youth, and to try to explain them with the right type of speech and to avoid hyperbole, useless words and ambiguities, which breed dissensions.' Keen, 141. 'Preface to *The Corpus of Christian Doctrine*, 1560.' *Praefatio Philippi Melanthonis.* '[M] e nihil appetivisse splendidius, ac pio studio, ut in Catechismo fieri decet, proposuisse materias iuventuti utiles, et conatum esse, proprio genere sermonis eas explicare et vitare hyperbolas, ἀκυρολογίας et ambigua, quae dissensiones pariunt.' MSA 6.9.9–14.

metaphysics into his theology and came out with a more Aristotelian and anthropocentric doctrine of the will. In Chapter 6 above, I have shown this argument to be false. Melanchthon always strictly separated philosophical metaphysics from theology. The second position in opposition to mine was (2) That Melanchthon was won over to the position expressed by Erasmus in *De libero arbitrio* and *Hyperaspistes*. Again, in the course of this book I have shown this position to be false. Whereas Erasmus argued for free choice in applying oneself to a life of grace-aided good works resulting in a transformational model of justification by congruous merit, Melanchthon argued for free choice in receiving God's grace by faith in Jesus resulting in a forensic model of justification by imputed merit. Erasmus advocated a scholastic, Roman Catholic free will (which was also the position of the post-Tridentine Roman Church). Melanchthon taught *evangelical* free will. Both preserved an element of choice, but Melanchthon attached that choice to salvation by faith alone, such that he could always say that he was in agreement with Luther and in opposition to Erasmus.

Theologian	Status of the will	Method of justification	Source of justifying merit
Luther	Bound	Faith alone	Imputed
Erasmus	Free	Faith *and* works	Intrinsic
Melanchthon	Free	Faith alone	Imputed

Specifically, evangelical free will can be defined as free will in choosing to accept personal faith in Jesus Christ upon hearing God's Word, which is always uniformly illumined by the Holy Spirit. This choice of faith is a free, passive action,[5] and it is non-meritorious (i.e. it is simple acquiescence to being forensically justified). The faith that results from this free choice is *instrumental* for salvation rather than *causative*.

Philipp Melanchthon was the first person in church history to articulate this doctrine of evangelical free will. He, however, did not think he was presenting a new opinion, but rather reiterating the old foundational (or foun*tain*-tional, if the reader will pardon the pun) doctrines of biblical and patristic antiquity. In the preface to the 1543 edition of the *Loci*, Melanchthon wrote, 'I am not presenting [bringing forth] new opinions; in fact I feel that there is no greater sin in the church of God than to toy with creating new opinions and to depart from the prophetic and apostolic scripture and the true commands of God's church. Rather, I am following and embracing the doctrine of the Wittenberg church

---

[5] The phrase 'passive action' sounds like an oxymoron, and it is ironic that Melanchthon's final position on free will, to which he arrived partially through an aversion to rational inconsistency, ended up very nearly (if not in fact) embracing an antinomy.

and her allies, which is without a doubt the consensus of Christ's catholic church, that is to say, of all learned men in Christ's church.'[6]

Yet Melanchthon's evangelical free will *was* something new. It was neither a Roman Catholic transformational model of justification, nor Luther's understanding of the bound will combined with imputed righteousness. In fact, it was a development *from within* the theological landscape of Luther's soteriology. It was a retention of Luther's *mechanism* of salvation (substitutionary atonement in Christ alone through faith alone), coupled with a deliberate departure from the negative consequences of a strong view of the governance of God.

In essence, Melanchthon's evangelical free will was a response to Luther in the same manner as Arminius' doctrine of the will was a response to Calvinism. Arminius and his popularizer John Wesley were not original—they had merely come to similar conclusions within a Reformed milieu as Melanchthon had already done within the Lutheran context.

Melanchthon's ideas, if not so much his name, have come to have great influence in the whole Western Christian tradition. Many modern evangelical Christians would probably hold to some form of Melanchthon's doctrine of evangelical free will. But to carry the story onward from Melanchthon's death to the debates between the Philippists and the Gnesio-Lutherans, the *Formula of Concord*, later Pietism, Evangelical Revivals, and out into the Reformed world would fill many more volumes—while our space here is done. Let us give Master Philipp the last word, penned on 16 February 1560:

I affirm that I have a desire to teach rightly, and a pious will; and I hope my labors and opinions are approved by many pious and learned men, and that I and all my opinions and works are subjected; and to this end I subject them to the judgments of all pious and learned men. For I know that I am not without a fault.... While this general calamity for the church has exercised me also for a long enough time now, may no judgment about doctrine come from my miseries and my multitude of enemies. For the confusion of life shows that it is all too true when it is said, 'The learned rabble is a terrible evil.'

I pray to the Son of God our Lord Jesus Christ, sitting at the right hand of the eternal Father, and bestowing gifts of mercy upon men, that he may always assemble his church in these regions, and govern me with clemency and bring it about that we may, as much as possible, be one in God. And thinking often of the cruelty of adversaries, I recite to

---

[6] Keen, 137. *Philippus Melanchthon Pio Lectori S. D.* 'Non gigno novas opiniones nec aliud maius scelus esse in Ecclesai Dei sentio, quam ludere fingendis novis opinionibus et discedere a Prophetica et Apostolica scriptura et consensu vero Ecclesiae Dei. Sequor autem et amplector doctrinam Ecclesiae Witebergensis et coniunctarum, quae sine ulla dubitatione consensus est Ecclesiae catholicae Christi, id est, omnium eruditorum in Ecclesai Christi.' MSA 2/1.166.1–8.

myself and to others this, from Tertullian: 'If you entrust your injuries to God, he is your avenger; if harm, he will restore; if sadness, he is a doctor; if dead, he will revive you.'[7] The pious know that this saying agrees with divine consolations, whoever thinks of them with regard to his own tribulations. Farewell, reader.[8]

---

[7] *De patientia* 15. CSEL 47.22.
[8] Keen, 141–2. MSA 6.10–11.

Timeline of Melanchthon's Life

1497	16 February	Philipp Schwarzerd (later 'Melanchthon') born in Bretton
1503		Julius II becomes pope
1509		Birth of John Calvin
1510		Student at Heidelberg University
1512		Graduate student at Tübingen University
1513		Leo X becomes pope
1514		Teaching at Tübingen University
1517		Luther's *95 Theses*
1518		Teaching at Wittenberg University
1519		Ferdinand Magellan's voyage to circumnavigate the globe departs from Seville
1519		Charles V becomes Holy Roman Emperor
1520		Marriage to Katherine Krapp
1521		Diet of Worms
1521		*Loci communes* (first edition)
1521–2		Wittenberg unrest
1522		Luther's *Invocavit* sermons, restoring order in Wittenberg
1522		*Loci communes* (first edition, revised)
1522		*Annotations on Romans*
1522		Hadrian VI becomes pope
1523		Clement VII becomes pope
1524		Erasmus: *De libero arbitrio*
1524		Peasant Wars in Germany
1525		Luther: *De servo arbitrio*
1525		Charles V defeats Francis I of France
1526		Erasmus: *Hyperaspistes*
1526		First Diet of Speyer
1527		The sack of Rome, by Charles V's troops
1527		*Dissertatio* on Colossians
1527		*Scholia* on Colossians (first edition)
1527–8		*Visitation Articles*
1528		*Scholia* on Colossians (second edition)
1529		*Dispositio* on Romans
1529		Second Diet of Speyer, term 'Protestant' first used
1529		*Schwabach Articles*
1529		*Marburg Articles*
1529		Ottoman siege of Vienna

1530		Diet of Augsburg
1530		John Eck's *404 Articles*
1530		*Augsburg Confession*
1530		*Confutation of the Augsburg Confession*
1531		*Apology to the Augsburg Confession*
1531		Death of Zwingli
1532		*Summary of Ethics*
1532		*Commentary on Romans* (first full exposition of evangelical free will)
1533		*Loci communes* (second edition)
1534		Paul III becomes pope
1534		Ignatius Loyola founds the Jesuits
1534		Henry VIII declares self head of Church of England
1536		Death of Erasmus
1536–7		Cordatus controversy
1540		*Augsburg Confession Variata*
1540		*Commentary on Romans*
1541		Regensburg Colloquy
1543		*The Elements of Rhetoric*
1543		*Loci communes* (third edition)
1543		Copernicus argues that the earth revolves around the sun
1545–7		Council of Trent begins
1546		Death of Luther
1547		Schmalkaldic War
1548		Augsburg Interim
1548		Leipzig Interim
1549–50		Criticism of Melanchthon from Matthias Flacius Illyricus
1550		Julius III becomes pope
1551		*The Saxon Confession*
1551–2		Calvin's falling-out with Melanchthon
1552		*The Examination of Ordinands* (first edition, German)
1553		*De anima*
1553		*Loci communes* (fourth edition)
1554		*The Examination of Ordinands* (second edition, Latin)
1555		Marcellus II becomes pope
1555		Paul IV ('Carafa') becomes pope
1556–60		Controversy with Gallus
1557		Katherine Melanchthon dies
1558		Report to Elector August
1558–9		*Response to the Bavarian Articles*
1559		Pius IV becomes pope
1559		A second report to Elector August
1560	19 April	†

Select Bibliography

Primary Sources

Acta reformationis Catholicae ecclesiam Germaniae concernentia saeculi XVI. Die Reformverhandlung des deutschen Episkopats von 1520 bis 1570, ed. Georg Pfeilschifter, 6 vols. (Regensburg: F. Pustet, 1959–).

Amsdorf, Nikolaus von, *De contingentia. Disputatione prima pars* (Dresden: Sächsische Landesbibliothek, Ms. Dres. A180, 1536), 752–70.

——*Annotationes quibus indicatur paucis quae in locis communibus Philippi Melanchthonis displicent per N.A.* (Weimar: Goethe-Schiller Archiv der Nationale Forschungs- und Gedenkstätten der klassischen deutschen Literatur: Ehemalige Thüringische Landesbibliothek folio Band XL, 1541), 301–9.

Aquinas, Thomas, *Summa Theologiae: Latin Text and English Translation, Introductions, Notes, Appendices and Glossaries*, ed. Cornelius Ernst et al., 61 vols. (London: Blackfriars, 1963–80).

Augustine, *On Free Choice of the Will*, trans. Thomas Williams (Indianapolis: Hackett, 1993).

Bekenntnisschriften der evangelisch-lutherisch Kirche / herausgegeben im Gedenkjahr der Augsburgischen Konfession 1930 (Göttingen: Vandenhoeck & Ruprecht, 1952).

Biel, Gabriel, *Canonis Misse Expositio*, ed. H. A. Oberman and W. J. Courtenay, 4 vols. (Wiesbaden: Steiner, 1963–).

——'De Circumcisione Domini', Sermo II, in ordine 14, in *Sermones de festivitatibus Christi* (Hagenau, 1510).

Book of Concord: The Confessions of the Evangelical Lutheran Church, ed. Theodore G. Tappert (Philadelphia: Fortress, 1959).

Book of Concord: The Confessions of the Evangelical Lutheran Church, ed. Robert Kolb and Timothy J. Wengert, trans. Charles Arand et al. (Minneapolis: Fortress, 2000).

Calvin, John, *The Bondage and Liberation of the Will: A Defence of the Orthodox Doctrine of Human Choice Against Pighius*, ed. A. N. S. Lane, trans. G. I. Davies (Grand Rapids: Baker, 1996).

——*Concerning the Eternal Predestination of God*, trans. J. K. S. Reid (Louisville: Westminster John Knox, 1961).

——*Ioannis Calvini opera quae supersunt omnia*, ed. Guilelmus Baum et al., 59 vols. (Brunsvigae: C. A. Schwetschke, 1863–1900).

——*Joannis Calvini opera selecta*, ed. Petrus Barth et al., 5 vols. (Monachii: C. Kaiser, 1926–62).

——*Sermons on Election and Reprobation*, ed. Ernie Springer, trans. Iohn Fielde (Audobon, NJ: Old Paths, 1996).

——*Traité de la prédestination éternelle de Dieu, par laquelle les uns sont éleuz à salut, les autres laissez en leur condemnation* (Geneva, 1560).

——*Treze sermons traitans de l'élection gratuite de Dieu en Iacob, et de la réiection en Esau* (Geneva, 1562).

Cochlaeus, Johannes, *De libero arbitrio hominis adversus locos communes Philippi Melanchthonis, libri duo* (Tübingen: Morhart, 1525).

Confutatio der Confessio Augustana vom 3. August 1530, ed. Herbert Immenkötter (Münster: Aschendorff, 1979).

Corpus Christianorum: Series Latina (Turnholt, 1953).

Corpus Scriptorum Ecclesiasticorum Latinorum (Vienna, 1886–).

Duns Scotus, John, *De Primo Principio*, ed. and trans. Allan B. Wolter (Chicago: Franciscan Herald Press, 1982).

——*God and Creatures: The Quodlibetal Questions*, ed. Felix Alluntis and Allan B. Wolter, trans. Felix Alluntis (Princeton: Princeton University Press, 1975).

——*Duns Scotus on the Will and Morality*, ed. and trans. Allan B. Wolter (Washington, DC: Catholic University of America Press, 1986).

——*Opera Omnia*, ed. C. Balic et al. (Vatican City: Typis Polyglottis Vaticanis, 1950–).

——*Opera Omnia*, ed. Luke Wadding, 12 vols. (Lyons: Durand, 1639).

——*Philosophical Writings: A Selection*, ed. and trans. Allan B. Wolter (Indianapolis: Hackett, 1987).

Eck, Joannes, *Sub Domini Ihesu et Mariae Patrocinio. Articulos 404 partim ad disputationes Lipsicam, Baden, & Bernen attinentes, partim vero ex scriptis pacem ecclesiae perturbantium extractos, Coram divo Caesare Carolo V. Ro. Imp. semp Augu. etc. ac proceribus Imperii, Ioan Eckius minimus ecclesiase minister, offert se disputturum, ut in scheda latius explicatur Augustae Vindelicorum* (Ingolstadt, 1530).

——'John Eck's Four Hundred Four Articles for the Imperial Diet at Augsburg', trans. Robert Rosin, in Robert Kolb and James A. Nestingen, eds., *Sources and Contexts of the Book of Concord* (Minneapolis: Fortress Press, 2001), 31–82.

Erasmus, Desiderius, *Ausgewählte Schriften: Ausgabe in acht Bänden: Lateinisch und Deutsch*, ed. Werner Welzig, 8 vols. (Darmstadt: Wissenschaftliche Buchgesellschaft, 1968–80).

——*Ausgewählte Werke*, ed. Hajo Holborn and Annemarie Holborn (Munich: C. H. Beck, 1964).

——*The Enchiridion of Erasmus*, ed. and trans. Raymond Himelick (Bloomington: Indiana University Press, 1963).

——*Opera omnia Desiderii Erasmi Roterodami*, ed. Joannes Clericus, 10 vols. (Lugduni Batavorum: 1703–6).

——*Opus epistolarum Des. Erasmi Roterodami*, ed. P. S. Allen et al., 12 vols. (Oxonii: Typographeo Clarendoniano, 1906–58).

——*Vom freien Willen*, trans. Otto Schumacher (Göttingen: Vandenhoeck & Ruprecht, 1956).

Flacius, Matthias, *Entschuldigung Matthiae Flacij Illyrici, geschrieben an die Universitet zu Wittemberg der Mittelding halben. Item sein brief an Philip. Melanthonem sampt etlichen andern schriften dieselbige sach belangend. Verdeudscht* (Magdeburg: Christian Rödinger, 1549).

Gallus, Nikolaus, *Bekentnis Vnterricht vnd vermanung/der Pfarrhern vnd Prediger/der Christlichen Kircehn zu Mageburgk. Anno 1550. Den. 13. Aprils* (Magdeburg: Michael Lotther, 1550).

—— *Confessio et Apologia pastorum & reliquorum ministrorum Ecclesiae Magdeburgensis. Anno 1550. Idibus Aprilis* (Magdeburg: Michael Lotther, 1550).

—— *Erklerung der Religions streite/zu nottu[e]rfftigem vnterricht der Kirche/vnd ablenung falscher Calumnien. Wider die verfelscher der waren Augspurgischen Confession* (Regensburg: Heinrich Geissler, 1559).

—— *Erklerung vnd Consens vieler Christlichen Kirchen/der Augspurgischen Confession/ auff die newe verfelschung der Lehre vom Freyen willen/wie die aus dem INTERIM von etlichen noch gefu[e]rt vnd verteidigt wird* (Regensburg: Heinrich Geissler, 1559).

—— Introduction to *Das der freie Wille nichts sey/Antwort/D. Martini Lutheri/an Erasmum Roterodamum/Verdeudscht durch D. Justum Jonam/Zuuor niemals allein im Druck ausgangen* (Regensburg: Heinrich Geissler, 1559).

—— *Qvaestio libero arbitrio, qvatenvs illa qvibvsdam nunc disceptatur in Ecclesijs Augustanae Confessionis. Cvm adsertione ex perpetva propheticae et apostolicae scripturae sententia, & ex sententia Lutheri instaratoris doctrinae, authoris & interprecis Augustanae Confessionis* (Regensburg: Heinrich Geissler, 1559).

—— *Religion streit vnd Einigkeit* (Regensburg: Heinrich Geissler, 1560).

—— *Tafel der verkerten/vnd gleich vmbgekerten etlicher Lere/bey der wahren Christlichen Augsp. Conf.* (Regensburg: Heinrich Geissler, 1560).

—— *Wa[e]chterstimme/Nic. Galli. Wo vnd in was Stücken/vnter dem Namen Lutheri/ der Augspurgischen Confession vnd H. Schrift/Wider Lutherum/wider die Augspur. Conf. H. Schrift jtzo gelehret wird* (Regensburg: Heinrich Geissler, n.d.).

Gregory of Rimini, *Gregorii Ariminensis OESA Lectura super primum et secundum Sententiarum*, ed. A. Damasus Trapp, 7 vols. (Berlin: W. de Gruyter, 1978).

—— *Gregorii Ariminensis: Super primum et secundum Sententiarum* (St Bonaventure, NY: Franciscan Institute, 1955).

Kolb, Robert and James A. Nestingen, eds., *Sources and Contexts of the Book of Concord* (Minneapolis: Fortress Press, 2001).

Kolde, Theodore, ed., *Die älteste Redaktion der Augsburger Konfession mit Melanchthons Einleitung* (Gütersloh, 1906).

Library of Christian Classics, ed. John Baillie et al., 26 vols. (Philadelphia: Westminister, 1950–69).

Lombard, Peter, *Sententiae in IV libris distinctae*, 3rd edn., ed. Ignatius C. Brady, 2 vols. (Grottaferrata: Collegii S. Bonaventurae ad Claras Aquas, 1971–81).

Luther, Martin, *D. Martin Luthers Werke: Kritische Gesamtausgabe*, 69 vols. (Weimar: H. Bölau, 1883–).

—— *D. Martin Luthers Werke: Kritische Gesamtausgabe. Briefwechsel*, 18 vols. (Weimar: H. Bölaus Nachfolger, 1930–85).

—— *D. Martin Luthers Werke: Kritische Gesamtausgabe. Deutsche Bibel*, 12 vols. (Weimar: H. Bölaus Nachfolger, 1906–61).

—— *D. Martin Luthers Werke: Kritische Gesamtausgabe. Tischreden*, 6 vols. (Weimar: H. Bölaus Nachfolger, 1912–21).

——*Das der freie Wille nichts sey/Antwort/D. Martini Lutheri/an Erasmum Roteroda-mum/Verdeudscht durch D. Justum Jonam/Zuuor niemals allein im Druck ausgangen* (Regensburg: Heinrich Geissler, 1559). (With an introduction by Nikolaus Gallus.)

——*Luther's Works: American Edition*, ed. Jaroslav Pelikan and Helmut Lehmann, 55 vols. (St Louis/Philadelphia: Concordia/Fortress, 1955–86).

——*Martin Luther: Ausgewählte Schriften*, ed. Karin Bornkamm and Gerhard Ebeling, 6 vols. (Frankfurt am Main: Insel Verlag, 1982–95).

——*Martin Luther: Studienausgabe*, ed. Hans-Ulrich Delius (Berlin: Evangelische Verlagsanstalt, 1979–99).

Markwald, R. K., ed. and trans., *A Mystic's Passion: The Spirituality of Johannes von Staupitz in his 1520 Lenten Sermons: Translation and Commentary* (New York: Peter Lang, 1990).

Mehlhausen, Joachim, ed., *Das Augsburger Interim von 1548*, 2nd edn. (Neukirchen: Neukirchener Verlag, 1996).

Melanchthon, Philipp, *Annotationes Philippi Melanchthonis in Epistola Pauli ad Romanos unam, et ad Corinthios duas* (Argent: Iohannem Heruagium, 1523).

ANNO || TATIONES PHILIPPI || Melanchthonis in Epistolā Pau || li ad Romanos unam, Et ad || Corintios duas. || ARGENTORATI APVD || Iohannem Heruagium. Anno || M.D.XXIII || Woodcut opposite title page, on title page, and on various pages. 144 leaves.

——*Commentary on Romans*, trans. Fred Kramer (St Louis: Concordia, 1992).

——'A Critical Translation of Philip Melanchthon's "Elementorum Rhetorices Libri Duo". (Latin Text)', trans. Mary Joan La Fontaine (unpublished dissertation) (Ann Arbor: University of Michigan, 1968).

——*Corpus Reformatorum: Philippi Melanthonis opera quae supersunt omnia*, ed. K. Bretschneider and H. Bindseil, 28 vols. (Halle: Schwetschke, 1834–60).

——*Die Epistel S. Pauli zun Colossern* (Michael Lotter, 1529). Or, with full detail:

Die Epi= || stel S. Pauli zun || Colossern durch Philip || pum Melanchton ym la= || tein zum andern mal || ausgelegt. || Verdeudscht durch Justum || Jonam mit einer schönen vor || rhede Martini Luther || an die deudschen || leser. || Gedruckt. || 1529 || Woodcut, 4º. Colophon: Hat gedruckt Michael Lotter. 1529. || [101 +1 blank] leaves.

——*Epitome ethices* (1532), in Hermann Heineck, ed., *Die älteste Fassung von Mel-anchthons Ethik: Zum ersten Mal herausgegeben* (Berlin: Philosophisch-Historischer Verlag von Dr. R. Silinger, 1893). This work can be found in English translation in *A Melanchthon Reader*, ed. and trans. Ralph Keen, 203–38 (see below).

——*Heubtartikel Christlicher Lere: Melanchthons deutsche Fassung seiner* Loci Theologici *nach dem Autograph und dem Originaldruck von 1553*, ed. Ralf Jennett and Johannes Schilling (Leipzig: Evangelische Verlagsanstalt, 2002).

——*Loci Communes 1543 Philip Melanchthon*, trans. Jacob Preus (St Louis: Concordia, 1992).

——*Melanchthon on Christian Doctrine: Loci Communes, 1555*, trans. Clyde L. Man-schreck (New York: Oxford University Press, 1965).

Melanchthon, Philipp, *A Melanchthon Reader*, ed. and trans. Ralph Keen, American University Studies, Series VII, Theology and Religion, 41 (New York: Peter Lang, 1988).

——*Melanchthon: Selected Writings*, trans. Charles Leander Hill, ed. Elmer Ellsworth Flack and Lowell J. Satre (Minneapolis: Augsburg, 1962).

——*Melanchthons Briefwechsel: Kritische und kommentierte Gesamtausgabe*, ed. Heinz Scheible, 10 vols. (Stuttgart: Frommann-Holzboog, 1977–).

——*Melanchthons Briefwechsel: Texte*, ed. Heinz Scheible, 8 vols. (Stuttgart: Frommann-Holzboog, 1977–).

——*Melanchthons Werke in Auswahl [Studiensausgabe]*, ed. R. Stupperich, 7 vols. (Gütersloh: Gerd Mohn, 1951–75).

——*Paul's Letter to the Colossians*, trans. D. C. Parker (Sheffield: Almond, 1989).

——*Philip Melanchthon: Orations on Philosophy and Education*, ed. Sachiko Kusukawa, trans. Christine F. Salazar (Cambridge: Cambridge University Press, 1999).

——*Philipp Melanchthonis epistolae, iudicia, consilia, testimonia aliorumque ad eum epistolae quae in Corpus Reformatorum desiderantur*, ed. Heinrich Ernst Bindseil (Halle, 1874).

——*Scholia in Epistolam Pauli ad Colosenses, recognita ab autore* (Wittenberg: Joseph Klug, 1528). Or, with full detail:

SCHO= || LIA IN EPISTO= || LAM PAVLI || ad Colossensses, re= ||cognita ab || autore. || PHIL. MELANCH. || Woodcut, 8°. Colophon: IMPRESSVM VVITTEN= || BERGAE PER IO= || SEPHVM KLVGK. || 106 + [1 + 1 blank] leaves, numbered 1–16, 16, 17–30, 32–40, 4[1], 42–8, 48, 49–56, 55, 58, 57, 60, 59, 62, 61, 64–100, 101, 102–5.

——*Supplementa Melanchthoniana. Werke Philipp Melanchthons die im Corpus Reformatorum vermisst werden*, ed. O. Clemen, 4 vols. (Leipzig, 1910–29).

——*Texte aus der Anfangszeit Melanchthons*, ed. E. Bizer (Neukirchen-Vluyn: Neukirchener-Verlag, 1966).

Nicene and Post-Nicene Fathers of the Christian Church: A Select Library, ed. P. Schaff (Edinburgh: T&T Clark, 1988–91).

Ockham, William, *Predestination, God's Foreknowledge, and Future Contingents*, ed. and trans. Marilyn McCord Adams and Norman Kretzmann (New York: Appleton-Century-Crofts, 1969).

——*Opera philosophica et theologica*, ed. Gedeon Gál et al., 17 vols (St Bonaventure, NY: St Bonaventure University, 1967–88).

——*Quodlibetal Questions*, trans. A. J. Freddoso and F. E. Kelley, 2 vols. (New Haven: Yale University Press, 1991).

Patrologia cursus completus, series Latina, ed. J. P. Migne, 221 vols. (Paris, 1844–79).

Philipp I, Langraf von Hessen, *Briefwechsel Langraf Philipps des Grossmüthigen von Hessen mit Bucer*, ed. Max Lenz (Leipzig: S. Hirzel, 1880–91).

Pighius, Albert, *De libero hominis arbitrio et divina gratia, Libri decem* (Cologne: Melchior Novesianus, 1542).

Scheurl, Christoph, *Christoph Scheurls Briefbuch, ein Beitrag zur Geschichte der Reformation und ihrer Zeit. Erster Band: Briefe von 1505–1516; Zweiter Band: Briefe von*

1517–1540) ed. Franz Freiherr Von Soden and Joachim Karl Friedrich Knaake (Potsdam, 1867–72; reprinted Aalen, 1962).

Schroeder, H. J., trans., *Canons and Decrees of the Council of Trent: Original Text With English Translation* (London: B. Herder, 1941).

Staupitz, Johann, *Johann von Staupitzens sämmtliche Werke. Erster Band: Deutsche Schriften*, ed. J. K. F. Knaake (Potsdam, 1867).

——*Johannis Staupitii, opera quae reperiri poterunt omnia: Deutsche Schriften*, ed. J. K. F. Knaake, vol. 1 (Potsdam, 1867).

——*Libellus de executione eterne predestinationis* (Nuremberg, 1517).

——*Salzburger Predigten 1512. Eine textkritische Edition*, ed. Wolfram Schneider-Lastin (Tübingen, 1990).

——*Sämtliche Schriften, Abhandlungen, Predigten, Zeugnisse. Tübinger Predigten*, ed. Lothar Graf zu Dohna and Richard Wetzel, vols. 1, 2, and 5 seem to be currently available (Berlin: De Gruyter, 1979–).

——*Staupitz, Tübinger Predigten, Quellen und Forschungen zur Reformationsgeschichte*, ed. Georg Buchwald and Ernst Wolf, vol. 8 (Leipzig, 1927).

——*Von dem heyligen rechten Christlichen glauben. Johannes Staubitz Nach seinem abschayden an tag kumen vnd außgangen* (Nuremberg: Jobst Gutknecht, 1525).

——*Von der lieb gottes* (1518), in English translation in John Joseph Stoudt, 'John Staupitz on God's Gracious Love', *Lutheran Quarterly* 8 (1956), 225–44.

Secondary Sources

Adams, Marilyn McCord, *William Ockham*, 2 vols. (Notre Dame: University of Notre Dame Press, 1987).

Bainton, Roland H., *Erasmus of Christendom* (London: Collins, 1969).

——*Here I Stand: A Life of Martin Luther* (New York: Mentor, 1950).

Baltzer, Otto, *Die Sentenzen des Petrus Lombardus: Ihre Quellen und ihre dogmengeschichtliche Bedeutung: Neudruck der Ausgabe Leipzig 1902* (Wiesbaden: Scientia Verlag Aalen, 1972).

Bayer, Oswald, 'Freedom? The Anthropological Concepts in Luther and Melanchthon Compared', *Harvard Theological Review* 91 (1998), 373–87.

Bornkamm, Heinrich, 'Melanchthons Menschenbild', in *Philipp Melanchthon: Forschungsbeiträge zur vierhundertsen Wiederkehr seines Todestages dargeboten in Wittenberg 1960*, ed. Walter Elliger (Göttingen: Vandenhoeck & Ruprecht, 1961), 76–90.

Boyle, Marjorie O'Rourke, *Erasmus on Language and Method in Theology* (Toronto: University of Toronto Press, 1977).

——*Rhetoric and Reform: Erasmus' Civil Dispute with Luther*, Harvard Historical Monographs 71 (Cambridge, MA: Harvard University Press, 1983).

——'Stoic Luther: Paradoxical Sin and Necessity', *Archiv für Reformationsgeschichte* 73 (1982), 69–93.

Brady, Ignatius C., 'Peter Lombard', in Berard L. Marthaler et al., eds., *New Catholic Encyclopedia*, 2nd edn., vol. 11 (Detroit: Thomson Gale, 2003), 190–1.

Brüls, Alfons, *Die Entwicklung der Gotteslehre beim jungen Melanchthon, 1518–1535, Untersuchungen zur Kirchengeschichte* (Bielefeld: Luther-Verlag, 1975).

Cameron, Euan, 'Philipp Melanchthon: Image and Substance', *Journal of Ecclesiastical History* 48 (1997), 705–22.

Colish, Marcia L., *Peter Lombard*, 2 vols. (Leiden: E. J. Brill, 1994).

——'Peter Lombard', in *The Medieval Theologians: An Introduction to Theology in the Medieval Period*, ed. G. R. Evans (Oxford: Blackwell, 2001), 168–83.

Cross, Richard, *Duns Scotus* (New York: Oxford University Press, 1999).

Davies, Brian, *The Thought of Thomas Aquinas* (Oxford: Clarendon Press, 1992).

Davies, G. I., *see Calvin, John, in Primary Sources, above.*

Dettloff, Werner, *Die Lehre von der Acceptatio Divina bei Johannes Duns Scotus mit besondere Berücksichtigung der Rechtfertigungslehre* (Werl: Dietrich Coelde-Verlag, 1954).

Engelland, Hans, 'Der Ansatz der Theologie Melanchthons', in *Philipp Melanchthon: Forschungsbeträge zur vierhundertsen Wiederkehr seines Todestages dargeboten in Wittenberg 1960*, ed. Walter Elliger (Göttingen: Vandenhoeck & Ruprecht, 1961), 56–75.

——*Melanchthon, Glauben und Handeln* (Munich: C. Kaiser, 1931).

——'Introduction' to *Melanchthon on Christian Doctrine: 1555 Loci Communes*, ed. and trans. Clyde L. Manschreck (New York: Oxford University Press, 1965), xxv–xlii.

Ernst, Wilhelm, *Gott und Mensch am Vorabend der Reformation: Eine Untersuchung zur Moralphilosophie und -theologie bei Gabriel Biel* (Leipzig: St Benno-Verlag, 1972).

Estes, James M., *Peace, Order and the Glory of God: Secular Authority and the Church in the Thought of Luther and Melanchthon, 1518–1559*, Studies in Medieval and Reformation Traditions—History, Culture, Religion, Ideas 111, ed. Andrew Colin Gow (Leiden: Brill, 2005).

——'The Role of Godly Magistrates in the Church: Melanchthon as Luther's Interpreter and Collaborator', *Church History* 67 (1998), 463–83.

Fenlon, Dermot, *Heresy and Obedience in Tridentine Italy: Cardinal Pole and the Counter Reformation* (London: Cambridge University Press, 1972).

Fraenkel, Peter, *Testimonia Patrum: The Function of the Patristic Argument in the Theology of Philip Melanchthon* (Geneva: Droz, 1961).

Geisler, Norman L., ed., *What Augustine Says* (Grand Rapids: Baker, 1982).

Gerhards, H., 'Die Entwicklung des Problems der Willensfreiheit bei Philipp Melanchthon', Ph.D. dissertation (Rheinischen Friedrich Wilhelms Universität, 1955).

Gerrish, B. A., *Grace and Reason: A Study in the Theology of Luther* (Oxford: Clarendon Press, 1962).

González, Justo L., *A History of Christian Thought*, 3 vols. (Nashville: Abingdon Press, 1971).

Green, Lowell C., *How Melanchthon Helped Luther Discover the Gospel: The Doctrine of Justification in the Reformation* (Fallbrook, CA: Verdict, 1980).

—— 'Melanchthon's Relation to Scholasticism', in *Protestant Scholasticism: Essays in Reassessment*, ed. Carl R. Trueman and R. S. Clark (Carlisle: Paternoster Press, 1999), 273–88.

Günther, Hartmut Oskar, 'Die Entwicklung der Willenslehre Melanchthons in der Auseinandersetzung mit Luther und Erasmus', Ph.D. dissertation (Friedrich-Alexander Universität, 1963).

Hägglund, Bengt, *De homine: människouppfattningen i äldre luthersk tradition* (Lund: C. W. K. Gleerup, 1959).

Hamm, Berndt, *Promissio, Pactum, Ordinatio: Freiheit und Selbstbindung Gottes in der scholastischen Gnadenlehre*, Beiträge zur historischen Theologie 54, ed. Gerhard Ebeling (Tübingen: J. C. B. Mohr (Paul Siebeck), 1977).

Hoffmann, Manfred, 'Rhetoric and Dialectic in Erasmus's and Melanchthon's Interpretation of John's Gospel', in *Philip Melanchthon (1497–1560) and the Commentary*, ed. Timothy J. Wengert and M. Patrick Graham (Sheffield: Sheffield Academic Press, 1997), 48–78.

Immenkötter, Herbert, and Gunther Wenz, *Im Schatten der Confession Augustana: Die Religionsverhandlungen des Augsburger Reichstages 1530 im historischen Kontext*, Reformationsgeschichtliche Studien und Texte 136 (Münster: Aschendorf, 1997).

Kaufman, Peter Iver, 'Charitas non est nisi a Spiritui Sancto: Augustine and Peter Lombard on Grace and Personal Righteousness', *Augustiniana* 30 (1980), 209–20.

Keen, Ralph, *A Checklist of Melanchthon Imprints* (St Louis: Center for Reformation Research, 1988).

—— 'Melanchthon and His Roman Catholic Opponents', *Lutheran Quarterly* 12 (1998), 419–29.

Kelly, J. N. D., *Early Christian Doctrines* (London: Adam & Charles Black, 1977).

Knowles, David, 'The Middle Ages: 604–1350', in Hubert Cunliffe-Jones, ed., *A History of Christian Doctrine* (Edinburgh: T&T Clark, 1978), 283ff.

Kolb, Robert, *Bound Choice, Election, and Wittenberg Theological Method* (Grand Rapids: Eerdmans, 2005).

—— *Luther's Heirs Define his Legacy: Studies on Lutheran Confessionalization* (Aldershot: Variorum, 1996).

—— 'Melanchthon's Influence on the Exegesis of His Students: The Case of Romans 9', in *Philip Melanchthon (1497–1560) and the Commentary*, ed. Timothy J. Wengert and M. Patrick Graham (Sheffield: Sheffield Academic Press, 1997), 194–215.

—— 'Nikolaus Gallus' Critique of Philip Melanchthon's Teaching on the Freedom of the Will', *Archiv für Reformationsgeschichte* 91 (2000), 87–110.

—— 'Nikolaus von Amsdorf on Vessels of Wrath and Vessels of Mercy: A Lutheran's Doctrine of Double Predestination', *Harvard Theological Review* 69 (1976), 325–43. Reprinted as chapter 2 in Kolb's *Luther's Heirs*.

Kuropka, Nicole, *Philipp Melanchthon: Wissenschaft und Gesellschaft. Ein Gelehrter im Dienst der Kirche (1526–1532)* (Tübingen: Mohr Siebeck, 2002).

Kusukawa, Sachiko, *The Transformation of Natural Philosophy: The Case of Philip Melanchthon* (Cambridge: Cambridge University Press, 1995).

Lane, A. N. S., 'Did Calvin Believe in Freewill?' *Vox Evangelica* 12 (1981), 72–90.

328 *Select Bibliography*

Leff, Gordon, *Gregory of Rimini: Tradition and Innovation in Fourteenth Century Thought* (Manchester: Manchester University Press, 1961).

—— *William of Ockham: The Metamorphosis of Scholastic Discourse* (Manchester: Manchester University Press, 1975).

Lexutt, Athina, *Rechtfertigung im Gespräch: Das Rechtfertigungsverständnis in den Religionsgesprächen von Hagenau, Worms und Regensburg 1540/41* (Göttingen: Vandenhoeck & Ruprecht, 1996).

Lohse, Bernhard, *Luthers Theologie in ihrer historischen Entwicklung und in ihrem systematischen Zusammenhang* (Göttingen: Vandenhoeck & Ruprecht, 1995).

—— *Martin Luther's Theology: Its Systematic Development*, ed. and trans. Roy A. Harrisville (Edinburgh: T&T Clark, 1999).

MacCulloch, Diarmaid, *The Reformation* (New York: Viking, 2004).

MacKinnon, James, *Luther and the Reformation*, 4 vols. (London: Longmans, 1929).

Manschreck, Clyde Leonard, *Melanchthon: The Quiet Reformer* (New York: Abingdon Press, 1958).

Matz, Wolfgang, *Der befreite Mensche: die Willenslehre in der Theologie Philipp Melanchthons* (Göttingen: Vandenhoeck & Ruprecht, 2001).

Maurer, Wilhelm, *Historical Commentary on the Augsburg Confession*, trans. H. George Anderson (Philadelphia: Fortress, 1986).

—— *Der junge Melanchthon: zwischen Humanismus und Reformation*, 2 vols. (Göttingen: Vandenhoeck & Ruprecht, 1967–9).

—— 'Melanchthons Anteil am Streit zwischen Luther und Erasmus', *Archiv für Reformationsgeschichte* 49 (1958), 89–114.

Maxcey, Carl E., *Bona Opera: A Study in the Development of the Doctrine in Philip Melanchthon* (Nieuwkoop: B. De Graaf, 1980).

McGrath, Alister E., *Christian Theology: An Introduction* (Oxford: Blackwell, 1998).

—— *Iustitia Dei: A History of the Christian Doctrine of Justification*, 2nd edn. (Cambridge: Cambridge University Press, 1998).

—— *Luther's Theology of the Cross: Martin Luther's Theological Breakthrough* (Oxford: Blackwell, 1985).

McSorley, Harry J., *Luthers Lehre vom unfreien Willen nach seiner Hauptschrift De servo arbitrio im Lichte der biblischen und kirchlichen Tradition* (Munich: Hueber, 1967).

—— *Luther: Right or Wrong? An Ecumenical-Theological Study of Luther's Major Work, The Bondage of the Will* (New York: Newman Press, 1969).

Mehlhausen, Joachim, ed., *Das Augsburger Interim von 1548* (Neukirchen-Vluyn: Neukirchener-Verlag, 1970).

Meijering, E. P., *Melanchthon and Patristic Thought: The Doctrines of Christ and Grace, the Trinity, and the Creation* (Leiden: E. J. Brill, 1983).

Mirković, Mijo, *Matija Vlačić Illirik*, 2 vols., 2nd edn. (Croatia: Pula and Rijeka, 1960–2). (Be advised—the text is written in Serbo-Croat!)

Mülhaupt, Erwin, 'Luther und Melanchthon: Die Geschichte einer Freundschaft', in *Luther im 20. Jahrhundert* (Göttingen: Vandenhoeck & Ruprecht, 1982), 121–34.

Neuser, Wilhelm H., *Der Ansatz der Theologie Philipp Melanchthons* (Neukirchen Kr. Moers: Verlag der Buchhandlung des Erziehungsvereins, 1957).

Noryskiewicz, J., 'Melanchthons ethische Prinzipienlehre und ihr Verhältnis zure Moral der Scholastik', dissertation (Münster, 1904).

Oberman, Heiko Augustinus, ed. and trans., *Forerunners of the Reformation: The Shape of Late Medieval Thought Illustrated by Key Documents* (Philadelphia: Fortress Press, 1966).

——*The Harvest of Medieval Theology: Gabriel Biel and Late Medieval Nominalism* (Cambridge, MA: Harvard University Press, 1963).

——'Headwaters of the Reformation', in *Luther and the Dawn of the Modern Era*, ed. Heiko Oberman (Leiden: E. J. Brill, 1974), 41–88.

Olson, Oliver K., *Matthias Flacius and the Survival of Luther's Reform* (Wiesbaden: Harassowitz Verlag, 2002).

Pannenberg, Wolfhart, *Die Prädestinationslehre des Duns Scotus* (Göttingen: Vandenhoeck & Ruprecht, 1954).

Pauck, Wilhelm, 'Luther und Melanchthon', in Vilmos Vajta, ed., *Luther and Melanchthon in the History and Theology of the Reformation* (Philadelphia: Muhlenberg Press, 1961).

Peters, Christian, *Apologia Confessionis Augustanae: Untersuchungen zur Textgeschichte einer lutherischen Bekenntnisschrift (1530–1584)* (Stuttgart: Calwer Verlag, 1997).

Plitt, G. L. and T. Kolde, *Die Loci communes Philipp Melanchthonis in ihrer Urgestalt*, 4th edn. (Leipzig: Deichert, 1925).

Portalié, Eugène, *A Guide to the Thought of Saint Augustine*, trans. Ralph J. Bastian (London: Burns & Oates, 1960).

Posset, Franz, *The Front-Runner of the Catholic Reformation: The Life and Works of Johann von Staupitz* (Aldershot: Ashgate, 2003).

Rabil, Albert, *Erasmus and the New Testament: The Mind of a Christian Humanist* (San Antonio: Trinity University Press, 1972).

Rosemann, Philipp W., *Peter Lombard* (Oxford: Oxford University Press), 2004.

Rogness, Michael, *Philip Melanchthon: Reformer without Honor* (Minneapolis: Augsburg, 1969).

Scheible, Heinz, 'Aristoteles und die Wittenberger Universitätsreform: Zum Quellenwert von Lutherbriefen', in *Humanismus und Wittenberger Reformation: Festgabe anlässlich des 500. Geburtstages des Praeceptor Germaniae Philipp Melanchthon am 16. Februar 1997: Helmar Junghans gewidmet*, ed. Michael Beyer and Günter Wartenberg (Leipzig: Evangelische Verlagsanstalt, 1996), 123–44.

——'Luther and Melanchthon', *Lutheran Quarterly* 4 (1990), 317–39.

——*Melanchthon: Eine Biographie* (Munich: C. H. Beck, 1997).

——'Melanchthon zwischen Luther und Erasmus', in *Melanchthon und die Reformation: Forschungsbeiträge*, ed. Gerhard May and Rolf Decot (Mainz: Philipp von Zabern, 1996), 171–97.

Schmidt, Martin Anton, 'Das Sentenzenwerk des Petrus Lombardus und sein Aufstieg zum Muster- und Textbuch der theologischen Ausbildung', in *Handbuch der Dogmen- und Theologiegeschichte*, ed. Carl Andresen (Göttingen: Vandenhoeck & Ruprecht, 1988), 1.587–615.

Schneider, John R., 'Melanchthon's Rhetoric as a Context for Understanding His Theology', in *Melanchthon in Europe: His Work and Influence Beyond Wittenberg*, ed. Karin Maag (Grand Rapids: Baker/Paternoster, 1999), 141–59.

——*Philip Melanchthon's Rhetorical Construal of Biblical Authority: Oratio Sacra* (Lewiston, NY: Mellen, 1990).

Schulze, Manfred, '"Via Gregorii" in Forschung und Quellen', in *Gregor von Rimini: Werk und Wirkung bis zur Reformation* (Berlin: Walter de Gruyter, 1981), 1–126.

Schwarzenau, Paul, *Der Wandel im theologischen Ansatz bei Melanchthon von 1525–1535* (Gütersloh: Carl Bertelsmann Verlag, 1956).

Sperl, Adolf, *Melanchthon zwischen Humanismus und Reformation* (Munich: Chr. Kaiser Verlag, 1959).

Steinmetz, David Curtis, *Luther and Staupitz: An Essay in the Intellectual Origins of the Protestant Reformation* (Durham, NC: Duke University Press, 1980).

——*Misericordia Dei. The Theology of Johann von Staupitz in its Late Medieval Setting* (Leiden: E. J. Brill, 1968).

——*Reformers in the Wings* (Philadelphia: Fortress, 2001).

Stupperich, Robert, *Melanchthon*, trans. Robert H. Fisher (London: Lutterworth, 1965).

TeSelle, Eugene, *Augustine the Theologian* (New York: Herder and Herder, 1970).

Thompson, W. D. J. Cargill, 'The "Two Kingdoms" and the "Two Regiments": Some Problems of Luther's *Zwei-Reiche-Lehre*', *Journal of Theological Studies* n.s. 20 (1969), 164–84. Reprinted in *idem, Studies in the Reformation: Luther to Hooker*, ed. C. W. Dugmore (London: Athlone Press, 1980), 42–59.

——*The Political Thought of Martin Luther*, ed. Philip Broadhead (Brighton: Harvester, 1984).

Tinkler, John F., 'Erasmus' Conversation with Luther', *Archiv für Reformationsgeschichte* 82 (1991), 59–81.

Watson, Philip S., *Let God Be God! An Interpretation of the Theology of Martin Luther* (London: Epworth, 1947).

Wengert, Timothy J., *Human Freedom, Christian Righteousness: Philip Melanchthon's Exegetical Dispute with Erasmus of Rotterdam* (New York: Oxford University Press, 1998).

——'Melanchthon and Luther/Luther and Melanchthon', *Lutherjahrbuch* 66 (1999), 54–88.

——'Philip Melanchthon's 1522 Annotations on Romans and the Lutheran Origins of Rhetorical Criticism', in Richard A. Muller and John L. Thompson, eds., *Biblical Interpretations in the Era of the Reformation: Essays Presented to David C. Steinmetz in Honor of His Sixtieth Birthday* (Grand Rapids: Eerdmans, 1996), 118–40.

——'Philip Melanchthon's Contribution to Luther's Debate with Erasmus over the Bondage of the Will,' in Joseph A. Burgess and Marc Kolden, eds., *By Faith Alone: Essays on Justification in Honor of Gerhard O. Forde* (Grand Rapids: Eerdmans, 2004), 110–24.

—— ' "We Will Feast Together in Heaven Forever": The Epistolary Friendship of John Calvin and Philip Melanchthon', in *Melanchthon in Europe: His Work and Influence Beyond Wittenberg*, ed. Karin Maag (Grand Rapids: Baker, 1999), 19–44.

Wiedenhofer, Siegfried, *Formalstrukturen humanistischer und reformatischer Theologie bie Philipp Melanchthon*, 2 vols. (Bern: Herbert Lang, 1976).

Wood, Rega, 'Ockham's Repudiation of Pelagianism', in *The Cambridge Companion to Ockham*, ed. Paul Vincent Spade (Cambridge: Cambridge University Press, 1999), 350–73.

Zumkeller, Adolar, *Johann von Staupitz und seine christliche Heilslehre* (Würzburg: Augustinus-Verlag, 1994).

zur Mühlen, Karl Heinz, 'Melanchthons Auffassung vom Affekt in den Loci communes von 1521', in *Humanismus und wittenberger Reformation: Festgabe anläßlich des 500. Geburtstag des Praeceptor Germaniae, Philipp Melanchthon, am 16. Februar 1997, Helmar Junghans gewidmet*, ed. Michael Beyer et al. (Leipzig: Evangelische Verlagsanstalt, 1997), 327–36.

Index